For

Julia E. Peacock,

Dean of Health Sciences, Technology,
Engineering Sciences and Computing

About the Authors

William H. Murray III and Chris H. Pappas have teamed up to write over 30 computer books on various programming languages. A few of their titles include *The Visual C++ Handbook*, *OLE Wizardry*, and *Cross-Platform Programming for Windows*. Both Murray and Pappas teach introductory and advanced C/C++ courses in the S.U.N.Y. system in Binghamton, New York.

Borland C++
In Depth

William H. Murray III
and
Chris H. Pappas

Osborne **McGraw-Hill**

Berkeley New York St. Louis San Francisco
Auckland Bogotá Hamburg London Madrid
Mexico City Milan Montreal New Delhi Panama City
Paris São Paulo Singapore Sydney
Tokyo Toronto

Osborne **McGraw-Hill**
2600 Tenth Street
Berkeley, California 94710
U.S.A.

For information on translations or book distributors outside the U.S.A., or to arrange bulk purchase discounts for sales promotions, premiums, or fundraisers, please contact Osborne McGraw-Hill at the above address.

Borland C++ In Depth

234567890 DOC 99876

ISBN 0-07-882216-5

Acquisitions Editor
  Wendy Rinaldi

Project Editor
  Claire Splan

Technical Editor
  Jeffrey Hsu

Copy Editor
  Ann Spivack

Proofreader
  Sally Engelfried

Indexer
  William H. Murray
  Chris H. Pappas

Computer Designer
  Peter Hancik

Illustrator
  Lance Ravella

Cover Design
  Ted Mader Associates

Quality Control Specialist
  Joe Scuderi

For information on translations or book distributors outside the U.S.A., or to arrange bulk purchase discounts for sales promotions, premiums, or fundraisers, please contact Osborne **McGraw-Hill** at the above address.

Contents at a Glance

Contents

Part I

The Borland Compiler and C/C++ Programming

Part II

C and C++ Programming Foundations

Part III

Foundations for Object-Oriented Programming in C++

Part IV

Special Libraries

Part V

Foundations for Win32 Programming

Part VI

Using Object Libraries for Win32 Programming

Introduction

This book highlights Borland's newest C/C++ compiler package, version 5. One package meets the needs of programmers working in the Windows 3.11, Windows 95, and Windows NT programming environments. The Borland package includes a C/C++ compiler, debuggers, various other development tools, and tools for creating Java components. As complete as the Borland compiler package is, you don't have to be a professional programmer to use it or this book. What you need is a genuine interest in learning the C/C++ language. This book teaches you C, C++, and Windows programming from the ground up and was designed for the novice and professional alike. If you are interested in learning more about procedure-oriented and object-oriented programming, this book is for you!

Borland C++ In Depth is a multifaceted book designed with you, the programmer, in mind. We will guide you through many traps and potential pitfalls encountered by program developers. By the time you reach the end of this book, you will be able to efficiently use your compiler package and write and debug sophisticated C, C++, and Windows code. Unlike quick-start books, this book was designed to lay a solid foundation for continued study.

How This Book Is Organized

This book can be used in a variety of ways, depending on your background and programming needs. The book can be divided into several major sections:

Chapters 1 through 4 introduce you to the programming tools contained in the Borland C/C++ compiler package.

Chapters 5 through 14 cover the foundations and programming concepts in the C and C++ languages. These are procedure-oriented chapters teaching traditional programming concepts.

Chapters 15 through 18 build upon the ideas introduced in earlier C and C++ chapters to teach you the concepts and definitions of object-oriented programming. Here you will learn how procedure-oriented and object-oriented programs differ and how to write a simple object-oriented program. The object-oriented programs developed in these chapters are similar to earlier programs using the procedure-oriented approach. The object-oriented concepts can be extended into the later chapters dealing with Windows 95 and Windows NT programs.

Chapters 19 is designed to show you how to utilize many features of the standard C and C++ libraries. In this chapter you will learn of language features that allow you to take advantage of C and C++ features.

Chapters 20 through 22 introduce you to Microsoft Windows concepts that apply to Windows 95 and Windows NT. In these chapters you will learn how to use the Borland compiler to develop applications that include GDI primitives, cursors, icons, menus, and dialog boxes. These successive chapters will give you a quick start in developing applications that are capable of running under all 32-bit Windows platforms.

Chapters 23 through 27 show you how to add object-oriented features to your Windows 95 and Windows NT applications. You will learn how to use both Borland's ObjectWindows library and Microsoft's MFC library to add advanced features to your programs. These features aid in making program maintenance a breeze. (Note: You must have access to the MFC library in order to use it with the Borland C/C++ compiler.)

Chapter 28 will teach you how to develop 32-bit applications using Borland's Experts. You'll gain a full understanding of how to use this hot code generator.

Appendix A is designed to introduce you to the concepts and definitions associated with Borland's tools for Java. Here you'll also learn simple programming techniques for this exciting new language.

Conventions Used in This Book

The following conventions have been used throughout this book:

■ When referring to items that apply equally to C and C++, the reference will be to C.

- Function names and other reserved words appear in boldface type.
- Keywords, variables, and constants appear in italic type.
- Program listings are shown in typewriter-style text.
- Text for you to enter from the keyboard is printed in boldface.

A Special Disk Offer

A disk is available containing all of the program listings in this book. To use the disk, you will need a computer running Windows 95 or Windows NT with the Borland compiler properly installed and running.

Send a check or money order (in U.S. currency) for $25 for a 3.5-inch disk to the address below. Please allow three weeks for personal checks to clear. No purchase orders, please. All foreign orders (outside North America) must have a check drawn on a U.S. bank in U.S. currency for $30 for a 3.5-inch disk. Foreign orders will be sent air mail.

Please send me the program listings included in *Borland C++ In Depth* by Pappas and Murray. Enclosed is a money order or check, for $25 ($30 for foreign orders) in U.S. funds, which covers the cost of the disk and all handling and postage. (Sorry, no purchase orders can be accepted! This coupon may be copied.) 3.5-inch 1.44M disk format only.

Name: _____

Address: _____

City: _____ State: _____ Zip: _____

Country: _____

Mail to:

Nineveh National Research
Borland C++ In Depth Disk Offer
P.O. Box 2943
Binghamton, N.Y. 13902

This is solely the offer of the authors. Osborne/McGraw-Hill takes no responsibility for the fulfillment of this offer.

PART ONE

The Borland Compiler and C/C++ Programming

Chapter One

Why You Need This Book

Have you ever tried to teach *yourself* something? What usually happens? Somewhere along the way you realize that you have developed some bad habits. And just who was it that pointed these facts out to you? Probably a teacher, a trainer, a "pro," or a known expert in that field. Why do you need this book? Because C and C++, unlike the computer languages that preceded them, can precipitate the worst kind of bad habits unless you know to watch out for them.

The crux of the matter involves C/C++'s *new* language features. Even if you are already a proficient programmer, you are still headed for trouble if you attempt to master C and C++ on your own, because C and C++ involve completely new ways of approaching tasks. Take for example, the analogy of learning a foreign language like French.

When do you get in trouble with your use of the French language? Only when you translate literally from English to French. In other words, it is just not enough to know the French equivalents to English words; you need to know how to syntactically and ideologically put them together. The same is true when mapping from whichever older high-level language you may already know to C/C++.

The authors of this book have been teaching programming for a combined total of over 26 years and have coauthored over 30 programming books! They have seen many inexperienced and many *very* experienced programmers tackle learning C/C++. Both categories of students have difficulties mastering these new languages. Novice programmers suffer from a general lack of knowledge about what any computer language can do. Experienced programmers suffer because they keep trying to make C/C++ fit what they *already* know about computer languages.

Think of C and C++ as a supersonic jet that you have parked in your driveway. Now which would you prefer? To have someone teach you how to switch on the auto-pilot so you can get that jet in the air TODAY? Or would you prefer to learn how to read the gauges, understand lift and drag, and practice takeoffs, flying, and landings with an experienced instructor? Alright, so the latter approach doesn't sound as appealing initially—it sounds as though it will take some effort before you actually get to fly the machine. However, if you take the time to learn what the machine can do, once you start flying on your own you will be able to go anywhere you want!

In each chapter of this book the authors point out the nuances of C/C++. Time is spent detailing those features of C/C++ that are identical in concept to older high-level languages such as PL/I, Pascal, COBOL, FORTRAN, and so on. The text also teaches, conceptually, then by coded example, those new concepts unique to C and C++. The book also details the sometimes confusing differences *between* C and C++. Most importantly, each chapter points out what you should *not* do with C/C++ so that you'll never have someone say behind your back, "Sure that person can fly, but someone should mention that the plane's upside down!"

Evolving Standards

There are two very important concepts you need to keep in the back of your mind when dealing with C and C++:

1. You will never be a true C/C++ programmer until you stop thinking in the computer language you already know.

2. Never stop your formal study of C and C++.

Unlike many older high-level languages in use today which have been around for many decades, C and C++ are relative fledglings. This situation generates a totally new problem—standardization. When you learned and started to use COBOL, FORTRAN, Basic, PL/I, Pascal, Modula-2, and so on, the theoretical matched the empirical. In the case of C and C++, you have two languages that are continuing to evolve. This presents a particularly difficult learning situation.

For example, many experienced programmers use reference materials when tackling new algorithm design. Why reinvent the wheel when you can find a previously written/debugged code segment that performs the exact function you need? In the case of documented C/C++ code, however, you could come across eight or more generations of code syntax:

1. Historic C

2. C

3. ANSI C

4. C++

5. ANSI C++

6. Microsoft Windows—Borland's way with OWL object libraries

7. Microsoft Windows—Microsoft's way with MFC object libraries

8. ANSI/ISO C (WG14) / C++ (WG21) Standard Libraries

9. As yet undefined generations

When referencing any documented C/C++ code, you need to make certain you are using the appropriate flavor of C/C++ for the application at hand. This does not mean you will always use the same C/C++ syntax—at some point you may need to fit a new code-segment into an older piece of C/C++ code. By the time you have finished reading, studying, and executing the examples in this book, you will have a fundamental understanding of both C and C++ and understand the generational differences.

Installing the Borland C++ Compiler

Borland has made installing your new C/C++ compiler as easy and straightforward as possible. To install Borland C++, simply run:

```
setup.exe
```

This file will either be found on Disk 1 or on the CD-ROM's setup subdirectory. We suggest that you select the default, *typical* install option. This will guarantee that you get all of the Help files and example programs that will make using your new compiler as enjoyable an experience as possible.

What's New?

From the computer industry's viewpoint, the most important recent development is Windows 95. Whether you like or don't like Bill Gates, Microsoft, and Windows, there's no denying the popularity of Microsoft Windows in any version (3.*x*, 95, or NT). For this reason alone, if you are developing a new application, you will undoubtedly want it to run under one of these versions of Microsoft Windows. The good news is that Borland has evolved their excellent C/C++ compilers to keep pace with this dynamically changing operating system environment.

Windows 95 Is Here

Borland C++ offers you a no-risk migration path to Windows 95. Borland C++ runs under Windows 95 today and includes unique Windows 95 header files and import libraries so you can create native Windows applications.

Target 16- and 32-Bit Applications from One Environment

Only Borland C++ lets you create powerful ANSI C and C++ applications for DOS, 16-bit Windows, and 32-bit Windows applications from a single IDE (Integrated Development Environment). Borland's OWL (Object Windows Library) allows you to develop true single-source 16-bit and 32-bit Windows applications. The Borland C/C++ compiler is also compatible with the Microsoft Foundation Class (MFC) Library as you'll learn in Chapters 16 and 27. That means less work, less frustration, and more free disk space on your way to Windows 95.

Scalability

Borland C++ provides full support for VBX (Visual Basic Custom) controls in both 16- and 32-bit applications, including Windows 95. A multi-target (platform or architecture) project manager handles complex dependencies, as well as multiple executables, DLLs (Dynamic Link Libraries), with a single build cycle. Borland C++ also incorporates full OLE. (OLE stands for Object Linking and Embedding support and scripting. A *script* file is an ASCII text file that allows you to redefine the Borland C/C++ IDE—Integrated Development Environment.) Each action you can take within the IDE is associated with a script file that you can view, enhance, or modify to fit your personal preferences.

System Recommendations

This section provides hardware and software recommendations that will help you get the most out of the Borland C++ compiler. Many of the suggestions are intended to improve overall system performance, whereas other tips make the product easier and more enjoyable to use.

Minimum Hardware and Software Requirements

The Borland C++ compiler package will operate on a wide range of Intel-based computers. The following is a list of *minimum* hardware and software requirements necessary to run the Borland C++ compiler package:

- 80386 Intel microprocessor
- 16 megabytes of RAM
- A high-density floppy disk drive
- A CD-ROM drive
- One 300-megabyte hard disk
- MS-DOS 5.0 or higher and Microsoft Windows 3.1 or higher
- Microsoft Windows NT 3.5 or higher for WIN32 development
- A VGA monitor

Recommended Hardware and Software Requirements

- A Pentium PC, running at 90 MHz or higher
- 16 to 32 megabytes of RAM
- A high-density floppy disk drive
- A CD-ROM drive
- A one-gigabyte hard disk
- Microsoft Windows 95 or Windows NT
- An SVGA monitor or better

How This Book Is Organized

A complete description of the layout of this book is in the Preface. If your programming goals are a little more selective, here are some suggestions about chapters to read:

- For a fast start on entering, editing, saving, compiling, and running simple programs, read Chapter 3.
- To learn more about just C and C++, read Chapters 3 and 5 through 14.
- To learn about Object-Oriented Programming in C++, read Chapters 15 through 18.
- To understand Microsoft Windows application development, read Chapters 20 through 22.
- To learn how to use Object-Oriented libraries, read Chapters 23 through 27.
- To use Borland Experts for auto-code generation, read Chapter 28.

In the Next Chapter...

Chapter 2 gives a high-level overview of the Borland C++ IDE (Integrated Development Environment). It is through the IDE that you access every feature of the Borland C++ compiler to generate, debug, and test code targeted for DOS, 16-bit Windows, and 32-bit Windows applications. This overview prepares you for Chapters 3 and 4, which provide gradual hands-on experience with each individual Borland C++ feature.

Chapter Two

Getting Started in the Integrated Development Environment

The Borland C++ IDE (Integrated Development Environment) allows you to easily create, open, view, edit, save, compile, and debug all of your C and C++ applications. The Borland C++ IDE also contains options for fine-tuning your work environment according to your personal preferences and for complying with application-specific hardware requirements. Many of the features discussed in the next sections are demonstrated in Chapter 3.

Starting the Borland C++ IDE

Launching the Borland C++ IDE is easy. If you are using a mouse, you can double-click on the Borland C++ icon, which is found in the Borland C++ group. Alternatively, you can access the Windows Run command from the keyboard, and then enter the following command:

```
C:BCW.EXE
```

Figure 2-1 shows the initial screen for the Borland C++ IDE.

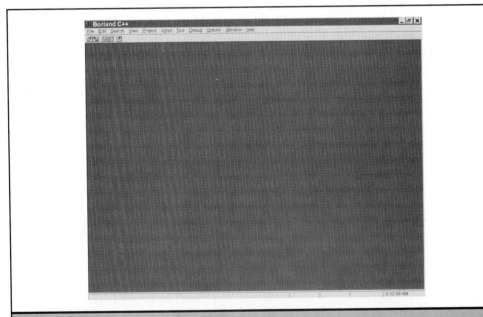

Figure 2-1.   *The initial screen for the Borland C++ compiler's IDE*

Accessing Context-Sensitive Help

Help for each Borland C++ IDE feature is easily accessed because all of the compiler's documentation is on-line. Tapping into this valuable resource is as simple as placing the cursor on the feature in question and pressing F1. However, context-sensitive help is not restricted to Borland C++ IDE features. If you place the cursor on a C/C++ language construct and press ALT-F1, the help utility will automatically display a description of the construct's syntax, an explanation of its use, and often a clarifying, executable example.

This chapter is designed to give you a broad overview of each Borland C++ IDE option. Do not become discouraged by the number of features and options available. You can use the default settings of many of the Borland C++ IDE's capabilities, which makes it easy to get an application up and running. As your experience grows and your application requirements increase in complexity, you will gradually gain hands-on experience with the more sophisticated capabilities of this powerful environment. While you are reading through this chapter, take a pencil and check those Borland C++ IDE features that sound interesting to you. When the need arises to use one of these features, you can easily refer back to this section for an explanation of how to use the option.

Understanding Menus

Before beginning a discussion of each Borland C++ IDE feature, let's examine a few traits that all menu items have in common. For example, there are two ways to access menu items. The most common approach is to place the mouse pointer over the preferred option and click the left mouse button. The second approach is to use the underscored hot key. For example, you can access the File menu directly from the keyboard by simultaneously pressing the ALT key and the letter F.

Menu items can be selected using the same sequences described above, and there is often one additional way to select them. You can directly activate some menu items from anywhere within the integrated environment by using their specific hot key combinations. If a menu item has this capability, the option's specific hot key combination is displayed to the right of the menu item on the menu. For example, you can invoke the File menu option Save immediately, avoiding the necessity of first selecting the File menu, simply by pressing ALT-FS.

Additional comments concerning menus: First, if a menu item is grayed, the integrated environment is alerting you to the fact that this particular option is currently unavailable. Basically, this means that the integrated environment is lacking some necessary prerequisite for that particular option to be valid. For example, the File menu's Save option will be grayed if the edit window is empty. The option knows that you cannot save something that does not exist, and it indicates this by deactivating and graying the Save command.

Second, any menu item followed by three periods (...) indicates an option that, when selected, will automatically display a dialog box or a submenu. For example, the File menu's Open... command, when selected, causes the Open dialog box to appear. Finally, you can activate some menu items by clicking on their associated buttons on the toolbars, which are located below the main menu bar. Let's look at the interesting IDE features that are usually available via a menu choice.

The File Menu

The Borland C++ IDE File menu, shown here, localizes the standard set of file manipulation commands common to many Windows applications.

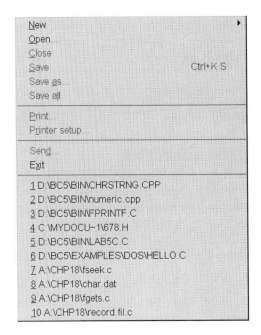

New	▶
Open...	
Close	
Save	Ctrl+K S
Save as...	
Save all	
Print...	
Printer setup...	
Send...	
Exit	
1 D:\BC5\BIN\CHRSTRNG.CPP	
2 D:\BC5\BIN\numeric.cpp	
3 D:\BC5\BIN\FPRINTF.C	
4 C:\MYDOCU~1\678.H	
5 D:\BC5\BIN\LAB5C.C	
6 D:\BC5\EXAMPLES\DOS\HELLO.C	
7 A:\CHP18\fseek.c	
8 A:\CHP18\char.dat	
9 A:\CHP18\fgets.c	
10 A:\CHP18\record.fil.c	

New...

The New... menu item opens a new edit dialog box window. You usually begin any new application at this point. The IDE automatically titles and numbers each window you open. Numbering begins at 00, so your first window title will always be *noname00*, your second window title *noname01*, and so on.

Open...

Unlike New..., which opens an edit dialog box window for a previously nonexistent file, the Open... menu item opens a dialog box that requests information on a previously saved file. This dialog box is the standard Open File dialog box, which displays the default drive, path, and file search parameters and allows you to select your own. The dialog box has a time-saving feature that automatically remembers your preferences, using these as defaults each time you use the Open... command.

Close

The Close command simply closes the current file.

Save

The Save menu item saves the contents of the currently selected or active window to the file specified. You can distinguish the previously saved contents of a window from the unsaved contents of a window by simply checking the window's title bar. If you see a default title, such as *xxx*1, you will know that the window's contents have never been given a valid filename and saved. Saving a previously unsaved file will automatically invoke the Save As dialog box.

Save As...

The Save As... menu item allows you to save a copy of the active window's contents under a new name. If you are wondering why you might choose this option, here's a possible scenario. You have just finished a project. You have a working program. However, you would like to try a few changes. For the sake of security, you do not want to tweak the current version. By choosing the Save As... option, you can copy the file's contents under a new name, and then you can tweak the duplicate. Should disaster ensue, you can always go back to your original file.

Save All

If you have never written a C, C++, Windows 95, or Windows NT application, you will be stunned at the actual number of files involved in creating a project's executable file. The problem with the Save option is that it only saves the active window's contents. The Save All menu item saves every window's contents. If any window contains previously unsaved text, the Save All command will automatically invoke the Save As dialog box, prompting you for a valid filename for each window.

Print...

Obtaining a hard copy of the active window's contents is as simple as selecting the Print... menu item. The Print dialog box provides you with several options. First, you can choose between printing the entire window's contents or printing only selected text by clicking on the appropriate radio button. You can also select which printer to use and configure the selected printer by choosing the Printer setup... option.

Printer Setup...

This option allows you to select a printer, along with its associated print characteristics.

Send

This command electronically mails the file in the active Edit Window, a file (node) highlighted in the Project Window, or a file referenced on a highlighted line in the Message Window. This command is available only if your system has a mail message service (MAPI) installed.

Exit

The Exit menu item allows you to quit the Borland C++ IDE. Don't worry if you have forgotten to save a window's contents before selecting Exit. The IDE will automatically display a warning message for each window containing unsaved text, allowing you to save the information before exiting.

Recent File List

Right below the Print setup... menu item is a list of the most recently edited files. The nice feature about such lists (often called *history lists*) are that they are context sensitive. History lists save you time by remembering the last several items you have selected for a particular option. For this menu, the items remembered are previously opened files. The first time you use the Borland C++ IDE, this portion of the File menu is empty, because there is no history of opened files. The File menu illustrated earlier shows a recent file history list with ten sample files.

The Edit Menu

Edit menu items allow you to quickly edit or search through an active window's contents in much the same way you would with any standard word processor. The next illustration shows the Borland C++ IDE Edit menu.

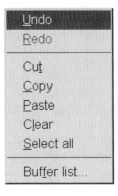

Undo

The Undo menu item allows you to reverse the most recent editing change you made.

Redo

The Redo menu item allows you to reverse the action of the last Undo. Use this option to reinstate a valid editing change that you thought was an incorrect change.

Cut

The Cut menu item copies the selected text in the active window to the Clipboard and then deletes the text from the active window. Selecting text is as simple as placing the mouse pointer on the first character in the text you want to cut and holding the left mouse button down while you drag the mouse to the right and/or down through the text. This causes the selected text to be displayed in reverse video.

The Cut command is often used in conjunction with the Paste command to move text from one location to another. When the cut text is placed on the Clipboard, all previous Clipboard contents are destroyed.

Copy

Like Cut, the Copy menu item places the selected text on the Clipboard. However, unlike Cut, Copy leaves the original selected text in place. A good use for this option would be to reproduce intricate code sequences or clarifying comments needed in multiple source files.

The Copy command is often used in conjunction with the Paste command to copy text from one location to another. When the copied text is placed on the Clipboard, all previous Clipboard contents are destroyed.

Paste

The Paste menu item is used to insert the contents of the Clipboard at the current cursor location. The Clipboard can only paste information that has been previously placed on the Clipboard by the Cut or Copy command.

Clear

The Clear menu item deletes selected text without copying the information to the Clipboard. Selecting text is as simple as placing the mouse pointer on the first character in the text you want to delete and holding the left mouse button down while you drag the mouse to the right and/or down through the text. This causes the selected text to be displayed in reverse video. Even though Cleared text is not copied to the Clipboard, you can still undo a Clear by choosing the Edit | Undo command.

Select All

The Select All menu item is used to select the entire contents of the active window for cutting, copying, or deleting.

Buffer List...

This command opens the Buffer List which lets you load a buffer (file held in memory) into an Edit window. The Buffer List displays a list of buffers. If a file has been changed since it was last saved, the label (modified) appears after the filename. Use the Buffer List to replace the contents of an Edit window without closing the original file. If the file you replace is not loaded in another Edit window, it is hidden. You can then later use the Buffer List to load the hidden buffer into an Edit window.

The Search Menu

The Search menu, shown here, provides commands to search for text and error locations in your files.

Find...	Ctrl+F
Replace...	Ctrl+Q Ctrl+A
Search again	F3
Browse symbol...	Ctrl+O Ctrl+B
Locate symbol...	
Previous message	Alt+F7
Next message	Alt+F8

Find.../Replace.../Search Again

These three commands perform the standard text processing search, replace, and repeat search/replace options found in most word processors. You can use this to find or change variable, constant, and function names. Remember that C/C++ is case-sensitive, so make certain you specify the correct search/replace options.

Browse Symbol

When you choose this command from an open Edit window, the dialog box contains selected text, or if no text is selected, it contains the word at the cursor. A symbol may be any class, function, or variable symbol which is defined in your source code (not only in the current file, but also in any source file that is compiled and linked as part of the same project).

Locate Symbol

You use the Locate symbol option by entering the symbol you want to locate and then choosing OK or pressing ENTER. The IDE positions the cursor in an Edit window at the line in the source code file that contains the symbol or function. If the file is not is loaded in an Edit window, a new Edit window opens with the file loaded. This command is only available while you are using the integrated debugger and your program is not running.

Previous Message/Next Message

These menu options allow you to quickly review previously viewed error diagnostics or to move to the next error message generated by the compiler.

The View Menu

The commands on the View menu, shown here, let you choose which windows display in the IDE.

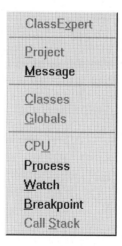

ClassExpert

The ClassExpert command displays the ClassExpert window where you can add and manage classes in a AppExpert application. This command is not available unless the current project is an AppExpert application that you generated by choosing the File | New | AppExpert command.

Project

The Project command opens the project tree where you can view a graphical representation of your project with project elements displayed as nodes (usually associated with files) in a collapsible/expandable hierarchy diagram. This command is not available until you have a project loaded in the IDE. If the Project window is closed, you can reopen it again with this command.

Message

The Message window displays status, warnings, and error messages. When you get error messages, the Message window opens and displays the output. If the Message window has been closed, you can reopen it again with the View | Message command. In the Message window you can scroll through the output messages, navigate to the program line referenced in the message, and track messages (highlight one program line after another in the source code as you view messages).

Classes

The Classes command displays all of the classes in your application arranged in a horizontal tree that shows parent-child relationships. The window is automatically sized to display as much of your class hierarchy as possible. You can highlight any class in the display by using the arrow keys or by clicking directly on the class name. You can then go to the source code that defines the highlighted class, inspect the functions and data elements of the highlighted class, or print the source code.

Globals

The Globals command opens a window listing every variable in your program in alphabetical order. You can highlight any variable in the display by using the arrow keys or by clicking directly on the variable name. You can then go to the source code that defines the highlighted variable or inspect the declaration of the highlighted variable.

CPU

The CPU option opens up the CPU window allowing you to inspect the microprocessor's register contents, memory buffers, and associated flags. This option is only available when you are debugging your application.

Process

The Process option opens the Process window, which displays a process/thread hierarchy tree. You can use this tree to visually track the hierarchy of program or task execution.

Watch

The Watch option opens the Watch window, which allows you to view the contents of variables while you are debugging an application. You can use the INSERT and DELETE keys to add or remove variables from the Watch window.

Breakpoint

The Breakpoint command opens a window that lists each set breakpoint and its line number. You can run your program full speed up to a breakpoint and then drop back to single-step execution mode for debugging purposes.

Call Stack

The Call Stack menu item opens the Call Stack dialog box. The window displays the sequence of function calls leading up to the current line of code highlighted by the debugger. This reverse-order list works like a data structure's stack: the last function called is at the top of the list, and the first function called is at the bottom.

The Project Menu

The Project menu, shown here, provides commands to create or modify a project and to make, build, or compile your programs.

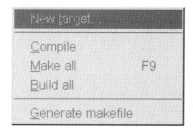

New Target...

The New target... option is used to add a new target node and specify target information for it. The node you create is added to the current project and placed at the bottom of the project tree. This new node is created as a standalone target. You can move it or make it a child of another node in the project tree by using the ALT-UP ARROW/ALT-DOWN ARROW, or ALT-LEFT ARROW/ALT-RIGHT ARROW keys. The options on the Add Target dialog box are Target Name, Target Type, AppExpert, Standard, and Source Pool.

This last option represents a collection of nodes in the project that are typically marked "exclude from parent" and not built. Source Pools act as a model or template from which you can create reference copies of code for use throughout your project. By using Source Pools, you can let different targets use common source code. If the target type is Source Pool, the target is added to the project, and you can add nodes to it immediately.

Compile

The Compile option signals the compiler to compile the source code in the active window. Compiling a file is a useful development phase, because it is here that you learn whether the file in question contains any syntax errors. For this reason it is possible to compile header (*.H) files, even though header files cannot be executed. If the compile process detects any syntax errors, either non-fatal warnings or fatal errors, these are displayed in the Output window.

Make All

Typical C/C++ programs are comprised of many files. Some of these files may be supplied by the compiler, the operating system, the programmer, or even third-party vendors. It can get even more complicated if the project's files are created by several programming teams. Because there can be so many files, and because the compile process can take a very long time, the Make all menu becomes an extremely useful tool. Make all examines all of the files in the project and then compiles and links only those dependent files displaying dates and times more recent than the project's executable file. If the Make all process detects any syntax errors, either non-fatal warnings or fatal errors, these are displayed in the Output window.

Build All

The only difference between Make all and Build all is that Build all ignores the dates of all of a project's files and painstakingly compiles and links all of them. Imagine the following scenario: Your company, for the sake of economy, has decided to go without any systems maintenance personnel. This decision, coupled with the seasonal time change, system downtime, and so on, results in your discovery that the systems on your network all have different system clock settings. Because of this, newly created files are being stamped with the previous day's date! Choosing the Make all option in this case could leave these current, updated files out of the final executable file. However, by choosing Build all, you avoid any date/time stamp checks, creating an executable file that truly reflects the current state of all included files. If the Build all process detects any syntax errors, either non-fatal warnings or fatal errors, these are displayed in the Output window. Use the Next Error or Previous Error menu items to search forward or backward through this list.

Generate makefile

The Generate makefile command generates a make file for the current project. It gathers information from the currently loaded project and produces a make file named [projectname].mak. You cannot convert make files to project files. The IDE displays the new make file in an Editor window.

The Script Menu

The Script menu provides access to commands that allow you to create, edit, save, and run *script* files. Typically you write a script in an editor, like the IDE editor, and save it to a file with an .spp extension. You then load and run the script file by entering its name in the Script Command window. The following instructions show you how to write and run a program that displays Welcome To C/C++ in a message window.

First, choose the Options | Environment | Scripting and add your script directory path to the Script Path so the IDE can find your scripts. For example, if your path already contains .;c:\bc5\script, it would look like this after you add a directory called c:\userscript: .;c:\bc5\script;c:\userscrpt.

Next, click Diagnostic Messages so the script processor will send scripting error messages and print statement output to the Script page. Hit the ENTER key to exit the Environment Settings dialog box. At this point select the View | Messages option and click the Script tab to open the Message window's Script page, then scroll to the end of the window. If you want to start with a clear page, you can delete the messages generated by the IDE startup by clicking the right mouse button within the Script page and choosing Delete All from the pop-up menu.

You are now ready to create the script file by choosing the File | New | Text Edit option to open a new file in the IDE editor, then entering the following script:

```
first( ) {
  import IDE; // Use the IDE object listed below
  IDE.Message ("Welcome To C/C++");
}
```

Save the file with *first.spp*. To run the script file, simply choose the Script | Run File option. Any statements that aren't in a function or other block will simply execute the first time you load the program. If you have a function called *_SetData()*, that function will also run when you load the program. If you have a function with the same name as the file, that will be the default function that runs when you load the program after any *_SetData()* function runs.

All Script files use the **IDE** object. This class represents the Borland C++ Interactive Development Environment (IDE). An **IDEApplication** object called **IDE** is instantiated when Borland C++ starts up. You typically use this class description to determine how to use or extend this **IDE** object:

```
//Syntax for IDEApplication Object

IDEApplication()

//Properties

xxx Application                      ReadOnly
string Caption                       ReadWrite
string CurrentDirectory              ReadOnly
xxx DefaultFilePath                  ReadWrite
Editor Editor                        ReadOnly
string FullName                      ReadOnly
int Height                           ReadWrite
int IdleTime                         ReadOnly
int IdleTimeout                      ReadWrite
int LoadTime                         ReadOnly
string KeyboardAssignmentFile        ReadWrite


KeyboardManager KeyboardManager      ReadOnly
xxx Left                             ReadWrite
string ModuleName                    ReadOnly
string Name                          ReadOnly
xxx Parent                           ReadOnly


bool RaiseDialogCreatedEvent         ReadWrite


xxx StatusBar                        ReadWrite
xxx Top                              ReadWrite
string Version                       ReadOnly
xxx Visible                          ReadWrite
xxx Width                            ReadWrite

//Methods

bool CloseWindow()
bool ScriptCommands()
bool ScriptCompileFile()
bool ScriptModules()
bool ScriptRun()
bool ScriptRunFile()
bool DebugAddBreakpoint()
```

```
bool DebugAddWatch()
bool DebugAnimate()
bool DebugAttach()
string DebugEvaluate()
bool DebugFindExecutionPoint()
bool DebugInspect()
bool DebugInstructionStepInto()
bool DebugInstructionStepOver()

bool DebugLoad()
bool DebugLoadSymbolTable()
bool DebugPauseProgram()
bool DebugResetThisProgram()
bool DebugRun()
bool DebugRunTo()
bool DebugStatementStepInto()
bool DebugStatementStepOver()
bool DebugTerminateProgram()
bool DebugToggleBreakpoint()
int DirectionDialog(string prompt)
string DirectoryDialog(string prompt, string initialValue[, string
pathSpecifier])

bool DoFileOpen(string filename, string toolName)
bool EditBufferList()
bool EditCopy()
bool EditCut()
bool EditPaste()
bool EditRedo()
bool EditSelectAll()
bool EditUndo()
void EndWaitCursor()
void EnterHelpContextMode()
void ExpandWindow()
bool FileClose([string fileName])
string FileDialog(string prompt, string initialValue)
bool FileExit( [int IDEReturn] )

string FileFirstFile(string filePattern)
bool FileNew([string toolName, string fileName])
bool FileOpen([string name, string toolName])
```

```
bool FilePrint(bool suppressDialog)
bool FilePrinterSetup()
bool FileSave()
bool FileSaveAll()
bool FileSaveAs([string newName])
int GetRegionBottom(string RegionName)
int GetRegionLeft(string RegionName)
int GetRegionRight(string RegionName)

int GetRegionTop(string RegionName)
bool GetWindowState()
void Help(string helpfile, int contextID, string  helpstring)
bool HelpAbout()
bool HelpContents()
bool HelpKeyboard()
bool HelpKeywordSearch([string keyword])
bool HelpOWLAPI()
bool HelpUsingHelp()
bool HelpWindowsAPI()
string KeyPressDialog(string prompt, string default)
string[ ] ListDialog(string prompt, bool multiSelect, bool sorted, string [ ]
initialValues)

void LocalMenu()
void Menu()
int Message(string text, int severity, int buttons)
int MessageCreate(string toolName, int messageType, int parentMessage, string
filename, int lineNumber, int columnNumber, string text, string helpFileName,
int helpContextId)
bool NextWindow(bool priorWindow)
bool OptionsEnvironment()
bool OptionsProject()
bool OptionsSave([int saveWhat])
bool OptionsStyleSheets()

bool OptionsTools()
bool ProjectAppExpert()
bool ProjectBuildAll([bool suppressOkay, string nodeName])
bool ProjectCloseProject()
bool ProjectCompile([string nodeName])
bool ProjectGenerateMakefile([string nodeName])
```

```
bool ProjectMakeAll([bool suppressOkay, string nodeName])
bool ProjectManagerInitialize()
bool ProjectNewProject([string pName])
bool ProjectNewTarget( [string nTarget, int targetType, int platform, int
libraryMask, int modelOrMode] )

bool ProjectOpenProject([string pName])
void Quit()

bool SaveMessages(string tabName, string fileName)

bool SearchBrowseSymbol([string sName])
bool SearchFind([string pat])
bool SearchLocateSymbol([string sName])
bool SearchNextMessage()
bool SearchPreviousMessage()
bool SearchReplace([string pat, string rep])
bool SearchSearchAgain()
bool SetRegion(string RegionName, int left, int top, int right, int bottom)
bool SetWindowState(int desiredState)
string SimpleDialog(string prompt, string initialValue [, int maxNumChars])

void StartWaitCursor()
string StatusBarDialog(string prompt, string initialValue [, int maxNumChars])
bool Tool([string toolName, string commandstring])
void Undo()
bool ViewBreakpoint()
bool ViewCallStack()
bool ViewClasses()
bool ViewClassExpert()
bool ViewCpu()
bool ViewGlobals()
bool ViewInformation()
bool ViewMessage()
bool ViewProcess()
bool ViewProject()

bool ViewWatch()
```

```
bool WindowArrangeIcons()
bool WindowCascade()
bool WindowCloseAll([string typeName])
bool WindowMinimizeAll([string typeName])
bool WindowRestoreAll([string typeName])
bool WindowTileHorizontal()
bool WindowTileVertical()
string YesNoDialog(string prompt, string default)

//Events

void BuildComplete(bool result)
void DialogCreated(string dialogName, int dialogHandle)
void Exiting()
void HelpRequested(string filename, int contextId)
void Idle()
void KeyboardAssignmentsChanging(string newFilename)
void KeyboardAssignmentsChanged(string newFilename)
void MakeComplete(bool result)
void ProjectClosed(string projectFileName)
void ProjectOpened(string projectFileName)

void SecondElapsed()
void Started(bool VeryFirstTime)
void SubsytemActivated(string systemName)
bool TransferOutputExists(TransferOutput output)
void TranslateComplete(bool result)
```

The Script menu provides the commands shown in the next illustration.

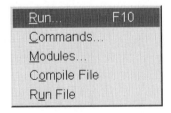

Run...

The Run... command runs an open script file.

Commands...

The Commands... command lists the various legal actions or methods available to all **IDEApplication**s.

Modules...

The Modules... command lists the modules or code segments, including all global variables currently accessible to the script file.

Compile File

The Compile File command compiles the script file.

Run File

The Run File command runs the script file.

The Tool Menu

The Tool menu, shown here, lets you run programs, tools, and utilities without leaving the IDE. To run a program from the Tool menu, choose the program you want from the list of available tools. The Tool List shows the three preinstalled programs, Turbo Debugger, Grep, and WinSight.

Turbo Debugger
Grep
WinSight

Turbo Debugger

The Turbo Debugger command activates the DOS-mode only integrated debugger used to single-step and examine individual program statements and variables.

Grep

Grep (Global Regular Expression Print) is a powerful text-search program derived from the UNIX utility of the same name. Grep searches for a text pattern in one or more files or in its standard input stream.

WinSight

WinSight gives you debugging information about window classes, windows, and messages. Using WinSight, you can study how any application creates classes and windows and monitor how windows send and receive messages.

The Debug Menu

The options listed in the Debug menu, shown here, are discussed next.

```
Run
Load...
Attach...

Run to...
Pause process
Reset this process
Terminate process

Find execution point

Add breakpoint...
Breakpoint Options...

Add watch...
Evaluate...
Inspect...
```

Run

The Run menu item is used to run your program. Depending on the program's target format, the Borland C++ IDE will automatically invoke an MS-DOS, Windows 95, or Windows NT environment to test the resulting application.

Load...

The Load...command opens the Load dialog box, which lets you run a program and optionally specify any command-line options to pass to the application you want to debug.

Attach...

The Attach... command opens the Attach To Program dialog box, which shows the programs currently in process and lets you attach them to the current debugging session or close and remove them from system memory. When you attach a program, it displays in the CPU view.

Run To...

The Run to... command opens the Run To dialog box, which lets you execute your program normally (not step by step) until it reaches the line and source file you specify.

Pause Process

The Pause process command halts execution of an application running in a debugging session. This command is only available while you are using the integrated debugger and your program is running.

Reset This Process

The Reset this process command returns the program to the state it was in at the beginning of the current debugging session. For example, use this command to restore all variables, members, and expressions modified during the current debugging session to their original values. This command is only available while you are using the integrated debugger.

Terminate Process

The Terminate process command stops the current debugging session. The command also releases memory your program has allocated and some of the memory used for debugging information, and it closes any open files that your program was using. This command is only available while you are using the integrated debugger.

Find Execution Point

The Find execution point command positions the cursor at the execution point in an Edit window. If you closed the Edit window containing the execution point, the IDE opens an Edit window displaying the source code at the execution point. This command is only available while you are using the integrated debugger and your program is not running.

Add Breakpoint...

The Add breakpoint... command opens the Breakpoint Properties dialog box, which lets you enter a conditional or unconditional breakpoint. When you choose this command from an active Edit window, the dialog box contains the name of the file loaded in the active Edit window and the line number at the cursor location. This command is not available if the debugger is stopped at an unrecoverable error.

Breakpoint Options...

The Breakpoint Options... command displays the BreakPoint/Conditions/Action Groups dialog box where you can set the properties that control the behavior of one or more breakpoints in a specified group.

Add Watch...

The Add watch... command opens the Watch Properties dialog box, which lets you set a watch expression. When you choose this command from an active Edit window, the dialog box contains selected text, or, if no text is selected, it contains the word at the cursor. After you add the watch, the Watch window displays. This command is not available if the debugger is stopped at an unrecoverable error.

Evaluate...

The Evaluate command opens the Expression Evaluator dialog box, which lets you evaluate a variable or expression, view the value of any variable or other data item, alter the value of simple data items, and use the Expression Evaluator as a calculator at any time.

Inspect...

The Inspect... command opens the Inspect Expression dialog box, which lets you enter a variable or expression you want to examine while debugging your program. This command is only available while you are using the integrated debugger and your program is not running.

The Options Menu

The Options menu, shown here, contains commands for changing various default settings for both your project and your environment (integrated development environment), installing or modifying tools, working with any Style Sheets that are available for your project, and specifying what gets saved when you exit BCW. Most of the commands in this menu lead to a dialog box. The Project and Environment commands both open a dialog box that lets you set options that affect your program and programming environment.

Project...

The Project... command displays the Project Options dialog box, where you set options for your entire project. The available topics are listed in Table 2-1.

Environment...

The Environment... command displays the Project Options dialog box, where you set options for the IDE in general.

This command works the same as the Set Options command on the Edit window. The available topics are listed in Table 2-2.

Tools...

The Tools... command opens the Tools dialog box, where you can install, delete, or modify the tools listed under the Tool menu. The Tool menu lets you run programming tools of your choice without leaving the Borland C++ IDE. Tools can be standalone programs (like Grep, Turbo Debugger, or an alternate editor), or they can be translators that are used for each file (or node) in a project. You can run a DOS program with the Windows IDE transfer.

Style Sheets...

The Style Sheets... command displays the Style Sheet dialog box where you can specify default compile and run-time option settings associated with a project. Style Sheets are predefined sets of options that can be associated with a node.

Save...

The Save... command opens the Save Options dialog box, where you save settings you have made for the C++ environment, desktop, and current project.

The Window Menu

The Window menu, shown here, contains window management commands. Most of the windows you manage from this menu have all the standard window elements, such as scroll bars, Minimize and Maximize buttons, and a Control menu box. To open windows, use the File | Open or File | New commands.

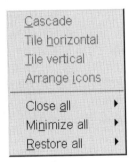

Cascade

The Cascade option will take all the windows currently open, and skew them down the display screen like a deck of cards. This visual arrangement allows you to easily see the number of windows open and their associated file names. The disadvantage to this visual arrangement is that you can only see the contents of the topmost window.

Tile Horizontal/Tile Vertical

The Tile commands instruct the integrated environment to equally subdivide the visual workspace so that each open window is the same shape and size. The advantage of this visual arrangement is that you can see the contents of all open windows simultaneously. The disadvantage is that this visual arrangement involves

Directories	Compiler	16-Bit Compiler	32-Bit Compiler
C++ Options	Optimizations	Messages	Linker
Librarian	Resources	Make	

Table 2-1. *Available Project Options*

Browser	Editor	Syntax Highlighting	SpeedBar
Scripting	Process Control	Preferences	Fonts
Project View	Debugger	Resource Editors	

Table 2-2. *Available Options*

too many open windows, which means each window is allocated only a postage stamp-sized portion of the screen. Options include horizontal or vertical sizing.

Arrange Icons

The Arrange icons command rearranges any icons on the desktop. The rearranged icons are evenly spaced, beginning at the lower left corner of the desktop. This command is useful when you resize your desktop that has minimized windows. It is unavailable when no windows are minimized.

Close All

The Close all command closes all open windows.

Minimize All

The Minimize option provides commands to minimize all or some open windows.

Restore All

The Restore all menu provides commands to restore some or all minimized windows to their former size.

The Help Menu

With such a rich, diverse, and sophisticated development environment, you would be lost without this last, but most important Main Menu option, namely, Help. Whether you are trying to understand a C/C++ language construct, understand a feature of the IDE, or understand how they all work together, the resources available to you through Help should answer your questions.

To speed up the time it takes to search this information database, the Help menu, shown here, subdivides the database into categories. Each command opens up a standard Help dialog box allowing you to specify search patterns, move forward and backward through nested help windows, and select high-level views of the help topics.

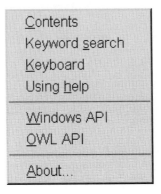

Contents

The Contents menu presents a high-level overview of Help categories.

Keyword Search

Keyword Search allows you to search for help on a specific topic by entering the keyword itself.

Keyboard

The Keyboard command lists alternate keystrokes provided to access various IDE features.

Using Help

The Using Help command discusses the various Help capabilities and how to access them.

Windows API

The Windows API command accesses specific help files for the Windows Application Programmer Interface.

OWL API

The OWL API command accesses specific help files for Borland C++'s Object Windows Libraries.

About...

The About... command details the current Borland C/C++ compiler version number.

In the Next Chapter...

In this chapter, you have been given a broad overview of each Borland C++ IDE feature. In the next chapter, you will learn how to write, compile, link, and test simple C/C++ programs. These programs will help you learn and apply the features learned in this chapter.

Chapter Three

Writing and Compiling Simple C/C++ Programs

T his chapter gives you hands-on experience with those commands and features of the Borland C/C++ compilers necessary to create, edit, save, compile, and run the sample standalone DOS-mode applications presented in this book. Because the integrated environment has so many ways to invoke the same operation, you might want to highlight the text anywhere you see the method you prefer, for example, keyboard commands versus mouse-menu interaction.

Your First Program

You start the Borland IDE (Integrated Development Environment) by first double-clicking on the Borland C++ icon found within the Borland C++ Group created when you installed the compiler. Once you have done this you should see a screen similar to Figure 3-1.

Starting the Borland IDE

To begin entering a new program, choose the File | New | Text Edit option found in the Main Menu, as highlighted in Figure 3-2. You use this option to create source code files, usually with *.C, or *.CPP file extensions, and to create your own header files. Header files have a *.H file extension. You select menu items by either clicking on

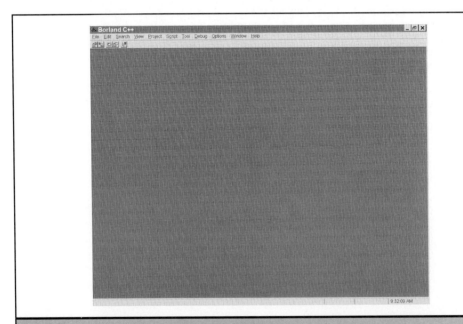

Figure 3-1.   *The initial Borland C++ IDE screen*

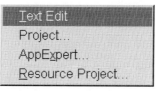

Figure 3-2. *Choosing the File\New\Text Edit option*

them with the mouse, highlighting them with the cursor keys and then pressing ENTER, or if available, by pressing their hot key(s). Hot keys allow you to quickly activate the associated option without the time-consuming sequence of selecting Main Menu items, followed by submenus, using either the keyboard or your mouse.

Beginning a New File

The following short program is included for you to practice entering, editing, saving, compiling, and running from within the Borland IDE:

```
/ * * * * * * * * * * * * * * * * * * * * * * * * * * * * * * * * * * * * * * * * * * * * * * * * *
      sample.c
      Use 'sample.c" to practice entering, editing,
      saving, compiling, linking, and running your first
      DOS-mode C program.
      Copyright (c) Chris H. Pappas and William H. Murray, 1996
* * * * * * * * * * * * * * * * * * * * * * * * * * * * * * * * * * * * * * * * * * * * * * * * */

#include <stdio.h>
#include <stdlib.h>

#define NUM_ELEMENTS 4

void DisplayArray( int int_Array[NUM_ELEMENTS]    )        ;

void main( void )
{
  int  offset                                             ;
  int  int_Array[ NUM_ELEMENTS ]                          ;
  char UserResponse;
```

```
    printf( "\nYour First C program!"                  )      ;
    printf( "\nWould you like to continue (Y/N): "  )      ;
    scanf ( "%c", &UserResponse                         )      ;

    if( UserResponse == 'Y' ) {
        printf(" \nThe uninitialized int_Array: "    )      ;
        DisplayArray( int_Array )                              ;
        for( offset = 0; offset < NUM_ELEMENTS; offset++ ) {
            printf( "\nEnter one integer value: "   )      ;
            scanf ( "%d",&int_Array[ offset ]       )      ;
        }
      printf( "\nThe initialized int_Array: "        )      ;
      DisplayArray( int_Array )                                ;
    }
    else
      exit( 1 )                                                ;
}

void DisplayArray( int int_Array[NUM_ELEMENTS]              )
{
  int offset                                                   ;

  for( offset = 0; offset < NUM_ELEMENTS; offset++          )
      printf( "\n%d",int_Array[ offset ] )                     ;
  printf( "\n\n" )                                             ;
}
```

After selecting the File I New I Text Edit option, enter the program just given exactly as you see it. The Borland IDE functions just like your word processor. If you make any typographical errors, simply use the standard editing keys (BACKSPACE, DELETE, INSERT, and so on) to make any necessary changes. When you feel the program is correct, save the file (as covered in the next section).

Saving a File

To save the contents of the active window, choose the File I Save option. Notice that this command, unlike File I New, has a hot key, F2. You might want to use your highlighting pen to remind yourself that the simple press of F2 saves your active file.

When you activate the Save option, the IDE opens up the Save File As dialog box shown in Figure 3-3. Save the sample program under the filename sample.c, then click on the Save button.

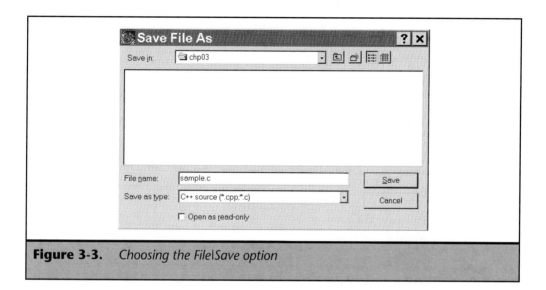

Figure 3-3. *Choosing the File\Save option*

Compiling the Program

With the program saved, it is time to compile the application. At this point, you have three options, all found in the Project Main Menu. You can choose to simply compile the active window's contents or you can perform a Make or Build. These options warrant individual explanations.

The Compile Option

Typical C/C++ applications are made up of two types of files: header files with .H file extensions and C or C++ source files with .C or .CPP file extensions, respectively.

 NOTE: There are many other types of files but, for now, this list is sufficient for the purpose of understanding the compile, Make, and Build options.

All three types of files can be compiled. In this sense, compiling requests the compiler to evaluate each file's respective syntax, making sure it follows the rules of C/C++. However, only .C and .CPP source files are executable. You cannot execute .H header files. The options Make and Build are reserved for generating executable files, and for this reason they are not used on .H header files.

The Make and Build Options

Both options, Make and Build, will attempt to generate an executable, *.EXE file. These options should be applied only to source files with either .C or .CPP file extensions, or when a specific Project file is open (see the "Starting a New Project" section later in this chapter). The difference between Make and Build is subtle.

For the moment, assume you are developing an advanced C/C++ application involving eight different files. When you generate the executable file, all eight support files are first converted to object format, then linked together. Now, suppose two days later you edit and streamline the source code within one of the original eight support files. Certainly, you would understand that the original executable file does not reflect the updated code. And here is the crux of the matter: file date-stamping.

The Make option first checks to see if an executable version of your program exists. If it does, Make checks the date of the executable file against all of the dates of the eight support files. If any support file has a more recent date, Make selectively compiles the newer file only, and then relinks all of the object files into an updated executable file.

Unlike Make, Build is more like a brute-force effort. Build ignores all file date-checks and simply recompiles and links all of the support files into an executable file. Of course, Builds will take more time than a Make whenever only a few of the support files are updated. With all this said, care is needed when deciding whether to perform a Make or a Build. Can you think of a real world scenario that could lead to disaster if a Make is chosen over a Build?

In the real world, factors outside of perfect code can affect how a program runs. If the support files just happen to be accessed across a company's network, different files could easily be stored across various computers. Are all of the clocks on each individual computer accurate? All you need is for one networked computer to be a minute behind everyone else's. The well-intended programmer retrieves a file from someone else's system, updates it, and then saves the file *with an older date* than the previously generated executable! Choosing Make would pass over this updated/old-dated file, leaving the previously generated executable file untouched! Had a Build been chosen, this situation would have been totally avoided. For this reason, the text rehearses you by illustrating the Build option. With sample.c saved, choose the Project Build option. You will see a window similar to the one shown in Figure 3-4. If you don't see this window, then double-check your source code against the listing in the book and correct any typographical errors.

Running a Program

To run the application after a successful Build, choose the Debug | Run command. Be careful: when running a DOS-mode application from within the IDE, the IDE automatically opens a DOS-compatibility box. You will have a few moments of confusion when this window is opened, and then the IDE returns to the main Edit window. Simply click on the OK button to let the IDE know you know it started the application, and then you can test the program. Figure 3-5 shows one complete run of sample.c.

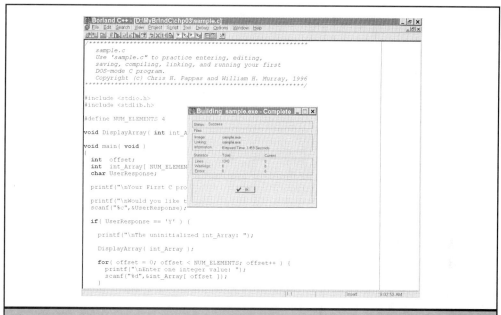

Figure 3-4.   *Choosing Project\Build (or Make)*

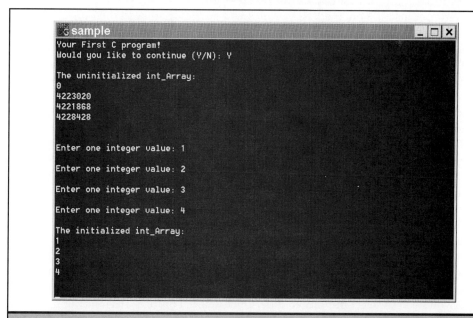

Figure 3-5.   *Choosing the Debug\Run option*

An Alternate Approach

The previous discussion demonstrated the easiest approach to entering, editing, saving, compiling, and running a DOS-mode application. However, the topics and example programs presented later in this book are object-oriented Window applications requiring many resource and support files. Compiling an application of this complexity requires the use of one of the IDE's more advanced capabilities, namely the Project utility. The following sections introduce you to this helpful file maintainer by reusing sample.c as an introductory example.

Beginners will undoubtedly find the previously discussed method easier. However, as the example programs become more complex, you may want to return to this chapter to review the use of the IDE's Project utility.

Starting a New Project

As already discussed, most C/C++ programs are made up of more than one file. These full-bodied applications require the inclusion of multiple source files, header files, and resource files. The Borland IDE contains the Project utility to methodically track and maintain what can easily become an overwhelming file maintenance nightmare. However, it takes time to learn the design philosophies and syntax necessary to write such applications.

To make learning C/C++ as easy and straightforward as possible, the example programs throughout the first part of this text use only one file. If you performed a default compiler installation, the IDE assumes you are going to need the Project utility. For this reason, the following section explains the somewhat cumbersome steps necessary to override this automatic default, until all of the Project utility's support file types have been discussed and practiced in later chapters.

To begin, you can consider a Project file as a specially encoded file that details the relationships between all of a program's support and source files, with their required interpretation. These file types can easily include all the C/C++ assembly language code, resources, bitmaps, and many other support files needed to generate the final executable file. Again, for our purposes there will be only one C/C++ file that needs its appropriate compiler. You start a Project file by choosing the Project | New Project... option. This opens up the New Target dialog box shown in Figure 3-6. The dialog box shown in Figure 3-6 has not yet been edited in and shows the initial IDE defaults.

For the majority of programs found in the first half of this text, follow these steps for defining each new project. First, give the Project file a name. Project files traditionally have an .IDE file extension. You can also include a path if you so choose. This allows each Project to reside in its own subdirectory. Figure 3-7 uses d:\mybrlndc\chp03\myfirst.ide. The IDE will automatically give the Target Name, the same name as the Project, in this case, myfirst.

Next, you need to select the Target Type. Once again, Figure 3-7 details the appropriate selection, Application[.exe]. Choose this option by simply clicking on it with your mouse. Your target Platform is DOS(Standard), and the Target Model is

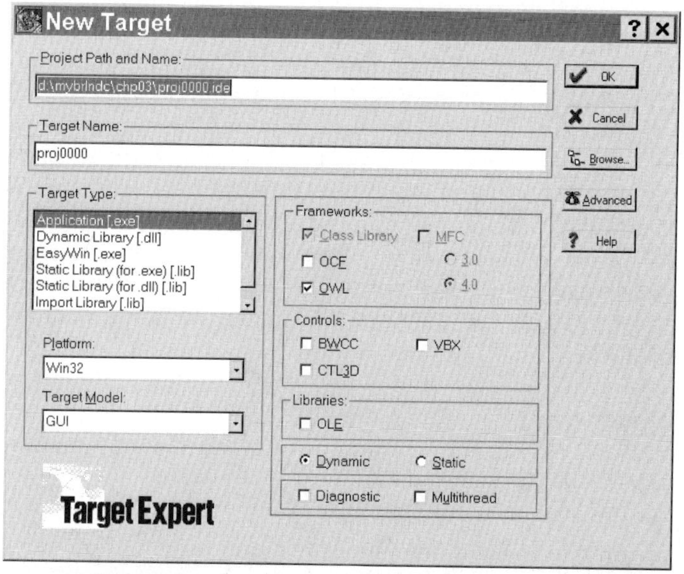

Figure 3-6.   *Starting a New Project file*

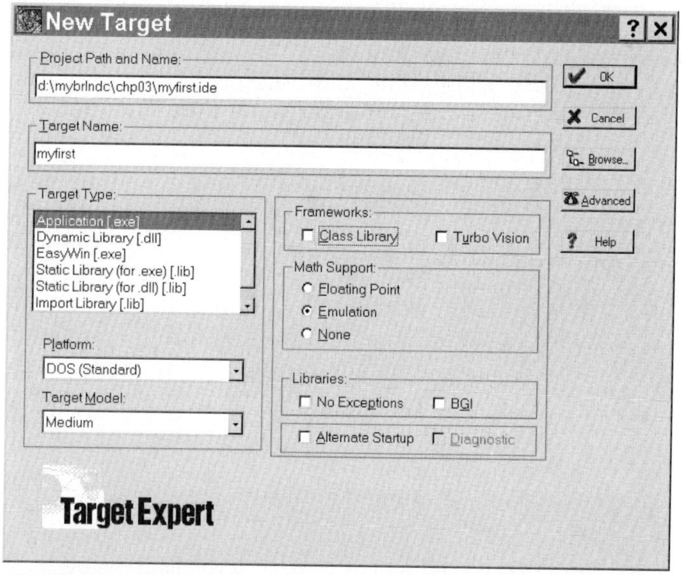

Figure 3-7.   *A completed New Target dialog window*

Medium. The last step you need to perform before clicking on OK is to go over to the Frameworks section of the New Target dialog window and click off the Class Library option. (Notice at the bottom of the dialog box the BGI Libraries option. Remember it, because this option allows you to use Borland's advanced graphics functions.) Before going any further, make certain that your New Target dialog box matches Figure 3-7.

Once you have clicked on the OK button, the IDE will automatically open up the Project Window, shown in the bottom of Figure 3-8. Unfortunately, there is a default installation problem. The IDE assumes you are using a *.CPP or C++ source file. Many of the initial example programs in the text start off with the C language. Under these circumstances, you will need to delete this file. Simply click your mouse on the file, myfirst[.cpp], and press the DELETE key. You should see a screen similar to the one shown in Figure 3-8. Click on the Yes button.

At this point, you are ready to add the appropriate file to the Project window. Simply press the INSERT key (make certain the Project window is active by clicking inside its window border). Figure 3-9 shows the resulting dialog box. Choose the file sample.c by double-clicking on it, then click on the OK button.

The Project file description is now complete. Your Project file window should look similar to the one shown in Figure 3-10.

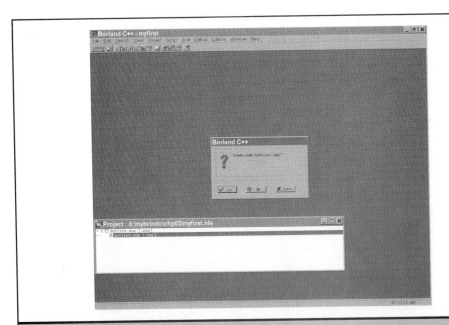

Figure 3-8. *Deleting the default C++ source file*

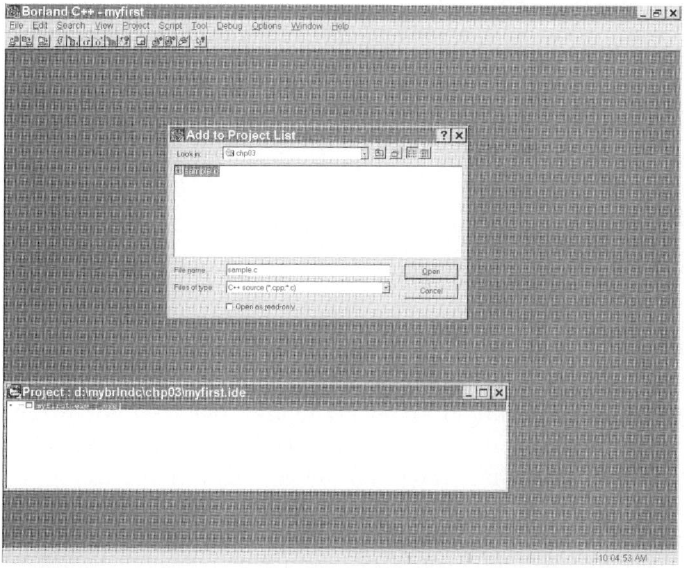

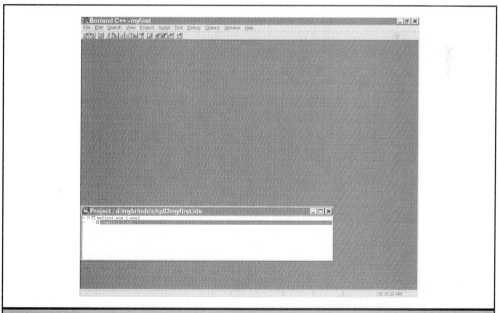

Figure 3-9.   *Adding sample.c to the Project file*

Figure 3-10.   *The completed Project file description*

Building the Project

Once you have defined a Project file, you need to instruct the IDE to go ahead and build all dependent relationships—for example, invoke the C compiler for related C source files, C++ compiler for its dependent C++ code, bring in the Assembler for *.ASM source files, and so on. You do this by choosing the Project | Build all option. Our example Project only has one source file, sample.c, so the Build all process only invokes the C compiler. To test the program you use the same procedure described previously in the "Running a Program" section of this chapter.

In the Next Chapter...

This chapter was designed to allow you to rehearse the simple steps necessary to enter, edit, save, compile or Build an application, and then to run it. In Chapter 4, you will learn how to use the Borland C/C++ IDE debug capabilities such as variable watches, inspections, breakpoints, and single-step execution modes.

Chapter Four

Debugging Programs

One of the most exciting features of the Borland C/C++ IDE is its integrated debugger. After an introduction to and experience with just a few simple command sequences, you can use the integrated debugger to shave 20 to 30 percent off the time it will take to debug an application. In Chapter 3, you learned how to use your Borland C/C++ compilers to enter, edit, save, and compile simple DOS-mode applications. This chapter shows you how to use the IDE's integrated debugging utilities to quickly detect, diagnose, and fix a program's syntax and logic errors. Mastering the basic concepts discussed in this chapter will have a tremendous payback in time saved in the long run. To begin using your Borland C/C++ compiler's IDE, enter the following C program, exactly as you see it.

NOTE: *If you already know a little C, you may detect errors in the source code. These errors were put there specifically to demonstrate the use of the IDE's integrated debugger, so please do not fix them.*

```
/**************************************************************
   fixme.c
   This C program is designed to give you hands-on experience
   with your compiler's debugger. If you enter the program
   exactly as you see it, it will not compile and run. Only
   after you follow the step-by-step instructions included
   within the text can you correct all of the syntax and
   logical mistakes necessary to execute the program.
   Copyright © Chris H. Pappas and William H. Murray, 1996
 **************************************************************/

#define MAX_ARRAY_ELEMENTS 4

void ShowArrayContents( int array_of_ints[ MAX_ARRAY_ELEMENTS ] ) ;

void main ( void )
{
  int   continue = 0, displacement                            ;
  float array_of_ints[ MAX_ARRAY_ELEMENTS ]                   ;

  Printf( "Welcome To: Learning How To Debug Programs"
);

  printf( \n\nReady To Begin? "                               );
  scanf ( "%d",continue                                       );

  if( continue = 1 )                                         {
```

```
    printf( "\nDefault \"array_of_ints\" contents: "
);
    ShowArrayContents( array_of_ints )                              ;
    for( displacement = 0; displacement < MAX_ARRAY_ELEMENTS;
                                        displacement++        ){
      printf( "Enter a single value for element[%2d] - "         ,
              displacement                                       );
      scanf ( "%d", array_of_ints[ displacement ]               );
    }
    printf( "\nUser-Defined \"array_of_ints\" contents: "        );
    ShowArrayContents( array_of_ints )                              ;
    printf( "\n\nCongratulations on a job well done!"            );
  }
  else
    printf( "Program Execution Over"                             );
}

void ShowArrayContents( int array_of_ints[ MAX_ARRAY_ELEMENTS ]    )
{
  int    displacement                                               ;

  printf( "\"array_of_ints\" contents: "                          );
  for    ( displacement = 0; displacement < MAX_ARRAY_ELEMENTS    ,
                          displacement++                          )
    printf( " %f -",array_of_ints[ displacement ]                );
  printf( "\n\n"                                                  );
}
```

Once you have entered the example program, fixme.c, make certain you have saved the program. (If choosing to use the Project utility discussed in Chapter 3, then also make certain that you have created the required project file and inserted the sample code.) At this point you are ready to perform a Project Compile.

Figure 4-1 shows a sample Message window and the program's first diagnosed error. Part of learning a new language involves the interaction between you and the compiler. You need to recognize which types of flagged error messages are right on the money or pretty close to being right, and which are totally off the wall. However, an experienced C/C++ programmer can glean some additional information about why a program is not compiling from all three categories! The good news is that more of the C/C++ compiler's diagnostic messages are right on the money than any diagnostic messages output by compilers in the past.

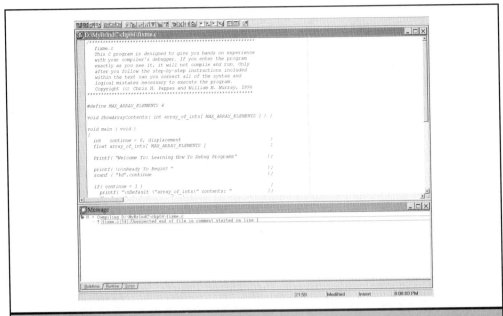

Figure 4-1. *Accurately diagnosed incorrectly terminated comment block message*

Surprises When Using New Languages

Figure 4-1 shows a correctly diagnosed problem: the comment block is not terminated with the required */ symbol pair. Using the editor, go back into fixme.c and close the comment block by adding */ at the end of the comment. Save the file, and execute another Compile. Figure 4-2 shows the new list of error diagnostics. Notice that the cursor is flashing after the identifier *continue*.

Even if you are *very* experienced programming in a language other than C/C++, you may discover a few coding problems in C/C++ not previously entered into your debugging bag of tricks. Case in point: the variable *continue*. The sample program specifically chose to use this identifier's name to hold the user's response to the question, "Ready To Begin?" The choice of the receiving variable's name, *continue*, then makes for readable, self-documenting source code. However, there is only one problem: in C/C++ *continue* is a reserved word: **continue**. Obviously, care needs to be taken when learning, using, or even translating an old algorithm from some other language into C/C++! As far as the error diagnostic message is concerned, in this case, although the message correctly flags the line of source code containing the problem, it does not correctly detail the error.

Notice however, that all of the *continue*'s are in **bold**. The IDE automatically **boldfaces** all C/C++ reserved or keywords. The better clue to this line of source code having a problem then, is the fact that the name of the integer variable *continue*, is

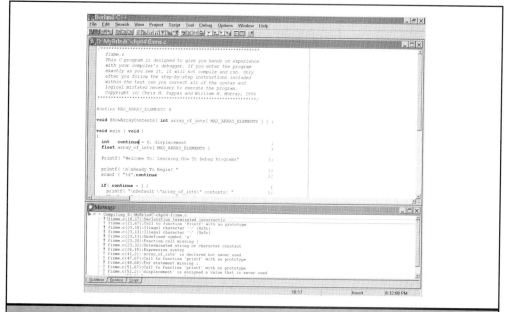

Figure 4-2.   *Vague error diagnostic of* continue*'s data declaration*

boldfaced, indicating the IDE's assumption you want the keyword **continue**, clearly not the case.

At this point you need to go through the source code and change every use of the variable *continue* to *continu* (minus the e). (Note: you could also change *continue* to *CONTINUE*. Because C and C++ are case sensitive, there is now no complaint from the compiler since *CONTINUE* has nothing to do with **continue**.) At this point save the program with your preferred changes and execute another Compile.

Learning a New Language Through Compiler Diagnostic Messages

So far you have looked at two error message diagnostics, one very accurate, the second slightly vague. Throughout the remaining discussion, pay attention to which error messages are correct, indiscriminate, or even completely wrong. Start building a knowledgeable interpretation of error diagnostics so that in the future you will not waste time trying to fix an incorrectly diagnosed or flagged problem. After performing the previous build, you should now have an error massage window that looks similar to the one shown in Figure 4-3.

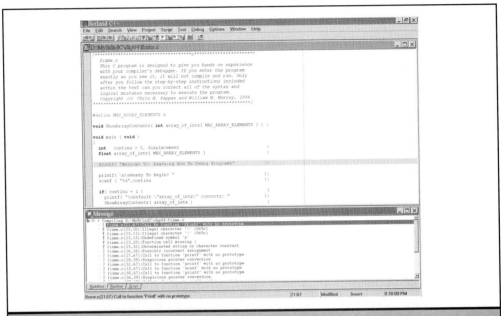

Figure 4-3.   *Printf() function correctly flagged but with one hidden cause!*

The error message flags the use of the function *Printf()*. Because C and C++ are case sensitive and stdio.h prototypes the function as **printf()**, the error message is correct: *Printf()* (a potentially defined user function) is not **printf()**. Using your editor, change *Printf()* in the source code, to the correct **printf()** casing. Save the program and execute another Compile. All fixed? Take a close look at Figure 4-4.

Now what's wrong? You have the same message except this second message has '*printf*' in single quotes, unlike the last message which had '*Printf*' single-quoted. You need to constantly remind yourself as to the cause of this second message: we did not **#include** the required header file necessary to make the declaration of **printf()** legal.

The first '*Printf*' error message said that there was no prototype for a possible user-defined function called *Printf()*. This second error message, a bit more confusing because it is now cased properly, says the same thing, *no prototype for 'printf'*. Because stdio.h provides this description, you need to edit the source program by going in under the comment block and inserting this line:

```
#include <stdio.h>
```

However, because this is a chapter dedicated to helping you learn about the compiler, including debugging and error diagnostics, remember the lesson: you must

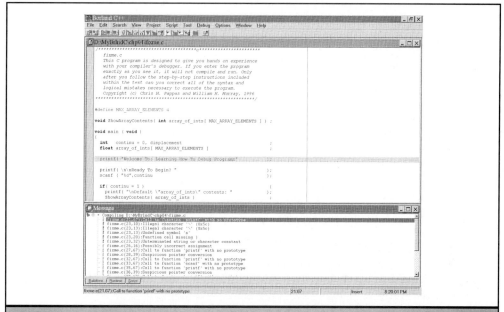

Figure 4-4. *The same line of code flagged again. Now what's wrong with printf()?*

always **#include** the proper header file when using a C/C++ compiler-supplied library function. This will include, in future chapters, header files such as math.h, stdlib.h, string.h, ctype.h, limits.h, and iostream.h. After **#include**(ing) the above statement, save the program and execute another Compile. Figure 4-5 shows the resulting diagnostics.

The error message says that the character \ is illegal. It isn't. The real problem is that the **printf()** statement isn't started properly. The following code sniglet details the incorrect and corrected solutions. This line:

```
printf( \n
```

should have been written this way:

```
printf( "\n
```

So, although the error message does target the correct line of code, the message is fairly useless to a novice C/C++ programmer. Make the necessary source code change, save the file, and execute a Build. Figure 4-6 contains the new message flagging the statement as a "possible assignment."

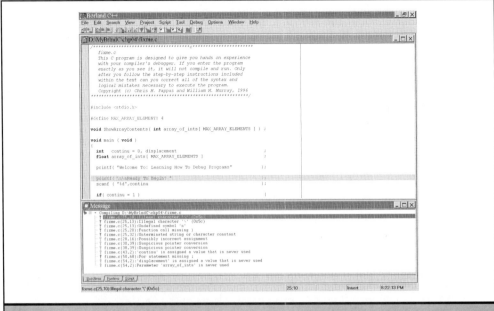

Figure 4-5. *An incorrect diagnostic noting \ as an illegal character*

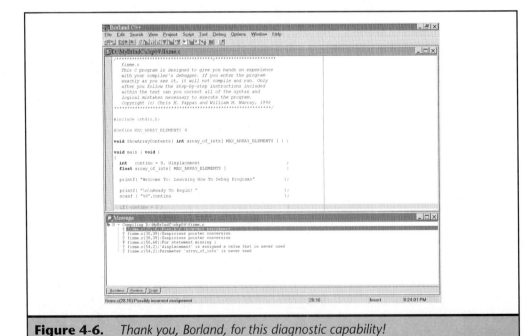

Figure 4-6. *Thank you, Borland, for this diagnostic capability!*

The message "Possibly incorrect assignment..." flagging the **if** statement will be one of your best assistants for avoiding a potentially devastating syntax and logical error. See if you can figure this error out on your own by looking at the following two statements:

```
if( continu = 1 )
```

versus

```
if( continu == 1 )
```

Did you catch it? The first **if** condition contains an *assignment statement* while the second **if** example contains a *logical comparison*! Now, some C/C++ compilers will not flag this mistake. The result is that you have a program that compiles and runs. However, it will run inconsistently depending on the logic following an **if** statement always evaluating to TRUE (which, to the C/C++ compilers, is any value not equal to zero), because the compiler sees this:

```
if( continu = 1 )
```

as this:

```
if( 1 )
```

which is *always* TRUE! Change the incorrect **if** condition so that it has the required double-equal symbol pair known as the logical equals operator, **==**.

*NOTE: The rather awkward selection of a value of 1 for a user response, instead of a more logical Y for yes, was chosen specifically to highlight how an incorrectly written **if** condition is viewed by the compilers.*

Save the program and execute a Compile. Figure 4-7 shows the updated message window.

The problem diagnosed by the compiler deals with the discrepancy between the function's formal argument description, which declares *array_of_ints* to be of type **int**, while the actual function call sends an array declared to be of type **float**. To fix this error, redefine the array (under **main()**) to be of type **int**, instead of type **float**. Save the change and execute another Compile.

Once again, the compiler has correctly diagnosed and flagged the appropriate line of offending code. The first two **for** loop statements should be terminated with a

Figure 4-7. *A correctly diagnosed incorrect variable declaration type*

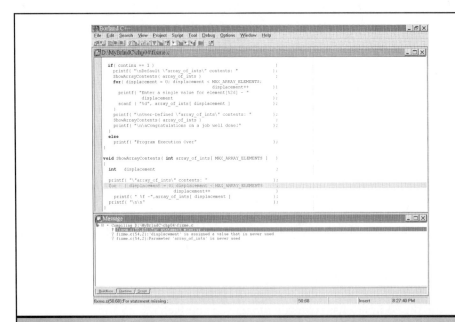

Figure 4-8. *A correctly diagnosed missing for statement semicolon*

semicolon. However, only the first statement has the semicolon; the second statement incorrectly terminates with a comma. You need to change this line:

```
displacement < MAX_ARRAY_ELEMENTS            ,
```

to this:

```
displacement < MAX_ARRAY_ELEMENTS            ;
```

Save the change and this time perform a Project | Build. Figure 4-9 shows the resulting message window.

You now have a program that's ready to run. But is it error free? The compiler has only given the algorithm an OK as far as syntax is concerned. Remember, C and C++, unlike any other previous language you may have used, can compile syntactically OK code that yields run-time chaos!

This language design capability also allows you to write code that is more difficult to debug than many other languages. However, don't let this news discourage you. Between the information presented in this text, the example programs, and the

Figure 4-9.   *Status: Success*

hands-on rehearsals provided, you will more than be able to "rise to the occasion!" So, at this point you are ready to execute the program.

Because this sample algorithm is a DOS-mode application, choose the Tool menu, followed by the Turbo Debugger option. This will switch your screen over to DOS emulation mode and get you ready to run/debug the program. Figure 4-10 shows the resulting Turbo Debugger screen.

To run the program, choose the Run menu (ALT-R), followed by the Run command ®, or use the alternative approach: the hot key F9. (Still have your highlighter out? Why not highlight the approach you like best!) Of course, you could use the mouse to click on Run, then the Run submenu command.

When you run the program, type **1** in response to the screen prompt "Ready To Begin?" then press ENTER. Your screen initially looks like Figure 4-11 until you press ENTER. After pressing the ENTER key, you will see a window similar to Figure 4-12.

What you see is pretty useless isn't it? All you are left looking at is the source code.

This initially confusing screen output was generated by a syntax problem on the **scanf()** statement attempting to input the 1 you just entered. The function **scanf()** was written to expect the address of the memory location to fill. This is accomplished by

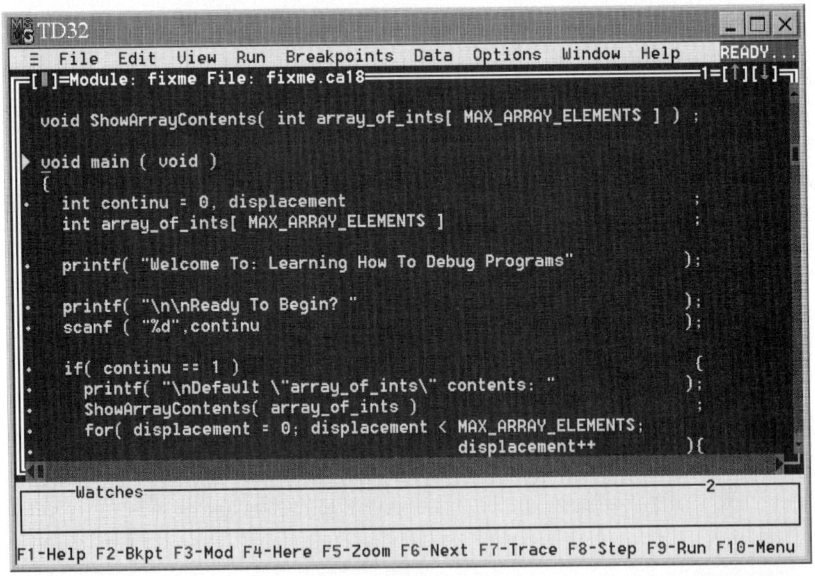

Figure 4-10.   *The initial Turbo Debugger screen displaying fixme.c*

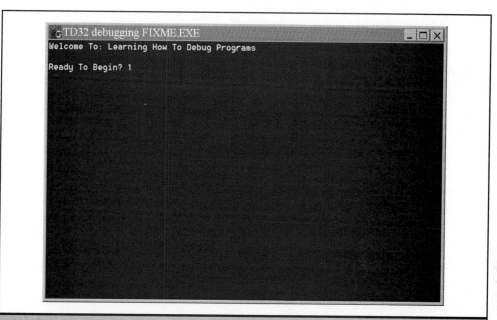

Figure 4-11.   *Running fixme.exe*

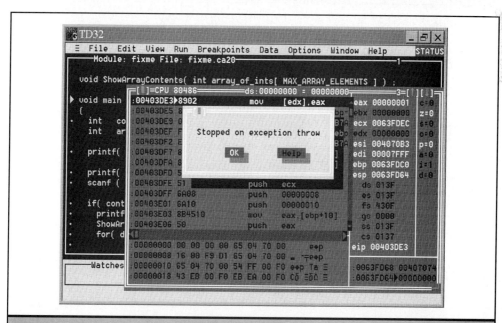

Figure 4-12.   *A confusing Turbo Debugger error message window*

placing the C/C++ address operator, **&,** in front of the variable being used. fixme.c's **scanf()** statement looks like this:

```
scanf ( "%d", continu
```

However, to work properly it needs to be corrected to include the address operator:

```
scanf (   "%d", &continu
```

Because the Turbo Debugger has no text-editing capabilities, you now need to quit the Turbo Debugger by choosing the File | Quit option. Next, use the IDE to fix the **scanf()** statement so that it looks like the corrected version above. Save the file and execute a Build. Now restart the Turbo Debugger by going to the Tools menu and type **1** followed by the ENTER key. You will now see a screen similar to Figure 4-13.

When you are trying to debug an application, running the program at full speed can still leave you confused, as in this last step. A better approach is to execute the algorithm step by step. To do this, the Borland C/C++ debuggers have two single-step modes: trace into, with a hot key of F7, or step over, with its hot key of F8. Both execute

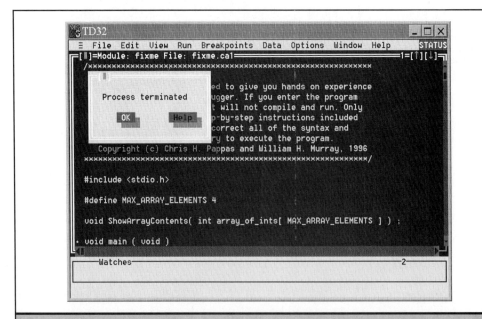

Figure 4-13. *Problems when running the Turbo Debugger at full speed*

your program one line at a time. The difference between trace into and step over only comes into play when the source code statement you are about to execute is a function call. Trace into follows your debugging single-step mode, *into* the function called, while step over, *steps over* the called function's body, with single-step execution continuing with whichever statement followed the function call.

Tracking Down Logical Errors with the Integrated Debugger

One could easily write an entire book on just how to use all of the features of Borland's integrated debuggers. Fortunately for you and I, under most circumstances we will need to only understand and use two of them. Basically, this is what we want to do: execute your program slowly, not at full speed, and look at the contents of your variables. Between these two steps you will be amazed at just how quickly you can locate *the* line of offending code. All of the other integrated debugger options discussed below are variations on these two themes.

Setting Watches

One of the most powerful punches provided by the integrated debugger is its ability to display any of your program variables' contents. You do this with what is called a watch. To place any of your program's variables into the Watch window you follow these steps:

1. Place the cursor on *any* use of the target variable: either its declaration or any use of it.
2. Press CTRL-F7.
3. Press the ENTER key.
4. Repeat from the first step as needed.

It's just that easy. Now, using these three steps, place the variable *continu* (or *CONTINUE* if you chose to change **continue** to *CONTINUE*) into the watches window as seen in Figure 4-14.

> *NOTE: If you have been following the example session, at this point you need to click on the OK button as shown in Figure 4-13.*

However, simply placing a variable into the Watches window would still be fairly useless if your program executed at full speed. No human is capable of watching the variables' contents change at today's processor speeds. What is needed is a way to slow down execution to single steps that humans can recognize.

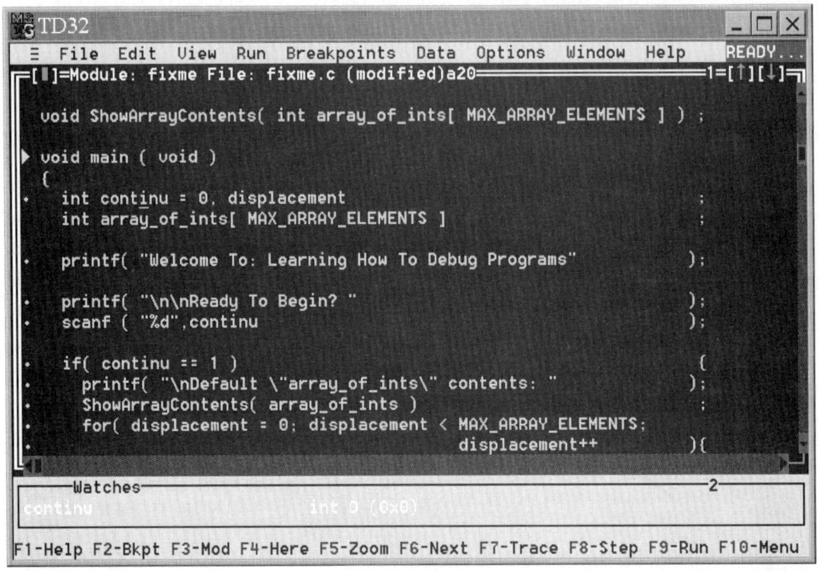

```
╔═╗TD32                                                    _ □ ×
╠═╣
 ≡  File  Edit  View  Run  Breakpoints  Data  Options  Window  Help   READY...
┌[■]=Module: fixme File: fixme.c (modified)a20═════════════════1=[↑][↓]┐

  void ShowArrayContents( int array_of_ints[ MAX_ARRAY_ELEMENTS ] ) ;

▶ void main ( void )
  {
 •  int continu = 0, displacement                          ;
    int array_of_ints[ MAX_ARRAY_ELEMENTS ]               ;

 •  printf( "Welcome To: Learning How To Debug Programs"        );

 •  printf( "\n\nReady To Begin? "                              );
 •  scanf ( "%d",continu                                        );

 •  if( continu == 1 )                                          {
 •    printf( "\nDefault \"array_of_ints\" contents: "          );
 •    ShowArrayContents( array_of_ints )                        ;
 •    for( displacement = 0; displacement < MAX_ARRAY_ELEMENTS;
                                          displacement++        ){
┌──Watches──────────────────────────────────────────────2──
│continu                        int 0 (0x0)
├────────────────────────────────────────────────────────────
F1-Help F2-Bkpt F3-Mod F4-Here F5-Zoom F6-Next F7-Trace F8-Step F9-Run F10-Menu
```

Figure 4-14.   *The variable* continu *placed into the Watches window*

Executing a Program Line by Line

The integrated debugger makes executing your program line by line very simple: you either press or click on F7 or F8. Both commands, listed at the bottom of your integrated debugger window, will execute your program one line at a time. The first time you activate either option, you will notice an arrow symbol, SYMBOL 216 \f "Wingdings" \s 12 appear to the left of **main()** in the source code. This *trace arrow* shows you which code statement will be executed *the next time* you select F7 or F8. (This is an important point—not this time, but the next time you select F7 or F8.) The only difference between F7, known as a trace into, and F8, known as step over, is what happens when you are about to execute a function call.

If the trace arrow is on a function call and you select F7, the integrated debugger will trace into the called function line by line, assuming you want to debug the called function. However, if the trace arrow is on a function call and you activate F8, the integrated debugger will assume you already know the about-to-be-called function is OK and that you do not need to waste your time debugging it. In this case the integrated debugger will execute the called function at full speed and stop execution at the line of code below the function call statement. Proper selection of either the trace into or step over options can make for very efficient debugging cycles. (What do you mean, you put the cap back on your highlighter?)

Setting Breakpoints

There will certainly be times when even continual selection of step over (F8) would be too time-consuming—for example, when you are incorporating hundreds of lines of previously written and debugged code into a new algorithm. Under these circumstances, to quickly skip over this known good code, you need to use a breakpoint.

A *breakpoint* is like a stop sign. The integrated debugger executes a program at full speed until it sees one of these breakpoints, at which point it stops and goes into single-step mode, awaiting an F7 or F8. Your program can have as many breakpoints as needed. To set a breakpoint follow these steps:

1. Place the cursor on the line of source code needing the breakpoint.

2. Press F2, or choose the Breakpoints, Toggle menu/submenu commands.

Yet another simple sequence. Repeat steps 1 and 2 above for fixme.c by placing a breakpoint on this statement:

```
scanf("%d", &continu);   /* or CONTINU if you chose this substitution option */
```

You can easily tell if your source code contains a breakpoint because the integrated debugger environment highlights these lines in red. At this point you are ready to run fixme.c full-speed up to, but not past, this statement.

Running to a Breakpoint

Running a program at full speed up to the first breakpoint, or any subsequent breakpoints, is just as easy as running a program straight through. You use the Run, Run menu/submenu options, or press F9. (Good, your highlighter is still in your hand!) Now before you try this, concentrate on the Watch window's display of *continu*'s contents, which should be garbage at this point. Whichever method you prefer, run the program. Notice that execution stops on the red breakpointed line. Now press F7 to execute the **scanf()** statement step by step.

When you get to the "Ready To Begin?" prompt again, type **1** and press ENTER. Because the **scanf()** statement is supposed to place the '1' into the variable *continu*, you can see from the Watch window's contents that the **scanf()** statement works.

At this point if you were to execute a trace into (F7) or step over (F8), the Turbo Debugger would flash you to the program output window and then instantly back to the Turbo Debugger screen shown in Figure 4-15. A program's Turbo Debugger output

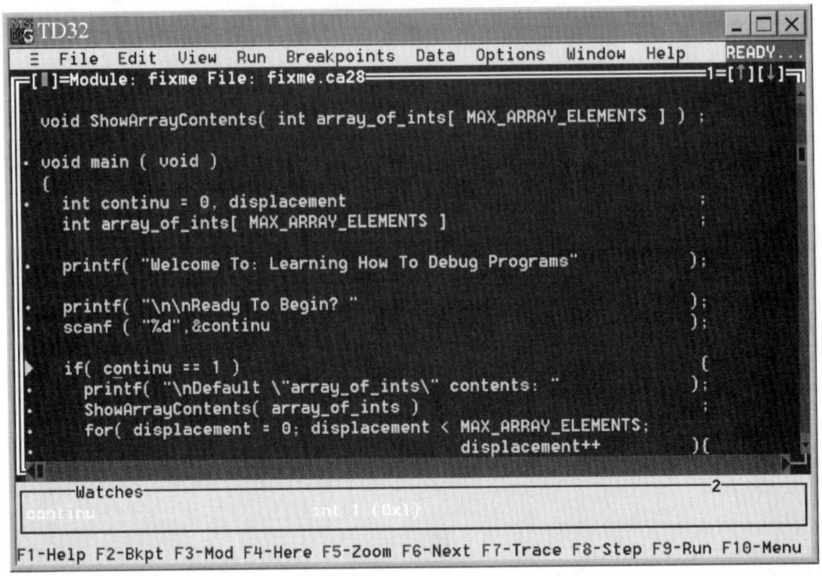

Figure 4-15. *Viewing the corrected scanf() statement's effect on the variable* continu

resides on the User Screen. Switch to the User Screen now by either pressing ALT-F5 or using the Window, User Screen, menu/submenu sequence. (Where's that highlighter?)

Try pressing F7 or F8 several times until you see a Program Termination message and then practice switching to the User screen. You will see a window similar to the one shown in Figure 4-16.

This run-time detected problem involves an incorrect **printf()** output format specification within the **ShowArrayContents()** function body. The following statement,

```
printf( " %f -",array_of_ints[ displacement ]
```

is attempting to output an integer array element with a float, **%f**, specification. Once again, you need to quit the Turbo Debugger and edit this statement so that it looks like this:

```
printf( " %d -",array_of_ints[ displacement ]
```

Remember to save the file, execute a Build, and run the Turbo Debugger from the IDE's Tools menu. Practice executing the program line by line by pressing F7 or F8 until you see the message window shown in Figure 4-17.

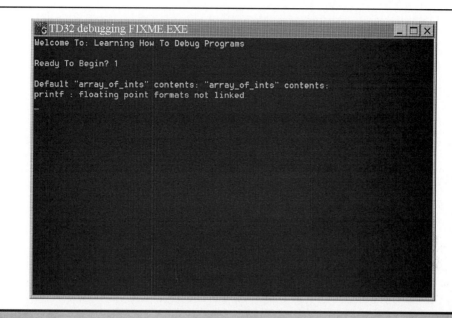

Figure 4-16.   *A "floating point formats not linked" error message*

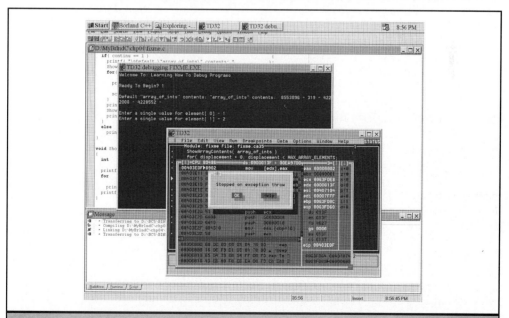

Figure 4-17.   *"Stopped on exception throw" error message*

The first integer value is correctly inserted into the array. However, after entering a second value and pressing the ENTER key, you see the error message displayed in Figure 4-17. Why? Once again, the Turbo Debugger has picked up a run-time error. This is the offending statement:

```
scanf ( "%d", array_of_ints[ displacement ]                    );
```

Once again, it is a **scanf()** function call. The problem is, again, the missing address operator. Remember, **scanf()** wants the address of the memory location in which to place the input data. Quit the Turbo Debugger, re-edit, save, and Build the application with the corrected statement, given here:

```
scanf ( "%d", &array_of_ints[ displacement ]                    );
```

This time when you run the Turbo Debugger with an F7 (trace into), F8 (step over), or F9 (full-speed execution), you will have a successful run!

Program Resets

There may be occasions in your debugging cycle when you will flash past a program statement too fast—either using F7 (trace into), F8 (step over), or F2 or F9 (set/run to a breakpoint). In these circumstances you will want to do an integrated debugger reset. This tells the integrated debugger that you still want to debug the program, but back from the beginning. Do this by pressing CTRL-F2 or selecting Run, Program reset menu/submenu commands.

Practice with Trace Into and Step Over

Now that you are more comfortable with using the Turbo Debugger, you should practice the two single-step options of trace into (F7) and step over (F8). Assuming you are still running the Turbo Debugger, execute a program reset as described in the previous section (try the CTRL-F2 keyboard approach). Continue pressing F7 to execute a trace into until the trace arrow is on the **ShowArrayContents()** function call:

```
ShowArrayContents( array_of_ints )                    ;
```

Now press F7 once more until you begin single-stepping the code inside the **ShowArrayContents()** function. Notice how trace into single-steps *into* the function. Now stop and perform a program reset (hint: CTRL-F2). This time continue pressing F8 (step over) until the trace arrow is once again on the call to the function **ShowArrayContents()**. Now press F8 (step over) once. Did you see the difference? Step over (F8) executed function **ShowArrayContents()** at full speed and then stopped on the **for** statement *below the function call*:

```
for( displacement = 0; displacement < MAX_ARRAY_ELEMENTS;
                                    displacement++          ){
```

To be efficient, you should always choose to step over any function that you positively know (probably from its use in previous programs) is error free.

CAUTION: Under the wrong circumstances, executing a program reset (CTRL-F2) can get you into serious trouble. The potentially devastating scenario involves a debugging phase where you have used F7, F8, or F2 (to set breakpoint) and F9 (to run to the breakpoint) past a statement that opens an external file. Should you at this point choose a Program reset, you can potentially lose the data file. If you know that your debugging cycle might involve this type of abortive execution, you will either need to move the file close statement or create an additional file close statement that you can single-step-over before performing the Program reset.

A Quick Review

In this chapter, you have learned several useful Turbo Debugger features. To review, you now know that you can execute your program, line by line, by simply pressing F7 or F8. Watching a variable's contents is as simple as putting the variable in a Watch window (by pressing CTRL-F7 with the cursor on the variable in question, then pressing the ENTER key). You learned that you can set a breakpoint by simply putting the cursor on the line in question and pressing F2. Finally, you saw how to run your program to a breakpoint by pressing F9. Table 4-1 reviews these function keys.

Function Key	Use
F2	Toggles a breakpoint on whichever line the cursor is flashing
CTRL-F2	Executes a program reset
F7	Executes your program step by step, including a trace into functions
CTRL-F7	Begins entering a variable into the Watch window; requires cursor to be on the variable in question
F8	Executes your program step by step, not with trace into but instead by stepping over the called function's code
F9	Runs a program full speed, or up to the next breakpoint if any exist

Table 4-1. *A Review of Basic Turbo Debugger Function Keys*

In the Next Chapter...

Now that you are more familiar with the tools provided by the Borland C/C++ IDE, you are ready to dive into the C/C++ languages themselves. Because a large portion of C syntax, logic, controls, and design, are so similar to C++, the following chapters concentrate on simpler C examples and explanations. For example, how you declare variables, what types of logic control statements are available (**if, if...else, for, while, do while**), how you declare and use arrays, and finally functions, are identical in C and C++.

PART TWO

C and C++ Programming Foundations

Chapter Five

Fundamentals of C and C++ Programming

Chapters 1 through 4 introduced you to those features of the Borland C++ compiler necessary to enter, edit, compile, and debug simple C and C++ programs. Beginning with this chapter, you will explore the origins, syntax, and usage of the C and C++ language. A study of C's history is worthwhile because it reveals the language's successful design philosophy and helps you understand why C and C++ will be the language of choice for years to come.

C's Evolution

The C language has a very interesting history that actually goes way back to a European language known as Algol 60, through to the codevelopment phase of C itself along with the UNIX operating system. Table 5-1 shows a comprehensive tracing of C's lineage.

Algol 60 was a language that appeared only a few years after FORTRAN was introduced. This new language was more sophisticated and had a strong influence on the design of future programming languages. Its authors paid a great deal of attention to the regularity of syntax, modular structure, and other features usually associated with high-level structured languages. Unfortunately, Algol 60 never really caught on in the United States. Many say this was due to the language's abstractness.

The inventors of CPL (Combined Programming Language) intended to bring Algol 60's lofty intent down to the realities of an actual computer. However, CPL proved just as difficult to learn and to implement as Algol 60; this led to its eventual downfall. The creators of BCPL (Basic Combined Programming Language) tried to boil CPL down to its basic good features.

When Ken Thompson designed the B language for an early implementation of UNIX, he was trying to further simplify CPL. He succeeded in creating a very sparse

Language	Developed By
Algol 60	An international committee in early 1960
CPL (Combined Programming Language)	Both Cambridge and the University of London in 1963
BCPL (Basic Combined Programming Language)	Martin Richards at Cambridge in 1967
B	Ken Thompson at Bell Labs in 1970
C	Dennis Ritchie at Bell Labs in 1972

Table 5-1. *C's Lineage*

language that was well suited for use on the hardware available to him. However, both BCPL and B may have become too streamlined—each became a limited language, useful only for dealing with certain kinds of problems.

For example, no sooner had Ken Thompson implemented the B language than a new machine, called the PDP-11, was introduced. UNIX and the B compiler were immediately transferred to this new machine. Although the PDP-11 was a larger machine than its PDP-7 predecessor, it was still quite small by today's standards. It had only 24K of memory, of which the system used 16K and one 512K fixed disk. Some thought was given to rewriting UNIX in B, but the B language was slow because of its interpretive design. There was another problem as well: B was byte-oriented, but the PDP-11 was word-oriented. For these reasons, work was begun in 1971 on a successor to B, appropriately named C.

Dennis Ritchie is credited with creating C, a language that restored some of the generality lost in BCPL and B. He accomplished this through a shrewd use of data types, while maintaining the simplicity and direct access to the hardware that were the original goal designs of CPL. Our journey through C's history continues with a discussion of the UNIX operating system, since both the system and most of the programs that run on it are written in C. However, this does not mean that C is tied to UNIX or any other operating system or machine.

C and UNIX

The UNIX/C codevelopment environment has given C a reputation for being a *system programming language* because it is useful for writing compilers and operating systems. C is also very useful for writing major programs in many different domains. UNIX was originally developed in 1969 on what would now be considered a small DEC PDP-7 at Bell Laboratories in Murray Hill, New Jersey. UNIX was written entirely in PDP-7 assembly language. By design, this operating system was intended to be "programmer friendly," providing useful development tools, lean commands, and a relatively open environment.

Many languages developed by a single individual (C, Pascal, Lisp, and APL) contain a cohesiveness that is missing from languages developed by large programming teams (Ada, PL/I, and Algol 68). It is also typical for a language written by one person to reflect the author's field of expertise. Dennis Ritchie was noted for his work in systems software—computer languages, operating systems, and program generators. Given Ritchie's areas of expertise, it is easy to understand why C is a language of choice for systems software design. C is a relatively low-level language that allows you to specify every detail in an algorithm's logic to achieve maximum computer efficiency. But C is also a high-level language that can hide the details of the computer's architecture, thereby increasing programming efficiency.

In 1983, the ANSI (American National Standards Institute) committee was formed for the purpose of creating ANSI C—a standardization of the C language. The C language continues to evolve with the ANSI C committee guaranteeing that the syntax and usage for each new feature be compatible across ANSI C compliant compilers. For example, the original C language did not contain exception handling. (This is a compiler's ability to generate error recovery code for conditions that would normally crash an application.) As C continues to evolve it adopts new and useful features such as exception handling.

C and Other Languages

Figure 5-1 displays C's relationship to other languages. If you start at the bottom of the continuum and move upward, you go from the tangible and empirical to the elusive and theoretical. The dots represent major advancements, with many steps left out:

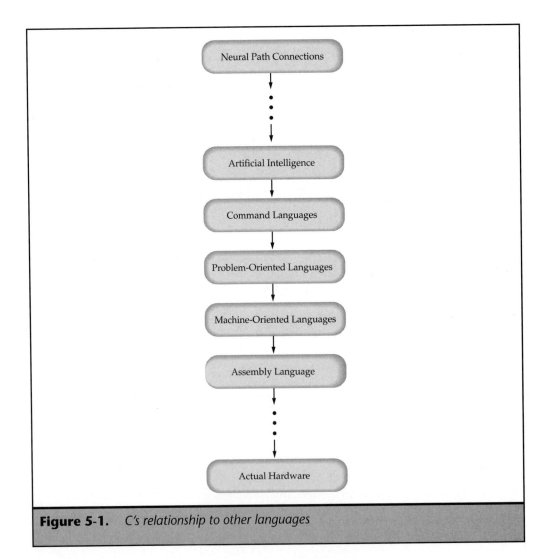

Figure 5-1.   *C's relationship to other languages*

Early ancestors of the computer, like the Jacquard loom (1805) and Charles Babbage's "analytical engine" (1834), were programmed in hardware. The day may well come when we will program a machine by plugging a neural path communicator into a socket implanted into the temporal lobe (language memory) or Broca's area (language motor area) of the brain's cortex.

In the earliest of days, electronic computers were programmed in assembly language. This first language works directly with a computer's built-in instruction set, and is fairly easy to learn. However, because assembly languages force you to think in terms of hardware, you have to specify every operation in the machine's terms. Therefore, you are always moving bits into or out of registers, adding them, shifting register contents from one register to another, and finally storing the results in memory. This is tedious and an error-prone endeavor. In contrast, the first high-level languages, such as FORTRAN, were created as alternatives to assembly languages.

High-level languages are much more general and abstract and allow you to think in terms of the problem at hand, rather than in terms of the computer's hardware. Unfortunately, the creators of high-level languages made the fallacious assumption that everyone who had been driving a standard, so to speak, would prefer driving an automatic. Excited about providing ease in programming, they left out some necessary options. FORTRAN and Algol are too abstract for systems-level work; they are *problem-oriented languages,* the kind used for solving problems in engineering, science, or business. Programmers who wanted to write systems software still had to rely on their machine's assembler. In reaction to this situation, a few systems software developers took a step backward—or lower, in terms of the continuum—and created the category of *machine-oriented languages.*

As you saw in C's genealogy, BCPL and B fit into this class of very low-level software tools. These languages were excellent for a specific machine but not much use for anything else; they were too closely related to a particular architecture. The C language is one step above machine-oriented languages but is still a step below most problem-solving languages. C is close enough to the computer to give you great control over the details of an application's implementation, yet far enough away to ignore the details of the hardware. This is why the C language is considered at once a high- and a low-level language.

Advantages of C

Computer languages, just like their human language counterparts, have a particular look and set of grammatical rules. APL has its hieroglyphic appearance, assembly language its columns of mnemonics, and Pascal its easily read syntax. And then there's C. Many programmers encountering C for the first time will find its syntax cryptic and perhaps intimidating.

C contains very few of the friendly English-like syntax structures found in many other programming languages. Instead, C presents the software engineer with unusual-looking operators and a plethora of pointers. New C programmers will soon discover a variety of language characteristics whose roots go back to C's original hardware/software progenitor. The following section lists several of C's major advantages.

Access to Pointer Variables

Any language considered for operating system and advanced application development must have the ability to address specific areas of memory. Used correctly this feature generates the most efficient algorithms. The C language meets these design requirements by using pointers. Although it is true that other languages implement pointers, C is noted for its ability to perform pointer arithmetic. For example, if the variable *offset* points to the first element of an array *DailyTemperature*, then *offset+1* will be the address of the second element of *DailyTemperature*.

C and Modular Programming

A typical Windows application can easily contain hundreds of included files, all necessary to create the executable. Some of these files come with the C compiler, some come with the operating system, while still others may have been written by different project teams. If C did not have a way to efficiently process this multitude of files, a simple recompile could easily take five to ten minutes, precious time that easily adds up when you do this a hundred times a day!

To address this potential bottleneck, C supports *modular programming*, which is the concept of separate compilation and linking. This allows you to recompile only the parts of a program that have been changed during development. This feature can be extremely important when you are developing large programs, or even medium-size programs on slow systems. Without support for modular programming, the amount of time required to compile a complete program can make the change, compile, test, and modify cycle prohibitively slow.

C as a Structured Language

Considering C's 1971 incubation period, which predated formal structured programming, you will be pleased to note that C contains all of the control structures you would expect of a modern day language. **For** loops, if and if-else constructs, case (switch) statements, and **while** loops are all incorporated into the language. C also provides for the compartmentalization of code and data by managing their scope. For example, C provides local variables for this purpose and calls-by-value for subroutine data privacy.

C Is Not Strongly Typed

Some languages are considered to be *strongly typed*. This means that the compiler enforces strict compatibility checks between a variable's formal data type declaration and any use of it within the program. For example, in Pascal the compiler flags any attempt to assign a character value to a variable defined as an integer. Unlike Pascal, which is a strongly typed language, C treats data types somewhat more loosely. C allows a programmer to assign a character value to a variable defined as type **int**. (Typing is explained in more detail in "Not a Strongly Typed Language," later in this chapter.) This is a carryover from the B language, which was also a loosely typed language. This looseness allows you to view data in different ways. For example, at one point in a program, the application may need to see a variable as a character and yet, for purposes of uppercasing (by subtracting 32), may want to see the same memory cell as the ASCII equivalent of the character.

Efficient Memory Use

For many of the same reasons that C programs tend to be fast, they tend to be very memory efficient. The lack of built-in functions saves programs from having to carry around support for functions that are not needed by that application. In addition, the C compiler recognizes repeated source-code segments and, instead of duplicating the translated code, simply sets a pointer to the first encoded instruction set. This can make for very disconcerting program traces as the novice C programmer watches the Integrated Debugger jump *backward* in their code, while single-stepping the program *forward*!

Function Libraries

One of the reasons C programs execute so quickly is that they never (if properly designed) carry along the excess baggage of unused functions. C programs only pull in those routines necessary to get the job done. However, to get the job done right, there are many commercial function libraries available for all C compilers. These libraries are available for graphics, file handling, database support, screen windowing, data entry, communications, and general support functions. By using these libraries, you can save a great deal of development time.

Manipulating Bits

Naturally, with C's origins so closely tied to the UNIX operating system, the language provides a rich set of bit-manipulation operators to handle this environment's need to manipulate objects at the bit level.

Portability

Long gone are the days when if you owned a PC it was an IBM PC. Today, there are hundreds of PC brands available, with the inevitability of even more unique platforms being developed as you read. In today's programming environment, for any language to be of any use, it must be portable. *Portability* is a measure of the ease of converting a program running on one computer or operating system to another computer or operating system. Programs written in C are among the most portable in the modern computer world. This is especially true in the mini- and microcomputer worlds.

Smaller Size

Another reason for C's lightening pace execution speeds is that it has fewer syntax rules than many other languages. You may be surprised to find out that you can write a top-quality C compiler that will operate in only 256K of total memory. Actually there are more operators and combinations of operators in C than there are keywords.

Speed

There are three main factors responsible for C programs executing so quickly:

- C is a small language.
- C has a small run-time system.
- The C language is close to the hardware.

For these reasons, C programs typically run at speeds close to their assembly language equivalents.

User-Defined Data Structures

C is considered a building block language, with application-specific definitions (which are nothing more than unique combinations of standard building blocks). For example, all arrays in C are one-dimensional. Multidimensional arrangements are built from combinations of these one-dimensional arrays. Arrays and structures (records) can be joined in any manner desired, creating database organizations that are limited only by the programmer's ability. This building block approach makes for efficient code generation, while providing the programmer with the flexibility to meet each application's specific needs.

Very Few Keywords

As you have already seen, the original C language, as developed by Dennis Ritchie, contained a mere 27 keywords. The ANSI C standard (discussed later in this chapter in "C and the ANSI C Standard") has added several reserved words. Borland further enhances the instruction set with even more. Few keywords means few compiler restrictions, since all of the functionality of the compiler must be written by you. However, if each programmer had to actually write the routines to perform the daily tasks, such as file I/O, performed by all programs, using C would be a programmer's nightmare. For example, C does not contain any built-in input and output capabilities, nor does it contain any arithmetic operations (beyond those of basic addition and subtraction) or string-handling functions.

Because any language missing these capabilities is of little use, C provides a rich set of library functions for input/output, arithmetic operations, and string manipulation. This agreed-upon library set is so commonly used that it can almost be seen as part of the language itself. One of the strengths of C, however, is its loose structure, which enables you to recode these functions easily.

Disadvantages of C

As you have seen from C's history, attempts to design an all-encompassing language have all failed. If this were not the case, C wouldn't exist. Typically, all-encompassing languages are too big, overbearing, hard to learn, and bring along much unneeded overhead. In today's programming environment different programming problems require different solutions, with the software engineer choosing the best language for a project. For any project, this is one of the first decisions you need to make, and it is nearly irrevocable once you start coding. The choice of a programming language can mean the difference between a project's success and failure. The following sections cover some of the weaknesses of the C language to give you a better idea of when to use and when *not* to use C for a particular application. Remember, even today, there are no perfect languages.

Not a Strongly Typed Language

You may be scratching your head at this moment. Yes, you were just told that not being strongly typed was one of C's *advantages*. So why then is this also listed as one of C's disadvantages? The fact that C is not strongly typed *is* one of its strengths, but it is also a weakness.

Technically, *typing* is a measure of how closely a language enforces the use of variable types. (For example, integer and floating-point are two different types of numbers.) In some languages it is illegal to assign one data type to another without invoking a conversion function. This protects the data from being compromised by unexpected roundoffs. As discussed earlier, C will allow an integer to be assigned to a character variable, and vice versa. What this means to you is that you are going to have to properly manage your variables.

For experienced programmers this will not be a problem. However, novice program developers may want to remind themselves that this can be the source of side effects. A *side effect* in a language is an unexpected change to a variable or other item. Because C is not a strongly typed language, it gives you great flexibility to view data different ways and, therefore, to accidentally generate code returning incorrect results.

For example, the assignment operator (=) can appear more than once in the same expression. This flexibility, which you can use to your advantage, means that expressions can be written that have no clear and definite value. To have restricted the use of the assignment and similar operators or to have eliminated all side effects and unpredictable results would have removed from C much of its power and appeal as a high-level assembly language.

Run-Time Checking

Although Borland's C++ compiler is exemplary in its advanced, nonstandard, run-time checking capabilities, a typical C compiler lacks checking in the run-time system. This can cause many mysterious and transient problems to go undetected. For example, the run-time system would not warn you if your application exceeded an array's bounds. This is one of the costs of streamlining a compiler for the sake of speed and efficiency.

Programming Discipline

When you scrutinize C's tremendous range of features, from bit manipulation to high-level formatted I/O, and its relative consistency from machine to machine, there is no mystery as to its acceptance in science, engineering, and business applications. Like any other powerful tool, however, C imposes a heavy responsibility on its users. C programmers need to acquire a discipline very quickly, adopting various rules and conventions in order to make their programs understandable both to themselves long after the programs were written and to others trying to analyze the code for the first time. In C, programming discipline is essential. The good news is that it comes almost automatically with practice.

C and the ANSI C Standard

In the beginning, there was only one C standard available. It was the book entitled *The C Programming Language* by Brian Kernighan and Dennis Ritchie (Prentice-Hall, 1988). This book was not specific on some language details, which led to a divergence among compilers. The ANSI C standard strives to remove these ambiguities. Although a few of the proposed changes could cause problems for some previously written programs, they should not affect most existing code. This section describes some of the significant changes suggested and implemented by the committee. Some of these changes are intended to increase the flexibility of the language, while others are attempts to standardize features previously left to the discretion of the compiler implementor.

NOTE: *The standard has not corrected all areas of confusion in the language. Because C interfaces efficiently with machine hardware, many programs will always require some revision when they are moved to a different environment.*

The ANSI C committee that developed the standard adopted as guidelines some phrases that collectively have been called the "spirit of C." In essence, these say: Trust the programmer. Don't prevent the programmer from doing what needs to be done. Keep the language small and simple. The ANSI C committee also contacted the international community to ensure that ANSI (American) standard C would be identical to the ISO (International Standards Organization) standard version. Because of these efforts, C is the only language that effectively deals with alternate collating sequences, enormous character sets, and multiple user cultures.

The Evolution of C into C++

You can think of C++ as being a more automatic, higher-level language. Technically speaking, C++ is a superset of C. C++ retains all of C's strengths, including its power and flexibility in dealing with the hardware/software interface; its low-level system programming; and its efficiency, economy, and powerful expressions. However, C++ brings the C language into the dynamic world of object-oriented programming and makes it a platform for high-level problem abstraction, going beyond even Ada in this respect. C++ accomplishes all of this with a simplicity and support for modularity similar to Modula-2 while maintaining the compactness and execution efficiency of C.

C++ bridges the gap between standard procedural language constructs familiar to so many programmers and the object-oriented model, which you can exploit fully to produce a purely object-oriented solution to a problem. In practice, a C++ application can reflect this duality by incorporating both the procedural programming model and the newer object-oriented model. This biformity in C++ presents a special challenge to the beginning C++ programmer; not only is there a new language to learn, but there is also a new way of thinking and problem solving.

C++'s Recent Past

Because C++ is a superset of C, it shares, to a large degree, C's historical development. However, although C and C++ are somewhat like BCPL and Algol 60, only C contains components of Simula 67. C++'s ability to overload operators and its flexibility to include declarations close to their first point of application are features found in Algol 68. The concept of subclasses (or derived classes) and virtual functions is taken from Simula 67. Like many other popular programming languages, C++ represents an evolution and refinement of some of the best features of previous languages. Of course, it is closest to C. Bjarne Stroustrup of Bell Labs developed the C++ language in the early 1980s. (Stroustrup credits Rick Mascitti with the naming of this new language.)

C++ was originally developed to solve some very rigorous event-driven simulations for which considerations of efficiency precluded the use of other languages. C++ was first used outside Dr. Stroustrup's language group in 1983, and by the summer of 1987, the language was still going through a natural refinement and evolution. One key design goal of C++ was to maintain compatibility with C. The idea was to preserve the integrity of millions of lines of previously written and debugged C code, the integrity of many existing C libraries, and the usefulness of previously developed C tools. Because of the high degree of success in achieving this goal, many programmers find the transition to C++ much simpler than when they first went from some other language, such as FORTRAN, to C.

Just like its C underpinnings, C++ supports large-scale software development. However, C++ is better for large-scale project development because its increased type checking eliminates many of the side effects experienced when writing loosely typed C applications is no longer possible.

Undoubtedly, the most significant C++ feature not found in C is its support for object-oriented programming (OOP). You will have to modify your approach to problem solving to derive all of the benefits of C++. For example, objects and their associated operations must be identified, and all necessary classes and subclasses must be constructed.

C++ Objects Can Streamline Code Design

By bundling data declarations with the functions that make the data do something meaningful, a C++ object can improve upon an older language's limited built-in constructs and features. For example, a FORTRAN software engineer may want to keep records on employees. You could accomplish this with multiple arrays of scalar data that represent each set of data. All of the arrays are necessarily tied together by a common index. If there are ten fields of information on each employee, ten array accesses would have to be made using the same index location in order to represent the array of records.

An object-oriented C++ solution involves the declaration of a simple object, *PersonnelFile*, that can receive messages to *Hire*, *Fire*, *ViewEmployeeData*, or *PrintEmployeeData* information contained within the object. The manipulation of the *PersonnelFile* object can then be performed in a natural manner. Inserting a new record into the *PersonnelFile* object becomes as simple as this:

```
PersonnelFile.Hire(NewEmployee)
```

Here the **Hire()** function is a method, or member function, suitably defined in the class that supports *PersonnelFile* objects, and the *NewEmployee* parameter is the specific information that is to be added. Note that the class of objects called *PersonnelFile* is not a part of the underlying language itself. Instead, the programmer extends the language to suit the problem. By defining a new class of objects or by modifying existing classes (creating a subclass), a more natural mapping from the problem space to the program space (or solution space) occurs. The biggest challenge comes in truly mastering this powerful enhancement.

Minor C++ Enhancements

Although C++ is a true superset of C, meaning that everything that works in a C program will work in a C++ program, there are subtle and sometimes glaring differences between the two languages. This next section details several of the minor enhancements made to C++.

An Unspecified Number of Parameters

One surprising feature, not seen in many other older high-level languages, is C++'s ability to define and use C++ functions with an unknown number and type of parameters. C++ accomplishes this task by using the ellipsis (...) operator. When you use this feature, parameter type checking is suppressed to allow flexibility in the interface to the function.

Anonymous Unions

An *anonymous union* is a union without a name. C++ allows you to define anonymous unions anywhere a variable or field can be defined. You can use this ability for the economy of memory storage by allowing the sharing of memory among two or more fields of a structure.

Block Declarations

Unlike C, which requires all variable declarations to be the first statement type found inside a function and then requires they be followed by the function's body, C++ allows data declarations anywhere within a block. This feature allows you to declare an identifier closer to its first point of application. It even permits the loop control variable to be declared within the formal definition of the control structure, as shown here:

```
void AnyFunction ( void )

{
  // all data declarations here;

  // executable statement;
  // executable statement;
  // executable statement;

  // notice ElementOffset's declaration below!
  for ( int ElementOffset = 0; ElementOffset < MAX_ELEMENTS;
                                        ElementOffset++ )
}
```

Comments

Although C allows multiline comments delimited by the comment symbol pair /* and */, C++ introduces the comment to end-of-line delimiter //. Because C++ does not have a unique opening and closing comment symbol pair, only the single //, C++ terminates the comment at the end of each line. This requires the programmer to remember that comment blocks must have the double slash at the beginning of each successive line.

Default Parameter Values

Unlike C, C++ allows you to define and initialize a function's dummy arguments. In this case, the function can be invoked using fewer than the total number of parameters. Any missing trailing parameters assume their default values.

Enumeration Names

C++ provides the programmer with a little bit of shorthand when defining enumerated type variables. In C++ the name of an enumeration is a type name. This streamlines the notation by not requiring the qualifier **enum** to be placed in front of the enumeration type name.

Explicit Type Conversions

C++ allows a programmer to use the name of a predefined type or user-defined type as a function to convert data from one type to another. Under certain circumstances, such an explicit type conversion can be used as an alternative to a cast conversion.

Function Declarations

Unlike the older, outdated C function header syntax, C++ permits the specification by name and type for each function's dummy argument *inside* the parentheses next to the function name. For example:

```
void * DuplicateMemory( void *Destination, int InitChar, unsigned int Bytes )
{
    .   .   .
}
```

C placed this information immediately inside the function body. The good news is that the equivalent C interface, under the ANSI C standard, would look exactly the same. In this case, C++ influenced the ANSI C standards committee. Just as in C, the C++ translator will perform type checking to ensure that the number and type of values sent into a function when it is invoked match the number and type of the formal arguments defined for the function. A check is also made to make certain that the function's return type matches the variable used in the expression invoking the function. This type of parameter checking is missing in most C systems.

Function Overloading

A powerful, fundamental construct facilitating the design of powerful objects is C++'s ability to define and use functions with the *same* name. This construct is known as *function overloading*. The C++ compiler distinguishes which overloaded function to invoke on the basis of the number and type of its parameters.

inline Specifier

Although you can use the C/C++ **#define** keyword to define macros, neither compiler performs any error checking when the macro is invoked with the wrong number or type of arguments. In C++ you can use the **inline** specifier to instruct the compiler to perform inline substitution of a given function at the location where the function is invoked, *with* error checking!

New and Delete Operators

Unlike the C functions **malloc()** and **free()**, which are not language keywords, C++ uses two new keywords **new** and **delete**, which allow for programmer-controlled allocation and deallocation of heap storage.

Reference Parameters in a Function

C programmers override the call-by-value argument passing convention by using pointer variables. However, within the referenced function, pointer variable syntax can be confusing to the novice. C++ uses the ampersand operator (&), to declare a reference parameter. For example:

```
int iValue;
AddOneInFunction ( iValue );
   .   .   .

void AddOneInFunction (int& iReferenced_Data)
{
   iReferenced_Data++;
}
```

Because *&iReferenced_Data* is defined as a reference parameter, its address is assigned to the address of *iValue* when **AddOneInFunction()** is invoked. The value of *iValue* that is sent in is incremented within function **AddOneInFunction()** and returned to variable *iValue* outside of function **AddOneInFunction()**. It is not necessary for the address of *iValue* to be explicitly passed into function **AddOneInFunction()** as it is in C.

Scope Qualifiers

C++ uniquely applies the scope qualifier operator :: to resolve name conflicts. For example, if a function has a local declaration for a variable *fValue* and there exists a global variable *fValue,* the qualifier *::fValue* allows the global variable to be accessed within the scope of the local function. The reverse is not possible.

The const Specifier

You can use the **const** specifier to lock the value of an entity within its scope. You can also use it to lock the data pointed to by a pointer variable, the value of the pointer address, or the values of both the pointer address and the data pointed to.

Structure and Class Names

In a similar fashion to the C++ shorthand applied to enumerated variable declarations, in C++ the name of a structure or class is a type name. This class construct does not exist in C. In C++ it is not necessary to use the qualifier **struct** or **class** in front of a structure or class name.

VOID Pointers and Functions Returning VOID

In C++, the type **void** is used to indicate that a function returns nothing. Pointer variables can be declared to point to **void**. Such pointers can then be assigned to any other pointer that points to an arbitrary base type.

Major C++ Enhancements

Of course, the biggest difference between C and C++ is that C++ is an object-oriented language. The discussion that follows highlights this major C++ component.

Class Constructs and Data Encapsulation

C++ uses the **class** keyword to declare objects. A **class** definition can encapsulate all of the data declarations, the initial values, and the set of operations, called *methods*, or *member functions*, for data abstraction. Objects can be declared to be of a given class, and messages can be sent to objects. Additionally, each object of a specified class can contain its own private set and public set of data representative of that class.

Constructors and Destructors

With most C++ objects being dynamically allocated and deallocated, some construct must exist to initialize and restore memory to the available pool. C++ uses constructors and destructors for this purpose. When an object is declared, the specified initialization constructor is activated. Destructors automatically deallocate storage for the associated object when the scope in which the object is declared is exited.

Derived or Child Classes

Sometimes known as a *child class*, a *derived class* can be considered a subclass of a specified class, thereby forming a hierarchy of abstractions. Derived class objects typically inherit all or some of the methods of the parent class. It is also common for a derived class to then incorporate these inherited methods with new methods specific to the subclass. All subclass objects contain the fields of data from the parent class as well as any of their own private data.

Friends

The concept of data hiding and data encapsulation implies a denied access to the inner structures that make up an object. The class's private section is normally completely off-limits to any function outside the class. C++ does allow other functions outside methods or classes to be declared to be a friend to a specified class. Friendship breaks down a normally impenetrable wall and permits access to the class' private data and methods.

Messages

If procedures are sent arguments, then in a similar fashion, objects are sent messages. You manipulate objects by sending them messages. The set of possible messages that can be sent to an object is specified in the class description for the object. Each object responds to a message by determining an appropriate action to take based on the nature of the message. For example, if *SetScreenResolution* represents an object, and *SetColumns* represents a method with a single integer parameter, sending a message to the object would be accomplished by using the following statement:

```
#define NUMBER_OF_COLUMNS 80
SetScreenResolution.SetColumns ( NUMBER_OF_COLUMNMS );
```

Operator Overloading

In a similar manner to function overloading, C++ allows the programmer to take the set of predefined or user-defined operators and functions supplied with the compiler and give them multiple meanings. This is known as *operator overloading*.

For example, different functions typically have different names, but for functions performing similar tasks on different types of objects, it is sometimes better to let these functions have the *same* name. When their argument types are different, the compiler can distinguish them and choose the right function to call. What follows is a coded example; you could have one function called **CalculateAverage()** that was overloaded for an array of integers, floating points, and double values.

```
int    CalculateAverage ( int NUMBER_OF_STUDENTS, int    iClassList[] );
float  CalculateAverage ( int NUMBER_OF_STUDENTS, float  fClassList[] );
double CalculateAverage ( int NUMBER_OF_STUDENTS, double dClassList[] );
```

Because you have declared the three different functions by the same name, the compiler can look at the invoking statement and automatically decide which function is appropriate for the formal parameter list's arguments:

```
CalculateAverage ( NUMBER_OF_STUDENTS,iClassList );
CalculateAverage ( NUMBER_OF_STUDENTS,fClassList );
CalculateAverage ( NUMBER_OF_STUDENTS,dClassList );
```

Polymorphism and Virtual Functions

Because child or derived classes inherit their parent class' methods, it is quite possible that there will exist many types of subclasses all using the same methods. *Polymorphism* involves a tree structure of parent classes and their subclasses. Each subclass within this tree can receive one or more messages with the same name. When an object of a class within this tree receives a message, the object determines the particular application of the message that is appropriate for an object of the specified subclass.

Stream Libraries

An additional library stream is included with the C++ language. The three classes **cin**, **cout**, and **cerr** are provided for terminal and file input and output. All of the operators within these three classes can be overloaded within a user-defined class. This capability allows the input and output operations to be easily tailored to an application's needs.

The C++ struct

In the purest sense, C++ allows you to define an object with the **struct** keyword. However, a *structure* in C++ is a subset of a class definition and has no private or protected sections. This subclass can contain both data (as is expected in ANSI C) and functions.

Basic Components of a C Program

In this section you will learn about the seven fundamental components of a "good" program. You may have heard that C is a difficult language to master. Although it is true that a brief encounter with C code may leave you scratching your head, this is only due to C's foreign syntax, structure, and indentation schemes. By the end of this chapter, you should have enough information to have developed a working knowledge of the C language that enables you to write short but meaningful code.

The Seven Key Elements

Some computer language design courses use a problem-solution format called an IPO diagram. IPO (Input Process Output) diagrams are one of many stylized approaches to the age old programming problem of input/process/output. The following list elaborates on these three fundamentals and encapsulates the entire application development cycle. All well-written programs must address these requirements:

1. All applications input information from some source.

2. All applications determine how this data is to be arranged and stored.

3. All applications use a set of instructions to manipulate the input using one of four types of statements:

    a. single statements

    b. conditional statements

    c. loops

    d. subroutines

4. All applications output the results of their data calculations.

5. All applications incorporate all of the fundamentals just listed, expressed by using good modular design.

6. All applications employ self-documenting code (meaningful variable names).

7. All applications employ a consistent indentation scheme.

A Simple C Program

The following C program illustrates the basic components of a C application. It is suggested that you enter each example as you read about it to help you understand new concepts as you encounter them.

```
/*
 *    simple.c
 *    The simplest C application.
 *    Copyright (c) Chris H. Pappas and William H. Murray, 1996
 */

#include <stdio.h>

void main( void )
{
  printf(" Welcome to the exciting world of C programming! ");
}
```

There is a lot happening in this short piece of code. Let's begin with the comment block:

```
/*
 *    simple.c
 *    The simplest C application.
 *    Copyright (c) Chris H. Pappas and William H. Murray, 1996
 */
```

The program begins with a clarifying comment. A meaningful comment is one that neither insults the intelligence of the programmer nor assumes too much. In C, comments begin /* and are terminated with */. Anything between these unique symbol pairs is ignored by the compiler. The next statement:

```
#include <stdio.h>
```

represents one of C's unique features, known as a preprocessor statement. A *preprocessor statement* is like a precompile instruction. In this case, the statement instructs the compiler to retrieve the code stored in the predefined stdio.h file into the source code on the line requested. (The stdio.h file is called a header file. *Header files* can include symbolic constants, identifiers, and function prototypes and have these declarations pulled out of the main program for purposes of modularity.) Following the **#include** statement is the main function declaration:

```
void main( void )
{
   .
   .
   .
}
```

Unlike older high-level languages, C does not have procedures, only functions. All C programs are made up of function calls. Every C program must have one called **main()**. The first use of the keyword **void** identifies the functions return type. (**void**, in this sense, means the function returns nothing. The second use of **void**, within the parentheses, indicates that the **main()** function has no formal arguments.)

The **main()** function is usually where program execution begins and ends. Following the **main()** function header is the body of the function itself. Notice the { and } symbol pairs. These are called *braces*. You use braces to encapsulate multiple statements. These braces may define the body for a function, or they may bundle together statements that are dependent on the same logic control statement, as is the case when several statements are executed based on the validity of an **if** statement. In this example, the braces define the body of the main program. The next line is the only statement in the body of the **main()** function and is the simplest example of an output statement:

```
printf(" Welcome to the exciting world of C programming! ");
```

The **printf()** function was previously prototyped in stdio.h. Because no other parameters are specified, the sentence will be printed to the display monitor.

A Simple C++ Program

This next program illustrates the simplest type of C++ program you can write. The example that follows performs the same function as the one just discussed, only it does so in C++ syntax:

```
//
// simple.cpp
```

```
//   The simplest C++ program.
//   Copyright (c) Chris H. Pappas and William H. Murray, 1996
//

#include <iostream.h>

void main( void )
{
   cout << " Welcome to the exciting world of C++ programming! ";
}
```

Basically, the C++ equivalent has three distinct differences. First, the comment designator has been changed from the /* */ pair to //. Second, the **#include** filename has been changed to iostream.h. The third change involves a different output operator call, **cout**. Many of the examples in the book will highlight the sometimes subtle and sometimes dazzling differences between C and C++.

Your Second C Program

This next example increases the previous program's complexity by adding variable declarations, and performing rudimentary input and output:

```
/*
 *   ioinc.c
 *   This C program translates the user-defined length,
 *   in meters and centimeters.
 *   Copyright (c) Chris H. Pappas and William H. Murray, 1996
 */

#include <stdio.h>

void main( void )
{
   float fUserDefinedFeet,
         fMeteredConversion,
         fCentimeterConversion;

   printf( "Length to convert: "   );
   scanf ( "%f", &fUserDefinedFeet );

   while ( UserDefinedFeet > 0 ) {

      fCentimeterConversion = feet * 12 * 2.54          ;
      fMeteredConversion    = fCentimeterConversion / 100;
```

```
      printf ( "English Measure   : %9.2f\n", fUserDefinedFeet       );
      printf ( "Metered Measure   : %9.2f\n", fMeteredConversion     );
      printf ( "Centimeter Measure: %9.2f\n", fCentimeterConversion );

      printf ( "\nEnter another value to be \n"                      );
      printf ( "converted (0 ends the program): "                    );
      scanf  ( "%f", &fUserDefinedFeet                               );

   }
   printf ( "Program Termination" );
}
```

Variable Declarations

The first feature new to this program is its variable declarations. C requires all of a function's variables (**main()** is no exception) to be declared immediately after the function's opening {. This program declares three **float** variables:

```
float fUserDefinedFeet,
      fMeteredConversion,
      fCentimeterConversion;
```

All C variables must be declared before they are used. One of the standard data types supplied by the C language is **float**. The syntax for declaring variables in C requires the definition of the variable's type before the name of the variable. In this example, the **float** type is represented by the keyword **float**, and the three variables *fUserDefinedFeet*, *fMeteredConversion*, and *fCentimeterConversion* are defined.

Input

The next unconventional-looking statement is used to input information from the keyboard:

```
printf( "Length to convert: "   );
scanf ( "%f", &fUserDefinedFeet );
```

Unlike the simplest use of the **printf()** statement, the **scanf()** function has a requirement called a format string. *Format strings* define how the input data is to be interpreted and represented internally. The "%f " function parameter instructs the compiler to interpret the input as **float** data.

Where To Put Input Data

Not only does the **scanf()** statement employ a format string argument, but it has an additional requirement. Officially, **scanf()** wants the address to the memory location receiving the input data. In the previous statement you may have noticed that the **float** variable *fUserDefinedFeet* was preceded by an ampersand symbol (&). The & is known as an *address operator*. Whenever a variable is preceded by this symbol, the compiler uses the address of the specified variable instead of the value stored in the variable. The **scanf()** function has been written to expect the address of the variable to be filled.

Simple Repetition

Most high-level languages provide the three standard forms of repetition, **for** loops, **while** loops, and **do-while** loops. One of the simplest loop structures to code in C is the **while** loop:

```
while( fUserDefinedFeet > 0 ) {

}
```

Technically, **while** loops are categorized as pretest loops. This pretest loop starts with the reserved word **while** followed by a Boolean expression that returns either a TRUE or a FALSE.

NOTE: *Both C and C++ consider a value of 0 as being a logical FALSE and any nonzero value to be TRUE. The latter is sometimes represented as !0, because the ! symbol represents the logical NOT.*

The opening brace ({) and closing brace (}) are optional; they are only needed when more than one executable statement is to be associated with the loop repetition.

Braced statements are sometimes referred to as *compound statements, compound blocks,* or *code blocks*. If you are using compound blocks, make certain you use the agreed upon brace style. Although it doesn't matter to the compiler where the braces are placed (in terms of skipped spaces or lines), programmers reading your code will certainly appreciate the style and effort. An opening loop brace is placed at the end of the test condition, and the closing brace is placed in the same column as the first character in the test condition.

Styling Simple Output

In analyzing the second program, you will notice more complex **printf()** function calls:

```
printf ( "English Measure   : %9.2f\n", fUserDefinedFeet      );
printf ( "Metered Measure   : %9.2f\n", fMeteredConversion    );
printf ( "Centimeter Measure: %9.2f\n", fCentimeterConversion );

printf ( "\nEnter another value to be \n"                      );
printf ( "converted (0 ends the program): "                    );
scanf  ( "%f", &fUserDefinedFeet                               );
```

Whenever a **printf()** function is invoked to print not only *literal strings* (any set of characters between double quote marks), but also values, a format string is required. The format string represents two things: a picture of how the output string is to look combined with the format interpretation for each of the values printed. Format strings are always between double quotation marks. Let's break down the first **printf()** format string ("English Measure : %9.2f\n", *fUserDefinedFeet*) into its separate components:

Control	Action
English Measure :	Output the literal string.
%9.2f	Take the value of *fUserDefinedFeet*, interpret it as a **float**, and print *it* in a field of spaces with 2 decimal places.
\n	Once the line is complete, execute a new line feed using an output control character.
,	The comma separates the format string from the variable name(s) used to satisfy all format descriptors. In this case there is only one %9.2f.

The C *escape sequences*, or *output control characters*, allow you to use a sequence of characters to represent special characters. Table 5-2 lists all of the output control symbols and describes how to use them in format strings.

All leading zeros are ignored by the compiler for characters notated in hexadecimal. The compiler determines the end of a hex-specified escape character when it encounters either a non-hex character or more than two hex characters, excluding leading zeros. Also on the subject of formatting, and even though the subject is a bit advanced, are the **scanf()** formatting controls.

Table 5-3 describes the **scanf()** formatting controls and their meanings. If you wish to input a string without automatically appending a terminating null character (\0), use %nc, where *n* is a decimal integer. In this case, the **c** type character indicates that

Escape Sequences	Value	Char	What It Does
\a	0x 07	BEL	Audible bell
\b	0x 08	BS	Backspace
\f	0x OC	FF	Formfeed
\n	0x OA	Lf	Newline (line feed)
\r	0x OD	Cf	Carriage return
\t	0x 09	HT	Tab (horizontal)
\v	0x OB	VT	Vertical tab
\\ (see NOTE)	0x 5C		Backslash
\'	0x 27	'	Single quote (apostrophe)
		"	Double quote
\?	0x 3F	?	Question mark
\O	0x	Any	0 = a string of up to three octal digits
\xH	0x	Any	H = a string of hex digits
\XH (uppercase)	0x	Any	H = a string of hex digits

NOTE: The \\ must be used to represent a real ASCII backslash, as used in DOS paths.

Table 5-2.   *Output Control Characters*

the argument is a pointer to a character array. The next n characters are read from the input stream into the specified location, and no null character (\0) is appended. If n is not specified, the default character array length is 1. As you learn more about the various C data types, you can refer back to Tables 5-2 and 5-3 for a reminder of how the various controls affect input and output.

Function	scanf	printf
Size of value (modifies data type):		
Specify short integer	%hd	
Specify long integer	%ld	%ld
Specify double	%lf	%lf
Use with **float** to indicate a long double	%Lf	%Lf
Type of data to be read or displayed:		
Single character	%c	%c
Signed integer	%d	%d
Signed double or **float** in exponential format	%e	%e
Signed double or **float** in decimal format	%f	%f
Octal (letter "O" not 0)	%O	%O
Character string	%s	%s
Unsigned decimal integer	%u	%u
Hexadecimal (%X for uppercase letters)	%x	%x
Prints percent symbol		%%
Decimal integer, six digits wide		%6d
Floating point, six digits wide		%6f
Floating point, two digits after decimal point		%.2f
Floating point, six digits wide, two after decimal	%6.2f	%6.2f

Table 5-3. *C Value Formatting Controls*

Using Borland's Integrated Debugger

To examine the actual operation of the C code presented in this section, you can use the integrated debugger. When you compile your program, make certain you have turned on debug information. This is done in conjunction with the Project utility. Once your application is compiled and linked, use the debugger to keep an eye on the variables *fUserDefinedFeet*, *fMeteredConversion*, and *fCentimeterConversion*.

Your Second C++ Program

The following C++ example is identical in function to the previous C example except for some minor variations in the syntax used:

```
//
//  ioincpp.cpp
//  This C++ program translates the user-defined length,
//  in meters and centimeters.
//  Copyright (c) Chris H. Pappas and William H. Murray, 1996
//

#include <iomanip.h>
#include <iostream.h>

void main( void )
{
  float fUserDefinedFeet,
        fMeteredConversion,
        fCentimeterConversion;

  cout << "Length to convert: ";
  cin  >> fUserDefinedFeet;

  while( fUserDefinedFeet > 0 ) {

    fCentimeterConversion = fUserDefinedFeet * 12 * 2.54;
    fMeteredConversion    = fCentimeterConversion/100    ;

    cout << "English measure:    "
         <<  setw         ( 9           )
         <<  setprecision ( 2           )
         <<  setiosflags  ( ios::fixed )
         <<  fUserDefinedFeet
         <<  "\n";
    cout << "Metered measure:    "
         <<  setw         ( 9           )
         <<  setprecision ( 2           )
         <<  fMeteredConversion
         <<  "\n";
```

```
    cout << "Centimeter measure: "
         <<   setw          ( 9           )
         <<   setprecision ( 2            )
         <<   fCentimeterConversion
         << "\n";

    cout << "\nEnter another value to be \n"   ;
    cout << "converted (0 ends the program): ";
    cin  >>  fUserDefinedFeet                  ;
  }
  cout    << "Program Termination"             ;
}
```

The first two changes in converting the application from C to C++ involve the use of **cin** and **cout** for I/O. These statements use the << ("put to," or insertion) and >> ("get from," or extraction) iostream operators. Both operators have been overloaded to handle the output/input of all the predefined types. They can also be overloaded to handle user-defined types such as rational numbers. The last four changes are all related to formatting C++ output.

To gain the same output precision easily afforded by C's "%9.2f" format string, the program requires four additional statements. The file iomanip.h is included in the program to give access to three specific class member inline functions: **setw()**, **setprecision()**, and **setiosflags()**. As you look at the code, you will notice that the calls to **setw()** and **setprecision()** are repeated. This is because their effect is only for the next output value, unlike **setiosflags()**, which makes a global change to **fixed** output. C++ programmers who like the power and flexibility of the C output function **printf()** can use **printf()** directly from library stdio.h. The next two statements show the C and C++ equivalents:

```
printf( "English measure    : %9.2f\n", fUserDefinedFeet );
cout << "English measure    :"

     << setw         ( 9            )
     << setprecision ( 2            )
     << setiosflags  ( ios::fixed )
     << fUserDefinedFeet
     << "\n";
```

Files

The following section quickly introduces you to those syntax requirements necessary to easily access external file information. The section, as before shows you both the C and C++ equivalents. First the C program.

```c
/*
 *   smplfile.c
 *   This C program
 *   demonstrates how to perform external I/O.
 *   Copyright (c) Chris H. Pappas and William H. Murray, 1996
 */

#include <stdio.h>

#define MIN_DISCOUNT .97
#define MAX_DISCOUNT .95

void main( void )
{
  FILE *fin,*fout                            ;
  float fRetailPrice, fWholesalePrice   ;

  fin  = fopen ( "a:\\Retail.sls" ,"r" );
  fout = fopen ( "a:\\Whlsale.sls","w" );

  while( fscanf( fin,"%f",&fRetailPrice ) != EOF ) {
    fprintf( fout,"Your order of \t\t$%9.2f\n", fRetailPrice );
    if( fRetailPrice < 10000 )
          fWholesalePrice = fRetailPrice * MIN_DISCOUNT;
      else fWholesalePrice = fRetailPrice * MAX_DISCOUNT;
    fprintf( fout,"is discounted to \t$%8.2f.\n\n",
                  fWholesalePrice                          );
  }
}
```

C programs require all external files to be associated with a file pointer. The *file pointer* is a pointer that points to information that defines various things about a file, including the path to the file, its name, and its status. A file pointer is a pointer variable of type **FILE** and is defined in stdio.h. The following statement from the example program declares two files, **fin* and **fout*:

```
FILE *fin,*fout;
```

The next two statements in the program open two separate streams and associate each file with its respective stream. The statements also return the file pointer for each file. Because these are pointers to files, your application should never alter their values:

```
fin  = fopen ( "a:\\Retail.sls" ,"r" );
fout = fopen ( "a:\\Whlsale.sls","w" );
```

The second parameter to the **fopen()** function is the file mode. Files may be opened in either text or binary mode. When in text mode, most C compilers translate carriage return/line feed sequences into newline characters on input. During output, the opposite occurs. However, binary files do not go through such translations. Table 5-4 lists all of the valid file modes.

Mode	Usage
"r"	Opens a text file for reading.
"w"	Opens a text file for writing.
"r+"	Opens a text file for update reading or writing.
"w+"	Creates a new file for update (if file exists it is overwritten).
"a"	Opens a file in append mode or creates a file for writing if the file does not exist.
	Opens a file in append mode for updating at the end of the file or creates a file for writing if the file does not exist.
"rb"	Opens a binary file for reading.
"wb"	Opens a binary file for writing.

Table 5-4.   *C Valid File Modes*

The r+, w+, and a+ file modes select both reading and writing. (The file is open for update.) When switching between reading and writing, you must remember to reposition the file pointer using either **fsetpos()**, **fseek()**, or **rewind()**. C does perform its own file closing automatically whenever the application closes. However, there may be times when you want direct control over when a file is closed. The following listing shows the same program modified to include the necessary closing function calls:

```c
/*
 *   smplfile.c
 *   This C program demonstrates how to perform external I/O
 *   including the manual fclose() statements.
 *   Copyright (c) Chris H. Pappas and William H. Murray, 1996
 */

#include <stdio.h>
#define MIN_DISCOUNT .97
#define MAX_DISCOUNT .95

void main( void )
{
  FILE *fin,*fout                 ;
  float fRetailPrice, fWholesalePrice  ;

  fin  = fopen ( "a:\\Retail.sls" ,"r" );
  fout = fopen ( "a:\\Whlsale.sls","w" );

  while( fscanf( fin,"%f",&fRetailPrice ) != EOF ) {
    fprintf( fout,"Your order of \t\t$%8.2f\n", fRetailPrice );
    if( fRetailPrice < 10000 )
         fWholesalePrice = fRetailPrice * MIN_DISCOUNT;
     else fWholesalePrice = fRetailPrice * MAX_DISCOUNT;
    fprintf( fout,"is discounted to \t$%8.2f.\n\n",
                  fWholesalePrice);
  }

  fclose( fin  );
  fclose( fout );
}
```

The following program performs the same function as the one just examined but is coded in C++:

```
//
//  smplfile.cpp
//  This C++ program demonstrates how to perform external I/O
//  and includes the manual file closing statements.
//  Copyright (c) Chris H. Pappas and William H. Murray, 1996
//

#include <fstream.h>
#include <iomanip.h>

#define MIN_DISCOUNT .97
#define MAX_DISCOUNT .95

void main ( void )
{
   ifstream fin ( "a:\\Retail.sls"  );
   ofstream fout( "a:\\Whlsale.sls"  );
   float fRetailPrice, fWholesalePrice;

   fin >> fRetailPrice;
   while( !fin.eof() ) {

     fout << setiosflags ( ios::fixed );

     fout << "Your order of \t\t$"
          << setprecision
          << setw ( 9 )
          << fRetailPrice
          << "\n";

     if( fRetailPrice < 10000 )
         fWholesalePrice = fRetailPrice * MIN_DISCOUNT;
       else fWholesalePrice = fRetailPrice * MAX_DISCOUNT;

     fout << "is discounted to \t$"
          << setprecision
          << setw ( 9 )
          << fWholesalePrice
          << ".\n\n";
```

```
    fin >> fRetailPrice;
  }

  fin.close  ( );
  fout.close ( );
}
```

Disk file input and output are slightly different in C++ than in C. C++ has a two-part design to its stream library; a **streambuf** object and a stream. This same model performs I/O for keyboard and terminal as well as disk I/O. The same operators and operations perform in precisely the same way. This greatly simplifies a programming task that has always been difficult and confusing. To facilitate disk file I/O, the stream library defines a **filebuf** object, which is a derivative of the standard **streambuf** type. Like its progenitor type, **filebuf** manages a buffer, but in this case, the buffer is attached to a disk file.

In the Next Chapter...

In this chapter you have learned all about C/C++'s interesting lineage and you wrote several simple C and C++ programs. In Chapter 6, you will learn about C/C++'s standard data types, operators, and new capabilities previously unavailable to older high-level languages.

Chapter Six

Working with Data

When creating a program, a programmer must make a host of decisions. Many of these decisions are the same whether the programmer is using C or C++ or any other programming language. This chapter examines some of these common decisions—for example, how you declare a variable, what makes for a legal variable name, and how to select a variable's precision. The standard data types, modifiers, and operators that can be used with C or C++ applications are primary reasons for the stability found in these applications.

Rules for Naming Variables, Constants, and Functions

Just as functions and procedures can be grouped under the category of subroutines, variable names, constant names, application-specific types, function names, and labels can all be grouped under the broad category called *identifiers*. C and C++ define an identifier as a sequence of one or more letters, digits, or underscores that begins with a letter or underscore. Identifiers can contain any number of characters, but only the first 31 characters are significant to the compiler. (However, other programs that read the compiler output, such as the linker, may recognize even fewer characters.)

You may at first be surprised to learn that C and C++ are *case-sensitive* languages. This means that the C compiler considers uppercase and lowercase letters to be distinct characters. For example, the compiler sees the variables *FIRSTNAME* and *FirstName* as two unique identifiers representing different memory cells. This feature enables you to create distinct identifiers that have the same spelling but different cases for one or more of the letters. The selection of case can also help you understand your code. For example, identifiers declared in **#include** header files are often created using only uppercase letters. Because of this, whenever you encounter an uppercase identifier in the source file, you have a visual clue as to where that particular identifier's definition can be found.

Technically speaking, a valid identifier may begin with the special underscore character _. However, although it is syntactically legal, you should not use leading underscores in identifiers you create. Identifiers beginning with an underscore can cause conflicts with the names of system routines or variables and produce errors. As a result, programs containing names beginning with leading underscores are not guaranteed to be portable.

NOTE: *Use of two sequential underscore characters (__) in an identifier is reserved for C++ implementations and standard libraries.*

Often, learning a new language's syntax is much easier than knowing how to fit these syntax rules into the unwritten set of rules-for-usage agreed upon by experts in the language. One example is the stylistic convention adopted by many C/C++ programmers of preceding all identifiers with an abbreviation of the identifier's data type. For instance, all integer identifiers would begin with an *i*, floats would begin with an *f*, null-terminated strings would begin with *sz*, pointer variables would begin with a *p*, and so on.

With this naming convention (which is neither a formal syntax requirement nor a guideline found written in manuals), you can easily look at a piece of code and not only see which identifiers are being used but also their data type. This approach makes it easier to learn how a particular section of code operates and to do line-by-line source debugging. The programs throughout this book use both variable naming conventions because many of the programs you encounter in real life will use one of these formats.

These are examples of identifiers:

```
fAverageTemperature
iNumber_of_Records
pszFileName
lElevation
iMaximumLength
iMAXIMUM_LENGTH
EOF
NULL
```

See if you can determine why the following identifiers are illegal:

```
1ST_Place_Winner
#lbs
STOP!
```

The first identifier is illegal because it begins with a decimal number. The second identifier begins with a # symbol, and the last identifier ends with an illegal character.

Take a look at the following identifiers. Are they legal or not?

```
O
OO
OOO
_____
```

Actually, all four identifiers are legal. The first three identifiers use the uppercase letter "O." Because each has a different number of O's, they are all unique. The fourth identifier is composed of five underscore (_) characters. Is it meaningful? Definitely not. Is it legal? Yes. Although these identifiers meet the "letter of the law," they greatly miss the "spirit of the law." The point is that all identifiers, functions, constants, and variables should have meaningful names. Because uppercase and lowercase letters are considered distinct characters, each of the following identifiers is unique:

```
MAXIMUM_FILES_OPEN
maximum_files_open
MaximumFilesOpen
```

When used properly, case-sensitivity helps a programmer know something about the identifiers category, and possibly, even where to find its declaration. However, this same case-sensitivity can create tremendous headaches for the novice C/C++ programmer. For example, trying to reference the **printf()** function when it was typed **PRINTF()** will invoke "unknown identifier" complaints from the compiler. In Pascal, however, a writeln is a WRITELN is a WriteLn. With experience, you would probably detect the preceding **printf()** error, but can you see what's wrong with this next statement?

```
Printf ( "%S", pszCustomerName );
```

Assuming that *pszCustomerName* was defined properly, you might think that nothing was wrong. Remember, however, that C is case sensitive—the %S print format has never been defined; only %s has. For more advanced applications, some linkers may further restrict the number and type of characters for globally visible symbols. Also, the linker, unlike the compiler, may not distinguish between uppercase and lowercase letters.

By default, the Borland C++ LINK sees all public and external symbols, such as *PROGRAM_IDENTIFIER*, *program_identifier*, and *Program_Identifier*, as the same. You can, however, make LINK case sensitive by using the /NOI option. This would force LINK to see the preceding three example variables as being unique. Use your Borland C++'s Help utility for additional information on how to use this switch. One last word on identifiers: an identifier cannot have the same spelling and case as a keyword of the language. The next section lists C and C++ keywords.

Using Reserved Words

Reserved words, or as they are sometimes called, *keywords*, are predefined identifiers that have special meanings to the C/C++ compiler. You can use them only as defined. Remember, the name of a program identifier cannot have the same spelling and case as a C/C++ keyword. The C/C++ language keywords are listed in Table 6-1. You cannot redefine keywords. However, you can specify text to be substituted for keywords before compilation by using preprocessor directives.

A	double	G
__asm	__ds	goto
_asm	_ds	
asm	dynamic_cast	**H**
auto		__huge
	E	_huge
B	else	huge
break	enum	
bool	__es	**I**
	_es	if
C	__except	__import
case	explicit	_import
catch	__export	inline
__cdecl	_export	int
_cdecl	extern	__interrupt
cdecl		_interrupt
char	**F**	interrupt
class	false	
const	__far	**L**
const_cast	_far	__loadds
continue	far	_loadds
__cs	__fastcall	long
_cs	_fastcall	
	__finally	**M**
D	float	mutable
__declspec	for	
default	friend	**N**
delete		namespace
do		__near

Table 6-1. *C/C++ Reserved Words*

_near	**S**	throw
near	__saveregs	true
new	_saveregs	__try
	__seg	try
O	_seg	typedef
operator	short	typeid
	signed	typename
P	sizeof	
__pascal	__ss	**U**
_pascal	_ss	union
pascal	static	unsigned
private	static_cast	using
protected	__stdcall	
public	_stdcall	**V**
	struct	virtual
R	switch	void
register		volatile
reinterpret_cast		
return	**T**	**W**
__rtti	template	wchar_t
	this	while
	__thread	

Table 6-1. *C/C++ Reserved Words* (continued)

Standard C and C++ Data Types

A variable's data type tells the compiler two things: how much memory to allocate and what type of interpretation it should make about the binary value placed into memory. All programs deal with information that you can usually represent by using one of the seven basic C and C++ types: text or **char**, integer values or **int**, floating-point values or **float**, double floating-point values or **double** (**long double**), enumerated or **enum**, valueless or **void**, and pointers. This next section explains the basic use of each.

Text	(data type **char**) is made up of single characters, such as a, Z, ?, 3, and strings, such as "There is more to life than increasing its speed". (Usually, 8 bits, or 1 byte per character, with the range of 0 to 255.)
Integer	values are those numbers you learned to count with (1, 2, 7, -45, and 1,345). (Usually, 16 bits wide, 2 bytes, or 1 word, with the range of -32,768 to 32,767.) (Under Windows 95 and Windows NT, integers are now 32 bits wide with a range from -2147483648 to 2147483647)
Floating point	values are numbers that have a fractional portion, such as pi (3.14159) and exponents (7.563x1021). These are also known as real numbers. (Usually, 32 bits, 4 bytes, or 2 words, with the range of +/- 3.4E-38 to 3.4E+38.)
Double floating point	values have an extended range. (Usually, 64 bits, 8 bytes, or 4 words, with the range of 1.7E-308 to 1.7E+308.) Long double floating-point values are even more precise. (Usually, 80 bytes, or 5 words, with the range of +/- 1.18E-4932 to 1.18E+4932.)
Enumerated	data types allow for user-defined types.
void	is used to signify values that occupy zero bits and have no value. (This type can also be used for the creation of generic pointers, as discussed in Chapter 10.)
Pointer	data type doesn't hold information in the normal sense of the other data types; instead, each pointer contains the address of the memory location holding the actual data.

Character Types

Undoubtedly, the simplest data type to use is character. Every language uses a set of characters to construct meaningful statements. For instance, all books written in English use combinations of 26 letters of the alphabet, the 10 digits, and the punctuation marks. Similarly, C and C++ programs are written using a set of characters consisting of:

26 lowercase letters of the alphabet	abcdefghijklmnopqrstuvwxyz
26 uppercase letters of the alphabet	ABCDEFGHIJKLMNOPQRSTUVWXYZ
10 digits	0 1 2 3 4 5 6 7 8 9
and the symbols	+ - * / =, . _ : ; ? \ " ' ~	! # % $ & ( ) [ ] { } ^ @

C and C++ also use the blank space, sometimes referred to as white space. Combinations of symbols, with no blank space between them, are also valid C and C++ characters. In fact, the following is a mixture of valid C and C++ symbols:

++ -- == && || << >> >= <= += -= *= /= ?: :: /* */ //

The following C program illustrates how to declare and use **char** data types:

```c
/*
 *   usechar.c
 *   A C program demonstrating the char data type and showing
 *   how a char variable can be interpreted as an integer.
 *   Copyright (c) Chris H. Pappas and William H. Murray, 1996
 */
#include <ctype.h>
#include <stdio.h>

void main( void )
{
  char cUserInputChar                          ,
       cConvertedToUpperCase                   ,
       cConvertedToUppercase                   ;

  printf ( "Please type a lower-case letter: "     );
  scanf  ( "%c", &cUserInputChar                   );

  cConvertedToUpperCase = toupper ( cUserInputChar );
  cConvertedToUppercase = tolower ( cUserInputChar );

  printf ( "The UPPERcase character \'%c\' has a decimal ASCII"
           " value of %d\n",cConvertedToUpperCase,
             cConvertedToUpperCase                     );

  printf ( "The ASCII value represented in hexadecimal"
           " is %x\n",cConvertedToUpperCase              );

  printf ( "If you add sixteen you will get \'%c\'\n",
           (cConvertedToUpperCase+16)                    );

  printf ( "The calculated ASCII value in hexadecimal"
           " is %x\n",(cConvertedToUpperCase+16)          );
```

```
    printf ( "The LOWERcase character \'%c\' has a decimal ASCII"
            " value of %d\n",cConvertedToUppercase,
              cConvertedToUppercase                            );
}
```

Running the program would look something like this:

```
Please type a lower-case letter: a
The UPPERcase character 'A' has a decimal ASCII value of 65
The ASCII value represented in hexadecimal is 41
If you add sixteen you will get 'Q'
The calculated ASCII value in hexadecimal is 51
The character 'a' has a decimal ASCII value of 97
```

Notice the use of \' in the format string to output the single quotes, and the use of the %x to interpret the associated variable's contents as a hexadecimal value.

Enumerated Types

Because enumerated types (sometimes referred to as *user-defined types*) cannot be read into a program or directly output, there *is* only one reason for using them: readability. So instead of relating to the days of the week as integers 1 through 5, your program can use a more readable, self-documenting enumeration, such as *MON, TUE, WED, THR,* and *FRI.*

Technically speaking, when an enumerated variable is defined, it is associated with a set of named integer constants called the *enumeration set.* The variable can contain any one of the constants at any time, and the constants can be referred to by name. For example, the following definition creates the enumerated type *air_reserve;* the enumerated constants *DEPLETED, IN_SERVICE,* and *CHARGED;* and the enumerated variable *InstructorTank*:

```
enum air_reserve { DEPLETED, IN_SERVICE,
                        CHARGED = 3 } InstructorTank;
```

All three constants (*DEPLETED, IN_SERVICE,* and *CHARGED*) and variables (*InstructorTank* and *RentalTank*—see upcoming code statement) are type **int**, and each constant is automatically provided a default initial value unless another value is specified. In the preceding example, the constant name *DEPLETED* has the integer value zero by default because it is the first in the list and was not specifically overridden. The value of *IN_SERVICE* is 1 because it occurs immediately after a constant with the value of zero. The constant *CHARGED* was specifically initialized to the value 3, and if another constant were included in the list after *CHARGED*, the new constant would have the integer value of 4. Having created *air_reserve*, you can later define another variable, *RentalTank*, as follows:

```
enum air_reserve RentalTank;
```

After this statement, it is legal to place the value 3 into the variable *InstructorTank* and the value of zero into the variable *RentalTank*:

```
InstructorTank = CHARGED ;
RentalTank     = DEPLETED;
```

NOTE: When defining additional enumerated variables in C++, it is not necessary to repeat the **enum** *keyword. However, both syntaxes are accepted by the C++ compiler.*

One common mistake is to think that *air_reserve* is a variable. It is a "type" of data that can be used later to create additional enumerated variables like *InstructorTank* or *RentalTank*. Because the name *InstructorTank* is an enumerated variable of type *air_reserve*, *InstructorTank* can be used on the left of an assignment operator and can receive a value. This occurred when the enumerated constant *CHARGED* was explicitly assigned to it. The names *DEPLETED*, *IN_SERVICE*, and *CHARGED* are names of constants; they are not variables and their values cannot be changed. Tests can be performed on the variables in conjunction with the constants. The following is a complete C program that uses the preceding definitions:

```
/*
 *   useenum.c
 *   A C program demonstrating the use of enumeration variables
 *   Copyright (c) Chris H. Pappas and William H. Murray, 1996
 */

#include <stdio.h>

void main( void )
  enum air_reserve { DEPLETED, IN_SERVICE,
                              CHARGED = 3 } InstructorTank;
  enum air_reserve RentalTank;
```

```
    InstructorTank = CHARGED;
    RentalTank     = DEPLETED;

    printf ( "The integral value stored in InstructorTank is %d\n",
             InstructorTank                                        );

    if ( RentalTank < IN_SERVICE )     {
      printf ( "CHARGE NOW!\n"       );
      printf ( "CHARGE TONIGHT\n"    );
      exit    ( 0                    );
    }

    if ( InstructorTank >= RentalTank )
      printf ( "Has SAFE margin\n"   );
    else
      printf ( "Bring SPARE tanks\n" );
}
```

In C, an **enum** type is equivalent to the type **int**. This technically allows a program to assign integer values directly to enumerated variables. C++ enforces a stronger type check and does not allow this mixed-mode operation.

Floating-Point Types

Borland C++ uses the three floating-point types **float**, **double**, and **long double**. Although the ANSI C standard does not specifically define the values and storage that are to be allocated for each of these types, the standard did require each type to hold a minimum of any value in the range 1E-37 to 1E+37. The Borland C/C++ environment has greatly expanded upon this minimum requirement.

Historically, most C compilers have always had the types **float** and **double**. The ANSI C committee added the third type, **long double**. You can use **long double** on any computer, even those that have only two types of floating-point numbers. However, if the computer does not have a specific data type of **long double**, then the data item will have the same size and storage capacity as a double. The following C++ program illustrates how to declare and use floating-point variables:

```
//
//   usefloat.cpp
//   A C++ program demonstrating using the float data type.
//   Copyright (c) Chris H. Pappas and William H. Murray, 1996
//
```

```cpp
#include <iostream.h>
#include <iomanip.h>

void main( void )
{
  float fUserInputValue                        ;
  long  lInitialFlagStatus = cin.flags ( );

  cout << "Value to convert: "        ;
  cin  >>   fUserInputValue           ;

  cout << "Standard Formatting:     "
       <<   fUserInputValue
       <<   endl                      ;

  cout.setf(ios::scientific);

  cout << "Scientific Formatting:   "
       << fUserInputValue
       << endl                        ;

  cout.setf(ios::fixed);

  cout << "Fixed Formatting:        "
       <<   setprecision ( 2 )
       <<   fUserInputValue           ;

  cout.flags ( lInitialFlagStatus );
}
```

Running the program looks similar to:

```
Value to convert: 987.54321
Standard Formatting:   987.654
Scientific Formatting:  9.876543e+002
Fixed Formatting:       9.8e+002
```

Notice the different value printed depending on the print format specification default, scientific or fixed.

Integer Types

Along with the standard type **int**, the compiler supports **short int** and **long int**. These are most often abbreviated to just **short** and **long**. Although the C language is not hardware dependent (syntax, etc.), data types used by the C language are. Thus, the actual sizes of **short**, **int**, and **long** depend upon the implementation. Across all C compilers, the only guarantee is that a variable of type **short** will not be larger than one of type **long**. Borland C/C++ allocates 2 bytes for both **short** and **int**. (Under Windows 95 and Windows NT integers are now 32 bits.) The type **long** occupies 4 bytes of storage.

Modifying Types

Currently, you can apply the **unsigned** modifier to four types: **char**, **short int**, **int**, and **long int**. When one of these data types is modified to be unsigned, you can think of the range of values it holds as representing the numbers displayed on a car odometer. An automobile odometer starts at 000..., increases to a maximum of 999..., and then recycles back to 000.... It also displays only positive whole numbers. In a similar way, an unsigned data type can hold only positive values in the range beginning with zero and running to the maximum number that can be represented.

Let's take a look at a hypothetical example. Suppose you are designing a new data type called *OCTAL* and have decided that *OCTAL* variables can hold only 3 bits. You have also decided that the data type *OCTAL* is signed by default. Because a variable of type *OCTAL* can only contain the bit patterns 000 through 111 (or 0 to 7 decimal) and you want to represent both positive and negative values, you have a problem. You can't have both positive and negative numbers in the range 0 to 7 because you need one of the three bits to represent the sign of the number. Therefore, *OCTAL*'s range is a subset. When the most significant bit is 0, the value is positive. When the most significant bit is 1, the value is negative. This gives an *OCTAL* variable the range of -4 to +3.

However, applying the **unsigned** data type modifier to an *OCTAL* variable would yield a range of 0 to 7, because the most significant bit can be combined with the lower two bits to represent a broader range of positive values instead of identifying the sign of the number. This simple analogy holds true for any of the valid C data types defined to be of type **unsigned**. The storage and range for the fundamental C data types are summarized in Table 6-2 (16-bit) and Table 6-3 (32-bit).

Access Modifiers

Many older high-level languages have the keyword **const**, which is used to declare constant values. However, both the **const** and **volatile** modifiers are new to C and

Type	Length	Range		
unsigned char	8 bits	0	to	255
char	8 bits	-128	to	127
enum	16 bits	-32,768	to	32,767
unsigned int	16 bits	0	to	65,535
short int	16 bits	-32,768	to	32,767
int	16 bits	-32,768	to	32,767
unsigned long	32 bits	0	to	4,294,967,295
long	32 bits	-2,147,483,648	to	2,147,483,647
float	32 bits	3.4 x 10-38	to	3.4 x 10+38
double	64 bits	1.7 x 10-308	to	1.7 x 10+308
long double	80 bits	3.4 x 10-4932	to	1.1 x 10+4932
near (pointer)	16 bits	NA		
far (pointer)	32 bits	NA		

Table 6-2. *Fundamental C Data Types (16-bit)*

C++. They were added by the ANSI C standard to help identify which variables will never change (**const**) and which variables can change unexpectedly (**volatile**).

The const Modifier

Whenever your program wants to guarantee that a variable's contents remain unchanged, it declares a *constant*. For example, if a program deals with the area and circumference of a circle, the constant value pi=3.14159 would be used frequently. In a financial program, an interest rate might be a constant. In such cases, you can improve the readability of the program by giving the constant a descriptive name. Using descriptive names can also help prevent errors.

Suppose that a constant value (not a constant variable) is used at many points throughout the program. A typographical error might result in the wrong value being typed at one or more of these points. However, if the constant is given a name, a typographical error would then be detected by the compiler because the incorrectly spelled identifier would probably not have been declared. Suppose you are writing a program that repeatedly uses the value pi. It might seem as though a *variable* called *pi* should be declared with an initial value of 3.14159. However, the program should not

Type	Length	Range		
unsigned char	8 bits	0	to	255
char	8 bits	-128	to	127
short int	16 bits	-32,768	to	32,767
unsigned int	32 bits	0	to	4,294,967,295
int	32 bits	-2,147,483,648	to	2,147,483,647
unsigned long	32 bits	0	to	4,294,967,295
enum	16 bits	-2,147,483,648	to	2,147,483,647
long	32 bits	-2,147,483,648	to	2,147,483,647
float	32 bits	3.4×10^{-38}	to	$3.4 \times 10^{+38}$
double	64 bits	1.7×10^{-308}	to	$1.7 \times 10^{+308}$
long double	80 bits	3.4×10^{-4932}	to	$1.1 \times 10^{+4932}$
near (pointer)	32 bits		NA	
far (pointer)	32 bits		NA	

Table 6-3.   *Fundamental C Data Types (32-bit)*

be able to change the value of a constant. For instance, if you inadvertently wrote "pi" to the left of an equal sign, the value of pi would be changed, causing all subsequent calculations to be incorrect. C and C++ provide mechanisms that prevent such an error from occurring: you can establish constants, the values of which cannot be changed.

The following four statements demonstrate how to define C/C++ constants. You declare a constant by writing "const" before the keyword (such as **int**, **float**, or **double**) in the declaration. Because a constant cannot be changed, it must be initialized in its declaration:

```
int     iSum                    =    100,
            iOffset             =      1,
            iHowMany                   ;
        double dMicrons         =      0,
            dAcceleration              ;
const int   iLowerLimit         =      1,
            iDISCOUNT_RATE      =     25;
const float fConversionFactor = 32.157;
```

The integer constants *iLowerLimit* and *iDISCOUNT_RATE* are declared with values 1 and 25, respectively; the constant *fConversionFactor* is of type **float** and has been initialized to 32.157. In addition, the integer (nonconstant) variables *iSum*, *iOffset*, and *iHowMany* have been declared. Initial values of 100 and 1 have been established for *iSum* and *iOffset*, respectively. Finally, *dMicrons* and *dAcceleration* have been declared to be (nonconstant) variables of type **double**. An initial value of 0 has been set up for *dMicrons*.

The only difference between the use of constants and variables is that the initial values assigned to the constants cannot be changed. That is, the constants are not *lvalues*; they cannot appear to the left of an equal sign. (Expressions that refer to memory locations are called *lvalue expressions*.)

Expressions referring to modifiable locations are modifiable *lvalues*. One example of a modifiable *lvalue* expression is a variable name declared without the **const** specifier. Normally, the assignment operation assigns the value of the right-hand operand to the storage location named by the left-hand operand. Therefore, the left-hand operand of an assignment operation (or the single operand of a unary assignment expression) must be an expression that refers to a modifiable memory location.

#define Constants

Actually, both C and C++ provide another method for establishing constants, the **#define** compiler directive. Let's look at an example. Suppose that at the beginning of a program, you have this statement:

```
#define NUMBER_OF_ACCOUNTS 10
```

The form of this statement is **#define** followed by two strings of characters separated by blanks. When the program is compiled, there are several passes made through the program. The first step is accomplished by the *compiler preprocessor*. The preprocessor does such things as carry out the **#include** and **#define** directives. When the preprocessor encounters the **#define** directive, it replaces every occurrence of *NUMBER_OF_ACCOUNTS* in the source file(s) with the number 10.

In general, when the preprocessor encounters a **#define** directive, it replaces every occurrence of the first string of characters, "*NUMBER_OF_ACCOUNTS*", in the program with the second string of characters, "10". Additionally, no value can be assigned to *NUMBER_OF_ACCOUNTS* because it has never been declared a variable. As a result of the syntax, *NUMBER_OF_ACCOUNTS* has all the attributes of a constant. Note that the **#define** statement is *not* terminated by a semicolon. If a semicolon followed the value 10, then every occurrence of *NUMBER_OF_ACCOUNTS* would be replaced with "10;". The directive's action is to replace the first string with *everything* in the second string. All of the programs that have been discussed so far are short and would usually be stored in a single file. If a statement such as the **#define** for *NUMBER_OF_ACCOUNTS* appeared at the beginning of the file, the substitution of "10" for "*NUMBER_OF_ACCOUNTS*" would take place throughout the program. Under these circumstances, the compiler directive would be effective only for the single file in which it is written.

You now understand that C and C++ provide two distinct approaches to defining program constants. In many programs, the action of each of these two methods is essentially the same. On the other hand, the use of the modifier keyword **const** results in a "variable," the value of which cannot be changed. Later in this chapter, in the "Storage Classes" section, you will see how variables can be declared in such a way that they exist only over certain regions of a program. The same can be said for constants declared with the keyword **const**. Thus, the **const** declaration is somewhat more versatile than the **#define** directive. Also, the **#define** directive is found in standard C and C++ and is therefore already familiar to C programmers.

The volatile Modifier

In a multitasking environment, it is quite possible that a value calculated by one program is passed to another. To help an application legalize such actions, it needs to declare the associated variable **volatile**. The **volatile** keyword signifies that a variable can unexpectedly change because of events outside the control of the program. For example, the following definition indicates that the variable *iExternallyReferencedVariable* can have its value changed without the knowledge of the program:

```
volatile int iExternallyReferencedVariable;
```

A definition like this is needed, for example, if *iExternallyReferencedVariable* is updated by hardware that maintains the current clock time. The program that contains the variable *iExternallyReferencedVariable* could be interrupted by the time-keeping hardware and the variable *iExternallyReferencedVariable* changed. A data object should be declared volatile if it is a memory-mapped device register or a data object shared by separate processes, as would be the case in a multitasking operating environment.

const and volatile Used Together

Both C and C++ allow your applications to use the **const** and **volatile** modifiers with any other data types (for example, **char** and **float**) and also with each other. The following definition specifies that the program does not intend to change the value in the variable *ciExternallyReferencedVariable*:

```
const volatile ciExternallyReferencedVariable;
```

Note that because of the second keyword, **volatile**, the compiler makes no assumptions about the variable's value from one moment to the next. Therefore, two things happen. First, an error message is issued by the compiler for any line of source code that attempts to change the value of the variable *ciExternallyReferencedVariable*. Second, the compiler will not remove the variable *ciExternallyReferencedVariable* from inside loops because an external process can also be updating the variable while the program is executing.

Modifiers: pascal, cdecl, near, far, and huge

Borland C++ allows you to write C/C++ programs that can easily call other routines written in different languages. The first two modifiers, **pascal** and **cdecl**, are used most frequently in these types of advanced applications. The opposite of this also holds true. For example, you can write a Pascal program that calls a C/C++ routine.

When you mix languages this way, you have to take two very important issues into consideration: identifier names and the way parameters are passed. When Borland C/C++ compiles your program, it places all of the program's global identifiers (functions and variables) into the resulting object code file for linking purposes. By default, the compiler saves those identifiers using the same case in which they were defined (uppercase, lowercase, or mixed). Additionally, the compiler appends to the front of the identifier an underscore (_). Because Borland C++'s integrated linking (by default) is case sensitive, any external identifiers you declare in your program are also assumed to be in the same form with a prepended underscore and the same spelling and case as defined.

pascal

Older high-level languages use a different calling sequence than C and C++. For example, FORTRAN and Pascal pass function arguments from left to right and do not allow variable-length argument lists. In Pascal, it is also the called function's responsibility to remove the arguments from the stack, rather than having the invoking function do so when control returns from the invoked function. A C and C++ program can generate this calling sequence in one of two ways. First, it can use a compile-time switch, which makes the Pascal calling sequence the default for all enclosed calls and function definitions. Second, the C program can override the default C calling sequence explicitly by using the **pascal** keyword in the function definition.

When C generates a function call, by default it appends an underscore to the function name and declares the function external. It also preserves the casing of the name. However, when the **pascal** keyword is used, the underscore is not prepended and the identifier (function or variable) is converted to uppercase. The following code segment demonstrates how to use the **pascal** keyword on a function. (The same keyword can be used to ensure FORTRAN code compatibility.)

```
float pascal piCalculateBill ( int    iNUMBER_OF_ACCOUNTS,
                               float fDiscountRate      )
{
   .    .    .
}
```

The following coded segment highlights the ability to use the Pascal modifier with variable declarations:

```
float pascal piCalculateBill ( int    iNUMBER_OF_ACCOUNTS,
                               float fDiscountRate      )
{
   .    .    .
}

int pascal piCustomerAccounts [ NUMBER_OF_ACCOUNTS ]  ;

void main( void )
{
  int iNUMBER_OF_ACCOUNTS 50, fDiscountRate = 15;

  piCustomerAccounts [ 0 ] =
           piCalculateBill ( iNUMBER_OF_ACCOUNTS,fDiscountRate );
}
```

Here *piCustomerAccounts* is globally defined with the **pascal** modifier. Function **main()** also shows how to make an external reference to a **pascal** function type. Since both functions, **main()** and *piCalculateBill()*, are in the same source file, the function *piCalculateBill()* is global to **main().**

cdecl

Should your application need to guarantee that certain identifiers remain case sensitive and keep the underscore at the front, the program uses the keyword **cdecl**. This is most often the case for identifiers being used in another C file. To maintain this C compatibility (preserving the case and having a leading underscore prepended), you can use the **cdecl** keyword. When the **cdecl** keyword is used in front of a function, it also affects how the parameters are passed. Note that all C and C++ functions prototyped in the header files of Borland C/C++—for example, stdio.h—are of type

cdecl. This ensures that you can link with the library routines. The following example shows how you would rewrite the previous example to maintain C compatibility:

```
#define NUMBER_OF_ACCOUNTS 30

float cdecl cfCalculateBill ( int    iNUMBER_OF_ACCOUNTS,
                              float fDiscountRate        )
{
    .
    .
    .
}

int cdecl ciCustomerAccounts [ NUMBER_OF_ACCOUNTS ]    ;

void main( void )
{
    int iNUMBER_OF_ACCOUNTS 50, fDiscountRate = 15;

    ciCustomerAccounts[0] =
            cfCalculateBill ( iNUMBER_OF_ACCOUNTS,fDiscountRate );
}
```

near, far, and huge

These three modifiers are now somewhat passé as a direct result of the newer 32-bit operating systems and matching 32-bit C/C++ compilers (all addresses under these environments are a full 32-bits). However, if you are still developing for the older 16-bit environments, you use the three modifiers **near**, **far**, and **huge** to affect the action of the indirection operator (*); in other words, they modify pointer sizes to data objects. A **near** pointer is only 2 bytes long, a **far** pointer is 4 bytes long, and a **huge** pointer is also 4 bytes long. The difference between the **far** pointer and the **huge** pointer is that the **huge** pointer has to deal with the form of the address.

Conversions—Data Type

Frequently, an application will employ what is called a *mixed-mode* calculation. This is where an equation uses combinations of the standard data types, such as **int** and **float**. You can write statements that perform operations involving variables of different types. In contrast to some other programming languages, C and C++ perform automatic conversions from one type to another. As you progress through the book, additional types will be introduced, and mixing of those types will be discussed.

All compilers encode each data type differently in memory. Suppose that the number 10 is being stored. Its representation will depend upon its type. That is, the pattern of zeros and ones in memory will be different when 10 is stored as an integer than when it is stored as a floating-point number. Suppose that the following operation is executed, where both *fFloatTypeResult* and *fUserInputValue* are of type **float**, and the variable *iIntegerTypeValue* is of type **int**. The statement is therefore a mixed-mode operation:

```
fFloatTypeResult = fUserInputValue * iIntegerTypeValue;
```

When the statement is executed, the value of *iIntegerTypeValue* will be converted into a floating-point number before the multiplication takes place. The compiler recognizes that a mixed-mode operation is taking place. Therefore, it generates code to perform the following operations. The integer value assigned to *iIntegerTypeValue* is read from memory. This value is then converted to the corresponding floating-point value, which is then multiplied by the real value assigned to *fUserInputValue,* and the resulting floating-point value is assigned to *fFloatTypeResult.* In other words, the compiler performs the conversion automatically. Note that the value assigned to *iIntegerTypeValue* is unchanged by this process and remains of type **int**.

You have seen that in mixed-mode operations involving a value of type **int** and another value of type **float**, the value of type **int** is converted into a value of type **float** for calculation. This is done without changing the stored integral value during the conversion process. Now let's consider mixed-mode operations between two different types of variables. Actually, before doing this, you need to know that there is in fact a *hierarchy of conversions,* in that the object of lower priority is temporarily converted to the type of higher priority for the performance of the calculation. The hierarchy of conversions takes the following structure, from highest priority to lowest: **double, float, long, int, short**. For example, the type **double** has a higher priority than the type **int**. When a type is converted, the value of the number and its accuracy are unchanged.

In this next example a conversion from type **float** to type **int** takes place. Suppose that the variables *iIntegerTypeValue1* and *iIntegerTypeValue2* have been defined to be of type **int**, while *fUserInputValue* and *fFloatTypeResult* have been defined to be of type **float**. Consider the following sequence of statements:

```
iIntegerTypeValue1 =    3;
iIntegerTypeValue2 =    4;

fUserInputValue    = 7.0;

fFloatTypeResult   = fUserInputValue +
                     iIntegerTypeValue1 / iIntegerTypeValue2 ;
```

In this example, the statement *iIntegerTypeValue1 / iIntegerTypeValue2* is *not* a mixed-mode operation; instead, it represents the division of two integers, and its result is zero because the fractional part (0.75, in this case) is *discarded* when integer division is performed. Therefore the value stored in *fFloatTypeResult* is 7.0. However, what if *iIntegerTypeValue2* had been defined to be of type **float**?

In this case, *fFloatTypeResult* would have been assigned the floating-point value 7.75 since the statement *iIntegerTypeValue1 / iIntegerTypeValue2* would be a mixed-mode operation. Under these circumstances, the value of *iIntegerTypeValue1* is temporarily converted to the floating-point value 3.0, and the result of the division is 0.75. When that is added to *fUserInputValue*, the result is 7.75. It is important to know that the type of the value to the left of the assignment statement determines the type of the result of the operation.

For example, suppose that *fx* and *fy* have been declared to be of type **float** and *iIntegerResult* has been declared to be of type **int**. Consider the following statements:

```
fx            = 7.0          ;
fy            = 2.0          ;
iIntegerResult = 4.0 + fx / fy ;
```

Here, you might think that the variable *iIntegerResult* is assigned *fx/fy* which is 3.5, added to 4.0, or a floating-point result of 7.5. However, this value cannot be assigned to *iIntegerResult* because *iIntegerResult* is of type **int**. The number 7.5 is therefore converted into an integer. When this is done, the fraction part is truncated. The resulting whole number is converted from a floating-point representation to an integer representation, and the value assigned to *iIntegerResult* is the integer number 7.

Converting One Data Type to Another Using the Cast Operator

Even though the C/C++ compilers automatically change the format of a variable in mixed-mode operations, there are circumstances where automatic conversion is *not* performed. For those occasions, you must specifically designate that a change of type is to be made. These explicit specifications also clarify to other programmers the statements involved. The C language provides several procedures that allow you to designate that type conversion must occur. One of these procedures is called the *cast operator*.

Whenever you want to temporarily change the format of a variable, you simply precede the variable's identifier with the parenthesized type you want it converted to. For example, if *iIntegerTypeValue1* and *iIntegerTypeValue2* were defined to be of type **int** and *fUserInputValue* and *fFloatTypeResult* have been defined to be of type **float**, the following three statements would perform the same operation. All three statements perform a floating-point conversion and division of the variables *iIntegerTypeValue1* and *iIntegerTypeValue2*:

```
fFloatTypeResult = fUserInputValue +
                    (float)iIntegerTypeValue1 / iIntegerTypeValue2 ;
fFloatTypeResult = fUserInputValue +
                    iIntegerTypeValue1/(float)iIntegerTypeValue2   ;
fFloatTypeResult = fUserInputValue +
                    (float)iIntegerTypeValue1 /
                    (float)iIntegerTypeValue2                      ;
```

Because of the usual rules of mixed-mode arithmetic discussed earlier, if either variable is cast to type **float**, a floating-point division occurs. The third statement explicitly highlights the operation to be performed.

Storage Classes

There are four ways to define or alter a variable's storage class. Borland C++ supports the four storage class specifiers: **auto**, **register**, **static**, and **extern**. The storage class precedes the variable's declaration and instructs the compiler how the variable should be stored. Items declared with the **auto** or **register** specifier have local lifetimes. Items declared with the **static** or **extern** specifier have global lifetimes. (An item with a local lifetime XXXXXXXX; an item with a global lifetime exists throughout the execution of the source program.)

Storage class specifiers also affect the visibility of a variable or function, as well as its storage class. *Visibility* (sometimes defined as scope) refers to that portion of the source program in which the variable or function can be referenced by name.

You can also change a variable's storage class and visibility by moving its declaration within the source file. Declarations outside all function definitions are said to appear at the *external level*, while declarations within function definitions appear at the *internal level*. The exact meaning of each storage class specifier depends on two factors: whether the declaration appears at the external or internal level and whether the item being declared is a variable or a function.

Variable Declarations at the External Level

The only storage classes legal at the external level (outside all functions) are **static** and **extern**, not **auto** or **register**. They are either definitions of variables or references to variables defined elsewhere. An external variable declaration that also initializes the variable (implicitly or explicitly) is a defining declaration:

```
static int iNumOne      ; // implicit 0 by default
static int iNumOne = 10  // explicit

int iNumTwo        = 20; // explicit
```

Once a variable is defined at the external level, it is visible throughout the rest of the source file in which it appears. The variable is not visible prior to its definition in the same source file. Also, it is not visible in other source files of the program unless a referencing declaration makes it visible, as described shortly. You can define a variable at the external level only once within a source file. If you give the **static** storage-class specifier, you can define another variable with the same name and the **static** storage-class specifier in a different source file. Because each **static** definition is visible only within its own source file, no conflict occurs.

When your application uses the **extern** storage-class specifier it is referencing a variable defined elsewhere. You can use an external declaration to make a definition in another source file visible or to make a variable visible above its definition in the same source file. The variable is visible throughout the remainder of the source file in which the declared reference occurs. For an external reference to be valid, the variable it refers to must be defined once, and only once, at the external level. The definition can be in any of the source files that form the program. The following C++ program demonstrates the use of the **extern** keyword:

```
//
//     FileA.c
//
#include <iostream.h>

extern int iAn_Int;                  // makes iAn_Int visible
                                     // above its declaration


void main( void )
{
    iAn_Int++;                       // uses the above extern
                                     // reference
    cout << iAn_Int << "\n";         // prints 11
    TestFunctionOne ( )   ;
}

int iAn_Int = 10;                    // actual definition of
```

```
                                    // iAn_Int

void TestFunctionOne( void )
{
  iAn_Int++               ;           // references iAn_Int
  cout << iAn_Int << "\n";            // prints 12
  TestFunctionTwo ( )     ;
}


/\/\/\/\/\/\/\/\/\/\/\/\/\/\/\/\/\/\/\/\/\/\/\/\/\/\/\
//
//      FileB.c
//

#include <iostream.h>

extern int iAn_Int;                  // references iAn_Int
                                     // declared in Source A

void TestFunctionTwo( void )
{
  iAn_Int++                ;
  cout << iAn_Int << "\n" ;          // prints 13
}
```

Variable Declarations at the Internal Level

All four storage class specifiers are legal at the internal level (inside function bodies). The default is **auto**. The **auto** storage-class specifier declares a variable with a local lifetime. It is visible only in the block in which it is declared and can include initializers.

Local variable declarations preceded by the **register** storage-class specifier instruct the compiler to give the variable storage in a register, if possible. This specifier speeds access time and reduces code size. It has the same visibility as an **auto** variable. If no registers are available when the compiler encounters a register declaration, the variable is given the **auto** storage class and stored in memory. Although ANSI C does not allow for taking the address of a register object, this restriction does not apply to C++. Applying the address operator (&) to a C++ register variable forces the compiler to store the object in memory because the compiler must put the object in a location for which an address can be represented.

When preceding a variable declaration at the internal level with the **static** storage-class specifier, you instruct the compiler to give the variable a global lifetime but visibility only within the block in which it is declared. Unlike **auto** variables, **static** variables keep their values when the block is exited. You can initialize a **static** variable with a constant expression. It is initialized to zero by default.

A variable declared with the **extern** storage-class specifier is a reference to a variable with the same name defined at the external level in any of the source files of the program. The internal **extern** declaration is used to make the external-level variable definition visible within the block. The next program demonstrates these concepts:

```
int iNumOne =  1;

void main( void )
{ // references the iNumOne defined above
     extern int iNumOne;

  // default initialization of 0, iNumTwo only visible
  // in main()
     static int iNumTwo;

  // stored in a register (if available), initialized
  // to 0
     register int rRegisterVariable = 0;

  // default auto storage class, iNumThree initialized
  // to 0
     int iNumThree = 0;

  // values printed are 1, 0, 0, 0:
     cout << iNumOne << rRegisterVariable
         <<iNumTwo  << iNumThree           ;
     TestFunctionOne ( )                   ;
}

void TestFunctionOne( void )
{
  // stores the address of the global variable iNumOne
     static int *piNumOne = &iNumOne;

  // creates a new local variable iNumOne making the
  // global iNumOne unreachable
     int iNumOne = 32;
```

```
    // new local variable iNumTwo
    // only visible within TestFunctionOne
       static int iNumTwo = 2;

       iNumTwo += 2;

    // the values printed are 32, 4, and 1:
       cout << iNumOne << iNumTwo

            << *piNumOne;
}
```

Because *iNumOne* is redefined in **TestFunctionOne()**, access to the global *iNumOne* is denied. However, by using the data pointer *piNumOne* (discussed in Chapter 10), the address of the global *iNumOne* was used to print the value stored there.

Visibility Rules--A Review

To summarize, C and C++ provide four ways to control a variable's visibility, or scope. The four scopes for a variable are: block, function, file, and program. A variable declared within a block or function is known only within the block or function. A variable declared external to a function is known within the file in which it appears, from the point of its appearance to the end of the file. A variable declared external in one source file and declared external in other files has program scope.

Function Declarations at the External Level

C and C++ demand all function declarations to be at the external level. These languages do not permit nesting of function bodies, as do many older high-level languages such as Pascal. When declaring a function at the external level, you can use either the **static** or the **extern** storage-class specifier. Functions, unlike variables, always have a global lifetime.

The visibility rules for functions vary slightly from the rules for variables. Functions declared to be static are visible only within the source file in which they are defined. Functions in the same source file can call the **static** function, but functions in *other* source files cannot. Also, you can declare another **static** function with the same name in a different source file without conflict. Functions declared external are visible throughout *all* source files that make up the program (unless you later redeclare such a function to be static). Any function can call an external function. Function declarations that omit the storage-class specifier are external by default.

C/C++ Operators

Although the good news is that C and C++ have many of the standard operators found in other high-level languages, you will be surprised at the number of operators *not* found in other languages. These include bitwise operators, increment and decrement operators, conditional operators, the comma operator, and assignment and compound assignment operators.

Arithmetic Operators

The most obvious and straightforward of the C/C++ operators are the standard set of arithmetic operators for addition (+), subtraction (-), multiplication (*), division (/), and modulus (%). The first four are straightforward and need no amplification. However, an example of the modulus operator will help you understand its usage and syntax. Here the modulus operator returns the remainder of integer division. The last assignment statement attempts to divide 8 by 0, resulting in an error message:

```
int iValue1 = 3,
    iValue2 = 8,
    iValue3 = 0,
    iResult   ;

iResult = iValue2 % iValue1;        // iResult = 2
iResult = iValue1 % iValue1;        // iResult = 3

iResult = iValue2 % iValue3;        // error condition
```

The Assignment Operator

Like other C operators, the result of an assignment operator is a value that is assigned. However, the assignment operator in C is different than the assignment statement in other languages. Assignment is performed by an assignment operator rather than an assignment statement. An expression with an assignment operator can be used in a large expression such as this:

```
iValue1 = 8 * ( iValue2 = 5 );
```

In this example, the variable *iValue2* is first assigned the value 5. This is multiplied by the 8, with *iValue1* receiving a final value of 40. Overuse of the assignment operator can rapidly lead to unmanageable expressions. There are two places in which this feature is normally applied. First, it can be used to set several variables to a particular value, as in, $X = Y = Z = 0$. The second use is most often seen in the condition of a

while loop, such as *while ((c = getchar()) != EOF)*. This assigns the value that **getchar()** returned to c and then tests the value against EOF. If it is EOF, the loop is not executed. The parentheses are necessary because the assignment operator has a lower precedence than the nonequality operator. Otherwise, the line would be interpreted as *c = (getchar() != EOF)*. The variable *c* would be assigned a value of 1 (TRUE) each time **getchar()** returned EOF.

Bitwise Operators

The C/C++ bitwise operators allow you to look at a variable's contents as binary values. They are useful in accessing the individual bits in memory, such as the screen memory for a graphics display. Bitwise operators can operate only on integral data types, not on floating-point numbers. Three bitwise operators act just like the logical operators, but on each bit in an integer. These are AND (&), OR (|), and XOR (^). An additional operator is the one's complement (~), which simply inverts each bit.

AND (&)

The bitwise AND operator compares two bits; if both bits are a 1, the result is a 1. Note that this is different from binary addition, where the comparison of two 1 bits would result in a sum flag set to zero and the carry flag set to 1. Very often the AND operation is used to select out, or *mask*, certain bit positions. For example:

0xF1	& 0x35	Returns 0x31 (hexadecimal)
0361	& 0065	Returns 061 (octal)
11110011	& 00110101	Returns 00110011 (bitwise)

OR (|)

The bitwise OR operator compares two bits and generates a 1 result if either or both bits are a 1. The OR operation is useful for setting specified bit positions. For example:

0xF1	| 0x35	Returns 0xF5 (hexadecimal)
0361	| 0065	Returns 0365 (octal)
11110011	| 00110101	Returns 11110111 (bitwise)

XOR (^)

The EXCLUSIVE OR operator compares two bits and returns a result of 1 when, and only when, the two bits are complementary. This logical operation can be very useful when it is necessary to complement specified bit positions, as in the case of computer graphics applications. Following is an example of using these operators with the hexadecimal and octal representation of constants. The bit values are shown for comparison.

0xF1 ^ 0x35	Returns 0xC4 (hexadecimal)
0361 ^ 0065	Returns 0304 (octal)
11110011 ^ 00110101	Returns 00000000 11000110 (bitwise)

NOT

The NOT operation performs a logical invert operation. For example:

~0xF1	Returns 0xFF0E (hexadecimal)
~0361	Returns 0177416 (octal)
~11110011	Returns 11111111 00001100 (bitwise)

The Comma Operator

C and C++ provide the comma operator, which allows two expressions to be evaluated where normally only one is syntactically legal. The value of the comma operator is the value of the right-hand expression. One place where the comma operator commonly appears is in a **for** loop, where more than one variable is being iterated. For example, *for(min=0, max=length-1; min < max; min++,max—)*.

Compound Assignment Operators

C and C++ allow you to easily abbreviate expressions with the use of compound assignment operators. This additional set of assignment operators allows for a more concise way of expressing certain computations. The following code segment shows the standard assignment syntax applicable in many high-level languages. If you look closely at these two code segments, you will quickly see the required syntax:

```
iOffset = iOffset + irow_increment;
ddepth = ddepth - d1_fathom;
fcalculate_tax = fcalculate_tax * 1.07;
fyards = fyards / ifeet_convert;
```

C's compound assignment statements would look like this:

```
iOffset += irow_increment;
ddepth -= d1_fathom;
fcalculate_tax *= 1.07;
fyards /= ifeet_convert;
```

Using a C compound assignment operator requires you to remove the redundant variable reference from the right-hand side of the assignment operator and place the operation to be performed immediately before the =.

The Conditional Operator

Another new operator just waiting to syntactically and logically confuse a novice C/C++ programmer is the conditional operator (?:). The operator has this syntax:

TestCondition ? *TRUE_Statement* : *FALSE_Statement*;

If the *TestCondition* is TRUE, the value of the conditional expression is *TRUE_Statement*. Otherwise, it is the value of *FALSE_Statement*. For example, look at the following statement:

```
if( 'A'  <=  c && c <= 'Z' )
    cout << ( 'a' + c - 'A' );
  else
      cout << c;
```

You could rewrite the statement using the conditional operator:

```
cout << ('A' <= c && c <= 'Z') ? ('a' + c - 'A') : c;
```

Both statements will make certain that the character printed, "c", is always lowercase.

The Increment and Decrement Operators

C and C++ have a special set of operators to add or subtract 1 from a number; these are the *increment* (++) and *decrement* (- -) *operators*. The two characters must be placed next to each other without any white space. They can be applied only to variables, not to constants. Instead of coding this way:

```
Sum + 1;
```

you can write this:

```
Sum++;
```

or

```
++Sum;
```

When these two operators are the sole operators in an expression, you will not have to worry about the difference between the different syntaxes. A **for** loop very often uses this type of increment for the loop control variable:

```
Total = 0;
for( times = 1; times <= 5; times++  )
  Total = Total + i;
```

A decrement loop would be coded this way:

```
Total = 0;
for( times = 5; times  >= 1; times -- )
  Total = Total + i;
```

If you use these operators in complex expressions, you have to consider *when* the increment or decrement actually takes place. The postfix increment, for example *times*++, uses the value of the variable in the expression first and then increments its value. However, the prefix increment, for example ++*times*, increments the value of the variable first and then uses the value in the expression. Assume the following data declarations:

```
int x = 3,
    y    ,
    z = 0;
```

See if you can figure out what happens in each of the following statements. For simplicity, assume the original initialized values of the variables for each statement:

Statement	x is assigned	y is assigned	z is assigned
z = ++x;	4		4
z = x++;	4		3
z = --x;	2		2
z = x--;	2		3
x = y = z--;	0	0	-1

Although the subtleties of these two different operations may currently elude you, they are included in the C language because of specific situations that cannot be eloquently handled in any other way.

The Left Shift and Right Shift Operators

C incorporates two shift operators, the left shift (<<) and the right shift (>>) operators. The left shift moves the bits to the left and sets the rightmost (least significant) bit to zero. The leftmost (most significant) bit shifted out is thrown away. In terms of unsigned integers, shifting the number one position to the left and filling the LSB with a zero doubles the number's value. The following C++ code segment demonstrates how this would be coded:

```
unsigned int value1 = 65;
value1 <<= 1    ;
cout    << value1;
```

If you were to examine *value1*'s lower byte you would see the following bit changes performed:

```
<<     0100     0001     ( Decimal 65  )

       1000     0010     ( Decimal 130 )
```

The right shift operator moves bits to the right. The lower order bits shifted out are thrown away. Halving an unsigned integer is as simple as shifting the bits one position to the right, filling the MSB position with a zero. A C coded example would look very similar to the preceding example except for the compound operator assignment statement (discussed later in the chapter) and the output statement:

```
unsigned int value1 = 10;
value1 >>= 1;
printf ( "%d", value1 ) ;
```

Examining just the lower byte of the variable *value1* would reveal the following bit changes:

```
<<     0000     1010     ( Decimal 10 )

       0000     0101     ( Decimal  5 )
```

Relational and Logical Operators

All relational operators are used to establish a relationship between the values of the operands. They always produce a value of !0 if the relationship evaluates to TRUE or a 0 value if the relationship evaluates to FALSE. Following is a list of the C and C++ relational operators:

Operator	Meaning
==	Equality (not assignment)
!=	Not equal
>	Greater than
<	Less than
>=	Greater than or equal
<=	Less than or equal

The logical operators AND (&&), OR (| |), and NOT (!) produce a TRUE (!0) or FALSE (zero) based on the logical relationship of their arguments. The simplest way to remember how the logical AND && works is to say that an ANDed expression will only return a true (!0) when both arguments are true (!0). The logical OR | | operation in turn will only return a FALSE (zero) when both arguments are FALSE (zero). The logical NOT ! simply inverts the value. Following is a list of the C and C++ logical operators:

Operator	Meaning
!	NOT
&&	AND
| |	OR

Have some fun with the following C program as you test the various combinations of relational and logical operators. See if you can predict the results ahead of time.

```
/*
 *   operator.c
 *   A C program demonstrating some of the subtleties of
 *   logical and relational operators.
 *   Copyright (c) Chris H. Pappas and William H. Murray, 1996
 */
```

```
#include <stdio.h>

void main( void )
{
  float fA, fB;

  printf ( "\nEnter fA and fB: " );
  scanf  ( "%f%f",&fA,&fB         );

  printf("\n  fA > fB is %d",
          (fA > fB)             );

  printf("\n  fA < fB is %d",
          (fA < fB)             );

  printf("\n  fA >= fB is %d",
          (fA >= fB)            );

  printf("\n  fA <= fB is %d",
          (fA <= fB)            );

  printf("\n  fA == fB is %d",
          (fA == fB)            );

  printf("\n  fA != fB is %d",
          (fA != fB)            );

  printf("\n  fA && fA is %d",
          (fA && fB)            );

  printf("\n  fA || fB is %d",
          (fA || fB)            );
}
```

You may be surprised at some of the results obtained for some of the logical comparisons. Remember, there is a very strict comparison that occurs for both data types **float** and **double** when values of these types are compared with zero—a number that is very slightly different from another number is still not equal. Also, a number that is just slightly above or below zero is still TRUE (!0).

The C++ equivalent of the program just examined follows:

```
//
//  operator.cpp
//  A C++ program demonstrating some of the subtleties of
//  logical and relational operators.
//  Copyright (c) Chris H. Pappas and William H. Murray, 1996
//

#include <iostream.h>

main()
{
  float fA, fB;

  cout << "\nEnter fA and fB: ";
  cin >> fA >> fB;

  cout << endl;

  cout << " fA  > fB is "
       << (fA  > fB)
       << endl;

  cout << " fA  < fB is "
       << (fA  < fB)
       << endl;

  cout << " fA >= fB is "
       << (fA >= fB)
       << endl;

  cout << " fA <= fB is "
       << (fA <= fB)
       << endl;

  cout << " fA == fB is "
       << (fA == fB)
       << endl;

  cout << " fA != fB is "
       << (fA != fB)
       << endl;
```

File Name	Compatibility	Description
io.h		Contains structures and declarations for low-level input/output routines.
iomanip.h	C++	Declares the C++ streams I/O manipulators and contains templates for creating parameterized manipulators.
iostream.h	C++	Declares the basic C++ streams (I/O) routines.
limits.h	ANSI C	Contains environmental parameters, information about compile-time limitations, and ranges of integral quantities.
locale.h	ANSI C	Declares functions that provide country- and language-specific information.
malloc.h		Declares memory-management functions and variables.
math.h	ANSI C	Declares prototypes for the math functions and math error handlers.
mem.h		Declares the memory-manipulation functions. (Many of these are also defined in string.h.)
memory.h		Contains memory-manipulation functions.
new.h	C++	Access to _new_handler, and set_new_handler.
_nfile.h		Defines the maximum number of open files.
_null.h		Defines the value of NULL.
process.h		Contains structures and declarations for the spawn... and exec... functions.
search.h		Declares functions for searching and sorting.
setjmp.h	ANSI C	Declares the functions **longjmp** and **setjmp** and defines a type jmp_buf that these functions use.
share.h		Defines parameters used in functions that make use of file-sharing.
signal.h	ANSI C	Defines constants and declarations for use by the signal and raise functions.

Table 6-5. *Standard C/C++ Libraries* (continued)

File Name	Compatibility	Description
stdarg.h	ANSI C	Defines macros used for reading the argument list in functions declared to accept a variable number of arguments (such as **vprintf**, **vscanf**, and so on).
stddef.h	ANSI C	Defines several common data types and macros.
stdio.h	ANSI C	Defines types and macros needed for the standard I/O package defined by Kernighan and Ritchie and extended under UNIX System V. Defines the standard I/O predefined streams stdin, stdout, stdprn, and stderr, and declares stream-level I/O routines.
stdiostr.h	C++	Declares the C++ (version 2.0) stream classes for use with stdio FILE structures. You should use iostream.h for new code.
stdlib.h	ANSI C	Declares several commonly used routines such as conversion routines and search/sort routines.
string.h	ANSI C	Declares several string-manipulation and memory-manipulation routines.
strstrea.h	C++	Declares the C++ stream classes for use with byte arrays in memory.
sys\locking.h		Contains definitions for mode parameter of locking function.
sys\stat.h		Defines symbolic constants used for opening and creating files.
sys\timeb.h		Declares the function **ftime** and the structure **timeb** that it returns.
sys\types.h		Declares the type time_t used with time functions.
thread.h	C++	Defines the thread classes.
time.h	ANSI C	Defines a structure filled in by the time-conversion routines asctime, localtime, and gmtime, and a type used by the routines ctime, difftime, gmtime, localtime, and stime. It also provides prototypes for these routines.

Table 6-5.   *Standard C/C++ Libraries* (continued)

File Name	Compatibility	Description
typeinfo.h	C++	Declares the run-time type information classes.
utime.h		Declares the **utime** function and the **utimbuf** struct that it returns.
values.h		Defines important constants, including machine dependencies; provided for UNIX System V compatibility.
varargs.h		Definitions for accessing parameters in functions that accept a variable number of arguments. Provided for UNIX compatibility; you should use stdarg.h for new code.

Table 6-5. *Standard C/C++ Libraries (continued)*

Check your reference manual for a detailed explanation of the individual functions provided by each library.

In the Next Chapter...

After reading this chapter, you should understand C's basic data types and operators, so it's time to move on to the topic of logic control. Chapter 7 introduces you to C's decision, selection, and iteration control statements.

Chapter Seven

Logic Control Statements

In Chapter 6, you learned about C/C++'s standard data types and their numeric ranges. You saw how to declare variables, initialize variables, change variable visibility, and you were introduced to older high-level language operators, new C/C++ operators, and C/C++ libraries. This chapter is dedicated to explaining C/C++ statements involved in a program's logic flow. All logic control statements are used the same way in both C and C++ programs. The good news is that many of these logic control statements are similar to other high-level language controls, such as **if**, **if-else**, and **switch-case** statements and **for**, **while**, and **do-while** loops.

C/C++ also have several new logic control constructs, such as **break**, **continue**, and several shorthand notations like the conditional operator ?: (made up of the question mark symbol and a colon). The difficulty with these new constructs lies not in their syntax, but in learning how to incorporate these new capabilities into a properly encoded C/C++ algorithm. For example, have you ever studied a foreign language? Which was easier, learning the rules of the language, or using them to the extent that you sounded like a native? Your instructor may have even told you that you would never correctly use the language until you learned to stop translating from your natural language into the new language. Well, the same holds true with C/C++.

You will never be a truly proficient C/C++ programmer until you stop translating from some other language to C/C++. Here's the reason: C and C++ have ideas, concepts, syntax, and constructs that are not available to many older high-level languages. Therefore, if all you are doing is translating, you will not be taking advantage of all that C/C++ have to offer! The same holds true if you are a C programmer making the jump to C++. A simple C to C++ translation does not a C++ program make. Fortunately, this book will teach you the proper way to use both languages.

Conditional Statements

There are four basic categories of conditional statements available to C/C++ programmers: the **if**, the **if-else**, the conditional ?:, and the **switch-case**. Before discussing the individual conditional statements, however, one general rule needs to be highlighted. You can use most of the conditional statements to selectively execute either a single line of code or multiple lines of related code. Multiple lines of related code are often referred to as *compound blocks*.

Whenever a conditional statement is associated with only one line of executable code, braces{} are not required around the executable statement. However, if the conditional statement is associated with executable statements, braces are required to relate the block of executable statements with the conditional test. For this reason, **switch-case** statements are required to have an opening and a closing brace.

Simple Conditional if

The C/C++ **if** statement allows your program to perform the conditional execution of a statement or statements, just the way it would in other high-level languages. The syntax for a simple **if** statement follows (notice that the expression must be enclosed in parentheses):

```
if( TestStatement )
  TrueStatementToExecute;
```

To execute an **if** statement, the *TestStatement* must evaluate to either TRUE or FALSE. If *TestStatement* is TRUE, *TrueStatementToExecute* will be performed and execution will continue on to the next statement following *TrueStatementToExecute*. However, if the expression evaluates to FALSE, *TrueStatementToExecute* will not be executed, and the statement following *TrueStatementToExecute* will be executed. For example, the following code segment will print the message "Put the roof down on the car!" whenever the variable *TodaysWeather* is greater than or equal to *NO_RAIN*:

```
if( TodaysWeather == NO_RAIN )
  cout << "Put the roof down on the car!";
```

The following code segment illustrates the syntax for an **if** statement associated with a compound block of executable statements. The syntax requires that all of the associated statements be enclosed by a pair of braces {} and that each statement within the block must end with a semicolon. (Note that there is no semicolon placed after the closing brace }.)

```
if( TestStatement ) {
   Statement1;
   Statement2;
   Statement3;
   Statementn;
}
```

One thing you need to understand is how C and C++ evaluate the meanings of TRUE and FALSE. To C/C++ any value of 0 is interpreted as a logical FALSE, and any nonzero value, represented as !0, as TRUE. Because neither C nor C++ are strongly typed languages, this allows you to generate many types of *TestStatements* from numeric comparisons to character comparisons, and so on. Just remember that when your *TestStatement* returns a nonzero value, C/C++ will interpret the result as a logical TRUE.

Simple Bi-Conditional if-else

The C/C++ **if-else** statement allows a program to take two separate actions based on the validity of a particular expression. The simplest syntax for an **if-else** statement looks like this:

```
if( TestStatement )
   TrueStatement;
else
   FalseStatement;
```

In this case, if *TestStatement* evaluates to TRUE, *TrueStatement* will be taken; otherwise, when *TestStatement* evaluates to FALSE, *FalseStatement* will be executed. Of course, either *TrueStatement*, *FalseStatement*, or both could be compound statements or blocks requiring braces. The syntax for these three combinations is straightforward:

```
if( TestStatement ) {
   TrueStatement1;
   TrueStatement2;
   TrueStatementn;
}
else
   FalseStatement;


if( TestStatement )
   TrueStatement;
else {
   FalseStatement1;
   FalseStatement2;
   FalseStatementn;
}


if( TestStatement ) {
   TrueStatement1;
   TrueStatement2;
   TrueStatementn;
}
```

```
else {
  FalseStatement1;
  FalseStatement2;
  FalseStatementn;
}
```

Just keep in mind that whenever a block action is being taken, you do not follow the closing brace } with a semicolon.

Nested if-else

Of course, C/C++ would not be complete without the ability to nest **if-else** statements. *Nesting* is where one **if** statement's **if** or **else** statement is in itself another **if** or **if...else** statement. Here the difficulty lies not in the syntax but in correctly matching each **else** with its appropriate **if**. Look at an example and see if you can figure out what will happen:

```
if( TodaysTemperature < FIFTY  )
if( TodaysTemperature < THIRTY ) cout << "Wear the down jacket!";
else cout << "Parka will do.";
```

Don't let the lack of indentation in this example bother you. The listing was purposely misaligned so as not to give any visual clues as to which statement went with which **if**. The question becomes: What happens if *TodaysTemperature* is *FIFTY*? Does the "Parka will do." message get printed? The answer is no. In this example, the **else** action is associated with the second **if** *TestStatement* because C/C++ matches each **else** with the first unmatched **if**. To make debugging as simple as possible under such circumstances, the C/C++ compilers associate each **else** with the closest **if** that does not already have an **else** associated with it. Of course, proper indentation will always help clarify the situation:

```
if( TodaysTemperature < FIFTY )
  if( TodaysTemperature < THIRTY ) cout << "Wear the down jacket!";
  else cout << "Parka will do.";
```

The same logic can also be represented by the alternate listing shown here:

```
if( TodaysTemperature < FIFTY )
  if( TodaysTemperature < THIRTY )
    cout << "Wear the down jacket!";
  else
    cout << "Parka will do.";
```

Each application you write will benefit most by one of the two styles, as long as you are consistent throughout the source code. See if you can figure out this next example:

```
if( TestStatement1 )
  if( TestStatement2 )
    TestStatement2_TrueAction;
else
  TestStatement1_FalseAction;
```

You may be thinking this is just another example of what has already been discussed. That's true, but what if you really did want *TestStatement1_FalseAction* to be associated with *TestStatement1* and not *TestStatement2*? The examples so far have all associated the **else** action with the second, or closest, **if**. (By the way, many a programmer has spent needless time debugging programs of this nature. They're indented to work the way you are logically thinking, as was the preceding example, but unfortunately, the compiler doesn't care about your "pretty printing.") Correcting this situation requires the use of braces:

```
if( TestStatement1 ) {
  if( TestStatement2 )
    TestStatement2_TrueAction;
  }
else
  TestStatement1_FalseAction;
```

The problem is solved by making *TestStatement2* and its associated *TestStatement2_TrueAction* a block associated with a TRUE evaluation of *TestStatement1*. This makes it clear that *TestStatement1_FalseAction* will be associated with the **else** clause of *TestStatement1*.

if-else-if Statements

The **if-else-if** statement combination is often used to perform multiple successive comparisons. Its general form looks like this:

```
if( TestStatement1 )
  TestStatement1_TrueAction;

else if( TestStatement2 )
  TestStatement2_TrueAction;
```

```
else if( TestStatement3 )
   TestStatement3_TrueAction;
```

Of course, each action could be a compound block requiring its own set of braces (with the closing brace not followed by a semicolon). This type of logical control flow evaluates each *TestStatement* until it finds one that is TRUE. When this occurs, all remaining test conditions are bypassed. In the preceding example if none of the *TestStatements* evaluated to TRUE, no action would be taken. Look at this next example and see if you can guess the result:

```
if( TestStatement1 )
   TestStatement1_TrueAction;

else if( TestStatement2 )
   TestStatement2_TrueAction;

else if( TestStatement3 )
   TestStatement3_TrueAction;
else
   Execute_Dropthrough_DefaultAction;
```

Unlike the previous example, this **if-else-if** statement combination will always perform some action. If none of the **if** *TestStatements* evaluate to TRUE, the **else** *Execute_Dropthrough_DefaultAction* will be executed.

An Introduction to the Conditional Operator (?:)

The conditional statement ?: provides a quick way to write a test condition. Associated actions are performed depending on whether *TestStatement* evaluates to TRUE or FALSE. The operator can be used to replace an equivalent **if-else** statement. The syntax for a conditional statement is shown here:

```
TestStatement ? TrueStatement : FalseStatement;
```

The ?: operator is also sometimes referred to as the *ternary* operator because it requires three operands. Examine this statement:

```
if( DataValue >= 0 )
   DataValue = DataValue;
```

```
else
  DataValue = -DataValue;
```

You can rewrite the statement using the conditional operator:

```
DataValue = ( DataValue >= 0 ) ? DataValue : -DataValue;
```

The code segment is designed to always return the absolute value of *DataValue*. The conditional operator has less priority than any of the other operators used in the expression, therefore, no parentheses are required in the example. (Nevertheless, parentheses are frequently used to enhance readability.) The following C++ program uses the ?: operator to cleverly format the program's output:

```
//
//  usecondt.cpp
//  A C++ program using the conditional operator, ?:
//  Copyright (c) Chris H. Pappas and William H. Murray, 1996
//

#include <math.h>
#include <iostream.h>

void main( void )
{
  float LoanBalance, LoanPayment;

  cout << "Loan balance: ";
  cin  >> LoanBalance;

  cout << "\Loan payment: ";
  cin  >> LoanPayment;

  cout << "\n\nYou have ";
  cout << ( (LoanPayment > LoanBalance) ? "overpaid by $" : "paid $");
  cout << ( (LoanPayment > LoanBalance) ? abs(LoanBalance - LoanPayment) :
                                   LoanPayment);
  cout << " on your loan of $" << LoanBalance << ".";
}
```

The program uses the first conditional statement inside a **cout** statement to decide which string—"overpaid by $" or "paid $"—is to be printed. The second conditional statement calculates and prints the appropriate dollar value.

Using switch-case Selection

Another alternative to nested **if-else-if** statements is the C/C++ **switch-case** statement. A **switch-case** statement allows you to easily code multiple logic paths based on a single variable's contents. Usually, the variable's contents fall into a specific, testable subset of values. Be very careful, though; unlike many other high-level language selection statements such as Pascal's case statement, the C/C++ **switch-case** statement has a few peculiarities. The general form of a C/C++ **switch-case** statement follows:

```
switch( TestValue ) {
  case constant1:
    statements1;
    break;
  case constant2:
    statements2;
    break;
      .
      .
      .
  case constantn:
    statementsn;
    break;
  default: statements; // default - optional
}
```

There is one keyword that a novice C/C++ programmer needs to pay particular attention to: **break**. If this example had been coded in Pascal and *constant1* equaled *TestValue*, *statements1* would have been executed, with program execution picking up with the next statement at the end of the case statement (below the closing brace). In C/C++ the situation is quite different.

In the preceding syntax, if the **break** statement had been removed from *constant1*'s section of code, a match similar to the one used in the preceding paragraph would have left *statements2* as the next statement to be executed. It is the **break** statement that causes the remaining portion of the **switch-case** statements to be skipped. Let's look at a few examples. Examine the following **if-else-if** code segment:

```
if( eMove == SMALL_CHANGE_UP )
   fYcoord =    8;

else if( eMove == SMALL_CHANGE_DOWN )
   fYcoord =   -8;
```

```
else if( eMove == LARGE_CHANGE_UP )
  fYcoord =    6;

else
  fYcoord =   -6;
```

You can rewrite this code using a **switch** statement:

```
switch( eMove ) {
  case   SMALL_CHANGE_UP:
    fYcoord =    8;
    break;
  case   SMALL_CHANGE_DOWN:
    fYcoord =   -8;
    break;
  case   LARGE_CHANGE_UP:
    fYcoord =    6;
    break;
  default:
    fYcoord =   -6;
}
```

In this example, the value of *eMove* is consecutively compared to each case value looking for a match. When one is found, *fYcoord* is assigned the appropriate value. Then the **break** statement is executed, skipping over the remaining **case**s of the switch statements. However, if no match is found, the default assignment is performed (*fYcoord* = -6). Because this is the last option in the **switch-case** statement, there is no need to include a **break**. A **switch-case default** is optional. Proper placement of the **break** statement within a **switch-case** statement allows you to create a set of **case**s, all performing the same operation as in this next program:

```
/*
 *   useswtch.c
 *   A C program demonstrating the
 *   drop-through capabilities of the switch statement.
 *   Copyright (c) Chris H. Pappas and William H. Murray, 1996
 */

void main( void )
{
```

```
char a_character       = 'U';
int NumberOfVowels     = 0 ,
    NumberOfConsonants = 0 ;

switch( a_character ) {
  case 'a' | 'A':
  case 'e' | 'E':
  case 'i' | 'I':
  case 'o' | 'O':
  case 'u' | 'U': NumberOfVowels++;
                    break;
  default  :       NumberOfConsonants++;
  }
}
```

Notice the use of the bit-wise OR operator used to combine tests for upper- and lowercase. Also note how the **switch-case** statement enumerates several test values that all execute the same code section and the drop-through characteristic of a purposefully missing **break** statement. Several other high-level languages have their own form of selection (the case statement in Pascal and the select statement in PL/I) which allows for several test values, all producing the same result to be included on the same selection line. C/C++, however, requires a separate case for each. But notice in this example how the same effect has been created by not inserting a **break** statement until all possible vowels have been checked. Should *a_character* contain a constant, all of the vowel case tests will be checked and skipped until the **default** statement is reached.

The following C++ program illustrates the similarity in syntax between a C switch statement and its C++ counterpart:

```
//
//   calendar.cpp
//   A C++ program using a switch statement
//   to print a yearly calendar.
//   Copyright (c) Chris H. Pappas and William H. Murray, 1996
//

#include <iostream.h>

void main( void )
{
```

```cpp
int January_1st,
    DaysPerMonth,
    Month,Date,
    IsALeapYear;

cout << "Please enter January 1's starting day;\n";
cout << "\nA 0 indicates January 1 is on a Monday,";
cout << "\nA 1 indicates January 1 is on a Tuesday, etc: ";
cin  >>  January_1st;

cout << "\nEnter the year you want the calendar generated: ";
cin  >>  IsALeapYear;

cout << "\n\n The calendar for the year " << IsALeapYear;

IsALeapYear = IsALeapYear % 4;
cout.width( 20 );

for( Month = 1; Month <= 12; Month++ ) {
  switch( Month ) {
    case 1:
      cout << "\n\n\n" << " January" << "\n";
      DaysPerMonth = 31;
      break;
    case 2:
      cout << "\n\n\n" << " February" << "\n";
      DaysPerMonth = IsALeapYear ? 28 : 29;
      break;
    case 3:
      cout << "\n\n\n" << "  March " << "\n";
      DaysPerMonth = 31;
      break;
    case 4:
      cout << "\n\n\n" << "  April " << "\n";
      DaysPerMonth = 30;
      break;
    case 5:
      cout << "\n\n\n" << "   May  " << "\n";
      DaysPerMonth = 31;
      break;
    case 6:
```

```
      cout << "\n\n\n" << "   June   " << "\n";
      DaysPerMonth = 30;
      break;
   case 7:
      cout << "\n\n\n" << "   July   " << "\n";
      DaysPerMonth = 31;
      break;
   case 8:
      cout << "\n\n\n" << " August " << "\n";
      DaysPerMonth = 31;
      break;
   case 9:
      cout << "\n\n\n" << "September" << "\n";
      DaysPerMonth = 30;
      break;
   case 10:
      cout << "\n\n\n" << " October " << "\n";
      DaysPerMonth = 31;
      break;
   case 11:
      cout << "\n\n\n" << "November " << "\n";
      DaysPerMonth = 30;
      break;
   case 12:
      cout << "\n\n\n" << "December " << "\n";
      DaysPerMonth = 31;
      break;
}

cout.width( 0 );
cout << "\nSun  Mon  Tue  Wed  Thu  Fri  Sat\n";
cout << "---  ---  ---  ---  ---  ---  ---\n";

for( Date = 1; Date <= 1 + January_1st * 5; Date++ )
   cout <<  " ";

for( Date = 1; Date <= DaysPerMonth; Date++ ) {
   cout.width( 2 );
   cout << Date;
   cout.width( 0 );
   if ( ( Date + January_1st ) % 7 > 0 )
```

```
      cout <<  "    ";
    else
      cout <<  "\n ";
  }
  January_1st=(January_1st + DaysPerMonth) % 7;
 }
}
```

The program begins by asking the user to enter an integer code representing the day of the week on which January 1st occurs (0 for Monday, 1 for Tuesday, and so on). The second prompt asks for the year for the calendar. The program can now print the calendar heading and use the year entered to generate an *IsALeapYear*. Using the modulus operator (%) with a value of 4 generates a remainder of zero whenever it is leap year and a nonzero value whenever it is not leap year. Next, a 12-iteration loop is entered, printing the current month's name and assigning *DaysPerMonth* the correct number of days for that particular month. All of this is accomplished by using a **switch** statement to test the current month integer value.

Outside the **switch-case** statement, after the month's name has been printed, day-of-the-week headings are printed, and an appropriate number of blank columns is skipped, depending on when the first day of the month was. The last **for** loop actually generates and prints the dates for each month. The last statement in the program prepares the day_code for the next month to be printed.

Combining if-else-if and switch-case

This next example combines the uses for **if-else-if** and **switch-case** statements with a clever use of enumerated types:

```
/*
 *   ifelswth.cpp
 *   A C program demonstrating the if-else-if statement
 *   used in a meaningful way with several switch-case statements.
 *   Copyright (c) Chris H. Pappas and William H. Murray, 1996
 */

typedef enum measures {YARDS, INCHES, CENTIMETERS,
                       METERS} MEASUREMENTS;
#include <stdio.h>

void main( void )
{
```

```
int          WantsToConvertTo,
             LengthToConvert ;
float        ConvertedLength ;
MEASUREMENTS SelectedMeasure ;

cout << "\nMeasurement to be converted : ";
cin  >>  LengthToConvert;

cout << "\nPlease enter :          \
        \n\t\t 0 for YARDS         \
        \n\t\t 1 for INCHES        \
        \n\t\t 2 for CENTIMETERS \
        \n\t\t 3 for METERS        \
        \n\n\t\tYour response -->> " ;

cin  << WantsToConvertTo;

switch( WantsToConvertTo ) {
  case 0  :  SelectedMeasure = YARDS;        break;
  case 1  :  SelectedMeasure = INCHES;       break;
  case 2  :  SelectedMeasure = CENTIMETERS; break;
  default :  SelectedMeasure = METERS;
}

if( SelectedMeasure == YARDS )
          ConvertedLength = LengthToConvert  /  3           ;
else if( SelectedMeasure  == INCHES )
          ConvertedLength = LengthToConvert  * 12           ;
else if( SelectedMeasure  == CENTIMETERS )
          ConvertedLength = LengthToConvert  * 12 * 2.54    ;
else if( SelectedMeasure  == METERS )
          ConvertedLength = (LengthToConvert * 12 * 2.54)/100;
else
  printf( "No translation needed." );

switch( SelectedMeasure ) {
  case YARDS      : cout << "\n"
                         <<  LengthToConvert
                         << " is "
                         <<  ConvertedLength
                         << " in yards      ";
```

```
                              break;
      case INCHES      : cout << "\n"
                              << LengthToConvert
                              << " is "
                              << ConvertedLength
                              << " in inches        ";
                              break;
      case CENTIMETERS : cout << "\n"
                              << LengthToConvert
                              << " is "
                              << ConvertedLength
                              << " in centimeters ";
                              break;
      default          : cout << "\n"
                              << LengthToCovert
                              << " is "
                              << ConvertedLength
                              << " in meters        ";

  }
}
```

The example program uses an enumerated type to perform the specified length conversion. In standard C, enumerated types exist only within the code itself (for reasons of readability) and cannot be input or output directly. The program uses the first **switch-case** statement to convert the input code to its appropriate *SelectedMeasure* type. The nested **if-else-if** statements perform the proper conversion. The last **switch-case** statement prints the converted value with its appropriate "literal" type. Of course, the nested **if-else-if** statements could have been implemented by using a **switch-case** statement.

Iterative Statements

C/C++ even have a few surprises when it comes to simple types of loop control statements. Actually, the loop types themselves are fairly standard in operation. What are interesting, however, are the ways in which you can alter the logic flow within a loop or exit a loop. C/C++ include the standard set of repetition control statements: **for** loops, **while** loops, and **do-while** loops (called **repeat-until** loops in several other high-level languages).

The basic difference between a **for** loop and a **while** or **do-while** loop has to do with the "known" number of repetitions. Typically, **for** loops are used whenever there is a definite predefined required number of repetitions, and **while** and **do-while** loops are reserved for an "unknown" number of repetitions.

C and C++ provide four methods for altering the repetitions in a loop. All loops can naturally terminate based on the expressed test condition. In C/C++, however, a loop can also terminate because of an anticipated error condition by using either a **break** (the other use for **break** statements, besides the **switch-case** use) or **exit()** statement. Loops can also have their logic control flow altered by a **break** statement or a **continue** statement.

Pre-Test for Loop

The syntax for a **for** loop looks very similar to most high-level languages:

```
for( Init_LoopControl; TestCondition; Increment_LoopControl )
```

for loop execution begins with the one-time-only initialization of the loop control variable, in this example, *Init_LoopControl*. This is done at the start of the loop, and it is never executed again. Following this, *TestCondition*, which is called the loop terminating condition, is tested. Whenever *TestCondition* evaluates to TRUE, the statement or statements within the loop are executed.

If the loop was entered, then after all of the statements within the loop are executed, *Increment_LoopControl* is executed. However, if *TestCondition* evaluates to FALSE, the statement or statements within the loop are ignored, along with *Increment_LoopControl*, and execution continues with the statement following the end of the loop.

To check yourself on the proper use of loop control variables, answer the following question: What is the value of the loop control variable *outside* the loop? Answer: undefined. Your program should never use the loop control variable anywhere else but *inside* the loop structure. Outside the loop, the variable's contents are volatile.

The indentation scheme applied to **for** loops with a compound block looks like this:

```
for( Init_LoopControl; TestCondition; Increment_LoopControl ) {
  Statement1;
  Statement2;
  Statement3;
  Statementn;
}
```

When several statements need to be executed, a pair of braces is required to tie their execution to the loop control structure. Let's examine a few examples of **for** loops. The following example sums up the first five integers. It assumes that *Total* and *ControlValue* have been predefined as integers:

```
Total = 0;
for( ControlValue = 1; ControlValue <= 5; ControlValue++ )
  Total += ControlValue;
```

After *Total* has been initialized to 0, the **for** loop is encountered. First, *ControlValue* is initialized to 1 (this is done only once); second, *ControlValue*'s value is checked against the loop terminating condition <= 5. Because this is TRUE, a 1 is added to *Total*. Once the statement is executed, the loop control variable (*ControlValue*) is incremented by 1. This process continues four more times until *ControlValue* is incremented to 6 and the loop terminates. In C++, the same code segment could be written as follows. See if you can detect the subtle difference:

```
for( int ControlValue=1; ControlValue <= 5; ControlValue++ )
  Total += ControlValue;
```

C++ allows the loop control variable to be declared and initialized within the **for** loop. This brings up a very sensitive issue among structured programmers—the proper placement of variable declarations. In C++, you can declare variables right before the statement that actually uses them. In the preceding example, because *ControlValue* is used only to generate a *Total* with *Total* having a larger scope than *ControlValue*, the local declaration for *ControlValue* is harmless. However, look at the following code segment:

```
int Total = 0;
for( int ControlValue=1; ControlValue <= 5; ControlValue++ )
  Total += ControlValue;
```

This would obscure the visual "desk check" of the variable *Total*, because it was not declared below the function head. For the sake of structured design and debugging, it is best to localize all variable declarations. It is the rare code segment that can justify the usefulness of moving a variable declaration to a nonstandard place in sacrifice of easily read, easily checked, and easily modified code.

The value used to increment **for** loop control variables does not always have to be 1 or ++. The following example sums all the odd numbers up to 9:

```
OddTotal = 0;
for( OddNumber = 1; OddNumber <= 9; OddNumber += 2 );
  OddTotal += OddNumber;
```

In this example, the loop control variable *OddNumber* is initialized to 1 and is incremented by 2. Of course, **for** loops don't always have to go from a smaller value to a larger one. The following example uses a **for** loop to read into an array of characters and then print the character string backward:

```
//
//  palindrm.cpp
//  A C++ program that uses a for loop to input a character array.
//  Copyright (c) Chris H. Pappas and William H. Murray, 1996
//

#include <stdio.h>

#define PALINDROME_SIZE 25

void main( void )
{
  int Offset;
  char Palindrome[ PALINDROME_SIZE ];

  for( Offset = 0; Offset < PALINDROME_SIZE; Offset++ )
    Palindrome[ Offset ] = getchar();

  for( Offset = PALINDROME_SIZE - 1; Offset >= 0; Offset--)
    putchar( Palindrome[ Offset ] );
}
```

In this example, the first **for** loop initialized *Offset* to zero (necessary because all array indexes are offsets from the starting address of the first array element), and while there is room in *Palindrome*, reads characters in one at a time. The second **for** loop initializes the loop control variable *Offset* to the offset of the last element in the array and, while *Offset* contains a valid offset, prints the characters in reverse order. This process could be used to parse an infix expression, such as 5 + 3, that was being converted to prefix notation: +5 3.

Pre-Test while Loop

while loops are also pre-test loops, which means that the program evaluates *TestCondition* before entering the statement or statements within the body of the loop. Because of this, pre-test loops may be executed from zero to many times. This is the syntax for a C/C++ **while** loop:

```
while( TestCondition )
   statement;
```

This is the syntax for a C/C++ **while** loop for compound blocks:

```
while( TestCondition ) {
   statement1;
   statement2;
   statement3;
   statementn;
}
```

Usually, **while** loop control structures are used whenever an indefinite number of repetitions is expected. The following C program uses a **while** loop to control the number of times *ValueToconvert* is shifted to the right. The program prints the binary representation of a signed integer:

```
/*
 *    usewhile.c
 *    A C program using a pre-test while loop with flag.
 *    Copyright (c) Chris H. Pappas and William H. Murray, 1996
 */

#include <stdio.h>

#define A_BYTES_SIZE  8
#define A_WORDS_SIZE 16

void main( void )
```

```
{
  int         ValueToConvert     = 256,
              CurrentBitPosition =   1;
  unsigned int BitMask           =   1;

  printf( "The following value %d,\n",ValueToConvert );
  printf( "in binary form looks like: "            );

  while( CurrentBitPosition <= A_WORDS_SIZE ) {
    if( ( ValueToConvert >> (A_WORDS_SIZE - CurrentBitPosition) )
                         &    BitMask)                /*shift each*/
      printf( "1" );                                  /*bit to 0th*/
    else                                              /*position &*/
      printf( "0" );                                  /*compare to*/

    if( CurrentBitPosition == A_BYTES_SIZE )          /*BitMask    */
      printf( " " );
    CurrentBitPosition++;
  }
}
```

The program begins by defining two constants, *A_WORDS_SIZE* and
A_BYTES_SIZE, that can be easily modified for different architectures.
A_WORDS_SIZE will be used as a flag to determine when the **while** loop will
terminate. Within the **while** loop, *ValueToConvert* is shifted, compared to *BitMask*, and
printed from most significant bit to least. This allows the algorithm to use a simple
printf() statement to output the results.

Post-Test do-while Loop

The post-test **do-while** loop is the only loop always entered at least once, with the loop
condition being tested at the end of the first iteration. In contrast, **for** loops and **while**
loops may execute from zero to many times, depending on the loop control variable.
This is the syntax for a **do-while** loop:

```
do
  Statement ;
while( TestStatement );
```

For compound blocks this is the syntax:

```
do {
 action1;
 action2;
 action3;
 actionn;
} while(test_condition);
```

Because **do-while** loops always execute at least once, they are best used whenever there is no doubt you want the particular loop entered. For example, if your program needs to present a menu to the user, even if all the user wants to do is immediately quit the program, he or she needs to see the menu to know which key terminates the application. The following C++ program uses a **do-while** loop to print a menu and obtain a valid *user response*. It is a DOS mode only application.

```
//
//     A C++ program using a do-while loop to print a menu
//     and obtain a valid user response.
//     Copyright (c) Chris H. Pappas and William H. Murray, 1996
//

#include <conio.h>
#include <iostream.h>

void main( void )
{
   int Xcoord, Ycoord, MenuSelection;

   clrscr();
   do {
     cout << "\t\t\t>>> Electronic Teller <<<\n\n"   ;

     cout << "\t\t\t    Balance Inquiry : 1\n"        ;
     cout << "\t\t\t    Transfer Funds  : 2\n"        ;
     cout << "\t\t\t    Savings Account : 3\n"        ;
     cout << "\t\t\t    Checking Account: 4\n"        ;
     cout << "\t\t\t    Loan Rates      : 5\n"        ;
     cout << "\t\t\t    Quit:             6\n"        ;
     cout << "\n\t\t\tPlease enter your selection: ";

     Xcoord = wherex();              Ycoord = wherey();
```

```
do {

    gotoxy(Xcoord,Ycoord); cout << "    "          ;

    gotoxy(Xcoord,Ycoord); cin >> MenuSelection   ;

    } while ( ( MenuSelection < 1 ) || ( MenuSelection > 6 ) );

  } while( MenuSelection != 6 );
}
```

The header file *conio.h* contains many useful functions for controlling the monitor. The program uses four of these functions: **clrscr(), wherex(), wherey(),** and **gotoxy().** Before discussing the two **do-while** loops used in the program, let's take a look at these functions. **clrscr()** erases all information on the display monitor. The two functions **wherex()** and **wherey()** return the current screen coordinates of the cursor. The **gotoxy()** function positions the cursor to the specified screen coordinates for either input or output. The program uses a **do-while** loop to print the menu items and continues to reprint the menu items until the user has selected option 6 to quit.

The program employs two **do-while** loops. Notice the use of the nested inner **do-while** loop. It is the responsibility of this loop to make certain the user has entered an acceptable response (a number from 1 to 6, inclusive). Because you don't want the user's incorrect guesses to be "newlined" all the way down the display screen, the inner loop uses the **gotoxy()** statements to keep the cursor on the same line as the first response.

The program accomplishes this by obtaining the cursor's original position after the input prompt "...enter your selection:" is printed. The functions **wherex()** and **wherey()** are designed for this specific purpose. Once the user has typed a response, however, the cursor's x and y coordinates change; this requires their original values to be stored in the variables *Xcoord* and *Ycoord* for repeated reference.

Once inside the inner **do-while loop**, the first **gotoxy()** statement blanks out any previously entered values and then obtains the next number entered. This process continues until an acceptable *MenuSelection* is obtained. When the inner **do-while** loop is exited, control returns to the outer **do-while** loop, which repeats the menu again until the user enters a 6 to quit.

An Introduction to the break Keyword

You have already seen the **break** keyword used to exit a **switch-case** statement after executing the matching **case**. However, the C/C++ **break** statement can also be used to exit a loop before the test condition becomes FALSE. The **break** statement is similar in many ways to a **goto** statement, only the point jumped to is not known directly.

When breaking out of a loop, program execution continues with the next statement following the loop itself. Look at a very simple example:

```c
/*
 *    usebreak.c
 *    A C program demonstrating the use of the break statement.
 *    Copyright (c) Chris H. Pappas and William H. Murray, 1996
 */

#define MAX_LETTERS 10

void main( void )
{
  int UserInput, Offset = 0;


 char BuildWord[ MAX_LETTERS ];

  while( ((UserInput = getchar()) != EOF )  &&
         (Offset < MAX_LETTERS) )               {
    if( (UserInput >= 48) || (UserInput <= 57) )
      break;
    BuildWord[ Offset ] = UserInput;
  }
}
```

This program allows the user to enter any character from the keyboard building a word; however, as soon as the user enters a digit (ASCII decimal equivalents 48 through 57) the loop is exited, terminating the word build. Try using the integrated debugger to single-step the program. Pay particular attention to what happens when you enter a numeric digit at the keyboard. Notice that the trace line drops to the **main()**'s closing brace }.

An Introduction to the continue Keyword

In some ways the C/C++ **continue** statement works just like a loop **break** statement. For example, when a **continue** statement is encountered within a loop, just like with a **break**, all of the statements below either keyword within the loop body are ignored. However, although the **break** causes the loop to terminate execution altogether, the **continue** does not circumvent incrementing the loop control variable or the loop control test condition. In other words, if the loop control variable still satisfies the loop test condition, the loop *will* continue to iterate. The following program demonstrates this concept, using a guess-my-weight amusement park game:

```
/*
*    usecntnu.c
*    A C program demonstrating the use of the continue
*    statement.
*    Copyright (c) Chris H. Pappas and William H. Murray, 1996
*/

#include <stdio.h>

#define YES  1
#define NO   0

void main( void )
{
  int ActualWeight    = 185,
      GuessedWeight,
      HowManyGuesses  =   0,
      GetsTheCupyDoll =  NO;

  while( !GetsTheCupyDoll ){

    printf( "Guess my weight: "  );
    scanf(  "%d",&GuessedWeight  );

    HowManyGuesses++;

    if( GuessedWeight  == ActualWeight )
       GetsTheCupyDoll = YES;
    else
      continue;

    printf( "It took you %d tries to guess my weight!",
            HowManyGuesses);
  }
}
```

The **continue** statement leaves the visibility of the **printf()** conditional, but does not circumvent iterating the loop until the user makes a correct guess. Only when the user guesses the correct weight is *GetsTheCupyDoll* set equal to *YES*, skipping the **else continue** statements and printing the number of guesses. Use your integrated debugger to enter the preceding program and trace the variables *GuessedWeight*, *HowManyGuesses*, and *GetsTheCupyDoll*. Pay particular attention to which statements are executed after *GuessedWeight* is compared to *ActualWeight*.

Combining break and continue

The **break** and **continue** statements can be combined to solve some interesting program problems. Look at the following C++ example:

```
//
//  brkcntnu.cpp
//  A C++ program demonstrating the usefulness of combining
//  the break and continue statements.
//  Copyright (c) Chris H. Pappas and William H. Murray, 1996
//

#include <ctype.h>
#include <iostream.h>

#define CARRIAGE_RETURN '\n'

void main( void )
{
  int a_character;

  while( (a_character = getchar()) != EOF )
  {
    if( isascii(a_character) == 0 ) {
      cout << "Not an ASCII character; ";
      cout << "not going to continue/n";
      break;
    }

    if( ispunct(a_character) || isspace(a_character) ) {
      putchar( CARRIAGE_RETURN );
      continue;
    }

    if( isprint(a_character) == 0 ) {
      a_character = getchar();
```

```
        continue;
    }

    putchar( a_character );
  }
}
```

Before seeing how the program functions, take a look at the input to the program:

```
word control ^B exclamation! apostrophe' period.
```

```
^Z
```

Also, examine the output produced:

```
word
control
B
exclamation

apostrophe

period
```

The program continues to read character input until the EOF character ^Z is typed. It then examines the input, removing any nonprintable characters, and places each "word" on its own line. It accomplishes all of this by using some very interesting functions defined in *ctype.h*, including **isascii()**, **ispunct()**, **isspace()**, and **isprint()**. Each of the functions is passed a character parameter and returns either a zero or some other value indicating the result of the comparison.

The function **isascii()** indicates whether the character passed falls into the acceptable ASCII value range; **ispunct()** indicates whether the character is a punctuation mark; **isspace()** indicates whether the character is a space; and **isprint()** reports whether the character parameter is a printable character. Using these functions, the program determines whether to continue the program at all and, if it is to continue, what it should do with each of the characters input.

The first test within the **while** loop evaluates whether the file is even in readable form. For example, the input data could have been saved in binary format, rendering the program useless. If this is the case, the associated **if** statements are executed, printing a warning message and breaking out of the **while** loop permanently.

If all is well, the second **if** statement is encountered; it checks whether the character input is either a punctuation mark or a blank space. If either of these conditions is TRUE, the associated **if** statements are executed. This causes a blank line to be skipped in the output and executes the **continue** statement. The **continue** statement efficiently jumps over the remaining test condition and output statement but does not terminate the loop. It merely indicates that the character's form has been diagnosed properly and that it is time to obtain a new character.

If the file is in an acceptable format and the character input is not punctuation or a blank, the third **if** statement asks whether the character is printable or not. This test takes care of any control codes. Notice that the example input to the program included a control ^B. Because ^B is not printable, this **if** statement immediately obtains a new character and then executes a **continue** statement. Similarly, this **continue** statement indicates that the character in question has been diagnosed, the proper action has been taken, and it is time to get another character. The **continue** statement also causes the **putchar()** statement to be ignored while not terminating the **while** loop.

Program Termination Using the exit() Function

Under certain circumstances, it is proper for a program to terminate long before all of the statements in the program have been examined and/or executed. For these specific circumstances, C incorporates the **exit()** library function. The function **exit()** expects one integer argument, called a status value. The UNIX and MS-DOS operating systems interpret a status value of zero as signaling a normal program termination, while any nonzero status values signify different kinds of errors.

The particular status value passed to **exit()** can be used by the process that invoked the program to take some action. For example, if the program were invoked from the command line and the status value indicated some type of error, the operating system might display a message. In addition to terminating the program, **exit()** writes all output waiting to be written and closes all open files. The following C++ program averages a list of up to 30 grades. The program will exit if the user requests to average more than SIZE number of integers.

```
//
// exit.cpp
// A C++ program demonstrating the use of the exit function.
// Copyright (c) Chris H. Pappas and William H. Murray, 1996
//

#include <iostream.h>
#include <process.h>

#define NUMBER_OF_GRADES 30
```

```
void main( void )
{
  int    Row                      ,
         HowMany                  ,
         Grades[ NUMBER_OF_GRADES ];
  float  Total              =    0,
         TopScore           =    0,
         LowScore           = 100,
         ClassAverage           ;

  cout << "\nEnter the number of Grades to average: ";
  cin  >>    HowMany;

  if( HowMany > NUMBER_OF_GRADES ) {
    cout << "\nYou can only enter up to " << NUMBER_OF_GRADES << \
            " scores" << " to be averaged.\n" ;
    cout << "\n        >>> Program was exited. <<<\n";
    exit( 1 );
  }

  for( Row = 0; Row < HowMany; Row++ ) {
    cout << "\nPlease enter a grade " << Row+1 << ":   ";
    cin  >>    Grades[ Row ];
  }

  for(Row = 0; Row < HowMany; Row++)
    Total = Total + Grades[ Row ];

  ClassAverage = Total/(float)HowMany;

  for( Row = 0; Row < HowMany; Row++ ) {
    if( Grades[ Row ] > TopScore ) TopScore = Grades[ Row ];
    if( Grades[ Row ] < LowScore ) LowScore = Grades[Row];
  }

  cout << "\nThe maximum grade is " << TopScore     ;
  cout << "\nThe minimum grade is " << LowScore     ;
  cout << "\nThe average grade is " << ClassAverage;
}
```

The program begins by including the *process.h* header file. Either *process.h* or *stdlib.h* can be included to prototype the function **exit()**. The constant

NUMBER_OF_GRADES is declared to be 30 and is used to dimension the array of integers, *Grades*. After the remaining variables are declared, the program prompts the user for the number of *Grades* to be entered. For this program, the user's response is to be typed next to the prompt.

The program inputs the requested value into the variable *HowMany* and uses this for the **if** comparison. When the user wants to average more numbers than will fit in *Grades*, the two warning messages are printed, and then the **exit()** statement is executed. This terminates the program altogether.

See if you can detect the two subtle differences between the preceding program and the one that follows:

```
cout << "\nEnter the number of scores to be averaged: ";
cin  >>   HowMany;

if( HowMany > NUMBER_OF_GRADES ) {
   cout << "\nYou can only enter up to " << NUMBER_OF_GRADES << \
           " scores" << " to be Averaged.\n";
   cout << "\n        >>> Program was exited. <<<\n";
   exit( EXIT_FAILURE );
```

By including the *stdlib.h* header file instead of *process.h*, two additional definitions became visible: **EXIT_SUCCESS** (which returns a value of zero) and **EXIT_FAILURE** (which returns an unsuccessful value). This code segment was rewritten to take advantage of the **EXIT_SUCCESS** definition for a more readable parameter to the function **exit()**.

Registering Exit Code Using the atexit() Function

Whenever a program invokes the **exit()** function or performs a normal program termination, it can also call any registered "exit functions" posted with **atexit()**. The following C program demonstrates this capability:

```
/*
 *   atexit.cpp
 *   A C program demonstrating the relationship between the
 *   function atexit() and the order in which the functions
 *   declared are executed.
 *   Copyright (c) Chris H. Pappas and William H. Murray, 1996
 */
```

```
#include <iostream.h>
#include <stdlib.h>

void atexit_RegisteredFunction1( void );
void atexit_RegisteredFunction2( void );
void atexit_RegisteredFunction3( void );

void main( void )
{

  atexit( atexit_RegisteredFunction1 );
    atexit( atexit_RegisteredFunction2 );
      atexit( atexit_RegisteredFunction3 );

  cout << "Atexit program begins.\n"  ;
  cout << "Atexit program ends.\n\n" ;
  cout << "=======================\n\n";
}

void atexit_RegisteredFunction1( void )
{
  cout << "atexit_RegisteredFunction1 executed.\n";
}

void atexit_RegisteredFunction2( void )
{
  cout << "atexit_RegisteredFunction2 executed.\n";
}

void atexit_RegisteredFunction3( void )
{
  cout << "atexit_RegisteredFunction3 executed.\n";
}
```

The output from the program looks like this:

```
Atexit program begins.
Atexit program ends.
```

```
========================

atexit_RegisteredFunction3 executed.
atexit_RegisteredFunction2 executed.
atexit_RegisteredFunction1 executed.
```

The **atexit()** function uses the name of a function as its only parameter and registers the specified function as an **exit()** function. Whenever the program terminates normally, as in the preceding example, or invokes the **exit()** function, all **atexit()** declared functions are executed. Technically, each time the **atexit()** statement is encountered in the source code, the specified function is added to a list of functions to execute when the program terminates.

When the program terminates, any functions that have been passed to **atexit()** are executed, with the last function added being the first one executed. This explains why the *atexit_RegisteredFunction3* output statement was printed before the similar statement in *atexit_RegisteredFunction1()*. **atexit()** functions are normally used as cleanup routines for dynamically allocated objects. Because one object (B) can be built upon another (A), **atexit()** functions execute in reverse order. This would delete object B before deleting object A.

In the Next Chapter...

In this chapter, you have explored those logic control constructs similar to older high-level languages, as well as several unique C/C++ options. Chapter 8 explains the nuances of C/C++ functions including their syntax, argument passing defaults, and once again, unique C/C++ capabilities.

Chapter Eight

Functions

Technically speaking, there are two types of subroutines: procedures and functions. *Procedure* subroutines can be passed from zero to many arguments and may return zero to several arguments. *Function* subroutines, like their procedure counterparts, can also be passed from zero to many arguments, but always return one argument. For example, functions usually calculate one value, such as an employee's overtime hours, whereas calling many functions to generate an employee's paycheck would involve a more complex procedure. C and C++ do not have the category of subroutines called procedures. All processing must be done in functions.

Because there is a formal difference between the two subroutine categories, you need to learn how to properly use C/C++ functions to do both. This chapter introduces you to the concept of a function and how it is prototyped under the latest ANSI C/C++ standard. Using many example programs, you will examine the different types of functions and how arguments are passed. These programming examples show you how to create and implement a wide range of functions. Many of the example programs also use built-in C and C++ library functions that give your program extended power.

You will also learn how to use the standard C/C++ variables *argc* and *argv* to pass command-line arguments to the **main()** function. Additionally, the chapter explores several unique function capabilities available only in C++.

What Are Functions?

Functions are the main building blocks of C and C++ programs. Separating and coding parts of your program in separate modules, called functions, allows the program to be broken down into workable parts. For example, one function might be used to capture input data, another to print information, and yet another to write data to the disk. As a matter of fact, all C and C++ programming is done within a function. The one function every C or C++ program has is **main()**.

Function Prototyping and Style

One of the biggest problems in understanding algorithms written in historic C involved the way functions were written. Historic C hid formal argument descriptions within the function's body. This made desk checks, or walkthroughs, very difficult in large projects. To make matters worse, the historic C compiler failed to perform any compile-time checks between a function call's actual argument list and the function's formal argument list. C, assuming that "programmers know what they are doing," would faithfully go off and try to execute functions called with the wrong number or wrong types of arguments.

It should be no surprise then to discover that this was *the* area addressed by the ANSI C committee. When the ANSI C standard was implemented for C, it was the C functions that underwent the greatest change. The ANSI C standard for functions is based upon the function prototype that has already been extensively used in C++. The C programs in this book conform to the ANSI C standard.

Prototyping

At this point you probably have a few questions. What does a C/C++ function look like? Where do functions go in a program? How are functions declared? What constitutes a function? Where is type checking performed? Beginning with the ANSI C standard, all functions must be prototyped. The prototyping can take place in the C or C++ program itself or in a header file. For the programs in this book, most function prototyping is contained within the program itself.

Function declarations begin with the C and C++ function prototype. The function prototype is simple, and it is usually included at the start of program code to notify the compiler of the type and number of arguments that a function will use. Prototyping enforces stronger type checking than was previously possible when C standards were less strongly enforced. Although other prototyping style variations are legal, this book recommends the function prototype form that is a replication of the function's declaration line, with the addition of a semicolon at the end, whenever possible. For example:

```
TYPE_RETURNED FunctionName( ARGUMENT_TYPE ArgumentName
                          [,ARGUMENT_TYPE ArgumentName, ...] );
```

Starting from the left and working to the right, you see that a function prototype begins with the function's *TYPE_RETURNED* argument. The function can return the type **void**, **int**, **float**, and so on. The *FunctionName()* is any meaningful name you choose to describe the function. If any information is passed to the function, an *ARGUMENT_TYPE* followed by an *ArgumentName* should also be given. Arguments can also be of type **void**, **int**, **float**, and so on. You can pass many values to a function by repeating the argument type and name separated by a comma. It is also correct to list just the argument type (without specifying a dummy argument name). This style of function prototype is frequently used when prototyping lNumTworary routines, where no assumption can be made about the readability relationship between actual and dummy arguments.

Although function prototypes traditionally go into an application's header file, function bodies are placed either below **main()** or, in larger projects, in their own **.c* or **.cpp* file. The function itself is actually an encapsulated piece of C or C++ program code in this format:

```
TYPE_RETURNED FunctionName(ARGUMENT_TYPE ArgumentName
                          [,ARGUMENT_TYPE ArgumentName, ...])
{
```

```
        .
        .
     (data declarations and body of function)
        .
        .
     return( );
  }
```

Function headers are usually identical to function prototypes with one important exception: they do not end with a semicolon. A function prototype and function used in a program are shown in the following C example:

```
/*
 *    prototyp.c
 *    A C program to illustrate function prototyping.
 *    Function adds two integers
 *    and returns an integer result.
 *    Copyright (c) Chris H. Pappas and William H. Murray, 1996
 */

#include <stdio.h>

int AddThem(int NumOne,int NumTwo); /* function prototype  */

void main( void )
{
  int NumOne = 10,
      NumTwo = 20,
      Result   ;

  Result = AddThem( NumOne,NumTwo    );
  printf( "The sum is: %d\n", Result );
}

int AddThem(int NumOne,int NumTwo ) /* function declaration */
{
  int LocalResult;

  LocalResult = NumOne + NumTwo;
  return( LocalResult );                /* function return    */
}
```

In this example, the function is called *AddThem()*. The prototype defines two
formal arguments: **int** *NumOne*, and **int** *NumTwo*, and a return type of **int**. Actually, the
ANSI C standard suggests that all functions be prototyped in a separate header file.
This, as you might guess, is how header files are associated with their appropriate
C/C++ libraries. For simple programs, as already mentioned, including the function
prototype within the body of the program is acceptable. The same function written for
C++ takes on an almost identical appearance:

```cpp
//
//  prototyp.cpp
//  A C++ program to illustrate function prototyping.
//  Function adds two integers
//  and returns an integer result.
//  Copyright (c) Chris H. Pappas and William H. Murray, 1996
//

#include <iostream.h>

int AddThem(int NumOne,int NumTwo);   // function prototype

void main( void )
{
  int NumOne = 10,
      NumTwo = 20,
      Result    ;

  Result = AddThem( NumOne,NumTwo );
  cout << "The sum is: "
       << Result
       << endl;
}

int AddThem(int NumOne,int NumTwo)    // function declaration
{
  int LocalResult;

  LocalResult = NumOne + NumTwo;
  return( LocalResult );                // function return
}
```

Call-by-Value and Call-by-Reference

Programmers know that there are two ways to pass actual arguments to functions: call-by-value or call-by-reference (sometimes referred to as call-by-variable). In the previous two examples, arguments have been passed by value to the functions. When variables are passed *call-by-value*, a copy of the variable's actual contents is passed to the function. Because a copy of the variable is passed, the variable in the calling function itself is not altered. Calling a function by value is the most popular means of passing information to a function, and it is the default method in C and C++. The major drawback to the call-by-value method is that the function typically returns only one value.

On the other hand, when you use *call-by-reference*, the address of the argument, rather than the actual value, is passed to the function. This approach also requires less program memory than a call-by-value. When you use call-by-reference, the variables in the calling function can be altered. Another advantage to a call-by-reference is that more than one value can be returned by the function.

The following program is identical to the C version just discussed, except that it overrides the default call-by-value with call-by-reference. In C, you accomplish a call-by-reference by using a pointer as an argument, as shown here. This same method can be used with C++:

```c
/*
 *    callbref.c
 *    A C program to illustrate call-by-reference.
 *    Copyright (c) Chris H. Pappas and William H. Murray, 1996
 */

#include <stdio.h>

void AddThem(int NumOne,int NumTwo,int *PointerToResult);

void main( void )
{
  int NumOne = 10,
      NumTwo = 20,
      Result    ;

  AddThem( NumOne,NumTwo,&Result );
  printf("The sum is: %d\n", Result);
}

void AddThem(int NumOne,int NumTwo,int *PointerToResult)
{
```

```
    *PointerToResult = NumOne + NumTwo;
}
```

In the original C version, this program printed *Result* from **main()** after the function *AddThem()* calculated the sum, stored, and then returned the sum in the *LocalResult* variable. This program eliminates *AddThem()*'s *LocalResult* data declaration, and, instead, returns the calculated sum right in the **main()**'s *Result* variable. All of this was accomplished with call-by-reference.

Basically, there are three syntax changes required for call-by-reference to override a default call-by-value. First, you need to change the formal argument's data type to that of a pointer, for example:

```
int                becomes          int *
char               becomes          char *
float              becomes          float *
```

Second, when you invoke the function, you need to change what you are sending over. Because you are no longer sending data copies but addresses to memory locations holding data, you need to place the address operator, &, in front of the actual argument's name. For example:

```
FunctionName( IntValue   ); becomes   FunctionName( &IntValue   );
FunctionName( CharValue  ); becomes   FunctionName( &CharValue  );
FunctionName( FloatValue ); becomes   FunctionName( &FloatValue );
```

The third syntax change involves how you use the pointer variable within the function body. Because the function receives an address to a memory location instead of the data itself, you need to use a special syntax to gain access to the variable's storage. For example:

```
*PointerToResult = NumOne + NumTwo;
```

This statement illustrates the use of the variables *NumOne* and *NumTwo* as the normal syntax needed for call-by-value. However, because *PointerToResult* holds the address to **main()**'s *Result*, it needs to be dereferenced within the function body. This explains the asterisk (*) in front of the variable's name. Now when **PointerToResult* is assigned a new value, it is actually taking place in **main()**'s *Result* because both variables share the same memory address. As you have learned, in C, you can use variables and pointers as arguments in function declarations. C++ uses variables and pointers as arguments in function declarations and adds a third type.

In C++, the third argument type is called a reference type. The reference type specifies a location but does not require a dereferencing operator. Many advanced C++ programs use this syntax to simplify the use of pointer variables within called subroutines. Examine the following syntax carefully and compare it with the previous example:

```
//
//  reftype.cpp
//  A C++ program to illustrate an equivalent
//  call-by-reference, using the C++ reference type.
//  Copyright (c) Chris H. Pappas and William H. Murray, 1996
//

#include <iostream.h>

void AddThem(int NumOne,int NumTwo, int &RefToResult);

void main( void )
{
    int NumOne = 10,
        NumTwo = 20,
        Result    ;

    AddThem( NumOne,NumTwo,Result );
    cout << "The sum is: "

        << Result

        << endl;
}

void AddThem(int NumOne,int NumTwo,  int &RefToResult)
{
    RefToResult = NumOne + NumTwo;
}
```

When you examined the listing, did you notice the lack of pointers in the C++ program code? The reference type in this example is *RefToResult*. Notice the much simpler syntax when using reference types. The only change in this program, from the original C version, is the function's formal argument type for *RefToResult*, which instead of being

```
int          // default call-by-value
```

or

```
int *        // call-by-reference using pointer notation
```

becomes

```
int &        // call-by-reference using the C++ exclusive reference type
```

In C++, references to references, references to bit-fields, arrays of references, and pointers to references are not allowed. Regardless of whether you use call-by-reference or a reference type, C++ always uses the address of the argument.

Scope

A variable's scope, or range of visibility, is similar for C and C++ variables used with functions. Variables can have a local, file, or class scope. You may use a local variable completely within a function definition. Its scope is then limited to the function itself. The variable is said to be accessible, or visible, only within the function and has a local scope. Variables with a file scope are declared outside of individual functions or classes. These variables have visibility or accessibility throughout the file in which they are declared and are global in range.

A variable may be used with a file scope and later within a function definition with a local scope. When this is done, the local scope takes precedence over the file scope. C++ offers a new programming feature called the scope resolution operator (::). When the C++ resolution operator is used, a variable with local scope is changed to one with file scope. In this situation, the variable would possess the value of the "global" variable. This is the syntax for referencing the global variable:

```
::GlobalAccessRequest
```

Scope rules allow unique programming errors. Various scope rule errors are discussed at the end of this chapter.

Recursion

If you have never heard the clever definition for recursion, here it is: Recursion - see
Recursion. *Recursion* occurs in a program when a function calls itself. Initially, this
might seem like an endless loop, but it is not. Both C and C++ support recursion.
Recursive algorithms allow for creative, readable, and terse problem solutions. For
example, the next program uses recursion to generate the factorial of a number. (The
factorial of a number is defined as the number multiplied by all successively lower
integers.) For example:

```
8 * 7 * 6 * 5 * 4 * 3 * 2 * 1    = 40320
```

Care must be taken when choosing data types because the product increases very
rapidly. The factorial of 15 is 1307674368000.

```c
/*
 *   recurson.c
 *   A C program illustrating recursive function calls.
 *   Calculation of the factorial of a number.
 *   Example:  7! = 7 x 6 x 5 x 4 x 3 x 2 x 1 = 5040
 *   Copyright (c) Chris H. Pappas and William H. Murray, 1996
 */

#include <stdio.h>

double RecursiveFactorial(double danswer);

void main( void )
{
  double ValueToFactor = 105.0, TheFactorialIs;

  TheFactorialIs = RecursiveFactorial( ValueToFactor );

  printf( "The factorial of %10.0lf is: %15.0lf\n"      ,
          ValueToFactor,TheFactorialIs                  );
}

double RecursiveFactorial(double CurrentValue)
{
  if( CurrentValue <= 1.0 )
```

```
    return( 1.0 );
  else
    return( CurrentValue * RecursiveFactorial(CurrentValue-1.0));
}
```

RecursiveFactorial() is recursive because within its function body it has a call to itself. Notice too that the **printf()** function uses a new format code for printing a double value: %...lf. Here the *l* is a modifier to the *f* and specifies a double instead of a **float**.

Function Arguments

Now that you know how to pass information call-by-value or call-by-reference, it is time to take a closer look at different function argument types. As it turns out, not all data types are passed call-by-value by default, requiring a manual-override to call-by-reference when needed. For example, by default, all array types are passed call-by-reference! (Note that strings—arrays-of-**chars**—are no exception. In this section, you will learn more about passing function arguments to functions. These arguments go by many different names. Some programmers call them arguments, while others refer to them as parameters or dummy variables.

Of course, function arguments are optional. Some functions you design may receive no arguments, while others may receive many. Function argument types can be mixed; that is, you can use any of the standard data types as a function argument. Many of the following examples illustrate passing various data types to functions. For your edification, these programs employ functions from the various C and C++ libraries.

Formal and Actual Arguments

All function headers contain an argument list called the *formal argument list*. Items in the list are optional, so the actual list may be empty or it may contain any combination of data types, such as **int**eger, **float**, and **char**acter. When the function is called by the program, an argument list is also passed to the function. This list is called the *actual argument list*. In general, there is usually a one-to-one match, when writing ANSI C code, between the formal and actual argument lists, although in reality no strong enforcement is used. Examine the following coded C example:

```
printf( "Integer precision %d, float precision %f,ValueToOutput );
```

In this case, only one argument is being passed to **printf()**, although two are expected. When fewer arguments are supplied, the missing arguments are initialized to meaningless values.

C++ overcomes this problem, to a degree, by permitting a default value to be supplied with the formal argument list. When an argument is missing in the actual argument list, the default argument is automatically substituted. For example, in C++, the function prototype might appear as this:

```
void Display(float ScaleFactor,int Xcoordinate = MIN_X,int Ycoord = MIN_Y);
```

Here, if either *Xcoord* or *YCoord* is not specified in the call to the function *Display()*, the values associated with the symbolic constant *MIN_X* or *MIN_Y* are used. C++ requires that all formal arguments using default values be listed at the end of the formal argument list. In other words, *Display(0.75)*, *Display(0.50,70)*, and *Display(0.30, 128,359)* are all valid function calls.

Type void as an Argument

One of the purposes of the **void** data type is to explicitly and formally declare nothing. In ANSI C **void** should be used to explicitly state the absence of function arguments. The following program has a simple function named *PrintSquareRoot()* that receives no arguments and does not return a value. The **main()** function calls the function *PrintSquareRoot()*. When the *PrintSquareRoot()* function is finished, control is returned to the **main()** function. This is one of the simplest types of functions you can write:

```
/*
 *    void.c
 *    A C program that will print a message with a function.
 *    The function uses a type void argument and sqrt() function
 *    from the standard C library.
 *    Copyright (c) Chris H. Pappas and William H. Murray, 1996
 */

#include <stdio.h>
#include <math.h>

void PrintSquareRoot( void );

void main( void )
{
  printf("This program calls a function with zero arguments, \n\n");
```

```
    printf("and calculates the square root of the value 98765.0: " );

    PrintSquareRoot( );
}

void PrintSquareRoot( void )
{
    double ValueToUse = 98765.0, CalculatedSquareRoot;

    CalculatedSquareRoot = sqrt( ValueToUse );
    printf("The square root of %lf is %lf\n", ValueToUse,
                                    CalculatedSquareRoot);

}
```

Notice that *PrintSquareRoot()* makes a call to the function **sqrt()**, prototyped in *math.h*. **sqrt()** expects a **double** as an argument and returns the square root as a double value.

Characters as Arguments

This next program demonstrates how to pass a single character to a function. Character data types, by default, are passed to a function's call-by-value. In this program the single character is intercepted from the keyboard in the function **main()** and passed to the function *Print_A_char()*. The **getch()** function reads the character.

There are other functions that are closely related to **getch()** in the standard C library: **getc()**, **getchar()**, and **getche()**. These functions can also be used in C++, but in many cases a better choice will probably be **cin**. Additional details for using **getch()** are contained in your Borland C++ reference manuals and are available as online help. The **getch()** function intercepts a character from the standard input device (keyboard) and returns a character value, without echo to the screen, as shown here:

```
/*
 *   char.c
 *   This C program will accept a character from the keyboard,
 *   pass it to a function, and print a message using
 *   the character.
 *   Copyright (c) Chris H. Pappas and William H. Murray, 1996
 */

#include <stdio.h>
#include <ctype.h>
```

```
void Print_A_char(char LetterToPrint);

void main( void )
{
  char UserInput_char;

  printf("Letter to print:  \n");
  UserInput_char = getch(      );
  Print_A_char( UserInput_char );
}

void Print_A_char(char LetterToPrint)
{
 printf("The UP-cased LetterToPrint is %c",
        toupper( LetterToPrint )       ;
}
```

After obtaining the *UserInput_char*, the program passes the single character to the function *Print_A_char*. Using the function **toupper()**, prototyped in ctype.h, the program outputs the up-cased character equivalent. Just remember, character data is passed to functions, by default, call-by-value.

Integers as Arguments

The next program passes a single integer to a function. The *CalculateValues()* function uses the supplied length to calculate and print the area of a square, the volume of a cube, and the surface area of a cube:

```
/*
 *    int.c
 *    This C program will calculate values given a length.
 *    The function uses a type int argument, accepts length
 *    from keyboard with the scanf() function.
 *    Copyright (c) Chris H. Pappas and William H. Murray, 1996
 */

#include <stdio.h>

void CalculateValues(int ValueToUse);
```

```
 void main( void )
{
  int TestValue;

  printf( "Enter the TestValue: " );
  scanf ( "%d",&TestValue          );
  CalculateValues( TestValue       );
}

void CalculateValues(int ValueToUse)
{
  float Area,Volume,SurfaceArea;
  const float PI = 3.14159;

  Area        = PI * ValueToUse * ValueToUse    ;
  Volume      = PI * 4.0/3.0    * ValueToUse
                   * ValueToUse * ValueToUse     ;
  SurfaceArea = PI * 4.0        * ValueToUse
                                * ValueToUse     ;

  printf( "Side Length : %d  \n\n",ValueToUse  );
  printf( "Area        : %f \n",Area           );
  printf( "Volume      : %f \n",Volume         );
  printf( "Surface Area: %f \n",SurfaceArea    );
}
```

Even though *ValueToUse* is of type **int**, the calculated values are all of type **float**. Note: just like **char** data types, **int** data types are passed, by default, call-by-value.

Floats and Doubles as Arguments

You use **int** argument types the same way you use **float** and **double** argument types. You simply declare them, place the variable name within the function call, correctly define and match their number and data type with the function prototype/header, and then use their dummy argument name counterpart within the function body. Because these concepts are straightforward, it is now time to concentrate on a less obvious use for array argument types.

Arrays as Arguments

Because Chapter 9 is dedicated exclusively to the topic of arrays, the use of them in this chapter is a bit advanced. However, we include a discussion of arrays here because they are valid argument types. Unlike **int**, **char**, **float**, and **double** data types, which are passed to functions call-by-value by default, arrays are passed, by default, call-by-reference. In the following example, the contents of an array are passed to a function as a call-by-reference. In this case, the address of the first array element is passed using an unsized array syntax:

```c
/*
 *    array.c
 *    This C program will call a function with an array.
 *    The function uses a pointer to pass array information.
 *    Copyright (c) Chris H. Pappas and William H. Murray, 1996
 */

#include <stdio.h>
#define TEN 10

void FillTheArray(int TestArray[]);

void main( void )
{
  int offset, TestArray[ TEN ];

  FillTheArray( TestArray );

  for( offset = 0; offset < TEN; offsett++ )
    printf( "%d",TestArray[ offset ] );
}

void Print_A_char(int TestArray[])
{
  int offset;

  for( offset = 0; offset < TEN; offsett++ )
    scanf( "%d",TestArray[ offset ] );
}
```

To pass an array to a function, you simply use its name, in this example, *Print_A_char(TestArray);*. By specifying the name of the array, you are providing the address of the first element in the array. It is also possible to pass the address

information by using an unsized array syntax. The next example shows how you
can do this:

```
/*
 *    array.c
 *    This C program will call a function with an array.
 *    The function uses a pointer to pass array information.
 *    Copyright (c) Chris H. Pappas and William H. Murray, 1996
 */

#include <stdio.h>
#define TEN 10

void FillTheArray(int *PointerToElement);

void main( void )
{
  int offset, TestArray[ TEN ];

  FillTheArray( TestArray );

  for( offset = 0; offset < TEN; offsett++ )
    printf( "%d",TestArray[ offset ] );
}

void Print_A_char(int *PointerToElement)
{
  int Count;

  for( Count = 0; Count < TEN; Count++ ) {
    scanf( "%d",PointerToElement );
    PointerToElement++;
  }
}
```

Because *TestArray* is an array of integers, it is possible to pass the array by
specifying a pointer of the element type, *int **. Notice that within the function
Print_A_char(), it is *not* necessary to dereference the *PointerToElement*, since **scanf()**
wants the memory location's address, not access to its contents. If *Print_A_char* had
wanted to then print each filled array element, it *would* have to dereference the pointer
variable, like this:

```
printf( "Integer just input is: %d", *PointerToElement);
```

The statement *PointerToElement++;* increments the address to point to the next **int** array element before repeating the loop.

Function Types

The previous section concentrated on formal argument types. In order not to confuse you, none of the examples in the last section returned information from the function and thus were of type **void**. In this section, you will review the concepts and syntax necessary to return values from functions.

To begin, remember that C and C++ do not have procedures, only functions. This means that you will have to make clever use of call-by-value, call-by-reference, and the data type **void** to accomplish the same things older high-level language procedures and functions do. For example, a Pascal procedure can return zero arguments. So how do you accomplish this in C/C++? You simply define the function as officially returning nothing by using the data type **void** (Note: functions returning type **void** do not use **return();** statements):

```
void Function_Returning_Nothing( .... );
```

That was easy. Now how about translating a procedure that returns several values into C/C++'s restricted use of functions? To accomplish this feat, you use a mix of call-by-reference with a return type:

```
int Function_Working_Like_Procedure(char *c,int *i,float *f,char Name[]);
```

or in C++ only, using the reference type:

```
int Function_Working_Like_Procedure(char &c,int &i,float &f,char Name[]);
```

In this function prototype, *Function_Working_Like_Procedure()* returns five values. The first three dummy arguments *c*, *i*, and *f*, were all received as pointers, giving the function the ability to change their calling argument's call-by-reference. *Name*, an array-of-**char**s, is passed, by default, call-by-reference, so it is the fourth variable passed as such. Finally, the function returns the fifth variable as an integer.

A final word about **return();** statements. Any function not returning the type **void** must have a **return();** statement with the enclosing parentheses containing a value or equation that is, or can be translated to, the specified return type. However, a function can have more than one **return();** statement. This will generate compiler warning messages, but a warning message does not necessarily mean you have written incorrect code. Warning messages are just meant to alert the programmer, so he or she is certain that the coding on a particular line is truly what is desired.

The following function body illustrates one way of using multiple **return();** statements:

```
float PerformCalculation( char Operator, float NumOne, float NumTwo)
{
  switch( Operator ) {
    case '+' : return ( NumOne + NumTwo );
    case '-' : return ( NumTwo - NumOne );
    case '*' : return ( NumOne * NumTwo );
    case */' : return ( NumOne / NumTwo );
}
```

The **switch-case** appears to be missing the required **break;** statements; however, in this syntax, the **return();** statements perform the same function.

Arguments for Function main()

There may be an occasion when you will need to write a program that accepts command-line arguments. For example, take the MS-DOS copy program. To run this program you type the program name, *copy*, followed by a source filename and a destination name. These last two entries are officially known as *command-line arguments*.

Traditionally, writing a program to access this information has been very tedious. C and C++ share the ability to easily intercept these command-line arguments. This allows you to pass arguments directly to your program without additional program prompts. For example, a program might pass four arguments from the command line:

```
List a:\myfil.dat LPT1:
```

In this example, three values are passed from the command line to the program *List*. Actually, it is **main()** that is given specific information. One argument received by **main()**, *argc*, is an integer giving the number of command-line terms plus 1. Since DOS 3.0, the program title is counted as the first term passed from the command line.

The second argument is a pointer to an array of string pointers called *argv*. All arguments are strings of characters, so *argv* is of type **char** *[*argc*]. Because all programs have a name, *argc* is always one greater than the number of command-line arguments. In the following examples, you will learn different techniques for retrieving various data types from the command line. The argument names *argc* and *argv* are the commonly agreed upon variable names used in all C/C++ programs.

Strings

No matter which data type you would like to enter on the command line, all arguments are passed as strings of characters, and thus they are the easiest to work with. In the next example, the C program expects that the user will enter several names on the command line. To ensure that the user enters several names, if *argc* isn't greater than 2, the user will be returned to the command line with a rejoinder to try again:

```c
/*
 *   string.c
 *   This C program illustrates how to read string data
 *   into the program with a command-line argument.
 *   Copyright (c) Chris H. Pappas and William H. Murray, 1996
 */

#include <stdio.h>
#include <process.h>

#define DOES_NOT_MEET_MINIMUM_REQUIREMENTS 2

void main(int argc,char *argv[])
{
  int offset;

  if( argc < DOES_NOT_MEET_MINIMUM_REQUIREMENTS ) {
    printf( "Enter several names on the command line\n" );
    printf( "when executing this program!\n"           );
    printf( "Please try again.\n"                       );
    exit  ( 1 );
  }
```

```
   for( offset = 1; offset < argc; offset++)
      printf("String #%d is %s\n",offset,argv[ offset ]   );
}
```

The program demonstrates how to use *argv*'s elements as simple null-terminated string data types by printing the names entered on the command line to the screen in the same order. If numeric data values are entered on the command line, they will also be interpreted as an ASCII string of individual characters and must be printed as such.

Integers

Programs frequently need to accept integer data from the command line. For example, consider a program that finds the average of a student's test scores. In such a case, the ASCII character information must be converted to an integer value. The C++ example in this section will accept a single integer number on the command line.

Because the number is actually a character string, it will be converted to an integer with the **atoi()** library function. The command-line value *ValueToConvert* is passed to a function called *ConvertToBinary()*. The function will convert the number in *ValueToConvert* to a string of binary digits and print them to the screen. When control is returned to **main()**, the *ValueToConvert* will be printed in octal and hexadecimal formats:

```
//
//  intargv.cpp
//  This C++ program illustrates how to read an integer
//  into the program with a command-line argument.
//  Copyright (c) Chris H. Pappas and William H. Murray, 1996
//

#include <iostream.h>
#include <stdlNumTwo.h>
#include <process.h>

void ConvertToBinary(int ValueToConvert);

void main(int argc, char *argv[])
{
  int ValueToConvert;

  if( argc != 2 ) {
```

```
   cout << "Enter a decimal number on the command line.\n";
   cout << "It will be converted to binary, octal and\n";
   cout << "hexadecimal.\n";
   exit( 1 );
 }

 ValueToConvert = atoi( argv[1]  );

 ConvertToBinary( ValueToConvert );

 cout << "Octal Radix: "
      << oct << ValueToConvert
      << endl;

 cout << "Hexadecimal Radix: "
      << hex << ValueToConvert
      << endl;
}

void ConvertToBinary(int ValueToConvert)
{
  int Position = 0, HoldConversion[ 50 ];

  while( ValueToConvert != 0 ) {
    HoldConversion[ Position ] = ( ValueToConvert % 2 );
    ValueToConvert /= 2;
    Position++;
  }

  Position--;
  cout << "Binary Radix: ";
  for(; Position >= 0; Position-- )
    cout << dec << HoldConversion[ Position ];
        << endl;
}
```

Notice the formatting of each base type conversion. You can convert base ten numbers to another base by dividing the number by the new base a successive number of times. In the case of conversion to a binary number, a 2 is repeatedly divided into a base ten number. The base ten number becomes the quotient from the previous division. The remainder after each division is either 1 or 0. The remainder becomes the binary digit. The individual array bits, which form the binary result, must be unloaded in reverse order. Study the **for** loop used in the function:

```
cout << dec << HoldConversion [ Position ];
```

This is the statement to print the number in octal format:

```
cout << "The octal value is: "
     << oct << ValueToConvert << endl;
```

It is also possible to print the hexadecimal equivalent by substituting hex for oct, as shown here:

```
cout << "The hexadecimal value is: "
     << hex << ValueToConvert << endl;
```

Floats

Translating *argv* null-terminated strings to **float** types is just as easy as in the last program. The only difference is that instead of using the **atoi()** function, you use **atof()**, which stands for alpha-to-float. The following C example will allow several angles to be entered on the command line. The cosine of the angles will be extracted and printed to the screen. Because the angles are of type **float**, they can take on values such as 12.0, 45.78, 0.12345, or 15:

```c
/*
 *    flotargv.c
 *    This C program illustrates how to read float data types
 *    into the program with a command-line argument.
 *    Copyright (c) Chris H. Pappas and William H. Murray, 1996
 */

#include <stdio.h>
#include <math.h>
#include <process.h>

const double PI = 3.14159;

void main(int argc, char *argv[])
{
```

```
   int     CurrentArgument;
   double  Angle;

   if( argc < 2 ) {
     printf( "Type several angles on the command line.\n" );
     printf( "Program will calculate and print\n"          );
     printf( "the cosine of the angles entered.\n"         );
     exit  ( 1 );
   }

   for ( CurrentArgument = 1; CurrentArgument < argc;

                           CurrentAragument++  )         {
     Angle = atof( argv[ CurrentArgument ]               );
     printf( "The cosine of %f is %15.14lf\n",
             Angle,cos( (PI/180.0) * Angle )             );

   }
 }
```

The program translates each successive angle, stored as a null-terminated string, into its **float** equivalent with a call to the function **atof()**. The program uses the **cos()** function within the **printf()** function to retrieve the cosine information.

Important C++ Features

C++ provides two special function capabilities not available to C programmers: **inline** functions and overloaded functions. When a C++ function header is preceded by the **inline** keyword, the C++ compiler inserts the function's body inline. This does away with the normal overhead involved in calling functions. Normal function calls force the compiler to generate additional time-consuming code, copy actual arguments, keep track of the calling function's return address, pass actual arguments, generate passed argument pop-stack code, and then reverse the process when the called function terminates. Invoking an **inline** function avoids all of this.

Overloading permits several function prototypes to be given the same function name. The numerous prototypes are then recognized by their distinguishing argument lists, not just by their name. Overloading is very useful when a function is required to perform the same logical sequence but work with different data types. For example, the logical steps required to average an array of ten integers is identical to the code necessary to average an array of ten **float**s, except for the data types.

inline

Think of the **inline** keyword as a directive or, better yet, a suggestion to the C++
compiler to insert the function inline. The compiler may ignore this suggestion for any
of several reasons. For example, the function might be too long. **inline** functions are
used primarily to save time when short functions are called many times within a
program. The following program defines the two functions *FindMinimum()* and
FindMaximum() as **inline** functions:

```cpp
//
//  inline.cpp
//  This C++ program illustrates the C++ inline function declaration.
//  Copyright (c) Chris H. Pappas and William H. Murray, 1996
//

#include <iostream.h>

inline int FindMinimum( int NumOne, int NumTwo )
{
  if( NumOne < NumTwo ) return( NumOne );
    else return( NumTwo );
}

inline int FindMaximum( int NumOne, int NumTwo )
{
  if( NumOne > NumTwo ) return( NumOne );
    else return( NumTwo );
}

void main( void )
{
  int NumOne = 1, NumTwo = 2;

  cout << "The minimum value is "
       << FindMinimum( NumOne, NumTwo );
       << endl;

cout << "The maximum value is "
       << FindMaximum( NumOne, NumTwo );
       << endl;
}
```

In this example, each function call is literally substituted with a duplicate inline copy of the respective function body. By eliminating the function call-stack, performance is improved while maintaining readability.

Overloading

The following program demonstrates C++'s ability to prototype and define multiple functions all having the same function name. Notice in the example that follows that the two overloaded functions are prototyped within the same scope. The C++ compiler selects which function to invoke based on the arguments provided. A function call to *AverageArrayElements()* will process **int**eger or **float** data correctly.

```cpp
//
//  overload.cpp
//  This C++ program illustrates function overloading.
//  The overloaded function receives an array of integers or
//  floats and returns either an integer or float product.
//  Copyright (c) Chris H. Pappas and William H. Murray, 1996
//

#include <iostream.h>
#define FIVE 5

int   AverageArrayElements( int   iGrades[] );
float AverageArrayElements( float fGrades[] );

void main( void )
{
  int   IntegerAverage,
        iGrades[ FIVE ] = {  100,    90,    78,    92, 87    };
  float FloatAverage,
        fGrades[ FIVE ] = { 97.6, 87.3, 76.1, 88.9, 97.6 };

  IntegerAverage = AverageArrayElements( iGrades );
  FloatAverage   = AverageArrayElements( fGrades );

  cout << "The Integer Average equals: "
       << IntegerAverage << endl;

  cout << "The Float Average equals   : "
       << FloatAverage << endl;
}
```

```
int AverageArrayElements( int iGrades[] )
{
  int offset, TempResult = 0;

  for( offset = 0; offseti < FIVE; offset++ )
    TempResult += iGrades[ offset ];
  return( TempResult );
}

float AverageArrayElements( float fGrades[] )
{
  int offset;
  float TempResult;

  for( offset = 0; offset < FIVE; offset++ )
    TempResult += fGrades[ offset ];
  return( TempResult );
}
```

For the C++ compiler to accept an overloaded function definition, one thing must be true: each overloaded version must contain a unique formal argument list. This means that the formal argument lists will either vary in the number of arguments or the types of arguments, or both. For example, if a function differs only in the function's return type and not in the formal argument list, the function cannot be overloaded:

```
int OverloadedFunctionName  ( int A_Value );

float OverloadedFunctionName( int A_Value );
```

This syntax is not allowed, because each prototype would accept the same type of arguments. Despite these limitations, overloading is a very important topic in C++ and is fully explored starting with Chapter 14.

Ellipsis (...)

You use the ellipsis when the number of arguments is not known. As such, they can be specified within the function's formal argument statement. For example:

```
RETURN_TYPE FunctionName( DATA_TYPE [,DATA_TYPE],... );
```

This syntax tells the C compiler that other arguments may or may not follow the required *DATA_TYPE*(s). Naturally, type checking is suspended with the ellipsis. The following C program demonstrates how to use the ellipsis. You may want to delay an in-depth study of the algorithm, however, until you have a thorough understanding of C string pointer types (see Chapters 9 and 10).

```c
/*
 *   ellipsis.c
 *   A C program demonstrating the use of ... and its support
 *   macros va_arg(), va_start(), and va_end().
 *   Copyright (c) Chris H. Pappas and William H. Murray, 1996
 */

#include <stdio.h>
#include <stdarg.h>
#include <string.h>

void PrintThem( char *String, ... );

void main( void )
{
  PrintThem("Print %d integers, %d %d %d",10,4,1);
}

void PrintThem( char *String, ... )
{
  int NumberOf_d_s = 0;
  va_list Ellipsis_TYPE;
  int d_Format = 'd';
  char *PointerToChar;
  PointerToChar = strchr( String,d_Format );

  while( *++PointerToChar != '\0' ) {
    PointerToChar++;
    PointerToChar = strchr( PointerToChar,d_Format );
    NumberOf_d_s++;
  }
  printf( "Output %d integers,",NumberOf_d_s );
```

```
va_start( Ellipsis_TYPE,String );

while( NumberOf_d_s-- )
  printf( " %d",va_arg(Ellipsis_TYPE,int) );

va_end(Ellipsis_TYPE);
}
```

The function *PrintThem()* has been prototyped to expect two arguments, a string pointer and an argument of type ..., or a varying length argument list. Naturally, functions using a varying length argument list are not omniscient. Something within the argument list must give the function enough information to process the varying part. In ellipsis.c, this information comes from the string argument. In a very crude approach, *PrintThem()* attempts to mimic the **printf()** function.

The subroutine scans the *String* format string to see how many %ds it finds. It then uses this information to make a calculated fetching and printing of the information in the variable argument. This may seem straightforward, but the algorithm requires a sophisticated sequence of events. The **strchr()** function returns the address of the location containing the "d" in %d. The first %d can be ignored, since this is required by the output message. The **while** loop continues processing the remainder of the String string looking for the variable number of %ds and counting them (*NumberOf_d_s*). With this accomplished, the beginning of the output message is printed.

The **va_start()** macro sets the *Ellipsis_TYPE* pointer to the beginning of the variable argument list. The **va_arg()** support macro retrieves the next argument in the variable list. The macro uses its second parameter to know what data type to retrieve; for the example program, this is type **int**. The function *PrintThem()* terminates with a call to **va_end()**. The last of the three standard C ellipsis support macros, **va_end()**, resets the pointer to null.

Problems Encountered with Scope Rules

If variables are used with different scope levels you may run into completely unexpected programming results, called side effects. For example, you have learned that it is possible to use a variable of the same name with both file and local scopes. The scope rules state that the variable with a local scope (called a local variable) will take precedence over the variable with a file scope (called a global variable). That all seems easy enough, but let's now consider some less obvious problem areas you might encounter in programming.

An Undefined Symbol in a C Program

In the following example, four variables are given a local scope within the function **main()**. Copies of the variables *NumOne* and *NumTwo* are passed to the function *Sum()*. This does not violate scope rules. However, when the *Sum()* function attempts to use the variable *NumThree*, it cannot find the variable. Why? Because the scope of the variable was local only to **main()**:

```
/*
 *    scope.c
 *    A C program to illustrate problems with scope rules.
 *    The function is supposed to form a product of three numbers.
 *    The compiler signals problems because variable n isn't known
 *    to the function multiplier.
 *    Copyright (c) Chris H. Pappas and William H. Murray, 1996
 */

#include <stdio.h>

int Sum( int NumOne, int NumTwo );

void main( void )
{
  int NumOne   = 1,
      NumTwo   = 2,
      NumThree = 3,
      Result   = 0;

  Result = Sum( NumOne, NumTwo                     );
  printf(  "The sum of the numbers is: %d\n", Result );
}

int Sum(int NumOne, int NumTwo )
{
  int LocalSum;

  LocalSum = NumOne + NumTwo + NumThree;
  return( LocalSum );
}
```

The C compiler issues a warning and an error message. It first reports a warning that the *NumThree* variable is never used within the function and then the error message that *NumThree* has never been declared in the function *Sum()*. One way around this problem is to give *NumThree* file scope by moving its declaration above **main()**.

Use a Variable with File Scope

This example gives the variable file scope. Making *NumThree* global to the whole file allows both **main()** and *Sum()* to use it. Also, note that both **main()** and *Sum()* can change the value of the variable. It is good programming practice not to allow functions to change global program variables if they are created to be truly portable.

```c
/*
 *   scope.c
 *   A C program to illustrate problems with scope rules.
 *   The function is supposed to form a product of three numbers.
 *   The compiler signals problems because variable n isn't known
 *   to the function multiplier.
 *   Copyright (c) Chris H. Pappas and William H. Murray, 1996
 */

#include <stdio.h>

int Sum( int NumOne, int NumTwo );


int NumThree = 3;

void main( void )
{
  int NumOne   = 1,
      NumTwo   = 2,
      Result   = 0;

  Result = Sum( NumOne, NumTwo                    );
  printf(  "The sum of the numbers is: %d\n", Result );
}


int Sum(int NumOne, int NumTwo )
{
  int LocalSum;

  LocalSim = NumOne + NumTwo + NumThree;
  return( LocalSum );
}
```

This program will compile correctly and print the *Result* to the screen.

Overriding a Variable with File Scope by a Variable with Local Scope

Should a program use the same variable name at both the external and internal levels, scope rules dictate that the function's internal declaration take precedence over any global reference. Here is a small program that illustrates this point:

```c
/*
 *    scope.c
 *    A C program to illustrate problems with scope rules.
 *    The function is supposed to form a product of three numbers.
 *    The compiler signals problems because variable n isn't known
 *    to the function multiplier.
 *    Copyright (c) Chris H. Pappas and William H. Murray, 1996
 */

#include <stdio.h>

int Sum( int NumOne, int NumTwo );

int NumThree = 3;

void main( void )
{
   int NumOne   = 1,
       NumTwo   = 2,
       Result   = 0;

   Result = Sum( NumOne, NumTwo                       );
   printf(  "The sum of the numbers is: %d\n", Result );
}

int Sum(int NumOne, int NumTwo )
{
   int LocalResult, NumThree = 10;

   LocalSum = NumOne + NumTwo + NumThree;
   return( LocalSum );
}
```

In this example, the variable *NumThree* has both file and local scope. When *NumThree* is used within the function *Sum()*, the local scope takes precedence and the sum of 1 + 2 + 10 = 13 is returned.

A Scope Problem in C++

In the following C++ example, everything works fine up to the point of printing the information to the screen. The **cout** statement prints the values for *NumOne* and *NumTwo* correctly. When selecting the *NumThree* value, it chooses the global variable with file scope. The program reports the sum (1 + 2 + 3 =) 10, clearly a mistake. You know that in this case the *Sum()* function used the local value of *NumThree*.

```
//
//   scope.cpp
//   A C++ program to illustrate problems with scope rules.
//   The function forms a product of three numbers. The n
//   variable is of local scope and used by the function
//   product. However, main() reports that the n value is 10.
//   What is wrong here?
//   Copyright (c) Chris H. Pappas and William H. Murray, 1996
//

#include <iostream.h>

int Sum(int NumOne,int NumOne);

int NumThree = 3;

void main( void )
{
   int NumOne = 1,
       NumTwo = 2,
       Result = 0;

   Result = Sum( NumOne,NumTwo );

   cout << "The sum of " << NumOne <<" + " << NumTwo
        << " + " << NumThree << " is: " << Result << endl;
}

int Sum( int NumOne,int NumOne )
{
   int LocalResult, NumThree = 10;
```

```
        LocalResult = NumOne + NumTwo + NumThree;
        return( LocalResult );
    }
```

If you actually wanted to form the sum with the global value of *NumThree*, how could this conflict be resolved? C++ would permit you to use the scope resolution operator. All you would need to do is change the syntax in the function body as was done in this next example program.

The C++ Scope Resolution Operator

In this example, the scope resolution operator (::) is used to avoid conflicts between a variable with both file and local scope. The last program reported an incorrect product because the local value was used in the calculation. Notice in the following listing that the *Sum()* function uses the scope resolution operator:

```
//
//  gscope.cpp
//  A C++ program to illustrate problems with scope rules.
//  The Function forms a product of three numbers. The n
//  variable is of local scope and used by function
//  product. However, main() reports that the n value is 10.
//  What is wrong here?
//  Copyright (c) Chris H. Pappas and William H. Murray, 1996
//

#include <iostream.h>

int Sum(int NumOne,int NumOne);

int NumThree = 3;

void main( void )
{
    int NumOne = 1,
        NumTwo = 2,
        Result = 0;

    Result = Sum( NumOne,NumTwo );
```

```
   cout << "The sum of " << NumOne <<" + " << NumTwo
       << " + " << NumThree << " is: " << Result << endl;
}

int Sum( int NumOne, int NumOne )
{
   int LocalResult, NumThree = 10;

   LocalResult = NumOne + NumTwo + ::NumThree;
   return( LocalResult );
}
```

Now the value of the global variable, with file scope, will be used in the calculation. When the results are printed to the screen, you will see that $1 + 2 + 3 = 6$. The scope resolution operator is very important in C++. Additional examples illustrating the resolution operator are given starting with Chapter 16.

In the Next Chapter...

Having fully investigated the standard and unique ways C and C++ deal with the subject of subroutines, it is time to take a closer look at the subject of C/C++ array types. Once again, you will discover that there are C/C++ array concepts very similar to most older high-level languages, but that there are also several new capabilities unique to C/C++.

Chapter Nine

Arrays

From having read these last few chapters, you are undoubtedly aware that C and C++ take programming fundamentals, common to most older high-level languages and greatly expand upon them. This certainly holds true when it comes to arrays. In C/C++, the topics of arrays, pointers, and strings are all related.

In this chapter, you will learn how to define and use arrays. Many C/C++ books combine the topics of arrays and pointers into one discussion. This is unfortunate, because there are many uses for arrays in C/C++ that are not dependent on a detailed understanding of pointers. Also, because there is a great deal of material to cover about arrays in general, it is best not to confuse the topic with a discussion of pointers. Pointers, however, allow you to comprehend fully just how an array is processed. Chapter 10 examines the topic of pointers and completes this chapter's discussion of arrays.

What Is an Array?

From the compiler's point of view, an array is like-sized elements stored linearly in consecutive memory locations. You access each individual data item by using a subscript, or index, to select one of the elements. In the C/C++ language, an array is not a standard data type; instead, it is an aggregate type made up of any other type of data. In C, it is possible to have an array of anything: characters, integers, floats, doubles, arrays, pointers, structures, and so on. Basically, the concept of arrays and their use is the same in both C and C++.

Because all elements are assumed to be the same size, arrays cannot be defined by using mixed data types (actually, if an array element is a structure, then mixed data types can exist in the array by existing inside the structure member). Without this assumption, it would be very difficult to determine where any given element was stored. Because the elements are all the same size and because that fact is used to help determine how to locate a given element, it follows that the elements are stored contiguously in the computer's memory (with the lowest address corresponding to the first element, the highest address to the last element). This means that there is no filler space between elements and that they are physically adjacent in the computer. C/C++ also support nested arrays, or arrays within arrays, referred to as *multidimensional* arrays.

From a C/C++ programmer's perspective, the most important fundamental to keep in mind when using arrays is this: the name of an array internally is viewed by the compiler as a pointer-*constant* to the array's first element. This is very important: the name of an array is A) viewed as a pointer type, and more specifically, B) a constant pointer—meaning a locked memory address to the array's first element. For example, even though an array's declaration takes the generic form:

```
ArrayElement_Type ArrayName[ NumberOfElements ];
```

the compiler views the declaration as:

```
ArrayElement_Type * const ArrayName = &ArrayName[ 0 ];
```

For this reason, an array's identifier can never be used as an lvalue. *lvalues* represent *variables* that can have their contents altered by the program; they frequently appear to the left of assignment statements. For example:

```
Salary = 45739.00;
```

If array names were legal *lvalues,* your program could change their contents:

```
float EmployeeSalaries[ MAX_EMPLOYEES ];
.
.
.
EmployeeSalaries = 45739.00;
```

The effect would be to change the starting address of the array itself, in effect, losing it. This may seem like a small thing, but some forms of expressions that might appear valid on the surface are not allowed in C/C++. All C/C++ programmers eventually learn these subtleties, but it helps if you understand structurally why these differences exist.

Array Declarations

All variable declarations in C/C++ begin with their data type; this is also true when defining an array. The syntax continues with a valid array name and a pair of matching square brackets enclosing a constant expression. The following are examples of array declarations:

```
int  ScreenCoordinates[ 5 ];    /* an array of twelve integers   */
char CompanyID[ 20 ];           /* an array of twenty characters */
```

Figure 9-1 illustrates the array *ScreenCoordinates*.

The constant expression defines the size of the array. It is illegal to use a variable name inside the square brackets. For this reason, it is not possible to avoid specifying the array size until the program executes. The expression must reduce to a constant value so that the compiler knows exactly how much storage space to reserve for the array.

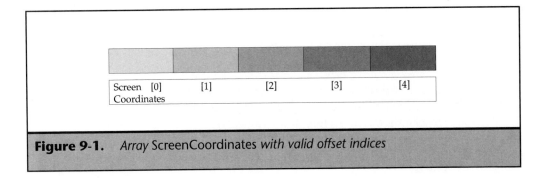

Figure 9-1.   *Array* ScreenCoordinates *with valid offset indices*

For the sake of proper design and ease of modification, it is best to use symbolic constants to specify the size of the array:

```
#define MAX_COORDINATES     20
#define MAX_COMPANY_ID_SIZE 15

int  ScreenCoordinates[ MAX_COORDINATES    ];
char CompanyID         [ MAX_COMPANY_ID_SIZE ];
```

Use of defined constants guarantees that subsequent references to the array will not exceed the defined array size. For example, it is very common to use a **for** loop to access array elements:

```
#define MAX_COORDINATES 20

void main( void )
{
   int Offset, ScreenCoordinates[ MAX_COORDINATES ];

   for( Offset = 0; Offset < MAX_COORDINATES; Offset++ ) {
   .   .   .
   }

}
```

The encoded statement *Offset < MAX_COORDINATES;* is a much safer keystroke entry than a compiler-overlooked mistake such as this: *Offset < 21;*. In addition, by using the symbolic constant throughout your program, one simple code change:

```
#define MAX_COORDINATES 20
```

to

```
#define MAX_COORDINATES 25
```

alters all related references in the entire project. The time-consuming alternative would be a search-and-replace of every *20* in your program with a *25*, assuming that the original *20*s had no *other* meaning and that there were no accidental *21*s or *19*s hanging around.

Array Initialization

C/C++ provide three techniques for initializing array elements:

Technique	Description
By default	When they are created—this applies only to global and static arrays.
Explicitly	When they are created—by supplying constant initializing data.
Run-Time	During program execution when you assign or copy data into the array.

You can only use *constant* data to initialize an array when it is created. If the array elements must receive their values from *variables*, you must initialize the array by writing explicit statements as part of the program code.

Default Initialization

C/C++ array declarations are either global, defined outside of **main()** and any other function; or local, inside a function. Global array elements are initialized to 0 (pointer arrays are initialized to null), whereas local array elements are assumed to contain garbage.

*NOTE: By preceding a local array's declaration with the storage class **static**, you change its storage class from local to global and, in this case, obtain the advantages of global storage initialization to 0.*

Explicit Initialization

C/C++ allow you to simultaneously declare and initialize variables of type **char**, **int**, **float**, and **double**. The same holds true for array declarations. The ANSI C/C++ standard lets you supply initialization values for any array, global or otherwise, defined anywhere in a program. The following code segment illustrates how to define and initialize four arrays:

```
int Status       [  3 ] = {  -1,0,1                                        };
static int Radix10 [ 10 ] = {   0,1,2,3,4,5,6,7,8,9                          };
float FloatRanges  [  3 ] = {   1.141579,0.75,55E0,-.33E1                    };
char AllVowels     [    ] = { 'A','a','E','e','I','i','O','o','U','u' };
```

Status is declared as an array of three integers and provides the values of the elements, separated by commas, in curly braces. As usual, a semicolon ends the statement. The effect of this is that after the compiled program loads into the memory of the computer, the reserved space for the *Status* array will already contain the initial values, so they won't need assignments when the program executes. It is important to realize that this is more than just a convenience—it happens at a different time. If the program goes on to change the values of the *Status* array, they stay changed. Many compilers permit you to initialize arrays only if they are global or **static**, as in the second example. This statement initializes the array *Radix10* when the entire program loads.

The third example illustrates putting the wrong count in the array declaration. Many compilers consider this an error, while others reserve enough space to hold whichever is greater—the number of values you ask for or the number of values you provide. This example will draw complaints from the Borland C++ compiler by way of an error message indicating too many initializers. In the opposite case, when you ask for more space than you provide values for, the values go into the beginning of the array and the extra elements contain either 0s or garbage (depending on the location and any keywords used in the array's declaration).

The last coded example highlights C/C++'s ability to automatically dimension an array based on the program-supplied initialization data. This also means that you do not need to count the values when you provide all of them. If the count is empty, as in the fourth example, the number of values determines the size of the array.

Unsized Initialization

As an absolute minimum, all C/C++ compilers require an array's declaration to have either an explicit number of elements declared or the initialization set. Although you can include both details, sometimes this leads to trouble. For example, a program will frequently want to define its own set of error messages. This can be done in either of two ways. Here is the first method:

```
char InputError   [ 37 ] = "Please enter a value between 0 - 9:\n",
     DeviceError  [ 16 ] = "Disk not ready\n",
     MonitorError [ 32 ] = "Program needs a color monitor.\n",
     Warning      [ 44 ] = "This operation will erase the active file!\n";
```

Supplying both the actual count and initialization data requires you to count the number of characters in the string, remembering to add 1 to the count for the unseen null-string terminator \0. This can become tedious at best, straining the eyes as you count the number of characters, and will probably be very error prone. The second method allows C/C++ to automatically dimension the arrays through the use of unsized array declaration syntax, as shown here:

```
char InputError   [ ] = "Please enter a value between 0 - 9:\n",
     DeviceError  [ ] = "Disk not ready\n",
     MonitorError [ ] = "Program needs a color monitor.\n",
     Warning      [ ] = "This operation will erase the active file!\n";
```

There are a few major pitfalls that await the inexperienced C/C++ programmer when initializing arrays. For example, an array with an empty size declaration and no list of values has a null length. If there are any data declarations after the array, then the name of the null array refers to the same address, and storing values in the null array puts them in addresses allocated to other variables.

Unsized array initializations are not restricted to one-dimensional arrays. For multidimensional arrays, you must specify all but the leftmost dimension for C/C++ to properly index the array. With this approach you can build tables of varying lengths, with the compiler automatically allocating enough storage.

Accessing Array Elements

If you are going to make a mistake when using arrays in C/C++, it's practically guaranteed that it will involve array element access, for the simple reason that an array's first element is at an *offset* of 0, not an *index* of 1! Also, because the first element is at an offset of 0, the last element is at an offset of *MAX_ARRAY_ELEMENTS* - 1. So, assuming the following declaration:

```
int Status[ MAX_STATUS_RANGE ] = { -1, 0, 1 };
```

the following statement accesses *-1*:

```
Status[ 0 ]
```

with

```
Status[ 2 ]
```

referencing 1, and

```
Status[ 3 ]
```

being your worst nightmare, because there is no fourth element.

The actual syntax for array element access is straightforward; you simply use the array's name followed by a set of square brackets. Within the square brackets is a constant expression representing the relative displacement to move from the beginning of the array (remember, an array's name *is* the address to the first element). The subscript is an instruction to the compiler on how much to add to that address to get to the beginning of the element in question. The actual number of bytes added to the address is *offset_value* * **sizeof(*array_element*)**.

One final note: array offsets can either be integral values or expressions evaluating down to integral values:

```
#define ARRAY_FIRST_ELEMENT_OFFSET 0
const   int   One               = 1;
const   int   Two               = 2;

Status[ ARRAY_FIRST_ELEMENT_OFFSET ]
Status[ Two        ]
Status[ Two - One ]
Status[ One - Two ]    // LOOK OUT!
```

Pop Quiz: 1) Is the last statement syntactically legal (YES/NO)? 2) Will the last statement execute (YES/NO)? The last statement is both syntactically correct, and it will execute. *One-Two* returns an offset of *-1*, causing the compiler to multiply *-1* times the **sizeof(int)**, with the resulting numeric value being subtracted from the array's name, *Status*, which holds the address to *Status*'s first element. Result: a nefarious bug plaguing you for the entire weekend!

If executed, the last statement would reference the memory locations for any variables formally defined above *Status*'s declaration. What if the preceding variable declaration was the loop control variable for a **for** loop:

```
int LoopControlVariable = 0;
int Status[ MAX_STATUS_RANGE ] = { -1, 0, 1 };
  .      .      .
Status[ One - Two ] = -1;
```

You wouldn't want to do that to your worst enemy. However, the C/C++ compiler, assuming "you are the experienced programmer," faithfully tries to execute the statement. So, here's a quote worth remembering: "If you are going to make a mistake when using arrays in C/C++, it's practically guaranteed that it will involve array element access...."

Calculating Array Dimensions (sizeof())

Applications make frequent use of the **sizeof()** operator to calculate the amount of storage needed by an object (actual, as in a declared variable, or hypothetical, as in the case of a standard data type like **int** or user-defined **typedef**). You have already seen how an integer can be either 2 or 4 bytes depending on the machine being used. If an additional amount of memory to hold seven integers will be requested from the operating system, some way is needed to determine whether 14 bytes (7 x 2 bytes/integer) or 28 bytes (7 x 4 bytes/integer) are needed. The following program automatically takes this into consideration (and prints a value of 14 for systems allocating 2 bytes per integer cell):

```
/*
 *   arraysiz.c
 *   A C program applying sizeof to determine an array's size.
 *   Copyright (c) Chris H. Pappas and William H. Murray, 1996
 */

#include <stdio.h>

#define MAX_DAYS_IN_WEEK 7


void main( void )
{
  int DailyHourMaximums [ MAX_DAYS_IN_WEEK ]
                   = { 5, 40, 40, 40, 40, 40, 10 };

  printf( "There are %d number of bytes in the array "
          "DailyHourMaximums: \n", (int) sizeof(DailyHourMaximums) );
}
```

This concept becomes essential when the program must be portable and independent of any particular hardware. If you are wondering why there is an **int** type cast on the result returned by **sizeof()**, it's because the ANSI C standard **sizeof()** does not return an **int** type. Instead, **sizeof()** returns a data type, **size_t**, that is large enough to hold the return value. The ANSI C/C++ standard added this to C/C++ because on certain computers an integer is not big enough to represent the size of all data items. In the example, casting the return value to an integer allows it to match the %**d** conversion character of the **printf()** function. Otherwise, if the returned value had been larger than an integer, the **printf()** function would not have worked properly. By changing the preceding array's data type, you can explore how various data types are stored internally:

```
//
//   exploresz.cpp
//   A C++ program illustrating contiguous array storage.
//   Copyright (c) Chris H. Pappas and William H. Murray, 1996
//

#include <iostream.h>

#define MAX_DAYS_IN_WEEK 7

void main( void)
{
  int    Offset,  DailyHourMaximums[ MAX_DAYS_IN_WEEK    ];

  cout << "sizeof(int) is "<< (int)sizeof(int) << "\n\n";

  for( Offset = 0; Offset < MAX_DAYS_IN_WEEK; Offset++ )
    cout << "&DailyHourMaximums["
         << Offset
         << "] = "
         << hex
         << &DailyHourMaximums[ Offset ]
         << endl;
}
```

If the program is run on a machine with a word length of 2 bytes, the output will look similar to this:

```
sizeof(int) is 2

&DailyHourMaximums[ 0 ] = 2F32
&DailyHourMaximums[ 1 ] = 2F34
&DailyHourMaximums[ 2 ] = 2F36
&DailyHourMaximums[ 3 ] = 2F38
&DailyHourMaximums[ 4 ] = 2F3A
&DailyHourMaximums[ 5 ] = 2F3C
&DailyHourMaximums[ 6 ] = 2F3E
```

Here the **&** (address) operator is applied to each successive array element, illustrating that an array element can be treated like any other variable; its value can form an expression, it can be assigned a value, and it can be passed as an argument (or parameter) to a function. In this example, you can see how the array elements' addresses are exactly 2 bytes apart (4 bytes for 32-bit applications). You will see the importance of this contiguous storage when you use arrays in conjunction with pointer variables.

Array Index Out of Bounds

Because C and C++ were designed to replace assembly language code, error checking was left out of the compiler to keep the code lean. Without any compiler error checking, you must be very careful when dealing with array boundaries. For example, the following program elicits no complaints from the compiler:

```c
/*
 *   dontrun.c
 *   Do NOT run this C program.
 *   Copyright (c) Chris H. Pappas and William H. Murray, 1996
 */

#include <stdio.h>

#define MAX          10
#define OUT_OF_RANGE 20

void main( void )
{
  int Offset, Going_TOO_FAR [ MAX ];

  for( Offset = 0; Offset < OUT_OF_RANGE; Offset++ )
    Going_TOO_FAR[ Offset ] = Offset;
}
```

yet it can change the contents of other variables or even crash the program by writing beyond the array's boundary. Notice that *offset < OUT_OF_RANGE;* compiles, generating a test condition allowing the loop to repeat 10 additional times. This gives *Offset* values 10 through 19. However, array *Going_TOO_FAR* only has legal *Offset*s of 0 through 9.

Output and Input of Strings

Although C and C++ do supply the data type **char**, they do not have a data type for character strings, as does Pascal, for example. Instead, the C/C++ programmer must represent a string as a special case of an array of characters. The array uses one cell for each character in the string, with the final cell holding the null character \0 (two keystrokes, but viewed as a single character by the compilers).

The following program shows how you can represent the three major types of transportation as a character string. The array *Method1* is initialized character by character through the use of the assignment operator, the array *Method2* is initialized by use of the function **scanf()**, and the array *Method3* is initialized in the following definition:

```
/*
 *    usestrng.c
 *    This C program demonstrates the use of strings.
 *    Copyright (c) Chris H. Pappas and William H. Murray, 1996
 */

#include <stdio.h>

void main( void )
{
  char        Method1[4]          ,        /* car    */
              Method2[6]          ;        /* plane */
  static char Method3[5] = "ship";         /* ship   */

  Method1[0] =  'c';
  Method1[1] =  'a';
  Method1[2] =  'r';
  Method1[3] =  '\0';

  printf( "\n\n\tPlease enter the mode --> plane " );
  scanf ( "%s",Method2                        );

  printf( "%s\n",Method1                       );
  printf( "%s\n",Method2                       );
  printf( "%s\n",Method3                       );
}
```

The next definitions show how C treats character strings as arrays of characters:

```
char    Method1[4]                    ,         /* car   */
        Method2[6]                    ;         /* plane */
static char Method3[5] = "ship";                /* ship  */
```

Even though the *Method1* "car" has three characters, the array *Method1* has four cells—one cell for each letter in the mode "car" and one for the null character. Remember, \0 counts as one character. Similarly, the *Method2* "plane" has five characters ("ship" has four) but requires six storage cells (five for *Method3*), including the null character. Remember, you could also have initialized the *Method3*[5] array of characters by using braces:

```
static char Method3[5] = {'s','h','i','p','\0'};
```

When you use double quotation marks to list the initial values of the character array, the system will automatically add the null terminator \0. Also, remember that the same line could have been written like this:

```
static char Method3[] = "ship";
```

This uses an unsized array. Of course, you could have chosen the tedious approach to initializing an array of characters that was done with *Method1*. A more common approach is to use the **scanf()** function to read the string directly into the array, as was done with *Method2*. The **scanf()** function uses a **%s** conversion specification. This causes the function to skip white space (blanks, tabs, and carriage returns) and then to read into the character array *Method2* all characters up to the next white space. The system will then automatically add a null terminator. Remember, the array's dimension must be large enough to hold the string along with a null terminator. Look at this statement one more time:

```
scanf( "%s",Method2 );
```

Are you bothered by the fact that *Method2* was not preceded by the address operator **&**? Although it is true that **scanf()** was written to expect the address of a variable, as it turns out, an array's name, unlike simple variable names, is an address expression—the address of the first element in the array.

When you use the **printf()** function in conjunction with a **%s**, the function is expecting the corresponding argument to be the address of some character string. The string is printed up to, but not including, the null character. The following listing illustrates these principles by using an equivalent C++ algorithm:

```
//
//   usestrng.cpp
//   This C++ program demonstrates the use of strings.
//   Copyright (c) Chris H. Pappas and William H. Murray, 1996
//

#include <iostream.h>

void main( void )
{
  char         Method1[4]            ,       // car
               Method2[6]            ;       // plane
  static char Method3[5] = "ship";          // ship

  Method1[0]  =   'c';
  Method1[1]  =   'a';
  Method1[2]  =   'r';
  Method1[3]  =   '\0';

  cout << "\n\n\tPlease enter the mode --> plane ";
  cin  >>   Method2                          ;

  cout << Method1 << "\n"                     ;
  cout << Method2 << "\n"                     ;
  cout << Method3 << "\n"                     ;
}
```

The output from the program looks like this:

```
car
plane
ship
```

Multidimensional Arrays

All of the arrays discussed so far have been one-dimensional and require only one index to access an element. The term *dimension* represents the number of indexes used to reference a particular element in an array. By looking at an array's declaration, you can tell how many dimensions it has. If there is only one set of brackets [ ], the array is one-dimensional; two sets of brackets [ ][ ] indicate a two-dimensional array; and so on. Arrays of more than one dimension are called multidimensional arrays. For real-world modeling, the working maximum number of dimensions is usually three. The following declarations set up a two-dimensional array that is initialized while the program executes:

```
//
//  twodimen.cpp
//  A C program demonstrating the use of a two-dimensional array.
//  Copyright (c) Chris H. Pappas and William H. Murray, 1996
//

#include <iostream.h>

#define NUM_ROWS    4
#define NUM_COLUMNS 5

void main( void )
{
  int RowOffset, ColumnOffset, Displacement, Multiple    ,
      CalculateOffsets [ NUM_ROWS ][ NUM_COLUMNS ]        ;

  for( RowOffset = 0; RowOffset < NUM_ROWS; RowOffset++   )

    for( ColumnOffset = 0; ColumnOffset < NUM_COLUMNS     ;
                                ColumnOffset++ )           {
      Displacement = NUM_COLUMNS - ColumnOffset            ;
      Multiple = RowOffset                                 ;
      CalculateOffsets[ RowOffset ][ ColumnOffset ]        =
        ( RowOffset+1 ) * ColumnOffset +
          Displacement  * Multiple                         ;
    }

  for( RowOffset = 0; RowOffset < NUM_ROWS; RowOffset++ ) {
    cout << "CURRENT ROW: "    << RowOffset << endl         ;
    cout << "RELATIVE DISTANCE FROM BASE:" << endl          ;

    for( ColumnOffset = 0; ColumnOffset < NUM_COLUMNS      ;
                                ColumnOffset++             )
      cout << " "
             << CalculateOffsets[ RowOffset ][ ColumnOffset ]
```

```
             << " "                                              ;
     cout << "\n\n"                                              ;
    }
}
```

The program uses two **for** loops to calculate and initialize each of the array elements to its respective "*RELATIVE DISTANCE FROM BASE:*". The created array has 4 rows (*NUM_ROWS) and 5 columns (NUM_COLUMNS)* per row, for a total of 20 integer elements.

Multidimensional arrays are stored in linear fashion in the computer's memory. Elements in multidimensional arrays are grouped from the rightmost index inward. In the preceding example, row 1, column 1 would be element three of the storage array. Although the calculation of the offset appears a little tricky, note how easily each array element itself is referenced:

```
CalculateOffsets[ RowOffset ][ ColumnOffset ] = . . .
```

The output from the program looks like this:

```
CURRENT ROW: 0
RELATIVE DISTANCE FROM BASE:


  0   1   2   3   4

CURRENT ROW: 1
RELATIVE DISTANCE FROM BASE:
  5   6   7   8   9


CURRENT ROW: 2
RELATIVE DISTANCE FROM BASE:
 10   11   12   13   14


CURRENT ROW: 3
RELATIVE DISTANCE FROM BASE:
 15   16   17   18   19
```

Arrays as Function Arguments

Just like other C/C++ variables, arrays can be passed from one function to another. Because arrays as function arguments can be discussed in full only after an introduction to pointers, this chapter begins the topic and Chapter 10 expands upon this base.

Passing Arrays to C/C++ Functions

There are only three things you need to remember when using C/C++ arrays as function arguments. First, all arrays, regardless of type, are passed call-by-reference. This should come as no surprise, since an array's name is the address to the first element. When the called function dereferences this address, it gains access to the actual array elements. Therefore, any changes made to the elements by the called function are reflected in the calling routine when the called function terminates. Second, because the array is passed call-by-reference by default, it would be incorrect for the called function to return the array in a **return();** statement. This is overkill.

The third thing to remember is that all array elements are passed to functions call-by-value (by default), meaning a copy of the array element is passed, not the address to the element. In this case, if the called function attempts to change the value, it is only a local copy. Of course, you can override this by passing the address to the individual element.

The following program demonstrates the first two array concepts and sends the entire array to a function:

```
//
//   cbrarray.cpp
//   This C++ program passes an entire array to a function call-by-reference.
//   Copyright (c) Chris H. Pappas and William H. Murray, 1996
//

#include <ctype.h>
#include <iostream.h>

#define ARRAY_MAX 5

void UPCaseArray( char Array[ ARRAY_MAX ] );

void main ( void )
{
  int offset;
  char Array[ ARRAY_MAX ] = { 'a' , 'e', 'i', 'o', 'u' };

  for( offset = 0; offset < ARRAY_MAX; offset++ )
      cout << Array[ offset ];

  UPCaseArray( Array );

  for( offset = 0; offset < ARRAY_MAX; offset++ )
      cout << Array[ offset ];
```

```
    }

    void UPCaseArray( char Array[ ARRAY_MAX ] )
    {
     for( int offset = 0; offset < ARRAY_MAX; offset++ )
          Array[ offset ] = toupper( Array[ offset ] );
     // NOTE: at this point - return( Array ); would be incorrect
    }
```

The output from the program demonstrates that the array is passed call-by-reference, because the first **for** loop outputs the original non-upcased contents:

```
    aeiou
```

while the second **for** loop in **main()** outputs the *Array*'s contents after calling the function *UPCaseArray()*:

```
    AEIOU
```

Clearly, the function *UPCaseArray()*, within its function body, has changed the *Array* back in function **main()**. The next program is a simple modification of this algorithm, only instead of passing the entire array, each individual element is passed:

```
    //
    //   cbvarray.cpp
    //   This C++ program passes individual array elements call-by-value.
    //   Copyright (c) Chris H. Pappas and William H. Murray, 1996
    //

    #include <ctype.h>
    #include <iostream.h>

    #define ARRAY_MAX 5

    void UPCaseArrayElements( char a_char );

    void main ( void )
    {
      int offset;
      char Array[ ARRAY_MAX ] = {  'a' ,  'e', 'i', 'o', 'u' };

      for( offset = 0; offset < ARRAY_MAX; offset++ )
          cout << Array[ offset ];
```

```
    for( offset = 0; offset < ARRAY_MAX; offset++ )
        UPCaseArrayElements( Array[ offset ] );

    for( offset = 0; offset < ARRAY_MAX; offset++ )
        cout << Array[ offset ];
}

void UPCaseArrayElements( char a_char )
{
  a_char = toupper( a_char );
}
```

Notice that the output from the program:

```
aeiou
```

does not change when the second **for** loop executes:

```
aeiou
```

illustrating that array elements, by default, are passed call-by-value, because the
function *UPCaseArrayElements()*, had no effect in function **main()**. This last program
highlights the code changes required to override the array element's call-by-value
convention, turning it into call-by-reference. See if you spot the three main changes:

```
//
//   ecbraray.cpp
//   This C++ program passes individual array elements call-by-value.
//   Copyright (c) Chris H. Pappas and William H. Murray, 1996
//

#include <ctype.h>
#include <iostream.h>

#define ARRAY_MAX 5

void UPCaseArrayElements( char *a_char_ptr );

void main ( void )
{
    int offset;
    char Array[ ARRAY_MAX ] = {  'a' ,   'e', 'i', 'o', 'u' };
```

```
   for( offset = 0; offset < ARRAY_MAX; offset++ )
        cout << Array[ offset ];

   for( offset = 0; offset < ARRAY_MAX; offset++ )
        UPCaseArrayElements( &Array[ offset ] );

   for( offset = 0; offset < ARRAY_MAX; offset++ )
        cout << Array[ offset ];
}

void UPCaseArrayElements( char *a_char_ptr )
{
 *a_char_ptr = toupper( *a_char_ptr );
}
```

The first change involves the *UPCaseArrayElements()* formal argument, which changed from the type **char**, to **char** *. The second change involves how the individual elements are passed, so instead of passing *Array[offset]*, the actual argument becomes *&Array[offset]*. The final syntax requirement revolves around the use of the passed element's address within the function *UPCaseArrayElements()*, which changes from:

```
a_char = toupper( a_char );
```

to

```
*a_char_ptr = toupper( *a_char_ptr );
```

The output from this program matches the first example, with each individual array element being upcased by the function:

```
aeiou
```

to

```
AEIOU
```

Three-Dimensional Arrays

The following C++ program incorporates many of the array features discussed so far, including multidimensional array initialization, referencing, and arguments:

```
//
//  threeD.cpp
//  A C++ program that demonstrates how to define, pass,
//  and walk through the different dimensions of an array.
//  Copyright (c) Chris H. Pappas and William H. Murray, 1996
//

#include <iostream.h>

#define TWO     2
#define THREE   3
#define FOUR    4
#define FIVE    5

void Arrays_and_sizeof( char Array[ ][ THREE ][ FOUR ] );

char Global_char_Array[ FIVE ][ FOUR ][ FIVE ] = {
                {
                  { 'P','L','A','N','E' },
                  { 'Z','E','R','O',' ' },
                  { ' ',' ',' ',' ',' ' },
                  { 'R','O','W',' ','3' },
                },
                {
                  { 'P','L','A','N','E' },
                  { 'O','N','E',' ',' ' },
                  { 'R','O','W',' ','2' }
                },
                {
                  { 'P','L','A','N','E' },
                  { 'T','W','O',' ',' ' }
                },
                {
                  { 'P','L','A','N','E' },
                  { 'T','H','R','E','E' },
                  { 'R','O','W',' ','2' },
                  { 'R','O','W',' ','3' }
                },
                {
                  { 'P','L','A','N','E' },
                  { 'F','O','U','R',' ' },
                  { 'r','o','w',' ','2' },
```

```
                          { 'a','b','c','d','e' }
                    }
};

int Matrix[ FOUR ][ THREE ] = { { 1 },{ 2 },{ 3 },{ 4 } };

void main( void )
{
  int PlaneIndex, RowOffset, ColumnOffset;
  char LocalCube[ TWO ][ THREE ][ FOUR ] ;

  cout << "sizeof LocalCube                     = "
       <<  sizeof(LocalCube)
       <<  endl                                 ;
  cout << "sizeof LocalCube[ 0 ]                = "
       <<  sizeof(LocalCube[ 0 ])
       <<  endl                                 ;
  cout << "sizeof LocalCube[ 0 ][ 0 ]           = "
       <<  sizeof(LocalCube[ 0 ][ 0 ])
       <<  endl                                 ;
  cout << "sizeof LocalCube[ 0 ][ 0 ][ 0 ]      = "
       <<  sizeof(LocalCube[ 0 ][ 0 ][ 0 ])
       <<  endl                                 ;

  Arrays_and_sizeof( LocalCube )                ;

  cout << "Global_char_Array[ 0 ][ 1 ][ 2 ] is    = "
       <<  Global_char_Array [ 0 ][ 1 ][ 2 ] << endl ;
  cout << "Global_char_Array[ 1 ][ 0 ][ 2 ] is    = "
       <<  Global_char_Array [ 1 ][ 0 ][ 2 ] << endl ;

  cout << "\nprint part of the Global_char_Array's plane 0\n";

  for( RowOffset=0; RowOffset < 4; RowOffset++ ) {
    for( ColumnOffset=0; ColumnOffset < 5; ColumnOffset++ )
      cout << Global_char_Array[ 0 ][ RowOffset ][ ColumnOffset ];
    cout << "\n";
  }

  cout << "\nprint part of the Global_char_Array's plane 4\n";

  for( RowOffset=0; RowOffset < 4; RowOffset++ ) {
```

```
      for( ColumnOffset=0; ColumnOffset < 5; ColumnOffset++ )
        cout << Global_char_Array[ 4 ][ RowOffset ][ ColumnOffset ];
      cout << "\n";
    }

  cout << "\nprint all of Matrix\n";

  for( RowOffset=0; RowOffset < 4; RowOffset++ ) {
    for( ColumnOffset=0; ColumnOffset < 3; ColumnOffset++ )
      cout << Matrix[ RowOffset ][ ColumnOffset ];
    cout << "\n";
  }
}


void Arrays_and_sizeof( char Array[ ][ THREE ][ FOUR ] )
{
cout << "sizeof Array                            = "
    <<   sizeof(Array)
    <<   endl                                         ;
cout << "sizeof  Array[0]                         = "
    <<   sizeof(Array[0])
    <<   endl                                         ;
cout << "sizeof  Global_char_Array                = "
    <<   sizeof(Global_char_Array)
    <<   endl                                         ;
cout << "sizeof Global_char_Array[ 0 ]            = "
    <<   sizeof(Global_char_Array[0])
    <<   endl                                         ;
}
```

First, note how *Global_char_Array* is defined and initialized. Braces are used to group the characters together so that they have a form similar to the dimensions of the array. This helps in visualizing the form of the array. The braces are not required in this case because you are not leaving any gaps in the array with the initializing data. If you were initializing only a portion of any dimension, various sets of the inner braces would be required to designate which initializing values should apply to which part of the array. The easiest way to visualize the three-dimensional array is to imagine five layers, each having a two-dimensional, four-row by five-column array (see Figure 9-2).

The first four lines of the program output show the size of the *LocalCube* array, various dimensions, and an individual element. The output illustrates how the total size of the multidimensional array is the product of all the dimensions times the size of the array data type, that is, $2 * 3 * 4 * sizeof(char)$, or 24.

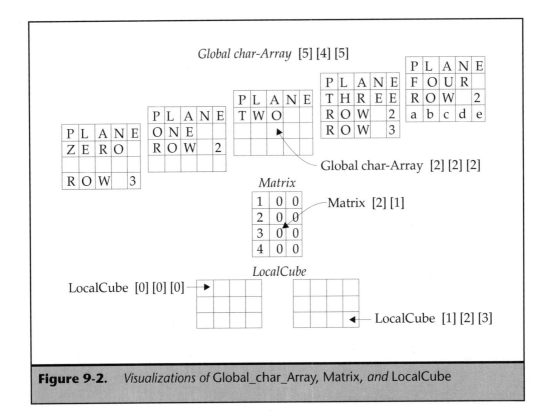

Figure 9-2. *Visualizations of* Global_char_Array, Matrix, *and* LocalCube

Notice how the array element *LocalCube[0]* is in itself an array that contains a two-dimensional array of *[THREE][FOUR]*, thereby giving *LocalCube[0]* the size of 12. The size of *LocalCube[0][0]* is 4, which is the number of elements in the final dimension because each element has a size of 1, as the *sizeof(LocalCube[0][0][0])* shows.

In order to fully understand multidimensional arrays, it is important to realize that *LocalCube[0]* is both an array name and a pointer constant. Because the program did not subscript the last dimension, the expression does not have the same type as the data type of each fundamental array element. Because *LocalCube[0]* does not refer to an individual element but rather to another array, it does not have the type of **char**. Because *LocalCube[0]* has the type of pointer constant, it is not a legal lvalue and cannot appear to the left of an assignment operator in an assignment expression.

Something very interesting happens when you use an array name in a function argument list, as was done when the function *Arrays_and_sizeof()* was invoked with

LocalCube. While inside the function, if you perform a **sizeof()** operation against the formal parameter that represents the array name, you do not correctly compute the actual size of Array. What the function sees is only a copy of the address of the first element in the array. Therefore, the function **sizeof()** will return the size of the address, not the item to which it refers.

The **sizeof()** *Array[0]* in function *Arrays_and_sizeof()* is 12, because it was declared in the function that the formal parameter was an array whose last two dimensions were [*THREE*] and [*FOUR*]. You could not have used any values when you declared the size of these last two dimensions because the function prototype defined them to be [*THREE*] and [*FOUR*]. Without a prototype, the compiler would not be able to detect the difference in the way the array was dimensioned. This would let you redefine how you viewed the array's organization. The function *Arrays_and_sizeof()* also outputs the size of the global *Global_char_Array*. This points out that while a function may have access to global data directly, it has access only to the address of an array that is passed to a function as an argument.

In regard to the **main()** function, the next two statements executed demonstrate how to reference specific elements in *Global_char_Array*. *Global_char_Array[0][1][2]* references the zero layer, second row, third column, or "R." *Global_char_Array[1][0][2]* references the second layer, row zero, third column, or "A."

The next block of code in **main()** contains two nested **for** loops demonstrating that the arrays are stored in plane-row-column order. As we've already seen, the rightmost subscript (column) of the array varies the fastest when you view the array in a linear fashion. The first **for** loop pair hardwires the output to the zero layer and selects a row, with the inner loop traversing each column in *Global_char_Array*. The program continues by duplicating the same loop structures but printing only the fifth layer (plane [4]) of the *Global_char_Array*.

The last **for** loop pair displays the elements of *Matrix* in the form of a rectangle, similar to the way many people visualize a two-dimensional array. The output from the program looks like this:

```
sizeof LocalCube                      = 24
sizeof LocalCube[ 0 ]                 = 12
sizeof LocalCube[ 0 ][ 0 ]            = 4
sizeof LocalCube[ 0 ][ 0 ][ 0 ]       = 1
sizeof Array                          = 2
sizeof Array[0]                       = 12
sizeof Global_char_Array              = 100
sizeof Global_char_Array[ 0 ]         = 20
Global_char_Array[ 0 ][ 1 ][ 2 ] is = R
Global_char_Array[ 1 ][ 0 ][ 2 ] is = A
```

This prints part of the *Global_char_Array*'s plane 0:

```
PLANE
ZERO

ROW 3
```

This prints part of the *Global_char_Array*'s plane 4:

```
PLANE
FOUR
row 2
abcde
```

This prints all of *Matrix:*

```
100
200
300
400
```

Are you bothered by the output? Look at the initialization of *Matrix*. Because each inner set of braces corresponds to one row of the array and enough values were not supplied inside the inner braces, the system padded the remaining elements with zeros. Remember, C automatically initializes all undefined static automatic numeric array elements to zero.

String Functions and Character Arrays

Because of the way C handles string data, many of the functions that use character arrays as function arguments were not discussed. Specifically, these functions are **gets()**, **puts()**, **fgets()**, **fputs()**, **sprintf()**, **stpcpy()**, **strcat()**, **strncmp()**, and **strlen()**. Understanding how these functions operate will be much easier now that you are familiar with the concepts of character arrays and null-terminated strings. One of the easiest ways to explain these functions is to show a few program examples.

gets(), puts(), fgets(), fputs(), and sprintf()

The following program demonstrates how you can use **gets()**, **puts()**, **fgets()**, **fputs()**, and **sprintf()** to format I/O:

```
/*
 *    strio.c
 *    A C program using several string I/O functions.
 *    Copyright (c) Chris H. Pappas and William H. Murray, 1996
 */

#include <stdio.h>

#define STRING_SIZE 20

void main( void )
{
  char TestString[ STRING_SIZE ];

  fputs   ( "Please enter the first string   : ",stdout );
  gets    (   TestString                              );
  fputs   ( "The first string entered is     : ",stdout );
  puts    (   TestString                              );

  fputs   ( "Please enter the second string : ",stdout );
  fgets   ( TestString,STRING_SIZE,stdin              );
  fputs   ( "The second string entered is    : ",stdout );
  fputs   ( TestString,stdout                         );

  sprintf( TestString,"This was %s a test","just");
  fputs   ( "sprintf() created               : ",stdout );
  fputs   ( TestString,stdout                         );
}
```

Here is the output from the first run of the program:

```
Please enter the first string   : string one
The first string entered is     : string one
Please enter the second string : string two
The second string entered is    : string two
sprintf() created                : This was just a test
```

Because the strings that were entered were less than the size of *TestString*, the program works fine. However, when you enter a string longer than *TestString*, something like the following can occur when the program is run a second time:

```
Please enter the first string  : one two three four five
The first string entered is    : one two three four five
Please enter the second string : six seven eight nine ten
The second string entered is   : six seven eight ninsprintf() created
  : This was just a testPlease enter the first string  : The first string
 entered is    :e ten
The second string entered is   :
```

Take care when running the program. The **gets()** function receives characters from standard input (**stdin**, the keyboard by default for most computers) and places them into the array whose name is passed to the function. When you press the ENTER key to terminate the string, a newline character is transmitted. When the **gets()** function receives this newline character, it changes it into a null character, thereby ensuring that the character array contains a string. No checking occurs to ensure that the array is big enough to hold all the characters entered.

The **puts()** function echoes to the terminal just what was entered with **gets()**. It also adds a newline character on the end of the string in the place where the null character appeared. The null character, remember, was automatically inserted into the string by the **gets()** function. Therefore, strings that are properly entered with **gets()** can be displayed with **puts()**.

When you use the **fgets()** function, you can guarantee a maximum number of input characters. This function stops reading the designated file stream when one fewer character is read than the second argument specifies. Because *TestString* size is 20, only 19 characters will be read by **fgets()** from **stdin**. A null character is automatically placed into the string in the last position; and if a newline were entered from the keyboard, it would be retained in the string. (It would appear before the null debug example.) The **fgets()** function does not eliminate the newline character like **gets()** did; it merely adds the null character at the end so that a valid string is stored. In much the same way as **gets()** and **puts()** are symmetrical, so too are **fgets()** and **fputs()**. **fgets()** does not eliminate the newline, nor does **fputs()** add one.

To understand how important the newline character is to these functions, look closely at the second run output given. Notice the phrase "sprintf() created..."; it follows immediately after the numbers six, seven, eight, and nine that had just been entered. The second input string actually had five more characters than the **fgets()** function read in (one fewer than *STRING_SIZE* of 19 characters). The others were left in the input buffer. Also dropped was the newline that terminated the input from the keyboard. (It is left in the input stream because it occurs after the 19th character.) Therefore, no newline character was stored in the string. Because **fputs()** does not add one back, the next **fputs()** output begins on the line where the previous output ended. The program relied was on the newline character read by **fgets()** and printed by **fputs()** to help control the display formatting.

The function **sprintf()** stands for "string printf()". It uses a control string with conversion characters in exactly the same way as does **printf()**. The additional feature is that **sprintf()** places the resulting formatted data in a string rather than immediately sending the result to standard output. This can be beneficial if the exact same output must be created twice—for example, when the same string must be output to both the display monitor and the printer. To review:

- **gets()** converts newline to a null.
- **puts()** converts null to a newline.
- **fgets()** retains newline and appends a null.
- **fputs()** drops the null and does not add a newline; instead, it uses the retained newline (if one was entered).
- **sprintf() varies, depending on user-supplied control string**

strcpy(), strcat(), strncmp(), and strlen()

All of the functions discussed in this section are predefined in the string.h header file. Whenever you wish to use one of these functions, make certain you include the header file in your program. Remember, all of the string functions prototyped in string.h expect null-terminated string parameters. The following program demonstrates how to use the **strcpy()** function:

```
//
//  strcpy.cpp
//  A C++ program using the strcpy() function.
//  Copyright (c) Chris H. Pappas and William H. Murray, 1996
//

#include <string.h>
#include <iostream.h>

#define STRING_SIZE 20

void main( void )
{
  char SourceString[ STRING_SIZE ] = "Initialized String!",
       DestinationString[ STRING_SIZE ];

  strcpy( DestinationString,"String Constant" );
  cout << DestinationString << endl          ;
```

```
      strcpy(  DestinationString,SourceString       );
      cout  << DestinationString << endl           ;
   }
```

The function **strcpy()** copies the contents of one string, *SourceString*, into a second string, *DestinationString*. The preceding program initializes *SourceString* with the message, "Initialized String!" The first **strcpy()** function call actually *copies "String Constant"* into the *DestinationString*, while the second call to the **strcpy()** function copies *SourceString* into *DestinationString* variable. The program outputs this message:

```
String Constant
Initialized String!
```

The **strcat()** function appends two separate strings. Both strings must be null terminated and the result itself is null terminated. The following program builds on your understanding of the **strcpy()** function and introduces **strcat()**:

```
//
//    strcat.cpp
//    A C++ program demonstrating how to use strcat().
//    Copyright (c) Chris H. Pappas and William H. Murray, 1996
//

#include <string.h>
#include <iostream.h>

#define STRING_SIZE 35

void main( void )
{
   char Greeting[           ] = "Good morning",
        Name     [           ] = " Carolyn, "   ,
        Message [ STRING_SIZE ]                  ;

   strcpy( Message,Greeting       );
   strcat( Message,Name           );
   strcat( Message,"how are you?" );
   cout  << Message << endl       ;
}
```

In this example, both *Greeting* and *Name* are initialized, while *Message* is not. The first thing the program does is to use the function **strcpy()** to copy the *Greeting* into *Message*. Next, the **strcat()** function is used to concatenate *Name* (*" Carolyn, "*) to *"Good morning"*, which is stored in *Message*. The last **strcat()** function call demonstrates how a string constant can be concatenated to a string. Here, *"how are you?"* is concatenated to the now current contents of *Message* (*"Good morning Carolyn, "*). The program outputs the following:

```
Good morning Carolyn, how are you?
```

The next program demonstrates how to use **strncmp()** to decide if two strings are identical:

```
/*
 *      strncmp.c
 *      A C program that uses strncmp() to compare two strings
 *      with the aid of the strlen() function.
 *      Copyright (c) Chris H. Pappas and William H. Murray, 1996
 */

#include <string.h>
#include <stdio.h>

void main( void )
{
  char String_A[ ] = "Adam",
       String_B[ ] = "Abel";
  int  Matches      = 0     ,
       LengthString_A       ;

  LengthString_A = strlen( String_A );

  if( strlen( String_B ) >= strlen( String_A ) )
     Matches = strncmp( String_A,String_B,LengthString_A );

  printf("The string %s found", Matches == 0 ? "was" : "wasn't");
}
```

The **strlen()** function is very useful; it returns the number of characters, not including the null-terminator, in the string pointed to. In the preceding program it is used in two different forms just to give you additional exposure to its use. The first call to the function assigns the length of *String_A* to the variable *LengthString_A*. The second invocation of the function is actually encountered within the **if** condition. Remember, all test conditions must evaluate to a TRUE (not 0 or !0) or FALSE (0). The **if** test takes the results returned from the two calls to **strlen()** and then asks the relational question >=. If the length of *String_B* is >= to that of *String_A*, the **strncmp()** function is invoked.

You are probably wondering why the program used a >= test instead of an = =. To know the answer you need a further explanation of how **strncmp()** works. The function **strncmp()** compares two strings, starting with the first character in each string. If both strings are identical, the function returns a value of zero. However, if the two strings aren't identical, **strncmp()** will return a value less than zero if *String_A* is less than *String_B* or a value greater than zero when *String_A* is greater than *String_B*. The relational test >= was used in case you wanted to modify the code to include a report of equality, greater than, or less than for the compared strings.

The program terminates by using the value returned by *Matches*, along with the conditional operator (?:), to determine which string message is printed. This is the program output for the example:

```
The string wasn't found
```

In the Next Chapter...

Before moving on to the next chapter, remind yourself that two of the most frequent causes for irregular program behavior are exceeding array boundaries and forgetting that character arrays used as strings must end with \0, a null-string terminator. Both errors can sit dormant for months until that one user enters a response that is one character too long. Chapter 10 ties together the topics of C/C++ pointers and arrays by demonstrating another legal syntax for accessing arrays and array elements via pointers.

Chapter Ten

Pointers

In C/C++, the topics of pointers, arrays, and strings are closely related. Consequently, you can consider Chapter 10 to be an extension of Chapter 9. Learning about pointers—what they are and how to use them—can be a challenging experience to the novice programmer. However, by mastering the concept of pointers, you will be able to create extremely efficient, powerful, and flexible C/C++ applications.

It is common practice for most introductory-level programs to use only the class of variables known as static. *Static* variables, in this sense, are variables declared in the variable declaration block of the source code. While the program is executing, the application can neither obtain more of these variables nor deallocate storage for a variable. In addition, you have no way of knowing the address in memory for each variable or constant. Accessing one of these static variables is a straightforward process—you simply use the variable's name. For example, in C, if you want to increment the **int** variable *decade* by 10, you access *decade* by name:

```
decade += 10;
```

Defining Pointer Variables

Another often more convenient and efficient way to access a variable is through a second variable that holds the address of the first variable (Chapter 8 introduced the concept of pointer variables, which are covered in more detail in this chapter). For example, suppose you have an **int** variable called *RAMContents* and another variable called *RAMAddress* (admittedly verbose, but highly symbolic) that can hold the address of a variable of type **int**. In C/C++, you have already seen that preceding a variable with the **&** address operator returns the address of the variable instead of its contents. Therefore, the syntax for assigning the address of a variable to another variable of the type that holds addresses should not surprise you:

```
RAMAddress = &RAMContents;
```

A variable that holds an address, such as *RAMAddress*, is called a pointer variable, or simply a pointer. Figure 10-1 illustrates this relationship. The variable *RAMContents* has been placed in memory at address 7751.

After the preceding statement is executed, the address of *RAMContents* will be assigned to the pointer variable *RAMAddress*. This relationship is expressed in English by saying that *RAMAddress* points to *RAMContents*. Figure 10-2 illustrates this relationship. The arrow is drawn from the cell that stores the address to the cell whose address is stored.

Accessing the contents of the cell whose address is stored in *RAMAddress* is as simple as preceding the pointer variable with an asterisk: **RAMAddress*. What you

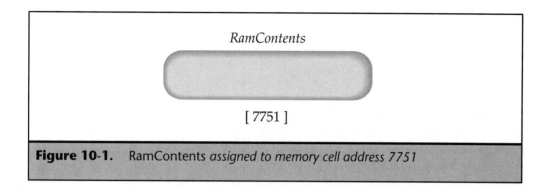

Figure 10-1.   RamContents *assigned to memory cell address 7751*

have done is dereferenced the pointer *RAMAddress*. For example, if you execute the following two statements, the value of the cell named *RAMContents* will be 20 (see Figure 10-3):

```
RAMAddress  = &RAMContents;
*RAMAddress = 20;
```

You can think of the * as a directive to follow the arrow (see Figure 10-3) to find the cell referenced. Notice that if *RAMAddress* holds the address of *RAMContents*, then

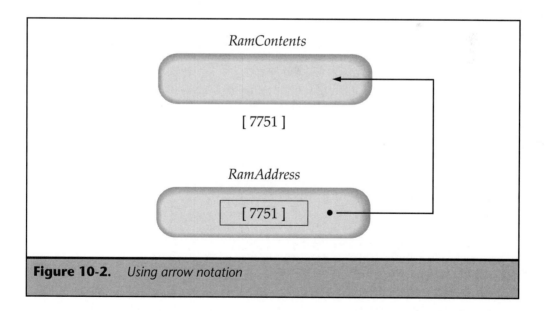

Figure 10-2.   *Using arrow notation*

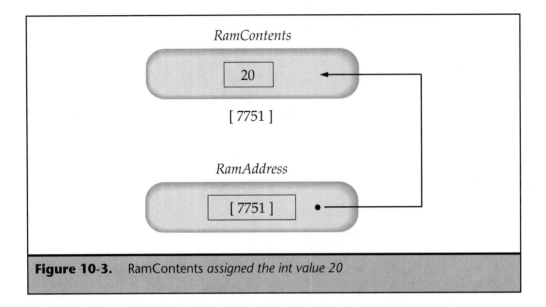

Figure 10-3.   RamContents *assigned the int value 20*

both of the following statements will have the same effect; that is, both will store the
value of 20 in *RAMContents*:

```
RAMContents = 20;
*RAMAddress = 20;
```

Pointer Variable Declarations

C/C++, like any other language, requires a definition for each variable. To define a
pointer variable *RAMAddress* that can hold the address of an **int** variable, you write

```
int *RAMAddress;
```

Actually, there are two separate parts to this declaration. The data type of
RAMAddress is

```
int *
```

and the identifier for the variable is

```
RAMAddress
```

The asterisk following int means "pointer to." That is, the following data type is a pointer variable that can hold an address to an **int**:

```
int *
```

This is an important concept. In C/C++, unlike many other languages, a pointer variable holds the address of a particular data type.

Let's look at an example:

```
char *RAM_char_Address;
int  *RAM_int_Address ;
```

The data type of *RAM_char_Address* is distinctly different from the data type of the pointer variable *RAM_int_Address*. Run-time errors and compile-time warnings may occur in a program that defines a pointer to one data type and then uses it to point to some other data type. It would be poor programming practice to define a pointer in one way and then use it in some other way. For example, look at the following code segment:

```
int   *RAM_int_Address;
float A_float    =   98.26;

RAM_int_Address = &A_float;
```

Here *RAM_int_Address* is defined to be of type **int ***, meaning it can hold the address of a memory cell of type **int**. The third statement attempts to assign *RAM_int_Address* the address of a declared float variable, *&A_float*.

Simple Statements Using Pointer Variables

The following code segment exchanges the contents of the variables *RAM_int_A* and *RAM_int_B* but uses the address and dereferencing operators to do so:

```
int  RAM_int_A = 15, RAM_int_B = 37, RAM_int_Temp;
int *RAM_int_Address;

RAM_int_Address  = &RAM_int_A     ;
RAM_int_Temp     = *RAM_int_Address;
*RAM_int_Address =  RAM_int_B     ;
RAM_int_B        =  RAM_int_Temp  ;
```

The first line of the program contains standard definitions and initializations. The statement allocates three cells to hold a single integer, gives each cell a name, and initializes two of them (see Figure 10-4). For discussion purposes, assume that the cell named *RAM_int_A* is located at address 5328, the cell named *RAM_int_B* is located at address 7916, and the cell named *RAM_int_Temp* is located at address 2385.

The second statement in the program defines *RAM_int_Address* to be a pointer to an **int** data type. The statement allocates the cell and gives it a name (placed at address

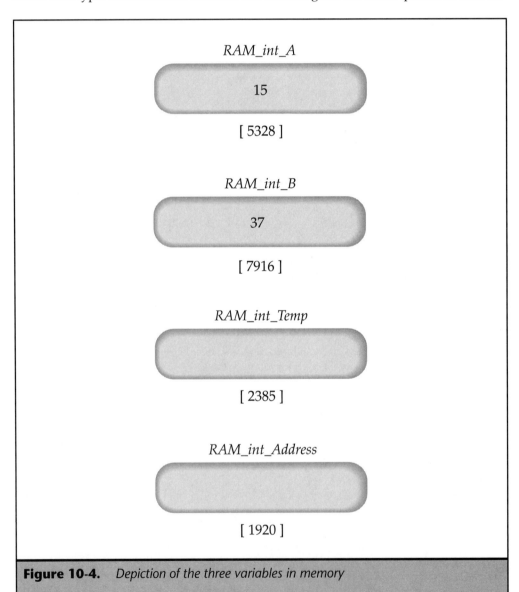

Figure 10-4. *Depiction of the three variables in memory*

1920). Remember, when the * is combined with the data type (in this case, **int**), the variable contains the address of a cell of the same data type. Because *RAM_int_Address* has not been initialized, it does not point to any particular **int** variable. If your program were to try to use *RAM_int_Address*, the compiler would not give you any warning and would try to use the variable's garbage contents to point with. The fourth statement assigns *RAM_int_Address* the address of *RAM_int_A* (see Figure 10-5).

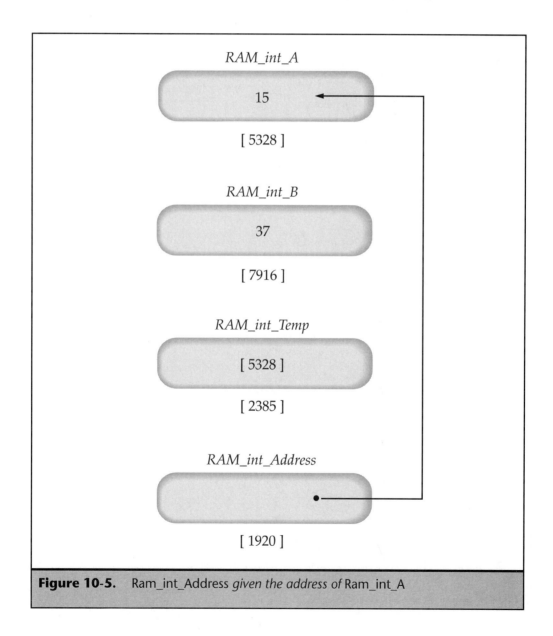

RAM_int_A

15

[5328]

RAM_int_B

37

[7916]

RAM_int_Temp

[5328]

[2385]

RAM_int_Address

[1920]

Figure 10-5. Ram_int_Address *given the address of* Ram_int_A

The next statement in the program uses the *expression* *RAM_int_Address* to access the contents of the cell to which *RAM_int_Address* points—*RAM_int_A*:

```
RAM_int_Temp = *RAM_int_Address;
```

Therefore, the integer value 15 is stored in the variable *RAM_int_Temp* (see Figure 10-6). If you left off the * in front of *RAM_int_Address*, the assignment statement would

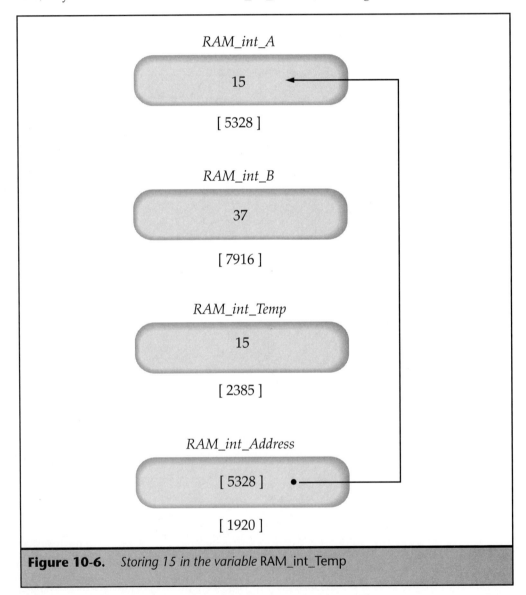

Figure 10-6. *Storing 15 in the variable* RAM_int_Temp

illegally store the contents of *RAM_int_Address*—the address 5328—in the cell named *RAM_int_Temp*, but *RAM_int_Temp* is supposed to hold an integer, not an address. This can be a very annoying bug to locate because many compilers will not issue any warnings/errors. (The Borland C/C++ compiler issues the warning, "different levels of indirection.")

To make matters worse, most pointers are near, meaning they occupy 2 bytes (4 bytes for 32-bit applications), the same data size as a PC-based integer.

The fifth statement in the program copies the contents of the variable *RAM_int_B* into the cell pointed to by the address stored in *RAM_int_Address* (see Figure 10-7):

```
*RAM_int_Address = RAM_int_B;
```

The last statement in the program simply copies the contents of one integer variable, *RAM_int_Temp*, into another integer variable, *RAM_int_B* (see Figure 10-8). Make certain you understand the difference between what is being referenced when a pointer variable is preceded (**RAM_int_Address*) and when it is not preceded (*RAM_int_Address*) by the dereference operator *.

For this example, the first syntax is a pointer to a cell that can contain an integer value. The second syntax references the cell that holds the address to another cell that can hold an integer. The following short program illustrates how to manipulate the addresses in pointer variables. Unlike the previous example, which swapped the program's data within the variables, this program swaps the addresses to where the data resides:

```
char   Code1 = 'A'   ,
       Code2 = 'B'   ;
char *Code1_Address,
     *Code2_Address,
     *Temp_Address ;

Code1_Address   = &Code1        ;
Code2_Address   = &Code2        ;
Temp_Address    = Code1_Address;
Code1_Address   = Code2_Address;
Code2_Address   = Temp_Address ;
printf( "%c%c", *Code1_Address, *Code2_Address );
```

Figure 10-9 shows the cell configuration and values after the execution of the first four statements of the program.

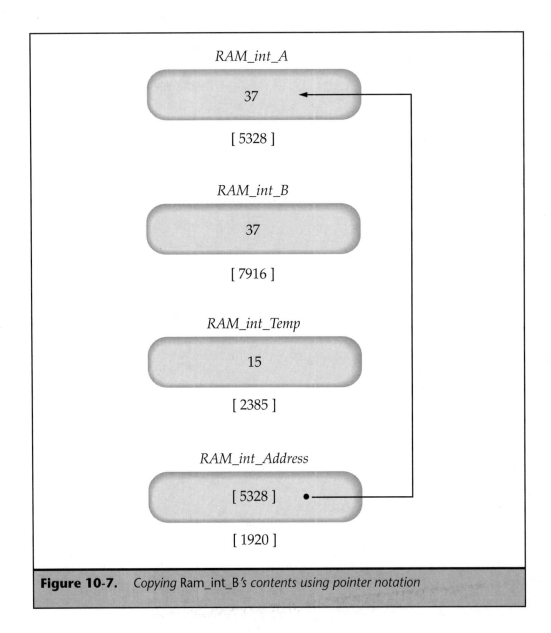

Figure 10-7. *Copying Ram_int_B's contents using pointer notation*

When the fifth statement is executed, the contents of *Code1_Address* are copied into *Temp_Address* so that both *Code1_Address* and *Temp_Address* point to *Code1* (see Figure 10-10).

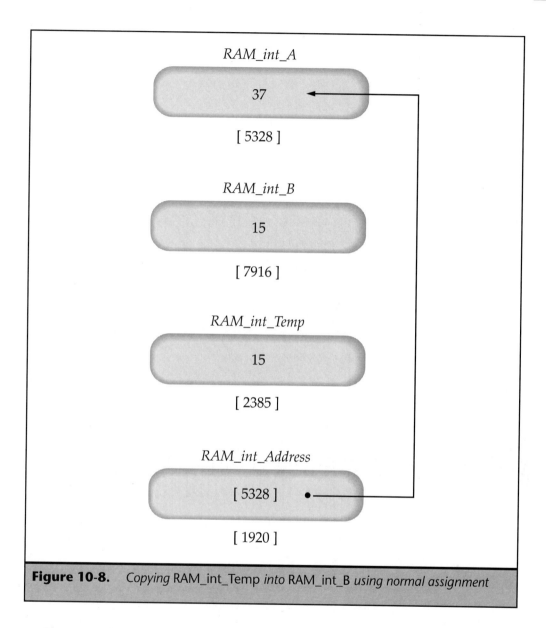

RAM_int_A

37

[5328]

RAM_int_B

15

[7916]

RAM_int_Temp

15

[2385]

RAM_int_Address

[5328]

[1920]

Figure 10-8.   *Copying* RAM_int_Temp *into* RAM_int_B *using normal assignment*

Executing the following statement copies the contents of *Code2_Address* into *Code1_Address* so that both pointers point to *Code2* (see Figure 10-11):

```
Code1_Address = Code2_Address;
```

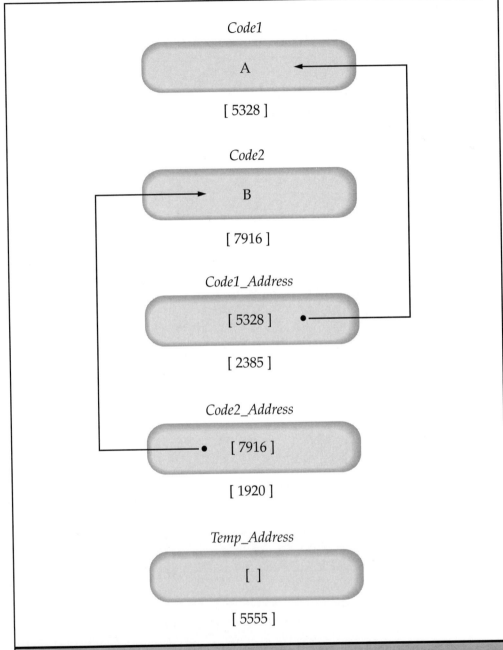

Figure 10-9. *Depiction of the five variables after executing program code*

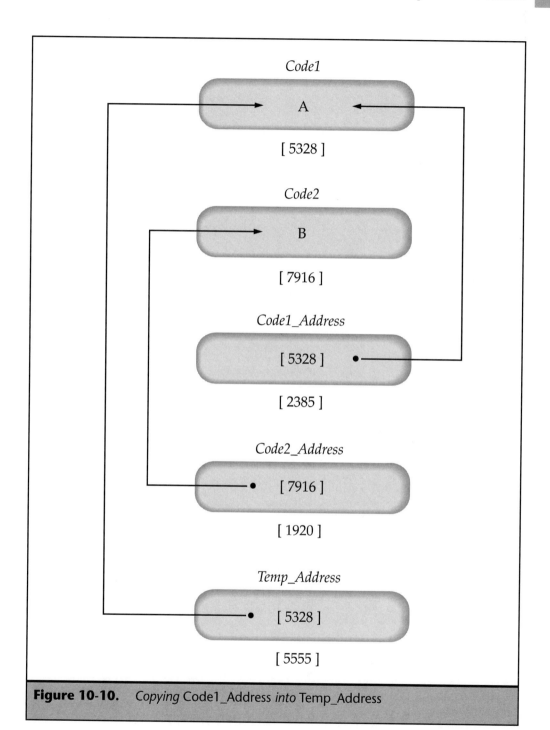

Figure 10-10. *Copying* Code1_Address *into* Temp_Address

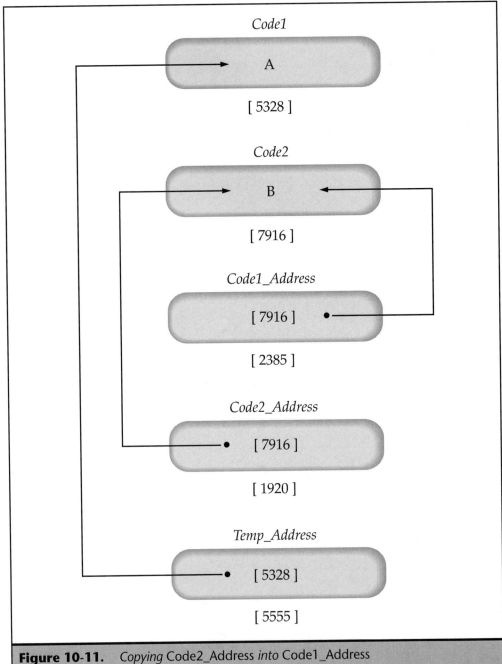

Figure 10-11. *Copying* Code2_Address *into* Code1_Address

Notice that if the code had not preserved the address to *Code1* in a temporary location, *Temp_Address*, there would be no pointer access to *Code1*.

The next to last statement copies the address stored in *Temp_Address* into *Code2_Address* (see Figure 10-12).

When the **printf()** statement is executed, because the value of **Code1_Address* is *"B"* and the value of **Code2_Address* is *"A"*, you will see

```
BA
```

Notice how the actual values stored in the variables *Code1* and *Code2* haven't changed from their original initializations. However, because you have swapped the contents of their respective pointers, **Code1_Address* and **Code2_Address*, it appears that their order has been reversed. This is an important concept to grasp. Depending on the size of a data object, moving a pointer to the object can be much more efficient than copying the entire contents of the object.

Pointer Variable Initialization

Pointer variables can be initialized in their definitions, just like many other variables in C/C++. For example, the following two statements allocate storage for the two cells *RAM_int* and *RAM_int_Address*:

```
int RAM_int;
int *RAM_int_Address = &RAM_int;
```

The variable *RAM_int* is an ordinary integer variable and *RAM_int_Address* is a pointer to an integer. Additionally, the code initializes the pointer variable *RAM_int_Address* to the address of *RAM_int*. Be careful: the syntax is somewhat misleading; you are not initializing **RAM_int_Address* (which would have to be an integer value) but *RAM_int_Address* (which must be an address to an integer). The second statement in the preceding listing can be translated into the following two equivalent statements:

```
int *RAM_int_Address;
RAM_int_Address = &RAM_int;
```

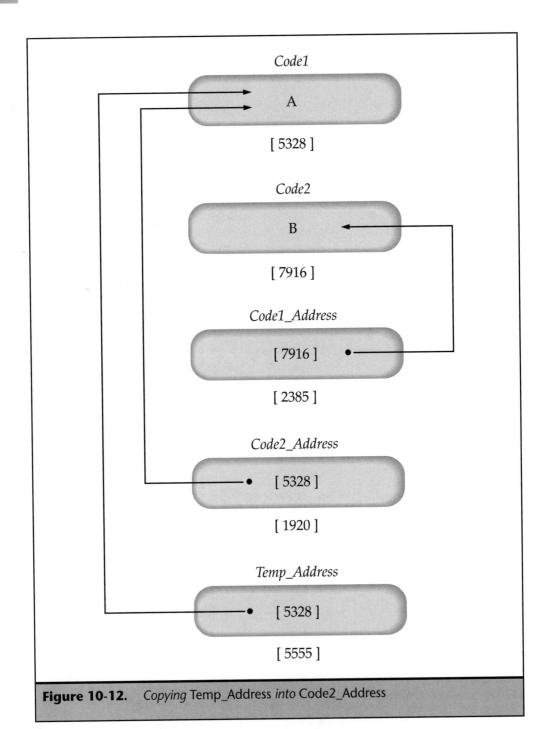

Figure 10-12.   *Copying* Temp_Address *into* Code2_Address

The following code segment shows how to declare a string pointer and then initialize it:

```
//
// strngptr.cpp
// A C++ program that initializes a string pointer and
// then prints the palindrome backwards then forwards.
// Copyright (c) Chris H. Pappas and William H. Murray, 1996
//

#include <string.h>
#include <iostream.h>

void main( void )
{
  char *Palindrome = "MADAM I'M ADAM";

  for( int offset  = strlen(Palindrome)-1; offset >= 0; offset-- )
    cout << Palindrome[ offset ];

  cout << "\n" << Palindrome    ;
}
```

Technically, the C/C++ compiler stores the address of the first character of the string *"MADAM I'M ADAM"* in the variable *Palindrome*. While the program is running, it can use *Palindrome* like any other string. This is because all C/C++ compilers create a string table which is used internally by the compiler to store the string constants a program is using.

The **strlen()** function prototyped in string.h calculates the length of a string. The function expects a pointer to a null-terminated string and counts all of the characters up to, but not including, the null character itself. The index variable *offset* is initialized to one less than the value returned by **strlen()** because the **for** loop treats the string *Palindrome* like an array of characters. The *Palindrome* has 14 letters. If *Palindrome* is treated as an array of characters, each element is indexed from 0 to 13. This example program highlights the somewhat confusing relationship between pointers to character strings and arrays of characters. However, if you remember that an array's name is actually the address of the first element, you should understand why the compiler issues no complaints.

Improper Use of the Address Operator

You cannot use the address operator on every C/C++ expression. The following examples demonstrate those situations where the & address operator cannot be applied:

```
CantStoreAddressOfConstant          = &37                    ;

int RAM_int = 5                                              ;
CantStoreAddressOfTempExpression = &( RAM_int + 15 );

CantStoreAddressOfRegisterVar       = &RegisterVar           ;
```

The first statement tries to illegally obtain the address of a hardwired constant value. Because the 37 has no memory cell associated with it, the statement is meaningless.

The second assignment statement attempts to return the address of the expression *RAM_int + 15*. Because the expression itself is actually a stack manipulation process, there is no address associated with the expression.

Normally, the last example honors the programmer's request to define *RegisterVar* as a register rather than as a storage cell in internal memory. Therefore, no memory cell address could be returned and stored. The C/C++ compiler gives the variable memory, not register storage.

Pointers to Arrays

As mentioned, pointers and arrays are closely related topics. Remember from Chapter 9 that an array's name is a constant whose value represents the address of the array's first element. For this reason, the value of an array's name cannot be changed by an assignment statement or by any other statement. Given the following data declarations, the array's name, *SeedDensity*, is a constant whose value is the address of the first element of the array of 20 floats:

```
#define NUMBER_OF_SAMPLES 10

float SeedDensity[ NUMBER_OF_SAMPLES ];
float *PtrToASeed;
```

The following statement assigns the address of the first element of the array to the pointer variable *PtrToASeed*:

```
PtrToASeed = SeedDensity;
```

An equivalent statement looks like this:

```
PtrToASeed = &SeedDensity[ 0 ];
```

However, if *PtrToASeed* holds the address of a float, the following statements are illegal:

```
SeedDensity       = PtrToASeed;
&SeedDensity[ 0 ] = PtrToASeed;
```

These statements attempt to assign a value to the constant *SeedDensity* or its equivalent *&SeedDensity[0]*, which makes about as much sense as

```
7 = PtrToASeed;
```

Pointers to Pointers

In C/C++, it is possible to define pointer variables that point to other pointer variables, which in turn point to the data, such as an integer. Figure 10-13 illustrates this relationship; *PtrToPtrToRAM_int* is a pointer variable that points to another pointer variable whose contents can be used to point to 10.

You may be wondering why this is necessary. The arrival of Windows and the Windows NT programming environment signals the development of multitasking operating environments designed to maximize the use of memory. To compact the use of memory, the operating system has to be able to move objects in memory. If your program points directly to the physical memory cell where the object is stored and the operating system moves it, disaster will strike. Instead of pointing directly to a data object, your application points to a memory cell address that will not change while your program is running (for example, let's call this a *VirtualRAMAddress*, and the *VirtualRAMAddress* memory cell holds the *PhysicalRAMAddress* of the data object). Now, whenever the operating environment wants to move the data object, all the operating system has to do is update the *PhysicalRAMAddress* pointed to by the *VirtualRAMAddress*. As far as your application is concerned, it still uses the unchanged address of the *VirtualRAMAddress* to point to the updated address of the *PhysicalRAMAddress*.

To define a pointer to a pointer in C, you simply increase the number of asterisks preceding the identifier:

```
int **PtrToPtrTo_int;
```

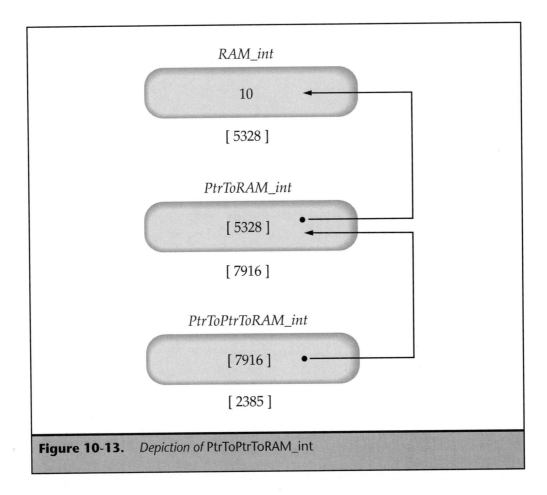

Figure 10-13.   *Depiction of* PtrToPtrToRAM_int

In this example, the variable *PtrToPtrTo_int* is defined to be a pointer to a pointer that points to an **int** data type. *PtrToPtrTo_int*'s data type is

```
int **
```

Each asterisk is read "pointer to." The number of pointers that must be followed to access the data item or, equivalently, the number of asterisks that must be attached to the variable to reference the value to which it points is called the *level of indirection* of the pointer variable. A pointer's level of indirection determines how much dereferencing must be done to access the data type given in the definition. Figure 10-14 illustrates several variables with different levels of indirection.

The first four lines of code in Figure 10-14 define four variables: the integer variable *RAM_int*, the *PtrToRAM_int* pointer variable that points to an integer (one

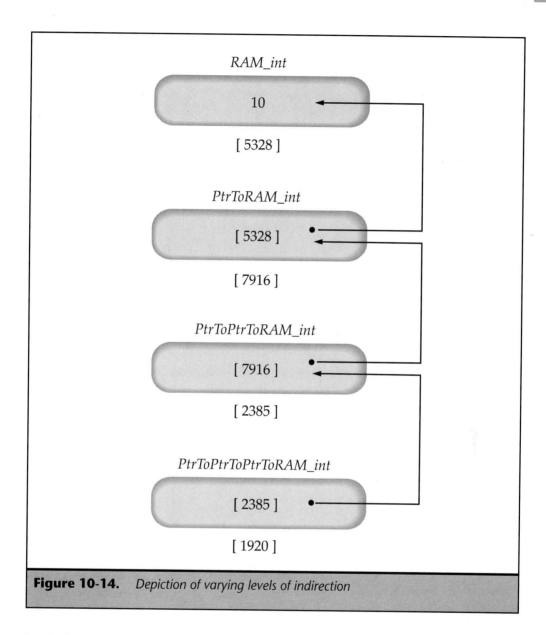

Figure 10-14. *Depiction of varying levels of indirection*

level of indirection), *the PtrToPtrToRAM_int* variable that points to a pointer that points to an integer (two levels of indirection), and *PtrToPtrToPtrToRAM_int*, illustrating that this process can be extended beyond two levels of indirection. The fifth line of code is

```
PtrToRAM_int = &RAM_int;
```

This is an assignment statement that uses the address operator. The expression assigns the address of *&RAM_int to PtrToRAM_int*. Therefore, *PtrToRAM_int*'s contents contain 1111. Notice that there is only one arrow from *PtrToRAM_int* to *RAM_int*. This indicates that *RAM_int*, or 10, can be accessed by dereferencing *PtrToRAM_int* just once. The next statement illustrates double indirection:

```
PtrToPtrToRAM_int = &PtrToRAM_int;
```

Because *PtrToPtrToRAM_int*'s data type is **int ****, to access an integer you need to dereference the variable twice. After the preceding assignment statement, *PtrToPtrToRAM_int* holds the address of *PtrToRAM_int* (not the contents of *PtrToRAM_int*), so *PtrToPtrToRAM_int* points to *PtrToRAM_int*, which in turn points to *RAM_int*. Notice that you must follow two arrows to get from *PtrToPtrToRAM_int* to *RAM_int*.

The last statement demonstrates three levels of indirection:

```
PtrToPtrToPtrToRAM_int = &PtrToPtrToRAM_int;
```

It also assigns the address of *PtrToPtrToRAM_int* to *PtrToPtrToPtrToRAM_int* (not the contents of *PtrToPtrToRAM_int*). Notice that the accompanying illustration shows that three arrows are now necessary to reference *RAM_int*.

To review, *PtrToPtrToPtrToRAM_int* is assigned the address of a pointer variable that indirectly points to an integer, as in the preceding statement. However, ****PtrToPtrToPtrToRAM_int* (the cell pointed to) can only be assigned an integer value, not an address, because ****PtrToPtrToPtrToRAM_int* is an integer:

```
***PtrToPtrToPtrToRAM_int = 10;
```

C/C++ allows pointers to be initialized like any other variable. For example, *PtrToPtrToPtrToRAM_int* could have been defined and initialized using the following single statement:

```
int ***PtrToPtrToPtrToRAM_int = &PtrToPtrToRAM_int;
```

Pointers to Strings

A string constant such as *"File not ready"* is actually stored as an array of characters with a null terminator added as the last character.

Because a **char** pointer can hold the address of a character, it is possible to define and initialize it. For example:

```
char *ErrorMessage = "File not ready";
```

This statement defines the char pointer *ErrorMessage* and initializes it to the address of the first character in the string.

Additionally, the storage is allocated for the string itself. The same statement could have been written as follows:

```
char *ErrorMessage;
ErrorMessage = "File not ready";
```

Again, care must be taken to realize that *ErrorMessage* was assigned the address, not *ErrorMessage, which points to the "F". The second example helps to clarify this by using two separate statements to define and initialize the pointer variable.

The following example highlights a common misconception when dealing with pointers to strings and pointers to arrays of characters:

```
char *ErrorMessage          = "File not ready" ;
char ErrorMessageAsArray[ ] = "Drive not ready";
```

The main difference between these two statements is that the value of *ErrorMessage* can be changed (because it is a pointer variable), but the value of *ErrorMessageAsArray* cannot be changed (because it is a pointer constant). In the same vein, the following assignment statement is illegal:

```
// Incorrect
char ErrorMessageAsArray[ 16 ];
ErrorMessageAsArray = "Drive not ready";
```

Although the syntax looks similar to the correct code in the preceding example, the assignment statement attempts to copy the address of the first cell of the storage for the string *"Drive not ready"* into *ErrorMessageAsArray*. Because *ErrorMessageAsArray* is a pointer constant, not a pointer variable, an error results.

The following input statement is incorrect because the pointer *ErrorMessage* has not been initialized:

```
// Incorrect
char *ErrorMessage;
cin >> ErrorMessage;
```

Correcting the problem is as simple as reserving storage for and initializing the pointer variable *ErrorMessage*:

```
char Buffer[ 10 ];

char *ErrorMessage = Buffer;

cin.get( ErrorMessage,10  );
```

Because the value of *Buffer* is the address of the first cell of the array, the second statement in the code not only allocates storage for the pointer variable, it also initializes it to the address of the first cell of the array *Buffer*. At this point, the **cin.get()** statement is satisfied because it is passed the valid address of the character array storage.

Pointer Arithmetic

If you are familiar with assembly language programming, then you are already comfortable with using actual physical addresses to reference information stored in tables. For those of you who are only accustomed to using subscript indexing into arrays, believe it or not, you have been effectively using the same assembly language equivalent. The only difference is that in the latter case you were allowing the compiler to manipulate the addresses for you.

Remember that one of C/C++'s strengths is their closeness to the hardware. In C/C++, you can actually manipulate pointer variables. Many of the example programs seen so far have demonstrated how one pointer variable's address, or address contents, can be assigned to another pointer variable of the same data type. C/C++ allows you to perform only two arithmetic operations on a pointer address—namely, addition and subtraction. Let's look at two different pointer variable types and perform some simple pointer arithmetic:

```
//
//  ptrarith.cpp
//  A C++ program demonstrating pointer arithmetic.
//  Copyright (c) Chris H. Pappas and William H. Murray, 1996
//

#include <iostream.h>

void main( void )
{
   int    *RAM_int_Address              ;
```

```
    float *RAM_float_Address        ;


    int    An_int                   ;
    float A_float                   ;

    RAM_int_Address    = &An_int    ;
    RAM_float_Address = &A_float    ;

    RAM_int_Address++               ;
    RAM_float_Address++             ;
}
```

Let's also assume that an integer is 2 bytes and a float is 4 bytes. Also, *An_int* is stored at memory cell address 2000, and *A_float* is stored at memory cell address 4000. When the last two lines of the program are executed, *RAM_int_Address* will contain the address 2002 and *RAM_float_Address* will contain the address 4004. But wait a minute—didn't you think that the increment operator ++ incremented by 1? This is true for character variables but not always for pointer variables.

In Chapter 6, you were introduced to the concept of operator overloading. Increment (++) and decrement (- -) are examples of this C/C++ construct. For the immediate example, because *RAM_int_Address* was defined to point to integers (which for the system in this example are 2 bytes), when the increment operation is invoked, it checks the variable's type and then chooses an appropriate increment value. For integers, this value is 2, and for floats, the value is 4 (on the example system). This same principle holds true for whatever data type the pointer is pointing to. Should the pointer variable point to a structure of 20 bytes, the increment or decrement operator would add or subtract 20 from the current pointer's address.

You can also modify a pointer's address by using integer addition and subtraction, not just the ++ and - - operators. For example, moving four float values over from the one currently pointed to can be accomplished with the following statement:

```
RAM_float_Address = RAM_float_Address + 4;
```

Look at the following program carefully and see if you can predict the results. Does the program move the *float* pointer *RAM_float_Address* one number over?

```
//
//  incorect.cpp
//  A C++ program using sizeof() and pointer arithmetic.
```

```
//  Copyright (c) Chris H. Pappas and William H. Murray, 1996
//

#include <iostream.h>
#include <stddef.h>

void main( void )
{
  float  floatArray[ ] = {15.38,12.34,91.88,11.11,22.22},
         *RAM_float_Address                                 ;
  size_t floatWidth                                         ;

  RAM_float_Address = &floatArray[ 0 ]                      ;

  floatWidth = sizeof( float )                              ;

  RAM_float_Address = RAM_float_Address + floatWidth    ;
}
```

Try using the integrated debugger to single-step through the program. Use the Trace window to keep an eye on the variables *RAM_float_Address* and *floatWidth*.

Assume that the debugger has assigned *RAM_float_Address* the address of *floatArray* and that *RAM_float_Address* contains an FFCA. The variable *floatWidth* is assigned the *sizeof(float)* that returns a 4. When you executed the final statement in the program, what happened? The variable *RAM_float_Address* changed to FFDA, not FFDE. Why? You forgot that pointer arithmetic takes into consideration the size of the object pointed to (4 * (4-byte floats) = 16). The program actually moves the *RAM_float_Address* pointer over four *float* values to 22.22.

Actually, you were intentionally misled by the naming of the variable *floatWidth*. To make logical sense, the program should have been written like this:

```
//
//  thiswrks.cpp
//  The same C++ program using meaningful variable names.
//  Copyright (c) Chris H. Pappas and William H. Murray, 1996
//

#include <iostream.h>

void main( void )
{
```

```
    float floatArray[ ] = {15.38,12.34,91.88,11.11,22.22}      ,
         *RAM_float_Address                                    ;
    int   HowMany_floats_ToSkip                                ;

    RAM_float_Address      = floatArray                        ;

    HowMany_floats_ToSkip = 1                                  ;

    RAM_float_Address = RAM_float_Address + HowMany_floats_ToSkip;

}
```

Pointer Arithmetic and Arrays

The following two programs index into a ten-character array. Both programs read in ten characters and then print out the same ten characters in reverse order. The first program uses the more conventional high-level language approach of indexing with subscripts. The second program is identical except that the array elements are referenced by address, using pointer arithmetic. Here is the first program:

```
/*
 *    offset.c
 *    A C program using normal array subscripting.
 *    Copyright (c) Chris H. Pappas and William H. Murray, 1996
 */

#include <stdio.h>

#define MAX_charS 10

void main( void )
{
  char Buffer[ MAX_charS ]                    ;
  int  offset                                 ;

  for( offset = 0; offset < MAX_charS; offset++    )
    Buffer[ offset ] = getchar( )                  ;

  for( offset = MAX_charS-1; offset >= 0; offset-- )
    putchar( Buffer[ offset ] )                    ;
}
```

Here is the second example:

```
/*
 *   pointers.c
 *   A C program using pointer arithmetic to access elements.
 *   Copyright (c) Chris H. Pappas and William H. Murray, 1996
 */

#include <stdio.h>

#define MAX_charS 10

void main( void )
{
  char  Buffer[ MAX_charS ]                    ,
  char *RAM_char_Address                       ;
  int lcv                                      ;

  RAM_char_Address = Buffer                    ;

  for( lcv = 0; lcv < MAX_charS; lcv++ )       {
    *RAM_char_Address=getchar( )               ;
    RAM_char_Address++                         ;
  }

  RAM_char_Address = Buffer + ( MAX_charS - 1 );

  for( lcv = 0; lcv < MAX_charS; lcv++ )       {
    putchar( *RAM_char_Address                 );
    RAM_char_Address−                          ;
  }
}
```

Because the first example is straightforward, the discussion will revolve around the second program, which uses pointer arithmetic. *RAM_char_Address* has been defined to be of type **char ***, which means it is a pointer to a character. Because each cell in the array *Buffer* holds a character, *RAM_char_Address* is suitable for pointing to each. The following statement stores the address of the first cell of *Buffer* in the variable *RAM_char_Address*:

```
RAM_char_Address = Buffer;
```

The **for** loop reads *MAX_charS* characters and stores them in the array *Buffer*. The following statement uses the dereference operator * to ensure that the target, the left-hand side of this assignment (another example of an *lvalue*), will be the cell to which *RAM_char_Address* points, not *RAM_char_Address* (which itself contains just an address).

```
*RAM_char_Address = getchar( );
```

The idea is to store a character in each cell of *Buffer*, not to store it in *RAM_char_Address*.

To start printing the array backwards, the program first initializes the *RAM_char_Address* to the last element in the array:

```
RAM_char_Address=Buffer + ( MAX_charS - 1 );
```

By adding 9 (*MAX_charS - 1*) to the initial address of *Buffer*, *RAM_char_Address* points to the tenth element. Remember, these are offsets. The first element in the array is at offset zero. Within the **for** loop, *RAM_char_Address* is decremented to move backward through the array elements. Make certain you use the integrated debugger to trace through this example if you are unsure of how *RAM_char_Address* is modified.

Problems with the Operators ++ and - -

Just as a reminder, the following two statements do not perform the same cell reference:

```
*RAM_char_Address++ = getchar( );

*++RAM_char_Address = getchar( );
```

The first statement assigns the character returned by **getchar()** to the current cell pointed to by *RAM_char_Address* and then increments *RAM_char_Address*. The second statement increments the address in *RAM_char_Address* first and then assigns the character returned by the function to the cell pointed to by the updated address.

Comparing Pointers

You have already seen examples demonstrating the effect of incrementing and decrementing pointers using the ++ and - - operators and the effect of adding an integer to a pointer. There are other operations that may be performed on pointers. These include:

- Subtracting an integer from a pointer
- Subtracting two pointers (usually pointing to the same object)
- Comparing pointers using a relational operator such as <=, =, or >=

Because (pointer - integer) subtraction is so similar to (pointer + integer) addition (these have already been discussed by example), it should be no surprise that the resultant pointer value points to a storage location integer element before the original pointer.

Subtracting two pointers yields a constant value that is the number of array elements between the two pointers. This assumes that both pointers are of the same type and initially point into the same array. Subtracting pointers that are not of the same type or that initially point to different arrays will yield unpredictable results.

NOTE: No matter which pointer arithmetic operation you choose, there is no check to see if the pointer value calculated is outside the defined boundaries of the array.

Pointers of like type (that is, pointers that reference the same kind of data, like **int** and **float**) can also be compared to each other. The resulting TRUE (!0) or FALSE (0) can either be tested or assigned to an integer, just like the result of any logical expression. Comparing two pointers tests whether they are equal, not equal, greater than, or less than each other. One pointer is less than another pointer if the first pointer refers to an array element with a lower number subscript. (Remember that pointers and subscripts are virtually identical.) This operation also assumes that the pointers reference the same array.

Finally, pointers can be compared to zero, the null value. In this case, only the test for equal or not equal is valid because testing for negative pointers makes no sense. The null value in a pointer means that the pointer has no value or does not point to anything. Null, or zero, is the only numeric value that can be directly assigned into a pointer without a type cast.

It should be noted that pointer conversions are performed on pointer operands. This means that any pointer may be compared to a constant expression evaluating to zero and any pointer may be compared to a pointer of type void *. (In this last case, the pointer is first converted to void *.)

Pointer Portability

The examples in this section have represented addresses as integers. This may suggest to you that a C pointer is of type **int**. It is not. A pointer holds the address of a particular type of variable, but a pointer itself is not one of the primitive data types **int**, **float**, and the like. A particular C system may allow a pointer to be copied into an **int** variable and an **int** variable to be copied into a pointer; however, C does not guarantee that pointers can be stored in **int** variables. To guarantee code portability, the practice should be avoided. Also, not all arithmetic operations on pointers are allowed. For example, it is illegal to add two pointers, to multiply two pointers, or to divide one pointer by another.

Pointers to Functions

All the examples so far have shown you how various items of data can be referenced by a pointer. As it turns out, you can also access portions of code by using a pointer to a function. Pointers to functions serve the same purpose as do pointers to data; that is, they allow the function to be referenced indirectly, just as a pointer to a data item allows the data item to be referenced indirectly.

A pointer to a function can have a number of important uses. For example, consider the **qsort()** function. The **qsort()** function has as one of its parameters a pointer to a function. The referenced function contains the necessary comparison that is to be performed between the array elements being sorted. The reason **qsort()** has been written to require a function pointer has to do with the fact that the comparison process between two elements can be a complex process beyond the scope of a single control flag. It is not possible to pass a function by value, that is, pass the code itself. C/C++, however, does support passing a pointer to the code or a pointer to the function.

The concept of function pointers is frequently illustrated by using the **qsort()** function supplied with the compiler. Unfortunately, in many cases the function pointer is declared to be of a type that points to other built-in functions. The following C++ programs demonstrate how to define a pointer to a function and how to "roll your own" function to be passed to the stdlib.h function **qsort()**. Here is the C++ program:

```
//
//  qsort.cpp
//  A C program illustrating how to declare your own
//  function and function pointer to be used with qsort().
//  Copyright (c) Chris H. Pappas and William H. Murray, 1996
//

#include <iostream.h>
#include <stdlib.h>

#define MAX_ELEMENTS 10

int    SortingOrder          ( const void   *RAM_int_A        ,
                               const void   *RAM_int_B        );
```

```
int ( *RAM_function_Address )( const void *, const void *      );

void main( void )
{
   int offset, Array[ MAX_ELEMENTS ] = { 0,5,3,2,8,7,9,1,4,6    };

   RAM_function_Address = SortingOrder                            ;
   qsort( Array,MAX_ELEMENTS,sizeof( int ), _function_Address  );

   for( offset = 0; offset < MAX_ELEMENTS; offset++ )
     cout <<[{|"|}]" << Array[offset]                            ;
}

int SortingOrder( const void *RAM_int_A, const void *RAM_int_B )
{
   return( (*(int *)RAM_int_A) - (*(int *)RAM_int_B)            );
}
```

The function *SortingOrder()* (which will be called the reference function) was prototyped to match the requirements for the fourth parameter to the function **qsort()** (which will be called the invoking function).

To digress slightly, the fourth parameter to the function **qsort()** must be a function pointer. This reference function must be passed two **const void** * parameters and it must return a type **int**. This is because **qsort()** uses the reference function for the sort comparison algorithm. Now that you understand the prototype of the reference function *SortingOrder()*, take a minute to study the body of the reference function.

If the reference function returns a value < 0, then the reference function's first parameter value is less than the second parameter's value. A return value of zero indicates parameter value equality, with a return value > 0 indicating that the second parameter's value was greater than the first's. All of this is accomplished by the single statement in *SortingOrder()*:

```
return( (*(int *)RAM_int_A) - (*(int *) RAM_int_B) );
```

Because both of the pointers were passed as type **void** *, they were cast to their appropriate pointer type **int** *, and then they were dereferenced (*). The result of the subtraction of the two values pointed to returns an appropriate value to satisfy **qsort()**'s comparison criterion.

Although the prototype requirements for *SortingOrder()* are interesting, the meat of the program begins with the pointer function declaration below the *SortingOrder()* function prototype:

```
int    SortingOrder           ( const void    *RAM_int_A        ,
                                const void    *RAM_int_B        );
int ( *RAM_function_Address )( const void *, const void *      );
```

A function's type is determined by its return value and argument list signature. A pointer to *SortingOrder()* must specify the same signature and return type. You might therefore think the following statement would accomplish this:

```
int *RAM_function_Address     ( const void *, const void *     );
```

That is almost correct. The problem is that the compiler interprets the statement as the definition of a function *RAM_function_Address()* taking two arguments and returning a pointer of type **int ***. The dereference operator unfortunately is associated with the type specifier, not *RAM_function_Address()*. Parentheses are necessary to associate the dereference operator with *RAM_function_Address()*.

The corrected statement declares *RAM_function_Address()* to be a pointer to a function taking two arguments and with a return type int—that is, a pointer of the same type required by the fourth parameter to **qsort()**.

In the body of **main()**, the only thing left to do is to initialize *RAM_function_Address()* to the address of the function *SortingOrder()*. The parameters to **qsort()** are the address to the base or zero element of the table to be sorted (*Array*), the number of entries in the table (*MAX_ELEMENTS*), the size of each table element (*sizeof(int)*), and a function pointer to the comparison function (*RAM_function_Address()*).

Learning to understand the syntax of a function pointer can be challenging. Let's look at a few examples. Here is the first one:

```
int *                    (*(*RAM_int_func_Address)(int))[5]        ;
float                    (*(*RAM_float_func_Address)(int,int))(float);
typedef double           (*(*(*RAM_double_func_Address)())[5])()    ;
RAM_double_func_Address  A_RAM_double_func_Address                  ;
(*(*func_array_func_Addresses())[5])()                             ;
```

The first statement defines *RAM_int_func_Address()* to be a function pointer to a function that is passed an integer argument and returns a pointer to an array of five **int** pointers.

The second statement defines *RAM_float_func_Address()* to be a function pointer to a function that takes two integer arguments and returns a pointer to a function taking a float argument and returning a float.

By using the **typedef** declaration, you can avoid the unnecessary repetition of complicated declarations. The **typedef** is read as follows: *RAM_double_func_Address* is defined as a pointer to a function that is passed nothing and returns a pointer to an array of five pointers that point to functions that are passed nothing and returns a **double**.

The last statement is a function declaration, not a variable declaration. The statement defines *func_array_func_Addesses()* to be a function taking no arguments and returning a pointer to an array of five pointers that point to functions taking no arguments and returning integers. The outer functions return the default C and C++ type **int**.

The good news is that you will rarely encounter complicated declarations and definitions like these. However, by making certain you understand these declarations, you will be able to confidently parse the everyday variety.

Dynamic Memory

When a C program is compiled, the computer's memory is broken down into four zones that contain the program's code, all global data, the stack, and the heap. The heap is an area of free memory (sometimes referred to as the free store) that is manipulated by using the dynamic allocation functions **malloc()** and **free()**.

When **malloc()** is invoked, it allocates a contiguous block of storage for the object specified and then returns a pointer to the start of the block. The function **free()** returns previously allocated memory to the heap, permitting that portion of memory to be reallocated.

The argument passed to **malloc()** is an integer that represents the number of bytes of storage that is needed. If the storage is available, **malloc()** will return a **void ***, which can be cast into whatever type pointer is desired. The concept of **void** pointers was introduced in the ANSI C standard and means a pointer of unknown type, or a generic pointer. A **void** pointer cannot itself be used to reference anything (because it doesn't point to any specific type of data), but it can contain a pointer of any other type. Therefore, any pointer can be converted into a **void** pointer and converted back without any loss of information.

The following code segment allocates enough storage for 100 float values:

```
float *RAM_float_Address;
int HowMany_floats = 100;

RAM_float_Address = (float *) malloc(HowMany_floats * sizeof(float));
```

The **malloc()** function has been instructed to obtain enough storage for 100 * the current size of a float. The cast operator *(float *)* is used to return a **float** pointer type. Each block of storage requested is entirely separate and distinct from all other blocks of storage. Absolutely no assumption can be made about where the blocks are located.

Blocks are typically "tagged" with some sort of information that allows the operating system to manage the location and size of the block. When the block is no longer needed, it can be returned to the operating system by using the following statement:

```
free( (void *) RAM_float_Address );
```

Just as in C, C++ allocates available memory in two ways. When variables are declared, they are created on the stack by pushing the stack pointer down. When these variables go out of scope (for instance, when a local variable is no longer needed), the space for that variable is freed automatically by moving the stack pointer up. The size of stack-allocated memory must always be known at compilation.

Your application may also have to use variables with an unknown size at compilation. Under these circumstances, you must allocate the memory yourself on the free store. The free store can be thought of as occupying the bottom of the program's memory space and growing upward, while the stack occupies the top and grows downward.

Your C and C++ programs can allocate and release free store memory at any point.

CAUTION: It is important to realize that free-store-allocated memory variables are not subject to scoping rules, as other variables are. These variables never go out of scope, so once you allocate memory on the heap, you are responsible for freeing it. If you continue to allocate free store space without freeing it, your program could eventually crash.

Most C compilers use the library functions **malloc()** and **free()**, just discussed, to provide dynamic memory allocation, but in C++ these capabilities were considered so important they were made a part of the core language. C++ uses **new** and **delete** to allocate and free free store memory. The argument to new is an expression that returns the number of bytes to be allocated; the value returned is a pointer to the beginning of this memory block. The argument to delete is the starting address of the memory block to be freed. The following two programs illustrate the similarities and differences between a C and C++ application using dynamic memory allocation. Here is the C example:

```
/*
 *   usemaloc.c
 *   A simple C program using malloc() and free().
 *   Copyright (c) Chris H. Pappas and William H. Murray, 1996
 */

#include <stdio.h>
#include <stdlib.h>
```

```
#define MAX_intS 512

void main( void )
{
  int * RAM_int_Address                                    ;

  RAM_int_Address = malloc( MAX_intS * sizeof( int ) );

  if( RAM_int_Address == NULL )
    printf( "Insufficient memory\n"                        );
  else
    printf( "Memory allocated\n"                           );

  free( RAM_int_Address                                    );
}
```

The first point of interest in the program begins with the second **#include** statement that brings in the stdlib.h header file, containing the definitions for both functions, **malloc()** and **free()**. After the program defines the **int *** pointer variable *RAM_int_Address*, the **malloc()** function is invoked to return the address to a memory block that is *MAX_intS * sizeof(int)* big. A robust algorithm will always check for the success or failure of the memory allocation, and it explains the purpose behind the **if-else** statement. The function **malloc()** returns a null whenever insufficient memory is available to allocate the block. This simple program ends by returning the allocated memory to the free store by using the function **free()** and passing it the beginning address of the allocated block. The C++ program does not look significantly different:

```
//
// usenwdl.cpp
// A simple C++ program using new and delete.
// Copyright (c) Chris H. Pappas and William H. Murray, 1996
//

#include <iostream.h>
// #include <stdlib.h> not needed for malloc(), free()

#define MAX_intS 512

void main( void )
{
```

```
   int *RAM_int_Address                    ;

   RAM_int_Address = new int[ MAX_charS ];

   if( RAM_int_Address == NULL )
     cout << "Insufficient memory\n"       ;
   else
     cout << "Memory allocated\n"          ;

   delete( RAM_int_Address                 );
}
```

The only major difference between the two programs is the syntax used with the function **free()** and the operator **new**. Whereas the function **free()** requires the **sizeof()** operator to ensure proper memory allocation, the operator **new** has been written to automatically perform the **sizeof()** function on the declared data type it is passed. Both programs will allocate 512 2-byte blocks of consecutive memory (on systems that allocate 2 bytes per integer).

Using void Pointers

Now that you have a detailed understanding of the nature of pointer variables, you can begin to appreciate the need for the pointer type **void**. To review, the concept of a pointer is that it is a variable that contains the address of another variable. If you always knew how big a pointer was, you wouldn't have to determine the pointer type at compile time. You would therefore also be able to pass an address of any type to a function. The function could then cast the address to a pointer of the proper type (based on some other piece of information) and perform operations on the result. This process would enable you to create functions that operate on a number of different data types.

That is precisely the reason C++ introduced the **void** pointer type. When **void** is applied to a pointer, its meaning is different from its use to describe function argument lists and return values (which mean "nothing"). A **void** pointer means a pointer to any type of data. The following C++ program demonstrates this use of **void** pointers:

```
//
//  usevoid.cpp
//  A C++ program using void pointers.
//  Copyright (c) Chris H. Pappas and William H. Murray, 1996
//
```

```
#include <iostream.h>


#define MAX_LETTERS 50

void PrintAnyDataType( void *RAM_Address, char DataType          );

void main( void )
{
  int    *RAM_int_Address                                        ;
  char   *RAM_char_Address                                       ;
  float  *RAM_float_Address                                      ;
  char    UserWantsToCreate                                      ,

          CarriageReturn                                         ;

  cout << "Please enter the dynamic data type\n"                 ;
  cout << "    you would like to create.\n\n"                    ;
  cout << "Use (s)tring, (i)nt, or (f)loat "                     ;
  cin  >>  UserWantsToCreate                                     ;
    cin.get( CarriageReturn                                      );
      switch( UserWantsToCreate )                                {
        case 's':
          RAM_char_Address = new char[ MAX_LETTERS ]             ;
          cout << "\nPlease enter a string: "                    ;
          cin.get( RAM_char_Address,MAX_LETTERS                  );
          PrintAnyDataType( RAM_char_Address,UserWantsToCreate   );
          break                                                  ;
        case 'i':
          RAM_int_Address = new int                              ;
          cout << "\nPlease enter an integer: "                  ;
          cin  >> *RAM_int_Address                               ;
          PrintAnyDataType( RAM_int_Address,UserWantsToCreate    );
          break                                                  ;
        case 'f':
          RAM_float_Address = new float                          ;
          cout << "\nPlease enter a float: "                     ;
          cin  >> *RAM_float_Address                             ;
          PrintAnyDataType( RAM_float_Address,UserWantsToCreate  );
          break                                                  ;
        default:
          cout << "\n\n  Object type not implemented!"           ;
```

```
        }
    }
void PrintAnyDataType( void *RAM_Address, char DataType        )
{
  switch(DataType)                                               {
      case 's':
        cout << "\nThe string read in:  " << (char *) RAM_Address  ;
        delete RAM_Address                                        ;
        break                                                     ;
      case 'i':
        cout << "\nThe integer read in: "
             << *((int *) RAM_Address)                            ;
        delete RAM_Address                                        ;
        break                                                     ;
      case 'f':
        cout << "\nThe float value read in: "
             << *((float *) RAM_Address)                          ;
        delete RAM_Address                                        ;
        break                                                     ;
      }
  }
```

The first statement of interest in the program is the *PrintAnyDataType()* function prototype. Notice that the function's first formal parameter, *RAM_Address*, is of type **void *** or a generic pointer. Moving down to the data declarations, you will find three pointer variable types: **int ***, **char ***, and **float ***. These will eventually be assigned valid pointer addresses to their respective memory cell types.

The action in the program begins with a prompt asking the user to enter the data type he or she would like to dynamically create. You may be wondering why the two separate input statements are used to handle the user's response. The first **cin** statement reads in the single-character response but leaves the \n line feed hanging around. The second input statement, *cin.get(CarriageReturn)*, remedies this situation.

The switch statement takes the user's response and invokes the appropriate prompt and pointer initialization. The pointer initialization takes one of three forms:

```
RAM_char_Address  = new char ;
RAM_int_Address   = new int  ;
RAM_float_Address = new float;
```

The following statement is used to input the character string, and in this example it limits the length of the string to *MAX_LETTERS* (*50*) characters:

```
cin.get ( RAM_char_Address,MAX_LETTERS );
```

Because the **cin.get()** input statement expects a string pointer as its first parameter, there is no need to dereference the variable when the *PrintAnyDataType()* function is invoked:

```
PrintAnyDataType ( RAM_char_Address,UserWantsToCreate );
```

Things get a little quieter if the user wants to input an integer or a float. The last two case options are the same except for the prompt and the reference variable's type.

Notice how the three invocations of the function *PrintAnyDataType()* have different pointer types:

```
PrintAnyDataType ( RAM_char_Address , UserWantsToCreate );
PrintAnyDataType ( RAM_int_Address  , UserWantsToCreate );
PrintAnyDataType ( RAM_float_Address, UserWantsToCreate );
```

Function *PrintAnyDataType()* accepts these parameters only because the matching formal parameter's type is **void** *. Remember, to use these pointers, you must first cast them to their appropriate pointer type. When using a string pointer with **cout**, you must first cast the pointer to type **char** *.

Just as creating integer and float dynamic variables was similar, printing their values is also similar. The only difference between the last two case statements is the string and the cast operator used.

Although it is true that all dynamic variables pass into bit oblivion whenever a program terminates, each of the case options takes care of explicitly deleting the pointer variable. When and where your program creates and deletes dynamic storage is application dependent.

Pointers and Arrays

The following sections include many example programs that deal with the topic of arrays and how they relate to pointers.

Strings (Arrays of Type char)

Many string operations in C are generally performed by using pointers and pointer arithmetic to reference character array elements. This is because character arrays or strings tend to be accessed in a strictly sequential manner. Remember, all strings in C are terminated by a null (\0). The following C++ program is a modification of a program used earlier in this chapter to print palindromes and illustrates the use of pointers with character arrays:

```cpp
//
//  chararay.cpp
//  A C++ program that prints a character array backwards
//  using a character pointer and the decrement operator.
//  Copyright (c) Chris H. Pappas and William H. Murray, 1996
//

#include <iostream.h>
#include <string.h>

void main( void )
{
  char  Palindrome[ ] = "POOR DAN IN A DROOP"      ,
        *RAM_char_Address                          ;

  RAM_char_Address = Palindrome + (strlen(Palindrome)-1 );

  do {

    cout << *RAM_char_Address                      ;
    RAM_char_Address--                             ;

  } while( RAM_char_Address >= Palindrome          );
}
```

After the program declares and initializes the *Palindrome* palindrome, it creates a *RAM_char_Address* of type **char ***. Remember that the name of an array is in itself an address variable. The body of the program begins by setting the *RAM_char_Address* to the address of the last character in the array. This requires a call to the function **strlen()**, which calculates the length of the character array.

NOTE: *The **strlen()** function counts just the number of characters. It does not include in the count the null terminator \0.*

You were probably thinking that was the reason for subtracting the 1 from the function's returned value. This is not exactly true; the program has to take into consideration the fact that the first array character's address is at offset zero.

Therefore, you want to increment the pointer variable's offset address to one less than the number of valid characters.

Once the pointer for the last valid array character has been calculated, the **do-while** loop is entered. The loop simply uses the pointer variable to point to the memory location of the character to be printed and prints it. It next calculates the next character's memory location and compares this value with the starting address of *Palindrome*. As long as the calculated value is >=, the loop iterates.

Arrays of String Pointers

One of the easiest ways to keep track of an array of strings is to define an array of pointers to strings. This is much simpler than defining a two-dimensional array of characters. The following program uses an array of string pointers to keep track of three function error messages:

```c
/*
 *   ptrarays.c
 *   A C program that demonstrates how to define and use
 *   arrays of pointers.
 *   Copyright Chris H. Pappas and William H. Murray, 1996
 */

#include <ctype.h>
#include <stdio.h>

#define NUMBER_OF_ERRORS 3

char *ErrorMessageAsArray[ NUMBER_OF_ERRORS ] =
        {
           "\nFile not available.\n"              ,
           "\nNot an alpha character.\n"          ,
           "\nValue not between 1 and 10.\n"
        }                                          ;

FILE *GetA_file ( char *RAM_char_Address          );
char  GetA_char ( void                            );
int   GetAn_int ( void                            );

FILE *FILE_Addess                                  ;

void main( void                                    )
{
   char A_char                                      ;
```

```
  int   An_int                                             ;

  GetA_file( "input.dat"                                  );
  A_char = GetA_char( )                                    ;
  An_int = GetAn_int( )                                    ;

}

FILE *GetA_file( char *RAM_char_Address                   )
{
  const FILE_Address_Error = 0                             ;

  FILE_Addess = fopen( RAM_char_Address,"r"               );
  if( !FILE_Addess                                        )
    printf( "%s",ErrorMessageAsArray[ FILE_Address_error ] );
  return( FILE_Addess                                     );
}

char GetA_char( void                                      )
{
  char  A_char                                             ;
  const GetA_char_Error = 1                                ;

  printf( "\nEnter a character: "                         );
  scanf(  "%c",&A_char                                    );
  if( !isalpha( A_char )                                  )
    printf( "%s",ErrorMessageAsArray[ GetA_char_error ]   );
  return( A_char                                          );
}

int GetAn_int( void                                       )
{
  int   An_int                                             ;
  const GetAn_int = 2                                      ;
  printf( "\nEnter an integer between 1 and 10: "         );
  scanf(  "%d",&An_int                                    );
  if( (An_int < 1) || (An_int > 10)                       )
    printf( "%s",ErrorMessageAsArray[ GetAn_int ]         );
  return( An_int                                          );
}
```

The *ErrorMessageAsArray* is initialized outside all function declarations. This gives it a global lifetime. For large programs, an array of this nature could be saved in a separate source file dedicated to maintaining all error message control. Notice that each function, *GetA_file()*, *GetA_char()*, and *GetAn_int()*, takes care of defining its own constant index into the array. This combination of an error message array and unique function index makes for a very modular solution to error exception handling. If a project requires the creation of a new function, the new piece of code selects a vacant index value and adds one error condition to *ErrorMessageAsArray*. The efficiency of this approach allows each code segment to quickly update the entire application to its peculiar I/O requirements without having to worry about an elaborate error detection/alert mechanism.

The C++ Reference Type

C++ provides a form of call-by-reference that is even easier to use than pointers. First, let's examine the use of reference variables in C++. As with C, C++ enables you to declare regular variables or pointer variables. In the first case, memory is actually allocated for the data object; in the second case, a memory location is set aside to hold an address for an object that will be allocated at another time. C++ has a third kind of declaration, the reference type. Like a pointer variable, a reference variable refers to another variable location, but like a regular variable, it requires no special dereferencing operators. The syntax for a reference variable is straightforward:

```
int  RAM_int_A        = 5         ;
int& RAM_int_A_alias = RAM_int_A;  // valid
int& RAM_int_B_alias            ;  // invalid: uninitialized
```

This example sets up the reference variable *RAM_int_A_alias* and assigns it to the existing variable *RAM_int_A*. At this point, the referenced location has two names associated with it—*RAM_int_A* and *RAM_int_A_alias*. Because both variables point to the same location in memory, they are, in fact, the same variable. Any assignment made to *RAM_int_A_alias* is reflected through *RAM_int_A*; the inverse is also true, and changes to *RAM_int_A* occur through any access to *RAM_int_A_alias*. Therefore, with the reference data type, you can create what is sometimes referred to as an alias for a variable.

The reference type has a restriction that serves to distinguish it from pointer variables, which, after all, do something very similar. The value of the reference type must be set at declaration, and it cannot be changed during the run of the program. After you initialize this type in the declaration, it always refers to the same memory location. Therefore, any assignments you make to a reference variable change only the data in memory, not the address of the variable itself. In other words, you can think of a reference variable as a pointer to a constant location.

For example, using the preceding declarations, the following statement doubles the contents of *RAM_int_A* by multiplying 5 * 2:

```
RAM_int_A_alias *= 2;
```

The next statement assigns *CopyOf_int* (assuming it is of type **int**) a copy of the value associated with *RAM_int_A_alias*:

```
CopyOf_int = RAM_int_A_alias;
```

The next statement is also legal when using reference types:

```
int *RAM_int_A_alias_Address = &RAM_int_A_alias;
```

This statement assigns the address of *RAM_int_A_alias* to the **int** * variable *RAM_int_A_alias_Address*.

The primary use of a reference type is as an argument or a return type of a function, especially when applied to user-defined class types.

Functions Returning Addresses

When you return an address from a function using either a pointer variable or a reference type, you are giving the user a memory address. The user can read the value at the address, and if you haven't declared the pointer type to be **const**, the user can always write the value. By returning an address, you are giving the user permission to read and, for non-**const** pointer types, write to private data. This is a significant design decision. See if you can anticipate what will happen in this next program:

```
//
//   dontdo.cpp
//   A C++ program showing what NOT to do with address
//   variables.
//   Copyright (c) Chris H. Pappas and William H. Murray, 1996
//

#include <iostream.h>

int *TestFunctionOne( void );
int *TestFunctionTwo( void );
```

```
void main( void )
{
  int *RAM_int_Address = TestFunctionOne( )    ;
  TestFunctionTwo( )                            ;
  cout << "Correct value? " << *RAM_int_Address;
}

int *TestFunctionOne( void )
{
  int LocalOne_int = 11;
  return &LocalOne_int ;
}

int *TestFunctionTwo( void )
{
  int LocalTwo_int = 44;
  return &LocalTwo_int ;
}
```

Using the Integrated Debugger

To examine the operation of this C++ code under actual operation, you can use the integrated debugger. Use the Trace window to keep an eye on the variable *RAM_int_Address*.

What has happened? When the *TestFunctionOne()* is called, local space is allocated on the stack for the variable *LocalOne_int*, and the value 11 is stored in it. At this point the *TestFunctionOne()* returns the address of this local variable (very bad news). The second statement in the main program invokes the *TestFunctionTwo()*. *TestFunctionTwo()* in turn allocates local space for *LocalTwo_int* and assigns it a value of 44. So how does the **printf()** statement print a value of 44 when it was passed the address of *LocalOne_int* when *TestFunctionOne()* was invoked?

Actually, what happened was this: when the address of the *TestFunctionOne()* local variable *LocalOne_int* was assigned to *RAM_int_Address* by T*estFunctionOne()*, the address to the *LocalOne_int* location was retained even after *LocalOne_int* went out of scope. When *TestFunctionTwo()* was invoked, it also needed local storage. Because *LocalOne_int* was gone, *LocalTwo_int* was given the same storage location as its predecessor. With *RAM_int_Address* hanging onto this same busy memory cell, you can see why printing the value it now points to yields a 44. Extreme care must be taken not to return the addresses of local variables.

When Should You Use Reference Types?

To review, there are four main reasons for using C++ reference types:

- Reference types lend themselves to more readable code by allowing you to ignore details of how a parameter is passed.

- Reference types put the responsibility for argument passing on the programmer who writes the functions, not on the individual who uses them.

- Reference types are a necessary counterpart to operator overloading.

- Reference types are also used with passing classes to functions so constructors and destructors are not called.

In the Next Chapter...

As you can see, the topic of pointers involves new C/C++ syntax and, more importantly, logical design requirements. Remember that it is C/C++'s use of pointer variables that allows you to create very efficient algorithms, albeit at the cost of easily written, debugged, and maintained code.

At this point in the book, you now know the fundamental components of a simple C/C++ program, and you have studied the building block constructs necessary to develop more advanced applications. Chapter 11 fleshes out the details of C/C++ I/O.

Chapter Eleven

Complete I/O in C

Many commonly used high-level languages have restrictive input and output mechanisms. As a result, programmers generate convoluted algorithms to perform sophisticated data retrieval and display. This is not the case with C, which has a very complete I/O (input/output) function library, although historically I/O was not even part of the C language itself. However, if you have used only simple I/O statements like Pascal's **readln** and **writeln** statements, you're in for a surprise.

This chapter discusses the many different ways to perform I/O in C. The standard C library I/O routines allow you to read and write data to files and devices. However, the C language itself does not include any predefined file structures. C treats all data as a sequence of bytes. There are three basic types of I/O functions: stream, console and port, and low-level.

Stream I/O

All of the stream I/O functions treat a data file or data items as a stream of individual characters. By selecting the appropriate stream function, your application can process data in any size or format required, from single characters to large, complicated data structures. Technically, when a program opens a file for I/O using the stream functions, the opened file is associated with a structure of type **FILE** (predefined in stdio.h) that contains basic information about the file. Once the stream is opened, a pointer to the file structure is returned. The file pointer, sometimes called the stream pointer or the stream, is used to refer to the file for all subsequent I/O.

All stream I/O functions provide buffered, formatted, or unformatted input and output. A buffered stream provides an intermediate storage location for all information that is input from the stream and output that is being sent to the stream. Because disk I/O is such a time-consuming operation, stream buffering streamlines the application. Instead of inputting stream data one character at a time or one structure's worth at a time, stream I/O functions access data a block at a time. As the application needs to process the input, it merely accesses the buffer, a much less time-consuming process. When the buffer is empty, another disk block access is made.

The reverse situation holds true for stream output. Instead of all data being physically output at the time the output statement is executed, all output data is put into the buffer. When the buffer is full, the data is written to the disk. However, most high-level languages have a problem with buffered I/O that you need to take into consideration. For example, if your program has executed several output statements that do not fill the output buffer, causing it to dump to the disk, that information is lost when your program terminates. The solution usually involves making a call to an appropriate function to flush the buffer.

Unlike other high-level languages, C solves this problem with buffered I/O by automatically flushing the buffer's contents whenever the program terminates. Of course, a well-written application should not rely on these automatic features but should always explicitly detail every action the program is to take.

CAUTION: If the application terminates abnormally when you use stream I/O, the output buffers may not be flushed, resulting in loss of data.

Console and Port I/O

Similar in function are the console and port I/O routines, which can be seen as an extension of the stream routines. They allow you to read or write to a terminal (console) or an input/output port (such as a printer port). The port I/O functions simply read and write data in bytes. Console I/O functions provide several additional options. For example, you can detect whether a character has been typed at the console and whether or not the characters entered are echoed to the screen as they are read.

Low-Level I/O

The third type of input and output provided by the C language is known as low-level I/O. None of the low-level I/O functions perform any buffering and formatting; instead, they invoke the operating system's input and output capabilities directly. These routines let you access files and peripheral devices at a more basic level than the stream functions. Files opened in this mode return a file handle. This handle is an integer value that is used to refer to the file in subsequent operations.

CAUTION: In general, it is very bad practice to mix stream I/O functions with low-level routines. Because stream functions are buffered and low-level functions are not, attempting to access the same file or device by two different methods leads to confusion and eventual loss of data in the buffers. Therefore, either stream or low-level functions should be used exclusively on a given file.

Table 11-1 lists the most commonly used C stream I/O functions, prototyped in stdio.h.

Table 11-2 lists the constants, types, and **struct**ures defined for the stdio.h prototyped input and output routines.

Understanding Files

To use any of the functions listed in Table 11-1, an application simply includes the header file, stdio.h. This file contains definitions for constants, types, and **struct**ures used in the stream functions (see Table 11-2) and contains function prototypes and macro definitions for the stream routines. Many of the constants predefined in stdio.h can be useful in your application. For example, **EOF** is defined to be the value

clearerr()	_fstrncpy()	spawnlp()
fclose()	ftell()	spawnlpe()
fcloseall()	fwrite()	spawnv()
fdopen()	getc()	spawnve()
feof()	getchar()	spawnvp()
ferror()	gets()	spawnvpe()
fflush()	getw()	sprintf()
fgetc()	_pclose()	sscanf()
fgetchar()	perror()	strerror()
fgetpos()	_popen()	_strerror()
fgets()	printf()	strncpy()
fileno()	putc()	tempnam()
flushall()	putchar()	tmpfile()
fopen()	puts()	tmpnam()
fprintf()	putw()	ungetc()
fputc()	remove()	unlink()
fputchar()	rename()	vfprintf()
fputs()	rewind()	vfscanf()
fread()	rmtmp()	vprintf()
freopen()	scanf()	vscanf()
fscanf()	setbuf()	vsprintf()
fseek()	setvbuf()	vsscanf()
fsetpos()	spawnl()	
_fsopen()	spawnle()	

Table 11-1. *Standard C Input and Output Routines*

returned by input functions at end-of-file, and **NULL** is the null pointer. Also, **FILE** defines the **struct**ure used to maintain information about a stream, and **BUFSIZ** defines the default size, in bytes, of the stream buffers.

buffering modes	_F_TERM	SEEK_CUR
BUFSIZ	_F_WRIT	SEEK_END
EOF	FILE	SEEK_SET
_F_BIN	fpos_t	size_t
_F_BUF	fseek/lseek modes	**stdaux**
_F_EOF	_IOFBF	**stderr**
_F_ERR	_IOLBF	**stdin**
_F_IN	_IONBF	**stdout**
_F_LBUF	L_ctermid	**stdprn**
_F_OUT	L_tmpnam	SYS_OPEN
_F_RDWR	NULL	TMP_MAX
_F_READ	FOPEN_MAX	

Table 11-2.   *stdio.h Constants, Types, and Structure Definitions*

Opening Files

Your program can use one of three functions to open a stream before input and output can be performed on the stream: **fopen()**, **fdopen()**, or **freopen()**. The file mode and form are set when the stream is opened. The stream file can be opened for reading, writing, or both and can be opened in either text or binary mode (in Chapter 5, Table 5-4 lists the possible file modes).

All three functions return a file pointer, which is used to refer to the stream. For example, if your program contains the following line, you can use the file pointer variable *pfinfile* to refer to the stream:

```
pfinfile = fopen( "input.dat", "r" );
```

NOTE: To give you additional exposure to coding style variations, this chapter uses Hungarian notation. Remember that Hungarian notation uses acronyms, or mnemonics to abbreviate an identifier's data type. For example, a file pointer variable like infile *is preceded by the letters* pf *to indicate the variable's data type—pointer to file.*

When your application begins execution, five streams are automatically opened. These streams are the standard input **stdin**, standard output **stdout**, standard error **stderr**, standard printer **stdprn**, and standard auxiliary **stdaux**. By default, the standard input, standard output, and standard error refer to the user's console. This means that whenever a program expects input from the standard input, it receives that input from the console. Likewise, a program that writes to the standard output prints its data to the console.

Any error messages that are generated by the library routines are sent to the standard error stream, meaning that error messages appear on the user's console. The standard auxiliary and standard print streams usually refer to an auxiliary port and a printer, respectively.

You can use the five file pointers in any function that requires a stream pointer as an argument. Some functions, such as **getchar()** and **putchar()**, are designed to use **stdin** or **stdout** automatically. Because the pointers **stdin**, **stdout**, **stderr**, **stdprn**, and **stdaux** are constants, not variables, do not try to reassign them to a new stream pointer value.

Changing File Buffering

All files opened using the **stdin**, **stdout**, and **stdprn** stream functions are buffered by default except for the preopened streams **stderr** and **stdaux**. The two streams **stderr** and **stdaux** are unbuffered by default unless they are used in either the **printf()** or **scanf()** family of functions. In this case, they are assigned a temporary buffer.

You can buffer **stderr** and **stdaux** with **setbuf()** or **setvbuf()**. The **stdin**, **stdout**, and **stdprn** streams are flushed automatically whenever they are full. You can use the two functions **setbuf()** and **setvbuf()** to make a buffered stream unbuffered, or to associate a buffer with an unbuffered stream. Note that buffers allocated by the system are not accessible to the user, but buffers allocated with the functions **setbuf()** and **setvbuf()** are named by the user and can be manipulated as if they were variables. These user-defined stream buffers are very useful for checking input and output before any system-generated error conditions.

You can define a buffer to be of any size; if you use the function **setbuf()**, the size is set by the constant **BUFSIZ** defined in stdio.h. The syntax for **setbuf()** looks like this:

```
void setbuf( FILE *stream, char *buffer );
```

The following example program uses **setbuf()** and **BUFSIZ** to define and attach a buffer to **stderr**. A buffered **stderr** gives an application greater control over error-exception handling. Using the integrated debugger, single-step the application exactly as you see it.

```
/*
 *   setbuf.c
 *   A C program demonstrating how to define and attach
 *   a buffer to the unbuffered stderr.
 *   Copyright (c) Chris H. Pappas and William H. Murray, 1996
 */

#include <stdio.h>

char cmyoutputbuffer[ BUFSIZ ];

void main( void )
{
    /*   associate a buffer with the unbuffered output stream */
    setbuf( stderr, cmyoutputbuffer ); /* line to comment out */

    /*                  insert into the output stream buffer */
    fputs( "Sample output inserted into the\n", stderr        );
    fputs( "output stream buffer.\n", stderr                  );

    /*                        dump the output stream buffer */
    fflush( stderr );
}
```

Try running the program a second time with the **setbuf()** statement commented out. This will prevent the program from associating a buffer with **stderr**. When you ran the program, did you see the difference? Without a buffered **stderr**, the integrated debugger outputs each **fputs()** statement as soon as the line is executed. The next application uses the function **setvbuf()**. The syntax for **setvbuf()** looks like this:

```
int setvbuf( FILE *stream, char *buffer, int buftype, size_t bufsize );
```

Here, the program determines the size of the buffer instead of using **MYBUFSIZ** defined in stdio.h:

```
/*
 *   setvbuf.c
 *   A C program demonstrating how to use setvbuf().
 *   Copyright (c) Chris H. Pappas and William H. Murray, 1996
 */

#include <stdio.h>

#define MYBUFSIZ 512
```

```
void main( void )
{
    char   ichar,      cmybuffer[ MYBUFSIZ   ]                      ;
    FILE *pfinfile, *pfoutfile                                      ;

    pfinfile  = fopen( "sample.in",  "r"  )                         ;
    pfoutfile = fopen( "sample.out", "w"  )                         ;

    if( setvbuf( pfinfile, cmybuffer, _IOFBF, MYBUFSIZ ) != 0 )
        printf( "pfinfile buffer allocation error\n"   )       ;
      else
        printf( "pfinfile buffer created\n"                )       ;

    if( setvbuf( pfoutfile, NULL, _IOLBF, 132 ) != 0   )
        printf( "pfoutfile buffer allocation error\n" )       ;
      else
        printf( "pfoutfile buffer created\n"              )       ;

    while( fscanf( pfinfile,"%c",&ichar ) != EOF        )
        fprintf( pfoutfile,"%c",ichar                  )       ;

    fclose( pfinfile  )                                          ;
    fclose( pfoutfile )                                          ;
}
```

The program creates a user-accessible buffer pointed to by *pfinfile* and a **malloc()**-allocated buffer pointed to by *pfoutfile*. This last buffer is defined as *buftype*, **_IOLBF**, or line buffered. Other options defined in stdio.h include **_IOFBF**, for fully buffered, and **_IONBF**, for no buffer.

Remember, both **setbuf()** and **setvbuf()** cause the user-defined buffer to be used for I/O buffering instead of an automatically allocated buffer. With **setbuf()**, if the buffer argument is set to **NULL**, I/O will be unbuffered. Otherwise, it will be fully buffered. With **setvbuf()**, if the buffer argument is **NULL**, a buffer will be allocated using **malloc()**. The **setvbuf()** buffer will use the *bufsize* argument as the amount allocated and automatically free the memory upon closing.

Closing Files

The two functions **fclose()** and **fcloseall()** close a stream or streams, respectively. The **fclose()** function closes a single file, whereas **fcloseall()** closes all open streams except **stdin**, **stdout**, **stderr**, **stdprn**, and **stdaux**. However, if your program does not explicitly close a stream, the stream is automatically closed when the application terminates. Because the number of streams that can be open at a given time is limited, it is a good practice to close a stream when you are finished with it.

Low-Level Input and Output in C

Table 11-3 lists the most commonly used low-level input and output functions used by an application.

Low-level input and output calls do not buffer or format data. Files opened by low-level calls are referenced by a file handle (an integer value used by the operating system to refer to the file). You use the **open()** function to open files. You can use the **sopen()** macro to open a file with file-sharing attributes.

Low-level functions are different from their stream counterparts because they do not require the inclusion of the stdio.h header file. However, some common constants that are predefined in stdio.h, such as **EOF** and **NULL**, may be useful. Declarations for the low-level functions are given in the io.h header file.

This second disk-file I/O system was originally created under the UNIX operating system. Because the ANSI C standard committee has elected not to standardize this low-level UNIX-like unbuffered I/O system, it cannot be recommended for future use. Instead, the standardized buffered I/O system described throughout this chapter is recommended for all new projects.

Character Input and Output

The ANSI C standard defines a set of character input and output routines that are supplied with all ANSI C-compliant compilers. These functions provide standard input and output and are considered to be high-level routines (as opposed to low-level routines, which access the machine hardware more directly). I/O in C is implemented through vendor-supplied functions rather than keywords defined as part of the language.

Function	Definition
close()	Closes a disk file
lseek()	Seeks to the specified byte in a file
open()	Opens a disk file
read()	Reads a buffer of data
unlink()	Removes a file from the directory
write()	Writes a buffer of data

Table 11-3. *Commonly Used C Low-Level Input and Output Routines*

Using getc(), putc(), fgetc(), and fputc()

The most basic of all I/O functions are those that input and output one character. The **getc()** function inputs one character from a specified file stream, like this:

```
int   ic         ;
ic = getc( stdin );
```

The input character is passed back in the name of the function **getc()** and then assigns the returned value to *ic*. (By the way, if you are wondering why *ic* isn't of type **char**, it is because the function **getc()** has been prototyped to return an **int** type. This is necessary because of the possible system-dependent size of the end-of-file marker, which might not fit in a single **char** byte size.) Function **getc()** converts the integer into an unsigned character.

This use of an unsigned character preserved as an integer guarantees that the ASCII values above 127 are not represented as negative values. Therefore, negative values can be used to represent unusual situations like errors and the end of the input file. For example, the end-of-file has traditionally been represented by *-1*, although the ANSI C standard states only that the constant **EOF** represent some negative value.

Because **getc()** returns an integer data type, the data item that inputs the value from **getc()** must also be defined as an integer. Although it may seem odd to be using an integer in a character function, the C language actually makes very little distinction between characters and integers. If a character is provided when an integer is needed, the character will be converted to an integer. The complement to the **getc()** function is **putc()**.

The **putc()** function outputs one character to the file stream represented by the specified file pointer. To send the same character that was just input to the standard output, use the following statement:

```
putc( ic, stdout );
```

The **getc()** function is normally buffered, which means that when a request for a character is made by the application, control is not returned to the program until a carriage return is entered into the standard input file stream. All the characters entered before the carriage return are held in a buffer and delivered to the program one at a time.

The application invokes the **getc()** function repeatedly until the buffer has been exhausted. After the carriage return has been sent to the program by **getc()**, the next request for a character results in more characters accumulating in the buffer until a carriage return is again entered. This means that you cannot use the **getc()** function for one-key input techniques that do not require pressing the carriage return. One final note: **getc()** and **putc()** are actually implemented as macros rather than as true functions. The functions **fgetc()** and **fputc()** are identical to their macro **getc()** and **putc()** counterparts.

Using getchar(), putchar(), fgetchar(), and fputchar()

The two macros **getchar()** and **putchar()** are actually specific implementations of the **getc()** and **putc()** macros, respectively. They are always associated with standard input **stdin** and standard output **stdout**. The only way to use them on other file streams is to redirect either standard input or standard output from within the program. The same two coded examples used earlier could be rewritten this way:

```
int  ic      ;
ic = getchar( );
```

and

```
putchar( ic   );
```

Like **getc()** and **putc()**, **getchar()** and **putchar()** are implemented as macros. The function **putchar()** has been written to return an **EOF** value whenever an error condition occurs. The following code can be used to check for an output error condition. Because of the check for **EOF** on output, it tends to be a bit confusing, although it is technically correct.

```
if( putchar( ic ) == EOF )
   printf( "An error has occurred writing to stdout" );
```

Both **fgetchar()** and **fputchar()** are the function equivalents of their macro **getchar()** and **putchar()** counterparts.

Using getch() and putch()

getch() and **putch()** are true functions, but they do not fall under the ANSI C standard because they are low-level functions that interface closely with the hardware. For PCs, these functions do not use buffering, which means that they immediately input a character typed at the keyboard. They can be redirected, however, so they are not associated exclusively with the keyboard. You can use the functions **getch()** and **putch()** exactly like **getchar()** and **putchar()**. Usually, a program running on a PC will use **getch()** to trap keystrokes ignored by **getchar()**—for example, PGUP, PGDN, HOME, and END.

The function **getchar()** sees a character entered from the keyboard as soon as the key is pressed; a carriage return is not needed to send the character to the program. This ability allows the function **getch()** to provide a one-key technique that is not available with **getc()** or **getchar()**. On a PC, the function **getch()** operates very differently from **getc()** and **getchar()**. This is partly due to the fact that the PC can easily determine when an individual key on the keyboard has been pressed.

Other systems, such as the DEC and VAX C, do not allow the hardware to trap individual keystrokes. These systems typically echo the input character and require the pressing of a carriage return, with the carriage return character not seen by the program unless no other characters have been entered. The carriage return, under such circumstances, returns a null character or a decimal zero. Additionally, the function keys are not available, and if they are pressed, produce unreliable results.

String Input and Output

String processing is the next step up from character I/O. In many applications, it is more natural to handle input and output in larger pieces than characters. For example, a file of salespeople may contain one record per line, with each record consisting of four fields: the salesperson's name, base pay, commission, and number of products sold, with white space separating the fields. It would be very tedious to use character I/O. Because of the organization of this type of file, it would be better to treat each record as a single character string and read or write it as a unit.

Using gets(), puts(), fgets(), and fputs()

The function **fgets()**, which reads whole strings rather than single characters, is suited to this task. In addition to the function **fgets()** and its inverse **fputs()**, there are also the macro counterparts **gets()** and **puts()**. The function **fgets()** expects three arguments: the address of an array in which to store the character string, the maximum number of characters to store, and a pointer to a file to read. The function will read characters into the array until the number of characters read in is one less than the size specified, all of the characters up to and including the next newline character have been read, or the end-of-file is reached, whichever comes first. If **fgets()** reads in a newline, the newline will be stored in the array. If at least one character was read, the function will automatically append the null string terminator \0. Suppose the file boatsale.dat looks like this:

```
Pat Pharr 32767 0.15 30
Beth Mollen 35000 0.12 23
Gary Kohut 40000 0.15 40
```

Assuming a maximum record length of 40 characters including the newline, the following program will read the records from the file and write them to the standard output:

```
/*
 *    fgets.c
 *    A C program that demonstrates how to read
 *    in whole records using fgets() and prints
 *    them out to stdout using fputs().
 *    Copyright (c) Chris H. Pappas and William H. Murray, 1996
 */

#include <stdio.h>

#define INULL_CHAR      1
#define IMAX_REC_SIZE 40

void main( void )
{
  FILE *pfinfile;
  char   crecord[ IMAX_REC_SIZE + INULL_CHAR ];

  pfinfile = fopen( "a:\\sales.dat", "r" );

  while( fgets( crecord, IMAX_REC_SIZE +INULL_CHAR,pfinfile) != NULL )
    fputs( crecord,stdout );
  fclose( pfinfile );
}
```

Because the maximum record size is 40, you must reserve 41 cells in the array; the extra cell is to hold the null terminator \0. The program does not generate its own newline when it prints each record to the terminal but relies instead on the newline read into the character array by **fgets()**. The function **fputs()** writes the contents of the character array, *crecord*, to the file specified by the file pointer, **stdout**. If your program happens to be accessing a file on a disk drive other than the one where the compiler is residing, it may be necessary to include a path in your filename. Notice this description in the preceding program; the double backslashes (\ \) are necessary syntactically to indicate a subdirectory. Remember that a single \ usually signals that an escape or line continuation follows.

Although the functions **gets()** and **fgets()** are very similar in usage, the functions **puts()** and **fputs()** operate differently. The function **fputs()** writes to a file and expects two arguments: the address of a null-terminated character string and a pointer to a file; **fputs()** simply copies the string to the specified file. It does not add a newline to the end of the string. The macro **puts()**, however, does not require a pointer to a file because the output automatically goes to **stdout**, and it automatically adds a newline character to the end of the output string.

Integer Input and Output

The C language incorporates two functions for reading and writing stream, or buffered, integer data: **getw()** and **putw()**. The complementary functions **getw()** and **putw()** are very similar to the functions **getc()** and **putc()** except that they input and output integer data instead of character data to a file.

Using getw() and putw()

You should use both **getw()** and **putw()** only on files that are opened in binary mode. The following program opens a binary file, writes ten integers to it, closes the file, and then reopens the file for input and echo print:

```
/*
 *    badEOF.c
 *    A C program that uses the functions getw() and putw() on
 *    a file created in binary mode.
 *    Copyright (c) Chris H. Pappas and William H. Murray, 1996
 */

#include <stdio.h>
#include <stdlib>

#define ISIZE 10

void main( void )
{
  FILE *pfi                                      ;
  int   ivalue, ivalues[ ISIZE ], i              ;
  pfi = fopen( "a:\\integer.dat", "wb"   )       ;
  if( pfi == NULL )                              {
      printf( "File could not be opened" )       ;
      exit ( 1  )                                ;
  }

  for( i = 0; i < ISIZE; i++ )                   {
    ivalues[ i ] = i + 1                         ;
    putw( ivalues[ i ], pfi  )                   ;
  }
```

```
    fclose( pfi )                                    ;

    pfi = fopen( "a:\\integer.dat", "r+b"    );
    if( pfi == NULL )                                {
        printf( "File could not be re-opened" );
        exit  ( 1 )                                  ;
    }

      while( !feof( pfi ) )                          {
        ivalue = getw( pfi      )                    ;
        printf( "%3d", ivalue )                      ;
      }
    }
```

Can you determine why the output from this program is incorrect?

```
1  2  3  4  5  6  7  8  9 10 -1
```

It is quite possible that the last value input within the **while** loop may be equal to EOF; the program uses the function **feof()** to check this end-of-file marker. However, the function does not perform a look-ahead operation as do some other high-level language end-of-file functions. In C, an actual read of the end-of-file value must be performed in order to flag the condition. To correct this situation, the program needs to be rewritten using what is called a *priming read statement*:

```
    .
    .
    .
  ivalue = getw( pfi )    ;
  while( !feof( pfi ) )    {
    printf( "%3d",ivalue );
    ivalue = getw( pfi    );
  }
    .
    .
    .
```

Before the program enters the final **while** loop, the priming read is performed to check to see if the file is empty. If it is not, a valid integer value is stored in *ivalue*. If the file is empty, however, the function **feof()** will acknowledge this, preventing the **while** loop from executing. Also notice that the priming read necessitated a rearrangement of the statements within the **while** loop. If the loop is entered, then *ivalue* contains a valid integer. Had the statements within the loop remained the same as the original program, an immediate second **getw()** function call would be performed. This would overwrite the first integer value. Because of the priming read, the first statement within the **while** loop must be an output statement. This is next followed by a call to **getw()** to get another value.

For example, suppose the **while** loop has been entered nine times. At the end of the ninth iteration, the integer numbers *1* through *8* have been echo printed and *ivalue* has been assigned a *9*. The next iteration of the loop prints the *9* and inputs the *10*. Because *10* is not **EOF**, the loop iterates, causing the *10* to be echo printed and **EOF** to be read. At this point the **while** loop terminates because the function **feof()** sees the end-of-file condition.

> **CAUTION:** *Writing code that is based on the function **feof()** is a peculiarly frustrating programming task because each high-level language tends to treat the end-of-file condition in a different way. Some languages read a piece of data and at the same time look ahead to see the end-of-file; others, like C, do not.*

Formatting Output

C makes it very easy for an application to output neatly printed graphs, reports, or tables. The two main functions that accomplish this formatted output are **printf()** and the file equivalent form, **fprintf()**. These functions can use any of the format specifiers shown in Tables 11-4 and 11-5. The format specification uses the following form:

```
%[flags] [width] [.precision] [h | l | L]type
```

Anything between [ ] is optional. The *type* of the specification is a character or a number that gives a format option. The simplest form can be just a percent sign and a type. For example, *%type* is used to determine if the argument is to be interpreted as a character, a string, or a number. *flags* are used to control the printing of signs, blanks, decimal points, radix of output, and so on. *width* refers to the minimum number of characters to print. *precision* refers to the maximum number of characters that are printed for the output. *h | l | L* are optional prefixes for giving the argument size.

Using printf() and fprintf()

The following example programs define four variable types: character, array-of-characters, integer, and real, and then demonstrate how to use the appropriate format controls on each variable. (The source code has been heavily

TYPE Character	FIELD Type	Format of Output
c	int or wint_t	printf means a single-byte character. wprintf means a wide character.
c	int or wint_t	printf means a wide character. wprintf means a single-byte character.
d	int	Signed decimal integer.
e	double	Signed number of the form [-]*d*.*ddd e* [*sign*]*dddd*. Here *d* is a single decimal digit, *ddd* is one or more decimal digits, *dddd* is exactly four decimal digits, and the sign is a + or -.
E	double	The same as *e*, except E is used in front of an exponent.
f	double	Signed number of the form [-]*ddd*.*ddd*. Here *ddd* is one or more decimal digits. The number of digits after the decimal point depends upon the precision.
g	double	Signed number in *f* or *e* format. The most compact format is used. No trailing zeros. No decimal point if no digits follow it.
G	double	The same as *g* format, except E is used in front of an exponent.
i	int	Signed decimal integer.
n	Pointer to integer	Number of characters written to the stream or buffer. Address of buffer given as integer argument.
o	int	Unsigned octal integer.
p	Pointer to void	Address (given by argument) is printed.

Table 11-4. ***printf()*** *and* ***fprintf()*** *Type Specifiers (Also Applies to* ***scanf()***, ***fscanf()***, *and* ***sscanf()***)*

TYPE Character	FIELD Type	Format of Output
s	String	printf gives a single-byte character string. wprintf gives a wide character string. (print to NULL or max precision)
S	String	printf gives a wide character string. wprintf gives a single-byte character string. (print to NULL or max precision)
u	int	Unsigned decimal integer.
x	int	Unsigned hexadecimal integer.

Table 11-4. *printf()* and *fprintf()* Type Specifiers (Also Applies to *scanf()*, *fscanf()*, and *sscanf()*) (continued)

commented to make associating the output generated with the statement that created it as simple as possible.) The first program formats **char** and string data types:

```
/*
 *    cprintf.c
 *    A C program demonstrating advanced char and string
 *    formatting.
 *    Copyright (c) Chris H. Pappas and William H. Murray, 1996
 */

#include <stdio.h>

void main( void )
{
    char c       =   'A'                                        '
         psz1[]  =   "In making a living today many no ",
         psz2[]  =   "longer leave any room for life."   ;
    int iln      =   0                                          ;

    /* print the c                            */
    printf("\n[%2d] %c",++iln,c);
```

FLAG	FIELD
Flag	**Meaning**
-	Left-align the result.
	(right alignment is the default)
+	Use a leading sign (+ or -) if number is a signed type.
	(sign used with negative number only is the default)
0	When width has 0 prefix, zeros will be added until the minimum width is reached.
	(no padding is the default)
blank (' ')	Output is prefixed with a blank. If positive and signed the blank will be ignored.
	(no appearing blanks is the default)
#	Prefixes nonzero output value with 0, 0x, or 0X.
	(no appearing blank is the default)
.	For e, E, or f formats, a # makes the output value contain a decimal point in all cases.
	(point appears only if digits follow is the default)

Table 11-5.   *printf()* and *fprintf()* Flags

```
/* print the ASCII code for c      */
printf("\n[%2d] %d",++iln,c);

/* print character with ASCII 90   */
printf("\n[%2d] %c",++iln,90);

/* minimum width 1                 */
printf("\n[%2d] %c",++iln,c);

/* minimum width 5, right-justify  */
printf("\n[%2d] %5c",++iln,c);
```

```
    /* minimum width 5, left-justify    */
    printf("\n[%2d] %-5c",++iln,c);

    /* 33 non-null, automatically        */
    printf("\n[%2d] %s",++iln,psz1);

    /* 31 non-null, automatically        */
    printf("\n[%2d] %s",++iln,psz2);

    /* minimum 5 overridden, auto 33    */
    printf("\n[%2d] %5s",++iln,psz1);

    /* minimum width 38, right-justify */
    printf("\n[%2d] %38s",++iln,psz1);

    /* minimum width 38, left-justify    */
    printf("\n[%2d] %-38s",++iln,psz2);

    /* minimum width 19, print all 17    */
    printf("\n[%2d] %19.19s",++iln,psz1);

    /* prints first 2 chars              */
    printf("\n[%2d] %.2s",++iln,psz1);

    /* prints 2 chars, right-justify     */
    printf("\n[%2d] %19.2s",++iln,psz1);

    /* prints 2 chars, left-justify      */
    printf("\n[%2d] %-19.2s",++iln,psz1);

    /* using printf arguments            */
    printf("\n[%2d] %*.*s",++iln,19,6,psz1);
}
```

The output generated by the program looks like this:

```
[ 1] A
[ 2] 65
[ 3] Z
[ 4] A
[ 5]     A
```

```
[ 6] A
[ 7] In making a living today many no
[ 8] longer leave any room for life.
[ 9] In making a living today many no
[10]         In making a living today many no
[11] longer leave any room for life.
[12] In making a living
[13] In
[14]                    In
[15] In
[16]                  In mak
```

The next example formats **int** data:

```c
/*
 *   iprintf.c
 *   A C program demonstrating advanced integer conversions
 *   and formatting.
 *   Copyright (c) Chris H. Pappas and William H. Murray, 1996
 */
#include <stdio.h>

void main( void )
{
  int iln    =   0  ,
      ivalue =   1234;

  /* print ivalue as octal value     */
  printf("\n[%2d] %o",++iln,ivalue);

  /* print lower-case hexadecimal     */
  printf("\n[%2d] %x",++iln,ivalue);

  /* print uppercase hexadecimal      */
  printf("\n[%2d] %X",++iln,ivalue);

  /* default ivalue width, 4          */
  printf("\n[%2d] %d",++iln,ivalue);

  /* printf ivalue with + sign        */
  printf("\n[%2d] %+d",++iln,ivalue);
```

```
   /* minimum 3 overridden, auto 4    */
   printf("\n[%2d] %3d",++iln,ivalue);

   /* minimum width 10, right-justify */
   printf("\n[%2d] %10d",++iln,ivalue);

   /* minimum width 10, left-justify  */
   printf("\n[%2d] %-d",++iln,ivalue);

   /* right justify with leading 0's  */
   printf("\n[%2d] %010d",++iln,ivalue);
}
```

The output from this program looks like this:

```
[ 1] 2322
[ 2] 4d2
[ 3] 4D2
[ 4] 1234
[ 5] +1234
[ 6] 1234
[ 7]       1234
[ 8] 1234
[ 9] 0000001234
```

This last example formats **float** data:

```
/*
 *   fprintf.c
 *   A C program demonstrating advanced float conversions and
 *   formatting.
 *   Copyright (c) Chris H. Pappas and William H. Murray, 1996
 */

#include <stdio.h>

void main( void )
{
   int    iln =   0          ;
```

```
    double dPi =   3.14159265;

    /* using default number of digits  */
    printf("\n[%d] %f",++iln,dPi);

    /* minimum width 20, right-justify */
    printf("\n[%d] %20f",++iln,dPi);

    /* right-justify with leading 0's  */
    printf("\n[%d] %020f",++iln,dPi);

    /* minimum width 20, left-justify  */
    printf("\n[%d] %-20f",++iln,dPi);

    /* width 10, 8 to right of '.'     */
    printf("\n[%2d] %10.8f",++iln,dPi);

    /* width 20, 2 to right-justify    */
    printf("\n[%2d] %20.2f",++iln,dPi);

    /* 4 decimal places, left-justify  */
    printf("\n[%2d] %-20.4f",++iln,dPi);

    /* 4 decimal places, right-justify */
    printf("\n[%2d] %20.4f",++iln,dPi);

    /* width 20, scientific notation   */
    printf("\n[%2d] %20.2e",++iln,dPi);
}
```

You can neatly format your application's output by studying the preceding examples and selecting those combinations that apply to your program's data types.

Formatting Input

Formatted input can be obtained for a C program by using the very versatile functions **scanf()** and **fscanf()**. The main difference between the two functions is that the latter requires that you specifically designate the input file from which the data is to be obtained. Table 11-4 lists all of the possible control string codes that can be used with the functions **scanf()**, **fscanf()**, and **sscanf()**.

Using scanf(), fscanf(), and sscanf()

You can use all three input functions, **scanf()**, **fscanf()**, and **sscanf()**, for extremely sophisticated data input. For example, look at the following statement:

```
scanf( "%2d%5s%4f", &ivalue, psz, &fvalue );
```

The statement inputs only a two-digit integer, a five-character string, and a real number that occupies a maximum of four spaces (2.97, 12.5, and so on). See if you can figure out what this next statement does:

```
scanf( "%*[ \t\n]\"%[^A-Za-z]%[^\"]\"", ps1 ,ps2 );
```

The statement begins by reading and not storing any white space. This is accomplished with the following format specification: "%*[\t\n]". The * symbol instructs the function to obtain the specified data but not to save it in any variable. As long as only a space, tab, or newline is on the input line, **scanf()** will keep reading until it encounters a double quote ("). This is accomplished by the \" format specification, which says the input must match the designated symbol. However, the double quotation mark is not input.

Once **scanf()** has found the double quotation mark, it is instructed to input all characters that are digits into *ps1*. The %[^A-Za-z] format specification accomplishes this with the caret ^ modifier, which says to input anything not an uppercase letter *A* through *Z* or lowercase letter *a* through *z*. Had the caret been omitted, the string would have contained only alphabetic characters. It is the hyphen between the two symbols *A* and *Z* and *a* and *z* that indicates the entire range is to be considered.

The next format specification, %[^\"], instructs the input function to read all remaining characters up to but not including a double quotation mark into *ps2*. The last format specification, \", indicates that the string must match and end with a double quotation mark. You can use the same types of input conversion control with the functions **fscanf()** and **sscanf()**. The only difference between the two functions **scanf()** and **fscanf()** is that the latter requires that an input file be specified. The function **sscanf()** is identical to **scanf()** except that the data is read from an array rather than a file.

The next example shows how you can use **sscanf()** to convert a string (of digits) to an integer. If *ivalue* is of type **int** and *psz* is an array of type **char** that holds a string of digits, then the following statement will convert the string *psz* into type **int** and store it in the variable *ivalue*:

```
sscanf( psz, "%d", &ivalue );
```

Very often, the functions **gets()** and **sscanf()** are used in combination because the function **gets()** reads in an entire line of input and the function **sscanf()** goes into a string and interprets it according to the format specifications. One problem often encountered with **scanf()** occurs when programmers try to use it in conjunction with various other character input functions such as **getc()**, **getch()**, **getchar()**, **gets()**, and so on.

The typical scenario goes like this: **scanf()** is used to input various data types that would otherwise require conversion from characters to something else. Then the programmer tries to use a character input function such as **getch()** and finds that **getch()** does not work as expected. The problem occurs because **scanf()** sometimes does not read all the data that is waiting to be read, and the waiting data can fool other functions (including **scanf()**) into thinking that input has already been entered. To be safe, if you use **scanf()** in a program, don't also use other input functions in the same program. Chapter 12 introduces you to the basics of C++ I/O. Chapters 13 through 16 explain the concepts necessary to do advanced C++ I/O, and Chapter 17 completes the subject of I/O in C++.

Manually Manipulating File Pointers

You can use the functions **fseek()**, **ftell()**, and **rewind()** to determine or change the location of the file position marker. The function **fseek()** resets the file position marker in the file pointed to by *pf* to the number of *ibytes* from the beginning of the file *ifrom = 0*, from the current location of the file position marker *ifrom = 1*, or from the end of the file *ifrom = 2*. C has predefined three constants that also can be used in place of the variable *ifrom*: **SEEK_SET** (offset from beginning-of-file), **SEEK_CUR** (current file marker position), and **SEEK_END** (offset from the end-of-file). The function **fseek()** will return zero if the seek is successful and **EOF** otherwise. The general syntax for the function **fseek()** looks like this:

```
fseek( pf, ibytes, ifrom );
```

The function **ftell()** returns the current location of the file position marker in the file pointed to by *pf*. This location is indicated by an offset, measured in bytes, from the beginning of the file. The syntax for the function *ftell()* looks like this:

```
long_variable = ftell( pf );
```

The value returned by *ftell()* can be used in a subsequent call to *fseek()*. The function **rewind()** simply resets the file position marker in the file pointed to by *pf* to the beginning of the file. The syntax for the function **rewind()** looks like this:

```
rewind( pf );
```

The following C program illustrates the functions **fseek()**, **ftell()**, and **rewind()**:

```c
/*
 *   fseek.c
 *   A C program demonstrating the use of fseek(),
 *   ftell(), and rewind().
 *   Copyright (c) Chris H. Pappas and William H. Murray, 1996
 */

#include <stdio.h>

void main( void )
{
  FILE *pf       ;
  char  c        ;
  long  llocation;

  pf = fopen( "test.dat", "r+t" );

  c = fgetc( pf );
  putchar  (  c );

  c = fgetc( pf );
  putchar  (  c );

  llocation = ftell( pf     );

  c = fgetc( pf );
  putchar  (  c );

  fseek( pf, llocation, 0  );

  c = fgetc( pf );
  putchar  (  c );

  fseek( pf , llocation, 0 );
  fputc( 'E', pf            );

  fseek( pf , llocation, 0 );

  c = fgetc( pf );
  putchar  (  c );
```

```
   rewind   ( pf );

   c = fgetc( pf );
   putchar   ( c );
}
```

The variable *llocation* has been defined to be of type **long**. This is because C supports files larger than 64K. The input file test.dat contains the string *ABCD*. After the program opens the file, the first call to **fgetc()** gets the letter *A* and prints it to the video display. The next statement pair inputs the letter *B* and prints it. When the function **ftell()** is invoked, *llocation* is set equal to the file position marker's current location. This is measured as an offset, in bytes, from the beginning of the file. Because the letter *B* has already been processed, *llocation* contains a 2. This means that the file position marker is pointing to the third character, which is 2 bytes over from the first letter, "*A*". Another I/O pair of statements now reads the letter *C* and prints it to the video display. After the program executes this last statement pair, the file position marker is 3 offset bytes from the beginning of the file, pointing to the fourth character, *D*.

At this point in the program, the function **fseek()** is invoked. It is instructed to move location offset bytes (or 2 offset bytes) from the beginning of the file (because the third parameter to the function **fseek()** is 0, as defined earlier). This repositions the file position marker to the third character in the file. The variable *c* is again assigned the letter *C*, and it is printed a second time. The second time the function **fseek()** is invoked, it uses parameters identical to the first invocation. The function **fseek()** moves the pointer to the third character, *C* (2 offset bytes into the file). However, the statement that follows doesn't input the *C* a third time but instead writes over it with a new letter, *E*. Because the file position marker has now moved past this new *E*, to verify that the letter was indeed placed in the file the function **fseek()** is invoked still another time.

The nest statement pair inputs the new *E* and prints it to the video display. With this accomplished, the program invokes the function **rewind()**, which moves the *pf* back to the beginning of the file. When the function **fgetc()** is then invoked, it returns the letter *A* and prints it to the file. The output from the program looks like this:

ABCCEA

You can use the same principles illustrated in this simple character example to create a random-access file of records.

Suppose you have the following information recorded for a file of individuals: social security number, name, and address. Suppose also that you are allowing 11 characters for the social security number, in the form *ddd-dd-dddd*, with the name and address being given an additional 60 characters (or bytes). So far, each record would be 11 + 60 bytes long, or 71 bytes.

All of the possible contiguous record locations on a random-access disk file may not be full; the personnel record needs to contain a flag indicating whether or not that disk record location has been used or not. This requires adding one more byte to the personnel record, bringing the total for one person's record to 72 bytes, plus 2 additional bytes to represent the record number, for a grand total record byte count of 74 bytes. One record could look like the following:

```
1 U111-22-3333Linda Lossannie, 521 Alan Street, Anywhere, USA
```

Record 1 in the file would occupy bytes 0 through 73; record 2 would occupy bytes 74 through 147; record 3, 148 through 221; and so on. If you use the record number in conjunction with the **fseek()** function, any record location can be located on the disk. For example, to find the beginning of record 2, use the following statements:

```
loffset = ( iwhich_record - 1 ) * sizeof( stA_PERSON );
fseek    ( pfi, loffset, 0   )                             ;
```

Once the file position marker has been moved to the beginning of the selected record, the information at that location can either be read or written by using various I/O functions such as **fread()** and **fwrite()**. With the exception of the comment block delimiter symbols /* and */ and the header stdio.h, the program just discussed would work the same in C++. Just substitute the symbol // for both /* and */ and change stdio.h to iostream.h.

Using the Integrated Debugger

Try entering this next program and printing out the value stored in the variable *stcurrent_person.irecordnum* after you have asked to search for the 25th record:

```
/*
 *    random.c
 *    A C random-access file program using fseek(), fread(),
 *    and fwrite().
 *    Copyright (c) Chris H. Pappas and William H. Murray, 1996
 */

#include <stdio.h>
#include <string.h>

#define iFIRST      1
#define iLAST       50
#define iSS_SIZE    11
```

```
    #define iDATA_SIZE   60
    #define cVACANT       'V'
    #define cUSED         'U'

    typedef struct strecord          {
      int   irecordnum               ;
      char cavailable                ,    /* V free, U used */
           csoc_sec_num[ iSS_SIZE   ],
           cdata        [ iDATA_SIZE ];
    } stA_PERSON;

    void main( void )
    {
      FILE        *pfi                                           ;
      stA_PERSON  stcurrent_person                               ;
      int         i, iwhich_record                               ;
      long int    loffset                                        ;

      pfi = fopen( "A:\\sample.fil", "r+"                   );

      for( i = iFIRST; i <= iLAST; i++ )                       {
        stcurrent_person.cavailable = cVACANT                   ;
        stcurrent_person.irecordnum = i                         ;
        fwrite( &stcurrent_person,sizeof(stA_PERSON), 1, pfi   );
      }

      printf( "Please enter the record you would like to find." );
      printf( "\nYour response must be between 1 and 50: "      );
      scanf ( "%d", &iwhich_record                             );

      loffset = (iwhich_record - 1) * sizeof(stA_PERSON         );
      fseek ( pfi,loffset,0                                    );
      fread ( &stcurrent_person,sizeof(stA_PERSON), 1, pfi     );

      fclose( pfi                                              );
    }
```

The **typedef** has defined *stA_PERSON* as a structure that has a 2-byte *irecordnum*, a 1-byte *cavailable* character code, an 11-byte character array to hold a *csoc_sec_num* number, and a 60-byte *cdata* field. This brings the total structure's size to 2 + 1 + 11 + 60, or 74 bytes. Once the program has opened the file in read-and-update text mode, it creates and stores 50 records, each with its own unique *irecordnum* and all initialized to *cVACANT*.

The **fwrite()** statement wants the address of the structure to output, the size in bytes of what it is outputting, how many to output, and which file to send it to. With this accomplished, the program next asks the user which record he or she would like to search for. Finding the record is accomplished in two steps. First, an offset address from the beginning of the file must be calculated. For example, record 1 is stored in bytes 0 to 73, record 2 is stored in bytes 74 to 148, and so on. By subtracting 1 from the record number entered by the user, the program multiplies this value by the number of bytes occupied by each structure and calculates the *loffset*.

For example, finding record 2 is accomplished with the following calculation: (2-1) x 74. This gives the second record a starting byte offset of 74. Using this calculated value, the **fseek()** function is then invoked and moves the file position marker *loffset* bytes into the file. As you are tracing through the program asking to view records 1 through 10, all seems fine. However, when you ask to view the 11th record, what happens? You get garbage.

The reason for this is that the program opened the file in text mode. Records 1 through 9 are all exactly 74 bytes, but records 10 and up take 75 bytes. Therefore, the 10th record starts at the appropriate *loffset* calculation but it goes 1 byte further into the file. Therefore, the 11th record is at the address arrived at by using the following modified calculation:

```
loffset = ( (iwhich_record - 1) * sizeof(stA_PERSON) ) + 1;
```

However, this calculation won't work with the first nine records. The solution is to open the file in binary mode:

```
pfi = fopen( "A:\\sample.fil", "r+b" );
```

In character mode, the program tries to interpret any two-digit number as two single characters, increasing records with two-digit *record_numbers* by 1 byte. In binary mode, the integer *record_number* is interpreted properly. Exercise care when deciding how to open a file for I/O.

In the Next Chapter...

In this chapter you learned about advanced C input and output capabilities. In Chapter 12 you will learn how to perform similar operations in C++ that will be expanded upon in Chapters 13 and 14 as you move on to object-oriented I/O in C++.

Chapter Twelve

An Introduction to I/O in C++

This chapter is a brief introduction to C++ I/O. The topic of advanced C++ input and output is continued in Chapter 17. The division of the topic is necessary because of the diverse I/O capabilities available to C++ programmers. Chapters 15 and 16 teach the fundamentals of object-oriented programming. Once you understand how objects are created, it will be much easier to understand advanced object-oriented C++ I/O. Chapter 17 looks at C++'s ability to effortlessly manipulate objects.

Streamlining I/O with C++

In many cases, the C++ equivalent of a C program streamlines how the program inputs and outputs data. For example, C++ does not require the use of format string arguments with **cin** or **cout**. However, this is not always true. Very often advanced I/O formatting in C++ requires more statements than the C equivalents. The software supplied with the Borland C++ compiler includes a standard library that contains functions commonly used by the C++ community. The standard I/O library for C, described by the header file stdio.h, is still available in C++. However, C++ introduces its own header file, called iostream.h, which implements its own collection of I/O functions.

The C++ stream I/O is described as a set of classes in iostream.h. These classes overload the "put to" and "get from" operators, << and >>. To better understand why the stream library in C++ is more convenient than its C counterpart, let's first review how C handles input and output.

First, recall that C has no built-in input or output statements; functions such as **printf()** are part of the standard library but not part of the language itself. Similarly, C++ has no built-in I/O facilities. The absence of built-in I/O gives you greater flexibility to produce the most efficient user interface for the data pattern of the application at hand.

The problem with the C solution to input and output lies with its implementation of these I/O functions. There is little consistency among I/O functions in terms of return values and parameter sequences. Because of this, programmers tend to rely on the formatted I/O functions **printf()**, **scanf()**, and so on—especially when the objects being manipulated are numbers or other noncharacter values. These formatted I/O functions are convenient and, for the most part, share a consistent interface, but they are also big and unwieldy because they must manipulate many kinds of values.

In C++, the class provides modular solutions to your data manipulation needs. The standard C++ library provides three I/O classes as an alternative to C's general-purpose I/O functions. These classes contain definitions for the same pair of operators—<< (insertion or put to) and >> (extraction or get from)—that are optimized for all kinds of data. (Chapter 16 discusses classes.)

cin Is To stdin As cout Is To stdout

The C++ stream counterparts to **stdin**, **stdout**, and **stderr**, prototyped in stdio.h, are **cin**, **cout**, and **cerr**, which are prototyped in iostream.h. These three streams are opened automatically when your program begins execution and become the interface between the program and the user. The **cin** stream is associated with the terminal keyboard. The **cout** and **cerr** streams are associated with the video display.

>> Is To scanf() As << Is To printf()

One of the major enhancements that C++ added to C was *operator overloading*. Operator overloading allows the compiler to determine which like-named function or operator is to be executed based on the associated variables' data types. The extraction >> ("get from") and insertion << ("put to") operators are good examples of this new C++ capability. Each operator has been overloaded so it can handle all of the standard C++ data types, including classes. Input and output in C++ have been significantly enhanced and streamlined by these overloaded stream library operators. The following two code segments illustrate the greater ease of use for basic I/O operations in C++. First, take a quick look at a C output statement using **printf()**:

```
printf( "Char Value    : %c, String     : %s   ,
         Integer value: %d, Float value: %f"  ,
         cvalue, svalue, ivalue, fvalue      );
```

Here is the C++ equivalent:

```
cout <<    "Char value   : " << cvalue
     << ", String value : " << svalue
     << ", Integer value: " << ivalue
     << ", Float value   : " << fvalue;
```

The C++ equivalent will reveal how the insertion operator has been overloaded to handle the four separate data types: char, string, integer, and float. If you are like many C programmers, you are not going to miss having to hunt down the *%type* symbols needed for your **printf()** and **scanf()** format specifications. As a result of operator overloading, the insertion operator will examine the data type you have passed to it and determine an appropriate format. An identical situation exists with the extraction operator, which performs data input. Look at the following C example:

```
scanf( "%c%S%d%f", &cvalue, svalue, &ivalue, &fvalue );
```

and its equivalent C++ counterpart:

```
cin >> cvalue >> svalue >> ivalue >> fvalue;
```

You no longer need to precede your input variables with the **&** address operator, or in the case of string data (*svalue*), to remember *not* to use the address operator. In C++, the extraction operator takes care of calculating the storage variable's address, storage requirements, and formatting. Having looked at two examples of the C++ operators << and >>, you might be slightly confused as to why they are named the way they are.

The simplest way to remember which operator performs output and which performs input is to think of these two operators as they relate to the stream I/O files. When you want to input information, you extract it >> from the input stream, **cin**, and put the information into a variable—for example, >> *cvalue*. To output information, you take a copy of the information from the variable *ivalue* and insert it << into the output stream: **cout <<**.

C++ will allow a program to expand upon the insertion and extraction operators using the syntax for operator overloading. The following code segment illustrates how the insertion operator can be overloaded to print the new type **stclient**:

```
ostream& operator << ( ostream& osout, stclient staclient )
{
  osout << "Name    : " << staclient.pszname    ;
  osout << "Address: " << staclient.pszaddress;
  osout << "Phone   : " << staclient.pszphone   ;
}
```

As a direct result of this new definition for the insertion operator, and assuming the structure variable *staclient* has been initialized, printing the information becomes a simple one-line statement!

```
cout << staclient;
```

Not only does this make structure output a straightforward process, but the insertion and extraction operators have an additional advantage—their final code size. The general-purpose I/O functions **printf()** and **scanf()** carry along code segments into the final executable version of a program that are often unused. In C, even if you are dealing only with integer data, you still pull along all of the conversion code for the additional standard data types. In contrast, the C++ compiler incorporates only those routines actually needed. The following program demonstrates how to use the input, or extraction, operator >> to read different types of data:

```
//
//   insert.cpp
//   A C++ program demonstrating how to use the
```

```
//   extraction >> operator to input a char,
//   string, integer, float, and double.
//   Copyright (c) Chris H. Pappas and William H. Murray, 1996
//

#include <iostream.h>

#define INUMCHARS 45
#define INULL_CHAR 1

void main( void )
{
  char    canswer                                              ;
  int     ivalue                                               ;
  float   fvalue                                               ;
  double  dvalue                                               ;
  char    svalue[ INUMCHARS + INULL_CHAR ]                     ;

  cout << "This program allows you to enter various data types.";
  cout << "Would you like to try it? << "\n\n"                 ;
  cout << "Please type a Y for yes and an N for no: "          ;

  cin  >>  canswer                                             ;

  if( canswer == 'Y' )                                         {

    cout << "\nEnter your first name: "                        ;
    cin  >>   svalue                                           ;
    cout << "\n\n"                                             ;

    cout << "Enter an integer value : "                        ;
    cin  >>  ivalue                                            ;
    cout << "\n\n"                                             ;

    cout << "Enter a float value    : "                        ;
    cin  >>  fvalue                                            ;
    cout << "\n\n"                                             ;

    cout << "Enter a double value   : "                        ;
    cin  >>  dvalue                                            ;
  }
}
```

In this example, the insertion operator << is used in its simplest form to output literal string prompts. Notice that the program uses four different data types and yet each input statement, **cin** >>, looks identical except for the variable's name. For those of you who are fast typists but are tired of trying to find the infrequently used %, ", and & symbols (required by **scanf()**), you can give your fingers and eyes a rest. The C++ extraction operator makes code entry much simpler and less error prone.

There is one more fact you need to know when inputting string information. The extraction operator >> is written to stop reading in information as soon as it encounters white space. White space can be a blank, tab, or newline. Therefore, when *svalue* is printed, only the first name entered is output. You can solve this problem by rewriting the program and using the **cin.get()** function:

```
cout << "\nEnter your first and last name: " ;
cin.get( svalue, INUMCHARS )                  ;
cout << "Thank you, " << svalue               ;
```

The output from the program now looks like this:

```
Enter your first and last name: Tammy Williams
Thank you, Tammy Williams
```

The **cin.get()** function has two additional parameters. Only one of these, the number of characters to input, was used in the previous example. The function **cin.get()** will read everything, including white space, until the maximum number of characters specified has been read in, or up to the next newline, whichever comes first. The optional third parameter, not shown, identifies a terminating symbol. For example, the following line would read into *svalue*, INUMCHARS characters, all of the characters up to but not including a * symbol, or a newline, whichever comes first.

```
cin.get( svalue, INUMCHARS, "*" );
```

This next example demonstrates how to use the output, or insertion, operator << in its various forms:

```
//
//  extract.cpp
//  A C++ program demonstrating how to use the
//  insertion << operator to input a char,
//  integer, float, double, and string.
//  Copyright (c) Chris H. Pappas and William H. Murray, 1996
```

```
//

#include <iostream.h>

void main( void )
{
  char    c          = 'A'                                ;
  int     ivalue     =  10                                ;
  float   fvalue     =  45.67                             ;
  double  dvalue     =  2.3e32                            ;
  char    svalue[ ] = "For all have..."                  ;

  cout << "Once upon a time there were "                 ;
  cout << ivalue << " people. " << endl                  ;

  cout << "Some of them earned " <<   fvalue             ;
  cout << " dollars per hour."    << "\n"                ;

  cout << "While others earned " << dvalue << " per year!"  ;
  cout << "\n\n" << "But you know what they say: "       ;

  cout << svalue << "\n\n"                                ;
  cout << "So, none of them get an "                     ;
  cout << c                                              ;
  cout << "!"                                            ;
}
```

The output from the program looks like this:

```
Once upon a time there were 10 people.
Some of them earned 45.67 dollars per hour.
While others earned 2.3e+32 per year!

But you know what they say: "For all have..."

So, none of them get an A!
```

When comparing the C++ source code with the output from the program, one thing you should immediately notice is that the insertion operator << does not automatically generate a newline. You still have complete control over when this occurs by including the newline symbol \n or **endl** when necessary.

endl is very useful for outputting data in an interactive program because it not only inserts a newline into the stream but also flushes the output buffer. You can also use **flush**; however, this does not insert a newline. Also notice that although the insertion operator very nicely handles the formatting of integers and floats, it isn't very helpful with doubles.

From stream.h to iostream.h

One of the most exciting enhancements to the compiler is the new C++ I/O library, referred to as the **iostream** library. By not including input/output facilities within the C++ language itself, but rather implementing them in C++ and providing them as a component of a C++ standard library, I/O can evolve as needed. At its lowest level, C++ interprets a file as a sequence, or stream, of bytes. At this level, the concept of a data type is missing. The I/O library aids in the transfer of these bytes.

From the user's perspective, however, a file is composed of a series of intermixed alphanumerics, numeric values, or, possibly, class objects. A second component of the I/O library takes care of the interface between these two viewpoints. The **iostream** library predefines a set of operations for handling reading and writing of the built-in data types. The library also provides for user-definable extensions to handle class types.

Basic input operations are supported by the **istream** class and basic output via the **ostream** class. Bidirectional I/O is supported via the **iostream** class, which is derived from both **istream** and **ostream**. There are four stream objects predefined for the user:

- **cin**   An **istream** class object linked to standard input.
- **cout**   An **ostream** class object linked to standard output.
- **cerr**   An unbuffered output **ostream** 0class object linked to standard error.
- **clog**   A buffered output **ostream** 0class object linked to standard error.

Any program using the **iostream** library must include the header file iostream.h. Because iostream.h treats stream.h as an alias, programs written using stream.h may or may not need alterations, depending on the particular structures used. You can also use the new I/O library to perform input and output operations on files. You can tie a file to your program by defining an instance of one of the following three class types:

- **fstream**   Derived from **iostream**, this links a file to your application for both input and output.
- **ifstream**   Derived from **istream**, this links a file to your application for input only.
- **ofstream**   Derived from **ostream**, this links a file to your application for output only.

Operators and Member Functions

The >> extraction operator and the << insertion operator have been modified to accept arguments of any of the built-in data types, including **char** *. They also can be extended to accept class argument types. Each **iostream** library class object maintains a format state that controls the details of formatting operations, such as the conversion base for integral numeric notation or the precision of a floating-point value. You can manipulate the format state flags by using the **setf()** and **unsetf()** functions. The **setf()** member function sets a specified format state flag. There are two overloaded instances:

```
setf( long       );
setf( long,long );
```

The first argument can be either a format bit flag or a format bit-field. Table 12-1 lists the format flags you can use with the **setf(long)** instance (using just the format flag).

Table 12-2 lists some of the format bit-fields you can use with the **setf(long,long)** instance (using a format flag and format bit-field).

There are certain predefined defaults. For example, integers are written and read in decimal notation. You can change the base to octal, hexadecimal, or back to decimal. By default, a floating-point value is output with six digits of precision. You can modify

Format Flag	Meaning
ios::showbase	display numeric base
ios::showpoint	display decimal point
ios::dec	decimal numeric base
ios::hex	hexadecimal numeric base
ios::oct	octal numeric base
ios::fixed	decimal notation
ios::scientific	scientific notation

Table 12-1. *Format Flags*

Bit-Field	Meaning	Flags
ios::basefield	Integral base	ios::hex,
		ios::oct,
		ios::dec
ios::floatfield	Floating-point	ios::fixed,
		ios::scientific

Table 12-2. *Format Bit-Fields*

this by using the precision member function. The following C++ program uses these new member functions:

```
//
//   numeric.cpp
//   A C++ program demonstrating advanced conversions and
//   formatting member functions.
//   Copyright (c) Chris H. Pappas and William H. Murray, 1996
//

#include <string.h>
#include <strstrea.h>

#define INULL_TERMINATOR 1

void row ( void );

void main( void )
{
  int    iln    =   0            ,
         ivalue =   1234         ;
  double dPi    =   3.14159265;

  // print ivalue as octal value
  row(); // [ 1]
  cout << oct << ivalue;

  // print lower-case hexadecimal
```

```
row(); // [ 2]
cout << hex << ivalue;

// print upper-case hexadecimal
row(); // [ 3] cout.setf( ios::uppercase );
cout << hex << ivalue;
cout.unsetf( ios::uppercase );   // turn uppercase off
cout << dec;                     // return to decimal base

// default ivalue width
row(); // [ 4]
cout << ivalue;

// printf ivalue with + sign
row(); // [ 5]
cout.setf( ios::showpos );       // don't want row number with +
cout << ivalue;
cout.unsetf( ios::showpos );

// minimum 3 overridden, auto
row(); // [ 6]
cout.width( 3 ); // don't want row number padded to width of 3
cout << ivalue;

// minimum width 10, right-justify
row(); // [ 7]
cout.width( 10 );    // only in effect for first value printed
cout << ivalue;

// minimum width 10, left-justify
row(); // [ 8]
cout.width( 10 );
cout.setf( ios::left );
cout << ivalue;
cout.unsetf( ios::left );

// right-justify with leading 0's
row(); // [ 9]
cout.width( 10 );
cout.fill( '0' );
cout << ivalue;
```

```
cout.fill( ' ' );

// using default number of digits
row(); // [10]
cout << dPi;

// minimum width 20, right-justify
row(); // [11]
cout.width( 20 );
cout << dPi;

// right-justify with leading 0's
row(); // [12]
cout.width( 20 );
cout.fill( '0' );
cout << dPi;
cout.fill(' ');

// minimum width 20, left-justify
row(); // [13]
cout.width( 20 );
cout.setf( ios::left );
cout << dPi;

// left-justify with trailing 0's
row(); // [14]
cout.width( 20 );
cout.fill('0');
cout << dPi;
cout.unsetf( ios::left );
cout.fill(' ');

// width 10, 8 to right of '.'
row(); // [15]
cout.precision( 9 );
cout << dPi;

// width 20, 2 to right-justify
row(); // [16]
cout.width( 20 );
cout.precision( 2 );
```

```
   cout << dPi;

   // 4 decimal places, left-justify
   row(); // [17]
   cout.precision( 4 );
   cout << dPi;

   // 4 decimal places, right-justify
   row(); // [18]
   cout.width( 20 );
   cout << dPi;

   // width 20, scientific notation
   row(); // [19] cout.setf( ios::scientific );
   cout.width( 20 );
   cout << dPi; cout.unsetf( ios::scientific );
}

void row ( void )
{
   static int ln = 0    ;

   cout << "\n["        ;
   cout.width( 2 )      ;
   cout << ++ln << "] " ;
}
```

You can use the output from the program to help write advanced output statements of your own:

```
[ 1] 2322
[ 2] 4d2
[ 3] 4d2
[ 4] 1234
[ 5] +1234
[ 6] 1234
[ 7]         1234
[ 8] 1234
[ 9] 0000001234
[10] 3.14159
[11]                   3.14159
```

```
[12]  00000000000003.14159
[13]  3.14159
[14]  3.141590000000000000
[15]  3.14159265
[16]                       3.1
[17]  3.142
[18]                      3.142
[19]  3.142
```

This next program demonstrates character and string formatting:

```cpp
//
//  chrstrng.cpp
//  A C++ program demonstrating advanced conversions and
//  formatting member functions.
//  Copyright (c) Chris H. Pappas and William H. Murray, 1996
//

#include <string.h>
#include <strstrea.h>

#define INULL_TERMINATOR 1

void row ( void );

void main( void )
{
  char c        =   'A'                                        ,
       psz1[]   =   "In making a living today many no "  ,
       psz2[]   =   "longer leave any room for life."    ;

  char psz_padstring5 [  5 + INULL_TERMINATOR ]              ,
       psz_padstring38[ 38 + INULL_TERMINATOR ]              ;

  // print the c
  // Notice that << has been overloaded to output char
  row(); // [ 1]
  cout << c;

  // print the ASCII code for c
  row(); // [ 2]
```

```
cout << (int)c;

// print character with ASCII 90
row(); // [ 3]
cout << (char)90;

// minimum width 1
row(); // [ 4]
cout << c;

// minimum width 5, right-justify
row(); // [ 5]
ostrstream( psz_padstring5, sizeof(psz_padstring5) )
     << "     " << c << ends;
cout << psz_padstring5;

// minimum width 5, left-justify
row(); // [ 6]
ostrstream( psz_padstring5, sizeof(psz_padstring5) )
     << c << "     " << ends;
cout << psz_padstring5;

// 33 automatically
row(); // [ 8]
cout << psz1;

// 31 automatically
row(); // [ 9]
cout << psz2;

// minimum 5 overriden, auto
// notice that the width of 5 cannot be overridden!
row(); // [10]
cout.write( psz1, 5 );

// minimum width 38, right-justify
// notice how the width of 38 ends with garbage data
row(); // [11]
cout.write( psz1, 38 );

// the following is the correct approach
```

```
  cout << "\n\nCorrected approach:\n";
  ostrstream( psz_padstring38, sizeof(psz_padstring38) )
        << "       " << psz1 << ends;
  row(); // [12]
  cout << psz_padstring38;

  // minimum width 38, left-justify
  ostrstream( psz_padstring38, sizeof(psz_padstring38) )
        << psz2 << "        " << ends;
  row(); // [13]
  cout << psz_padstring38;

  // minimum width 19, print all 17
  row(); // [14]
  cout << psz1;

  // prints first 2 chars
  row(); // [15]
  cout.write( psz1, 2 );

  // prints 2 chars, right-justify
  row(); // [16]
  cout << "               ";
  cout.write( psz1, 2 );

  // prints 2 chars, left-justify
  row(); // [17]
  cout.write( psz1, 2 );

  // using printf arguments
  row(); // [18]
  cout << "             ";
  cout.write( psz1, 6 );
}

void row (void)
{
  static int ln = 0    ;

  cout << "\n["          ;
```

```
    cout.width( 2 )         ;
    cout << ++ln << "] " ;
}
```

The output from this program looks like this:

```
[ 1] A
[ 2] 65
[ 3] Z
[ 4] A
[ 5]     A
[ 6] A
[ 7] In making a living today many no
[ 8] longer leave any room for life.
[ 9] In ma
[10] In making a living today many no . . .(b

Corrected approach:

[11]      In making a living today many no
[12] longer leave any room for life.
[13] In making a living today many no
[14] In
[15]                    In
[16] In
[17]            In mak
```

The following section highlights those output statements used in the preceding program that need special clarification. One point needs to be made: iostream.h is automatically included by strstream.h, which is needed to perform string output formatting. If your application needs to output numeric data or simple character and string output, you will need to include only iostream.h.

C++ Character Output

In the new I/O library (since Release 2.0), the insertion operator << has been overloaded to handle character data. With the earlier release, the following statement would have output the ASCII value of *c*:

```
cout << c;
```

In the current I/O library, the letter itself is output. For those programs needing the ASCII value, a cast is required:

```
cout << (int)c;
```

C++ Base Conversions

There are two approaches to outputting a value using a different base:

```
cout << hex << ivalue                    ;
```

and

```
cout.setf( ios::hex, ios::basefield );
cout <<    ivalue                        ;
```

Both approaches cause the base to be permanently changed from the statement forward (not always the effect you want). Each value output will now be formatted as a hexadecimal value. Returning to some other base is accomplished with the **unsetf()** function:

```
cout.unsetf( ios::hex,ios::basefield );
```

If you are interested in uppercase hexadecimal output, use the following statement:

```
cout.setf  ( ios::uppercase          );
```

When it is no longer needed, you will have to turn this option off:

```
cout.unsetf( ios::uppercase          );
```

C++ String Formatting

Printing an entire string is easy in C++. One approach to string formatting is to declare an array of characters and then select the desired output format, printing the string buffer:

```
pszpadstring38[ 38 + INULL_TERMINATOR ];
   .
   .
```

```
.
ostrstream( pszpadstring38, sizeof(pszpadstring38) )
    << "        "   << psz1;
```

The **ostrstream** member function is part of strstream.h and has three parameters: a pointer to an array of characters, the size of the array, and the information to be inserted. This statement appends leading blanks to right justify *psz1*. Portions of the string can be output using the write form of **cout**:

```
cout.write( psz1, 5 );
```

This statement will output the first five characters of *psz1*.

C++ Numeric Formatting

You can easily format numeric data with right- or left-justification, varying precisions, varying formats (floating-point or scientific), leading or trailing fill patterns, and signs. There are certain defaults. For example, the default for justification is right and for floating-point precision is six. The following code segment outputs *dPi* left-justified in a field width of 20, with trailing zeros:

```
cout.width( 20          );
cout.setf ( ios::left );
cout.fill ( '0'         );
cout <<     dPi         ;
```

Had the following statement been included, *dPi* would have been printed with a precision of two:

```
cout.precision( 2 );
```

With many of the output flags such as left-justification, selecting uppercase hexadecimal output, base changes, and many others, it is necessary to unset these flags when they are no longer needed. The following statement turns left-justification off:

```
cout.unsetf( ios::left      );
```

Selecting scientific format is a matter of flipping the correct bit flag:

```
cout.setf  ( ios::scientific );
```

You can print values with a leading + sign by setting the **showpos** flag:

```
cout.setf  ( ios::showpos    );
```

There are many minor details of the current I/O library functions that will initially cause some confusion. This has to do with the fact that certain operations, once executed, make a permanent change until turned off, while others take effect only for the next output statement. For example, an output width change, as in *cout.width(20);*, affects only the next value printed. That is why the function *row()* has to repeatedly change the width to get the output row numbers formatted within two spaces, as in [1]. However, other formatting operations like base changes, uppercase, precision, and floating-point/scientific remain active until specifically turned off.

C++ File Input and Output

All of the examples so far have used the predefined streams **cin** and **cout**. It is possible that your program will need to create its own streams for I/O. If an application needs to create a file for input or output, it must include the fstream.h header file (fstream.h includes iostream.h). The classes **ifstream** and **ofstream** are derived from **istream** and **ostream** and inherit the extraction and insertion operations, respectively. The following C++ program demonstrates how to declare a file for reading and writing using **ifstream** and **ofstream**, respectively:

```
//
//   ifofstrm.cpp
//   A C++ program demonstrating how to declare an
//   ifstream and ofstream for file input and output.
//   Copyright (c) Chris H. Pappas and William H. Murray, 1996
//

#include <fstream.h>

void main( void )
{
  char c                                              ;

  ifstream ifsin( "a:\\text.in",ios::in )             ;
  if( !ifsin )
    cerr << "\nUnable to open 'text.in' for input."   ;
```

```
    ofstream ofsout( "a:\\text.out",ios::out )              ;
    if( !ofsout )
      cerr << "\nUnable to open 'text.out' for output." ;

    while( ofsout && ifsin.get(c) )
      ofsout.put( c )                                        ;

    ifsin.close (    )                                       ;
    ofsout.close(    )                                       ;
}
```

The program declares *ifsin* to be of class **ifstream** and is associated with the file *text.in* stored in the A drive. It is always a good idea for any program dealing with files to verify the existence or creation of the specified file in the designated mode. By using the handle to the file *ifsin*, a simple **if** test can be generated to check the condition of the file. A similar process is applied to *ofsout*, except the file is derived from the **ostream** class. The **while** loop continues inputting and outputting single characters while the *ifsin* exists and the character read in is not **EOF**. The program terminates by closing the two files. Closing an output file can be essential to dumping all internally buffered data.

There may be circumstances when a program will want to delay a file specification or when an application may want to associate several file streams with the same file descriptor. The following code segment demonstrates this concept:

```
ifstream ifsin             ;
.
.
.
ifsin.open ( "week1.in" );
.
.
.
ifsin.close(             );
ifsin.open ( "week2.in" );
.
.
.
ifsin.close(             );
```

Whenever an application wishes to modify the way in which a file is opened or used, it can apply a second argument to the file stream constructors. For example:

```
ofstream ofsout( "week1.out", ios::app|ios::noreplace );
```

This statement declares *ofsout* and attempts to append it to the file named *week1.out*. Because **ios::noreplace** is specified, the file will not be created if *week1.out* doesn't already exist. The **ios::app** parameter appends all writes to an existing file. Table 12-3 lists the second argument flags to the file stream constructors that can be logically ORed together.

An **fstream** class object also can be used to open a file for both input and output. For example, the following definition opens the file *update.dat* in both input and append mode:

```
fstream io( "update.dat", ios::in|ios::app );
```

You can reposition all **iostream** class types by using either the **seekg()** or **seekp()** member function, which can move to an absolute address within the file or move a byte offset from a particular position. Both **seekg()** (sets or reads the get pointer's position) and **seekp()** (sets or reads the put pointer's position) can take one or two arguments. When used with one parameter, the **iostream** is repositioned to the specified pointer position. When it is used with two parameters, a relative position is calculated. The following listing highlights these differences, assuming the preceding declaration for **io**:

Mode Bit	Action
ios::in	Opens for reading
ios::out	Opens for writing
ios::ate	Seeks to EOF after file is created
ios::app	All writes added to end of file
ios::trunc	If file already exists, truncates
ios::nocreate	Unsuccessful open if file does not exist
ios::noreplace	Unsuccessful open if file does exist
ios::binary	Opens file in binary mode (default text)

Table 12-3.   *File Stream Constructor Flags*

```
streampos current_position = io.tellp( );
io << obj1 << obj2 << obj3            ;
io.seekp( current_position           );
io.seekp( sizeof(MY_OBJ), ios::cur   );
io << objnewobj2                     ;
```

The pointer *current_position* is first derived from *streampos* and initialized to the current position of the put-file pointer by the function **tellp()**. With this information stored, three objects are written to **io**. Using **seekp()**, the put-file pointer is repositioned to the beginning of the file. The second **seekp()** statement uses the **sizeof()** operator to calculate the number of bytes necessary to move one object's width into the file. This effectively skips over *obj1*'s position, permitting a new *obj2* to be written. If a second argument is passed to **seekg()** or **seekp()**, it defines the direction to move: **ios::beg** (from the beginning), **ios::cur** (from the current position), and **ios::end** (from the end of the file). For example, this line will move into the *get_file* pointer file 5 bytes from the current position:

```
io.seekg( 5, ios::cur  );
```

The next line will move the *get_file* pointer 7 bytes backward from the end of the file:

```
io.seekg( -7, ios::end );
```

C++ File Condition States

Associated with every stream is an error state. When an error occurs, bits are set in the state according to the general category of the error. By convention, inserters ignore attempts to insert things into an **ostream** with error bits set, and such attempts do not change the stream's state. The **iostream** library object contains a set of predefined condition flags which monitor the ongoing state of the stream. Table 12-4 lists the six member functions that can be invoked.

You can use these member functions in various algorithms to solve unique I/O conditions and to make the code more readable:

```
ifstream pfsinfile( "sample.dat", ios::in );
if( pfsinfile.eof( ) )
    pfsinfile.clear( ); // sets the state of pfsinfile to 0

if( pfsinfile.fail( ) )
    cerr << ">>> sample.dat creation error <<<";
```

Member Function	Action
eof()	Returns a nonzero value on end-of-file
fail()	Returns a nonzero value if an operation failed
bad()	Returns a nonzero value if an error occurred
good()	Returns a nonzero value if no state bits are set
rdstate()	Returns the current stream state
clear()	Sets the stream state (int=0)

Table 12-4. *Stream State Functions*

```
if( pfsinfile.good( ) )
    cin >> my_object   ;

if( !pfsinfile ) // shortcut
    cout << ">>> sample.dat creation error <<<";
```

In the Next Chapter...

This chapter has served as an introduction to C++ I/O concepts. To really understand various formatting capabilities, you'll need to learn about C++ classes and various overloading techniques. Chapters 13 and 14 teach object-oriented programming concepts. After you've received this information, you'll be introduced to additional C++ I/O techniques in Chapter 15.

Chapter Thirteen

Structures, Unions, and Miscellaneous Items

In this chapter you will investigate several advanced C and C++ types, such as structures, unions, and bit-fields, along with other miscellaneous topics. You will learn how to create and use structures in programs. The chapter also covers how to pass structure information to functions, use pointers with structures, create and use unions in programs, and use other important features, such as **typedef** and enumerated type **enum**.

The main portion of the chapter concentrates on two important features common to C and C++, the structure and the union. The C or C++ *structure* is conceptually an array or vector of closely related items. Unlike an array or vector, however, a structure permits the contained items to be of assorted data types. The structure is very important to C and C++. Structures serve as the flagship of a more advanced C++ type called the class. If you become comfortable with structures, it will be much easier for you to understand C++ classes, because classes share and expand upon many of the features of a structure. Chapters 16 and 18 are devoted to the C++ class.

Unions, another advanced type, allow you to store different data types at the same place in your system's memory. These advanced data types serve as the foundation of most spreadsheet and database programs. In the section that follows, you learn how to build simple structures, create arrays of structures, pass structures and arrays of structures to functions, and access structure elements with pointers.

C and C++ Structures

The notion of a data structure is a very familiar idea in everyday life. A card file containing friends' addresses, telephone numbers, and so on, is a structure of related items. A file of favorite CDs or LP records is a structure. A computer's directory listing is a structure. These are examples that use a structure, but what is a structure? A structure can be thought of as a group of variables which can be of different types held together in a single unit. The single unit is the structure.

Syntax and Rules for C and C++ Structures

In C or C++, you form a structure by using the keyword **struct**, followed by an optional tag field, and then a list of members within the structure. The optional tag field is used to create other variables of the particular structure's type. The syntax for a structure with the optional tag field looks like this:

```
struct tag_field {
    member_type member1;
    member_type member2;
    member_type member3;
        .
        .
        .
```

```
    member_type member n;
};
```

A semicolon terminates the structure definition because it is actually a C and C++ statement. Several of the example programs in this chapter use a structure similar to the following:

```
struct stboat {
    char      sztype [ iSTRING15 + iNULL_CHAR ];
    char      szmodel[ iSTRING15 + iNULL_CHAR ];
    char      sztitle[ iSTRING20 + iNULL_CHAR ];
    int       iyear                           ;
    long int  lmotor_hours                    ;
    float     fsaleprice                      ;
};
```

The structure is created with the keyword **struct** followed by the tag field or type for the structure. In this example, *stboat* is the tag field for the structure. This structure declaration contains several members; *sztype, szmodel,* and *sztitle* are null-terminated strings of the specified length. These strings are followed by an integer, *iyear; a long integer, lmotor_hours;* and a float, *fsaleprice.* The structure will be used to save sales information for a boat.

So far, all that has been defined is a new hypothetical structure type called *stboat.* However, no variable has been associated with the structure at this point. In a program, you can associate a variable with a structure by using a statement similar to the following:

```
struct stboat stused_boat;
```

The statement defines *stused_boat* to be of the type **struct** *stboat.* Notice that the declaration required the use of the structure's tag field. If this statement is contained within a function, then the structure, named *stused_boat,* is local in scope to that function. If the statement is contained outside of all program functions, the structure will be global in scope. It is also possible to declare a structure variable using this syntax:

```
struct stboat {
    char      sztype [ iSTRING15 + iNULL_CHAR ];
    char      szmodel[ iSTRING15 + iNULL_CHAR ];
    char      sztitle[ iSTRING20 + iNULL_CHAR ];
```

```
    int        iyear                                ;
    long int lmotor_hours                           ;
    float      fsaleprice                           ;
} stused_boat                                       ;
```

Here, the variable declaration is sandwiched between the structure's closing brace
(}) and the required semicolon (;). In both examples, *stused_boat* is declared as structure
type *stboat*. Actually, when only one variable is associated with a structure type, the tag
field can be eliminated, so it would also be possible to write:

```
struct {
    char       sztype [ iSTRING15 + iNULL_CHAR ];
    char       szmodel[ iSTRING15 + iNULL_CHAR ];
    char       sztitle[ iSTRING20 + iNULL_CHAR ];
    int        iyear                                ;
    long int lmotor_hours                           ;
    float      fsaleprice                           ;
} stused_boat                                       ;
```

Notice that this structure declaration does not include a tag field and creates what
is called an anonymous structure type. Although the statement does define a single
variable, *stused_boat*, there is no way the application can create another variable of the
same type somewhere else in the application. Without the structure's tag field, there is
no syntactically legal way to refer to the new type. However, it is possible to associate
several variables with the same structure type without specifying a tag field, as shown
in the following listing:

```
struct {
    char       sztype [ iSTRING15 + iNULL_CHAR ];
    char       szmodel[ iSTRING15 + iNULL_CHAR ];
    char       sztitle[ iSTRING20 + iNULL_CHAR ];
    int        iyear                                ;
    long int lmotor_hours                           ;
    float      fsaleprice                           ;
} stboat1, stboat2, stboat3                         ;
```

The C and C++ compiler allocates all necessary memory for the structure
members, as it does for any other variable. To decide if your structure declarations
need a tag field, ask yourself the following questions: "Will I need to create other
variables of this structure type somewhere else in the program?" and "Will I be passing
the structure type to functions?" If the answer to either of these questions is yes, you
need a tag field.

Syntax and Rule Extensions for C++ Structures

In many cases, C++ can be described as a superset of C. In general, this means that what works in C should work in C++. (However, using C design philosophies in a C++ program often ignores C++'s streamlining enhancements.) The structure declaration syntax styles just described all work with both the C and C++ compilers. However, C++ has one additional method for declaring variables of a particular structure type. This exclusive C++ shorthand notation eliminates the need to repeat the keyword **struct**. The following example highlights this subtle difference:

```
/* legal C and C++ structure declaration syntax */
struct stboat stused_boat;

// exclusive C++ structure declaration syntax
stboat stused_boat;
```

Using Structure Members

It is possible to reference the individual members within a structure by using the dot or member operator (.). The syntax is shown here:

```
stname.mname
```

In this line, *stname* is the variable associated with the structure type, and *mname* is the name of any member variable in the structure. In C, for example, information can be placed in the *szmodel* member with a statement such as this:

```
gets(stused_boat.szmodel);
```

Here, *stused_boat* is the name associated with the structure, and *szmodel* is a member variable of the structure. In a similar manner, you can use a **printf()** function to print information for a structure member:

```
printf( "%ld", stused_boat.lmotor_hours );
```

The syntax for accessing structure members is basically the same in C++:

```
cin >> stused_boat.sztype;
```

This statement will read the make of the *stused_boat* into the character array, while the next statement will print the *stused_boat* selling price to the screen:

```
cout << stused_boat.fsaleprice;
```

Structure members are handled like any other C or C++ variable except that the dot operator must always be used with them.

A Simple Structure

The example program for this section uses a structure similar to the *stboat* structure given earlier in this chapter. Examine the listing that follows to see if you understand how the various structure elements are accessed by the program:

```c
/*
 *   struct.c
 *   A C program illustrates how to construct a structure.
 *   The program stores data about your boat in a C structure.
 *   Copyright (c) Chris H. Pappas and William H. Murray, 1996
 */

#include <stdio.h>

#define iSTRING15 15
#define iSTRING20 20
#define iNULL_CHAR 1

struct stboat {
    char      sztype [ iSTRING15 + iNULL_CHAR ]      ;
    char      szmodel[ iSTRING15 + iNULL_CHAR ]      ;
    char      sztitle[ iSTRING20 + iNULL_CHAR ]      ;
    int       iyear                                  ;
    long int  lmotor_hours                           ;
    float     fsaleprice                             ;
} stused_boat                                        ;

void main( void )
{
    printf( "\nPlease enter the make of the boat: "  );
    gets  (   stused_boat.sztype                     );

    printf( "\nPlease enter the model of the boat: " );
```

```
      gets   (   stused_boat.szmodel                            );

      printf( "\nPlease enter the title number for the boat: "  );
      gets   (   stused_boat.sztitle                            );

      printf( "\nPlease enter the model year for the boat: "    );
      scanf  ( "%d", &stused_boat.iyear                         );

      printf( "\nPlease enter the current hours on "            );
      printf( "the motor for the boat: "                        );
      scanf  ( "%ld", &stused_boat.lmotor_hours                 );

      printf( "\nPlease enter the purchase price of the boat: " );
      scanf  ( "%f", &stused_boat.fsaleprice                    );

      printf( "\n\n\n"                                          );
      printf( "A %d %s %s with title number #%s\n"
              stused_boat.iyear,stused_boat.sztype              ,
              stused_boat.szmodel,stused_boat.sztitle           );
      printf( "currently has %ld motor hours"                   ,
              stused_boat.lmotor_hours                          );
      printf(" and was purchased for $%8.2f\n"                  ,
              stused_boat.fsaleprice                            );
}
```

The output from the preceding example shows how information can be manipulated with a structure:

```
A 1952 Chris Craft with title number #CC1011771018C
currently has 34187 motor hours and was purchased for $68132.98
```

You might notice, at this point, that *stused_boat* has a global file scope because it was declared outside of any function.

Passing Structures to Functions

There will be many occasions where it is necessary to pass structure information to functions. When a structure is passed to a function, the information is passed call-by-value. Because only a copy of the information is being passed in, it is impossible for the function to alter the contents of the original structure. You can pass a structure to a function by using the following syntax:

```
fname( stvariable );
```

If *stused_boat* was made local in scope to **main()**, and you move its declaration inside the function, it could be passed to a function named *vprint_data()* with this statement:

```
vprint_data( stused_boat );
```

The *vprint_data()* prototype must declare the structure type it is about to receive, as you might suspect:

```
/* legal C and C++ structure declaration syntax */
void vprint_data( struct stboat stany_boat );

// exclusive C++ structure declaration syntax
void vprint_data( stboat stany_boat );
```

Passing entire copies of structures to functions is not always the most efficient way of programming. Where time is a factor, the use of pointers might be a better choice. If saving memory is a consideration, the **malloc()** function can dynamically allocate structure memory in C when using linked lists instead of statically allocating memory. You'll see how this is done in the next chapter.

The next example shows how to pass a complete structure to a function. Notice that it is a simple modification of the last example. The next four example programs use the same basic approach. Each program modifies only that portion of the algorithm necessary to explain the current subject. This approach will allow you to easily view the code and syntax changes necessary to implement a particular language feature. Study the listing and see how the structure *stused_boat* is passed to the function *vprint_data()*.

```
/*
 *    passst.c
 *    A C program shows how to pass a structure to a function.
 *    Copyright (c) Chris H. Pappas and William H. Murray, 1996
 */

#include <stdio.h>

#define iSTRING15 15
#define iSTRING20 20
```

```
#define iNULL_CHAR 1

struct stboat {
  char     sztype [ iSTRING15 + iNULL_CHAR ]            ;
  char     szmodel[ iSTRING15 + iNULL_CHAR ]            ;
  char     sztitle[ iSTRING20 + iNULL_CHAR ]            ;
  int      iyear                                        ;
  long int lmotor_hours                                 ;
  float    fsaleprice                                   ;
}                                                       ;

void vprint_data( struct stboat stany_boat )            ;

void main( void )
{
  struct stboat stused_boat                             ;

  printf( "\nPlease enter the make of the boat: "     );
  gets  (    stused_boat.sztype                        );

  printf( "\nPlease enter the model of the boat: "    );
  gets  (    stused_boat.szmodel                       );

  printf( "\nPlease enter the title number for the boat: "  );
  gets  (    stused_boat.sztitle                       );

  printf( "\nPlease enter the model year for the boat: "   );
  scanf ( "%d",&stused_boat.iyear                      );

  printf( "\nPlease enter the current hours on"        );
  printf( " the motor for the boat:"                   );
  scanf ( "%ld", &stused_boat.lmotor_hours             );

  printf( "\nPlease enter the purchase price of the boat:"  );
  scanf ( "%f", &stused_boat.fsaleprice                );

  vprint_data(stused_boat                              );
}

void vprint_data( struct stboat stany_boat )
{
```

```
printf( "\n\n"                                                    );
printf( "A %d %s %s with title number#%s\n",stany_boat.iyear    ,.
        stany_boat.sztype,stany_boat.szmodel,stany_boat.sztitle);
printf( "currently has %ld motor hours",stany_boat.lmotor_hours);
printf( " and was purchased for $%8.2f"                          ,
        stany_boat.fsaleprice                                    );
}
```

In this example, an entire structure was passed by value to the function. The calling procedure simply invokes the function by passing the structure variable, *stused_boat*. Notice that the structure's tag field, *stboat*, was needed in the *vprint_data()* function prototype and declaration. As you will see later in this chapter, it is also possible to pass individual structure members by value to a function. The output from this program is similar to the previous example.

An Array of Structures

A structure is similar to a single card from a card file in that the real power in using structures comes from using a collection of structures (called an array of structures). In other words, a single card in a card file is of limited use, but the entire collection of cards is an irreplaceable tool. An array of structures is similar to the whole card file containing a great number of individual cards. If you maintain an array of structures, a database of information can be manipulated for a wide range of items.

This array of structures might include information on all of the boats at a local marina. It would be practical for a boat dealer to maintain such a file and be able to pull out of a database all boats on the lot selling for less than $45,000 or all boats with a minimum of one stateroom. Study the following example and note how the code has been changed from earlier examples:

```
/*
 *   stcary.c
 *   A C program uses an array of structures.
 *   This example creates a "used boat inventory" for
 *   Nineveh Boat Sales.
 *   Copyright (c) Chris H. Pappas and William H. Murray, 1996
 */

#include <stdio.h>

#define iSTRING15 15
#define iSTRING20 20
```

```
#define iNULL_CHAR 1
#define iMAX_BOATS 50
struct stboat {

  char      sztype   [ iSTRING15 + iNULL_CHAR ]              ;
  char      szmodel  [ iSTRING15 + iNULL_CHAR ]              ;
  char      sztitle  [ iSTRING20 + iNULL_CHAR ]              ;
  char      szcomment[ 80                      ]             ;
  int       iyear                                            ;
  long int  lmotor_hours                                     ;
  float     fretail                                          ;
  float fwholesale                                           ;
};

void main( void )
{
  int i, iinstock                                            ;
  struct stboat astNineveh[ iMAX_BOATS ]                     ;

  printf( "How many boats in inventory? "         );
  scanf ( "%d", &iinstock                         );

  for( i = 0; i < iinstock; i++ )                       {

    flushall( );                        /* flush keyboard buffer */
    printf( "\nPlease enter the make of the boat: "  );
    gets  (  astNineveh[ i ].sztype                  );

    printf( "\nPlease enter the model of the boat: " );
    gets  (  astNineveh[ i ].szmodel                 );

    printf( "\nPlease enter the title number for the boat: " );
    gets  (  astNineveh[ i ].sztitle                 );

    printf( "\nPlease enter a one line comment about the boat: ");
    gets  (  astNineveh[ i ].szcomment               );

    printf( "\nPlease enter the model year for the boat: "  );
    scanf ( "%d", &astNineveh[ i ].iyear             );

    printf( "\nPlease enter the current hours on "   );
    printf( "the motor for the boat: "               );
```

```
    scanf ( "%ld", &astNineveh[ i ].lmotor_hours                    );

    printf( "\nPlease enter the retail price of the boat :"         );
    scanf ( "%f", &astNineveh[ i ].fretail                          );

    printf( "\nPlease enter the wholesale price of the boat :"      );
    scanf ( "%f", &astNineveh[ i ].fwholesale                       );
  }

  printf( "\n\n\n"                                                  );

  for( i = 0; i < iinstock; i++ )                                   {
    printf( "A %d %s %s beauty with %ld low hours.\n"               ,
            astNineveh[ i ].iyear,astNineveh[ i ].sztype            ,
            astNineveh[ i ].szmodel,astNineveh[ i ].lmotor_hours  );
    printf( "%s\n",astNineveh[ i ].szcomment                        );
    printf(
            "Grab the deal by asking your Nineveh salesperson for");
    printf( " #%s ONLY! $%8.2f.\n", astNineveh[ i ].sztitle         ,
            astNineveh[ i ].fretail                                 );
    printf( "\n\n"                                                  );
  }
}
```

Here, Nineveh Boat Sales has an array of structures set up to hold information about the boats in the marina. The variable *astNineveh[iMAX_BOATS]* associated with the structure **struct** *stboat* is actually an array. In this case, *iMAX_BOATS* sets the maximum array size to *50*. This simply means that data on 50 boats can be maintained in the array of structures. It will be necessary to know which of the boats in the file you wish to view. The first array element is zero. Therefore, information on the first boat in the array of structures can be accessed with a statement such as this:

```
gets( astNineveh[ 0 ].sztitle );
```

As you study the program, notice that the array elements are accessed with the help of a loop. In this manner, element members are obtained with code, such as this:

```
gets( astNineveh[ i ].sztitle );
```

The **flushall()** statement inside the **for** loop is necessary to remove the newline left in the input stream from the previous **scanf()** statements (the one before the loop is entered and the last **scanf()** statement within the loop). Without the call to **flushall()**, the **gets()** statement would be skipped over. Remember, **gets()** reads everything up to and including the newline. Both **scanf()** statements leave the *newline* in the input stream. Without the call to **flushall()**, the **gets()** statement would simply grab the *newline* from the input stream and move on to the next executable statement.

The previous program's output serves to illustrate the small stock of boats on hand at Nineveh Boat Sales. It also shows how structure information can be rearranged in output statements:

```
A 1957 Chris Craft Dayliner 124876 low hours.
A great riding boat owned by a salesperson.
Grab the deal by asking your Nineveh salesperson for
#BS12345BFD ONLY! $36234.00.

A 1988 Starcraft Weekender a beauty with 27657 low hours.
Runs and looks great. Owned by successful painter.
Grab the deal by asking your Nineveh salesperson for
#BG7774545AFD ONLY! $18533.99.

A 1991 Scarab a wower with 1000 low hours.
A cheap means of transportation. Owned by grandfather.
Grab the deal by asking your Nineveh salesperson for
#156AFG4476 ONLY! $56999.99.
```

NOTE: When you are working with arrays of structures, be aware of the memory limitations of the system you are programming on--statically allocated memory for arrays of structures can require large amounts of system memory.

Pointers to Structures

In the next program, an array of structures is created in a similar manner to the last program. The arrow operator is used in this example to access individual structure members. The arrow operator can be used only when a pointer to a structure has been created.

```
/*
 * ptrstc.c
 * A C program uses pointers to an array of structures.
 * The Nineveh boat inventory example is used again.
```

```
 *  Copyright (c) Chris H. Pappas and William H. Murray, 1996
 */

#include <stdio.h>

#define iSTRING15 15
#define iSTRING20 20
#define iNULL_CHAR 1
#define iMAX_BOATS 50

struct stboat {
  char     sztype   [ iSTRING15 + iNULL_CHAR ]                    ;
  char     szmodel  [ iSTRING15 + iNULL_CHAR ]                    ;
  char     sztitle  [ iSTRING20 + iNULL_CHAR ]                    ;
  char     szcomment[ 80                     ]                    ;
  int      iyear                                                  ;
  long int lmotor_hours                                           ;
  float    fretail                                                ;
  float    fwholesale                                             ;
};

void main( void )
{
  int i, iinstock                                                 ;
  struct stboat astNineveh[ iMAX_BOATS ], *pastNineveh            ;
  pastNineveh = &astNineveh[ 0 ]                                  ;

  printf( "How many boats in inventory? "                        );
  scanf ( "%d", &iinstock                                        );
    for( i = 0; i < iinstock; i++ )                                {
      flushall( );                        /*  flush keyboard buffer */
      printf( "\nPlease enter the make of the boat: "            );
      gets  (   pastNineveh->sztype                              );

      printf( "\nPlease enter the model of the boat: "           );
      gets  (   pastNineveh->szmodel                             );

      printf( "\nPlease enter the title number for the boat: ");
      gets  (   pastNineveh->sztitle                             );

      printf(
          "\nPlease enter a one line comment about the boat: ");
```

```
        gets  ( pastNineveh->szcomment                         );

        printf( "\nPlease enter the model year for the boat: " );
        scanf ( "%d", &pastNineveh->iyear                      );
        printf( "\nPlease enter the current hours on "         );
        printf( "the motor for the boat: "                     );
        scanf ( "%ld",&pastNineveh->lmotor_hours               );

        printf( "\nPlease enter the retail price of the boat: " );
        scanf ( "%f", &pastNineveh->fretail                    );

        printf(
            "\nPlease enter the wholesale price of the boat: ");
        scanf ( "%f", &pastNineveh->fwholesale                 );

        pastNineveh++                                          ;
    }

  pastNineveh = &astNineveh[ 0 ]                               ;
  printf( "\n\n\n"                                             );

  for( i = 0; i < iinstock; i++ )                              {
    printf( "A %d %s %s beauty with %ld low hours.\n"          ,
            pastNineveh->iyear,    pastNineveh->sztype         ,
            pastNineveh->szmodel, pastNineveh->lmotor_hours    );
    printf( "%s\n", pastNineveh->szcomment                     );
    printf(
        "Grab the deal by asking your Nineveh salesperson for:");
    printf( "\n#%s ONLY! $%8.2f.\n",pastNineveh->sztitle       ,
                                    pastNineveh->fretail       );
    printf( "\n\n"                                             );
    pastNineveh++                                              ;
  }
}
```

The array variable *astNineveh[iMAX_BOATS]* and the pointer **pastNineveh* are associated with the structure by using the following statement:

```
struct stboat astNineveh[ iMAX_BOATS ],*pastNineveh;
```

The address of the array *astNineveh* is copied into the pointer variable *pastNineveh* with the following code:

```
pastNineveh = &astNineveh[ 0 ];
```

Although it is syntactically legal to reference array elements with the syntax that follows, it is not the preferred method:

```
gets( (*pastNineveh).sztype );
```

Because of operator precedence, the extra parentheses are necessary to prevent the dot (.) member operator from binding before the pointer *pastNineveh* is dereferenced. It is better to use the arrow operator, which makes the overall operation much cleaner:

```
gets( pastNineveh->sztype );
```

Although this is not a complex example, it does illustrate the use of the arrow operator. The example also prepares you for the real advantage in using pointers—passing an array of structures to a function.

Passing an Array of Structures to a Function

Earlier in the chapter it was mentioned that passing a pointer to a structure could be faster than simply passing a copy of a structure to a function. This fact becomes more evident when a program makes heavy use of structures. The next program shows how an array of structures can be accessed by a function with the use of a pointer:

```
/*
 *   psastc.c
 *   A C program shows how a function can access an array
 *   of structures with the use of a pointer.
 *   The Nineveh boat inventory is used again!
 *   Copyright (c) Chris H. Pappas and William H. Murray, 1996
 */

#include <stdio.h>

#define iSTRING15 15
#define iSTRING20 20
#define iNULL_CHAR 1
#define iMAX_BOATS 50

int iinstock;
```

```
struct stboat {
  char      sztype   [ iSTRING15 + iNULL_CHAR ]              ;
  char      szmodel  [ iSTRING15 + iNULL_CHAR ]              ;
  char      sztitle  [ iSTRING20 + iNULL_CHAR ]              ;
  char      szcomment[ 80                      ]             ;
  int       iyear                                            ;
  long int  lmotor_hours                                     ;
  float     fretail                                          ;
  float     fwholesale                                       ;
}                                                            ;

void vprint_data( struct stboat *stany_boatptr )             ;

void main( void )
{
  int i                                                      ;
  struct stboat astNineveh[ iMAX_BOATS ], *pastNineveh       ;
  pastNineveh = &astNineveh[ 0 ]                             ;

  printf( "How many boats in inventory?\n"                 );
  scanf ( "%d", &iinstock                                  );

  for( i = 0; i < iinstock; i++ )                            {

    flushall( );                         /*  flush keyboard buffer*/
    printf( "\nPlease enter the make of the boat: "        );
    gets  (   pastNineveh->sztype                          );

    printf( "\nPlease enter the model of the boat: "       );
    gets  (   pastNineveh->szmodel                         );

    printf( "\nPlease enter the title number for the boat: "   );
    gets  (   pastNineveh->sztitle                         );

    printf( "\nPlease enter a one line comment about the boat: ");
    gets  (   pastNineveh->szcomment                       );

    printf( "\nPlease enter the model year for the boat: " );
    scanf ( "%d", &pastNineveh->iyear                      );

    printf( "\nPlease enter the current hours on "         );
    printf( "the motor for the boat: "                     );
```

```
      scanf ( "%ld", &pastNineveh->lmotor_hours            );

      printf( "\nPlease enter the retail price of the boat: "    );
      scanf ( "%f", &pastNineveh->fretail                   );

      printf( "\nPlease enter the wholesale price of the boat: "  );
      scanf ( "%f", &pastNineveh->fwholesale                );

      pastNineveh++                                         ;
   }

   pastNineveh = &astNineveh[ 0 ]                           ;

   vprint_data( pastNineveh )                               ;
}

void vprint_data( struct stboat *stany_boatptr )
{
  int i                                                     ;
  printf( "\n\n\n"                                          );
  for( i = 0; i < iinstock; i++ )                           {
    printf( "A %d %s %s beauty with %ld low hours.\n"       ,
             stany_boatptr->iyear,stany_boatptr->sztype     ,
             stany_boatptr->szmodel,stany_boatptr->lmotor_hours );
    printf( "%s\n", stany_boatptr->szcomment                );
    printf(
           "Grab the deal by asking your Nineveh salesperson for");
    printf(" #%s ONLY! $%8.2f.\n",stany_boatptr->sztitle    ,
                                  stany_boatptr->fretail     );
    printf("\n\n"                                            );
    stany_boatptr++                                          ;
  }
}
```

The first indication that this program will operate differently from the last program comes from the *vprint_data()* function prototype:

```
void vprint_data( struct stboat *stany_boatptr );
```

This function expects to receive a pointer to the structure mentioned. In the function **main()**, the array *astNineveh[iMAX_BOATS]* and the pointer **pastNineveh* are associated with the structure with the following code:

```
struct stboat astNineveh[ iMAX_BOATS ],*pastNineveh;
```

Once the information has been collected for Nineveh Boat Sales, it is passed to the *vprint_data()* function by passing the pointer:

```
vprint_data( pastNineveh );
```

One major advantage of passing an array of structures to a function using pointers is that the array is now passed call-by-variable, or call-by-reference. This means that the function can now access the original array structure, not just a copy. With this calling convention, any change made to the array of structures within the function is global in scope. The output from this program is the same as for the previous examples.

C++ Structure Use

The following C++ program is similar to the last C program. In terms of syntax, both languages can handle structures in an identical manner. However, the example program takes advantage of C++'s shorthand structure syntax:

```
//
//   struct.cpp
//   A C++ program shows the use of pointers when
//   accessing structure information from a function.
//   Note:  Comment line terminates with a period (.)
//   Copyright (c) Chris H. Pappas and William H. Murray, 1996
//

#include <iostream.h>

#define iSTRING15  15
#define iSTRING20  20
#define iNULL_CHAR  1
#define iMAX_BOATS 50

int iinstock                                          ;
```

```
struct stboat {
  char      sztype [ iSTRING15 + iNULL_CHAR ]                       ;
  char      szmodel[ iSTRING15 + iNULL_CHAR ]                       ;
  char      sztitle[ iSTRING20 + iNULL_CHAR ]                       ;
  char      szcomment[ 80 ]                                         ;
  int       iyear                                                   ;
  long int  lmotor_hours                                            ;
  float     fretail                                                 ;
  float     fwholesale                                              ;
}                                                                   ;

void vprint_data( stboat *stany_boatptr )                           ;

void main ( void )
{
  int i                                                             ;
  char newline                                                      ;
  stboat astNineveh[ iMAX_BOATS ], *pastNineveh                     ;
  pastNineveh = &astNineveh[ 0 ]                                    ;

  cout << "How many boats in inventory? "                           ;
  cin  >>  iinstock                                                 ;

  for( i = 0; i < iinstock; i++ )                                   {
    cout << "\nPlease enter the make of the boat: "                 ;
    cin  >>   pastNineveh->sztype                                   ;

    cout << "\nPlease enter the model of the boat: "                ;
    cin  >>   pastNineveh->szmodel                                  ;

    cout << "\nPlease enter the title number for the boat: "        ;
    cin  >>   pastNineveh->sztitle                                  ;

    cout << "\nPlease enter the model year for the boat: "          ;
    cin  >>   pastNineveh->iyear                                    ;

    cout << "\nPlease enter the current hours on "
         << "the motor for the boat: "                              ;
    cin  >>  pastNineveh->lmotor_hours                              ;

    cout << "\nPlease enter the retail price of the boat: "         ;
```

```
    cin  >>    pastNineveh->fretail                              ;

    cout << "\nPlease enter the wholesale price of the boat: "  ;
    cin  >>    pastNineveh->fwholesale                           ;

    cout << "\nPlease enter a one line comment about the boat: ";
    cin.get(  newline                         )                  ;
    cin.get(  pastNineveh->szcomment,80,'.' )                    ;
    cin.get(  newline      )                                     ;

    pastNineveh++                                                ;
  }

  pastNineveh = &astNineveh[ 0 ]                                 ;
  vprint_data( pastNineveh )                                     ;
}

void vprint_data( stboat *stany_boatptr )
{
  int i                                                          ;
  cout << "\n\n\n"                                               ;
  for( i=0; i < iinstock; i++ )                                  {
    cout << "A[{|"|}]<< stany_boatptr->iyear <<[{|"|}]"
         << stany_boatptr->sztype <<[{|"|}]"
         << stany_boatptr->szmodel <<[{|"|}]beauty with "
         << stany_boatptr->lmotor_hours <<[{|"|}]low hours.\n"  ;
    cout << stany_boatptr->szcomment << endl                     ;
    cout << "Grab the deal by asking your Nineveh "
         << "salesperson for #"                                  ;
    cout << stany_boatptr->sztitle << "ONLY! $"
         << stany_boatptr->fretail << "\n\n"                     ;
    stany_boatptr++                                              ;
  }
}
```

One of the real differences between the C++ and C programs is how stream I/O is handled. Usually, simple C++ **cout** and **cin** streams can be used to replace the standard C **printf()** and **gets()** functions, as shown in this example:

```
cout << "\nPlease enter the wholesale price of the boat: ";
cin  >>    pastNineveh->fwholesale;
```

One of the program statements requests that the user enter a comment about each boat. The C++ input statement needed to read in the comment line uses a different approach for I/O. Recall that **cin** will read character information until the first white space. In this case, a space between words in a comment serves as white space. If **cin** were used, only the first word from the comment line would be saved in the *szcomment* member of the structure. Instead, a variation of **cin** is used so that a whole line of text can be entered:

```
cout << "\nPlease enter a one line comment about the boat: ";
cin.get(  newline                                )              ;
cin.get(  pastNineveh->szcomment,80,'.' )                       ;
cin.get(  newline                                )              ;
```

First, *cin.get(newline)* is used in a manner similar to the **flushall()** function of earlier C programs. In a buffered keyboard system, it is often necessary to strip the *newline* character from the input buffer. There are, of course, other ways to accomplish this, but they are not more eloquent. The statement *cin.get(newline)* receives the *newline* character and saves it in *newline*. (The variable *newline* is just a collector for the information and is not actually used by the program.) The comment line is accepted with the following code:

```
cin.get( pastNineveh->szcomment,80,'.' );
```

Here, *cin.get()* uses a pointer to the structure member, followed by the maximum length of the *szcomment*, 80, followed by a termination character (.). In this case, the comment line will be terminated when (*n-1*) or *80-1* characters are entered or a period is typed (the *n*th space is reserved for the null string terminator, \0). The period is not saved as part of the comment, so the period is added back when the comment is printed. Locate the code that performs this action.

Structure Manipulations

There are a few issues about structures that the past several examples have not illustrated. For example, it is also possible to pass individual structure members to a function. Another property allows the nesting of structures.

Nesting Structures Within Structures

You can nest structure declarations—that is, one structure can contain a member or members that are structure types. For example, the following structure could be included in yet another structure:

```
struct strepair {
  int ioilchange        ;
  int iplugs            ;
  int iairfilter        ;
  int ibarnacle_cleaning;
}                       ;
```

In the main structure, the *strepair* structure could be included as follows:

```
struct stboat {
  char            sztype   [ iSTRING15 + iNULL_CHAR ];
  char            szmodel  [ iSTRING15 + iNULL_CHAR ];
  char            sztitle  [ iSTRING20 + iNULL_CHAR ];
  char            szcomment[ 80                     ];
  struct strepair strepair_record                    ;
  int             iyear                              ;
  long int        lmotor_hours                       ;
  float           fretail                            ;
  float           fwholesale                         ;
} astNineveh[ iMAX_BOATS ]                           ;
```

If a particular member from *strepair_record* is desired, it can be reached by using the following code:

```
printf( "%d\n", astNineveh[0].strepair_record.ibarnacle_cleaning );
```

Passing Structure Members to a Function

Passing individual structure members is an easy and efficient means of limiting access to structure information within a function. For example, a function might be used to print a list of wholesale boat prices available on the lot. In that case, just the *fwholesale* price, which is a member of the structure, would be passed to the function. The call to the function would take this form:

```
vprint_price( astNineveh.fwholesale );
```

In this case, *vprint_price()* is the function name and *astNineveh.fwholesale* is the structure name and member.

Structures and Bit-Fields

C and C++ give you the ability to access individual bits within a larger data type, such as a byte. This is useful, for example, in altering data masks used for system information and graphics. The capability to access bits is built around the C and C++ structure. Consider, for example, that it might be desirable to alter the keyboard status register in a computer. This register contains flags for setting or querying the status of the extra keys on the computer keyboard. This eight-bit keyboard status register contains the following information where:

```
bit 0 = RIGHT SHIFT depressed (1)
      bit 1 = LEFT SHIFT  depressed (1)
      bit 2 = CTRL         depressed (1)
      bit 3 = ALT          depressed (1)
      bit 4 = SCROLL LOCK active    (1)
      bit 5 = NUM LOCK     active    (1)
      bit 6 = CAPS LOCK    active    (1)
      bit 7 = INS          active    (1)
```

In order to access and control this data, a structure could be constructed that uses the following form:

```
struct stkeybits {
  unsigned char
    ucrshift  : 1,        // lsb
    uclshift  : 1,
    ucctrl    : 1,
    ucalt     : 1,
    ucscroll  : 1,
    ucnumlock : 1,
    uccaplock : 1,
    ucinsert  : 1;        // msb
} stkey_register ;
```

The bits are specified in the structure starting with the least significant bit (*lsb*) and progressing toward the most significant bit (*msb*). You can specify more than one bit by just typing the quantity (in place of the 1). Only integer data types can be used for bit-fields. The members of the bit-field structure are accessed in the normal fashion.

Unions

A union is another data type that can be used in many distinctive ways. A specific union, for example, could be construed as an integer in one operation and a float or double in another operation. Although unions may look similar to structures, they actually are very dissimilar. A union can contain a group of many data types, as does a structure. In a union, however, those data types all share the same location in memory! Thus, a union can contain information on only one data type at a time. Many other high-level languages refer to this capability as a "variant record."

Syntax and Rules

A union is constructed by using the keyword **union** and the syntax that follows:

```
union tag_field {
   type field1;
   type field2;
   type field3;

        .

        .

        .

   type fieldn;
}                ;
```

A semicolon is used for termination because the structure definition is actually a C and C++ statement. Notice the declaration syntax similarities between structures and unions in the following example declaration:

```
union unmany_types {
   char   c    ;
   int    ivalue;
   float  fvalue;
   double dvalue;
} unmy_union   ;
```

The union is defined with the keyword **union** followed by the optional tag field, *unmany_types*. The union's optional tag field operates exactly the way its structure counterpart does. This union contains several members: a character, integer, float, and double. The union will allow *unmany_types* to save information on any one data type at a time. The variable associated with the union is *unmy_union*. If this statement is contained in a function, the union is local in scope to that function. If the statement is contained outside of all functions, the union will be global in scope. As with structures, it is also possible to associate several variables with the same union. Also, like a structure, members of a union are referenced by using the dot (.) operator. The syntax is shown here:

```
unname.mname
```

In this case, *unname* is the variable associated with the union type and *mname* is the name of any member of the union.

A Simple Union

To illustrate some concepts about unions, the following C++ program creates a union of the type just discussed. The purpose of this example is to show that a union can contain the definitions for many types but can hold the value for only one data type at a time.

```
//
//   unions.cpp
//   A C++ program demonstrates the use of a union.
//   A union is created with several data types.
//   Copyright (c) Chris H. Pappas and William H. Murray, 1996
//

#include <iostream.h>

union unmany_types {
  char    c                                              ;
  int     ivalue                                         ;
  float   fvalue                                         ;
  double dvalue                                          ;
} unmy_union                                             ;

void main( void )
{
  // valid I/O

  unmy_union.c = 'b'                                     ;
  cout << unmy_union.c << "\n"                           ;
  unmy_union.ivalue = 1990                               ;
```

```
   cout << unmy_union.ivalue << "\n"                         ;

   unmy_union.fvalue = 19.90                                 ;
   cout << unmy_union.fvalue << "\n"                         ;

   unmy_union.dvalue = 987654.32E+13                         ;
   cout << unmy_union.dvalue << "\n"                         ;

   // invalid I/O

   cout << unmy_union.c        << "\n"                       ;
   cout << unmy_union.ivalue << "\n"                         ;
   cout << unmy_union.fvalue << "\n"                         ;
   cout << unmy_union.dvalue << "\n"                         ;

   // union size
   cout << "The size of this union is: "
        << sizeof(unmany_types) <<[{|"|}]bytes." << "\n";
}
```

The first part of this program simply loads and unloads information from the union. The program works because the union is called upon to store only one data type at a time. In the second part of the program, however, an attempt is made to output each data type from the union. The only valid value is the double, because it was the last value loaded in the previous portion of code.

```
b
1990
19.9
9.876543e+18

−
-26216
-2.054608e+33
9.876543e+18
The size of this union is: 8 bytes.
```

Unions set aside storage room for the largest data type contained in the union. All other data types in the union share part, or all, of this memory location. By using the integrated debugger, you can get an idea of what is happening with storage within a union.

Miscellaneous Items

There are two further topics worth mentioning at this point: **typedef** declarations and enumerated types, **enum**. Both **typedef** and **enum** have the capability to clarify program code when used appropriately.

typedef

You can associate new data types with existing data types by using **typedef**. In a mathematically intense program, for example, it might be necessary to use the data type fixed, whole, real, or complex. These new types can be associated with standard C/C++ types with **typedef**. In the next program, two novel data types are created:

```c
/*
 *    typedf.c
 *    A C program shows the use of typedef.
 *    Two new types are created, "whole" and "real",
 *    which can be used in place of "int" and "float".
 *    Copyright (c) Chris H. Pappas and William H. Murray, 1996
 */
#include <stdio.h>

typedef int    whole;
typedef float real ;

void main( void )
{
  whole wvalue = 123                                    ;
  real  rvalue = 5.6789                                 ;

  printf( "The whole number is %d.\n", wvalue );
  printf( "The real number is %f.\n" , rvalue );
}
```

Be aware that using too many newly created types can adversely affect program readability and clarity. Use **typedef** carefully. You can use a **typedef** declaration to simplify declarations. Look at the next two coded examples and see if you can detect the subtle code difference introduced by the **typedef** keyword:

```c
struct stboat {
    char     sztype [ iSTRING15 + iNULL_CHAR ];
    char     szmodel[ iSTRING15 + iNULL_CHAR ];
```

```
   char      sztitle[ iSTRING20 + iNULL_CHAR ];
   int       iyear                            ;
   long int  lmotor_hours                     ;
   float     fsaleprice                       ;
} stused_boat                                 ;

typedef struct {
   char      sztype [ iSTRING15 + iNULL_CHAR ];
   char      szmodel[ iSTRING15 + iNULL_CHAR ];
   char      sztitle[ iSTRING20 + iNULL_CHAR ];
   int       iyear                            ;
   long int  lmotor_hours                     ;
   float     fsaleprice                       ;
} STBOAT                                      ;
```

Three major changes have taken place:

- The optional tag field has been deleted. (However, when using **typedef** you can still use a tag field, although it is redundant in meaning.)

- The tag field, *stboat*, has now become the new type *STBOAT* and is placed where structure variables have been defined traditionally.

- There now is no variable declaration for *stused_boat*.

The advantage of **typedef**s lies in their usage. For the remainder of the application, the program can now define variables of the type *STBOAT* using this simpler syntax:

```
STBOAT STused_boat;
```

The use of the uppercase letters is not syntactically required by the C/C++ compiler; however, it does illustrate an important coding convention. With all of the possible sources for an identifier's declaration, C/C++ programmers have settled on using uppercase to indicate the definition of a new type, constant, enumerated value, and macro, usually defined in a header file. The visual contrast between lowercase keywords and uppercase user-defined identifiers makes for more easily understood code because all uppercase usually means, "Look for this declaration in another file."

enum

The enumerated data type, **enum**, exists for one reason only: to make your code more readable. In other computer languages, this data type is referred to as a user-defined type. The general syntax for enumerated declarations looks like this:

```
enum op_tag_field { val1,. . .valn } op_var_dec ;
```

As you may have already guessed, the optional tag field operates exactly as it does in structure declarations. If you leave the tag field off, you must list the variable or variables after the closing brace. Including the tag field allows your application to declare other variables of the tag type. When declaring additional variables of the tag type in C++, it is not necessary to repeat the keyword **enum**.

Enumerated data types allow you to associate a set of easily understood human symbols—for example, Monday, Tuesday, Wednesday, and so on—with an integral data type. They also help you create self-documenting code. For example, instead of having a loop that goes from 0 to 4, it can now read from Monday to Friday:

```
enum eweekdays { Monday, Tuesday, Wednesday, Thursday, Friday };

/* C enum variable declaration   */
enum eweekdays ewToday;

/* Same declaration in C++       */
eweekdays ewToday;

/* Not using the enumerated type */
for( i = 0; i <= 4; i++ )
        .

        .

        .

/* Using the enumerated type     */
for( ewToday = Monday; ewToday <= Friday; ewToday++ )
```

Historically speaking, C compilers saw no difference between the data types **int** and **enum**. This meant that a program could assign an integer value to an enumerated type. In C++, the two types generate a warning message from the compiler without an explicit type cast:

```
/* legal in C not C++ */
ewToday = 1;/* correcting the problem in C++ */
ewToday = (eweekdays)1;
```

The use of **enum** is popular in programming when information can be represented by a list of integer values such as the number of months in a year or the number of days in a week. This type of list lends itself to enumeration.

The following example contains a list of the number of months in a year. These are in an enumeration list with a tag name *emonths*. The variable associated with the list is *emcompleted*. Enumerated lists will always start with zero unless forced to a different integer value. In this case, January is the first month of the year.

```
/*
 *    enum.c
 *    A C program shows the use of enum types.
 *    The program calculates elapsed months in year, and
 *    remaining months using enum type.
 *    Copyright (c) Chris H. Pappas and William H. Murray, 1996
 */

#include <stdio.h>

enum emonths {
   January = 1, February, March                           ,
   April        , May       , June                         ,
   July         , August    , September                    ,
   October      , November, December
} emcompleted                                             ;

void main( void )
{
   int ipresent_month
;
   int isum, idiff                                        ;

   printf( "\nPlease enter the present month (1 to 12): "  );
   scanf ( "%d", &ipresent_month                           );

   emcompleted =        December                          ;
   isum        =        ipresent_month                    ;
   idiff       = (int) emcompleted - ipresent_month        ;

    printf ( "\n%d month(s) past, %d months to go.\n", isum,idiff );
}
```

The enumerated list is actually a list of integer values from 1 to 12 in this program. Because the names are equivalent to consecutive integer values, integer arithmetic can be performed with them. The enumerated variable *emcompleted*, when set equal to December, is actually set to 12. This short program will simply perform some simple arithmetic and report the result to the screen:

```
Please enter the current month (1 to 12): 4
4 month(s) past, 8 months to go.
```

In the Next Chapter...

This chapter has detailed the nuances of C/C++ structures, unions, and enumerated types. Although all three concepts are identical in both C and C++, remember: there are subtle syntax and usage differences when implementing these concepts in either C or C++. Just because C++ is a superset of C (which means that anything that will work in a C program will work in a C++ algorithm), does not mean that you *should* write a C++ program the way you would a C application.

Chapter 14 completes the coverage of standard C and C++ programming features. After completing Chapter 14, you will be ready to launch into the fundamentals of object-oriented programming which are presented in Chapter 15.

Chapter Fourteen

Advanced C and C++ Programming Topics

This chapter deals with advanced programming concepts common to both C and C++. Many of the topics discussed, such as type compatibility and macros, will point out those areas of the language where you must use caution when designing your algorithm. Other topics discussed, like compiler-supplied macros and conditional preprocessor statements, will help you create more streamlined applications. The chapter ends by explaining the concepts and syntax necessary to create dynamic linked lists. Once you have completed Chapters 5 through 14, your knowledge of C/C++ will be sufficient to enable you to make the mental leap to the concept of object-oriented programming, which will be discussed in the remainder of the book.

Type Compatibility

As you now well know, C is not a strongly typed language, whereas C++ is only slightly more strongly typed (for example, **enum**erated types). You have also seen how C/C++ can perform automatic type conversions and explicit type conversions using the cast operator. The following section highlights the sometimes confusing way in which the C/C++ compiler interprets compatible types.

ANSI C Definition for Type Compatibility

The whole idea for the issue of compatible types came from the ANSI C committee. Many of the committee's recommendations added features to C, such as function prototyping, that made the language more readily maintained. In trying to define a set of rules or coded syntax that nailed down the language's automatic behind-the-scenes behavior, the ANSI C committee decided that for two types to be compatible, they must either be the same type or be pointers, functions, or arrays with certain properties, as described in the following sections.

Array Types

If two arrays have compatible array elements, the arrays are considered compatible. If only one array specifies a size, or neither does, the types are still compatible. However, if both arrays specify a size, both sizes must be identical for the arrays to be compatible. See if you can find all of the compatible arrays in the following declarations:

```
int        imax20    [ 20 ];
const int  cimax20   [ 20 ];
int        imax10    [ 10 ];
int        iundefined[    ];
```

The undimensioned integer array *iundefined* is compatible with both *imax20* and *imax10*. However, this last pair is incompatible because they use different array bounds. The arrays *imax20* (element type **int**) and *cimax20* (element type **const int**) are incompatible because their elements are not compatible. If either array specifies an array bound, the composite type of the compatible arrays has that size also. Using the preceding code segment, the composite type of *iundefined* and *imax20* is *int[20]*.

Enumerated Types

The ANSI C committee initially stated that each enumerated type be compatible with the implementation-specific integral type; this is not the case with C++. In C++, enumeration types are not compatible with integral types. In both C and C++, no two enumerated type definitions in the same source file are compatible. This rule is analogous to the tagged and untagged (anonymous) structures. This explains why *ebflag1* and *ebflag2* are compatible types, whereas *eflag1* is not a compatible type:

```
enum boolean {0,1} ebflag1;
enum         {0,1} eflag1 ;
enum boolean       ebflag2;
```

Function Types

There are three conditions that must be met in order for two prototyped functions to be considered compatible. The two functions must have the same return types and the same number of parameters, and the corresponding parameters must be compatible types. However, parameter names do not have to agree.

Multiple Source File Compatibility

Because the compiler views each declaration of a structure, a union, or an enumerated type as being a new noncompatible type, you might be wondering what happens when you want to reference these types across files within the same program. Multiple structure, union, and enumerated declarations are compatible across source files if they declare the same members, in the same order, with compatible member types. However, with enumerated types, the enumeration constants do not have to be declared in the same order, although each constant must have the same enumeration value.

Pointer Types

Two pointer types are considered compatible if they both point to compatible types. The composite type of the two compatible pointers is the same as the pointed-to composite type.

Structure and Union Types

Each new structure or union type that a program declares introduces a new type that is not the same as, nor compatible with, any other type in the same source file. For this reason, the variables *stanonymous1*, *stanonymous2*, and *stfloat1* in the following code segment are all different. However, a reference to a type specifier that is a structure, a union, or an enumerated type is the same type. You use the tag field to associate the reference with the type declaration. For this reason, the tag field can be thought of as the name of the type. This rule explains why *stfloat1* and *stfloat2* are compatible types.

```
struct              { float fvalue1, fvalue2; } stanonymous1;
struct              { float fvalue1, fvalue2; } stanonymous2;
struct sttwofloats { float fvalue1, fvalue2}   stfloat1    ;
struct sttwofloats                              stfloat2    ;
```

What Is an Identical Type?

The term composite type is associated with the subject of compatibility. The composite type is the common type that is produced by two compatible types. Any two types that are the same are compatible, and their composite type is the same type. Two arithmetic types are identical if they are the same type. Abbreviated declarations for the same type are also identical. In the following example, both *shivalue1* and *shivalue2* are identical types:

```
short       shivalue1;
short int  shivalue2;
```

And the type **int** is the same as **signed int** in this next example:

```
int          sivalue1;
signed int  sivalue2;
```

However, the types **int**, **short**, and **unsigned** are all different. When dealing with character data, the types **char**, **signed char**, and **unsigned char** are always different.

The ANSI C committee stated that any type preceded by an access modifier generates incompatible types. For example, the next two declarations are not compatible types:

```
int          ivalue1;
const int  ivalue2;
```

In this next set of declarations, see if you can guess which types are compatible:

```
char    *pc1, *pc2                                            ;
struct {int ix, iy;}         stanonymous_coord1, stanonymous_coord2;
struct  stxy {int ix, iy;} stanycoords                        ;
typedef struct stxy          STXY                             ;
STXY                         stmorecoords                     ;
```

Both *pc1* and *pc2* are compatible character pointers because the additional space between the * symbol and *pc2* in the declaration is superfluous. You are probably not surprised that the compiler sees *stanonymous_coord1* and *stanonymous_coord2* as the same type. However, the compiler does not see *stanycoords* as being the identical type to the previous pair of variables. Even though all three variables seem to have the same two integer fields, *stanonymous_coord1* and *stanonymous_coord2* are of an anonymous structure type, while *stanycoords* is of tag type *stxy*. Because of the **typedef** declaration, the compiler does see **struct** *stxy* as being the identical type to *STXY*. For this reason, *stanycoords* is identical to *stmorecoords*.

It is important to remember that the compiler sees **typedef** declarations as being synonymous for standard compiler-supplied types, not totally new types. The following code segment defines a new type called *MYFLOAT* that is the same type as **float**:

```
typedef float MYFLOAT;
```

Macros

In Chapter 6, you learned how to use the **#define** preprocessor to declare symbolic constants. You can use the same preprocessor to define macros. A *macro* is a piece of code that can look and act just like a function. The advantage of a properly written macro is in its execution speed. A macro is expanded (replaced by its **#define** definition) during preprocessing, creating what is called inline code. For this reason, macros do not have the overhead normally associated with function calls. However, each substitution lengthens the overall code size. Conversely, function definitions expand only once no matter how many times they are called. The trade-off between execution speed and overall code size can help you decide which way to write a particular routine.

There are other subtle differences between macros and functions that are based on when the code is expanded. These differences fall into three categories. In C/C++, a function name evaluates to the address of where to find the subroutine. Because macros sit inline and can be expanded many times, there is no one address associated with a macro. For this reason, a macro cannot be used in a context requiring a function pointer. Also, you can declare pointers to functions, but you cannot declare a pointer to a macro.

The C/C++ compiler sees a function declaration differently from a **#define** macro. Because of this, the compiler does not do any type checking on macros. The result is that the compiler will not flag you if you pass the wrong number or wrong type of arguments to a macro. Because macros are expanded before the program is actually compiled, some macros treat arguments incorrectly when the macro evaluates an argument more than once.

Defining Macros

You define macros the same way you define symbolic constants. The only difference is that the *substitution_string* usually contains more than a single value:

```
#define search_string substitution_string
```

The following example uses the preprocessor statement to define both a symbolic constant and a macro to highlight the similarities:

```
/* #define symbolic constant */
#define iMAX_ROWS 100

/* #define macro            */
#define NL putchar('\n')
```

The *NL* macro causes the preprocessor to search through the source code looking for every occurrence of *NL* and to replace it with *putchar('\n')*. Notice that the macro did not end with a semicolon. The reason for this has to do with how you invoke a macro in your source code:

```
void main( void )
{
    .
    .
    .
  NL;
```

The compiler requires that the macro call end with a semicolon. Suppose the *substitution_string* of the macro had ended with a semicolon:

```
#define NL putchar('\n');
```

Then, after the macro expansion had taken place, the compiler would see the following code:

```
void main( void )
{
    .
    .
    .
    putchar('\n');;
```

Macros and Parameters

C/C++ supports macros that take arguments. These macros must be defined with parameters, which serve a purpose similar to that of a function's parameters. The parameters act as placeholders for the actual arguments. The following example demonstrates how to define and use a paramaterized macro:

```
/* macro definition */
#define READ_RESPONSE(c) scanf("%c",(&c))
#define MULTIPLY(x,y) ((x)*(y))

int main(void)
{
  char cresponse;
  int a = 10, b = 20;
    .
    .
    .
  READ_RESPONSE(cresponse); /* macro expansions */
  printf("%d",MULTIPLY(a,b));
```

In this example *x*, *y*, and *c* serve as placeholders for *a*, *b*, and *cresponse*, respectively. The two macros, *READ_RESPONSE* and *MULTIPLY*, demonstrate the different ways you can invoke macros in your program. For example, *MULTIPLY* is substituted within a **printf()** statement, whereas *READ_RESPONSE* is stand-alone.

Problems with Macro Expansions

Macros operate purely by substituting one set of characters, or tokens, for another. The actual parsing of the declaration, expression, or statement invoking the macro occurs after the macro expansion process. This can lead to some surprising results if care is not taken. For example, the following macro definition looks perfectly legal:

```
#define SQUAREIT(x) x * x
```

However, suppose the statement is invoked with a value of 5, as shown here:

```
iresult = SQUAREIT(5);
```

The compiler sees the following statement:

```
iresult = 5 * 5;
```

On the surface everything looks fine. However, what if the same macro is invoked with this next statement:

```
iresult = SQUAREIT(x + 1);
```

It is seen by the compiler as

```
iresult = x + (1 * x) + 1;
```

instead of

```
iresult = (x + 1) * (x + 1);
```

As a general rule, it is safest to always parenthesize each parameter appearing in the body of the macro, as seen in the previous *READ_RESPONSE* and *MULTIPLY* macro definitions. And under those circumstances where the macro expansion may appear in a cast expression, for example:

```
dresult = (double)SQUAREIT(x + 1);
```

it is best to paramaterize the entire body of the macro:

```
#define SQUAREIT(x) ((x) * (x))
```

Most of the time, the C/C++ compiler is insensitive to additional spacing within standard C/C++ statements. This is not the case with macro definitions. Look closely at this next example and see if you can detect the error:

```
/* incorrect macro definition */
#define BAD_MACRO (ans) scanf("%d",(&ans))
```

Remember that the **#define** preprocessor searches for the *search_string* and replaces it with the *substitution_string*. These two strings are delineated by one or more blanks. The preceding definition, when expanded, will appear this way to the compiler:

```
(ans) scanf("%d",(&ans));
```

This creates an illegal statement. The problem has to do with the space between the macro name *BAD_MACRO* and (*ans*). That extra space made the parameter list part of the *substitution_string* instead of putting it in its proper place as part of the *search_string*. To fix the *BAD_MACRO* definition, you need to remove the extra space:

```
#define BAD_MACRO(ans) scanf("%d",(&ans))
```

To see if you really do understand the hidden problems that you can encounter when using macros, see if you can figure out what this statement would evaluate to:

```
int x = 5;
iresult = SQUAREIT(x++);
```

The situation gets worse when you use certain C/C++ operators like increment (++) and decrement (- -). The result of this expression may be 30, instead of the expected 25, because the implementations of C/C++ compilers are free to evaluate the expression in several different ways. For example, the macro could be expanded syntactically to read:

```
/* iresult = x * x; */
iresult = 5 * 5;
or
/* iresult = x * (x+1); */
iresult = 5 * 6;
```

Creating and Using Your Own Macros

Macros can include other macros in their definitions. You can use this feature to streamline your source code. For example, look at the following progressive macro definitions:

```
#define NL putchar('\n')
#define TAB putchar('\t')
#define FORMAT1 NL, NL, TAB
#define FORMAT2 NL, TAB, TAB
#define BEGIN_PROMPT FORMAT1, printf("Want to begin?"); \
                                printf("\nType 1 for yes, 0 for no")
#define READ_RESPONSE FORMAT2,scanf("%d",(&c))
#define FORMAT_PRINT(ccontrol,ivalue,fvalue) \
        printf("\n%c\t%d\t%8.2f",(ccontrol),(ivalue),(fvalue))
```

Now, instead of your main program including all of the code defined in the macro, your program looks like this:

```
void main( void )
{
  char   cresponse    ;
  int    ivalue = 23   ;
  float  fvalue = 56.78;

     .
     .
     .

  BEGIN_PROMPT;
  READ_RESPONSE( cresponse );
  FORMAT_PRINT(  cresponse, ivalue, fvalue );
```

However, remember that you are trading off automatic compiler type checking for source code readability, along with possibly causing side effects generated by the invoking statement's syntax.

Macros Shipped with the Compiler

The ANSI C committee has recommended that all C/C++ compilers define five special predefined macros that take no arguments. Each macro name begins and ends with two underscore characters, as listed in Table 14-1:

Macro Name	Meaning
_ _LINE_ _	A decimal integer constant representing the line number of the current source program line
_ _FILE_ _	A string constant representing the name of the current source file
_ _DATE_ _	A string constant representing the calendar date of the translation in the form *Mmm dd yyyy*
_ _TIMESTAMP_ _	A string constant representing the date and time of the last modification of the source file, in the form *Ddd Mmm hh:mm:ss yyyy*
_ _STDC_ _	Represents a decimal 1 if the compiler is ANSI C compatible

Table 14-1. *ANSI C/C++ Predefined Macros*

You invoke a predefined macro the same way you would a user-defined macro. For example, to print your program's name, date, and current line number to the screen, you would use the following statement:

```
printf( "%s | %s | Line number: %d", _ _FILE_ _, _ _DATE_ _, _ _LINE_ _ );
```

Advanced Preprocessor Statements

There are actually 12 standard preprocessor statements, sometimes referred to as directives. They are listed in Table 14-2. You are already familiar with two of the 12—**#include** and **#define**.

#include	#define	#ifdef	#endif
#undef	#ifndef	#if	#else
#elif	#line	#error	#pragma

Table 14-2. *Advanced Preprocessor Directives*

Remember that the C/C++ preprocessor processes a source file before the compiler translates the program into object code. By carefully selecting the correct directives, you can create more efficient header files, solve unique programming problems, and prevent combined files from crashing in on your declarations.

The following section explains the unique function of each of the ten new preprocessor directives not previously discussed. Some of the examples will use the code found in stdio.h in order to illustrate the construction of header files.

The #ifdef and #endif Directives

The **#ifdef** and **#endif** directives are two of several conditional preprocessor statements. You can use them to selectively include certain statements in your program. The **#endif** directive is used with all of the conditional preprocessor statements to signify the end of the conditional block. For example, if the name *LARGE_CLASSES* has been previously defined, the following code segment will define a new name called *MAX_SEATS*:

```
#ifdef LARGE_CLASSES
#define MAX_SEATS 100
#endif
```

Whenever a C++ program uses standard C functions, you can use the **#ifdef** directive to modify the function declarations so that they have the required **extern "C"** linkage, which inhibits the encoding of the function name. This usually calls for the following pair of directive code segments to encapsulate the translated code:

```
/*  used in graph.h  */
#ifdef _ _cplusplus
extern "C" {           /* allow use with C++ */
#endif

/* translation units */

#ifdef _ _cplusplus
}
#endif
```

The #undef Directive

The **#undef** directive tells the preprocessor to cancel any previous definition of the specified identifier. This next example combines your understanding of **#ifdef** with the use of **#undef** to change the dimension of *MAX_SEATS*:

```
#ifdef LARGE_CLASSES
#undef MAX_SEATS 30
#define MAX_SEATS 100
#endif
```

In case you were wondering, the compiler will not complain if you try to undefine a name not previously defined. Notice that once a name has been undefined, it may be given a completely new definition with another **#define** directive.

The #ifndef Directive

Undoubtedly, you are beginning to understand how the conditional directives operate. The **#ifndef** preprocessor checks to see if the specified identifier does not exist and then performs some action. The code segment that follows is taken directly from stdio.h:

```
#ifndef _SIZE_T_DEFINED
typedef unsigned int size_t;
#define _SIZE_T_DEFINED
#endif
```

In this case, the conditionally executed statements include both a **typedef** and **#define** preprocessor. This code takes care of defining the type **size_t**, specified by the ANSI C committee as the return type for the operator **sizeof()**. Make sure you read "The Proper Use of Header Files" section later in this chapter so you will understand what types of statements can go into header files.

The #if Directive

The **#if** preprocessor also recognizes the term **defined**. The code

```
#if defined(LARGE_CLASSES) && !defined (PRIVATE_LESSONS)
#define MAX_SEATS 30
#endif
```

shows how the **#if** directive, together with the **defined** construct, accomplishes what would otherwise require an **#ifndef** nested in an **#ifdef**:

```
#ifdef LARGE_CLASSES
#ifndef PRIVATE_LESSONS
```

```
#define MAX_SEATS 30
#endif
```

The two examples produce the same result, but the first is more immediately discerned. Both **#ifdef** and **#ifndef** directives are restricted to a single test expression. However, the **#if** combined with **define** allows compound expressions.

The #else Directive

The **#else** directive has the expected use. Suppose you know that a program is going to be run on a VAX computer and a PC. The VAX allocates 4 bytes, or 32 bits, to the type integer, whereas the PC allocates only 2 bytes, or 16 bits (for 16-bit compilers; or 4 bytes, or 32 bits, for 32-bit compilers). The following code segment uses the **#else** directive to make certain that an integer is viewed as the same on both systems:

```
#ifdef VAX_SYSTEM
#define INTEGER short int
#else
#define INTEGER int
#endif
```

Of course, the program will have to take care of defining the identifier *VAX_SYSTEM* when you run it on the VAX. As you can see, combinations of preprocessor directives make for interesting solutions.

The #elif Directive

The **#elif** directive is an abbreviation for "else if" and provides an alternate approach to nested **#if** statements. The following code segment checks to see which class size is defined and uniquely defines the *BILL* macro:

```
#if defined (LARGE_CLASSES)
     #define BILL printf("\nCost per student $100.00.\n")
  #elif defined (PRIVATE_LESSONS)
     #define BILL printf("\nYour tuition is $1000.00.\n")
   #else
     #define BILL printf("\nCost per student $150.00.\n")
#endif
```

Notice that the preprocessors don't have to start in column 1. The ability to indent preprocessor statements for readability is only one of the many useful recommendations made by the ANSI C committee and adopted by Borland C++.

The #line Directive

The **#line** directive overrides the compiler's automatic line numbering. You can use it to help in debugging your program. Suppose you have just merged a 50-line routine into a file of over 400 statements. All you care about are any errors that could be generated within the merged code. Normally, the compiler starts line numbering from the beginning of the file. If your routine had an error, the compiler would print a message with a line number of, say, 289. From your merged file's point of view, where is that? However, if you include a **#line** directive in the beginning of your freshly merged subroutine, the compiler would give you a line error number relative to the beginning of the function:

```
#line 1
int imy_mergefunction( void )
{
    .
    .
    .
}
```

The #error Directive

The **#error** directive instructs the compiler to generate a user-defined error message. It can be used to extend the compiler's own error-detection and message capabilities. After the compiler encounters an **#error** directive, it scans the rest of the program for syntax errors but does not produce an object file. For example, the following code prints a warning message *if _CHAR_UNSIGNED* is undefined:

```
#if !defined( if_CHAR_UNSIGNED )
#error /J option required.
#endif
```

The #pragma Directive

The **#pragma** directive gives the compiler implementation-specific instructions on how to interpret the source code and generate the executable. The Borland C++ compiler supports the following pragmas (see Table 14-3):

alloc_text	auto_inline	check_pointer
check_stack	code_seg	comment
data_seg	function	hdrstop
inline_depth	inline_recursion	init_seg
intrinsic	linesize	loop_opt
message	native_caller	optimize
pack	page	pagesize
skip	subtitle	title
warning		

Table 14-3. *#pragma Directives*

Conditional Compilation

You won't always find preprocessor statements in header files. You can use preprocessor directives in your source code to generate efficient compilations. Look at this next code segment and see if you can detect the subtle difference (hint: executable code size):

```
/* compiled if statement */
if(DEBUG_ON) {
  printf("Entering Example Function");
  printf("First argument passed has a value of %d",ifirst_arg);
}

/* comparison statement   */
#if defined(DEBUG_ON)
  printf("Entering Example Function");
  printf("First argument passed has a value of %d",ifirst_arg);
#endif
```

The first **if** statement is always compiled. This means that the debugging information is perpetually reflected in the executable size of your program. But what if you don't want to ship a product with your intermediate development-cycle code? The solution is to conditionally compile these types of statements.

The second portion of the code demonstrates how to selectively compile code with the **#if** defined directive. To debug your program, you simply define *DEBUG_ON*. This makes the nested **#if...#endif** statements visible to the compiler. However, when you are ready to ship the final product, you remove the *DEBUG_ON* definition. This makes the statements invisible to the compiler, reducing the size of the executable file.

Try the following simple test to prove to yourself how invisible the **#if...#endif** directives make the **printf()** statement pair. Copy the previous code segment into a simple C program that does nothing else. Include all necessary overhead (**#include**, **main()**, {, and so on). Do not define *DEBUG_ON*. Make certain that when you compile the program, there are no error messages. Now, remove the **#include** <stdio.h> statement from the program and recompile.

At this point, the compiler stops at the first **printf()** statement nested within the **if...printf()** block statement. The message printed is "Function 'printf' should have a prototype." You expect this because the **printf()** statement within the **if** is always visible to the compiler. Now, simply remove or comment out the **if...printf()** block statement and recompile.

The compiler does not complain about the **printf()** statements nested within the **#if...#endif** preprocessors. It never saw them. They would only become visible to the compilation phase of the compiler if *DEBUG_ON* is defined. You can use this selective visibility for more than executable statements. Look at this next code-streamlining option:

```
#if defined(DEBUG_ON)
  /*****************************************/
  /* The following code segment performs   */
  /* a sophisticated enough solution step  */
  /* to require a comment and debug output */
  /*****************************************/
  printf("    debug code goes here        ");
#endif
```

This example not only has a conditional output debug statement, but it also provides room for an explanatory comment. The little extra time it takes to write conditionally compiled code is easily justified by easily debugged code and small executable code size.

Advanced Preprocessor Operators

There are three operators that are available only to preprocessor directives. These are the *stringize* (#), *concatenation* (##), and *charizing* (#@) operators.

The Stringize Operator (#)

Placing a single # in front of a macro parameter causes the compiler to insert the name of the argument instead of its value. This has the overall effect of converting the argument name into a string. The operator is necessary because parameters are not replaced if they occur inside string literals that are explicitly coded in a macro. The following example demonstrates the syntax for the *stringize* operator:

```
#define STRINGIZE(ivalue) printf(#ivalue " is: %d",ivalue)
    .
    .
    .
int ivalue = 2;
   STRINGIZE(ivalue);
```

The output from the macro looks like this:

```
ivalue is: 2
```

The Concatenation Operator (##)

One use for the *concatenation* operator is for building variable and macro names dynamically. The operator concatenates the items, removing any white space on either side and forming a new token. When ## is used in a macro, it is processed after the macro parameters are substituted and before the macro is examined for any additional macro processing. For example, the following code shows how to create preprocessed variable names:

```
#define IVALUE_NAMES(icurrent_number) ivalue ## icurrent_number;
    .
    .
    .
int IVALUE_NAMES(1);
```

This is seen by the compiler as the following declaration:

```
int ivalue1;
```

Notice that the preprocessor removed the blanks so that the compiler didn't see *ivalue1* as *ivalue* 1. The operator can be combined with other preprocessor directives to form complex definitions. The following example uses the concatenation operator to generate a macro name, which causes the preprocessor to invoke the appropriate macro:

```
#define MACRO1 printf("MACRO1 invoked.")
#define MACRO2 printf("MACRO2 invoked.")
```

```
#define MAKE_MACRO(n) MACRO ## n
     .
     .
     .
MAKE_MACRO(1);
```

The output from the example looks like this:

```
MACRO1 invoked.
```

The Charizing Operator (#@)

The *charizing* preprocessor precedes formal parameters in a macro definition. This causes the actual argument to be treated as a single character with single quotation marks around it. For example:

```
#define CHARIZEIT(cvalue) #@cvalue
     .
     .
     .
cletter = CHARIZEIT(z);
```

This is seen by the compiler as:

```
cletter = 'z';
```

The Proper Use of Header Files

Because header files are made up of syntactically correct C/C++ ASCII text and are included in other files at the point of the #include directive, many beginning programmers misuse them. Sometimes they are incorrectly used to define entire functions or collections of functions. Although this approach does not invoke any complaints from the compiler, it is a logical misuse of the structure.

Header files are used to define and share common declarations with several source files. They provide a centralized location for the declaration of all external variables, function prototypes, class definitions, **struct**ures, **union**s, **enum**s, and inline functions. On the other hand, files that must *declare* a variable, function, or class include header files.

This provides two safeguards. First, all files are guaranteed to contain the same declarations. Second, should a declaration require updating, only one change needs to be made to the header file. The possibility of failing to update the declaration in a particular file is removed. Header files are frequently made up of:

- Preprocessor directives
- **const** declarations
- Function prototypes
- **typedef**s
- **struct**ure definitions
- **enum**erated types
- References to **extern**s

Some care should be taken in designing header files. The declarations provided should logically belong together. A header file takes time to compile. If it is too large or filled with too many disparate elements, programmers will be reluctant to incur the compile-time cost of including them.

A second consideration is that a header file should never contain a nonstatic definition. If two files in the same program include a header file with an external definition, most link editors will reject the program because of multiple defined symbols. Because constant values are often required in header files, the default linkage of a **const** identifier is **static**. For this reason, constants can be defined inside header files.

Making Header Files More Efficient

You make the compiling of header files more efficient by using combinations of preprocessor directives. The best way to learn how to construct an efficient header file is to look at an example:

```
#ifndef _INC_IOSTREAM
#define _INC_IOSTREAM

#if !defined(_INC_DEFS )
#include <_defs.h>
#endif

#if !defined(_INC_MEM )
#include <mem.h>     // to get memcpy and NULL
#endif

#endif  /* !_INC_IOSTREAM */
```

Before looking at the individual statements in the example, you need to know that the first pass of the compiler builds a symbol table. One of the entry types in a symbol table is the mangled names of header files. *Mangling* is something that the compiler does to distinguish one symbol from another. The C compiler mangles variable, constant, and function names by prepending an underscore to these symbols. The easiest way to control the compiled visibility of a header file is to surround the code within the header file with a tri-statement combination in this form:

```
#ifndef _INC_myheader
#define _INC_myheader    /* begin _INC_MYHEADER visibility */
    .
    .
    .
#endif /* end of conditional _INC_MYHEADER visibility */
```

This is exactly what was done with the previous coded example, where _INC_IOSTREAM was substituted for _INC_MYHEADER. The first time the compiler includes this header file, _INC_IOSTREAM is undefined. The code segment is included, making all of the nested statements visible. From this point forward, any additional **#include** <iostream.h> statements found in any of the other files used to create the executable file bypass the nested code.

limits.h and float.h

To help you write portable code, the ANSI C committee requires that all C/C+ compilers document the system-dependent ranges of integer and floating-point types. To see your compiler's limits.h or float.h, click on the File | Open command in the File Manager dialog box, locate the compiler's *include* subdirectory, then scan the file list for either file and double-click on the file's name (limits.h or float.h).

Your code can use these ranges to make certain your data will fit in the specified data type. For example, a VAX integer is 4 bytes, whereas a PC-based integer is only 2 (for 16-bit compilers). One solution to this storage-size problem looks like this:

```
if (PROGRAM_NEEDED_MAX > INT_MAX)
  pvoid = new llong_storage;
else
  pvoid = new iinteger_storage;
```

Handling Errors: perror()

One of the many interesting functions prototyped in stdio.h is a function called **perror()**. The **perror()** function prints to the **stderr** stream the system error message for the last library routine called that generated an error. It does this by using **errno** and **sys_errlist**, prototyped in stdlib.h. **sys_errlist** is an array of error message strings. **errno** is an index into the message string array and is automatically set to the index for the error generated. The number of entries in the array is determined by another constant, **sys_nerr**, also defined in stdlib.h.

The function **perror()** has only one parameter, a character string. Normally, the argument passed is a string representing the file or function that generated the error condition. The following example demonstrates the simplicity of the function:

```
/*
 *  perror.c
 *  A C program demonstrating the function perror()
 *  prototyped in stdio.h
 *  Copyright (c) Chris H. Pappas and William H. Murray, 1996
 */

#include <stdio.h>

void main( void )
{
    FILE *fpinfile;

    fpinfile = fopen("input.dat", "r");

    if ( !fpinfile )
        perror( "Could not open input.dat in file main() :" );
}
```

Here is the message:

```
Could not open input.dat in file main() : No such file or directory
```

Dynamic Memory Allocation: Linked Lists

Linked lists are often the best choice when you are trying to create memory-efficient algorithms. Previous example programs involving arrays of structures have all included definitions for the total number of structures used. For example, *MAX_BOATS* has been set to 50. This means that the program can accept data for a maximum of 50 boats. If 70 or 100 boats are brought onto the marina, the program itself will have to be altered to accommodate the increased number. This is because the structure allocation is static (not to be confused with the storage class modifier **static**). Static used in this sense means a variable that is created by the compiler at compile time. These types of variables exist for their normal scope, and you cannot create more of them or destroy any of them while the program is executing. You can immediately see the disadvantage of static allocation.

One way around the problem is to set the number of structures higher than needed. If *MAX_BOATS* is set to 5000, not even Nineveh Boat Sales could have a marina that large. However, 5000 means you are requiring the computer to set aside more than 100 times more memory than before. This is not an efficient way to program.

A better approach is to set aside memory dynamically as it is needed. With this approach, memory allocation for structures is requested as the inventory grows. Linked lists allow the use of dynamic memory allocation. A *linked list* is a collection of structures. Each structure in the list contains an element or pointer that points to another structure in the list. This pointer serves as the link between structures. The concept is similar to an array but enables the list to grow dynamically. Figure 14-1 shows a simple linked list for the Nineveh Boat Sales Program.

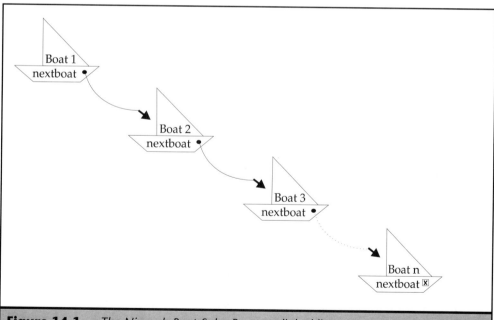

Figure 14-1. *The Nineveh Boat Sales Program linked list*

The linked list for this example includes a pointer to the next boat in the inventory:

```
struct stboat {
    char          sztype    [ 15 ];
    char          szmodel   [ 15 ];
    char          sztitle   [ 20 ];
    char          szcomment [ 80 ];
    int           iyear              ;
    long int      lmotor_hours       ;
    float         fretail            ;
    float         fwholesale         ;
    struct stboat *nextboat          ;
} Nineveh, *firstboat,*currentboat;
```

The user-defined structure type *stboat* is technically known as a *self-referential structure* because it contains a field that holds an address to another structure just like itself. The pointer *nextboat* contains the address of the next related structure. This allows the pointer *nextboat* in the first structure to point to the second structure, and so on. This concept is what makes a linked list of structures valuable.

Considerations When Using Linked Lists

To allow your program to dynamically reflect the size of your data, you need a means for allocating memory as each new item is added to the list. In C, memory allocation is accomplished with the **malloc()** function; in C++, **new** is used. In the next section, "A Simple Linked List," the complete program allocates memory for the first structure with this code:

```
firstboat=(struct stboat *) new (struct stboat);
```

The following code segment demonstrates how you can use a similar statement to achieve subsequent memory allocation for each additional structure. The **while** loop continues the entire process while there is valid data to be processed:

```
while( datain(&Nineveh) == 0 ) {
   currentboat->nextboat = (struct stboat *) new (struct stboat);
   if (currentboat->nextboat == NULL) return(1);
currentboat=currentboat->nextboat;

  *currentboat=Nineveh;

}
```

To give you some experience with passing structures, the **while** loop begins by sending **datain()** the address of the *stboat* structure, *&Nineveh*. The function **datain()** takes care of filling the structure with valid data or returns a value of 1 if the user has entered the letter *Q* indicating that he or she wants to quit. If **datain()** does not return a 1, the pointer *currentboat->nextboat* is assigned the address of a dynamically allocated *stboat* structure. Notice that the address returned by **new** was cast *(struct stboat *)* so that it matched the data type of the receiving variable. The **if** statement checks to see if the function call to **new** was successful or not. (**new** returns a NULL if unsuccessful.)

Because the logical use for *currentboat* is to keep track of the address of the last valid *stboat* structure in the list, the statement after the **if** updates *currentboat* to the address of the new end of the list, namely *currentboat*'s new *nextboat* address. The last statement in the loop copies the contents of the *stboat* structure *Nineveh* into the new dynamically allocated structure pointed to by **currentboat*. The last structure in the list will have its pointer set to NULL. Using NULL marks the end of a linked list. See if you can tell where this is done in the complete program that follows.

A Simple Linked List

The following program shows how to implement the Nineveh Boat Sales example using linked lists. Compare this program with the one given in Chapter 13 in the section "An Array of Structures." The C example in Chapter 13 is similar, except that it uses a static array implementation. Study the two listings and see which items are similar and which items have changed.

```
//
//      A C++ program is an example of a simple linked list.
//      Nineveh used boat inventory example is used again.
//      Copyright (c) Chris H. Pappas and William H. Murray, 1996
//

#include <stdlib.h>
#include <iostream.h>

struct stboat {
    char            sztype    [ 15 ]                    ;
    char            szmodel   [ 15 ]                    ;
    char            sztitle   [ 20 ]                    ;
    char            szcomment [ 80 ]                    ;
    int             iyear                               ;
    long int        lmotor_hours                        ;
    float           fretail                             ;
    float           fwholesale                          ;
    struct stboat   *nextboat                           ;
```

```
} Nineveh, *firstboat,*currentboat                          ;

void boatlocation( struct stboat *node        )             ;
void output_data ( struct stboat *boatptr     )             ;
int  datain       ( struct stboat *Ninevehptr )             ;

void main( void )
{
  firstboat = (struct stboat *) new ( struct stboat )       ;

  if( firstboat == NULL    )    exit(1)                     ;

  if( datain(&Nineveh) != 0 )    exit(1)                    ;

  *firstboat  = Nineveh                                     ;
  currentboat = firstboat                                   ;

  while( datain(&Nineveh)==0 )                              {
    currentboat->nextboat=
                (struct stboat *) new ( struct stboat )     ;
    if( currentboat->nextboat==NULL )    return( 1 )        ;
       currentboat = currentboat->nextboat                  ;
      *currentboat = Nineveh                                ;
  }

  currentboat->nextboat=NULL;          // signal end of list

  boatlocation( firstboat )                                 ;
}



void boatlocation( struct stboat *node )
{
  do {
    output_data( node )                                     ;
  } while( (node=node->nextboat) != NULL )                  ;
}

void output_data( struct stboat *boatptr )
{
```

```
    cout << "\n\n\n"                                              ;
    cout << "A[{|"|}]
          << boatptr->iyear
          <<[{|"|}]"
          << boatptr->sztype
          << boatptr->szmodel
          << [{|"|}]"
          << "beauty with[{|"|}]"
          << boatptr->lmotor_hours
          << [{|"|}]"
          << "low miles.\n";
    cout << boatptr->szcomment
          << ".\n"                                                ;
    cout << "Grab the deal by asking "
          << "your Nineveh salesperson for"                       ;
    cout << [{|"|}]#"
          << boatptr->sztitle
          << [{|"|}]ONLY! $"
          << boatptr->fretail << ".\n"                            ;
}

int datain( struct stboat *Ninevehptr )
{
    char newline;

    cout << "\n[Enter new boat information - a Q quits]\n\n";
    cout << "Enter the make of the boat.\n"                       ;
    cin  >>  Ninevehptr->sztype                                   ;

    if( *(Ninevehptr->sztype) == 'Q' ) return( 1 )               ;

    cout << "Enter the model of the boat.\n"                      ;
    cin  >>  Ninevehptr->szmodel                                  ;

    cout << "Enter the title number for the boat.\n"              ;
    cin  >>  Ninevehptr->sztitle                                  ;

    cout << "Enter the model year for the boat.\n"                ;
    cin  >>  Ninevehptr->iyear                                    ;

    cout << "Enter the number of hours on the boat motor.\n";
```

```
cin  >>  Ninevehptr->lmotor_hours                        ;

cout << "Enter the retail price of the boat.\n"          ;
cin  >>  Ninevehptr->fretail                             ;

cout << "Enter the wholesale price of the boat.\n"       ;
cin  >>  Ninevehptr->fwholesale                          ;

cout << "Enter a one line comment about the boat.\n"  ;
cin.get( newline );              // process carriage return
cin.get( Ninevehptr->szcomment,80,'.' )                  ;

cin.get( newline );              // process carriage return
return( 0 )                                              ;
}
```

Notice that the three functions are all passed pointers to an *stboat* structure:

```
void boatlocation( struct stboat *node      );

void output_data ( struct stboat *boatptr   );

int  datain      ( struct stboat *Ninevehptr );
```

The function *boatlocation()* checks the linked list for entries before calling the function *output_data()*. It does this with a **do...while** loop that is terminated whenever the node pointer is assigned a null address. This is true only when you have tried to go beyond the last *stboat* structure in the list. The *output_data()* function formats the output from each linked-list structure. In most high-level languages, linked lists provide program solutions that are very memory efficient and often the most difficult to debug. However, as you will learn throughout the remainder of the book, object-oriented C++ classes are even more efficient.

In the Next Chapter...

This chapter has completed your understanding of the structural underpinnings and unique C/C++ design considerations necessary to write professional C/C++ algorithms in a procedural environment. Beginning with Chapter 15, you will be introduced to the concept of object-oriented programming, and you will learn about C++ classes in Chapter 16. In Chapter 18, you will see how to combine the two concepts.

PART THREE

Foundations for Object-Oriented Programming in C++

Chapter Fifteen

Object-Oriented Programming—An Introduction

Chapters 1 through 14 have given you a fundamental working knowledge of those concepts common to both C and C++, along with constructs unique to the newer C++ language. Up to this point, all of the discussions and program examples have used a procedural design technique. In this chapter, you will be introduced to various object-oriented programming (OOP) concepts.

This chapter details the differences between a traditional procedure-oriented programming problem solution and an object-oriented approach. The chapter also discusses terms associated with C++ and object-oriented programming. These terms include, among others, "objects," "encapsulation," "hierarchy," "inheritance," and "polymorphism." Later in the chapter, simple examples show you how the C++ class type is an outgrowth of the C **struct** type. In the next chapter, you will learn the details of how the C++ class type forms the foundation for object-oriented programming.

An Old Concept Repackaged

Scott Guthery states that "object-oriented programming has been around since subroutines were invented in the 1940s" ("Are the Emperor's New Clothes Object-Oriented?", *Dr. Dobb's Journal*, December 1989). The article continues by suggesting that objects, the foundation of object-oriented programming, have appeared in earlier languages such as FORTRAN II. Considering these statements, why are we only hearing about object-oriented programming in the 1990s? Why is object-oriented programming being touted as the newest programming technique of the century? It seems that the bottom line is packaging.

OOP concepts may have been available in 1940, but they certainly weren't packaged in a usable container. Early programmers, growing up with the BASIC language, often wrote large programs without the use of structured programming concepts. Pages and pages of programming code were tied together with one- or two-letter variables that had a global scope, and **goto** statements abounded. The code was a nightmare to read, understand, and debug. Adding new features to such a program was like unlocking Pandora's box. The code, to say the least, was very difficult to maintain.

In the 1960s, structured programming concepts were introduced suggesting the use of meaningful variable names, global and local variable scope, and a procedure-oriented top-down programming approach. Applying these concepts made code easier to read, understand, and debug. Program maintenance was improved because the program could now be studied and altered one procedure at a time. Programming languages such as Ada, C, and Pascal encouraged a structured approach to programming problems.

Bjarne Stroustrup is considered the father of C++ because he developed the language at Bell Labs in the early 1980s. He may well be the father of object-oriented programming as we know it in the C++ language. Jeff Duntemann says, "Object-oriented programming is structured structured programming. It's the second derivative of software development, the Grand Unifying Theory of program structure"

("Dodging Steamships," *Dr. Dobb's Journal,* July 1989). Indeed, what you'll see is that object-oriented programming using C++ builds upon foundations established earlier in the C language. Even though C++ is the foundational language for object-oriented programming, it is still possible to write unstructured code or procedure-oriented code. The choice is yours.

This chapter introduces you to the most elegant packaging method for a programming concept you have ever seen. At last, with languages such as C++, we truly have the tools to enter the age of object-oriented programming.

Top-Down Design

Chapters 1 through 14 of this book were devoted to teaching traditional procedure-oriented structured programming techniques for solving C and C++ problems. These chapters introduced you to fundamental C and C++ syntax in a familiar programming environment. (If you have been programming in a language such as Pascal for any length of time, you have probably been using a structured procedure approach in solving programming problems. A procedural approach is common among all structured languages including C, C++, Pascal, and PL/I.) You have seen that a procedure-oriented C or C++ program is structured in such a way that there is typically a main function and possibly one or more functions (subroutines) that are called from the main function. This is a top-down approach. The main function is typically short, shifting the work to the remaining functions in the program.

Program execution flows from the top of the main function and terminates at the bottom of the same function. In this approach, code and data are separate. Procedures define what is to happen to data, but the two never become one. You'll see that this changes in object-oriented programming. The procedural approach suffers from several disadvantages, the chief of which is program maintenance. When additions or deletions must be made to the program code, such as in a database program, often the entire program must be reworked to include the new routines. This approach takes enormous amounts of time in both development and debugging. A better approach toward program maintenance is needed.

Object-Oriented Programming (OOP)

Object-oriented programs (OOPs) work differently from the traditional procedural approach. They require a new programming strategy that is often difficult for traditional procedure-oriented programmers to grasp. In the next four chapters, you will be introduced to the concepts that make up object-oriented programming in C++. If you have already written or examined program code for Microsoft Windows 3.x, Windows 95, or Windows NT, you have had a taste of one of the concepts used in object-oriented programming—that a program consists of a group of objects that are often related. With C++, you form objects by using the new class data type. A class provides a set of values (data) and the operations (methods or member functions) that act on those values. You can then manipulate the resulting objects by using messages. It is the message component of object-oriented languages that is also common to Windows and Presentation Manager programs.

In object-oriented programming, objects hold not only the data (called *member data*) but also the functions (called *member functions*, or *methods*) for working on that data. The two items have been combined into one working concept. Simply put, objects contain data and the methods for working on that data. Object-oriented programming offers three distinct advantages to the programmer. The first is program maintenance. Programs are easier to read and understand, and object-oriented programming minimizes program complexity by allowing only the necessary details to be viewed by the programmer.

The second advantage is program alteration (adding or deleting features). You can often make additions and deletions to programs, such as in a database program, by simply adding or deleting objects. New objects can inherit everything from a parent object, and they only need to add or delete items that differ. The third advantage is that you can use objects numerous times. You can save well-designed objects in a toolkit of useful routines that you can easily insert into new code, with few or no changes to that code. In the earlier chapters of this book, you discovered that you could convert many C programs to C++, and vice versa, by making simple program alterations. For example, **printf()** is switched to **cout** for I/O streams. This is an easy switch because the conversion is from and to a procedural programming structure.

However, object-oriented programming is exclusively in the C++ realm because C does not provide the vital link—the abstract data type class. It is therefore more difficult to convert a procedure-oriented program to object-oriented form. Programs have to be reworked, with traditional functions being replaced with objects. In some cases, it turns out to be easier to discard the old program and create an object-oriented program from the ground up. This can be considered a distinct disadvantage.

Object-Oriented C++ Programming

Object-oriented programming concepts cross language boundaries. Microsoft Quick Pascal, for example, was one of the first languages to allow the use of objects. What does C++ have that makes it a suitable language for developing object-oriented programs? The answer is, as previously mentioned, the class data type. It is C++'s class type, built upon C's **struct** type, that gives the language the ability to build objects. Also, C++ brings several additional features to object-oriented programming not included in other languages that simply make use of objects. C++'s advantages include strong typing, operator overloading, and less emphasis on the preprocessor.

It is true that you can do object-oriented programming with other products and in other languages, but with C++ the benefits are outstanding. This is a language that was designed, not retrofitted, for object-oriented programming. In the next section of this chapter, you will learn some object-oriented terminology. These terms and definitions will help you form a solid understanding of this programming technique. Be prepared; the new terminology will be your biggest hurdle as you enter the world of object-oriented programming.

OOP Terminology

Many OOP terms and concepts are language independent; that is, they are not associated with a specific language such as Pascal or C++. Therefore, many of the following definitions apply to the various implementations of object-oriented languages. Chapter 16 discusses terms that are more C++ specific. *Object-oriented programming* is a programming technique that allows you to view concepts as a variety of objects. You can use *objects* to represent the tasks that are to be performed, their interaction, and any given conditions that must be observed.

A *data structure* often forms the basis of an object; thus, in C or C++, the **struct** type can form an elementary object. Communicating with objects can be done through the use of *messages*, as mentioned earlier. Using messages is similar to calling a function in a procedure-oriented program. When an object receives a message, methods contained within the object respond. *Methods* are similar to the functions of procedure-oriented programming. However, methods are part of an object.

Explaining C++ Classes

The C++ *class* is an extension of the C and C++ **struct** type and forms the required abstract data type for object-oriented programming. The class can contain closely related items that share attributes. Stated more formally, an object is simply an instance of a class. In Figure 15-1, the Lincoln automobile class is illustrated.

```
Lincoln (parent class) --- |


                    |--Town Car (subclass)---A Town Car (instance)


                    |


                    |--Mark VIII (subclass)---A Mark VIII (instance)


                    |


                    |--Continental (subclass)---A Continental (instance)
```

Figure 15-1.   *Lincoln automobile class hierarchy diagram*

Assume that the Lincoln automobile class is described in the program's code. This class might include a description of items that are common to all Lincolns and data concerning maintenance intervals. At run time, three additional objects of the Lincoln class can be created. They could include the Lincoln Town Car, the Lincoln Mark VIII, and the Lincoln Continental. The additional objects might include details of features and data common to each individual model. For example, a Mark VIII is an object that describes a particular type of Lincoln automobile; therefore, it is in the Lincoln class of automobiles but is a specific type within that class. In other words, it is an instance of the Lincoln class. If a message is sent to the instance of the Lincoln class (similar to a call to a function) with instructions to dynamically adjust the air suspension on all four wheels during a sharp turn, that message could be utilized only by the Continental (at least in 1992 models) object of the class. Only the Lincoln Continental had an active air suspension in the 1992 model.

Ultimately, there should emerge class libraries containing many object types. You could use instances of those object types to piece together program code. You will see interesting examples of this when Windows class libraries are described in Chapters 24, 25, and 26. Before you examine these terms in closer detail, it is a good idea to become familiar with several additional concepts that relate to C++ and object-oriented programming, as described in the next few sections.

Data and Function Encapsulation

Encapsulation refers to the way each object combines its member data and member functions (methods) into a single structure. Figure 15-2 illustrates how you can combine data fields and methods to build an object.

Typically, an object's description is part of a C++ class and includes a definition for the object's internal structure, how the object relates with other objects, and some form of protection that isolates the functional details of the object from outside the class. The C++ class structure does all of this. In a C++ class, you control functional details of the object by using private, public, and/or protected descriptors.

In object-oriented programming, the public section is typically used for the interface information (methods) that makes the class reusable across applications. If data or methods are contained in the public section, they are available outside the class. The private section of a class limits the availability of data or methods to the class itself. A protected section containing data or methods is limited to the class and any derived subclasses.

Class Hierarchy

The C++ class actually serves as a template or pattern for creating objects. The objects formed from the class description are instances of the class. It is possible to develop a *class hierarchy* where there is a parent class and several child classes. In C++, the basis for doing this revolves around derived classes. Parent classes represent more generalized tasks, whereas *derived* child classes are given specific tasks to perform. For

```
Object Definition:

        data_type member_data_name;

        data_type member_data_name;

            .

            .


        return_type member_function_name(dummy_type dummy name);

        return_type member_function_name(dummy_type dummy name);

            .

            .

            .
```

Figure 15-2.   *Combining* member_data *and* member_function *(or method) in an object's definition*

example, the Lincoln class discussed earlier might contain data and methods common to the entire Lincoln line, such as engines, batteries, braking ability, and handling. Child classes derived from the parent, such as Town Car, Mark VIII, and Continental, could contain items specific to the class. For example, the 1992 Continental was the only car in the line with an active suspension system.

Inheritance

Inheritance in object-oriented programming allows a class to inherit properties from a class of objects. The parent class serves as a pattern for the derived class and can be altered in several ways. (In the next chapter, you will learn that member functions can be overloaded, new member functions can be added, and member access privileges can be changed.) If an object inherits its attributes from a single parent, it is called *single* inheritance. If an object inherits its attributes from multiple parents, it is called *multiple* inheritance. Inheritance is an important concept because it allows reuse of a class definition without requiring major code changes. Because child classes are extensions of parent classes, inheritance encourages the reuse of code.

Polymorphism

Another important object-oriented concept that relates to the class hierarchy is that common messages can be sent to the parent class objects and all derived subclass objects. This is called *polymorphism*. Polymorphism allows each subclass object to respond to the message format in a manner appropriate to its definition. Imagine a class hierarchy for gathering data. The parent class might be responsible for gathering the name, social security number, occupation, and number of years of employment for an individual. You could then use child classes to decide what additional information would be added based on occupation.

In one case a supervisory position might include yearly salary, while in another case a sales position might include an hourly rate and commission information. Thus, the parent class gathers general information common to all child classes, while the child classes gather additional information relating to specific job descriptions. Polymorphism allows a common data-gathering message to be sent to each class. Both the parent and child classes respond in an appropriate manner to the message. Polymorphism encourages extendability of existing code.

Virtual Functions

Polymorphism gives objects the ability to respond to messages from routines when the object's exact type is not known. In C++, this ability is a result of *late binding*. With late binding, the addresses are determined dynamically at run time rather than statically at compile time, as in traditional compiled languages. This static (fixed) method is often called *early binding*. Function names are replaced with memory addresses. You accomplish late binding by using virtual functions. Virtual functions are defined in the parent class when subsequent derived classes will overload the function by redefining the function's implementation. When you use virtual functions, instead of going directly to the object, messages are passed as a pointer that points to the object.

Virtual functions utilize a table for address information. The table is initialized at run time by using a constructor. A constructor is invoked whenever an object of its class is created. The job of the constructor here is to link the virtual function with the table of address information. During the compile operation, the address of the virtual function is not known; rather, it is given the position in the table (determined at run time) of addresses that will contain the address for the function.

Your First C++ Class

It has already been stated that the C++ class type is an extension of C's **struct** type. In this section, you learn how you can use the **struct** type in C++ to form a primitive class, complete with data and members. Next, you will examine the formal syntax for defining a class and see several simple examples of its implementation. The section discusses the differences between a primitive **struct** class type and an actual C++ class, and presents several simple examples to illustrate class concepts. (Chapter 16 gives a detailed analysis of the C++ class as it applies to object-oriented programming.)

But First, a C Class Object?

Chapter 13 discussed structures for C and C++. In many respects, the structure in C/C++ is an elementary form of a class. You use the keyword **struct** to define a structure. Examine the following code:

```
//
//  findsqrt.cpp
//  A C++ program using the keyword "struct" to illustrate a
//  primitive form of class. Here several member functions
//  are defined within the structure.
//  Copyright (c) Chris H. Pappas and William H. Murray, 1996
//

#include <iostream.h>
#include <math.h>

struct math_operations                                           {
  double data_value                                              ;

  void    set_value        ( double ang ) { data_value = ang;    }
  double get_square        ( void        ) { double answer;
                                             answer = data_value *
                                             data_value;
                                             return (answer);     }
  double get_square_root( void           ) { double answer       ;
                                             answer =
                                             sqrt(data_value)     ;
                                             return (answer);     }
} math                                                           ;

void main( void )
{
  // set numeric value to 35.63
  math.set_value( 35.63 )                                        ;

  cout << "The square of the data_value is      : "
       << math.get_square() << endl                              ;

  cout << "The square root of the data_value is : "
       << math.get_square_root() << endl                         ;
}
```

The first thing to notice in this code is that the structure definition contains member data and functions. Although you are used to seeing data declarations as part of a structure, this is probably the first time you have seen member functions defined within the structure definition. In the discussion of the **struct** type in Chapter 13 there was no mention of member functions because they are exclusive to C++.

These member functions can act upon the data contained in the structure (or class) itself. Recall that a class can contain member data and functions. By default, in a **struct** declaration in C++, member data and functions are public. (A public section is one in which the data and functions are available outside the structure.) Here is the output sent to the screen when the program is executed:

```
c:\findsqrt
The square of the data_value is        : 1269.5
The square root of the data_value is : 5.96909
```

In this example, the structure definition contains a single data value:

```
double data_value;
```

Next, three member functions are defined. Actually, the code for each function is contained within the structure:

```
    void    set_value      ( double ang ) { data_value = ang;    }
    double get_square      ( void        ) { double answer;
                                             answer = data_value *
                                             data_value;
                                             return (answer);     }
    double get_square_root( void         ) { double answer       ;
                                             answer =
                                             sqrt(data_value)     ;
                                             return (answer);     }
} math                                                            ;
```

The first member function is responsible for initializing the variable, *data_value*. The remaining two member functions return the square and square root of *data_value*. Notice that the member functions are not passed a value; *data_value* is available to them as members of the structure. Both member functions return a double. The program's **main()** function sets the value of *data_value* to 35.63 with a call to the member function, *set_value()*:

```
math.set_value( 35.63 );
```

Notice that the name "math" has been associated with the structure *math*. The remaining two member functions return values to the **cout** stream:

```
cout << "The square of the data_value is      : "
     << math.get_square() << endl;

cout << "The square root of the data_value is : "
     << math.get_square_root() << endl;
```

This example contains a structure with member data and functions. The functions are contained within the structure definition. You won't find an example simpler than this one. In the next program, the **struct** keyword is still used to develop a primitive class, but this time the member functions are written outside the structure. This is the way you will most commonly see structures and classes defined. This example contains a structure definition with one data member, *data_value*, and seven member functions. The member functions return information for various trigonometric values.

```
//
// degstruct.cpp
// A C++ program using the keyword "struct" to illustrate a
// primitive form of class. This program uses a structure
// to obtain trigonometric values for an angle.
// Copyright (c) Chris H. Pappas and William H. Murray, 1996
//

#include <iostream.h>
#include <math.h>

const double DEG_TO_RAD = 0.0174532925           ;

struct degree                                    {
  double data_value                              ;

  void   set_value      ( double )               ;
  double get_sine       ( void   )               ;
  double get_cosine     ( void   )               ;
  double get_tangent    ( void   )               ;
  double get_secant     ( void   )               ;
  double get_cosecant   ( void   )               ;
  double get_cotangent  ( void   )               ;
} deg                                            ;
```

```
void degree::set_value( double ang )
{
  data_value = ang                                    ;
}

double degree::get_sine( void )
{
  double answer                                       ;

  answer = sin( DEG_TO_RAD * data_value )             ;
  return( answer )                                    ;
}

double degree::get_cosine( void )
{
  double answer                                       ;

  answer = cos( DEG_TO_RAD * data_value )             ;
  return( answer )                                    ;
}

double degree::get_tangent( void )
{
  double answer                                       ;

  answer = tan( DEG_TO_RAD* data_value )              ;
  return( answer )                                    ;
}

double degree::get_secant( void )
{
  double answer                                       ;

  answer =1.0 / sin( DEG_TO_RAD * data_value )        ;
  return( answer )                                    ;
}

double degree::get_cosecant( void )
{
  double answer                                       ;
```

```
    answer = 1.0 / cos( DEG_TO_RAD * data_value );
    return( answer )                              ;
}

double degree::get_cotangent( void )
{
   double answer                                  ;

   answer = 1.0 / tan( DEG_TO_RAD * data_value );
   return( answer )                              ;
}

void main( void )
{
   // set angle to 25.0 degrees
   deg.set_value( 25.0 )                          ;

   cout << "The sine of the angle is: "
        << deg.get_sine( )        << endl         ;
   cout << "The cosine of the angle is: "
        << deg.get_cosine( )      << endl         ;
   cout << "The tangent of the angle is: "
        << deg.get_tangent( )    << endl          ;
   cout << "The secant of the angle is: "
        << deg.get_secant( )     << endl          ;
   cout << "The cosecant of the angle is: "
        << deg.get_cosecant( )  << endl           ;
   cout << "The cotangent of the angle is: "
        << deg.get_cotangent( ) << endl           ;
}
```

Notice that the structure definition contains the prototypes for the member functions. The variable, *deg*, is associated with the degree structure type:

```
struct degree {
  double data_value            ;

  void   set_value   ( double );
  double get_sine    ( void   );
  double get_cosine  ( void   );
  double get_tangent ( void   );
```

```
   double get_secant    ( void    );
   double get_cosecant ( void     );
   double get_cotangent( void     );
} deg                              ;
```

Immediately after the structure is defined, the various member functions are developed and listed. The member functions are associated with the structure or class by means of the scope operator (::). Except for the scope operator, the member functions look like normal functions. Examine the first part of the **main()** function:

```
// set angle to 25.0 degrees
deg.set_data( 25.0 );
```

Here the value 25.0 is being passed as an argument to the **set_value()** function. Observe the syntax for this operation. The **set_value()** function itself is very simple:

```
void degree::set_value( double ang )
{
   data_value = ang;
}
```

The function accepts the argument and assigns the value to the class variable, *data_value*. This is one way of initializing class variables. From this point forward in the class, *data_value* is accessible by each of the six member functions. The job of the member functions is to calculate the sine, cosine, tangent, secant, cosecant, and cotangent of the given angle. The respective values are printed to the screen from the **main()** function with statements similar to the following:

```
cout << "The sine of the angle is: "
     << deg.get_sine( ) << endl     ;
```

You can use the dot notation commonly used for structures to access the member functions. Pointer variables can also be assigned to a structure or class, in which case the arrow operator is used. You will see examples of this in Chapter 16.

C++ Class Syntax

The definition of a C++ class begins with the keyword **class**. The class name (tag type) immediately follows the keyword. The framework of the class is very similar to the struct type definition you have already seen.

```
class type {
   type var1;
   type var2;
   type var3;
       .
       .
       .
public:
   member_function_1;
   member_function_2;
   member_function_3;
   member_function_4;
       .
       .
       .
}name_associated_with_class_type;
```

Member variables immediately follow the class declaration. These variables are, by default, private to the class and can be accessed only by the member functions that follow. Member functions typically follow a public declaration. This allows access to the member functions from calling routines external to the class. All class member functions have access to public, private, and protected parts of a class. The following is an example of a class that is used in the next programming example:

```
class degree                       {
   double data_value               ;

public:
   void    set_value    ( double );
   double get_sine      ( void   );
   double get_cosine    ( void   );
   double get_tangent   ( void   );
   double get_secant    ( void   );
   double get_cosecant  ( void   );
   double get_cotangent ( void   );
} deg                              ;
```

This class has a type (tag name) *degree*. A private variable, *data_value*, will share degree values among the various member functions. Seven functions make up the function members of the class. They are *set_value()*, *get_sine()*, *get_cosine()*, *get_tangent()*, *get_secant()*, *get_cosecant()*, and *get_cotangent()*. The name that is associated with this class type is *deg*. Unlike this example, the association of a variable name with the class name is most frequently made in the **main()** function. Does this class definition look familiar? It is basically the structure definition from the previous example converted to a true class.

A Simple C++ Class

In a C++ class, the visibility of class members is, by default, private—that is, member variables are accessible only to member functions of the class. If the member functions are to have visibility beyond the class, you must explicitly specify that visibility. The conversion of the last program's structure to a true C++ class is simple and straightforward. First, the **struct** keyword is replaced by the **class** keyword. Second, the member functions that are to have public visibility are separated from the private variable of the class with the use of a public declaration. Examine the complete program:

```
//
//   smplclas.cpp
//   A C++ program illustrates a simple but true class and
//   introduces the concept of private and public.
//   This program uses a class to obtain the trigonometric
//   value for given angle.
//   Copyright (c) Chris H. Pappas and William H. Murray, 1996
//

#include <iostream.h>
#include <math.h>

const double DEG_TO_RAD = 0.0174532925 ;

class degree {
  double data_value                              ;

public:
  void   set_value     ( double )                ;
  double get_sine      ( void   )                ;
  double get_cosine    ( void   )                ;
  double get_tangent   ( void   )                ;
  double get_secant    ( void   )                ;
  double get_cosecant  ( void   )                ;
  double get_cotangent ( void   )                ;
} deg                                            ;
```

```
void degree::set_value( double ang )
{
  data_value = ang                              ;
}


double degree::get_sine( void )
{
  double answer                                 ;

  answer = sin( DEG_TO_RAD * data_value )       ;
  return( answer )                              ;
}

double degree::get_cosine( void )
{
  double answer                                 ;

  answer = cos( DEG_TO_RAD * data_value )       ;
  return( answer )                              ;
}

double degree::get_tangent( void )
{
  double answer                                 ;

  answer = tan( DEG_TO_RAD * data_value )       ;
  return( answer )                              ;
}

double degree::get_secant( void )
{
  double answer                                 ;

  answer = 1.0 / sin( DEG_TO_RAD * data_value ) ;
  return( answer )                              ;
}

double degree::get_cosecant( void )
{
```

```
    double answer                                      ;

    answer = 1.0 / cos( DEG_TO_RAD * data_value ) ;
    return( answer )                                   ;
}

double degree::get_cotangent( void )
{
    double answer                                      ;

    answer = 1.0 / tan( DEG_TO_RAD * data_value ) ;
    return( answer )                                   ;
}

void main( void )
{
    // set angle to 25.0 degrees
    deg.set_value( 25.0 )                              ;

    cout << "The sine      of the angle is : "
         << deg.get_sine( )        << endl             ;
    cout << "The cosine    of the angle is : "
         << deg.get_cosine( )      << endl             ;
    cout << "The tangent   of the angle is : "
         << deg.get_tangent( )     << endl             ;
    cout << "The secant    of the angle is : "
         << deg.get_secant( )      << endl             ;
    cout << "The cosecant  of the angle is : "
         << deg.get_cosecant( )    << endl             ;
    cout << "The cotangent of the angle is : "
         << deg.get_cotangent( )   << endl             ;
}
```

In this example, the body of the program remains the same. The structure definition has been converted to a true, but elementary, class definition with private and public parts. Note that the variable, *data_value*, is private to the class (by default) and as a result is accessible only by the member functions of the class. The member functions themselves have been declared public in visibility and are accessible from outside the class. Each class member, however, whether public or private, has access to all other class members, public or private. Here is the output from the program:

```
c:\smplclas
The sine        of the angle is : 0.422618
The cosine      of the angle is : 0.986308
The tangent     of the angle is : 0.466308
The secant      of the angle is : 2.3662
The cosecant    of the angle is : 1.18338
The cotangent of the angle is : 2.14451
```

Again, class member functions are usually defined immediately after the class has been defined and before the **main()** function of the program. Nonmember class functions are still defined after the function **main()** and are prototyped in the normal fashion.

In the Next Chapter...

The next chapter looks at the details of C++ classes more closely. In Chapter 16, you will learn how to automate classes that dynamically allocate and deallocate memory by using class constructors and destructors. You will also learn how to selectively override an object's private member visibility with the C++ keyword **friend**.

Chapter Sixteen

C++ Classes

In the last chapter, you learned that you could create a primitive C++ class by using the **struct** keyword. Next, several elementary C++ classes were created by using the **class** keyword. Both types of examples illustrated the simple fact that classes can contain member data and member functions that act on that data. In this chapter, you learn more about C++ classes.

This chapter discusses nesting of classes and structures, the use of constructors and destructors, overloading member functions, friend functions, operator overloading, derived classes, virtual functions, and other miscellaneous topics. These class structures create objects that form the foundation of object-oriented programs. Much of the programming flexibility offered to the C++ programmer is a result of the various data types discussed in earlier chapters.

The C++ **class** gives you another advantage: the benefits of a structure along with the ability to limit access to specific data to functions that are also members of the class. As a result, classes are one of the greatest contributions made by C++ to programming. The added features of the class over earlier structures include the ability to initialize and protect sensitive functions and data. In studying C and C++ programming, consider the increase in programming power you have gained with each new data type. Vectors or one-dimensional arrays allow a group of like data types to be held together.

Next, structures allow related items of different data types to be combined in a group. Finally, the C++ class concept takes you one step further with abstract data types. A class allows you to implement a member data type and associate member functions with the data. Using classes gives you the storage concept associated with a structure along with the member functions to operate on the member variables.

Advanced Object Concepts

In Chapter 15 you learned the syntax for creating an elementary C++ class. Classes have extended capabilities that go far beyond this simple syntax. This section explores these capabilities as they pertain to object-oriented programming. In Chapter 18, class objects will be woven into more complicated object-oriented programs.

The Basic Class Object

The following is a short review of a simple class based on the definitions from Chapter 15. Remember that a class starts with the keyword **class** followed by a class name (tag). In the following example, the class tag name is *car*. If the class contains member variables, they are defined at the start of the class. Their declaration type is private, by default. This example defines three member variables: *mileage*, *tire_pressure*, and *speed*. Class member functions follow the member variable list. Typically, the member functions are declared **public**. A **private** declaration limits accessibility of member variables to member functions within the class. This is often referred to as data hiding. A **public** declaration makes the member functions available outside of the class:

```
class car {
  int   mileage              ; // member data declarations
  int   tire_pressure        ;
  float speed                ;

public:
  int   maintenance   (int)  ; // member function prototypes
  int   wear_record   (int)  ;
  int   air_resistance(float);
} mycar                      ;
```

Here, three member functions are prototyped within the class definition. They are *maintenance()*, *wear_record()*, and *air_resistance()*. All three return an **int** type. Typically, however, the contents, or bodies of, the member functions are defined outside the class definition—usually immediately after the class itself. Let's continue the study of classes with a look at additional class features.

Nested Classes

Recall from Chapter 13 that structures can be nested. This also turns out to be true for C++ classes. When using nested classes, you must take care not to make the resulting declaration more complicated than necessary. The following examples illustrate the nesting concept.

Structures Within a Class

The following is a simple example of how two structures can be nested within a class definition. Using nesting in this fashion is both common and practical. You can also use the **class** keyword in this manner:

```
//
//   salary.cpp
//   A C++ program illustrates the use of nesting concepts
//   in classes. This program calculates the wages for
//   the named employee.
//   Copyright (c) Chris H. Pappas and William H. Murray, 1996
//

#include <iostream.h>

class employee                                    {
  struct emp_name                                 {
```

```
    char firstname [ 20 ]                              ;
    char middlename[ 20 ]                              ;
    char lastname  [ 20 ]                              ;
  } name                                               ;

  struct emp_hours                                     {
    double hours                                       ;
    double base_sal                                    ;
    double overtime_sal                                ;
  } hours                                              ;
public:
  void emp_input ( void )                              ;
  void emp_output( void )                              ;
}                                                      ;

void employee::emp_input( void )
{
  char cr                                              ;

  cout << "Enter first name of employee: "            ;
  cin  >>  name.firstname                              ;
  cin.get( cr );                  // flush carriage return

  cout << "Enter middle name of employee: "           ;
  cin  >>  name.middlename                             ;
  cin.get( cr )                                        ;

  cout << "Enter last name of employee:  "            ;
  cin  >>  name.lastname                               ;
  cin.get( cr )                                        ;

  cout << "Enter total hours worked:  "               ;
  cin  >>  hours.hours                                 ;

  cout << "Enter hourly wage (base rate):   "         ;
  cin  >>  hours.base_sal                              ;

  cout << "Enter overtime wage (overtime rate): "     ;
  cin  >>  hours.overtime_sal                          ;
```

```
    cout << "\n\n"                                    ;
}

void employee::emp_output( void )
{
  cout << name.firstname  << " "
       << name.middlename << " "
       << name.lastname    << endl          ;

  if( hours.hours <= 40 )
    cout << "Base Pay:  $"
         << hours.hours * hours.base_sal
         << endl                            ;
    else {
      cout << "Base Pay:   $"
           << 40 * hours.base_sal
           << endl                          ;
      cout << "Overtime Pay: $"
           << (hours.hours-40) * hours.overtime_sal
           << endl                          ;
    }
}

void main( void )
{
  employee acme_corp; // creates an acme_corp object

  acme_corp.emp_input ( )                        ;
  acme_corp.emp_output( )                        ;
}
```

In the next example, two classes are nested within the *employee* class definition. As you can see, the use of nesting can be quite straightforward:

```
class employee           {
  class emp_name         {
    char firstname [ 20 ];
    char middlename[ 20 ];
    char lastname  [ 20 ];
  } name                 ;
  class emp_hours        {
```

```
    double hours          ;
    double base_salary    ;
    double overtime_sal   ;
  } hours                 ;

public:
  void emp_input ( void) ;
  void emp_output( void) ;
};
```

The *employee* class includes two nested classes, *emp_name* and *emp_hours*. The nested classes, although part of the private section of the *employee* class, are actually available outside the class. In other words, the visibility of the nested classes is the same as if they were defined outside the employee class. The individual member variables, for this example, are accessed through the member functions (public, by default) *emp_input()* and *emp_output()*.

Both member functions, *emp_input()* and *emp_output()*, are of type **void** and do not accept arguments. The *emp_input()* function prompts the user for employee data that will be passed to the nested structures (classes). The data collected includes the employee's full name, the total hours worked, the regular pay rate, and the overtime pay rate. Output is generated when the *emp_output()* function is called. The employee's name, base pay, and overtime pay will be printed to the screen:

```
Enter first name of employee: Toni
Enter middle name of employee: Andre
Enter last name of employee: Williams
Enter total hours worked: 50
Enter hourly wage (base rate): 8.38
Enter overtime wage (overtime rate): 10.00
John James Jones
Base Pay:   $300.00
Overtime Pay: $120.00
```

The **main()** function in this program is fairly short. This is because most of the work is being done by the member functions of the class:

```
employee acme_corp    ; // creates an acme_corp object

acme_corp.emp_input ( );
acme_corp.emp_output( );
```

First, the variable *acme_corp*, representing the Acme Computer Corporation, is associated with the *employee* class. To request a member function, the dot operator is used. Next, *acme_corp.emp_input()* is called to collect the employee information, and then *acme_corp.emp_output()* is used to calculate and print the payroll results.

Alternate Structure Syntax

The following form of nesting is also considered acceptable syntax:

```
class cars              {
   int  mileage         ;
public:
   void trip ( int t   );
   int   speed( float s );
}                        ;

class contents          {
   int   count          ;
public:
   cars mileage         ;
   void rating( void )  ;
}                        ;
```

Here, *cars* becomes nested within the *contents* class. Nested classes, whether inside or outside, have the same scope.

Automating Classes

A *constructor* is a class member function. Constructors are useful for initializing class variables or allocating memory storage. The constructor always has the same name as the class it is defined within. Constructors have additional versatility: they can accept arguments and be overloaded. A constructor is executed automatically when an object of the class type is created. *Free store objects* are objects created with the new operator and serve to allocate memory for the objects created.

A *destructor* is a class member function typically used to return memory allocated from free store memory. The destructor, like the constructor, has the same name as the class it is defined in, preceded by the tilde character (~). Destructors are the logical complement to their constructor counterparts. A destructor is automatically called when the delete operator is applied to a class pointer or when a program passes beyond the scope of a class object. Destructors, unlike their constructor counterparts, cannot accept an argument and may not be overloaded.

Constructors and Destructors

In the first example involving the use of constructors and destructors, a constructor and destructor are used to signal the start and end of a coin conversion example. This program illustrates that constructors and destructors are called automatically:

```cpp
//
//   consdest.cpp
//   A C++ program illustrates the use of constructors and
//   destructors in a simple program.
//   This program converts cents into appropriate coins:
//   (quarters, dimes, nickels, and pennies).
//   Copyright (c) Chris H. Pappas and William H. Murray, 1996
//

#include <iostream.h>

const int QUARTER = 25                                      ;
const int DIME    = 10                                      ;
const int NICKEL  = 5                                       ;

class coins                                                 {
  int number                                                ;

public:
  coinsc() {cout << "Begin Conversion!\n";    } // constructor
  ~coins() {cout << "\nFinished Conversion!";} // destructor
  void get_cents         ( int  )                           ;
  int quarter_conversion( void )                            ;
  int dime_conversion    ( int  )                           ;
  int nickel_conversion ( int  )                            ;
}                                                           ;

void coins::get_cents( int cents )
{
  number=cents;
  cout << number
       << " cents, converts to:"
       << endl                                              ;
}

int coins::quarter_conversion( void )
{
```

```
    cout << number / QUARTER << " quarter(s), "              ;
    return( number % QUARTER )                               ;
}

int coins::dime_conversion( int dimes )
{
  cout << dimes / DIME << " dime(s), "                       ;
  return( dimes % DIME )                                     ;
}

int coins::nickel_conversion( int nickels )
{
  cout << nickels/NICKEL << " nickel(s), and "               ;

  return( nickels % NICKEL )                                 ;
}

void main( void )
{
  int coins, dimes, nickels, pennies                         ;

  cout << "Enter the cash, in cents, to convert: "           ;
  cin  >>  coins                                             ;

  // associate cash_in_cents with coins class
  coins cash_in_cents                                        ;

  cash_in_cents.get_cents                    ( coins   )     ;
  dimes   = cash_in_cents.quarter_conversion(         )      ;
  nickels = cash_in_cents.dime_conversion   ( dimes   )      ;
  pennies = cash_in_cents.nickel_conversion ( nickels )      ;
  cout << pennies << " penny(ies)."                          ;
}
```

This program uses four member functions. The first function passes the number of pennies to the private class variable *number*. The remaining three functions convert cash, given in cents, to the equivalent cash in quarters, dimes, nickels, and pennies. Notice in particular the placement of the constructor and destructor in the class definition. The constructor and destructor function descriptions contain nothing more than a message that will be printed to the screen. Constructors and destructors are not specifically called by a program. Their appearance on the screen is your key that the constructor and destructor were automatically called when the object was created and destroyed.

```
class coins                                                    {
   int number                                                  ;

public:
   coins () {cout << "Begin Conversion!\n";    }  // constructor
   ~coins() {cout << "\nFinished Conversion!";}  // destructor
   void get_cents        ( int  )                              ;
   int quarter_conversion( void )                              ;
   int dime_conversion    ( int  )                             ;
   int nickel_conversion ( int  )                              ;
};
```

Here is an example of the output from this program:

```
Enter the cash, in cents, to convert: 157
Begin Conversion!
157 cents, converts to:
6 quarter(s), 0 dime(s), 1 nickel(s), and 2 penny(ies).
Finished Conversion!
```

In this example, the function definition is actually included within the constructor and destructor. When the function definition is included with member functions, it is said to be implicitly defined. Member functions can be defined in the typical manner or declared explicitly as inline functions. You can expand this example to include dollars and half-dollars.

Initializing Member Variables

Another practical use for constructors is for initialization of private class variables. In the previous examples, class variables were set by utilizing separate member functions. In the next example, the original class of the previous program is modified slightly to eliminate the need for user input. In this case, the variable number will be initialized to 431 pennies.

```
class coins                                                    {
   int number                                                  ;

public:
   coins () {number=431;                       }  // constructor
```

```
    ~coins() {cout << "\nFinished Conversion!";}  // destructor
    int quarter_conversion ( void )                        ;
    int dime_conversion    ( int  )                        ;
    int nickel_conversion  ( int  )                        ;
}                                                          ;
```

The route to class variables should always be through class member functions. Remember that the constructor is considered a member function.

Dynamically Allocating and Deallocating Memory

Perhaps the most significant reason for using a constructor is in utilizing free store memory. In the next example, a constructor is used to allocate memory for the *string1* pointer with the **new** operator. A destructor is also used to release the allocated memory back to the system when the object is destroyed. This is accomplished with the use of the delete operator:

```
class string_operation                                    {
  char *string1                                           ;
  int   string_len                                        ;

public:
  string_operation ( char *) {string1=new char[string_len];};
  ~string_operation(        ) {delete string1;            };
  void input_data  ( char *)                              ;
  void output_data ( char *)                              ;
}                                                          ;
```

The memory allocated by **new** to the pointer *string1* can be deallocated only with a subsequent call to **delete**. For this reason, you will usually see memory allocated to pointers in constructors and deallocated in destructors. This also ensures that if the variable assigned to the class passes out of its scope, the allocated memory will be returned to the system. These operations make memory allocation dynamic and are most useful in programs that utilize linked lists. The memory used by standard data types, such as **int** and **float**, is automatically restored to the system.

Overloading Class Member Functions

Class member functions, like ordinary C++ functions, can be overloaded. Overloading functions means that more than one function can have the same function name in the current scope. It becomes the compiler's responsibility to select the correct function based upon the number and type of arguments used during the function call. The first example in this section illustrates the overloading of a class function, *angle*. The angle being converted is passed to member functions in one of two formats—a double or a string. With member function overloading, it is possible to process both types:

```
//
//   clasovrd.cpp
//   A C++ program illustrates overloading two class member
//   functions. The program allows an angle to be entered
//   in decimal or deg/min/sec format. One member function
//   accepts data as a double, the other accepts it as a string. The
//   program returns the sine, cosine, and tangent.
//   Copyright (c) Chris H. Pappas and William H. Murray, 1996
//

#include <iostream.h>
#include <math.h>
#include <string.h>

const double DEG_TO_RAD = 0.0174532925                          ;

class trigonometric                                             {
  double angle                                                  ;
  double answer_sine                                            ;
  double answer_cosine                                          ;
  double answer_tangent                                         ;

public:
  void trig_calc( double )                                      ;
  void trig_calc( char * )                                      ;
}                                                               ;

void trigonometric::trig_calc( double degrees )
{
  angle          = degrees                                      ;
  answer_sine    = sin( angle * DEG_TO_RAD )                    ;
  answer_cosine  = cos( angle * DEG_TO_RAD )                    ;
  answer_tangent = tan( angle * DEG_TO_RAD )                    ;

  cout << "\nFor an angle of " << angle
       << " degrees."              << endl;
```

```
  cout << "The sine is    "   << answer_sine    << endl      ;
  cout << "The cosine is  "   << answer_cosine  << endl      ;
  cout << "The tangent is "   << answer_tangent << endl      ;
}

void trigonometric::trig_calc( char *dat )
{
  char *deg, *min, *sec                                      ;

  deg   = strtok( dat,"ó " );               // make ó with alt-248
  min   = strtok( 0,"' "    )                                ;
  sec   = strtok( 0,"\""    )                                ;
  angle = atof(deg) + ( (atof(min))/60.0) + ((atof(sec) ) / 360.0);

  answer_sine    = sin( angle * DEG_TO_RAD )                 ;
  answer_cosine  = cos( angle * DEG_TO_RAD )                 ;
  answer_tangent = tan( angle * DEG_TO_RAD )                 ;

  cout << "\nFor an angle of "
       <<  angle << " degrees." << endl                      ;

  cout << "The sine    is " << answer_sine    << endl        ;
  cout << "The cosine  is " << answer_cosine  << endl        ;
  cout << "The tangent is " << answer_tangent << endl        ;
}

void main( void )
{
  trigonometric data                                         ;

  data.trig_calc(  75.0            )                         ;
  data.trig_calc( "356 75' 20\"" )                           ;
  data.trig_calc(  145.72          )                         ;
  data.trig_calc( "656 45' 30\"" )                           ;
}
```

This program makes use of a very powerful built-in function, **strtok()**, prototyped in string.h. The syntax for using **strtok()** is straightforward:

```
    char *STRTOK( string10, string20 );  // locates token in string1
    char *STRING10               ;  // STRING THAT HAS TOKEN(S)
const char *0STRING20            ;  // STRING WITH DELIMITER CHARS
```

The **strtok()** function will scan the first string, *string1*, looking for a series of character tokens. For this example, the tokens representing degrees, minutes, and seconds are used. The actual length of the tokens can vary. The second string, *string2*, contains a set of delimiters. Spaces, commas, or other special characters can be used for delimiters. The tokens in *string1* are separated by the delimiters in *string2*. Because of this, all of the tokens in *string1* can be retrieved with a series of calls to the **strtok()** function. **strtok()** alters *string1* by inserting a null character after each token is retrieved. The function returns a pointer to the first token the first time it is called. Subsequent calls return a pointer to the next token, and so on. When there are no more tokens in the string, a null pointer is returned.

This example permits *angle* readings formatted as decimal values or in degrees, minutes, and seconds of arc. For the latter case, **strtok()** uses the degree symbol (ó) to find the first token. For minutes, a minute symbol (') will pull out the token containing the number of minutes. Finally, the \" symbol is used to retrieve seconds. The last delimiter uses two symbols because the double quotation mark by itself is used for terminating strings. This program produces the following formatted output, for an angle of 75 degrees:

```
The sine    is 0.965926
The cosine  is 0.258819
The tangent is 3.732051
```

Class member function overloading gives programs and programmers flexibility when dealing with different data formats. If you are not into math or engineering programs, can you think of any applications that interest you where this feature might be helpful? Consider this possibility: if you are the cook in your household, you could develop an application that modifies recipes. You could write a program that would accept data as a decimal value or in mixed units. For example, the program might allow you to enter "3.75 cups, 1 pint 1.75 cups" or "1 pint 1 cup 2 tbs".

Accessing Private Members with Friends

One important feature of classes is their ability to hide data. Recall that member data is private by default in classes—that is, sharable only with member functions of the class. It is almost ironic, then, that there exists a category of functions specifically designed to override this feature. Functions of this type are called friend functions. *Friend functions* allow the sharing of private class information with nonmember functions. Friend functions, not defined in the class itself, can share the same class resources as member functions. Friend functions offer the advantage that they are external to the class definition, as shown here:

```
//
//   friend.cpp
//   A C++ program illustrates the use of friend functions.
//   The program will collect a string of date and time
//   information from system. Time information will
//   be processed and converted into seconds.
//   Copyright (c) Chris H. Pappas and William H. Murray, 1996
//

#include <iostream.h>
#include <time.h>      // for tm & time_t structure
#include <string.h>    // for strtok function prototype
#include <stdlib.h>    // for atol function prototype

class time_class                                          {
  long secs                                               ;
  friend char * present_time( time_class );  //friend
public:
  time_class( char * )                                    ;
}                                                         ;

time_class::time_class( char *tm )
{
  char *hours, *minutes, *seconds                         ;

  // data returned in the following string format:
  // (day month date hours:minutes:seconds year)
  // Thus, need to skip over three tokens, ie.
  // skip day, month and date
  hours   = strtok( tm," " )                              ;
  hours   = strtok( 0," " )                               ;
  hours   = strtok( 0," " )                               ;

  // collect time information from string
  hours   = strtok( 0,":" )                               ;
```

```
   minutes = strtok( 0,":" )                           ;
   seconds = strtok( 0," " )                           ;

   // convert data to long type and accumulate seconds.
   Secs  = atol( hours   ) * 3600                       ;
   secs += atol( minutes ) * 60                         ;
   secs += atol( seconds )                              ;
}

char * present_time(time_class);          // prototype

void main( void )
{
   // get the string of time & date information
   struct tm *ptr                                       ;
   time_t     ltime                                     ;
   ltime = time     ( NULL   )                          ;
   ptr   = localtime( &ltime )                          ;

   time_class tz( asctime( ptr ) )                      ;

   cout << "The date/time string information: "
        << asctime(ptr) << endl                         ;
   cout << "The time converted to seconds: "
        << present_time(tz) << endl                     ;
}

char * present_time( time_class tz )
{
   char *  ctbuf                                        ;
   ctbuf = new char[ 40 ]                               ;
   long int seconds_total                               ;

   seconds_total = tz.secs                              ;
   ltoa( seconds_total, ctbuf ,10 )                     ;
   return( ctbuf )                                      ;
}
```

Notice in the class definition the use of the keyword **friend** along with the description of the *present_time()* function. When you examine the program listing, you will notice that this function, external to the class, appears after the **main()** function description. In other words, it is written as a traditional C++ function, external to member functions of the defined class.

This program has a number of additional interesting features. In the function **main()**, the system's time is obtained with the use of *time_t* and its associated structure *tm*. In this program, *ltime* is the name of the variable associated with *time_t*. Local time is initialized and retrieved into the pointer, *ptr*, with the next two lines of code. By using *asctime(ptr)*, the pointer will point to an ASCII string of date and time information.

```
struct tm *ptr                   ;
time_t ltime                     ;
ltime = time( NULL )             ;
ptr    = localtime( &ltime )     ;

time_class tz( asctime( ptr ) );
```

The date and time string is formatted in this manner:

day month date hours:minutes:seconds year \n \0

For example:

```
Tue Jan 11   14:23:19 1996
```

There is a more detailed discussion of built-in functions, including those prototyped in time.h, in Chapter 19. The string information that is retrieved is sent to the class by associating *tz* with the class *time_class*:

```
time_class tz( asctime( ptr ) );
```

A constructor, *time_class(char *)*, is used to define the code required to convert the string information into integer data. This is accomplished by using the **strtok()** function. The date/time information is returned in a rather strange format. To process this information, **strtok()** must use a space as the delimiter in order to skip over the day, month, and date information in the string. In this program, the variable *hours* initially serves as a junk collector for unwanted tokens. The next delimiter is a colon (:), which is used in collecting both hour and minute tokens from the string. Finally, the number of seconds can be retrieved by reading the string until another space is encountered. The string information is then converted to a long type and converted to the appropriate number of seconds. The variable *secs* is private to the class but accessible to the friend function. The friend function takes the number of accumulated seconds, *tz.seconds*, and converts it back to a character string. The memory for storing the string is allocated with the **new** operator. This newly created string is a result of using the friend function. The program prints two pieces of information:

```
The date/time string information: Mon May 25 16:01:55 1992
The time converted to seconds: 57715
```

First, **cout** sends the string produced by **asctime()** to the screen. This information is obtainable from the *time_t()* function and is available to the **main()** function. Second, the system time is printed by passing *present_time* to the **cout** stream. Although friend functions offer some interesting programming possibilities when programming with C++ classes, they should be used with caution. Incorrect logical use of **friend**s leaves your objects open to unwanted side effects.

The this Pointer

The keyword **this** is used to identify a self-referential pointer that is implicitly declared in C++, as follows:

```
class_name *this;   //class_name is class type.
```

The **this** pointer is used to point to the object for which the member function is invoked. Here is an example, used in a **class** definition:

```
class class_name {
   char chr                                        ;

public:
   void begin_conv( char k ) { chr = k;            };
   char conv_chr  ( void  ) { return (this -> chr);};
}                                                  ;
```

In this case, the pointer **this** is used to access the private class variable member *chr*. There are additional uses for the **this** pointer. You can use it to include a link on a doubly linked list or when writing constructors and destructors involving memory allocations. Examine the following example:

```
class class_name {
  int  x, y, z                              ;
  char chr                                  ;

public:
  class_name ( size ) { this = new( size ); };
  ~class_name( void ) { delete( this );      };
};
```

Overloading Operators

Earlier in this chapter, you learned that it is possible to overload member functions in a class. In this section, you will learn that it is also possible to overload C++ operators. In C++, new definitions can be applied to such familiar operators as +, -, *, and / in a given class.

The idea of operator overloading is common in numerous programming languages, even if it is not specifically implemented. For example, all compiled languages make it possible to add two integers, two floats, or two doubles (or their equivalent types) with the + operator. This is the essence of operator overloading—using the same operator on different data types. In C++, it is possible to extend this simple concept even further. In most compiled languages it is not possible, for example, to take a complex number, matrix, or character string and add them together with the + operator. These operations are valid in all programming languages:

3 + 8
3.3 + 7.2

These operations are typically not valid operations:

(4 - j4) + (5 + j10)
(15ó 20' SY45"SY) + (53Ó 57' 40")
"combine " + "strings"

If the last three operations were possible with the + operator, the workload of the programmer would be greatly reduced when designing new applications. The good news is that in C++, the + operator can be overloaded, and the previous three operations can be made valid. Many additional operators can also be overloaded. Operator overloading is used extensively in C++. You will find examples throughout the various Borland C++ libraries.

Overloading Operators and Function Calls

In C++, the following operators can be overloaded:

+	-	*0	/	=	<	>	+=	-=
*0=	/=	<<	>>	>>=	<<=	= =	!=	<=
>=	+	- -	%	&	^^	!	|	~
&=	^=	|=	&&	||	%=	[]	()	new

delete

The main restrictions are that the syntax and precedence of the operator must remain unchanged from its originally defined meaning. Another important point is that operator overloading is valid only within the scope of the class in which overloading occurs.

THE SYNTAX OF OVERLOADING   In order to overload an operator, the operator keyword is followed by the operator itself:

type operator opr(param list)

For example:

```
angle_value operator +( angle_argument );
```

Here, *angle_value* is the name of the class type, followed by the operator keyword, then the operator itself (+) and a parameter to be passed to the overloaded operator. Within the scope of a properly defined class, several angles specified in degrees / minutes / seconds could be directly added together:

```
angle_value angle1( "376 15' 56\"" )            ;
angle_value angle2( "106 44' 44\"" )            ;
angle_value angle3( "756 17' 59\"" )            ;
angle_value angle4( "1306 32' 54\"" )           ;
angle_value sum_of_angles                       ;

sum_of_angles = angle1 + angle2 + angle3 + angle4;
```

As you know from earlier examples, the symbol for seconds is the double quotation mark ("). This symbol is also used to signal the beginning and end of a character string. The quote symbol can be printed to the screen if it is preceded with a backslash. This book uses this format for data input.

There is another problem that must be taken into account in programs such as this: the carry information from seconds-to-minutes and from minutes-to-hours must be handled properly. A *carry* occurs in both cases when the total number of seconds or minutes exceeds 59. This doesn't have anything to do with operator overloading directly, but the program must take this fact into account if a correct total is to be produced, as shown here:

```
//
//   opover.cpp
//   A C++ program illustrates operator overloading.
//   The program will overload the "+" operator so that
//   several angles, in the format degrees minutes seconds,
//   can be added directly.
//   Copyright (c) Chris H. Pappas and William H. Murray, 1996
//

#include <strstrea.h>
#include <stdlib.h>
#include <string.h>

class angle_value {
  int degrees, minutes, seconds                        ;

  public:
  angle_value() {degrees = 0,
                 minutes = 0,
                 seconds = 0; }         // constructor
  angle_value( char * )                                ;
  angle_value operator + ( angle_value )               ;
  char * info_display(void);
}                                                      ;

angle_value::angle_value(char *angle_sum)
{
  degrees = atoi( strtok( angle_sum,"ó" ) )            ;
  minutes = atoi( strtok( 0,"' "        ) )            ;
  seconds = atoi( strtok( 0,"\""        ) )            ;
```

```
   }

angle_value angle_value::operator+(angle_value angle_sum)
{
  angle_value ang                                             ;
  ang.seconds = (    seconds +angle_sum.seconds ) % 60  ;
  ang.minutes = ( ( seconds +angle_sum.seconds ) / 60 +
                    minutes +angle_sum.minutes ) % 60  ;
  ang.degrees = ( ( seconds +angle_sum.seconds ) / 60 +
                    minutes +angle_sum.minutes ) / 60  ;
  ang.degrees +=    degrees +angle_sum.degrees          ;
  return ang                                            ;
}

char * angle_value::info_display( void )
{
  char *ang[ 15 ]                                       ;
  // strstream.h required for incore formatting
  ostrstream(*ang,sizeof(ang)) << degrees << "ó"
                               << minutes << "′ "
                               << seconds << "\""
                               << ends                  ;
  return *ang                                           ;
}

void main( void )
{
  angle_value angle1( "376 15′ 56\""  )                 ;
  angle_value angle2( "106 44′ 44\""  )                 ;
  angle_value angle3( "756 17′ 59\""  )                 ;
  angle_value angle4( "1306 32′ 54\"" )                 ;
  angle_value sum_of_angles                             ;

  sum_of_angles = angle1 + angle2 + angle3 + angle4     ;
  cout << "the sum of the angles is "
       << sum_of_angles.info_display() << endl          ;
}
```

The details of how the mixed units are added together are included in the small piece of code that declares that the + operator is to be overloaded:

```
angle_value angle_value::operator+(angle_value angle_sum)
{
  angle_value ang;
  ang.seconds  =(    seconds + angle_sum.seconds )% 60  ;
  ang.minutes  =( ( seconds + angle_sum.seconds )/ 60 +
                    minutes + angle_sum.minutes )% 60  ;
  ang.degrees  =( ( seconds + angle_sum.seconds )/ 60 +
                    minutes + angle_sum.minutes )/ 60  ;
  ang.degrees +=    degrees + angle_sum.degrees      ;
  return ang                                          ;
}
```

Here, division and modulus operations are performed on the sums to ensure correct carry information. Although further details of the program's operation have been left out here—because you have seen most of the functions and modules in earlier examples—it is important to remember that when you overload operators, proper operator syntax and precedence must be maintained. The output from this program shows the sum of the four angles:

```
the sum of the angles is 2536 51' 33"
```

Derived Classes

As you saw in Chapter 15, a derived class can be considered an extension or inheritance of an existing class. The original class is known as a base or parent class and the derived class as a subclass or child class. As such, a derived class provides a simple means for expanding or customizing the capabilities of a parent class, without the need for re-creating the parent class itself. With a parent class in place, a common interface is possible to one or more of the derived classes.

Any C++ class can serve as a parent class, and any derived class will reflect its description. The derived class can add additional features to the parent class. For example, the derived class can modify access privileges, add new members, or overload existing ones. When a derived class overloads a function declared in the parent class, it is said to be a *virtual member function*. You will see that virtual member functions are very important to the concept of object-oriented programming.

The Syntax of a Derived Class

You describe a derived class by using the following syntax:

```
class derived-class-type :(public/private/protected) . . .
       parent-class-type { . . . .};
```

For example, in creating a derived class, you might write:

```
class retirement:public consumer { . . . .};
```

In this case, the derived class tag is *retirement*. The parent class has public visibility, and its tag is "consumer". A third visibility specifier is often used with derived classes—protected. A protected specifier is the same as a private specifier with the added feature that class member functions and friends of derived classes are given access to the class.

Creating Derived Classes

The next program depicts the concept of a derived class. The parent class collects and reports information on a consumer's name, address, city, state, and zip code. Two similar child classes are derived. One child class maintains information on a consumer's accumulated airline mileage, while the second derived child class reports information on a consumer's accumulated rental car mileage. Both derived child classes inherit information from the parent class. Study the listing and see what you can discern about these derived classes:

```
//
//  drvclass.cpp
//  A C++ program illustrates derived classes.
//  The parent class contains name, street, city,
//  state, and zip information. Derived classes add
//  either airline or rental car mileage information
//  to parent class information.
//  Copyright (c) Chris H. Pappas and William H. Murray, 1996
//

#include <iostream.h>
#include <string.h>

char cr                                          ;

class consumer                                   {
  char name  [ 60 ]                              ,
       street[ 60 ]                              ,
       city  [ 20 ]                              ,
       state [ 15 ]                              ,
       zip   [ 10 ]                              ;
  public:
```

```
  void data_output( void );
  void data_input ( void );
}                                         ;

void consumer::data_output( )
{
  cout << "Name  : " << name   << endl     ;
  cout << "Street: " << street << endl     ;
  cout << "City  : " << city   << endl     ;
  cout << "State : " << state  << endl     ;
  cout << "Zip   : " << zip    << endl     ;
}

void consumer::data_input( )
{
  cout << "Enter The Consumer's Full Name: ";
  cin.get( name,59, '\n' )                 ;
  cin.get( cr );       //flush carriage return
  cout << "Enter The Street Address: "     ;
  cin.get( street,59, '\n' )               ;
  cin.get( cr )                            ;
  cout << "Enter The City: "               ;
  cin.get( city,19, '\n')                  ;
  cin.get( cr )                            ;
  cout << "Enter The State: "              ;
  cin.get( state,14, '\n' )                ;
  cin.get( cr )                            ;
  cout << "Enter The Five Digit Zip Code: " ;
  cin.get( zip,9, '\n' )                   ;
  cin.get( cr )                            ;
}

class airline:public consumer            {
  char  airline_type[ 20 ]                ;
  float acc_air_miles                     ;
public:
  void airline_customer( )                ;
  void disp_air_mileage( )                ;
}                                         ;
```

```
void airline::airline_customer( )
{
  data_input( )                                 ;
  cout << "Enter Airline Type: "                ;
  cin.get( airline_type, 19, '\n' )             ;
  cin.get( cr )                                 ;
  cout << "Enter Accumulated Air Mileage: "     ;
  cin  >>  acc_air_miles                        ;
  cin.get( cr );          //flush carriage return
}

void airline::disp_air_mileage()
{
  data_output( )                                ;

  cout << "Airline Type: " << airline_type
       << endl                                  ;
  cout << "Accumulated Air Mileage: "
       << acc_air_miles << endl                 ;
}

class rental_car:public consumer               {
  char  rental_car_type[ 20 ]                   ;
  float acc_road_miles                          ;
public:
  void rental_car_consumer( )                   ;
  void disp_road_mileage  ( )                   ;
};

void rental_car::rental_car_consumer( )
{
  data_input( )                                 ;
  cout << "Enter Rental_car Type: "             ;
  cin.get( rental_car_type,19, '\n' )           ;
  cin.get( cr );       //flush carriage return
  cout << "Enter Accumulated Road Mileage: ";
  cin  >>  acc_road_miles                       ;
  cin.get( cr )                                 ;
}
```

```
void rental_car::disp_road_mileage( )
{
  data_output( )                              ;

  cout << "Rental Car Type: "
       << rental_car_type << endl              ;
  cout << "Accumulated Mileage: "
       << acc_road_miles << endl               ;
}

void main( void )
{
  //associate variable names with classes
  airline jetaway                             ;
  rental_car varooom                          ;

  //get airline information
  cout << "\n--Airline Consumer--\n"           ;
  jetaway.airline_customer( )                  ;


  //get rental_car information
  cout << "\n--Rental Car Consumer--\n"        ;
  varooom.rental_car_consumer( )               ;

  //now display all consumer information
  cout << "\n--Airline Consumer--\n"           ;
  jetaway.disp_air_mileage( )                  ;
  cout << "\n--Rental Car Consumer--\n"        ;
  varooom.disp_road_mileage( )                 ;
}
```

In the example, the parent class is type *consumer*. The private part of this class accepts consumer information for name, address, city, state, and zip code. The public part describes two functions, *data_output()* and *data_input()*. You have seen functions similar to these to gather class information in earlier programs. The first derived child class is airline:

```
class airline:public customer  {
  char  airline_type[ 20 ]     ;
  float acc_air_miles          ;
```

```
public:
  void airline_customer( void );
  void disp_air_mileage( void );
};
```

This derived child class contains two functions, *airline_customer()* and *disp_air_mileage()*. The first function, *airline_customer()*, uses the parent class to obtain name, address, city, state, and zip code and attaches the airline type and accumulated mileage.

```
void airline::airline_customer( )
{
  data_input( )                                ;
  cout << "Enter Airline Type: ";
  cin.get( airline_type, 19, '\n' )            ;
  cin.get( cr )                                ;
  cout << "Enter Accumulated Air Mileage: ";
  cin  >>  acc_air_miles                       ;
  cin.get( cr );      //flush carriage return
}
```

Do you understand how the derived class is being used? A call to the function *data_input()* is a call to a member function that is part of the parent class. The remainder of the derived class is involved with obtaining the additional airline type and accumulated mileage. The information on accumulated air mileage can be displayed for a consumer in a similar manner. The parent class function, *data_output()*, prints the information gathered by the parent class (name, address, and so on), while *disp_air_mileage()* attaches the derived child class' information (airline type and mileage) to the output. The process is repeated for the rental car consumer. Thus, one parent class serves as the data-gathering base for two derived child classes, each obtaining its own specific information. The following is a sample output from the program:

—Airline Consumer—

```
Name: Sandy M. Wright
Street: 222 Twain Street
City: Birmingham
State: Washington
Zip: 12345
Airline Type: TWA
Accumulated Air Mileage: 98722.5
```

—Rental Car Consumer—

```
Name: Howard W. Strewby
Street: 47 High Acres Drive
City: Poughkeepsie
State: New York
Zip: 12242
Rental Car Type: Mark VIII
Accumulated Road Mileage: 12334.9
```

Experiment with this program by entering your own database of information. You might also consider adding additional member functions to the consumer class.

In the Next Chapter...

In this chapter, you have learned about the more advanced capabilities of C++ objects. The next chapter goes into the details of advanced I/O in C++ so that you will have all of the background information necessary to understand the object-oriented environment discussed in Chapter 18.

Chapter Seventeen

C++ I/O in Detail

Chapter 12 introduced you to the **iostream** objects **cin** and **cout**, along with the "put to" (insertion) operator, <<, and the "get from" (extraction) operator, >>. This chapter explains the classes behind C++ I/O streams. First, however, the chapter introduces several additional topics of concern when writing C++ code, such as how to use C library functions in a C++ program.

Enumerated Types

User-defined enumerated types behave differently in C++ than their C counterparts. In particular, C **enum** types are compatible with the type **int**. This means they can be cross-assigned with no complaints from the compiler. However, in C++ the two types are incompatible. The second difference between C and C++ enumerated types involves the syntax shorthand used when you define C++ **enum** variables. The following example program highlights the enumerated type differences between the two languages:

```
//
//  enumerat.cpp
//  This C++ program demonstrates how to use enumerated types and
//  how C++ enumerated types differ from C enumerated types.
//  Copyright (c) Chris H. Pappas and William H. Murray, 1996
//

#include <iostream.h>

enum boolean { FALSE, TRUE };

void main( void )
{
// enum boolean bflag       = 0; legal C, but illegal C++ statement
   boolean bcontinue, bflag = FALSE;

   bcontinue = (boolean)1;

   bflag = bcontinue;
}
```

The example starts off by defining the enumerated type *boolean*, which is a standard type in several other high-level languages. Because of the ordering of the definition—*FALSE*, then *TRUE*—the compiler assigns a zero to *FALSE* and a 1 to *TRUE*. This is perfect for their logical use in a program. The commented-out statement in the **main()** program represents a legal C statement. Remember, when you define enumerated variables in C, such as *bflag*, you must use the **enum** keyword with the enumerated type's tag field—in this case, *boolean*.

Because C **enum** types are compatible with **int** types, it is also legal to initialize a variable with an integer value. This statement would not get past the C++ compiler. The second statement in **main()** shows the legal C++ counterpart. The last two statements in the program show how to use enumerated types. Notice that in C++ an explicit cast *(boolean)* is needed to convert the 1 to a *boolean* compatible type. Also, remember that user-defined types cannot be directly input from a file or output to a file. Either they must go through a conversion routine or you must custom-overload the >> and << operators, as discussed in Chapter 12.

Reference Arguments

A feature of C++ you will grow to appreciate more and more is the reference variable, which simplifies the syntax and readability of the more confusing pointer notation. Remember that by using pointer parameters a program could pass something to a function either call-by-reference or call-by-variable, which would enable the function to change the item passed. In contrast, call-by-value sends a copy of the variable's contents to the function. Any change to the variable in this case is a local change not reflected in the calling routine.

The following program passes a *stStudent* structure to a function, using the three possible calling methods: call-by-value, call-by-reference with pointer notation, and call-by-reference using the simpler C++ reference type. If the program were sending the entire array to the subroutine, by default the array parameter would be passed call-by-reference. However, single structures within the array, by default are passed call-by-value:

```
//
//  diffcall.cpp
//  A C++ program demonstrating how the C++ reference type
//  eliminates the more confusing pointer notation.
//  This program also demonstrates how to pass a single
//  array element, call-by-value, variable, and reference.
//  Copyright (c) Chris H. Pappas and William H. Murray, 1996
//

#include <iostream.h>

struct stStudent                                    {
  char  pszName    [ 66 ]                            ,
        pszAddress[ 66 ]                             ,
        pszCity    [ 26 ]                            ,
```

```
        pszState   [  3 ]                          ,
        pszPhone   [ 13 ]                           ;
  int    icourses                                   ;
  float GPA                                         ;
}                                                   ;

void vByValueCall     (stStudent    stAStudent);
void vByVariableCall  (stStudent *pstAStudent);
void vByReferenceCall (stStudent &rstAStudent);

void main( void )
{
  stStudent astLargeClass[ 100 ]                     ;

  astLargeClass[0].icourses = 10                     ;

  vByValueCall     ( astLargeClass[ 0 ] )       ;
  cout << astLargeClass[0].icourses
       << "\n";              // icourses still 10

  vByVariableCall  ( &astLargeClass[ 0 ] )      ;
  cout << astLargeClass[0].icourses
       << "\n";              //     icourses = 20

  vByReferenceCall ( astLargeClass[ 0 ] )       ;
  cout << astLargeClass[0].icourses
       << "\n";              //     icourses = 30
}

void vByValueCall     ( stStudent    stAStudent   )
{
  // normal structure syntax
  stAStudent.icourses += 10                          ;
}

void vByVariableCall ( stStudent *pstAStudent )
{
  // pointer syntax
  pstAStudent->icourses += 10                        ;
}
```

```
void vByReferenceCall( stStudent &rstAStudent )
{
  // simplified reference syntax
  rstAStudent.icourses += 10                    ;
}
```

The following code section has spliced together each function's prototype, along with its matching invoking statement:

```
void vByValueCall      (   stStudent  stAStudent );
     vByValueCall      (   astLargeClass[ 0 ]    );

void vByVariableCall  (   stStudent *pstAStudent );
     vByVariableCall  ( &astLargeClass[ 0 ]      );

void vByReferenceCall (   stStudent &rstAStudent );
     vByReferenceCall (   astLargeClass[ 0 ]     );
```

The first thing you should notice is the simpler syntax needed to send a reference variable, *astLargeClass[0]* (the last statement), over the equivalent pointer syntax, *&astLargeClass[0]*. At this point, the difference may appear small. However, as your algorithms become more complicated, this simpler syntax can avoid unnecessary precedence-level conflicts with other operators such as the pointer dereference operator (*) and the period member operator (.), which qualifies structure fields.

The following three statements were pulled out of the program's respective functions to show the syntax for using the structure within each function:

```
stAStudent.icourses   += 10;  // normal structure syntax
pstAStudent->icourses += 10;  // pointer syntax
rstAStudent.icourses  += 10;  // simplified reference syntax
```

The last two statements make a permanent change to the passed *stStudent* structure because the structure was passed call-by-reference (variable). Notice that the last statement did not require the pointer operator. The difference between the first and third statements is dramatic. Although they look identical, the first statement references only a copy of the *stStudent* structure. In this case, when *stAstudent.icourses* is incremented, it is done only to the function's local copy. Exiting the function returns the structure to bit-oblivion, along with the incremented value. This explains why the program outputs 10, 20, 30, instead of 20, 30, 40.

Assigning Arguments Default Values

C++ allows you to prototype a function by using default arguments. This means that if the invoking statement omits certain fields, predefined default values will be supplied by the function. Default argument definitions cannot be spread throughout a function's prototype; they must be the last formal parameters defined. The following example program demonstrates how to define and use such a function:

```
//
//   aplydef.cpp
//   This C++ program demonstrates how to prototype functions
//   with default arguments. Default arguments must always
//   be the last formal parameters defined.
//   Copyright (c) Chris H. Pappas and William H. Murray, 1996
//

#include <iostream.h>

void fdefault_argument( char ccode    ='Q', int ivalue = 0,
                        float fvalue = 0                    );

void main( void )
{
  fdefault_argument( 'A',2,12.34 );
  fdefault_argument(             );

}

void fdefault_argument( char ccode, int ivalue, float fvalue )
{
  if( ccode == 'Q' )
    cout << "\n\nUsing default values only.";
  cout << "\nivalue = " << ivalue;
  cout << "\nfvalue = " << fvalue;
}
```

In this program, all three formal parameter types have been given default values. The function **fdefault_argument()** checks the *ccode* value to switch on or off an appropriate message. The output from the program is straightforward:

```
ivalue = 2
fvalue = 12.34
```

```
Using default values only.
ivalue = 0
fvalue = 0
```

Careful function prototyping using default argument assignment can be an important approach to avoiding unwanted side effects. This is one means of guaranteeing that dynamically allocated variables will not have garbage values if the user did not supply any. Another way to initialize dynamically allocated memory is with the function **memset()**.

Initializing Dynamically Allocated Memory

You can use **memset()** to initialize a dynamically allocated byte, or bytes, to a specific character. The prototype for **memset()** looks like this:

```
void *memset( void *dest, int cchar, size_t count );
```

After a call to **memset()**, *dest* points to *count* bytes of memory initialized to the character *cchar*. The following example program demonstrates the difference between a static and a dynamic structure declaration:

```
//
//  memset.cpp
//  A C++ program demonstrating the function memset(),
//  which can initialize dynamically allocated memory.
//  Copyright (c) Chris H. Pappas and William H. Murray, 1996
//

#include <iostream.h>

struct keybits                                {
  unsigned char rshift, lshift , ctrl    , alt    ,
             scroll, numlock, caplock, insert;
}                                              ;

void main( void )
{
```

```
keybits stkgarbage, *pstkinitialized              ;

pstkinitialized = new keybits                     ;
memset( pstkinitialized, 0, sizeof(keybits) ) ;
}
```

Thanks to **memset()**, the dynamically allocated structure pointed to by *pstkinitialized* contains all zeros, whereas the compiler left the statically created *stkgarbage* full of random data. The call to the function **memset()** also used the **sizeof()** operator instead of hardwiring the statement to a "magic number." The use of **sizeof()** allows the algorithm to automatically adjust to the size of any object passed to it. Also, remember that C++ does not require the **struct** keyword to precede a structure tag field (*keybits*) when defining structure variables, as is the case with *stkgarbage* and *pstkinitialized*.

More On Formatting Output

The following example programs continue the discussion of C++-formatted output introduced in Chapter 12. The first program demonstrates how to print a table of factorials using **long double**s with the default right-justification:

```
//
//   factrial.cpp
//   A C++ program that prints a table of
//   factorials for the numbers from 1 to 25.
//   The program uses the long double type.
//   Formatting includes precision, width, and fixed
//   with default of right-justification when printing.
//   Copyright (c) Chris H. Pappas and William H. Murray, 1996
//

#include <iostream.h>
#include <iomanip.h>

void main( void )
{
   long double number, factorial              ;

   number   = 1.0                              ;
   factorial = 1.0                             ;
```

```
   cout.precision( 0           );        // no decimal place
   cout.setf      ( ios::fixed );        // use fixed format

   for(int i = 0; i < 25; i++ )                              {
      factorial *= number                                   ;
      number = number + 1.0                                 ;
      cout.width( 30 );              // width of 30 characters
      cout << factorial << endl                              ;
   }
}
```

The output from the program looks like this:

```
                             1
                             2
                             6
                            24
                           120
                           720
                          5040
                         40320
                        362880
                       3628800
                      39916800
                     479001600
                    6227020800
                   87178291200
                 1307674368000
                20922789888000
               355687428096000
              6402373705728000
            121645100408832000
           2432902008176640000
          51090942171709440000
        1124000727777607680000
       25852016738884976640000
      620448401733239439360000
   15511210043330985984000000
```

The next program/output pair demonstrates how to vary output column width and override the default right-justification:

```
//
//  varyoput.cpp
//  A C++ program that prints a table of
//  factorials for the numbers from 1 to 15.
//  The program uses the long double type.
//  Formatting includes precision, width, alignment,
//  and format of large numbers.
//  Copyright (c) Chris H. Pappas and William H. Murray, 1996
//

#include <iostream.h>
#include <iomanip.h>

void main( void )
{
  long double number,factorial;

  number   = 1.0;
  factorial = 1.0;

  cout.precision( 0            ); //        no decimal point
  cout.setf     ( ios::left );   //   left-justify numbers
  cout.setf     ( ios::fixed ); //        use fixed format

  for( int i = 0; i < 25; i++ )                              {
    factorial *= number                                      ;
    number = number + 1.0                                    ;
    cout.width( 30 );              // width of 30 characters
    cout << factorial << endl;
  }
}
```

The left-justified output looks like this:

```
1
2
6
24
120
720
5040
```

```
40320
362880
3628800
39916800
479001600
6227020800
87178291200
1307674368000
20922789888000
355687428096000
6402373705728000
121645100408832000
2432902008176640000
51090942171709440000
1124000727777607680000
25852016738884976640000
620448401733239439360000
15511210043330985984000000
```

The third format example prints out a table of numbers, their squares, and their square roots. The program demonstrates how easy it is to align columns, pad with blanks, fill spaces with zeros, and control precision in C++:

```cpp
//
//   columns.cpp
//   A C++ program that prints a table of
//   numbers, squares, and square roots for the
//   numbers from 1 to 15. The program uses the type
//   double. Formatting aligns columns, pads blank
//   spaces with the '0' character, and controls
//   precision of the answer.
//   Copyright (c) Chris H. Pappas and William H. Murray, 1996
//

#include <iostream.h>
#include <iomanip.h>
#include <math.h>

void main( void )
{
```

```
double number, square, sqroot                                    ;

cout << "num\t" << "square\t\t" << "square root\n"               ;
cout << "_____\n"             ;

number = 1.0                                                      ;
cout.setf( ios::fixed    );              //          use fixed format

for( int i = 1; i < 16; i++ )                                    {
   square = number * number;             //              find square
   sqroot = sqrt( number  );             //         find square root

   cout.fill     ( '0'    );             //    fill blanks with zeros
   cout.width    (  2     );             // column 2 characters wide
   cout.precision(  0     );             //         no decimal place
   cout << number << "\t"  ;

   cout.width    (  6     );             // column 6 characters wide
   cout.precision(  1     );             //      print 1 decimal place
   cout << square << "\t\t";

   cout.width    (  8     );             // column 8 characters wide
   cout.precision(  6     );             //    print 6 decimal places
   cout << sqroot << endl  ;

   number+ = 1.0           ;
  }
}
```

The formatted table looks like this:

```
num     square          square root
_____

01      0001.0          1.000000
02      0004.0          1.414214
03      0009.0          1.732051
04      0016.0          2.000000
05      0025.0          2.236068
06      0036.0          2.449490
07      0049.0          2.645751
08      0064.0          2.828427
```

```
09        0081.0              3.000000
10        0100.0              3.162278
11        0121.0              3.316625
12        0144.0              3.464102
13        0169.0              3.605551
14        0196.0              3.741657
15        0225.0              3.872983
```

Advanced Input and Output Options for C++

Chapter 16 introduced you to the concepts and syntax for object-oriented classes, constructors, destructors, member functions, and operators. Now you are ready for a deeper understanding of C++ I/O. Just like C, C++ does not have any built-in I/O routines. Instead, all C++ compilers come bundled with object-oriented **iostream** classes.

These standard I/O class objects have a cross-compiler syntax consistency because they were developed by the authors of the C++ language. If you are trying to write a C++ application that is portable to other C++ compilers, you will want to use these **iostream** classes. The Borland C++ compiler provides the following five ways to perform C/C++ I/O:

- Unbuffered C library I/O: The C compiler provides unbuffered I/O through functions such as **_read()** and **_write()**. These functions are very popular with C programmers because of their efficiency and the ease with which they can be customized.

- ANSI C buffered I/O: C also supports buffered functions such as **fread()** and **fwrite()**. These stdio.h library functions perform their own buffering before calling the direct I/O base routines.

- C console and port I/O: C provides additional I/O routines that have no C++ equivalent, such as **_getch()**, **_ungetch()**, and **_kbhit()**. All non-Windows applications can use these functions, which give you direct access to the hardware.

- Borland **iostream** class library: The **iostream** class library provides C++ programs with object-oriented I/O. You can use them in place of functions such as **scanf()**, **printf()**, **fscanf()**, and **fprintf()**. However, while these **iostream** classes are not required by C++ programs, many of the character-mode objects, such as **cin**, **cout**, **cerr**, and **clog**, are incompatible with the Windows graphical user interface.

- Borland Object-Windows Library (OWL): The OWL provides C++ and especially Windows applications with objects for disk I/O. Using this library of routines guarantees that your application will be portable and easy to maintain.

An Introduction to the iostream Class

With the exception of the stream buffer classes, all of the I/O objects defined in the **iostream** class library share the same abstract stream base class, called **ios**. These derived classes fall into four categories, as listed in Table 17-1.

Input Stream Classses	
istream	General-purpose input or as parent class for other derived input streams
ifstream	File input
istream_withassign	cin input
istrstream	String input
Output Stream Classes	
ostream	General-purpose output or as parent class for other derived output streams
ofstream	File output
ofstream_withassign	cout, **cerr**, and **clog** output
ostrstream	String output
Input/Output Stream Classes	
iostream	General-purpose input and output or as parent class for other derived I/O streams
fstream	File input/output
strstream	String input/output
stdiostream	Standard input/output
Stream Buffer Classes	
streambuf	Parent class for derived objects
filebuf	Disk file stream buffer
strstreambuf	String stream buffer
stdiobuf	Standard file I/O stream buffer

Table 17-1. *The Four ios Classes*

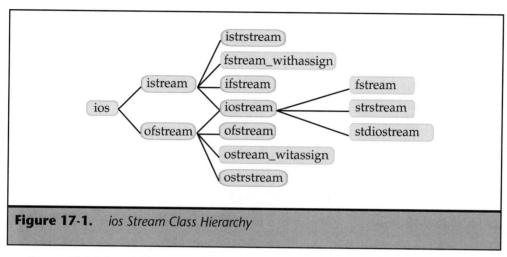

Figure 17-1.   *ios Stream Class Hierarchy*

Figure 17-1 (above) illustrates the interrelationship between these **ios** stream classes. All **ios**-derived **iostream** classes use a **streambuf** class object for the actual I/O processing.

The **iostream** class library uses the following three derived buffer classes with streams:

```
filebuf          Provides buffered disk file I/O
strstreambuf     Provides an in-memory array of bytes to hold
                 the stream data
stdiobuf         Provides buffered disk I/O with all buffering done
                 by the standard I/O system
```

Remember that all derived classes usually expand upon their inherited parent class definitions. This explains why you will often use an operator or member function for a derived class that doesn't appear to be in the derived class's definition. This means that if you are going to fully understand how any derived class operates, you will have to research back to the root or parent class definition. Because C++ derives so many of its classes from the **ios** class, a portion of ios.h follows. You will be able to use this as an easy reference for understanding any class derived from **ios**.

```
#ifndef EOF
#define EOF (-1)
#endif

class streambuf                                              ;
class ostream                                                ;
```

```
class ios                                                          {

public:
    enum io_state { goodbit    = 0x00                              ,
                    eofbit     = 0x01                              ,
                    failbit    = 0x02                              ,
                    badbit     = 0x04                          };

    enum open_mode { in        = 0x01                              ,
                     out       = 0x02                              ,
                     ate       = 0x04                              ,
                     app       = 0x08                              ,
                     trunc     = 0x10                              ,
                     nocreate  = 0x20                              ,
                     noreplace = 0x40                              ,
                     binary    = 0x80 }; // not in latest spec.

    enum seek_dir { beg=0, cur=1, end=2 }                          ;

    enum {          skipws     = 0x0001                            ,
                    left       = 0x0002                            ,
                    right      = 0x0004                            ,
                    internal   = 0x0008                            ,
                    dec        = 0x0010                            ,
                    oct        = 0x0020                            ,
                    hex        = 0x0040                            ,
                    showbase   = 0x0080                            ,
                    showpoint  = 0x0100                            ,
                    uppercase  = 0x0200                            ,
                    showpos    = 0x0400                            ,
                    scientific = 0x0800                            ,
                    fixed      = 0x1000                            ,
                    unitbuf    = 0x2000                            ,
                    stdio      = 0x4000                        };

    static const long basefield  ;     //        dec | oct | hex
    static const long adjustfield;     // left | right | internal
    static const long floatfield ;     //      scientific | fixed

    ios        ( streambuf* )  ;       //        differs from ANSI
    virtual ~ios(           )  ;
```

```
      inline long flags    (                       ) const          ;
      inline long flags    (long _l               )                 ;

      inline long setf      ( long _f, long _m )                     ;
      inline long setf      ( long _l              )                 ;
      inline long unsetf   ( long _l              )                  ;

      inline int width       (                       ) const          ;
      inline int width       (int _i               )                 ;
      inline ostream* tie ( ostream* _os      )                      ;
      inline ostream* tie (                       ) const          ;

      inline char fill       (                       ) const          ;
      inline char fill       ( char _c              )                 ;

      inline int precision( int _i              )                    ;
      inline int precision(                       ) const          ;

      inline int rdstate   (                       ) const          ;
      inline void clear     ( int _i = 0       )                     ;

      operator void *() const { if( state &( badbit|failbit ) )  \
                                return 0; return (void *)this; }
      inline int operator!(                       ) const          ;

      inline int   good       (                       ) const          ;
      inline int   eof         (                       ) const          ;
      inline int   fail        (                       ) const          ;
      inline int   bad        (                       ) const          ;
```

All of the example programs that follow use a derived class based on some parent class. Some of the example program code uses derived class member functions whereas other statements use inherited characteristics. These examples will help you understand the many advantages of derived classes and of inherited characteristics. Although these concepts may appear difficult or frustrating at first, you'll quickly appreciate how you can inherit functionality from a predefined class simply by defining a derived class based on the predefined one.

Input Stream Classes

The **ifstream** class used in the next example program is derived from **fstreambase** and **istream**. It provides input operations on a **filebuf**. The program concentrates on text stream input:

```
//
//   ifstream.cpp
//   A C++ program demonstrating how to use ifstream class,
//   derived from the istream class.
//   Copyright (c) Chris H. Pappas and William H. Murray, 1996
//
//   Valid member functions for ifstream include:
//           ifstream::open       ifstream::rdbuf
//
//   Valid member functions for istream include:
//           istream::gcount      istream::get
//           istream::getline     istream::ignore
//           istream::istream     istream::peek
//           istream::putback     istream::read
//           istream::seekg       istream::tellg

#include <fstream.h>
#define iCOLUMNS 80

void main( void )
{
  char cOneLine[ iCOLUMNS ]                          ;

  ifstream ifMyInputStream( "ifstream.cpp", ios::in );
  while( ifMyInputStream )                           {
    ifMyInputStream.getline( cOneLine, iCOLUMNS      );
    cout << '\n' << cOneLine                         ;
  }
  ifMyInputStream.close( )                           ;
}
```

The first statement in the program uses the **ifstream** constructor to create an **ifstream** object and connect it to an open file descriptor, *ifMyInputStream*. The syntax uses the name of a file, including a path if necessary (*"ifstream.cpp"*), along with one or more open modes (for example, **ios::in | ios::nocreate | ios::binary**). The default is text input. The optional **ios::nocreate** parameter tests for the file's existence. The *ifMyInputStream* file descriptor's integer value can be used in logical tests such as **if** and **while** statements and the value is automatically set to zero on **EOF**.

The **getline()** member function inherited from the **iostream** class allows a program to read whole lines of text up to a terminating null character. Function **getline()** has three formal parameters: a **char ***, the number of characters to input—including the null character—and an optional delimiter (default = '\n').

Because **char** array names are technically pointers to characters, *cOneLine* meets the first parameter requirement. The number of characters to be input matches the array's definition, or *iCOLUMNS*. No optional delimiter was defined. However, if you knew your input lines were delimited by a special character—for example, '*'—you could have written the **getline()** statement like this:

```
ifMyInputStream.getline( cOneLine, iCOLUMNS, '*' );
```

The example program continues by printing the string and then manually closes the file:

```
ifMyInputStream.close( );
```

Output Stream Classes

All **ofstream** classes are derived from **fstreambase** and **ostream** and allow a program to perform formatted and unformatted output to a **streambuf**. The output from this program is used later in this chapter in the section entitled "Text Versus Binary Files" to contrast text output with binary output. The program uses the **ofstream** constructor, which is very similar to its **ifstream** counterpart, described earlier. It expects the name of the output file, "*myostrm.out*", and the open mode, **ios::out**.

```
//
// ofstream.cpp
// A C++ program demonstrating how to use the ofstream class
// derived from the ostream class.
// Copyright (c) Chris H. Pappas and William H. Murray, 1996

// Valid ofstream member functions include:
//          ofstream::open      ofstream::rdbuf

// Valid ostream member functions include:
//          ostream::flush      ostream::ostream
//          ostream::put        ostream::seekp
//          ostream::tellp      ostream::write

#include <fstream.h>
#include <string.h>
#define iSTRING_MAX 40
```

```
void main( void )
{
  int  i = 0                                               ;
  long ltellp;
  char pszString[ iSTRING_MAX ] = "Sample test string\n"   ;

  // file opened in the default text mode
  ofstream ofMyOutputStream( "myostrm.out", ios::out )      ;

  // write string out character by character
  // notice that '\n' IS translated into 2 characters
  while( pszString[ i ] != '\0' )                           {
    ofMyOutputStream.put( pszString[ i ] )                  ;
    ltellp = ofMyOutputStream.tellp( )                      ;
    cout << "\ntellp value: " << ltellp                     ;
    i++                                                     ;
  }

  // write entire string out with write member function

  ltellp = ofMyOutputStream.tellp( )                        ;
  cout << "\ntellp's value before writing 2nd string: "
       << ltellp                                            ;
  ofMyOutputStream.write( pszString, strlen( pszString ) );
  ltellp = ofMyOutputStream.tellp( )                        ;
  cout << "\ntellp's updated value: " << ltellp             ;

  ofMyOutputStream.close( )                                 ;
}
```

The first **while** loop prints out the *pszString* character by character with the **put()** member function. After each character is output, the variable *ltellp* is assigned the current **put** pointer's position as returned by the call to the **tellp()** member function. It is important that you stop at this point to look at the output generated by the program, shown at the end of this section. The string variable *pszString* is initialized with 19 characters plus a '\0' null terminator, bringing the count to a total of 20. However, although the program output generates a *tellp* count of 1 . . . 20, the 20th character isn't the '\0' null terminator. This is because in text mode the *pszString*'s '\n' is translated into a 2-byte output, one for the carriage return (19th character) and the second for the line feed (20th character). The null terminator is not output.

The last portion of the program calculates the output pointer's position before and after using the **write()** member function to print *pszString* as a whole string. Notice that the *tellp* values printed show that the function **write()** also translates the single null terminator into a two-character output. If the character translation had not occurred, *tellp*'s last value would be 39 (assuming **put()** left the first count at 20, not 19). The abbreviated output from the program looks like this:

```
tellp value: 1
tellp value: 2
tellp value: 3

          .

          .

          .

tellp value: 17
tellp value: 18
tellp value: 20
tellp's value before writing 2nd string: 20
tellp's updated value: 40
```

Fortunately, **istream**-derived class member functions such as **get()** and **read()** automatically convert the 2-byte output back to a single '\n'. The program highlights the need for caution when dealing with file I/O. Were the file created by this program used later as an input file opened in binary mode, a disaster would occur because binary files do not use such translation; file positions and contents would be incorrect.

Buffered Stream Classes

The **streambuf** class is the foundation for C++ stream I/O. This general class defines all of the basic operations that can be performed with character-oriented buffers. The **streambuf** class is also used to derive file buffers (**filebuf** class) and the **istream** and **ostream** classes that contain pointers to **streambuf** objects. Any derived classes based on the **ios** class inherit a pointer to a **streambuf**. The **filebuf** class, as seen in Figure 17-2, is derived from **streambuf** and specializes the parent class to handle files.

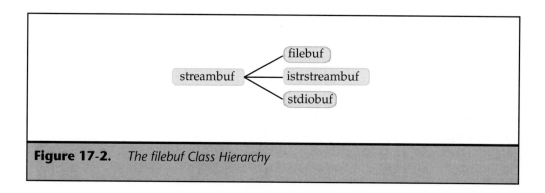

Figure 17-2.   *The filebuf Class Hierarchy*

The following program begins by defining two **filebuf** handles, *fbMyInputBuf* and *fbMyOutputBuf*, using the **open()** member function to create each text file. Assuming there were no file-creation errors, each handle is then associated with an appropriate **istream** (input) and **ostream** (output) object. With both files opened, the **while** loop performs a simple echo print from the input stream **is.get()** to the output stream **os.put()**, counting the number of line feeds, '\n'. The overloaded **close()** member function manually closes each file:

```cpp
//
//   filebuf.cpp
//   A C++ program demonstrating how to use filebuf class.
//   Copyright (c) William H. Murray and Chris H. Pappas, 1995
//
//   Valid member functions include:
//          filebuf::attach       filebuf::close
//          filebuf::fd           filebuf::~filebuf
//          filebuf::filebuf      filebuf::is_open
//          filebuf::open         filebuf::overflow
//          filebuf::seekoff      filebuf::setbuf
//          filebuf::sync         filebuf::underflow
//

#include <fstream.h>
#include <fcntl.h>
#include <process.h> // exit prototype

void main( void )
{
  char    ch                              ;
  int     iLineCount    = 0               ;
  filebuf fbMyInputBuf, fbMyOutputBuf      ;

  fbMyInputBuf.open( "17FILBUF.CPP", _O_RDONLY | _O_TEXT ) ;
  if( fbMyInputBuf.is_open( ) == 0 )                       {
    cerr << "Can't open input file"        ;
    exit( 1 )                              ;
  }

  istream is( &fbMyInputBuf )                              ;

  fbMyOutputBuf.open( "output.dat", _O_WRONLY | _O_TEXT )  ;
  if( fbMyOutputBuf.is_open( ) == 0 )                      {
    cerr << "Can't open output file"       ;
```

```
     exit( 2 )                                            ;
  }

  ostream os( &fbMyOutputBuf  )                           ;

  while( is )                                             {
    is.get( ch )                                          ;
    os.put( ch )                                          ;
    iLineCount += ( ch == '\n' )                          ;
  }

  fbMyInputBuf.close ( )                                  ;
  fbMyOutputBuf.close( )                                  ;

  cout << "You had " << iLineCount << " lines in your file";
}
```

String Stream Classes

You can use the **streambuf** class to extend the capabilities of the **iostream** class. Figure 17-1 illustrated the relationship between the **ios** and derived classes. It is the **ios** class that provides the derived classes with the programming interface and formatting features. However, it is the **streambuf** public members and virtual functions that do all the work. All derived **ios** classes make calls to these routines.

All buffered **streambuf** objects manage a fixed memory buffer called a reserve area. This reserve area can be divided into a get area for input and a put area for output. If your application requires, the get and put areas may overlap. Your program can use protected member functions to access and manipulate the two separate get and put pointers for character I/O. Each application determines the behavior of the buffers and pointers based on the program's implementation of the derived class. There are two constructors for **streambuf** objects. Their syntax looks like this:

```
streambuf::streambuf(                        );
streambuf::streambuf(char* pr, int nLength);
```

The first constructor is used indirectly by all **streambuf** derived classes. It sets all the internal pointers of the **streambuf** object to NULL. The second constructor creates a **streambuf** object that is attached to an existing character array. The following program demonstrates how to declare a string **strstreambuf** object derived from the **streambuf** base class. Once the *stbMyStreamBuf* object is created, the program outputs a single character using the **sputc()** member function and then reads the character back in with the **sgetc()** member function:

```
//
//  strembuf.cpp
//  A C++ program demonstrating how to use the streambuf class.
//  Copyright (c) Chris H. Pappas and William H. Murray, 1996
//

#include <strstrea.h>
#define iMYBUFFSIZE 1024

 void main( void )
{
  char c                                   ;

  strstreambuf stbMyStreamBuf( iMYBUFFSIZE );

  // output single character to buffer
  stbMyStreamBuf.sputc    ( 'A' )          ;
  c = stbMyStreamBuf.sgetc(    )           ;
  cout << c                                ;
}
```

Just remember that there are two separate pointers for **streambuf**-based objects, a put to and a get from. Each is manipulated independently of the other. The reason the **sgetc()** member function retrieves the 'A' is to return the contents of the buffer at the location to which the get pointer points. **sputc()** moves the put pointer but does not move the get pointer and does not return a character from the buffer. Table 17-2 gives the names and explanations for all **streambuf** public members and highlights which functions manipulate the put and get pointers.

Table 17-3 gives the names and explanations for all **streambuf** virtual functions.

Table 17-4 gives the names and explanations for all **streambuf** protected members.

As you can see, the **streambuf** class comes equipped with every function a program could possibly need for manipulating a stream buffer. Because the **streambuf** class is used to derive file buffers (**filebuf** class) and **istream** and **ostream** classes, they all inherit **streambuf** characteristics.

Text Versus Binary Files

Most of the example programs presented so far have used standard text files, or streams, as they are more appropriately called. This is not surprising because streams were originally designed for text, and text, therefore, is their default I/O mode. Standard text files, or streams, contain a sequence of characters including carriage returns and line feeds.

Public Member	Meaning
sgetc()	Returns the character pointed to by the get pointer. However, **sgetc()** does not move the pointer.
sgetn()	Gets a series of characters from the **streambuf()** buffer.
sputc()	Puts a character in the put area and moves the put pointer.
sputn()	Puts a sequence of characters into the **streambuf()** buffer and then moves the put pointer.
snextc()	Moves the get pointer and returns the next character.
sbumpc()	Returns the current character and then moves the get pointer.
stossc()	Advances the get pointer one position. However, **stossc()** does not return a character.
sputbackc()	Attempts to move the get pointer back one position. Character put back must match one from previous get.
out_waiting()	Reports the number of characters in the put area.
in_avail()	Reports the number of characters in the get area.
dbp()	Outputs **streambuf()** buffer statistics and pointer values.

Table 17-2.   *streambuf Public Member Functions*

Virtual Function	Meaning
seekoff()	Seeks to the specified offset
seekpos()	Seeks to the specified position
overflow()	Clears out the put area
underflow()	Fills the get area if necessary
pbackfail()	Extends the **sputbackc()** function
setbuf()	Tries to attach a reserve area to the **streambuf()**
sync()	Clears out the put and get area

Table 17-3.   *streambuf Virtual Functions*

allocate()	Allocates a buffer by calling **doalloc()**
doallocate()	Allocates a reserve area (virtual function)
base()	Returns a pointer to the beginning of the reserve area
ebuf()	Returns a pointer to the end of the reserve area
blen()	Returns the size of the reserve area
pbase()	Returns a pointer to the beginning of the put area
pptr()	Returns the put pointer
gptr()	Returns the get pointer
eback()	Returns the lower bound of the get area
epptr()	Returns a pointer to the end of the put area
egptr()	Returns a pointer to the end of the get area
setp()	Sets all the put area pointers
setg()	Sets all the get area pointers
pbump()	Increments/decrements the put pointer
gbump()	Increments/decrements the get pointer
setb()	Sets up the reserve area
unbuffered()	Sets or tests the **streambuf()** buffer state variable

Table 17-4.   *streambuf Protected Functions*

In text mode, there is no requirement that individual characters remain unaltered as they are written to or read from a file. This can cause problems for certain types of applications. For example, the ASCII value for the newline character is a decimal 10. However, it could also be written as an 8-bit, hexadecimal 0A. In a C/C++ program, it is considered to be the single character constant '\n'. As it turns out, under MS-DOS the newline is physically represented as a character pair—carriage return (decimal 13)/line feed (decimal 10).

Normally, this isn't a problem because the program automatically maps the two-character sequence into the single newline character on input, reversing the sequence on output. The problem is that a newline character occupies 1 byte, whereas the CR/LF pair occupies 2 bytes of storage. Binary files, or streams, contain a sequence of bytes with a one-to-one correspondence to the sequence found in the external device (disk, tape, or terminal).

In a binary file, no character translations will occur. For this reason, the number of bytes read or written will be the same as that found in the external device. If you are writing a program that needs to read an executable file, the file should be read as a binary file. You should also use binary files when reading or writing pure data files, like databases. This guarantees that no alteration of the data occurs except those changes performed explicitly by the application. The following program is identical to the program described earlier in the section entitled "Output Stream Classes," except that the output file mode has been changed from text to **ios::binary**:

```
//
// binary.cpp
// This program is a modification of 17OSTRM.CPP and
// demonstrates binary file output.
// Copyright (c) Chris H. Pappas and William H. Murray, 1996
// Valid ofstream member functions include:
//          ofstream::open      ofstream::rdbuf
// Valid ostream member functions include:
//          ostream::flush      ostream::ostream
//          ostream::put        ostream::seekp
//          ostream::tellp      ostream::write

#include <fstream.h>
#include <string.h>

#define iSTRING_MAX 40

void main( void )
{
  int  i =  0                                                ;
  long ltellp                                                ;
  char pszString[iSTRING_MAX] = "Sample test string\n"       ;

  // file opened in binary mode!
  ofstream ofMyOutputStream( "MYOSTRM.OUT",ios::out | ios::binary );

  // write string out character by character
  // notice that '\n' is NOT translated into 2 characters!

  while( pszString[ i ] != '\0' )
  {
    ofMyOutputStream.put( pszString[ i ] )                   ;
    ltellp = ofMyOutputStream.tellp(     )                   ;
    cout << "\ntellp value: " << ltellp                      ;
```

```
      i++                                                          ;
   }

   // write entire string out with write member function
   ltellp = ofMyOutputStream.tellp(          )                     ;
   cout << "\ntellp's value before writing 2nd string: " << ltellp ;
   ofMyOutputStream.write( pszString, strlen( pszString ) )        ;
   ltellp = ofMyOutputStream.tellp(          )                     ;
   cout << "\ntellp's updated value: " << ltellp                   ;

   ofMyOutputStream.close(          )                              ;
}
```

The abbreviated output, seen in the following listing, illustrates the one-to-one relationship between a file and the data's internal representation:

```
tellp value: 1
tellp value: 2
tellp value: 3

    .

    .

    .

tellp value: 17
tellp value: 18
tellp value: 19
tellp's value before writing 2nd string: 19
tellp's updated value: 38
```

The string *pszString*, which has 19 characters plus a '\0' null string terminator, is output exactly as stored, without the appended '\0' null terminator. This explains why **tellp()** reports a multiple of 19 at the completion of each string's output.

Combining C and C++ Code Using extern "C"

In previous discussions (in Chapter 6), you have seen how the **extern** keyword specifies that a variable or function has external linkage. This means that the variable or function referenced is defined in some other source file or later in the same file. However, in C/C++, you can use the **extern** keyword with a string. The string indicates that another language's linkage conventions are being used for the identifier(s) being defined. For C++ programs, the default string is "C++".

In C++, functions are overloaded by default. This causes the C++ compiler to assign a new name to each function. You can prevent the compiler from assigning a new name to each function by preceding the function definition with extern "C". This is necessary so that C functions and data can be accessed by C++ code. Naturally, this is only done for one of a set of functions with the same name. Without this override, the linker would find more than one global function with the same name. Currently, "C" is the only other language specifier supported by Borland C++. The syntax for using extern "C" looks like this:

```
extern "C" freturn_type fname(param_type(s) param(s))
```

The following listing demonstrates how extern "C" is used with a single-function prototype:

```
extern "C" int fprintf(FILE *stream, char *format, ...);
```

To modify a group of function prototypes, a set of braces, { }, is needed:

```
extern "C"
  {
        .
        .
        .
  }
```

The next code segment modifies the **getc()** and **putc()** function prototypes:

```
extern "C"
  {
      int getc(FILE *stream);
      int putc(int c, FILE *stream);
  }
```

The following example program demonstrates how to use extern "C":

```
//
//   extrnclk.cpp
//   A C++ program demonstrating how to link C++ code
//   to C library functions
//   Copyright (c) Chris H. Pappas and William H. Murray, 1996
//

#include <iostream.h>
#include <string.h>
#include <stdlib.h>

#define iMAX 9

extern "C" int imycompare( const void *pi1, const void *pi2 );

void main( void )
{
  int iarray[ iMAX ] = { 1, 9, 2, 8, 3, 7, 4, 6, 5 }          ;

  for( int i = 0; i < iMAX; i++ )
    cout << iarray[ i ] << " "                                ;

  qsort( iarray, iMAX, sizeof(int), imycompare )              ;

  for( i = 0; i < iMAX; i++ )
    cout << iarray[ i ] << " "                                ;
}

extern "C" int imycompare( const void *pi1, const void *pi2 )
{
  return( *(int *)pi1 - *(int *)pi2 )                         ;
}
```

All the Borland C include files use **extern** "C". This makes it possible for a C++ program to use the C run-time library functions. Rather than repeat extern "C" for every definition in these header files, the following conditional statement pair surrounds all C header file definitions:

```
// 3-statements found at the beginning of header file.

#ifdef __cplusplus
extern "C" {
#endif


// 3-statements found at the end of the header file.

#ifdef __cplusplus
}
#endif
```

When compiling a C++ program, the compiler automatically defines the **__cplusplus** name. This in turn makes the extern "C" { statement and the closing brace, }, visible only when needed.

Creating Your Own Manipulators

Chapter 12 introduced the concept of stream manipulators. You use manipulators with the insertion (<<) and extraction (>>) operators exactly as if they represented data for output or variables to receive input. As the name implies, however, manipulators can carry out arbitrary operations on the input and output streams. Several of the example programs used the built-in manipulators **dec, hex, oct, setw()**, and **setprecision()**. Now you will learn how to write your own custom manipulators. To gradually build your understanding of the syntax necessary to create your own manipulators, the example programs begin with the simplest type of manipulator, one with no parameters, and then move on to ones with parameters.

Without Parameters

You can create a custom manipulator anytime you need to repeatedly insert the same character sequence into the output stream. For example, maybe your particular application needs to flag an important piece of data for the user. You want to beep the speaker to get the user's attention just in case he or she isn't looking directly at the monitor. Without custom manipulators, your output statements would look like this:

```
cout << '\a' << "\n\n\t\tImportant data: "
     << fcritical_mass << endl;
```

Every time you wanted to grab the user's attention, you would repeat the bell prompt, '\a', and the "...Important data: " string. An easier approach is to define a manipulator, called beep, that automatically substitutes the desired sequence. The beep manipulator also makes the statement easier to read:

```
cout << beep << fcritical_mass << endl;
```

The following program demonstrates how to define and use the **beep()** function:

```
//
//   mybeep.cpp
//   This C++ program demonstrates how to create your own
//   non-parameterized manipulator.
//   Copyright (c) Chris H. Pappas and William H. Murray, 1996
//

#include <iostream.h>

ostream& beep( ostream& os )                              {
  return os << '\a' << "\n\n\t\t\tImportant data: ";
}

void main( void )
{
  double fcritical_mass = 12459876.12                     ;

  cout << beep << fcritical_mass                          ;
}
```

The globally defined **beep()** function uses an **ostream&** formal parameter and returns the same **ostream&**. **beep()** works because it is automatically connected to the stream's << operator. The stream's insertion operator, <<, is overloaded to accept this kind of function with the following inline function:

```
Inline ostream& ostream::operator<<(ostream& (*f)(ostream&)) {
  (*f)(*this);
  return *this;
}
```

The **inline** function associates the << operator with the custom manipulator by accepting a pointer to a function passed an **ostream&** type and that returns the same. This is exactly how **beep()** is prototyped. Now when << is used with **beep()**, the compiler dereferences the overloaded operator, finding where function **beep()** sits, and then executes it. The overloaded operator returns a reference to the original **ostream**. Because of this, you can combine manipulators, strings, and other data with the << operators.

With One Parameter

The Borland **iostream** class library, prototyped in iomanip.h, defines a special set of macros for creating parameterized macros. The simplest parameterized macro you can write accepts either one **int** or **long** parameter. The following listing shows a prototype for such a manipulator, *fc*. The example program demonstrates the syntax necessary to create a single-parameter custom manipulator:

```
//
//  mymanip.cpp
//  A C++ program demonstrating how to create and use
//  one-parameter custom manipulators.
//  Copyright (c) Chris H. Pappas and William H. Murray, 1996
//

#include <iostream.h>
#include <iomanip.h>
#include <string.h>
#define iSCREEN_WIDTH 80


ostream& fc( ostream& os, int istring_width )
{
  os << '\n'  ;
  for( int i=0; i < ((iSCREEN_WIDTH - istring_width)/2); i++ )
    os << ' '  ;
```

```
   return( os );
}

OMANIP(int) center( int istring_width )
{
   return OMANIP( int ) ( fc, istring_width );
}

void main( void )
{
   char *psz = "This is auto-centered text!" ;
   cout << center( strlen(psz) ) << psz      ;
}
```

The center custom-parameterized manipulator accepts a single value, *strlen(psz)*, representing the length of a string. iomanip.h defines a macro, **OMANIP(int)**, and expands into the class **__OMANIP_int**. The definition for this class includes a constructor and an overloaded **ostream** insertion operator. When function **center()** is inserted into the stream, it calls the constructor that creates and returns an **__OMANIP_int** object. The object's constructor then calls the **fc()** function.

With Multiple Parameters

You may think the next example looks somewhat familiar. Actually, it is the same code (columns.cpp) seen earlier in the chapter to demonstrate how to format numeric output. However, the program has been rewritten using a two-parameter custom manipulator to format the data. The first modification to the program involves a simple structure definition to hold the format manipulator's actual parameter values:

```
struct stwidth_precision {
   int iwidth    ;
   int iprecision;
};
```

When you create manipulators that take arguments other than **int** or **long**, you must use the **IOMANIP** declare macro. This macro declares the classes for your new data type. The definition for the format manipulator begins with the **OMANIP** macro:

OMANIP(stwidth_precision) format(int iwidth, int iprecision)

```
{
   stwidth_precision stWidth_Precision                        ;
   stWidth_Precision.iwidth     = iwidth                      ;
   stWidth_Precision.iprecision = iprecision                  ;
   return OMANIP( stwidth_precision )( ff, stWidth_Precision );
}
```

In this example, the custom manipulator is passed two integer arguments, *iwidth* and *iprecision*. The first value defines the number of spaces to be used by format, and the second value specifies the number of decimal places. Once format has initialized the *stWidth_Precision* structure, it calls the constructor, which creates and returns an **__OMANIP** object. The object's constructor then calls the *ff()* function, which sets the specified parameters:

```
static ostream& ff(ostream& os, stwidth_precision
                   stWidth_Precision)
{
   os.width     ( stWidth_Precision.iwidth     );
   os.precision( stWidth_Precision.iprecision );
   os.setf      ( ios::fixed                    );
   return os                                     ;
}
```

The complete program follows. All of the code replaced by the call to format has been left in the listing for comparison. Notice how the format custom manipulator streamlines each output statement:

```
//
//   maniptwo.cpp
//   This C++ program is the same as columns.cpp, except
//   for the fact that it uses custom-parameterized
//   manipulators to format the output.
//   A C++ program that prints a table of
//   numbers, squares, and square roots for the
//   numbers from 1 to 15. Program uses the type
//   double. Formatting aligns columns, pads blank
//   spaces with the '0' character, and controls the
//   precision of answer.
//   Copyright (c) Chris H. Pappas and William H. Murray, 1996
//
```

```
#include <iostream.h>
#include <iomanip.h>
#include <math.h>

struct stwidth_precision                                         {
  int iwidth                                                     ;
  int iprecision                                                 ;
}                                                                ;

IOMANIPdeclare( stwidth_precision              )                 ;

static ostream& ff( ostream& os, stwidth_precision
                    stWidth_Precision          )
{
  os.width     ( stWidth_Precision.iwidth      )                 ;
  os.precision( stWidth_Precision.iprecision )                   ;
  os.setf      ( ios::fixed                    )                 ;
  return os                                                      ;
}

OMANIP( stwidth_precision ) format( int iwidth, int iprecision )
{
  stwidth_precision stWidth_Precision                            ;
  stWidth_Precision.iwidth     = iwidth                          ;
  stWidth_Precision.iprecision = iprecision                      ;
  return OMANIP( stwidth_precision )( ff, stWidth_Precision )    ;
}

void main( void )
{
  double number, square, sqroot                                 ;

  cout << "num\t" << "square\t\t" << "square root\n"             ;
  cout << "_____\n"                   ;

  number = 1.0                                                   ;

//cout.setf( ios::fixed )   ;          //          use fixed format
  for(int i=1;i<16;i++)     {
```

```
   square = number*number ;          //              find square
   sqroot = sqrt( number );          //           find square root

   cout.fill      ( '0'  ) ;          //   fill blanks with zeros
// cout.width     ( 2    ) ;          // column 2 characters wide
// cout.precision( 0     ) ;          //           no decimal place
   cout << format( 2,0 ) << number << "\t"                   ;

// cout.width     ( 6    ) ;          // column 6 characters wide
// cout.precision( 1     ) ;          //    print 1 decimal place
   cout << format( 6,1 ) << square << "\t\t"                 ;

// cout.width     ( 8    ) ;          // column 8 characters wide
// cout.precision( 6     ) ;          //    print 6 decimal places
   cout << format( 8,6 ) << sqroot << endl                   ;

   number+ = 1.0                                             ;
 }
}
```

In the Next Chapter...

Now that you are more comfortable with advanced C++ object-oriented I/O, you are ready to move on to object-oriented design philosophies. Chapter 18 explains how important good class design is to a successful object-oriented problem solution.

```
//

#include <iostream.h>
#include <string.h>

#define maxlen 80

class stack                                             {
  char str1[ maxlen ]                                   ;
  int  first                                            ;

public:
  void clear( void      )                               ;
  char top  ( void      )                               ;
  int  empty( void      )                               ;
  int  full ( void      )                               ;
  void push ( char chr )                                ;
  char pop  ( void      )                               ;
}                                                       ;

void stack::clear( void )
{
  first = 0 ;
}

char stack::top( void )
{
  return( str1[ first ] )                               ;
}

int stack::empty( void )
{
  return( first == 0 )                                  ;
}

int stack::full( void )
{
  return( first == maxlen-1 )                           ;
}

void stack::push( char chr )
{
```

```
      str1[ ++first ] = chr                               ;
    }

  char stack::pop( void )
  {
    return( str1[ first-- ] )                             ;
  }

  void main( void )
  {
    stack mystack                                         ;
    char str[ 11 ] = "0123456789"                         ;

    // clear the stack
    mystack.clear( )                                      ;

    // load the string, char-by-char, on the stack
    cout << "\nLoad character data on stack" << endl      ;
    for( int i=0; i < strlen(str); i++ )                  {
      if( !mystack.full( ) )
        mystack.push( str[ i ] )                          ;
        cout << str[i] << endl                            ;
    }

    // unload the stack, char-by-char
    cout << "\nUnload character data from stack" << endl;
    while( !mystack.empty( ) )
      cout << mystack.pop( ) << endl                      ;

  }
```

In this program, characters from a string are pushed, one character at a time, onto the stack. Next, the stack is unloaded one character at a time. Loading and unloading are done from the stack top, so the first character information loaded on the stack is pushed down most deeply in the stack.

Observe in the following listing that the character for the number zero was pushed onto the stack first. It should be no surprise that it is the last character popped off the stack.

```
Load character data on stack
0
1
2
3
4
5
6
7
8
9

Unload character data from stack
9
8
7
6
5
4
3
2
1
0
```

Although this example lacks many of the more advanced object-oriented concepts such as memory management, inheritance, and polymorphism, it is nevertheless a simple object-oriented program. However, the power of object-oriented thinking becomes apparent as more and more of Meyer's seven points are actually implemented.

An Object-Oriented Linked List in C++

In Chapter 14, a linked-list program was developed in C++ using a traditional procedural programming approach. When using the traditional approach, you learned that the linked-list program is difficult to alter and maintain. This chapter traces the development of a linked-list program using objects that allows you to create a list of employee information and add and delete employees from the list. To limit the size of the linked-list program, no user interface will be used for gathering employee data. Data for the linked list has been hardwired in the **main()** function. Examples of how to make this program interactive and able to accept information from the keyboard have been shown in earlier chapters.

This program is slightly more difficult than the example in Chapter 14. You will find that it includes, in addition to linked-list concepts, all seven of the object-oriented concepts listed at the beginning of this chapter.

Creating a Parent Class

This program uses several child classes derived from a common parent class. The parent class for this linked-list example is named P_and_M_Auto_Dealership. The linked-list program is a database that will keep pertinent information and payroll data on company employees. The purpose of the parent class P_and_M_Auto_Dealership is to gather information common to all subsequent derived child classes. For this example, that common information includes an employee's last name, first name, occupation title, social security number, and number of years at the company. The parent class, P_and_M_Auto_Dealership, has three levels of isolation: public, protected, and private. The protected section of this class shows the structure for gathering data common to each derived child class. The public section (member functions) shows how that information will be intercepted from the function **main()**.

```
// PARENT CLASS
class P_and_M_Auto_Dealership {

friend class employee_list;

protected:
  char lastname[20];
  char firstname[15];
  char occupation[30];
  char social_security[12];
  int years_employed;
  P_and_M_Auto_Dealership *pointer;
  P_and_M_Auto_Dealership *next_link;

public:
  P_and_M_Auto_Dealership(char *lname,char *fname,char *ssnum,
      char *occup,int c_years_employed)
  {
    strcpy(lastname,lname);
    strcpy(firstname,fname);
    strcpy(social_security,ssnum);
    strcpy(occupation,occup);
    years_employed=c_years_employed;
```

```
    next_link=0;
}
    .
    .
    .
    .
```

The parent class and all derived child classes will use a friend class named employee_list. When you study the full program listing later in this chapter, notice that all derived child classes share this common variable, too. (Remember how the terms "private" and "public" relate to encapsulation concepts used by object-oriented programmers.)

A Derived Child Class

This program uses four derived child classes. Each of these is derived from the parent class P_and_M_Auto_Dealership shown in the last section. This segment presents one child class, salespersons, which represents the points common to all four derived classes. A portion of this derived class is shown next. The derived child class satisfies the object-oriented concept of inheritance.

```
//SUB OR DERIVED CHILD CLASS
class salespersons:public P_and_M_Auto_Dealership {

friend class employee_list;

private:
  float unit_sales_average;
  int comm_rate;

public:
  salespersons(char *lname,char *fname,char *ssnum,
               char *occup,int c_years_employed,
               float w_avg,int c_rate):
               P_and_M_Auto_Dealership(lname,fname,ssnum,
               occup,c_years_employed)
  {
    unit_sales_average=w_avg;
```

```
    comm_rate=c_rate;
}
        .
        .
        .
        .
```

In this case, the salespersons child class gathers information and adds it to the information already gathered by the parent class. This in turn forms a data structure composed of last name, first name, social security number, years worked, the total sales, and the appropriate commission rate.

Now take a look at the remainder of the child class description:

```
        .
        .
        .
        .

void fill_average(float w_avg)
{
   unit_sales_average=w_avg;
}

void fill_comm_rate(int c_rate)
{
   comm_rate=c_rate;
}

void add_data()
{
   pointer=this;
}

void send_info()
{
   P_and_M_Auto_Dealership::send_info();
   cout << "\n Weekly Sales Average (units): " << unit_sales_average;
   cout << "\n Commission Rate: " << comm_rate << "%";
}
};
```

Instead of **add_data()** setting aside memory for each additional linked-list node by using the **new** free store operator, the program uses each object's **this** pointer. The pointer is being assigned the address of an P_and_M_Auto_Dealership node.

Output information on a particular employee is constructed in a unique manner. In the case of the salespersons class, notice that **send_info()** makes a request to P_and_M_Auto_Dealership's **send_info()** function. P_and_M_Auto_Dealership's function prints the information common to each derived class; then the salespersons' **send_info()** function prints the information unique to the particular child class. For this example, this information includes the sales and the commission rate.

It also would have been possible to print the information about the salesperson completely from within the child class, but the method used allows another advantage of object-oriented programming to be illustrated—the use of virtual functions.

Using a Friend Class

The friend class, employee_list, contains the means for printing the linked list and for the insertion and deletion of employees from the list. Here is a small portion of this class:

```
//FRIEND CLASS
class employee_list {

private:
   P_and_M_Auto_Dealership *location;

public:
   employee_list()
   {
     location=0;
   }

   void print_employee_list();

   void insert_employee(P_and_M_Auto_Dealership *node);

   void remove_employee_id(char *social_security);

};
       .
       .
       .
       .
```

Notice that messages that are sent to the member functions **print_employee_list()**, **insert_employee()**, and **remove_employee_id()** form the functional part of the linked-list program.

Consider the function **print_employee_list()**, which begins by assigning the pointer to the list to the pointer variable present. While the pointer present is not zero, it will continue to point to employees in the linked list, direct them to **send_info()**, and update the pointer until all employees have been printed. The next section of code shows how this is achieved:

```
        .
        .
        .
        .

void employee_list::print_employee_list()
{
   P_and_M_Auto_Dealership *present=location;

   while(present!=0) {
      present->send_info();
      present=present->next_link;
   }
}
        .
        .
        .
```

You might recall from an earlier discussion that the variable pointer contains the memory address of nodes inserted via **add_data()**. This value is used by **insert_employee()** to form the link with the linked list. The insertion technique inserts data alphabetically by an employee's last name. Thus, the linked list is always ordered alphabetically by last name.

The program accomplishes a correct insertion by comparing the last name of a new employee with those already in the list. When a name (*node->lastname*), already in the list, is found that is greater than the *current_node->lastname*, the first **while** loop ends. This is a standard linked-list insert procedure that leaves the pointer variable, *previous_node*, pointing to the node behind where the new node is to be inserted and leaves *current_node* pointing to the node that will follow the insertion point for the new node.

When the insertion point is determined, the program creates a new link or node by calling *node->add_data()*. The *current_node* is linked to the new node's *next_link*. The last decision that must be made is whether the new node is to be placed as the front node in the list or between existing nodes. The program establishes this by examining the contents of the pointer variable *previous_node*. If the pointer variable is zero, it cannot be pointing to a valid previous node, so location is updated to the address of the new node. If *previous_node* contains a nonzero value, it is assumed to be pointing to a valid previous node. In this case, *previous_node->next_link* is assigned the address of the new node's address, or *node->pointer*.

```
                .
                .
                .
                .
void employee_list::insert_employee(P_and_M_Auto_Dealership *node)
{
    P_and_M_Auto_Dealership *current_node=location;
    P_and_M_Auto_Dealership *previous_node=0;

    while (current_node != 0 &&
            strcmp(current_node->lastname,node->lastname) < 0) {
        previous_node=current_node;
        current_node=current_node->next_link;
    }
    node->add_data();
    node->pointer->next_link=current_node;
    if (previous_node==0)
        location=node->pointer;
    else
        previous_node->next_link=node->pointer;
}
                .
                .
                .
                .
```

The program can remove items from the linked list only by knowing the employee's social security number. This technique adds a level of protection against accidentally deleting an employee.

As you examine **remove_employee_id()**, shown in the next listing, note that the structure used for examining the nodes in the linked list is almost identical to that of **insert_employee()**. However, the first **while** loop leaves the *current_node* pointing to the node to be deleted, not the node after the one to be deleted.

```
         .
         .
         .
         .
void employee_list::remove_employee_id(char *social_security)
{
  P_and_M_Auto_Dealership *current_node=location;
  P_and_M_Auto_Dealership *previous_node=0;

  while(current_node != 0 &&
        strcmp(current_node->social_security,
        social_security) != 0) {
    previous_node=current_node;
    current_node=current_node->next_link;
  }

  if(current_node != 0 && previous_node == 0) {
    location=current_node->next_link;
    delete current_node;
  }
  else if(current_node != 0 && previous_node != 0) {
    previous_node->next_link=current_node->next_link;
    delete current_node;
  }
}
```

The first compound **if** statement takes care of deleting a node in the front of the list. The program accomplishes this by examining the contents of *previous_node* to see if it contains a zero. If it does, then the front of the list, *location*, needs to be updated to the node following the one to be deleted. This is achieved with the following line:

```
current_node->next_link
```

The second **if** statement takes care of deleting a node between two existing nodes. This requires the node behind to be assigned the address of the node after the one being deleted:

```
previous_node->next_link=current_node->next_link.
```

Now that the important pieces of the program have been examined, the next section puts them together to form a complete program.

Examining the Complete Program

The following listing is the complete operational C++ object-oriented linked-list program. The only thing it lacks is an interactive user interface. When the program is executed, it will add eight employees, with their different job titles, to the linked list and then print the list. Next, the program will delete three employees from the list. This is accomplished by supplying their social security numbers. The altered list is then printed. The **main()** function contains information on which employees are added and deleted.

```cpp
//
//  P_and_M_Auto_Dealership.CPP
//  This C++ program illustrates object-oriented programming
//  with a linked list. This program keeps track of
//  employee data at the P_and_M_Auto_Dealership.
//  Copyright (c) Chris H. Pappas and William H. Murray, 1996
//

#include <iostream.h>
#include <string.h>

// PARENT CLASS
class P_and_M_Auto_Dealership {

friend class employee_list;

protected:
  char lastname[20];
  char firstname[15];
  char occupation[30];
  char social_security[12];
  int years_employed;
  P_and_M_Auto_Dealership *pointer;
  P_and_M_Auto_Dealership *next_link;

public:
  P_and_M_Auto_Dealership(char *lname,char *fname,char *ssnum,
      char *occup,int c_years_employed)
  {
    strcpy(lastname,lname);
    strcpy(firstname,fname);
    strcpy(social_security,ssnum);
    strcpy(occupation,occup);
```

```
    years_employed=c_years_employed;
    next_link=0;
  }

P_and_M_Auto_Dealership()
{
    lastname[0]=NULL;
    firstname[0]=NULL;
    social_security[0]=NULL;
    occupation[0]=NULL;
    years_employed=0;
    next_link=0;
  }

void fill_lastname(char *l_name)
{
    strcpy(lastname,l_name);
  }

void fill_firstname(char *f_name)
{
    strcpy(firstname,f_name);
  }

void fill_social_security(char *soc_sec)
{
    strcpy(social_security,soc_sec);
  }

void fill_occupation(char *o_name)
{
    strcpy(occupation,o_name);
  }

void fill_years_employed(int c_years_employed)
{
    years_employed=c_years_employed;
  }

virtual void add_data() {
  }
virtual void send_info()
```

```
   {
     cout << "\n\n" << lastname << ", " << firstname
        << "\n Social Security: #" << social_security;
     cout << "\n Job Title: " << occupation;
    cout << "\n Years With Company: " << years_employed;
   }
};

//SUB OR DERIVED CHILD CLASS
class deal_closer:public P_and_M_Auto_Dealership {

friend class employee_list;

private:
  float yearly_salary;

public:
  deal_closer(char *lname,char *fname,char *ssnum,
             char *occup,int c_years_employed,
             float y_salary):
             P_and_M_Auto_Dealership(lname,fname,ssnum,
             occup,c_years_employed)
  {
    yearly_salary=y_salary;
  }

  deal_closer():P_and_M_Auto_Dealership()
  {
    yearly_salary=0.0;
  }

  void fill_yearly_salary(float salary)
  {
    yearly_salary=salary;
  }

  void add_data()
  {
    pointer=this;
  }

  void send_info()
```

```
  {
    P_and_M_Auto_Dealership::send_info();
    cout << "\n Yearly Salary: $" << yearly_salary;
  }
};


//SUB OR DERIVED CHILD CLASS
class salespersons:public P_and_M_Auto_Dealership {

friend class employee_list;

private:
  float unit_sales_average;
  int comm_rate;

public:
  salespersons(char *lname,char *fname,char *ssnum,
               char *occup,int c_years_employed,
               float w_avg,int c_rate):
               P_and_M_Auto_Dealership(lname,fname,ssnum,
               occup,c_years_employed)
  {
    unit_sales_average=w_avg;
    comm_rate=c_rate;
  }

  salespersons():P_and_M_Auto_Dealership()
  {
    unit_sales_average=0.0;
    comm_rate=0;
  }

  void fill_average(float w_avg)
  {
    unit_sales_average=w_avg;
  }

  void fill_comm_rate(int c_rate)
  {
    comm_rate=c_rate;
```

```
    }

  void add_data()
  {
    pointer=this;
  }

  void send_info()
  {
    P_and_M_Auto_Dealership::send_info();
    cout << "\n Weekly Sales Average (units): "
         << unit_sales_average;
    cout << "\n Commission Rate: " << comm_rate << "%";
  }
};

//SUB OR DERIVED CHILD CLASS
class mechanics:public P_and_M_Auto_Dealership {

friend class employee_list;

private:
  float hourly_salary;

public:
  mechanics(char *lname,char *fname,char *ssnum,char *occup,
        int c_years_employed,float h_salary):
        P_and_M_Auto_Dealership(lname,fname,ssnum,
        occup,c_years_employed)
  {
    hourly_salary=h_salary;
  }

  mechanics():P_and_M_Auto_Dealership()
  {
    hourly_salary=0.0;
  }

  void fill_hourly_salary(float h_salary)
  {
    hourly_salary=h_salary;
  }
```

```
  void add_data()
  {
    pointer=this;
  }

  void send_info()
  {
    P_and_M_Auto_Dealership::send_info();
    cout << "\n Hourly Salary: $" << hourly_salary;
  }
};

//SUB OR DERIVED CHILD CLASS
class parts:public P_and_M_Auto_Dealership {

friend class employee_list;

private:
  float hourly_salary;

public:
  parts(char *lname,char *fname,char *ssnum,char *occup,
          int c_years_employed,float h_salary):
          P_and_M_Auto_Dealership(lname,fname,ssnum,
          occup,c_years_employed)
  {
    hourly_salary=h_salary;
  }

  parts():P_and_M_Auto_Dealership()
  {
    hourly_salary=0.0;
  }

  void fill_hourly_salary(float h_salary)
  {
    hourly_salary=h_salary;
  }

  void add_data()
  {
    pointer=this;
```

```
  }

  void send_info()
  {
    P_and_M_Auto_Dealership::send_info();
    cout << "\n Hourly Salary: $" << hourly_salary;
  }

};

//FRIEND CLASS
class employee_list {

private:
  P_and_M_Auto_Dealership *location;

public:
  employee_list()
  {
    location=0;
  }

  void print_employee_list();

  void insert_employee(P_and_M_Auto_Dealership *node);

  void remove_employee_id(char *social_security);

};

void employee_list::print_employee_list()
{
  P_and_M_Auto_Dealership *present=location;

  while(present!=0) {
    present->send_info();
    present=present->next_link;
  }
}

void employee_list::insert_employee(P_and_M_Auto_Dealership \
                                    *node)
```

```
{
  P_and_M_Auto_Dealership *current_node=location;
  P_and_M_Auto_Dealership *previous_node=0;
  while (current_node != 0 &&
          strcmp(current_node->lastname,node->lastname) < 0) {
    previous_node=current_node;
    current_node=current_node->next_link;
  }
  node->add_data();
  node->pointer->next_link=current_node;
  if (previous_node==0)
    location=node->pointer;
  else
    previous_node->next_link=node->pointer;
}

void employee_list::remove_employee_id(char *social_security)
{
  P_and_M_Auto_Dealership *current_node=location;
  P_and_M_Auto_Dealership *previous_node=0;

  while(current_node != 0 &&
      strcmp(current_node->social_security,
            social_security) != 0) {
    previous_node=current_node;
    current_node=current_node->next_link;
  }

  if(current_node != 0 && previous_node == 0) {
    location=current_node->next_link;
    // delete current_node; needed if new() used in add_data()
  }
  else if(current_node != 0 && previous_node != 0) {
    previous_node->next_link=current_node->next_link;
    // delete current_node; needed if new() used in add_data()
  }
}

main()
{
  employee_list workers;
```

```
cout.setf(ios::fixed);
cout.precision(2);

// static data to add to linked list
salespersons salesperson1("Friendly","Fran","212-98-7654",
                          "Salesperson",1,7.5,4.00);
salespersons salesperson2("Pest","Perry","567-45-3412",
                          "Salesperson",2,2.0,2.20);
salespersons salesperson3("Yourfriend","Yancy","213-44-9873",
                          "Salesperson",1,10.6,5.70);
mechanics mechanicperson1("Hardwork","Harriet","076-45-3121",
                          "Mechanic",7,10.34);
mechanics mechanicperson2("Lugwrench","Larry","886-43-1518",
                          "Mechanic",1,8.98);
deal_closer closerperson("Slick","Sally",
                         "111-22-4444","Closer",
                         10,40000.00);
parts partperson1("Muffler","Mike","555-66-7891",
                  "Parts",4,7.34);
parts partperson2("Horn","Hazel","345-77-7654",
                  "Parts",5,9.50);

// add the eight workers to the linked list
workers.insert_employee(&mechanicperson1);
workers.insert_employee(&closerperson);
workers.insert_employee(&salesperson1);
workers.insert_employee(&partperson1);
workers.insert_employee(&partperson2);
workers.insert_employee(&salesperson2);
workers.insert_employee(&mechanicperson2);
workers.insert_employee(&salesperson3);

// print the linked list
workers.print_employee_list();

// remove three workers from the linked list
workers.remove_employee_id("555-66-7891");
workers.remove_employee_id("111-22-4444");
workers.remove_employee_id("213-44-3412");

cout << "\n\n***********************************";
```

```
// print the revised linked list
workers.print_employee_list();

return (0);
}
```

Study the complete listing and see if you understand how employees are inserted and deleted from the list. If it is still a little confusing, go back and study each major section of code discussed earlier.

Linked-List Output

The linked-list program sends output to the monitor. The first section of the list contains the eight employee names that were used to create the original list. The last part of the list shows the list after three employees are deleted. Here is a sample output sent to the screen:

```
Friendly, Fran
  Social Security: #212-98-7654
  Job Title: Salesperson
  Years With Company: 1
  Weekly Sales Average (units): 7.50
  Commission Rate: 4%

Hardwork, Harriet
  Social Security: #076-45-3121
  Job Title: Mechanic
  Years With Company: 7
  Hourly Salary: $10.34

Horn, Hazel
  Social Security: #345-77-7654
  Job Title: Parts
  Years With Company: 5
  Hourly Salary: $9.50

Lugwrench, Larry
  Social Security: #886-43-1518
  Job Title: Mechanic
  Years With Company: 1
  Hourly Salary: $8.98
```

```
Muffler, Mike
  Social Security: #555-66-7891
  Job Title: Parts
  Years With Company: 4
  Hourly Salary: $7.34

Pest, Perry
  Social Security: #567-45-3412
  Job Title: Salesperson
  Years With Company: 2
  Weekly Sales Average (units): 2.00
  Commission Rate: 2%

Slick, Sally
  Social Security: #111-22-4444
  Job Title: Closer
  Years With Company: 10
  Yearly Salary: $40000.00

Yourfriend, Yancy
  Social Security: #213-44-9873
  Job Title: Salesperson
  Years With Company: 1
  Weekly Sales Average (units): 10.60
  Commission Rate: 5%


*********************************

Friendly, Fran
  Social Security: #212-98-7654
  Job Title: Salesperson
  Years With Company: 1
  Weekly Sales Average (units): 7.50
  Commission Rate: 4%

Hardwork, Harriet
  Social Security: #076-45-3121
  Job Title: Mechanic
  Years With Company: 7
  Hourly Salary: $10.34
```

```
Horn, Hazel
  Social Security: #345-77-7654
  Job Title: Parts
  Years With Company: 5
  Hourly Salary: $9.50

Lugwrench, Larry
  Social Security: #886-43-1518
  Job Title: Mechanic
  Years With Company: 1
  Hourly Salary: $8.98

Pest, Perry
  Social Security: #567-45-3412
  Job Title: Salesperson
  Years With Company: 2
  Weekly Sales Average (units): 2.00
  Commission Rate: 2%

Yourfriend, Yancy
  Social Security: #213-44-9873
  Job Title: Salesperson
  Years With Company: 1
  Weekly Sales Average (units): 10.60
  Commission Rate: 5%
```

In the Next Chapter...

If, in the course of this chapter, you have developed an interest in object-oriented programming, you will really be interested in the Windows applications developed in Chapters 23 and 28. These particular Windows applications make use of object libraries. These libraries contains the reusable classes that make programming under Windows 3.*x*, 95, and NT much easier. The next chapter looks at the power that libraries can give.

PART FOUR

Special Libraries

Chapter Nineteen

Using Important C and C++ Libraries

C and C++ programmers rely on functions built into the Borland C++ compiler libraries. These built-in functions save you from "reinventing the wheel" when you need a special routine. You'll find that both C and C++ offer extensive support for character, string, math, and special functions that allow you to address the hardware features of the computer. Most library functions are portable from one computer to another and from one operating system to another. There are some functions, however, that are system or compiler dependent. Using these functions efficiently requires you to know where to locate the library functions and how to call them properly. For example, only the Borland C++ compiler offers an extensive library of complex arithmetic functions, described in the complex.h header file.

Because many of the C and C++ functions have already been demonstrated in previous chapters, this chapter will concentrate on important features not yet covered or demonstrated.

Borland C++ Header Files

Do a directory listing of your Borland C++ include subdirectory. The frequently used header files, shown in Table 19-1, should be present.

There will be others, too, but these are the header files you will use repeatedly. Because these files are in ASCII format, you may want to print a copy of their contents for a future reference. You will find that some header files are short whereas others are quite long. All contain function prototypes and many contain built-in macros.

Header File	Description
bios.h	BIOS Interrupts
conio.h	Console and port I/O
ctype.h	Character functions
dos.h	DOS Interrupts
io.h	File handling and low-level I/O
math.h	Math Functions
stdio.h	Stream routines for C
stdlib.h	Standard Library Functions
iostream.h	Stream routines for C++
string.h	String Functions
time.h	Date and Time Functions

Table 19-1. *Frequently Used Borland C++ Header Files*

Examples throughout this chapter illustrate how to use many of these functions. We'll concentrate on the system-independent functions prototyped in ctype.h, math.h, stdlib.h, string.h, and time.

Character Functions (ctype.h)

In most languages, characters are defined as single bytes. Chinese is one language that requires 2 bytes to hold character information. The character macros and functions in C and C++, prototyped or contained in ctype.h, take integer arguments but utilize only the lower byte of the integer value. Automatic type conversion usually permits character arguments also to be passed to the macros or functions. These macros and functions allow characters to be tested for various conditions or to be converted between lowercase and uppercase characters, for example.

Finding Alphanumeric, Alpha, and ASCII Values

The three macros listed in Table 19-2 allow ASCII-coded integer values to be checked with the use of a lookup table.

The following program checks the ASCII integer values from 0 to 127 and reports which of the preceding three functions produce a TRUE condition for each case:

```
/*
 *    alpha.c
 *    A program demonstrating the use of the isalnum(), isalpha(),
 *    and isascii() library functions.
 *    Copyright (c) Chris H. Pappas and William H. Murray, 1996
 */

#include <stdio.h>
#include <ctype.h>

void main( void )
{
  int ch                                                       ;
  for( ch = 0; ch< = 127; ch++ )                               {
    printf( "The ASCII digit %d is an:\n",ch                   );
    printf( "%s",isalnum(ch) ? "  alpha-numeric char\n" : "" );
    printf( "%s",isalpha(ch) ? "  alpha char\n" : ""           );
    printf( "%s",isascii(ch) ? "  ascii char\n" : ""           );
    printf( "\n"                                                );
  }
}
```

Macro	Description
int isalnum(ch)	Checks for alphanumeric values A-Z, a-z, and 0-9. ch0 is integer.
int isalpha(ch)	Checks for alpha values A-Z and a-z. ch0 is integer.
int isascii(ch)	Checks for ASCII values 0-127 (0-7Fh). ch0 is integer.

Table 19-2.   *Determining Character Information*

A portion of the information sent to the screen is shown here:

```
The ASCII digit 0 is an:
  ascii char

The ASCII digit 1 is an:
  ascii char

            .

            .

            .

The ASCII digit 48 is an:
  alpha-numeric char
  ascii char

The ASCII digit 49 is an:
  alpha-numeric char
  ascii char

            .

            .

            .

The ASCII digit 65 is an:
  alpha-numeric char
  alpha char
  ascii char

The ASCII digit 66 is an:
  alpha-numeric char
  alpha char
  ascii char
```

These functions are very useful in checking the contents of string characters.

Finding Control, White Space, and Punctuation

The routines listed in Table 19-3 are implemented as both macros and functions.

These routines allow ASCII-coded integer values to be checked using a lookup table. A zero is returned for FALSE and a nonzero for TRUE. A valid ASCII character set is assumed. The value *ch* is an integer.

The next application checks the ASCII integer values from zero to 127 and reports which of the preceding nine functions give a TRUE condition for each value:

```
/*
 *   contrl.c
 *   A program demonstrating several character functions such as
 *   isprint(), isupper(), iscntrl(), etc.
 *   Copyright (c) Chris H. Pappas and William H. Murray, 1996
 */

#include <stdio.h>
#include <ctype.h>

void main( void )
{
  int ch;
  for( ch = 0; ch <= 127; ch++ )                               {
    printf( "The ASCII digit %d is a(n):\n",ch               );
    printf( "%s",isprint(ch)  ? "  printable char\n" : ""     );
    printf( "%s",islower(ch)  ? "  lowercase char\n" : ""     );
    printf( "%s",isupper(ch)  ? "  uppercase char\n" : ""     );
    printf( "%s",ispunct(ch)  ? "  punctuation char\n" : ""   );
    printf( "%s",isspace(ch)  ? "  space char\n" : ""         );
    printf( "%s",isdigit(ch)  ? "  char digit\n" : ""         );
    printf( "%s",isgraph(ch)  ? "  graphics char\n" : ""      );
    printf( "%s",iscntrl(ch)  ? "  control char\n" : ""       );
    printf( "%s",isxdigit(ch) ? "  hexadecimal char\n" : ""   );
    printf( "\n"                                              );
  }
}
```

A portion of the information sent to the screen is shown here:

```
The ASCII digit 0 is a(n):
  control char
```

```
The ASCII digit 1 is a(n):
  control char
          .
          .
          .
The ASCII digit 34 is a(n):
  printable char
  punctuation char
  graphics char
          .
          .
          .
The ASCII digit 65 is a(n):
  printable char
  uppercase char
  graphics char
  hexadecimal char
```

Routine	Description
int iscntrl(ch)	Checks for control character
int isdigit(ch)	Checks for digit 0-9
int isgraph(ch)	Checks for printable characters (no space)
int islower(ch)	Checks for lowercase a-z
int isprint(ch)	Checks for printable character
int ispunct(ch)	Checks for punctuation
int isspace(ch)	Checks for white space
int isupper(ch)	Checks for uppercase A-Z
int isxdigit(ch)	Checks for hexadecimal value 0-9, a-f, or A-F

Table 19-3.   *Determining Character Properties*

Conversions to ASCII, Lowercase, and Uppercase

The macros and functions listed in Table 19-4 allow ASCII-coded integer values to be translated.

The macro **toascii()** converts *ch* to ASCII by retaining only the lower 7 bits. The functions **tolower()** and **toupper()** convert the character value to the format specified. The macros **_tolower()** and **_toupper()** return identical results when supplied proper ASCII values. A valid ASCII character set is assumed. The value *ch* is an integer.

The next example shows how the macro **toascii()** converts integer information to correct ASCII values:

```
/*
 *   ascii.c
 *   A program demonstrating the use of the toascii() function.
 *   Copyright (c) Chris H. Pappas and William H. Murray, 1996
 */

#include <stdio.h>
#include <ctype.h>

int ch;

void main( void )
{
  for( ch = 0; ch <= 512; ch++ )               {
    printf( "The ASCII value for %d is %d\n",
            ch,toascii(ch)                       );
  }
}
```

Macro	Description
int toascii(ch)	Translates to ASCII character
int tolower(ch)	Translates ch0 to lowercase if uppercase
int _tolower(ch)	Translates ch0 to lowercase
int toupper(ch)	Translates ch0 to uppercase if lowercase
int _toupper(ch)	Translates ch0 to uppercase

Table 19-4. *Translating Character Properties*

Here is a partial list of the information sent to the screen:

```
The ASCII value for 0 is 0
The ASCII value for 1 is 1
The ASCII value for 2 is 2
                   .
                   .
                   .
The ASCII value for 256 is 0
The ASCII value for 257 is 1
The ASCII value for 258 is 2
                   .
                   .
                   .
The ASCII value for 384 is 0
The ASCII value for 385 is 1
The ASCII value for 386 is 2
```

The Math Functions (math.h)

The functions prototyped in the math.h header file permit a great variety of mathematical, algebraic, and trigonometric operations.

Borland also supplies a number of important constants in the math.h header file, as you can see in Table 19-5.

The math functions are relatively easy to use and understand for those familiar with algebraic and trigonometric concepts. Many of these functions were demonstrated in earlier chapters. When using trigonometric functions, remember that angle arguments are always specified in radians. The math functions are shown in Table 19-6.

If you program in C and need to use complex number arithmetic, you must resort to using **struct** complex and the **cabs()** function described in math.h. This is the only function available for complex arithmetic in C.

```
struct complex {double x,double y}
```

This structure is used by the **cabs()** function. The **cabs()** function returns the absolute value of a complex number.

To perform complex arithmetic operations in C++, programmers can take advantage of Borland's **complex** class. The **complex** class is described in the complex.h header file. Operator overloading is provided for +,, *, /, +=,=, *=, /=, =, ==, and !=. The stream operators, << and >>, are also overloaded.

Constant	Value
M_E	2.71828182845904523536
M_LOG2E	1.44269504088896340736
M_LOG10E	0.434294481903251827651
M_LN2	0.693147180559945309417
M_LN10	2.30258509299404568402
M_PI	3.14159265358979323846
M_PI_2	1.57079632679489661923
M_PI_4	0.785398163397448309616
M_1_PI	0.318309886183790671538
M_2_PI	0.636619772367581343076
M_1_SQRTPI	0.564189583547756286948
M_2_SQRTPI	1.12837916709551257390
M_SQRT2	1.41421356237309504880
M_SQRT_2	0.707106781186547524401

Table 19-5.   *Math Constants Found in math.h*

The following math.h functions, described in the previous section, are also overloaded:

```
friend double abs(complex&)
friend complex acos(complex&)
friend complex asin(complex&)
friend complex atan(complex&)
friend complex cos(complex&)
friend complex cosh(complex&)
friend complex exp(complex&)
friend complex log(complex&)
friend complex log10(complex&)
friend complex pow(complex& base,double expon)
fricnd complex pow(double base,complex& expon)
friend complex pow(complex& base,complex& expon)
```

```
double acos(double x)
double asin(double x)
double atan(double x)
double atan2(double y,double x)
double ceil(double x)
double cos(double x)
double cosh(double x)
double exp(double x)
double fabs(double x)
double floor(double x)
double fmod(double x,double y)
double frexp(double x,int *exponent)
double hypot(double x,double y)
double ldexp(double x,int exponent)
double log(double x)
double log10(double x)
double modf(double x,double *ipart)
double poly(double x,int degree,double coeffs[])
double pow(double x,double y)
double pow10(int p)
double sin(double x)
double sinh(double x)
double sqrt(double x)
double tan(double x)
double tanh(double x)
```

Table 19-6.   *Popular Math Functions*

```
friend complex sin(complex&)
friend complex sinh(complex&)
friend complex sqrt(complex&)
friend complex tan(complex&)
friend complex tanh(complex&)
friend complex acos(complex&)
friend complex asin(complex&)
friend complex atan(complex&)
friend complex log10(complex&)
friend complex tan(complex&)
friend complex tanh(complex&)
```

Here are some additional complex mathematical operations described in the complex.h header file:

```
friend double real(complex&)
friend double imag(complex&)
friend complex conj(complex&)
friend double norm(complex&)
friend double arg(complex&)
friend complex polar(double mag,double angle=0)
```

Because the standard functions prototyped in math.h have been used extensively in earlier chapters, the next several examples are devoted to the new functions described in the complex.h header file.

Real and Imaginary Parts of a Complex Result

The following program shows how to use the complex functions **real()** and **imag()** (for imaginary) to break apart a complex number:

```
//
//   break.cpp
//   A C++ program that demonstrates how to use the complex
//   function real() and imaginary() to break apart a complex number.
//   This program utilizes operator and function overloading.
//   Copyright (c) Chris H. Pappas and William H. Murray, 1996
```

```
//

#include <iostream.h>
#include <complex.h>

void main( void )
{
   double  x1 =  5.6, y1 = 7.2                     ;
   double  x2 =- 3.1, y2 = 4.8                     ;
   complex z1 =  complex( x1,y1 )                  ;
   complex z2 =  complex( x2,y2 )                  ;
   complex zt                                      ;

   zt = z1 + z2                                    ;
   cout << "The value of zt is: " << zt << "\n";
   cout << "The real part of the sum is: "
        << real(zt) << "\n"                        ;
   cout << "The imaginary part of the sum is: "
        << imag(zt) << "\n"                        ;
}
```

In this example, two complex numbers are added to form the complex sum *zt*. Adding numbers in rectangular coordinates is fairly easy for humans, but look at the simplicity of the program and appreciate what it is accomplishing. Here are the results for this example:

```
The value of zt is: (2.5, 12)
The real part of the sum is: 2.5
The imaginary part of the sum is: 12
```

Overloaded Operators with Complex Numbers

The fundamental mathematical operators +,, *, and / are *overloaded*. This means that you can use them to perform complex arithmetic directly. Examine the following program code:

```
//
//   complex.cpp
//   A C++ program that demonstrates how to use complex
//   arithmetic with overloaded operators.  Here complex
```

```
//    numbers are directly added, subtracted, multiplied, and
//    divided.
//    Copyright (c) Chris H. Pappas and William H. Murray, 1996
//

#include <iostream.h>
#include <complex.h>

void main( void )
{
  double   x1 =  5.6, y1 = 7.2                              ;
  double   x2 =- 3.1, y2 = 4.8                              ;
  complex z1 =   complex( x1,y1 )                           ;
  complex z2 =   complex( x2,y2 )                           ;

  cout << "The value of z1 + z2 is: " << z1+z2 << "\n";
  cout << "The value of z1 * z2 is: " << z1*z2 << "\n";
  cout << "The value of z1 z2 is: " << z1-z2 << "\n"   ;
  cout << "The value of z1 / z2 is: " << z1/z2 << "\n";
}
```

This example shows how various operators can be overloaded. The program prints the sum, product, difference, and division of two complex numbers:

```
The value of z1 + z2 is: (2.5, 12)
The value of z1 * z2 is: (-51.92, 4.56)
The value of z1 z2 is: (8.7, 2.4)
The value of z1 / z2 is: (0.5267994,1.506891)
```

This library opens new vistas for those inclined toward mathematics and engineering. Because **cout** can print the complex rectangular result, it must also be overloaded.

Rectangular to Polar Transformations

Complex numbers are often expressed in polar or rectangular forms. The following program adds two complex numbers in polar format and prints the result:

```
//
//    rectpol.cpp
```

```
//   A C++ program that demonstrates how to use complex
//   arithmetic with overloaded operators. Here rectangular
//   numbers are directly converted to their polar
//   equivalents. Arithmetic is also done directly on polar
//   numbers.
//   Copyright (c) Chris H. Pappas and William H. Murray, 1996
//

#include <iostream.h>
#include <complex.h>

void main( void )
{
  double m1 = 10.0, ang1 = M_PI/6;     // 60 deg in radians
  double m2 = 20.0, ang2 = M_PI_4;     // 45 deg in radians

  cout << "m1 and ang1 from polar to rectangular: "
       << polar(m1,ang1) << "\n"                      ;
  cout << "m2 and ang2 from polar to rectangular: "
       << polar(m2,ang2) << "\n"                      ;
  cout << "Add polar values then convert: "
       << polar(m1,ang1)+polar(m2,ang2) << "\n"    ;
 }
```

Use your calculator and check the results of these complex operations.

```
m1 and ang1 from polar to rectangular: (8.660254, 5)
m2 and ang2 from polar to rectangular: (14.14214, 14.14214)
Add polar values then convert: (22.80239, 19.14214)
```

If you work with complex numbers in mathematics or electrical engineering, these new features will be a big help.

REMEMBER: *The functions require all angles to be radians.*

Overloaded Functions and Complex Arithmetic

Many of the math.h functions are overloaded to let you use them with complex numbers. The following program illustrates several of these functions:

```
//
//   compover.cpp
//   A C++ program that demonstrates how to use complex
//   arithmetic with overloaded math.h functions. Here
//   the square root, cube, and absolute value of a number
//   in polar form is obtained.
//   Copyright (c) Chris H. Pappas and William H. Murray, 1996
//

#include <iostream.h>
#include <complex.h>

void main( void )
{
  double m1 =- 10.4, ang1 = M_PI/6;   // 30 deg in radians

  cout << "square root of polar m1  ang1: "
       << sqrt(polar(m1,ang1)) << "\n"        ;
  cout << "cube of polar m1  ang1: "
       << pow(polar(m1,ang1),3) << "\n"        ;
  cout << "absolute value of polar m1  ang1: "
       << abs(polar(m1,ang1)) << "\n"        ;
}
```

Imagine being able to take the square root of a complex number with nothing more than a call to the **sqrt()** function.

```
square root of polar m1  ang1: (0.8346663,3.115017)
cube of polar m1  ang1: (3.443789e-13,1124.864)
absolute value of polar m1  ang1: 10.4
```

Creating a Trigonometric Table

The final example for this section involves an application that will generate a table of sine, cosine, and tangent values for the angles from 0 to 45 degrees.

This application also takes advantage of the special C++ formatting abilities. Study the following listing to determine how the output will be sent to the screen:

```
//
//   math.cpp
```

```
//  A program that demonstrates the use of several
//  math functions.
//  Copyright (c) Chris H. Pappas and William H. Murray, 1996
//

#include <iostream.h>
#include <iomanip.h>
#include <math.h>

#define PI 3.14159265359

void main( void )
{
  int i                                                     ;
  double x, y, z, ang                                       ;

  for( i = 0; i <= 45; i++ )                                {
    ang = PI*i/180;           // convert degrees to radians
    x = sin( ang )                                          ;
    y = cos( ang )                                          ;
    z = tan( ang )                                          ;
    // formatting output columns
    cout << setiosflags( ios::left  ) << setw( 8 )
         << setiosflags( ios::fixed ) << setprecision( 6 );
    // data to print
    cout << i << "\t" << x << "\t"
         << y << "\t" << z << "\n"                          ;
  }
}
```

This application uses the **sin()**, **cos()**, and **tan()** functions to produce a formatted trigonometric table. The angles are stepped from 0 to 45 degrees and are converted to radians before being sent to each function.

The following is a partial output from this application:

```
0 0.000000 1.000000 0.000000
1 0.017452 0.999848 0.017455
2 0.034899 0.999391 0.034921
.    .       .         .
.    .       .         .
.    .       .         .
```

```
29  0.484810  0.874620  0.554309
30  0.500000  0.866025  0.577350
31  0.515038  0.857167  0.600861
 .      .         .          .
 .      .         .          .
 .      .         .          .
43  0.681998  0.731354  0.932515
44  0.694658  0.719340  0.965689
45  0.707107  0.707107  1.000000
```

Standard Library Functions (stdlib.h)

The standard library macros and functions comprise a powerful group of items for data conversion, memory allocation, and other miscellaneous operations. The prototypes for these functions are found in stdlib.h.

Data Conversions

One important group of functions described in stdlib.h are the data-converting functions. The principal job of these functions is to convert data from one data type to another. For example, the **atol()** function converts string information to a **long**.

The syntax of each function is shown in the following prototypes:

```
double atof(const char *s)
int atoi(const char *s)
long atol(const char *s)
char *ecvt(double value,int n,int *dec,int *sign)
char *fcvt(double value,int n,int *dec,int *sign)
char *gcvt(double value,int n,char *buf)
char *itoa(int value,char *s,int radix)
char *ltoa(long value,char *s,int radix)
double strtod(const char *s,char **endptr)
long strtol(const char *s,char **endptr,int radix)
unsigned long strtoul(const char *s,char **endptr,int radix)
char *ultoa(unsigned long value,char *s,int radix)
```

In these functions, *s points to a string, value is the number to be converted, *n* represents the number of digits in the string, *dec* locates the decimal point relative to the start of the string, *sign* represents the sign of the number, *buf* is a character buffer, *radix* represents the number base for the converted value, and *endptr* is usually NULL. If not, the function sets it to the character that stops the scan.

The use of several of these functions is illustrated in the following programs.

Converting a float to a string

The **fcvt()** function converts a **float** to a string. It is also possible to obtain information regarding the sign and location of the decimal point.

```c
/*
 *   fcvt.c
 *   A program demonstrating the use of the fcvt() function.
 *   Copyright (c) Chris H. Pappas and William H. Murray, 1996
 */

#include <stdio.h>
#include <stdlib.h>

void main( void )
{
  int   dec_pt, sign                                              ;
  char *ch_buffer                                                 ;
  int   num_char = 7                                              ;


  ch_buffer = fcvt( -234.5678, num_char, &dec_pt, &sign )    ;
  printf( "The buffer holds: %s\n",ch_buffer )                ;
  printf( "The sign (+=0,=1) is stored as a: %d\n",sign )    ;
  printf( "The decimal place is %d characters from right\n",
          dec_pt )                                              ;
}
```

The output from this program is shown here:

```
The buffer holds: 2345678000
The sign (+=0,=1) is stored as a: 1
The decimal place is 3 characters from right
```

Converting a string to a long

The **strtol()** function converts the specified string in the given base to its decimal equivalent. The following example shows a string of binary characters that will be converted to a decimal number:

```c
/*
 *   strto.c
```

```
*    A program demonstrating the use of the strtol() function.
*    Copyright (c) Chris H. Pappas and William H. Murray, 1996
*/

#include <stdlib.h>
#include <stdio.h>

void main( void )
{
  char *s = "101101", *endptr                        ;
  long  long_number                                  ;

  long_number = strtol( s, &endptr, 2 )              ;
  printf( "The binary value %s is equal to %ld decimal.\n",
          s, long_number )                           ;
}
```

In this example, "101101" is a string that represents several binary digits. The program produces the following results:

```
The binary value 101101 is equal to 45 decimal.
```

This is an interesting function because it allows a string of digits to be specified in one base and converted to another. This function would be a good place to start if you wanted to develop a general base change program.

Performing Searches and Sorts

The **qsort()** function performs a quick sort. You can use the **bsearch()** function to perform a binary search of an array. The **lfind()** function performs a linear search for a key in an array of sequential records, and the **lsearch()** function performs a linear search on a sorted or unsorted table.

```
void qsort(void *base,size_t nelem,size_t width,
    int(*fcmp)(const void *,const void *))
void *bsearch(const void *key,const void *base,
    size_t nelem,size_t width,int(*fcmp)(const void *,
    const void *))

void *lfind(const void *key,const void *base,
```

```
      size_t *,size_t width,int(*fcmp)
      (const void *,const void *))

void *lsearch(const void *key, void *base,
      size_t *,size_t width,int(*fcmp)
      (const void *,const void *))
```

Here, *key* represents the search key. *base* is the array to search. *nelem* contains the number of elements in the array. *width* is the number of bytes for each table entry. *fcmp* is the comparison routine used. *num* reports the number of records.

You'll see how to use the search and sort functions in the following applications.

The qsort() Function

In C and C++, as in any language, sorting data is very important. Borland C++ provides the **qsort()** function for sorting data. The following example is one application in which **qsort()** can be used:

```c
/*
 *    qsort.c
 *    A program demonstrating the use of the qsort() function.
 *    Copyright (c) Chris H. Pappas and William H. Murray, 1996
 */

#include <stdio.h>
#include <stdlib.h>

int int_comp( const void *i, const void *j )                    ;

int list[ 12 ] = { 95,53,71,86,11,28,34,53,10,11,74,-44 };

void main( void )
{
  int i                                                         ;

  qsort ( list, 12, sizeof(int), int_comp )                     ;

  printf( "The array after qsort:\n"       )                    ;
  for( i = 0; i < 12; i++ )
    printf( "%d ", list[ i ]               )                    ;
}
```

```
int int_comp( const void *i, const void *j )
{
   return( (*(int *)i)-(*(int *)j) )                          ;
}
```

The original numbers, in list, are signed integers. The **qsort()** function will arrange the original numbers in ascending order, leaving them in the variable list. Here, the original numbers are sorted in ascending order:
The array after **qsort()**:

--44 10 11 11 28 34 53 53 71 74 86 95

Can **qsort()** be used with **float**s? Why not alter the preceding program and see.

Searching an Array with bsearch()

You use the **bsearch()** function to perform a search in an integer array. The search value for this example is contained in *search_number*.

```
/*
 *    bsearh.c
 *    A program demonstrating the use of the bsearch() function.
 *    Copyright (c) Chris H. Pappas and William H. Murray, 1996
 */

#include <stdlib.h>
#include <stdio.h>

int int_comp( const void *i, const void *j  )                 ;

int data_array[ ] = {100, 200, 300, 400, 500,
                     600, 700, 800, 900      }                ;

void main( void )
{
   int *search_result                                         ;
   int  search_number = 400                                   ;

   printf( "Is 400 in the data_array? " )                     ;
   search_result = bsearch( &search_number, data_array, 9,
                           sizeof(int),int_comp);
   if( search_result ) printf( "Yes!\n" )                     ;
```

```
      else printf( "No!\n" )                          ;
}

int int_comp(const void *i,const void *j)
{
   return ((*(int *)i)-(*(int *)j));
}
```

This application sends a simple message to the screen regarding the outcome of the search, as shown here:

```
Is 400 in the data_array? Yes!
```

You can also use this function to search for a string of characters in an array.

Miscellaneous Operations

There are several miscellaneous functions in this library that perform a variety of diverse operations. These operations include calculating the absolute value of an integer and bit rotations. Bit rotation functions give you the ability to perform operations that were once just in the realm of assembly language programmers.

The Random Number Generator

Borland C++ provides a random number function. The random number generator can be initialized or seeded with a call to **srand()**. The seed function accepts an integer argument and starts the random number generator.

```
/*
 *   rand.c
 *   A program demonstrating the use of the srand() and rand()
 *   random number functions.
 *   Copyright (c) Chris H. Pappas and William H. Murray, 1996
 */

#include <stdlib.h>
#include <stdio.h>

void main( void )
{
   int x                                      ;
```

```
  srand( 3 )                                    ;

  for( x = 0; x < 8; x++ )
    printf( "Trial #%d, random number=%d\n" ,
            x,rand()                        );
}
```

An example of random numbers generated by **rand()** is shown here:

```
Trial #0, random number=48
Trial #1, random number=7196
Trial #2, random number=9294
Trial #3, random number=9091
Trial #4, random number=7031
Trial #5, random number=23577
Trial #6, random number=17702
Trial #7, random number=23503
```

Random number generators are important in programming for statistical work and for applications that rely on the generation of random patterns. A good random number generator will produce unbiased results. In other words, all numbers have an equal probability of appearing.

Bit Rotations

C and C++ provide a means of rotating the individual bits of integers and long values to the right and to the left. In the next example, two rotations in each direction are performed:

```
/*
 *   rotate.c
 *   A program demonstrating the use of the _rotl() and _rotr()
 *   bit rotate functions.
 *   Copyright (c) Chris H. Pappas and William H. Murray, 1996
 */

#include <stdio.h>
#include <stdlib.h>

void main( void )
```

```
{
  unsigned int val = 0x2345                                    ;

  printf( "rotate bits of %X to the left 2 bits and get %X\n" ,
          val,_rotl( val, 2 )                                  );
  printf( "rotate bits of %X to the right 2 bits and get %X\n",
          val,_rotr( val, 2 )                                  );
}
```

Here are the results:

```
rotate bits of 2345 to the left 2 bits and get 8D14
rotate bits of 2345 to the right 2 bits and get 48D1
```

Note that the original numbers are in hexadecimal format. The use of the bit rotation functions and the use of logical operators such as and, or, xor, and so on, give C and C++ the ability to manipulate data bit by bit.

String Functions (string.h)

Strings in C and C++ are usually considered one-dimensional character arrays terminated with a null character. The string functions, prototyped in string.h, typically use pointer arguments and return pointer or integer values. You can study the syntax of each command in the next section or in more detail in your Borland C++ reference manuals. Additional buffer-manipulation functions such as **memccpy()** and **memset()** are also prototyped in string.h. The memory and string functions provide flexible programming power to C and C++ programmers.

Working with Memory Functions

The memory functions, discussed in the previous section, are accessed with the following syntaxes:

```
void *memccpy(void *dest,void *source,int ch,unsigned count)

void *memchr(void *buf,int ch,unsigned count)

int memcmp(void *buf1,void *buf2,unsigned count)

void *memcpy(void *dest,void *source,unsigned count)
```

```
int memicmp(void *buf1,void *buf2,unsigned count)

void *memmove(void *dest,void *source,unsigned count)

void *memset(void *dest,int ch,unsigned count)
```

Here, *buf*, *buf1*, *buf2*, *dest*, and *source* are pointers to the appropriate string buffer. The integer *ch* points to a character value. The unsigned *count* holds the character count for the function.

You'll learn how to use a number of these functions in the following sections.

Finding a Character in a String

In this example, the buffer is searched for the occurrence of the lowercase character "f" using the **memchr()** function:

```
/*
 *   memchr.c
 *   A program demonstrating the use of the memchr() function,
 *   which finds a character in a buffer.
 *   Copyright (c) Chris H. Pappas and William H. Murray, 1996
 */

#include <string.h>
#include <stdio.h>

char buf[35];
char *ptr;

main()
{
  strcpy( buf, "This is a fine day for a search." );
  ptr = (char *)memchr( buf, 'f', 35            );
  if( ptr != NULL )
    printf( "character found at location: %d\n"   ,
            ptr-buf + 1                         );
  else
    printf( "character not found.\n"             );
}
```

For this example, if a lowercase *f* is in the string, the **memchr()** function will report the "character found at location: 11."

Comparing Characters in Strings with memicmp()

The following example highlights the **memicmp()** function, which compares two strings contained in *buf1* and *buf2*. This function is insensitive to the case of the string characters.

```
/*
 *   memcmp.c
 *   A program demonstrating the use of the memicmp() function
 *   to compare two string buffers.
 *   Copyright (c) Chris H. Pappas and William H. Murray, 1996
 */

#include <stdio.h>
#include <string.h>

char buf1[ 40 ]                                              ,
     buf2[ 40 ]                                              ;

void main( void )
{
  strcpy( buf1,"Well, are they identical or not?" );
  strcpy( buf2,"Well, are they identicle or not?" );
  /* 0 identical strings except for case */
  /* x any integer, means not identical */

  printf( "%d\n", memicmp( buf1, buf2, 40 )           );
  /* returns a non-zero value */
}
```

If it weren't for the fact that identical (or is it identicle?) was spelled incorrectly in the second string, both strings would have been the same. A nonzero value,1, is returned by **memicmp()** for this example.

The memset() Function

Often it is necessary to load or clear a buffer with a predefined character. In those cases you might consider using the **memset()** function, as shown here:

```
/*
 *   memset.c
```

```
*    A program demonstrating the use of the memset() function
*    to set the contents of a string buffer.

*    Copyright (c) Chris H. Pappas and William H. Murray, 1996
*/

#include <stdio.h>
#include <string.h>

char buf[20];

void main( void )
{
  printf( "The contents of buf: %s", memset( buf, '+', 15) );
  buf[ 15 ] = '\0'                                          ;
}
```

In this example, the buffer is loaded with 15 + characters and a null character. The program will print 15 + characters to the screen.

Working with String Functions

The prototypes for using several string manipulating functions contained in string.h are shown in Table 19-7.

Here, *s is a pointer to a string. *s1 and *s2 are pointers to two strings. Usually *s1 points to the string to be manipulated and *s2 points to the string doing the manipulation. ch is a character value.

Comparing the Contents of Strings with strcmp()

The following program uses the **strcmp()** function and reports how one string compares to another:

```
/*
*    strcmp.c
*    A program demonstrating the use of the strcmp() function
*    to compare two strings.
*    Copyright (c) Chris H. Pappas and William H. Murray, 1996
*/

#include <stdio.h>
#include <string.h>
```

```
char s1[ 45 ] = "A group of characters makes a good string.";
char s2[ 45 ] = "A group of characters makes a good string?";

int answer                                                        ;

void main( void )
{
  answer = strcmp( s1, s2                                 );
  if( answer > 0 ) printf( "s1 is greater than s2"         );
    else if( answer == 0 ) printf( "s1 is equal to s2"     );
      else printf( "s1 is less than s2"                    );
}
```

Can you predict which of the preceding strings would be greater? Can you do it without running the program? The answer is that *s1* is less than *s2*.

Searching Strings for Multiple Characters with strcspn()

The next program searches a string for the first occurrence of one or more characters:

```
/*
 *    strspn.c
 *    A program demonstrating the use of the strcspn() function to find
 *    the occurrence of one of a group of characters.
 *    Copyright (c) Chris H. Pappas and William H. Murray, 1996
 */

#include <stdio.h>
#include <string.h>

char s1[35];
int answer;

void main( void )
{
  strcpy( s1, "We are looking for great strings."   );
  answer = strcspn( s1, "abc"                         );
  printf( "The first a,b,c appeared at position %d\n",
          answer + 1                                  );
}
```

Function Name	Description
int strcmp(const char * s1,const char *s2)	Compares 2 strings
size_t strcspn(const char * s1,const char * s2)	Finds a substring in a string
char * strcpy(char * s1,const char * s2)	Copies a string
char * strerror(int errnum)	ANSI-supplied number
char * _strerror(char * s)	User-supplied message
size_t strlen(const char * s)	Null-terminated string
char * strlwr(char * s)	String to lowercase
char * strncat(char * s1, const char *s2,size_t n)	Appends *n* char *s2* to *s1*
int strncmp(const char * s1,const char * s2,size_t n)	Compares first *n* characters of two strings
int strnicmp(const char * s1,const char * s2,size_t n)	Compares first *n* characters of two strings (case insensitive)
char * strncpy(char * s1,const char * s2,size_t n)	Copies *n* characters of *s2* to *s1*
char * strnset(char * s,int ch,size_t n)	Sets first *n* characters of string to char setting
char * strpbrk(const char * s1 const char * s2)	Locates character from const *s2* in *s1*
char * strrchr(const char * s,int ch)	Locates last occurrence of *ch* in string
char * strrev(char * s)	Converts string to reverse
char * strset(char * s,int ch)	String to be set with *ch*
size_t strspn(const char * s1,const char * s2)	Searches *s1* with char set in *s2*
char * strstr(const char * s1,const char * s2)	Searches *s1* with *s2*
char * strtok(char * s1, const char * s2)	Finds token in *s1*. *s1* contains token(s), *s2* contains the delimiters
char * strupr(char * s)	Converts string to uppercase

Table 19-7. *String Manipulating Functions*

This program will report the position of the first occurrence of an "a", "b", or "c". A one is added to the answer because the first character is at index position zero. This program reports an "a" at position 4.

Finding the First Occurrence of a Character with strchr()

Have you ever wanted to check a sentence for the occurrence of a particular character? You might consider using the **strchr()** function. The following application looks for the first blank or space character in the string:

```
/*
 *    strchr.c
 *    A program demonstrating the use of the strchr() function to
 *    locate the first occurrence of a character in a string.
 *    Copyright (c) Chris H. Pappas and William H. Murray, 1996
 */


#include <stdio.h>
#include <string.h>

char   s1[ 20 ] = "What is a friend?"                   ;
char *answer                                            ;

void main( void )
{
  answer = strchr( s1, ' ' )                            ;
  printf( "After the first blank: %s\n", answer );
}
```

What is your prediction on the outcome after execution? Run the program and see.

Finding String Length with strlen()

The **strlen()** function reports the length of any given string. Here is a simple example:

```
/*
 *    strlen.c
 *    A program demonstrating the use of the strlen() function to
 *    determine the length of a string.
 *    Copyright (c) Chris H. Pappas and William H. Murray, 1996
 */
```

```
#include <stdio.h>
#include <string.h>

char *s1 = "String length is measured in characters!" ;

void main( void )
{
  printf( "The string length is %d", strlen( s1 )    );
}
```

In this example, the **strlen()** function reports on the total number of characters contained in the string. In this example, there are 40 characters.

Locating a String Within a String with strstr()

The **strstr()** function searches a given string within a group (a string) of characters, as shown here:

```
/*
 *   strstr.c
 *   A program demonstrating the use of the strstr() function to
 *   locate a string within a string.
 *   Copyright (c) Chris H. Pappas and William H. Murray, 1996
 */

#include <stdio.h>
#include <string.h>

void main( void )
{
  char *s1 = "There is always something you miss." ;
  char *s2 = "way"                                  ;

  printf( "%s\n", strstr( s1, s2 )                  );
}
```

This program sends the remainder of the string to the **printf()** function after the first occurrence of "way". The string printed to the screen is "ways something you miss".

Converting Characters to Uppercase with strupr()

A handy function to have in a case-sensitive language is one that can convert the characters in a string to another case. **strupr()** is a function that converts lowercase characters to uppercase, as shown here:

```
/*
 *    strupr.c
 *    A program demonstrating the use of the strupr() function to
 *    convert lowercase letters to uppercase.
 *    Copyright (c) Chris H. Pappas and William H. Murray, 1996
 */

#include <stdio.h>
#include <string.h>

char *s1 = "Uppercase characters are easier to read.";
char *s2                                                      ;

void main( void )
{
  s2 = strupr( s 1)                                           ;
  printf( "The results: %s", s2 )                             ;
}
```

This program converts each lowercase character to uppercase. Note that only lowercase letters will be changed.

Time Functions (time.h)

Table 19-8 shows some of the time and date function names in time.h.

These functions offer a variety of ways to obtain time and/or date formats for programs. A discussion of the syntax for each function is included in the next section.

Time and Date Structures and Syntax

Many of the date and time functions described in the previous section use the *tm* structure defined in time.h. This structure is shown here:

```
struct tm      {
   int   tm_sec  ;
   int   tm_min  ;
   int   tm_hour ;
   int   tm_mday ;
   int   tm_mon  ;
   int   tm_year ;
   int   tm_wday ;
   int   tm_yday ;
   int   tm_isdst;
}              ;
```

The syntax for calling each date and time function differs according to the function's ability. The syntax for each function is shown in Table 19-9.

Several of these functions are used in example programs in the next section.

Names	Description
asctime()	Converts date and time to an ASCII string and uses **tm0** structure
ctime()	Converts date and time to a string
difftime()	Calculates the difference between two times
gmtime()	Converts date and time to GMT using tm structure
localtime()	Converts date and time to tm structure
strftime()	Allows formatting of date and time data for output
time()	Obtains current time (system)
tzset()	Sets time variables for environment variable TZ

Table 19-8. *Time and Date Functions*

Function Name	Description
char * asctime(const struct tm * tblock)	Converts the structure into a 26-character string. For example: Wed Dec 13 10:18:20 1995
char * ctime(const time_ t *time)	Converts a time value, pointed to by * **time** into a 26-char string (see **asctime()**)
double difftime(time_ t time2,time_t time1)	Calculates the difference between time2 and time1 and returns a double
struct tm * gmtime(const time_t * timer)	Accepts address of a value returned by the function **time()** and returns a pointer to the structure with gmt information
struct tm * localtime (const time_t * timer)	Accepts address of a value returned by the function **time()** and returns a pointer to the structure with local time information
size_t strftime (char * s, size_t maxsize, const char * fmt, const struct tm * t)	Formats date and time information for output. *s* points to the string information, *maxsize* is maximum string length, *fmt* represents the format, and *t* points to a structure of type **tm**. The formatting options include: %a abbreviate weekday name %a full weekday name %b abbreviate month name %b full month name %c date and time information %d day of month (01 to 31) %h hour (00 to 23) %i hour (00 to 12) %j day of year (001 to 366) %m month (01 to 12) %m minutes (00 to 59) %p AM or PM

Table 19-9.   *Date and Time Functions*

Function Name	Description
	%s seconds (0 to 59)
	%u week number (00 to 51), Sunday is first day
	%w weekday (0 to 6)
	%w week number (00 to 51), Monday is first day
	%x date
	%x time
	%y year, without century (00 to 99)
	%y year, with century
	%z time zone name
	%% character %
time_t time(time_t *timer)	Returns the time in seconds since 00:00:00 gmt, January 1, 1970
void _tzset (void)	Sets the global variables daylight, *timezone*, and *tzname* based on the environment string. The **tz** environment string uses the following syntax: tz = zzz0[+/-]d [d]{lll} Here, zzz represents a three-character string with the local time zone—for example, "est" for eastern standard time. The [+/-]d [d] argument contains an adjustment for the local time zone's difference from gmt. Positive numbers are a westward adjustment, while negative numbers are an eastward adjustment. For example, a five would be used for est. The last argument, {lll}, represents the local time zone's daylight savings time—for example, edt for eastern daylight saving time.

Table 19-9.   *Date and Time Functions* (continued)

The localtime() and asctime() Functions

Many times it is necessary to obtain the time and date in a programming application. The next program returns these values by using the **localtime()** and **asctime()** functions:

```
/*
*    asctim.c
*    A program demonstrating the use of the localtime() and asctime()
*    functions.
*    Copyright (c) Chris H. Pappas and William H. Murray, 1996
*/

#include <time.h>
#include <stdio.h>

struct tm *date_time                          ;
time_t timer                                  ;

void main( void )
{
   time( &timer )                             ;
   date_time = localtime( &timer )            ;

   printf ( "The present date and time is: %s\n" ,
   asctime(  date_time )                             );
}
```

This program formats the time and date information in the manner shown here:

```
The present date and time is: Wed Dec 13 13:16:20 1995
```

The gmtime() Function

You can also use other functions to return time and date information. The next program is similar to the last example, except that the **gmtime()** function is used:

```
/*
*    gmtime.c
*    A program demonstrating the use of the gmtime() and asctime()
*    functions.
*    Copyright (c) Chris H. Pappas and William H. Murray, 1996
*/

#include <time.h>
#include <stdio.h>
```

```
void main( void )
{
  struct tm *date_time                    ;
  time_t timer                            ;

  time( &timer )                          ;
  date_time = gmtime( &timer )            ;

  printf( "%.19s\n", asctime( date_time ) );
}
```

The following date and time information was returned by this program:

```
Wed May 18 14:13:25
```

The strftime() Function

The **strftime()** function provides the greatest formatting flexibility of all the date and time functions. The following program illustrates several formatting options:

```
/*
 *    strtm.c
 *    A program demonstrating the use of the strftime() function.
 *    Copyright (c) Chris H. Pappas and William H. Murray, 1996
 */

#include <time.h>
#include <stdio.h>

void main( void )
{
  struct tm *date_time                    ;
  time_t    timer                         ;
  char      str[ 80 ]                     ;

  time( &timer )                          ;
  date_time = localtime( &timer )         ;
  strftime( str, 80, "It is %X on %A, %x",
            date_time )                   ;
  printf( "%s\n", str )                   ;
}
```

Here is a sample of the output for this program:

```
It is 17:18:45 on Wednesday, 12/13/95
```

 NOTE: *You may find that the **strftime()** function is not portable from one system to another. Use it with caution if portability is a consideration.*

The ctime() Function

The following C++ program illustrates how to make a call to the **ctime()** function. This program shows how easy it is to obtain date and time information from the system:

```cpp
//
//   ctime.cpp
//   A program demonstrating the use of the ctime() function.
//   Copyright (c) Chris H. Pappas and William H. Murray, 1996
//

#include <time.h>
#include <iostream.h>

time_t longtime                           ;

void main( void )
{
  time( &longtime )                        ;
  cout << "The time and date are " <<
          ctime( &longtime ) <<   "\n";
}
```

The output sent to the screen would appear in the following format:

```
The time and date are Wed Dec 13 14:23:27 1995
```

Creating a Delay Routine

Usually you want programs to execute as quickly as possible. However, there are times when slowing down information makes it easier for the user to view and understand what is happening. The **time_delay()** function in the following application delays program execution. The delay variable is in seconds. For this example, there is a two-second delay between each line of output to the screen:

```c
/*
 *   tdelay.c
 *   A C program that demonstrates how to create a delay
 *   function for slowing program output.
 *   Copyright (c) Chris H. Pappas and William H. Murray, 1996
 */

#include <stdio.h>
#include <time.h>

void time_delay( int )                 ;

void main( void )
{
   int i                       ;

   for( i = 0; i < 25; i++ )           {
      time_delay( 2 )                  ;
      printf( "The count is %d\n", i );
   }
}

void time_delay( int t )
{
   long initial, final ;
   long ltime                          ;

   initial = time( &ltime )            ;
   final = initial + t                 ;

   while( time( &ltime ) < final )     ;
   return                              ;
}
```

What other uses might the **time_delay()** function have? One case might be where the computer is connected to an external data-sensing device, such as a thermocouple or strain gauge. The function could be used to take readings every minute, hour, or day.

In the Next Chapter...

The best way to become proficient with the functions discussed in this chapter is to experiment with them. With Chapters 1 through 19 behind you, you are now well versed in the critical fundamentals of the correct usage of both C and C++. At this point, you are ready to easily understand how these concepts are more automatically combined to help you write true multi-tasking, object-oriented Windows applications. In the next chapter, you will begin working with this exciting development environment and all of its fundamental components.

PART FIVE

Foundations for Win32 Programming

Chapter Twenty

Windows: Concepts and Tools

Microsoft's primary development language for Windows 3.1, Windows 95, and Windows NT applications is C or C++. All major applications, save for the most time-sensitive components, are written in C or C++. The Borland C++ compiler provides all of the necessary tools for developing 16-bit and 32-bit Windows applications with the C or C++ programming language.

This chapter will discuss those Windows features that are common to both the 16- and 32-bit Windows platforms. Features specific to WIN32, used by Windows 95 and NT, will be discussed in Chapters 23 through 28. The Windows applications developed in the remainder of this book are all designed with the development tools provided with the Borland C++ compiler. When installing your Borland C++ compiler, make sure that the setup program includes all of the available tools for Windows development.

The first section of this chapter deals with the language, definitions, and terms used with both 16- and 32-bit Windows. You'll also learn about working in a graphics-based environment. The second section of this chapter discusses Windows items most frequently encountered and used by developers. These items include borders, icons, bitmaps, menus, and so on. The third section of this chapter describes Windows resources, including icons, cursors, bitmaps, menus, hot keys, dialog boxes, fonts, and so on. The final section of this chapter discusses the specific tools provided with your Borland C++ compiler for designing and building these applications.

This book will use the term Windows when referring to all Windows environments. If a specific environment or operating system is referenced, the terms Windows 3.*x*, Windows 95, or Windows NT will be used.

The Advantages of Windows

There are numerous advantages to Windows users and programmers alike compared to the older DOS text-based environment. Windows provides several major programming capabilities that include a standardized graphics interface, a multitasking capability, an OOP approach in programming, memory control, hardware independence, and the use of dynamic link libraries (DLLs).

Applications can be developed for both 16- and 32-bit versions of Microsoft Windows. Traditionally, the 16-bit version of Windows is the graphics-based operating environment that functions over DOS. Newer versions, such as Windows 95 and NT, are complete 32-bit operating systems. All environments bring together point-and-shoot control, pop-up menus, and the ability to run applications written specially for Windows, as well as standard applications that are DOS specific. The purpose of this portion of the chapter is to introduce you to Windows concepts and vocabulary.

A Consistent Look and Command Structure

Windows is a graphics-based multitasking operating environment. Applications written for Windows all have a consistent look and command structure. This makes learning each successive Windows application easier.

Windows provides numerous built-in functions that allow the easy implementation of menus, scroll bars, dialog boxes, icons, and other features that contribute to a user-friendly interface. Windows programs can access an extensive graphics programming language and draw graphics and output text in a variety of fonts and pitches.

Windows permits the application's treatment of the video display, keyboard, mouse, printer, serial port, and system timers in a hardware-independent manner. Device or hardware independence allows the same application to run identically on a variety of computers with differing hardware configurations. For example, systems with VGA and SVGA displays are adjusted automatically by Windows.

GUI—a Graphics User Interface

The standardized graphics user interface is perhaps the most noticeable Windows feature. This GUI (Graphics User Interface) is very important to the user. Even Windows 95, which sports a new screen style, is based on the standardized GUI interface. The GUI interface uses pictures, or icons, to represent disk drives, files, subdirectories, and many of the operating system commands and actions. Figure 20-1 shows a typical Windows 95 application—Microsoft Excel.

The program name is identified on the caption bar. Many of the basic spreadsheet functions are accessed through the program's menus by pointing and clicking with the mouse. Excel, like most Windows programs, provides both a keyboard and a mouse interface. Although you can access most Windows functions by using the keyboard, most GUI users prefer to use the mouse.

A similar look and feel is common to all Windows applications. Once a user learns how to manipulate common Windows commands, each new application becomes easier to master. For example, a Microsoft Word screen is shown in Figure 20-2. Notice the similar icons and appearance of these applications.

The consistent user interface provides advantages for the programmer, too. For example, you can tap into built-in Windows functions for constructing menus, toolbars and dialog boxes. All menus have the same style keyboard and mouse interface because Windows, rather than the programmer, handles the interface.

A Multitasking Environment

Windows is a multitasking environment, which means the user can have several applications or several instances of the same application running at the same time. Figure 20-3 shows several Windows applications running at the same time.

With multitasking, each application can occupy its own rectangular window on the screen. At any given time, the user can move the windows on the screen, switch between different applications, change the windows' sizes, and exchange information from one window to another.

The multitasking example shown in Figure 20-3 looks like four concurrently running processes, but it's not really. Actually, only one application can use the

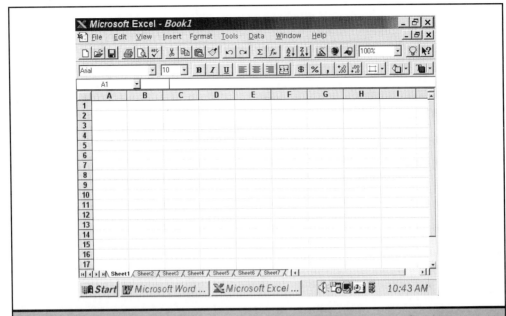

Figure 20-1. *A Microsoft Excel spreadsheet is a typical Windows application*

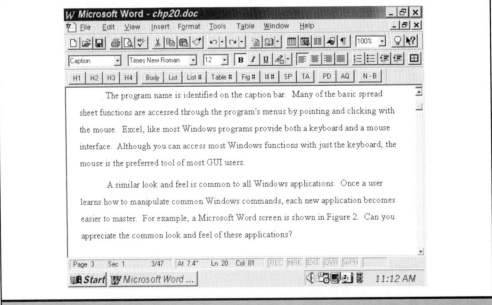

Figure 20-2. *A Microsoft Word application has the same "look and feel" as an Excel application*

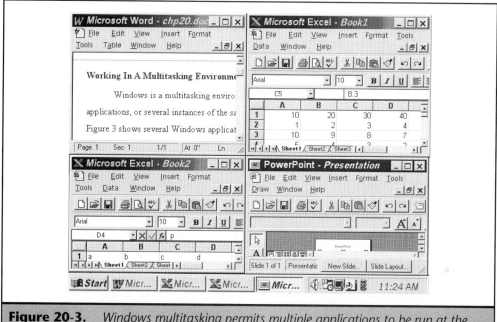

Figure 20-3.   *Windows multitasking permits multiple applications to be run at the same time*

processor at any one time. The distinction between a task that is processing and one that is merely running is important. There is also a third state to consider. An application may be in the active state. An active application is one that is receiving the user's attention. Just as there can be only one application that is processing at any given instant, so too can there be only one active application at a time. However, there can be any number of concurrently running tasks. Partitioning of the microprocessor's processing time, called *time slicing*, is also the responsibility of Windows. It is Windows that controls the sharing of the microprocessor by using queued input or messages.

Under DOS, applications assumed they had exclusive control of all the computer's resources, including the input and output devices, memory, the video display, and even the CPU itself. Under Windows, all of these resources are shared between applications. For example, memory management is controlled by Windows instead of by the application.

Working with a Queued Input

As you have just learned, memory is a shared resource, but so are most input and output devices such as the keyboard, mouse, and printer. Although a Windows program is written in C or C++, it is no longer possible to read directly from the keyboard with a **getchar()** function call or by using the **cin** I/O stream. With Windows, an application does not make explicit calls to read from the keyboard or mouse.

Windows processes all input requests in the system queue. It becomes the queue's responsibility to redirect the input to the appropriate application when multiple programs are running. This is achieved by transferring the message from the system queue to the application's queue. Now, when the application is ready to process the input, it reads from its queue and dispatches a message to the correct window.

An *input message* provides a uniform format for input. Input messages provide the system time, state of the keyboard, scan code of any depressed key, position of the mouse, and which mouse button has been pressed (if any), as well as information specifying which device generated the message.

Keyboard, mouse, and timer messages, for example, have identical formats and are processed in a similar manner. Windows also provides a device-independent virtual keycode that identifies the key, regardless of which keyboard it is on, and the device-dependent scan code generated by the keyboard, as well as the status of other keys on the keyboard, including ALT, CTRL, NUMLOCK, and SHIFT.

The keyboard and mouse are a shared resource. One keyboard and one mouse must supply all the input information for each application running under Windows. Windows sends all keyboard input messages directly to the currently active window. Mouse messages, on the other hand, are sent to the window that is physically underneath the mouse cursor.

Another shared resource are timer messages. Timer messages are similar to keyboard and mouse messages. Windows allows a program to set a system timer so that one of its windows receives a message at periodic intervals. This timer message is directly placed in the application's message queue. Other messages can to be passed into an application's message queue with the use of specific Windows functions.

Messages

Windows operates in a pseudo-OOPs (object-oriented programming) environment. You have learned that the message system is the underlying structure used to disseminate information in the multitasking environment. From the application's point of view, a message is a notification that some event has occurred that may or may not need a specific action. The user can initiate events by clicking or moving the mouse, changing the size of a window, or making a menu selection. Events can also be initiated by the application. For example, an Excel spreadsheet could finish a recalculation that results in the need to update a graphics bar chart. In this case, Excel would send an "update window" message to the chart.

Windows can also generate messages. For example, the "close session" message is used by Windows to inform each application of its intent to shut down.

Remember the following points concerning messages. It is the message system that allows Windows to achieve its multitasking capabilities. The message system makes it possible for Windows to share the processor among different applications. Each time Windows sends a message to the application, it also grants processor time to the application. The only way an application can get access to the microprocessor is when it receives a message. Messages enable an application to respond to events in the environment. These events can be generated by the application itself, by other concurrently running applications, by the user, or by Windows. Each time an event occurs, Windows makes a note and distributes an appropriate message to the interested applications.

Memory Management

When multitasking applications are involved, system memory is one of the most important shared resources. It is important, in a multitasking environment, that each application cooperate to share memory in order not to exhaust the total resources of the system. It is also important to keep memory defragmented as new programs are started and old ones are terminated. Windows is capable of consolidating free memory space by moving blocks of code and data in memory.

It is also possible to overcommit memory. For example, an application can contain more code than can actually fit into memory at one time. Windows can discard unused code from memory and later reload the code from the program's executable file.

Windows applications can share routines located in other executable files. The files that contain shareable routines are called dynamic link libraries (DLLs). Windows includes the mechanism to link the program with the DLL routines at run time. Windows itself is a set of dynamic link libraries. Windows programs make the connection with DLLs by using a new executable file format. This new format is called the *New Executable format*. The New Executable format provides the information Windows needs to manage the code and data segments and to perform the dynamic linking.

DLLs—Dynamic Link Libraries

Dynamic link libraries provide much of Windows' functionality; they enhance the base operating system by providing a powerful and flexible graphics user interface. Dynamic link libraries contain predefined functions that are linked with an application program when it is loaded (dynamically), instead of when the executable file is generated (statically). Dynamic link libraries use the .DLL file extension.

Storing frequently used routines in libraries was not an invention of the Windows product. For example, the C/C++ language depends heavily on libraries to implement standard functions for different systems. The linker makes copies of run-time library functions, such as **getchar()** and **printf()**, into a program's executable file. Libraries of functions save each programmer from having to re-create a new procedure for a common operation such as reading in a character or formatting output. Programmers can easily build their own libraries to include additional capabilities, such as changing a character font or justifying text. Making the function available as a general tool eliminates redundant design—a key feature in OOP.

Windows libraries are dynamically linked. In other words, the linker does not copy the library functions into the program's executable file. Instead, while the program is executing, it makes calls to the function in the library. Naturally, this conserves memory. No matter how many applications are running, there is only one copy of the library in RAM at a given time, and this library can be shared.

When a call is made to a Windows function, the C/C++ compiler must generate machine code for a far intersegment call. The call is to a function located in a code segment in one of the Windows libraries. This presents a problem because, until the program is actually running inside Windows, the address of the Windows function is unknown. Doesn't this sound suspiciously similar to the concept of late binding, discussed in the OOP section of this book? The solution to this problem in Windows is called *delayed binding* or dynamic linking. Starting with Windows 3.0 and Microsoft C 6.0, the linker allows a program to have calls to functions that cannot be fully resolved at link time. Only when the program is loaded into memory to be run are the far function calls resolved.

Special Windows import libraries are included with the C/C++ compiler; they are used to properly prepare a Windows program for dynamic linking. For example, the import library slibcew.lib is the import library that will be used for small-model 16-bit Windows programs. slibcew.lib contains a record for each Windows function that your program can call. This record defines the Windows module that contains this function and, in many cases, an ordinal value that corresponds to the function in the module.

Windows applications typically make a call to the Windows **PostMessage()** function. When your application is linked at compile time, the linker finds the **PostMessage()** function listed in slibcew.lib. The linker obtains the ordinal number for the function and embeds this information in the application's executable file. When the application is run, Windows connects the call your application makes with the actual **PostMessage()** function.

Freedom from Hardware Constraints

Windows also provides hardware or device independence, freeing you from having to build programs that take into consideration every possible monitor, printer, and input device available for computers. A non-Windowed application must be written to include drivers for every possible device. Likewise, to make a non-Windowed application capable of printing on any printer, you must furnish a different driver for each printer. This requires many software companies to write essentially the same device driver over and over again—a LaserJet driver for Microsoft Word for DOS, one for Microsoft Works, and so on.

Under Windows, a device driver for each hardware device is written once. This device driver can be supplied by Microsoft, the application vendor, or the user. Microsoft includes many drivers with Windows.

It is hardware independence that makes programming a snap for the application developer. The application interacts with Windows rather than with any specific device. It doesn't need to know what printer is hooked up. The application instructs Windows to draw a filled rectangle, and Windows worries about how to accomplish it on the installed hardware. Likewise, each device driver works with every Windows application. Developers save time, and users do not have to worry about whether each new Windows application will support their hardware configuration.

You achieve hardware independence by specifying the minimum capabilities the hardware must have. These capabilities are the minimum specifications required to ensure that the appropriate routines will function correctly. Every routine, regardless of its complexity, is capable of breaking itself down into the minimal set of operations required for a given device. This is a very impressive feature. For example, not every plotter is capable of drawing a circle by itself. As an application developer, however, you can still use the routines for drawing a circle, even if the plotter has no specific circle capabilities. Because every plotter connected to Windows must be capable of drawing a line, Windows is capable of breaking down the circle routine into a series of small lines.

Windows can specify a set of minimum capabilities to ensure that your application will receive only valid, predefined input. Windows has predefined the set of legal keystrokes allowed by applications. The valid keystrokes are very similar to those produced by the IBM-compatible keyboard. Should a manufacturer produce a keyboard that contains additional keys that do not exist in the Windows list of acceptable keys, the manufacturer would also have to supply additional software that would translate these illegal keystrokes into Windows' legal keystrokes. This predefined Windows legal input covers all the input devices, including the mouse. Therefore, even if someone should develop a four-button mouse, the users of the new mouse wouldn't have to worry. The manufacturer would supply the software necessary to convert all mouse input to the Windows predefined possibilities of mouse-button clicks.

The Windows Executable Format

An executable file format has been developed for Windows called the New Executable format. This new format includes a new style header capable of holding information about dynamic link library functions.

For example, DLL functions are included for the KERNEL, USER, and GDI (graphics device interface) modules. These libraries contain routines that help programs carry out various chores, such as sending and receiving messages. The library modules provide functions that can be called from the application program or from other library modules. To the module that contains the functions, the functions are known as exports. The New Executable format identifies these exported functions with a name and an ordinal number. Included in the New Executable format is an Entry Table section that indicates the address of each of these exported functions within the module.

From the perspective of the application program, the library functions that an application uses are known as imports. These imports use the various relocation tables and can identify the far calls that the application makes to an imported function. Almost all Windows programs contain at least one exported function. This window function is usually located in one of the library modules and is the one that receives window messages. It is important that the application indicate that this function is exported so Windows can properly allow the function to be called from an external module.

This new format also provides the additional information on each of the code and data segments in a program or library. Typically, code segments are flagged as moveable and discardable, while data segments are flagged as moveable. This allows Windows to move code and data segments in memory and even discard code segments if additional memory is needed. If Windows later decides it needs a discarded code segment, it can reload the code segment from the original executable file. Windows has another category called "load on call." This defines a program or library code segment that will not be loaded into memory at all unless a function in the code segment is called from another code segment. Through this sophisticated memory management scheme, Windows can simultaneously run several programs in a memory space that would normally be sufficient for only one program.

Windows Terminology

Windows includes new programming concepts and a unique vocabulary. These concepts and vocabulary can be divided into two categories:

- The features of Windows that are visible to the user, such as menus, dialog boxes, icons, and so on.

- The invisible features such as messages, function access, and so on.

There is a standard vocabulary associated with Windows programming development designed to give application developers the ability to communicate effectively with one another. For example, all Windows features have been given a name and an associated usage. In this section you will learn a number of Windows terms that will give you the ability to confidently discuss and develop applications.

The Windows Window

A Windows window appears to the user as a rectangular portion of the display device; its appearance is independent of the particular application at hand. To an application, however, the window is a rectangular area of the screen that is under the direct control of the application. The application has the ability to create and control everything about this window, including its size, shape, and position. When the user starts the application, a window is created. Each time the user clicks a window option, the application responds. Closing a window causes the application to terminate. By partitioning the screen into different windows, the user can direct input to a specific application within the multitasking environment by using the keyboard or a mouse. Windows then intercepts the user's input and allocates any necessary resources, such as memory, as needed.

Window Components

Features such as borders, control boxes, About boxes, and so on, are common to almost all Windows applications. It is this common interface that gives Windows a comforting predictability from one application to another. Figure 20-4 illustrates the fundamental components of a Windows 95 window.

The Border

A window typically has a border surrounding it. The border is made up of lines that frame the window. To the beginner, the border may appear only to delineate one application's screen from another. However, upon closer examination you'll see that the border not only serves as a screen boundary but also changes width to indicate which window is active. Also, by positioning the mouse pointer over a border and holding down the left mouse button, the user can change the size of the window.

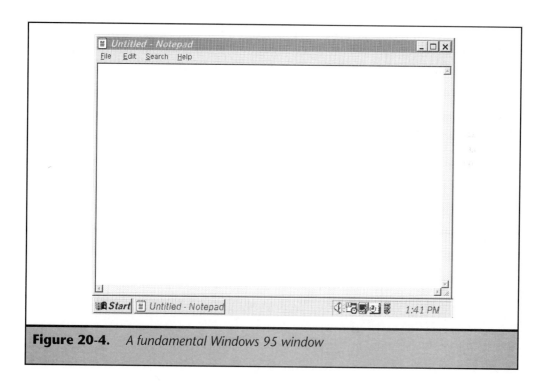

Figure 20-4. *A fundamental Windows 95 window*

The Client Area

The client area usually occupies the largest portion of each window. The client area is the primary output area for the application. Managing the client area is the responsibility of the application program. Additionally, only the application can output to the client area.

The Control Box

A control box is used by each Windows application. The control box is a small square box with a line through it in each window's upper-left corner. Clicking the mouse pointer on the control box causes Windows to display the system menu.

 NOTE: *This control box has been replaced, under Windows 95, with a small icon.*

The Horizontal Scroll Bar

Horizontal scroll bars, when displayed, are located at the bottom of each window. The horizontal scroll bar is used to select which of multiple columns of information you would like displayed. Clicking the mouse on either scroll bar arrow causes the screen image to be shifted one column at a time. Clicking the mouse on the transparent window block to the right of the left-pointing arrow, and dragging it causes the screen output to be quickly updated to any horizontally shifted portion of the application's screen output. One of the best uses for the horizontal scroll bar is for quickly moving through the multiple columns of a spreadsheet application, where the number of columns of information cannot fit into one screen width. Microsoft's Excel spreadsheet, shown earlier, uses this feature.

The Maximize Box

The maximize box is in the upper-right corner of each window. This box displays an upward-pointing arrow. You use the maximize box to make an application's window fill the entire screen. If this box is selected, all other application windows will be covered. Under Windows 95, the arrow has been replaced with a rectangular icon. The rectangular icon means maximize.

The Menu Bar

A menu bar, when used, is located just beneath the title bar. The menu bar is used for making menu selections. Users can select by pointing and clicking the menu command or by using a hot-key combination. Hot-key combinations often use the ALT key in conjunction with the underlined letter in a command. For example, ALT-E accesses the Edit menu.

The Minimize Box

Each Windows 3.1 or NT application displays two vertical arrows in the upper-right corner of the screen. The minimize box uses the downward-pointing arrow. This button causes the window to be shrunk to a small picture called an icon. Under Windows 95, the arrow has been replaced with a dash icon. The dash icon means minimize.

The System Menu

The system menu is activated by clicking the mouse pointer on the control box or icon. The system menu provides standard application options such as Restore, Move, Size, Minimize, Maximize, and Close.

The Title Bar

The name of the application program is displayed at the top of the window in the title bar. Title bars are located at the top of each associated window. They are left-justified under Windows 95, but centered under Windows 3.1 and Windows NT. Title bars can be very useful in helping to remember which applications are currently running.

The Vertical Scroll Bar

The vertical scroll bar, when used, is located directly below each window's maximize box and has opposite-pointing arrows at its extremes, a colored band, and a transparent window block. The transparent window block is used to visually represent the orientation between the currently displayed contents and the overall document (the colored band). You use the vertical scroll bar to select which of multiple pages of output you would like displayed. Clicking the mouse on either arrow shifts the display one line at a time. Clicking the mouse on the transparent window block below the up arrow and dragging it causes screen output to be quickly updated to any portion of the application's screen output. One of the best uses of the vertical scroll bar is for quickly moving through a multipage word processing document. Microsoft Word for Windows is one application that takes advantage of this feature.

A Pseudo-Class for Windows

Multiple instances of the same application, say, Microsoft Word, are said to be of the same window class. However, each instance's window can take on different characteristics. These windows may be different sizes, placed in different areas of the display, have different text in the caption bars, have different display colors, or use different mouse cursors.

Each instance creates a window based on a specific window class. With applications developed in C using traditional function calls, five window classes are registered by the Windows application during its initialization phase. Your application may register additional classes of its own. In order to allow several windows to be created and based on the same window class, Windows specifies some of a window's characteristics as parameters to the **CreateWindow()** or **CreateWindowEx()** functions, while others are specified in a window class structure. Also, when a window class is registered, the class becomes available to all programs running under Windows. For C++ Windows applications utilizing Borland's Object-Windows Library (OWL) or Microsoft's Foundation Class library (MFC), much of this registration work is already done through the use of predefined objects. In Chapters 21 and 22, you'll learn how to write Windows applications in C using traditional function calls in procedure-oriented applications. Chapters 23 through 28 are designed to teach you how to write similar applications with object libraries in an object-oriented environment.

Windows of similar appearance and behavior can be grouped together into classes, thereby reducing the amount of information that needs to be maintained. The word "class" as it is used here does not have the same meaning as a C++ class. Because each window class has its own shareable window class structure, there is no needless replication of the window class' parameters. Also, two windows of the same class use the same function and any of its associated subroutines. This feature saves time and storage because there is no code duplication.

Resources

Windows applications have always had several object-oriented components. Recall that in object-oriented programming, an object is an abstract data type that consists of a data structure and various functions that act on the data structure. Likewise, objects can receive messages that can cause them to function differently.

A Windows graphics object, for example, is a collection of data that can be manipulated as a whole entity and that is presented to the user as part of the visual interface. In particular, a graphics object implies both the data and the presentation of data. Menus, title bars, control boxes, push buttons, and scroll bars are examples of graphics objects. The next sections describe several Windows graphics objects that affect the user's view of an application.

Bitmaps

Bitmaps are actually a photographic image of the display. These pixel images are stored in memory. Bitmaps are used whenever an application must display a graphics image quickly. Because bitmapped images are transferred directly from memory, they can be "snapped" to the screen more quickly than by executing the code necessary to re-create the image. There are two basic uses for bitmaps. First, bitmaps are used to draw pictures on the display. For example, Windows uses many small bitmaps for drawing arrows in scroll bars; displaying the check marks when selecting pop-up menu options, drawing the system menu box, the size box, and many others. Second, bitmaps are used for creating brushes. Brushes allow you to paint and fill objects on the screen.

There are two disadvantages to using bitmaps. First, depending on the size of the bitmap, bitmaps can occupy an unpredictably large portion of memory. For each pixel that is being displayed, there needs to be an equivalent representation in memory.

Displaying the same bitmap on a color monitor versus a monochrome monitor would also require more memory. On a monochrome monitor, one bit can be used to define when a single pixel is turned on or off. However, on a color monitor that can display 16 colors, each pixel would require 4 bits to represent all of its color characteristics. Also, as the resolution of the display device increases, so does the memory requirement for the bitmap. Another disadvantage of bitmaps is that they contain only a *static* picture. For example, if an automobile is represented by a bitmap, there is no way to access the picture's various components, such as tires, hood, window, and so on as individual components. However, if the automobile had been constructed from a series of primitive drawing routines, an application would be able to change the data sent to these routines and modify individual items in the picture. For example, an application could modify the roof line and convert the sedan to a convertible. You can create or modify bitmaps with Borland's Resource Workshop.

Brushes

Windows uses brushes to paint colors and fill areas with predefined patterns. Brushes have a minimum size of 8x8 pixels and have three basic characteristics: size, pattern, and color. With their 8x8-pixel minimum size, brushes are said to have a pattern, not a style as pens do. The pattern may be a solid color, hatched, diagonal, or any other user-definable combination.

Carets

Carets are symbols the application places in a window to show the user where input will be received. Carets are distinguished from other screen markers because they blink. Most of the time, mouse input is associated with a cursor and keyboard input with a caret. However, the mouse can move or change the input emphasis of a caret. To help clarify the difference between a cursor and a caret, Windows carets behave most similarly to the old DOS cursor. Unlike in the cases of icons and cursors, an application must create its own carets using special functions. There are no stock carets.

Cursors

Cursors are graphics symbols and also differ from the old DOS blinking underscore. The cursor actually follows the movement of the pointing device. The graphics symbol is capable of changing shapes to indicate particular Windows actions. For example, the standard Windows arrow cursor changes to the small hourglass cursor to indicate a pause while a selected command is being executed. Windows provides several stock cursors: a diagonal arrow, a vertical arrow, an hourglass, a cross hair, an I-beam, and so on. You can also use Borland's Resource Workshop to create your own cursors.

Dialog Boxes

A dialog box is a pop-up window. Dialog boxes are primarily used to receive input from the user rather than to just present output. A dialog box allows an application to receive information one field at a time or one dialog box's worth of information at a time, rather than a character at a time. Figure 20-5 shows a typical Windows dialog box. The graphic design of a dialog box is done automatically for you by Windows. The layout of a dialog box is normally done with Borland's Resource Workshop.

Fonts

Fonts are graphics objects that define a complete set of characters from one typeface. These characters are all of a certain size and style that can be manipulated to give text a variety of appearances. A typeface is a basic character design, defined by certain serifs and stroke widths. For instance, your application can use any of the different fonts provided with Windows including System, Courier, and Times Roman, or custom fonts that you define and include in the application program's executable file. By using built-in routines, Windows allows for the dynamic modification of a font, including boldface, italics, underline, and changing the size of the font. Windows provides all of the necessary functions for displaying text anywhere within the client area. Additionally, because of Windows device independence, an application's output will have a consistent appearance from one output device to the next when using TrueType fonts. TrueType font technology, first supplied with Windows 3.1, provides improved fonts for the screen and printer.

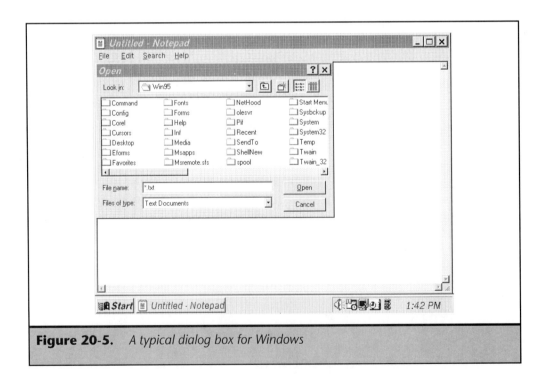

Figure 20-5. *A typical dialog box for Windows*

Icons

An icon is a small graphics object used to remind the user of a particular operation or idea. For example, whenever a spreadsheet application is minimized, an icon can be used to display a very small histogram icon. This icon would remind the user that the application is running. Double-clicking the mouse on the histogram would then cause Windows to bring the application to active status. Icons can be very powerful tools. They are good for gaining the user's attention, as in the case of an error warning, and also for presenting choices to the user. Windows provides several stock icons including a question mark, an exclamation point, an asterisk, and an upturned palm icon. It is also possible to design your own device-independent color icons with Borland's Resource Workshop.

Message Boxes

The message box is similar, but simpler, to that of a dialog box. Message boxes are pop-up windows that contain a title, an icon, and a message. Figure 20-6 shows an example of a message box.

The application supplies the message title, the message itself, and instructions on which stock icon to use (if any). Stock responses, such as an OK button, are allowed if needed. Additional stock user responses include Yes/No, Yes/No/Cancel,

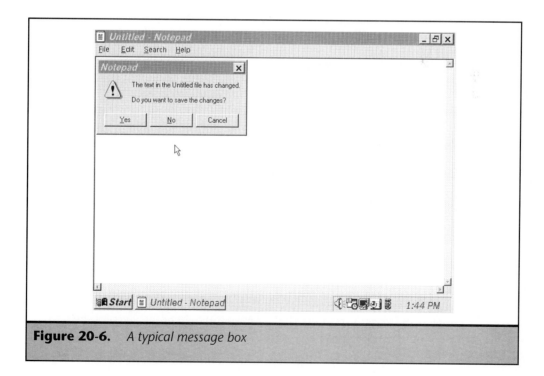

Figure 20-6. *A typical message box*

OK/Cancel, and Retry/Cancel. Stock icons include IconHand, IconQuestion, IconExclamation, and IconAsterisk.

Pens

When Windows draws a shape on the screen, it uses information on the current pen and brush. Pens are used to draw lines and to outline shapes. They have three basic characteristics: line width, style (dotted, dashed, solid), and color. Windows always has a pen for drawing black lines and one for drawing white lines available to each application. It is also possible to create your own pens. For example, you might want to create a thick light-gray line to outline a portion of the screen or a dot-dash-dot line for spreadsheet data analysis.

Processing Messages

You have learned that an application does not write directly to the screen, process any hardware interrupts, or output directly to the printer. Instead, the application uses the appropriate Windows functions or waits for an appropriate message to be delivered. Applications must incorporate, in their code, a method of processing these messages.

The Windows application must now be totally oriented toward the processing of messages. It must be capable of awakening, determining the appropriate action based on the type of message received, taking that action to completion, and returning to sleep.

Windows applications are significantly different from their older DOS counterparts. Windows provides an application program with access to hundreds of function calls directly or, through foundation classes, indirectly. These function calls are handled by three main modules called the KERNEL, GDI, and USER modules. The KERNEL is responsible for memory management, loading and running an application, and scheduling. The GDI contains all of the routines to create and display graphics. The USER module takes care of all other application requirements.

The next section takes a closer look at the message system by examining the format and sources of messages and looking at several common message types and the ways in which both Windows and your application process messages.

The Windows Message Format

Messages notify a program that an event of interest has occurred. Technically, a message is not just of interest to the application, but also to a specific window within that application. Therefore, every message is addressed to a window.

Windows has only one message system—the system message queue. However, each program currently running under Windows also has its own program message queue. Each message in the system message queue must eventually be transferred by the USER module to a program's message queue. The program's message queue stores all messages for all windows in that program.

For Windows applications, messages have four parameters regardless of the type of message: a window handle, a message type, one *wParam* (WORD) parameter, and one *lParam* (LONG) parameter.

The first parameter is the handle of the window to which the message is addressed. This is a 16-bit value under Windows 3.1 and a 32-bit value under Windows 95 and Windows NT. In an object-oriented programming environment, a handle is just the identifier of an object, which for the current syntax is the identifier of the particular window to which the message is addressed. This handle will reference an object that is located in a moveable portion of memory. Even though the portion of memory can be moved, the handle remains the same. This fact allows Windows to manage memory efficiently while leaving the relocation invisible to the application. Because multiple windows can be created based on the same window class, a single window function can process messages for more than one window within a single program. Here, the application can use the handle to determine which window is receiving the message.

The second parameter in a message is its message type. This is one of the identifiers specified in the windows.h header file or in one of the associated header files. With Windows, each message type begins with a two-character mnemonic, followed by the underscore character and finally a descriptor. The most frequently encountered type of message in traditional C Windows applications is the window message starting with the letters WM_. Windows messages include WM_CREATE, WM_PAINT, WM_CLOSE, WM_COPY, WM_PASTE, etc. Other message types include control window messages (BM_), edit control messages (EM_), and list box messages (LB_). An application can also create and register its own message type. This permits the use of private message types.

The last two parameters provide additional information necessary to interpret the message. The contents of these last two parameters will therefore vary depending on the message type. Examples of the types of information that would be passed include which key was just struck, the position of the mouse, the position of the vertical or horizontal scroll bar elevators, and the selected pop-up menu item. The *wParam* value is 16 bits under Windows 3.1 and 32 bits under Windows 95 and Windows NT. The *lParam* value is 32 bits under all versions of Windows.

Creating Messages

Windows is multitasking as the result of using messages. Thus, all messages must be processed by Windows. As you have learned, there are four basic sources for a message. An application can receive a message from the user, from Windows itself, from the application, or from other applications.

User messages include keystroke information, mouse movements, point-and-click coordinates, any menu selections, the location of scroll bar elevators, and so on. The application program will devote a great deal of time to processing user messages. User-originated messages indicate that the person running the program wishes to change the way the application is viewed.

A message is sent to an application whenever a state change is to take effect. An example of this would be when the user clicks an application's icon indicating that he or she wants to make that application the active application. Windows tells the application that its main window is being opened, that its size and location are being modified, and so on. Windows messages can be processed or ignored, depending on the current state of an application.

In Chapters 21 and 22, you will learn how to write simple Windows applications in C. What you will see is that a program is broken down into specific procedures, with each procedure processing a particular message type for a particular window. One procedure, for example, will deal with resizing the application's window. It is quite possible that the application may even want to resize itself. In other words, the source of the message is the application itself.

Currently, most applications written for Windows do not fully use the fourth type of message source, inter-task communication. However, this category will become increasingly important as more and more applications take advantage of this Windows integration capability. To facilitate this type of message, Microsoft has developed the dynamic data exchange protocol (DDE).

Responding to Messages

Procedure-oriented Windows applications, such as those you'll see in Chapters 21 and 22, use a procedure for processing each type of message they may encounter. Different windows can respond differently to messages of the same type. For example, one application may have created two windows that respond to a mouse-button click in two different ways. The first window could respond to a mouse-button click by changing the foreground color, while the second window may respond to the mouse-button click by moving a cursor in a word processor's document. It is because the same message can be interpreted differently by different windows that Windows addresses each message to a specific window within an application. The application will not only have a different procedure to handle each message type, it will also need a procedure to handle each message type for each window. The window procedure groups together all the message type procedures for an application.

The Message Loop

A basic component of all Windows applications is the message-processing loop. C applications contain procedures to create and initialize windows, followed by the message-processing loop and, finally, some code required to close the application. The message loop is responsible for processing a message delivered by Windows to the main body of the program. The program will acknowledge the message and then request Windows to send it to the appropriate window procedure for processing. When the message is received, the window procedure executes the desired action.

There are two factors that can affect the sequence in which a message is processed; the message queue and the dispatching priority. Recall that messages can be sent from one of two queues—either the system queue or the application's message queue. Messages are first placed in the system queue. When a given message reaches the front of the queue, it is sent to the appropriate application's message queue. This dual-mode action allows Windows to keep track of all messages and permits each application to concern itself with only those messages that pertain to it.

Messages are placed in the queues in a first-in-first-out order. These messages are called synchronous messages. Most Windows applications use this type of dispatching method. However, there are occasions when Windows will push a message to the end of the queue, thereby preventing it from being dispatched. Messages of this type are called *asynchronous* messages. Care must be taken when sending an asynchronous message that overrides the application's normal sequence of processing.

Three types of asynchronous messages exist: paint, timer, and quit. A timer message, for example, causes a certain action to take effect at a specified time, regardless of the messages to be processed at that moment. A timer message has priority and will cause all other messages to be pushed back in the queue.

A few asynchronous messages can be sent to other applications. What is unique is that the receiving application doesn't put the message into its queue. Rather, the received message directly calls the application's appropriate window procedure, where it is immediately executed.

How does Windows dispatch messages that are pending for several applications at the same time? Windows handles this problem in one of two ways. One method of message processing is called *dispatching priority*. Whenever Windows loads an application, it sets the application's priority to zero. Once the application is running, however, the application can change its priority from a -15 to a +15. With everything else being equal, Windows will settle any message-dispatching contention by sending messages to the highest priority application.

One example of a high-priority program would be a data communications application. Tampering with an application's priority level is very uncommon. Windows has another method for dispatching messages to concurrent applications of the same priority level. Whenever Windows sees that a particular application has a backlog of unprocessed messages, it hangs onto the new message while continuing to dispatch other new messages to the other applications.

Gaining Access to Windows Functions

Windows provides the developer with hundreds of functions. Examples of these functions include **DispatchMessage()**, **PostMessage()**, **RegisterWindowMessage()**, and **SetActiveWindow()**.

A Special Calling Convention

Function declarations in Windows 3.*x* include the **pascal** modifier, which was more efficient under 16-bit DOS. Windows 95 and NT do not use this modifier. Recall that all parameters passed to Windows functions are passed via the system stack. In a traditional C program, function parameters are first pushed onto the stack and then the function is called. Normally, the parameters are pushed from the right-most parameter to the left-most parameter. Upon return from the function, the calling procedure must adjust the stack pointer to a value equal to the number of bytes originally pushed onto the stack.

The Pascal parameter-passing sequence pushes parameters onto the stack from left to right. It is the called function's responsibility to adjust the stack before the return. Windows uses this calling convention because it turns out to be more space efficient. Therefore, the compiler understands that any function declared with the reserved word **pascal** is to use the more efficient calling convention.

The windows.h Header File

The windows.h header file contains (under Windows 3.1) or winuser.h (under Windows 95 and NT) provides a path to over a thousand constant declarations, typedef declarations, and hundreds of function prototypes. One of the main reasons a Windows application takes longer to compile than a traditional C or C++ program is the size of this file. The windows.h header file (or its associated header files) is an integral part of all Windows programs.

 TIP: Because of the importance of this information, print a hard copy of the windows.h header file to keep as a convenient reference.

Usually, the **#define** statements found in windows.h associate a numeric constant with a text identifier. For example:

```
#define WM_CREATE 0x0001
```

In this case, the compiler will use the hexadecimal constant 0x0001 as a replacement for WM_CREATE during preprocessing.

Other **#define** statements may appear a bit unusual. For example:

```
#define NEAR near
#define VOID void
```

In Borland C++, both **near** and **void** are reserved words. Your applications should use the uppercase NEAR and VOID for one very good reason: if you port your application to another compiler, it will be much easier to change the **#define** statements within the header file than to change all of the occurrences of a particular identifier in the application.

Windows Application Components

There are several important steps that are common in developing all procedure-oriented Windows applications:

- Create **WinMain()** and any associated Windows functions in C.
- Create the menu, dialog box, and any additional resource descriptions and put them into a resource script file.
- (Optional) Use the Borland Resource Workshop to create unique cursors, icons, and bitmaps.
- (Optional) Use the Borland Resource Workshop to create dialog boxes.
- Create any module definitions (Windows 3.1 applications only) and place them in the module definition file.
- Build (compile and link) all C/C++ language sources.
- Compile the resource script file and add it to the executable file.

The actual creation of a Windows application requires the use of several new development tools. You'll need a brief overview of these tools before developing applications in C or C. The next section discusses the tools supplied with the Borland C++ compiler as they relate to creating a Windows application.

Borland C++ Windows Tools

The Borland C++ compiler contains several resource editors packaged in the Resource Workshop. The individual editors are available by selecting the Resource Workshop icon from the Borland C++ Group Box or by selecting the File | New | Resource Project... sequence from within the C++ compiler's editor. (To distinguish a dialog box choice from ordinary selections in a menu, three dots (an ellipsis) follow the dialog option name.) These editors allow for the quick definition of icons, cursors, and bitmaps. They also provide a convenient method for creating menus and dialog box descriptions for data entry. The HotSpot Editor allows the developer to specify hotspot locations and formats.

Resources have the capability of turning ordinary Windows applications into truly exciting graphical presentations. When you develop custom icons, cursors, menus, bitmaps, and more, you'll add graphical flair to your projects. Resources also let you add user-interactive components to your program such as menus, keyboard accelerators, and dialog boxes.

Graphics objects such as icons, cursors, carets, message boxes, dialog boxes, fonts, bitmaps, pens, and brushes are all examples of resources. A *resource* represents data that is included in an application's executable file. Technically speaking, however, it does not reside in a program's normal data segment. When Windows loads a program into memory for execution, it usually leaves all of the resources on the disk. For example, when the user first requests to see an application's About box, Windows must first access the disk to copy this information from the program's executable file into memory.

Applications typically define their resources as read only and discardable. The attributes allow Windows to discard the resource whenever additional memory is required. If the resource is requested again, Windows will simply read the disk and reload the data back into system memory.

> **NOTE:** *Under Windows 3.x, multiple instances of the same application share the application's program code and resource definitions.*

The resource compiler is a compiler designed to compile Windows resources. Many times a Windows application will use its own resources, such as dialog boxes, menus, and icons. Each one of these resources must be predefined in a file called a resource file or resource script file. These files are created with the editors mentioned previously. Resource script files can be compiled into resource files by the resource compiler. This information is then added to the application's final executable file. This method allows Windows to load and use the resources from the executable file.

The use of resources and additional compilers adds an extra layer of complexity to application development, but one that is easily incorporated with the use of a project utility.

Why Create a Project?

The Project utility provides an efficient means of overseeing the compilation of resources and program code as well as keeping the executable version of an application up to date. The Project utility accomplishes its incremental operation by keeping track of the times and dates of the various source code files.

Project files include information about the compile and link process for the particular application. Developers have the choice of changing libraries, hardware platforms, software platforms, and so on. Project files are created within the integrated Borland C++ editing environment. In many cases, the default project file setup can be used with just minor adjustments for program titles and a file list to include in the build operation.

The Project utility includes support for incremental compiles and links. For example, say you have created a Windows application that simulates the flight of an airliner. Later you decide to create a unique cursor. Instead of pointing with the standard arrow provided by Windows, you decide to create a cursor that looks like a jet airplane. When the application is recompiled, the program only really needs to accommodate the changes in the cursor resource file, plane.cur. The Project utility can ensure that only the information about the new cursor is updated during recompilation. As you might imagine, this can save a lot of development time.

Including Resources

Customizing a Windows application with your own icons, pointers, and bitmaps is easy when you use the resource editors. These editors, in conjunction with the Borland C++ compiler, give you a complete environment in which to develop graphical resources. The editors will also help you create menus and dialog boxes—the basic means of data entry in Windows. In this section you learn how to use these editors to create icons, cursors, menus, and dialog boxes. The editors can also help you manipulate individual bitmaps, keyboard accelerators, and strings. The cursor, menu, and dialog box created separately in this chapter will be assembled into a presentation-quality pie chart program in Chapter 22.

The Resource Editors

Each resource editor included within the Borland Resource Workshop is an integral part of the compiler. As such, each editor is a completely integrated resource development environment designed to run under Windows. You can start each editor by first selecting File | New | Resource Project... and then selecting the appropriate resource type. Let's examine the use of several of these editors.

Designing Icons, Cursors, and Bitmaps

This section describes the general operation of the editors capable of producing images such as icons, cursors, and bitmaps. Although each is a separate editor, they share many common features. As an example of the use of these image editors, we'll create a simple icon. Icons and cursors are both really small bitmaps. The icon and cursor editors allow you to design device-independent bitmap images. The icons and cursors created with these editors are functionally device independent in respect to resolution.

Initially, Icon Image (*.ico) is selected from the New Project dialog box, as shown in Figure 20-7.

A color palette, tool box, and drawing surface appear. Use these tools and colors to design a new icon, as shown in Figure 20-8.

A large editing area is provided when designing icons, cursors, or bitmaps. An icon normally occupies a 32x32 grid. Windows 95 now uses a smaller icon, occupying a 16x16 grid. Grid lines are added to the main drawing canvas to aid in figure alignment, but they will not be present in the final icon. As you can see in Figure 20-8, the editor also provides a small View window to allow you to view the icon in true size.

The first time you select the Save option from the File menu, the editor will prompt you for a filename. If you are creating an icon, the file system will automatically append an .ico file extension. The .cur file extension is used for cursors. If you are creating multiple icons, make certain you choose the Save As... option, not Save. Save overwrites your original file, but Save As... allows you to create multiple images. This resource will be saved in a file named myicon.ico, as shown in Figure 20-9.

When you are creating cursors, you can select an optional hotspot from the cursor toolbox. The hotspot on cursors is a point that will be used to return the current screen coordinates during the application's use. A good location for the hotspot on an arrow cursor would be on the tip of the arrow head.

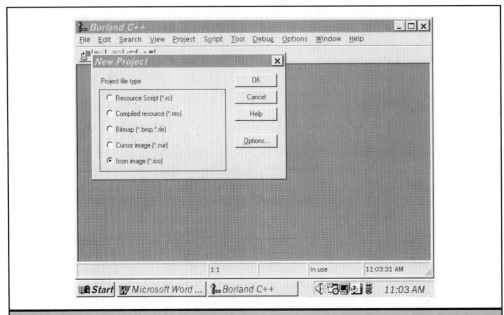

Figure 20-7. *Enter the icon editor by selecting Icon image from within the New Project dialog box*

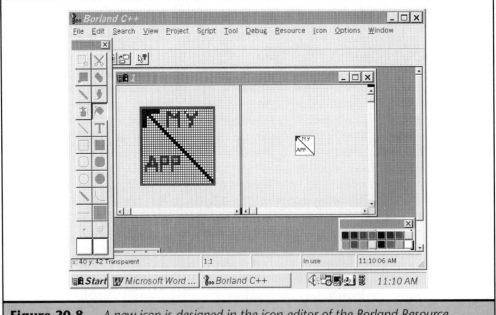

Figure 20-8. *A new icon is designed in the icon editor of the Borland Resource Workshop*

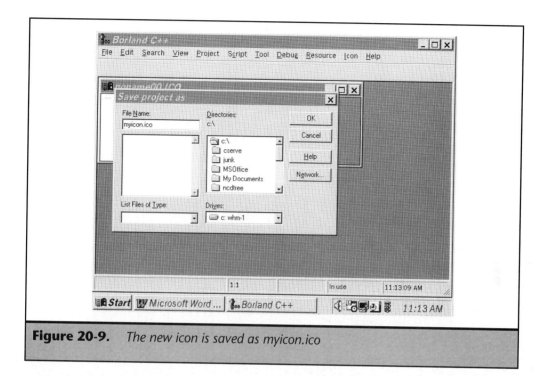

Figure 20-9. *The new icon is saved as myicon.ico*

Designing Menus

Menus are one of Windows' most important tools for creating interactive programs. Menus form the gateway that allows a consistent interfacing across applications. Menus allow the user to point and click selections that have been predefined. These selections can include screen color choices, sizing options, and file operations.

What is a menu? A menu is a list of items or names that represent options that an application can take. In some cases, the items in a menu can even be bitmaps. The user can select an option by using the mouse, the keyboard, or a hot key. Windows, in turn, responds by sending a message to the application stating which command was selected.

More advanced menu options allow the user to select dialog boxes from the menu list. Dialog boxes permit data entry from the keyboard, allowing users to enter string, integer, and even real number information in applications. However, before you can get to a dialog box, you must pass through a menu.

Let's look at the creation of a simple menu resource. If you start the Resource Workshop directly from the Borland C++ Group Box, you'll be able to create a menu resource by selecting File | New... The New Project dialog box will appear. Select to .RC file option to create a resource script file (a file you can read), as shown in Figure 20-10.

A default menu will be outlined in the editor, as shown in Figure 20-11.

If you examine Figure 20-11, you'll see the default menu in the right portion of the window. Double-click on any default menu item to allow that item to be changed. The

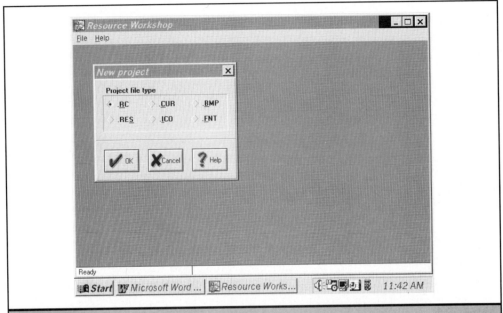

Figure 20-10. *Use the .RC option to create a text file for this resource*

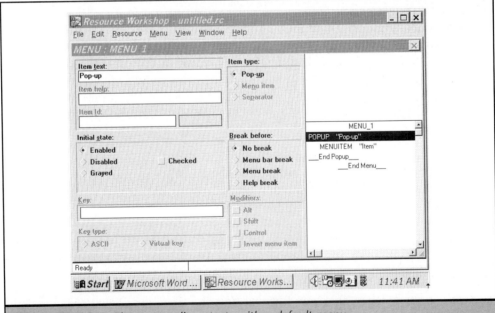

Figure 20-11. *The menu editor starts with a default menu*

name of the default menu is "Pop-up". Simply change that name by editing the name in the Item text edit box. Menu items, initially named "Item", can be changed in a similar manner. If you wish to add an additional menu item, select Menu | New menu item. Figure 20-12 shows how the default menu was changed to a menu named "Microprocessors". This menu now includes six menu items.

Notice in Figure 20-12 that the Resource Workshop automatically adds a default Item Id to each menu item. The Windows application references the menu item by using this ID value.

Select the Save option from the File menu to save this menu.

Dialog Boxes

In the previous section, you learned how to create a simple menu. Although menus are considered a means for simple data entry, the dialog box is the most powerful data entry tool for Windows. Data can be entered directly into the application's client area, but dialog boxes are the preferred entry form for maintaining consistency across all Windows programs.

Dialog boxes allow the user to check items in a window list, set push buttons for various choices, directly enter strings and integers from the keyboard, and indirectly enter real numbers (floats). Starting with Windows 3.0, dialog boxes can also contain combo boxes. *Combo boxes* allow a combination of a single-line edit fields and list

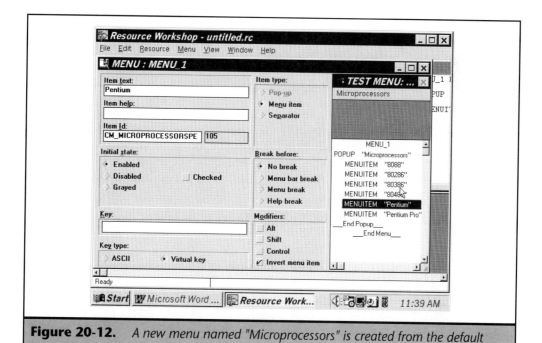

Figure 20-12. *A new menu named "Microprocessors" is created from the default menu*

boxes. The dialog box is the programmer's key to serious data entry in Windows programs. The dialog box is also the programmer's secret for ease of programming, because Windows handles all necessary overhead.

Dialog boxes can be called when selected as a choice from a menu and appear as a pop-up window to the user. To distinguish a dialog box choice from ordinary selections in a menu, three dots (an ellipsis) follow the dialog option name.

Dialog boxes are usually designed in the Dialog Editor. The Dialog Editor is designed to read and save resource files in either the text (.RC file extension) or the compiled format (.RES file extension).

CONCEPTS   Dialog boxes are actually "child" windows that pop up when selected from the user's menu. Windows provides the means necessary for processing the message information when various dialog box controls are selected.

Dialog boxes can be produced in two basic styles—modal and modeless. Modal dialog boxes are the most popular and are used throughout this book. When a *modal dialog box* is created, no other options within the current program will be available until the user ends the modal dialog box by clicking an OK or Cancel button. The OK button will process any new information selected by the user, while the Cancel button will return the user to the original window without processing new information.

Modeless dialog boxes are more closely related to ordinary windows. Just as a pop-up window can be created from a parent window, letting the user switch back and forth between the two, so can a modeless dialog box. Modeless dialog boxes are preferred when a certain option must remain on the screen, such as a color select dialog box.

CONTROLS   By far the most important aspect of using the Dialog Editor is an understanding of the various controls that are provided for the user in the toolbox. Here is a brief explanation of the most frequently used controls.

- The *check box control* creates a small square box, called a check box, with a label to its right. Check boxes are usually marked or checked by clicking with the mouse, but they can also be selected with the keyboard. Several check boxes usually appear together in a dialog box; they allow the user to check one or more features at the same time.

- The *radio button control* creates a small circle, called a radio button, with a label to its right. Radio buttons, like check boxes, typically appear in groups. However, unlike check boxes, only one radio button can be selected at a time in any particular group.

- The *push button control*, sometimes called simply a button, is a small rectangular button with rounded corners. The push button control can be sized. The push button contains a label within it. Push buttons are used for an immediate choice such as accepting or canceling the dialog box selections made by the user.

■ The *group box control* creates a rectangular outline within a dialog box to enclose a group of controls that are to be used together. The group box contains a label on its upper-left edge.

■ The *horizontal scroll bar* and *vertical scroll bar* controls allow horizontal and vertical scroll bars to be created for the dialog box. These are usually used in conjunction with another window or control that contains text or graphics information.

■ The *list box control* creates a rectangular outline with a vertical scroll bar. List boxes are useful when scrolling is needed to allow the user to select a file from a long directory listing.

■ The *edit text control* creates a small interactive rectangle on the screen in which the user can enter string information. The Edit box can be sized to accept short or long strings. This string information can be processed directly as character or numeric integer data and indirectly as real-number data in the program. The Edit box is the most important control for data entry.

■ The *static text control* allows the insertion of labels and strings within the dialog box. These can be used, for example, to label an Edit box.

■ The *icon control* is used for the placement of a dialog box icon. The icon control creates the rectangular space for the icon.

■ The *combo box* is made up of two elements. It is a combination of a single-line edit field (which is also called "static text") and a list box. With a combo box, the user has the ability to enter something into the Edit box or scroll through the List box looking for an appropriate selection. Windows provides several styles of combo boxes.

Controls can be placed by selecting the appropriate control from the toolbox, positioning the mouse pointer in the dialog box, and clicking the mouse button. If the placement is not where you desire it, you can use the mouse for repositioning.

USING THE DIALOG BOX EDITOR   Select the Resource Workshop icon from the Borland C++ Group Box. To create a new dialog box resource, select File | New... to gain access to the New resource dialog box. Select DIALOG from the Resource Type list box, shown in Figure 20-13.

Next, pick the Dialog type from the DialogExpert dialog box, as shown in Figure 20-14.

Once this selection is made, the screen will contain the initial outline for the new dialog box. This initial dialog box can be moved about the screen and sized to fit your needs. The screen in Figure 20-15 shows the initial dialog box.

As you study Figure 20-15, you will notice additional features supplied by the dialog box editor. The alignment tools allow controls to be aligned vertically or horizontally. The tool box provides a complete collection of frequently used dialog box controls.

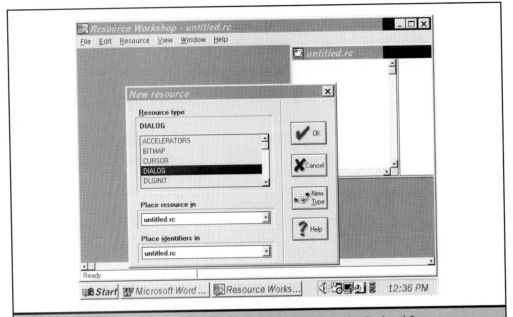

Figure 20-13. *Dialog boxes can be created from within the Borland Resource Workshop*

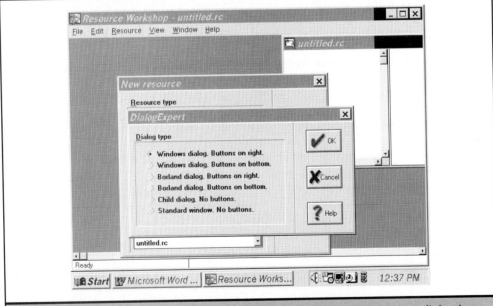

Figure 20-14. *The initial style of dialog box is set with the DialogExpert dialog box*

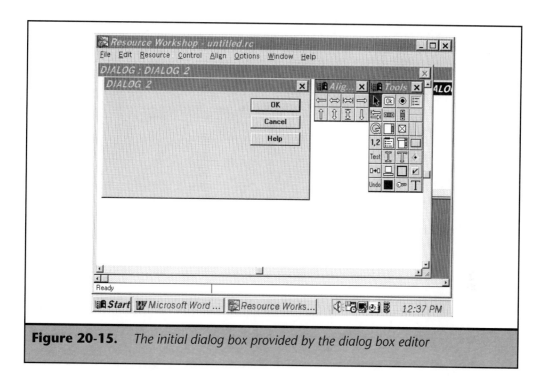

Figure 20-15.   *The initial dialog box provided by the dialog box editor*

In Figure 20-16, you will see that a static text control has been moved from the tool box to the dialog box.

Static text controls are most frequently used for labels. This control was stretched, by dragging its edge with the mouse, to the size shown in the figure. If you double-click the left mouse button when the cursor is positioned over the control, you will be able to edit the control's properties. Figure 20-17 shows the default properties for the static text box.

With a little editing, as shown in Figure 20-18, the control's caption is changed and the text is centered within the control.

Notice that the control is assigned an ID value of -1. All static text controls use an ID value of -1, because they never have to be referenced individually from within the application.

Add an edit box control just below the static text control. Size the control to match the static text control then double-click on the edit control to examine its properties, as shown in Figure 20-19.

No caption will be used, because we want the edit box to appear empty. Notice that the editor assigns a Control ID value of IDC_EDIT1. This simply refers to the ID value for the first edit box. If your application wants to access this control, it must refer to this ID value.

Figure 20-20 shows the final dialog box form while it is being tested within the dialog box editor.

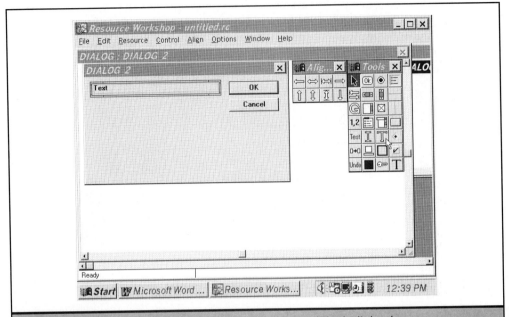

Figure 20-16. *A static text control is added to the default dialog box*

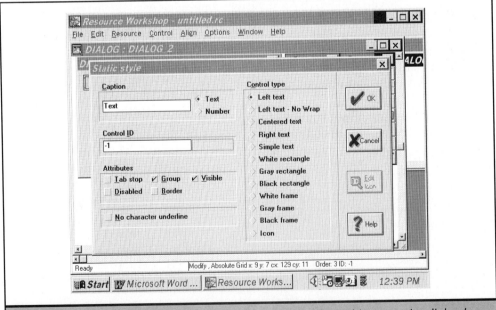

Figure 20-17. *Various control styles can be changed from this properties dialog box*

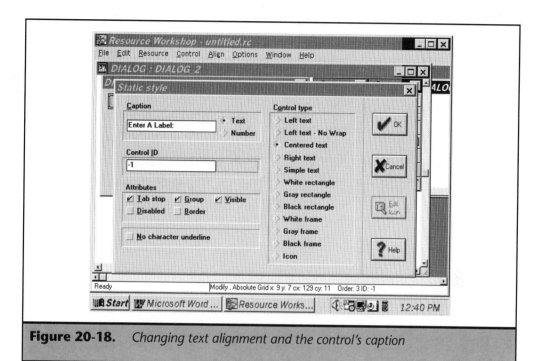

Figure 20-18.   *Changing text alignment and the control's caption*

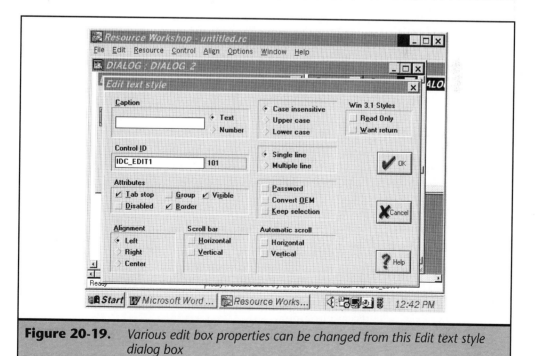

Figure 20-19.   *Various edit box properties can be changed from this Edit text style dialog box*

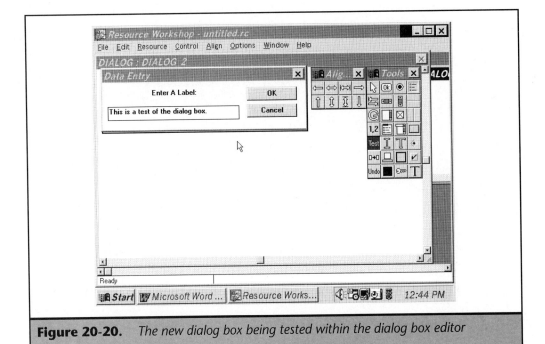

Figure 20-20.   *The new dialog box being tested within the dialog box editor*

Notice that the caption has been changed for the dialog box and that it has been resized. During the test mode, selected from Options | Test, text can actually be entered into the edit box as shown earlier in Figure 20-20.

You learn how to incorporate many of these resources into your Windows applications starting in Chapter 22.

More Resource Information

In addition to the information contained in this chapter, the Borland user's guides provide a wealth of information on each of these topics. While using the various resource editors, avail yourself of the extensive built-in help engine that is available with the Borland C++ compiler.

In the Next Chapter...

In Chapters 21 and 22 you'll learn how to write simple Windows applications in C using traditional function calls in procedure-oriented applications. Chapters 23 through 28 are designed to teach you how to write similar applications with object libraries in an object-oriented environment.

Chapter Twenty-One

Procedure-Oriented
C Programming

607

The last chapter presented you with many new terms and concepts and gave you an idea of how Windows has evolved. You've discovered that three of Microsoft Windows' most powerful objectives involve developing applications with a common graphical interface that can concurrently share system resources with other applications, all in a device-independent format. In this chapter, you will learn how to develop procedure-oriented Windows applications that include many of these features.

A Simple Windows Program

This Windows application will be named SWP, which is a mnemonic for *Simple Windows Program*. This Windows template will demonstrate many of the Windows components necessary to create and display an application window including all of the basic components discussed in the previous chapter. The SWP application will also demonstrate how to draw a simple graphics figure and print a text message to the screen. The SWP template contains Windows programming code that can be used over and over again.

Most Windows applications need the minimal capabilities illustrated in the SWP application. Later, you'll learn how the SWP application can be used as *boilerplate code* for developing future Windows applications. By boilerplating the code, you will save time and help develop an understanding of how Windows applications are put together and how they work.

Before jumping directly into a coded example, take a minute to study the standard Windows data types and structures shown in Tables 21-1 and 21-2.

Data Type	Description
HANDLE	Defines a handle.
HWND	Defines a handle to a window.
HDC	Defines a handle to a device context.
LONG	A 32-bit signed integer.
LPSTR	Defines a linear pointer.
NULL	An integral 0 under Windows 3.x. Defined as ((void *)0) under Windows 95 and NT.
UINT	A Win32 data type that automatically casts an *lParam* into a 16-bit value for Windows 3.x applications and a 32-bit value in Win32.
WCHAR	16-bit UNICODE character used to represent all of the symbols known for all of the world's written languages.

Table 21-1. *Commonly Used Windows Data Types*

Structure	Description
MSG	Defines the fields of an input message structure.
PAINTSTRUCT	Defines the paint structure used when drawing inside a window's client area.
RECT	Defines a rectangle structure.
WNDCLASS	Defines a window class structure.

Table 21-2. *Commonly Used Windows Structures*

To thoroughly understand Windows application development you must start with the basics. This means that you need to understand the least-common denominator to all Windows function calls. The information presented in Tables 21-1 and 21-2 provides the necessary background. Knowing the types of variables going in and out of a function call will make understanding that function's purpose easier. Table 21-1 lists common data types used in Windows.

Table 21-2 shows frequently used structures for Windows.

Handles

A *handle* is a unique number that identifies many different types of objects, such as windows, controls, menus, icons, pens and brushes, memory allocation, output devices, and even window instances. (In Windows terminology, each loaded copy of a program is called an *instance*.) Writing a Windows application always involves the use of handles.

Windows allows you to run more than one copy of the same application simultaneously. Under Windows 3.1, there needs to be a way to keep track of each of these instances. Windows keeps track by attaching a unique instance handle to each running copy of the application.

The instance handle is used as an index into an internally maintained table. Having the handle reference a table element, rather than an actual memory address, allows Windows to dynamically rearrange all resources simply by inserting a new address into the resource's identical table position. For example, if Windows associates a particular application's resource with table look-up position 7, then no matter where Windows moves the resource in memory, table position 7 will contain the resource's current location.

Windows conserves memory resources by the way it manages multiple instances of the same application. Several multitasking environments such as Windows 95 and NT load each duplicate instance of an application just as if each were an entirely new application. However, Windows 3.1 can conserve system resources by using the same code for all instances of an application. The only portion of each instance that is usually unique is the instance's data segment.

The first instance of an application has a very important role, because it defines all of the objects necessary for the functioning of the application. This can include controls, menus, dialog boxes, and much more, along with new window classes. A Windows application can even be instructed to allow other applications to share these new definitions.

Developing a Template (SWP) Application

In the following section is a complete listing of the simplest code required to get a Windows application up and running. This application is named swp.c. Study the listing and make a mental note of each major programming section.

```
//
//  SWP.c
//  A template that can be used to develop
//  additional Windows applications.
//  Copyright (c) Chris H. Pappas and William H. Murray, 1996
//

#include <windows.h>

LRESULT CALLBACK WndProc(HWND,UINT,WPARAM,LPARAM);

char szProgName[]="ProgName";

int WINAPI WinMain(HINSTANCE hInst,HINSTANCE hPreInst,
                   LPSTR lpszCmdLine,int nCmdShow)
{
  HWND hWnd;
  MSG  lpMsg;
  WNDCLASS wcApp;

  wcApp.lpszClassName=szProgName;
  wcApp.hInstance     =hInst;
  wcApp.lpfnWndProc   =WndProc;
  wcApp.hCursor       =LoadCursor(NULL,IDC_ARROW);
  wcApp.hIcon         =0;
  wcApp.lpszMenuName  =0;
  wcApp.hbrBackground=GetStockObject(WHITE_BRUSH);
  wcApp.style         =CS_HREDRAW|CS_VREDRAW;
  wcApp.cbClsExtra    =0;
```

```
   wcApp.cbWndExtra    =0;
   if (!RegisterClass (&wcApp))
     return 0;

   hWnd=CreateWindow(szProgName,"A SWP Template",
                     WS_OVERLAPPEDWINDOW,CW_USEDEFAULT,
                     CW_USEDEFAULT,CW_USEDEFAULT,
                     CW_USEDEFAULT,(HWND)NULL,(HMENU)NULL,
                     (HANDLE)hInst,(LPSTR)NULL);
   ShowWindow(hWnd,nCmdShow);
   UpdateWindow(hWnd);
   while (GetMessage(&lpMsg,NULL,0,0)) {
     TranslateMessage(&lpMsg);
     DispatchMessage(&lpMsg);
   }
   return(lpMsg.wParam);
}

LRESULT CALLBACK WndProc(HWND hWnd,UINT messg,
                         WPARAM wParam,LPARAM lParam)
{
  HDC hdc;
  PAINTSTRUCT ps;

  switch (messg)
  {
    case WM_PAINT:
      hdc=BeginPaint(hWnd,&ps);
//--------- your routines below ---------

      Rectangle(hdc,100,100,300,300);
      TextOut(hdc,350,200,"<- A Rectangle",14);

//--------- your routines above ---------
      ValidateRect(hWnd,NULL);
      EndPaint(hWnd,&ps);
      break;

    case WM_DESTROY:
      PostQuitMessage(0);
      break;
```

```
   default:
      return(DefWindowProc(hWnd,messg,wParam,lParam));
 }
  return(0);
}
```

 NOTE: *You will be able to experiment with other drawing functions by placing the function calls between the two comment lines:*

```
//--------- your routines below ---------


//--------- your routines above ---------
```

This will save you initial development time while you master the use of basic drawing functions.

The following sections will examine all important aspects of swp.c.

Application Elements

All Windows applications must contain two essential elements, the **WinMain()** function and a window function, often called the callback function. The C/C++ compiler requires that you name the main body of your program **WinMain()**. **WinMain()** serves as the entry point for the Windows application and component-wise acts in a similar way to the **main()** function in standard C/C++ programs.

The required window function, not to be confused with **WinMain()**, has a unique role. To appreciate the window function's purpose, you need to know that a Windows application never directly accesses any Windows functions. Instead, when a Windows application attempts to execute a standard Windows function, it makes a request to Windows to carry out the specified task. For this reason, all Windows applications must have a callback window function. The callback function is registered with Windows and it is called back whenever Windows executes an operation on a window.

The WinMain() Function

As you have learned, the C/C++ compiler requires all Windows applications to have a **WinMain()** function. This is where program execution begins and usually ends. The **WinMain()** function is responsible for:

- Initiating and creating the application's message-processing loop (which accesses the program's message queue).
- Performing required initializations.
- Registering the application's window class type.
- Terminating the program, usually when a WM_QUIT message is received.

The **WinMain()** function is passed four parameters from Windows. The following code segment illustrates these required parameters as they are used in the SWP application:

```
int WINAPI WinMain(HINSTANCE hInst,HINSTANCE hPreInst,
                   LPSTR lpszCmdLine,int nCmdShow)
```

The first formal parameter to **WinMain()** is *hInst* which contains the instance handle of the current instance of the application. This number uniquely identifies the program when it is running under Windows.

The second formal parameter, *hPreInst*, will contain a NULL value under Windows 95 and NT. This indicates that there are no previous instances of this application. Under Windows 3.x, *hPreInst* was used to indicate if there were or were not any previous copies of the program loaded. Under Windows 95 and NT, each application runs in its own separate address space. For this reason, *hPreInst* will never return a valid previous instance, just NULL.

The third parameter, *lpszCmdLine*, is a pointer to a null-terminated string that represents the application's command line arguments. Normally, *lpszCmdLine* contains a NULL if the application was started using the Windows Run... command.

The fourth and last formal parameter to **WinMain()** is *nCmdShow*. The **int** value stored in *nCmdShow* represents one of the many Windows predefined constants defining the possible ways a window can be displayed, such as SW_SHOWNORMAL, SW_SHOWMAXIMIZED, or SW_MINIMIZED.

Window Class Registration

Windows requires that every window class you create be based on a predefined window class. **WinMain()** is responsible for registering the application's main window class. Each window class is based on a combination of user-selected styles, fonts, caption bars, icons, size, placement, and so on. The window class serves as a template that defines these attributes.

Registered window classes are available to all programs running under Windows. For this reason, the programmer should use caution when naming and registering classes to make certain that the names used do not conflict with any other application's window classes. Windows requires that every instance (loaded copy of a program), register its own window classes.

All window class definitions use the standard C/C++ structure type. As an illustration, the following example is taken directly from winuser.h. The header file contains a **typedef** statement defining the structure type WNDCLASSW (a UNICODE-compatible definition) from which WNDCLASS is derived under Win32:

```
typedef struct tagWNDCLASSW {
    UINT        style;
    WNDPROC     lpfnWndProc;
    int         cbClsExtra;
    int         cbWndExtra;
    HANDLE      hInstance;
    HICON       hIcon;
    HCURSOR     hCursor;
    HBRUSH      hbrBackground;
    LPCWSTR     lpszMenuName;
    LPCWSTR     lpszClassName;
} WNDCLASSW, *PWNDCLASSW, NEAR *NPWNDCLASSW, FAR *LPWNDCLASSW;

#define WNDCLASS WNDCLASSW
```

Although Windows does provide several predefined window classes, most applications define their own window class. Your application does this by defining a structure of the appropriate type and then filling the structure's fields with the information about the window class.

Table 21-3 explains the various fields within the WNDCLASS structure. As you become more familiar with writing a Windows application, you will notice the frequent use of "0" for a parameter's value. This usually tells Windows to use a predefined default setting; otherwise, a specific value or constant must be used.

Field Name	Description	
style	Specifies the class style. Styles can be combined by using the bitwise logical OR operator. Values for the style field include:	

Value	Meaning
CS_BYTEALIGNCLIENT	Uses byte boundaries in the X direction, aligns a window's client area.
CS_BYTEALIGNWINDOW	Uses byte boundaries in the x direction, aligns the window.
CS_CLASSDC	Assigns a window class its own display context that can be shared by instances.
CS_DBCLKS	Sends a double-click message to a window.
CS_GLOBALCLASS	Defines a global window class.
CS_HREDRAW	If the horizontal size of a window changes, will redraw the entire window.
CS_KEYCVTWINDOW	Performs a virtual key conversion.
CS_NOCLOSE	Deactivates the close option on the system menu.
CS_NOKEYCVT	Deactivates virtual key conversion.
CS_OWNDC	Assigns each window instance its own display context.
CS_PARENTDC	Gives the parent window's display context to the window class.

Table 21-3.   *WNDCLASS Structure Field Definitions*

Field Name	Description	
	Value	**Meaning**
	CS_SAVEBITS	Saves the portion of the screen image that is obscured by a window.
	CS_VREDRAW	If the vertical size of a window changes, will redraw the entire window.
lpfnWndProc	Is a pointer to the window function that will carry out all of the tasks for the window.	
cbClsExtra	Defines the number of extra bytes to allocate for the WNDCLASS structure (usually is NULL).	
cbWndExtra	Defines the number of extra bytes to allocate for all additional structures created using this window class (usually is NULL).	
hInstance	Defines the instance of the application registering the window class.	
hIcon	Specifies the icon to be used whenever the window is minimized (usually is NULL).	
hCursor	Identical to hIcon, only it defines the cursor to be used for the window (usually is NULL).	
hbrBackground	Defines a brush to be used for painting the window's background. This can be the handle to a physical brush or it can be a color value. If a color value is used it must be one of the following standard system colors listed, and a 1 must be added to the chosen color:	

Table 21-3. *WNDCLASS Structure Field Definitions* (continued)

Field Name	Description
	COLOR_SCROLLBAR
	COLOR_BACKGROUND
	COLOR_ACTIVECAPTION
	COLOR_INACTIVECAPTION
	COLOR_MENU
	COLOR_WINDOW
	COLOR_WINDOWFRAME
	COLOR_MENUTEXT
	COLOR_WINDOWTEXT
	COLOR_CAPTIONTEXT
	COLOR_ACTIVEBORDER
	COLOR_INACTIVEBORDER
	COLOR_APPWORKSPACE
	COLOR_HIGHLIGHT
	COLOR_HIGHLIGHTTEXT
	COLOR_BTNFACE
	COLOR_BTNSHADOW
	COLOR_GRAYTEXT
	COLOR_BTNTEXT
	COLOR_INACTIVECAPTIONTEXT
	COLOR_BTNHIGHLIGHT
lpszMenuName	A long pointer to a null-terminated string, indicating the resource name of a menu (can be NULL).
lpszClassName	A long pointer to a null-terminated string, indicating the name of the window class. This name must be unique in order to avoid confusion when sharing a window class among applications.

Table 21-3.   *WNDCLASS Structure Field Definitions* (continued)

The listing that follows is from the SWP application and demonstrates how the WNDCLASS structure has been defined and initialized for Windows 95 and NT applications:

```
char szProgName[]="ProgName";
        .
        .
        .
  WNDCLASS wcApp;
        .
        .
        .
  wcApp.lpszClassName=szProgName;
  wcApp.hInstance     =hInst;
  wcApp.lpfnWndProc   =WndProc;
  wcApp.hCursor       =LoadCursor(NULL,IDC_ARROW);
  wcApp.hIcon         =0;
  wcApp.lpszMenuName =0;
  wcApp.hbrBackground=GetStockObject(WHITE_BRUSH);
  wcApp.style         =CS_HREDRAW|CS_VREDRAW;
  wcApp.cbClsExtra   =0;
  wcApp.cbWndExtra   =0;
  if (!RegisterClass (&wcApp))
      return 0;
```

Although the previous portion of code will also work with Windows 3.*x*, it would be wise to check for previous instances of the application in order to conserve memory resources. So if you are developing applications specifically for Windows 3.*x*, modify the code in the following manner:

```
char szProgName[]="ProgName";
        .
        .
        .
  WNDCLASS wcApp;
        .
        .
        .
  if (!hPreInst) {
    wcApp.lpszClassName=szProgName;
    wcApp.hInstance     =hInst;
    wcApp.lpfnWndProc   =WndProc;
    wcApp.hCursor       =LoadCursor(NULL,IDC_ARROW);
```

```
    wcApp.hIcon          =0;
    wcApp.lpszMenuName =0;
    wcApp.hbrBackground=GetStockObject(WHITE_BRUSH);
    wcApp.style          =CS_HREDRAW|CS_VREDRAW;
    wcApp.cbClsExtra     =0;
    wcApp.cbWndExtra     =0;
    if (!RegisterClass (&wcApp))
      return 0;
}
```

In this example, the template assigned a generic name, "ProgName", to the window's *wcApp.lpszClassName*. You should assign a unique class name for each new window class you define.

The second WNDCLASS field, *hInstance*, is assigned the value returned in *hInst* after **WinMain()** is invoked, indicating the current instance of the application. *lpfnWndProc* is assigned the pointer address to the window function that will carry out all of the window's tasks. For the SWP application, the function is called **WndProc()**. (Note that **WndProc()** is a user-defined function name, not a Windows function name.) The function must be prototyped before the assignment statement.

The *wcApp.hCursor* field is assigned a handle to the instance's cursor, which in this example is IDC_ARROW (representing the default tilted arrow cursor). This assignment is accomplished through a call to the **LoadCursor()** function. Because the SWP has no default icon, *wcApp.hIcon* is assigned a 0 value.

When *wcapp.lpszMenuName* is assigned a 0 value, Windows understands that the class has no menu. If it did, the menu would have a name and it would appear between quotation marks. The **GetStockObject()** function returns a handle to a brush used to paint the background color of the client area of windows created from this class. For the SWP application, the function returns a handle to one of Windows predefined brushes, WHITE_BRUSH.

The *wcApp.style* window class style has been set to CS_HREDRAW ored with CS_VREDRAW. All window class styles have identifiers that begin with CS- in windows.h or winuser.h. Each identifier represents a bit value. The bit-wise OR operation | is used to combine these bit flags. The two parameters used (CS_HREDRAW or CS_VREDRAW) instruct Windows to redraw the entire client area whenever the horizontal or vertical size of the window is changed.

The last two fields, *wcApp.cbClsExtra* and *wcApp.cbWndExtra,* are frequently assigned a 0 value. These fields are used to optionally indicate the count of extra bytes that may have been reserved at the end of the window class structure and the window data structure used for each window class.

You have probably noticed a couple of lines of code from the previous example that have not been explained, namely:

```
        .
        .
        .
    if (!RegisterClass (&wcApp))
      return 0;
```

This **if** statement registers the new window class. It does this by sending **RegisterClass()** a pointer to the window class structure. If Windows cannot register the window class, possibly due to lack of memory, **RegisterClass()** will return a 0, terminating the program.

Under Windows 95, the **RegisterClassEx()** function can be used in place of the **RegisterClass()** function. **RegisterClassEx()** allows the inclusion of the small Windows 95 icons via the WNDCLASSEX structure. This is the syntax for **RegisterClassEx()**:

```
ATOM RegisterClassEx(CONST WNDCLASSEX FAR *lpwcx);
```

Here, *lpwcx* is a pointer to the WNDCLASSEX structure. The WNDCLASSEX structure is similar to WNDCLASS, as you can see:

```
UINT     style;
WNDPROC  lpfnWndProc;
int      cbClsExtra;
int      cbWndExtra;
HANDLE   hInstance;
HICON    hIcon;
HCURSOR  hCursor;
HBRUSH   hbrBackground;
LPCTSTR  lpszMenuName;
LPCTSTR  lpszClassName;
HICON    hIconSm;
```

The only addition of the WNDCLASSEX structure is the *hIconSm* member, which is the handle of the small icon associated with a window class.

Creating a Window

Defining and then registering a window class has nothing to do with actually displaying a window in a Windows application. As mentioned, all windows are of some predefined and registered class type. Now that you know how to define and register a window class, you need to see the steps necessary in creating an actual window.

A window is created with a call to the Windows **CreateWindow()** function. Although the window class defines the general characteristics of a window which allow the same window class to be used for many different windows, the parameters to **CreateWindow()** specify more detailed information about the window.

The **CreateWindow()** function uses the information passed to it to describe the window's class, title, style, screen position, parent handle, menu handle, and instance handle. The call to **CreateWindow()** for the SWP application uses the following actual parameters:

```
hWnd=CreateWindow(szProgName,"A SWP Template",
                  WS_OVERLAPPEDWINDOW,CW_USEDEFAULT,
                  CW_USEDEFAULT,CW_USEDEFAULT,
                  CW_USEDEFAULT,(HWND)NULL,(HMENU)NULL,
                  (HANDLE)hInst,(LPSTR)NULL);
```

The first field *szProgName* defines the window's class, followed by the title to be used for the window. The style of the window is the third parameter, WS_OVERLAPPEDWINDOW. This standard Windows style represents a normal overlapped window with a caption bar, a system menu box, minimize and maximize icons, and a window frame.

The next six parameters (either CW_USEDEFAULT or NULL) represent the initial X and Y positions and X and Y size of the window, along with the parent window handle and window menu handle. Each of these fields has been assigned a default value. The *hInst* field contains the instance handle of the program, followed by no additional parameters (NULL).

CreateWindow() returns the handle of the newly created window if it was successful. Otherwise, the function returns NULL.

Showing and Updating a Window

You now know how to define and register a window class and create its instance. This, however, is still not enough to actually see the application's main window. To display a window, you need to make a call to the Windows **ShowWindow()** function. The following example is from the SWP application:

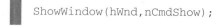

```
ShowWindow(hWnd,nCmdShow);
```

As described above, the *hWnd* parameter holds the handle of the window created by the call to **CreateWindow()**. The second parameter to **ShowWindow()**, *nCmdShow*, determines how the window is initially displayed (also referred to as the window's visibility state).

The value of *nCmdShow* can specify that the window be displayed as a normal window (SW_SHOWNORMAL) or can indicate several other possibilities. For example, substituting *nCmdShow* with the winuser.h constant SW_SHOWMINNOACTIVE causes the window to be drawn as an icon:

```
ShowWindow(hWnd,SW_SHOWMINNOACTIVE);
```

Other possibilities include SW_SHOWMAXIMIZED, which causes the window to be active and fill the entire display, along with its counterpart SW_SHOWMINIMIZED.

The last step in displaying a window requires a call to Windows' **UpdateWindow()** function:

```
UpdateWindow(hWnd);
```

If a call is made to the **ShowWindow()** function with a SW_SHOWNORMAL parameter, the function will erase the window's client area with the background brush specified in the window's class. It is the call to **UpdateWindow()** that causes the client area to be painted by generating a WM_PAINT message (WM_PAINT is explained later in the chapter).

Creating a Message Loop

Now that the application's window has been created and displayed, the program is ready to perform its main task: the processing of messages. Remember, Windows does not send input from the mouse or keyboard directly to an application. Instead, it places all input into the application's message queue. The message queue can contain messages generated by Windows or messages posted by other applications.

Once the call to **WinMain()** has taken care of creating and displaying the window, the application needs to create a message-processing loop. The most common approach is to use the standard C/C++ **while** loop:

```
while (GetMessage(&lpMsg,NULL,0,0))
{
  TranslateMessage(&lpMsg);
  DispatchMessage(&lpMmsg);
}
```

GetMessage()

A call to the **GetMessage()** function is used to retrieve the next message to be processed from the application's message queue. The **GetMessage()** function copies the message into the message structure pointed to by the long pointer, *lpMsg*, and sends it to the main body of the program.

The first NULL parameter instructs the function to retrieve any of the messages for any window that belongs to the application. The last two parameters (0,0) tell **GetMessage()** not to apply any message filters. Message filters can restrict retrieved messages to specific categories such as keystrokes or mouse moves. These filters are referred to as *wMsgFilterMin* and *wMsgFilterMax* and specify the numeric filter extremes to apply.

An application can normally return control to Windows any time before starting the message loop. For example, an application will normally make certain that all steps leading up to the message loop have executed properly. This can include making sure each window class is registered and has been created. However, once the message loop has been entered, only one message can terminate the loop. Whenever the message to be processed is WM_QUIT, the value returned is FALSE. This causes the processing to proceed to the main loop's closing routine. The WM_QUIT message is the only way for an application to get out of the message loop.

TranslateMessage()

Windows' **TranslateMessage()** function translates virtual-key messages into character messages. The function call is only required by applications that need to process character input from the keyboard. For example, this can be very useful for allowing the user to make menu selections without having to use the mouse.

Technically, the **TranslateMessage()** function creates an ASCII character message (WM_CHAR) from a WM_KEYDOWN and WM_KEYUP message. As long as this function is included in the message loop, the keyboard interface will be in effect.

DispatchMessage()

The **DispatchMessage()** function is used to send the current message to the correct window procedure. This function makes it easy to add additional windows and dialog boxes to your application, allowing **DispatchMessage()** to automatically route each message to the appropriate window procedure.

The Required Window Function

As you have learned, all Windows applications must include a **WinMain()** function and a Windows callback function. Because a Windows application never directly accesses any Windows functions, each application must make a request to Windows to carry out any specified operations.

NOTE: *Remember that a callback function is registered with Windows, and it is called back whenever Windows executes an operation on a window. The actual code size for the callback function will vary with each application. The window function itself may be very small, only processing one or two messages, or it may be large and complex.*

This concept of an operating system making a call to the application can be surprising to a beginning Windows programmer. The following code segment (minus application-specific statements) highlights the callback window function **WndProc()**, used in the SWP application:

```
LRESULT CALLBACK WndProc(HWND hWnd,UINT messg,
                         WPARAM wParam,LPARAM lParam)
{
  HDC hdc;
  PAINTSTRUCT ps;

  switch (messg)
  {
    case WM_PAINT:
      hdc=BeginPaint(hWnd,&ps);
//--------- your routines below ---------


         .

         .

         .


//--------- your routines above ---------
      ValidateRect(hWnd,NULL);
      EndPaint(hWnd,&ps);
      break;

    case WM_DESTROY:
      PostQuitMessage(0);
      break;

    default:
      return(DefWindowProc(hWnd,messg,wParam,lParam));
  }
  return(0);
}
```

One subtle detail that must not be overlooked is that Windows expects the name referenced by the *wcApp.lpfnWndProc* field of the window class structure definition to match the name used for the callback function. **WndProc()** will be the name used for the callback function for all subsequent windows created from this window class.

The following code segment reviews the placement and assignment of the callback function's name within the window class structure:

```
            .
            .
            .
    wcApp.lpszClassName=szProgName;
    wcApp.hInstance     =hInst;
    wcApp.lpfnWndProc   =WndProc;
            .
            .
            .
```

Windows has several hundred different messages it can send to the window function. All of them are labeled with identifiers that begin with "WM_". These identifiers are known as symbolic constants. The **#define** preprocessor statement is used to associate unique numeric values with each easily understood label. These symbolic constants are much easier to read and convey more information than their numeric counterparts. Table 21-4 contains a partial list of "WM_" messages found in the windows.h or winuser.h header files.

Message	Value
#define WM_ACTIVATE	0x0006
#define WM_ACTIVATEAPP	0x001C
#define WM_ASKCBFORMATNAME	0x030C
#define WM_CANCELMODE	0x001F
#define WM_CHANGECBCHAIN	0x030D
#define WM_CHAR	0x0102
#define WM_CHARTOITEM	0x002F
#define WM_CHILDACTIVATE	0x0022
#define WM_CLEAR	0x0303
#define WM_CLOSE	0x0010

Table 21-4.   *WM_ Windows Messages Defined in winuser.h*

Message	Value
#define WM_COMMAND	0x0111
#define WM_COMMNOTIFY	0x0044
#define WM_COMPACTING	0x0041
#define WM_COMPAREITEM	0x0039
#define WM_COPY	0x0301
#define WM_CREATE	0x0001
#define WM_CTLCOLORBTN	0x0135
#define WM_CTLCOLORDLG	0x0136
#define WM_CTLCOLOREDIT	0x0133
#define WM_CTLCOLORLISTBOX	0x0134
#define WM_CTLCOLORMSGBOX	0x0132
#define WM_CTLCOLORSCROLLBAR	0x0137
#define WM_CTLCOLORSTATIC	0x0138
#define WM_CUT	0x0300
#define WM_DEADCHAR	0x0103
#define WM_DELETEITEM	0x002D
#define WM_DESTROY	0x0002
#define WM_DESTROYCLIPBOARD	0x0307
#define WM_DEVMODECHANGE	0x001B
#define WM_DRAWCLIPBOARD	0x0308
#define WM_DRAWITEM	0x002B
#define WM_DROPFILES	0x0233
#define WM_ENABLE	0x000A
#define WM_ENDSESSION	0x0016
#define WM_ENTERIDLE	0x0121
#define WM_ERASEBKGND	0x0014
#define WM_FONTCHANGE	0x001D
#define WM_FULLSCREEN	0x003A

Table 21-4. *WM_ Windows Messages Defined in winuser.h* (continued)

Message	Value
#define WM_GETDLGCODE	0x0087
#define WM_GETFONT	0x0031
#define WM_GETHOTKEY	0x0033
#define WM_GETTEXT	0x000D
#define WM_GETTEXTLENGTH	0x000E
#define WM_HOTKEY	0x0312
#define WM_HOTKEYEVENT	0x0045
#define WM_HSCROLL	0x0114
#define WM_HSCROLLCLIPBOARD	0x030E
#define WM_ICONERASEBKGND	0x0027
#define WM_INITDIALOG	0x0110
#define WM_INITMENU	0x0116
#define WM_INITMENUPOPUP	0x0117
#define WM_KEYDOWN	0x0100
#define WM_KEYFIRST	0x0100
#define WM_KEYLAST	0x0108
#define WM_KEYUP	0x0101
#define WM_KILLFOCUS	0x0008
#define WM_LBUTTONDBLCLK	0x0203
#define WM_LBUTTONDOWN	0x0201
#define WM_LBUTTONUP	0x0202
#define WM_MBUTTONDBLCLK	0x0209
#define WM_MBUTTONDOWN	0x0207
#define WM_MBUTTONUP	0x0208
#define WM_MDIACTIVATE	0x0222
#define WM_MDICASCADE	0x0227
#define WM_MDICREATE	0x0220
#define WM_MDIDESTROY	0x0221

Table 21-4.   *WM_ Windows Messages Defined in winuser.h* (continued)

Message	Value
#define WM_MDIGETACTIVE	0x0229
#define WM_MDIICONARRANGE	0x0228
#define WM_MDIMAXIMIZE	0x0225
#define WM_MDINEXT	0x0224
#define WM_MDIREFRESHMENU	0x0234
#define WM_MDIRESTORE	0x0223
#define WM_MDISETMENU	0x0230
#define WM_MDITILE	0x0226
#define WM_MEASUREITEM	0x002C
#define WM_MENUCHAR	0x0120
#define WM_MENUSELECT	0x011F
#define WM_MOUSEACTIVATE	0x0021
#define WM_MOUSEFIRST	0x0200
#define WM_MOUSELAST	0x0209
#define WM_MOUSEMOVE	0x0200
#define WM_MOVE	0x0003
#define WM_NCACTIVATE	0x0086
#define WM_NCCALCSIZE	0x0083
#define WM_NCCREATE	0x0081
#define WM_NCDESTROY	0x0082
#define WM_NCHITTEST	0x0084
#define WM_NCLBUTTONDBLCLK	0x00A3
#define WM_NCLBUTTONDOWN	0x00A1
#define WM_NCLBUTTONUP	0x00A2
#define WM_NCMBUTTONDBLCLK	0x00A9
#define WM_NCMBUTTONDOWN	0x00A7
#define WM_NCMBUTTONUP	0x00A8

Table 21-4. *WM_ Windows Messages Defined in winuser.h* (continued)

Message	Value
#define WM_NCMOUSEMOVE	0x00A0
#define WM_NCPAINT	0x0085
#define WM_NCRBUTTONDBLCLK	0x00A6
#define WM_NCRBUTTONDOWN	0x00A4
#define WM_NCRBUTTONUP	0x00A5
#define WM_NEXTDLGCTL	0x0028
#define WM_NULL	0x0000
#define WM_OTHERWINDOWCREATED	0x0042
#define WM_OTHERWINDOWDESTROYED	0x0043
#define WM_PAINT	0x000F
#define WM_PAINTCLIPBOARD	0x0309
#define WM_PAINTICON	0x0026
#define WM_PALETTECHANGED	0x0311
#define WM_PALETTEISCHANGING	0x0310
#define WM_PARENTNOTIFY	0x0210
#define WM_PASTE	0x0302
#define WM_POWER	0x0048
#define WM_QUERYDRAGICON	0x0037
#define WM_QUERYENDSESSION	0x0011
#define WM_QUERYNEWPALETTE	0x030F
#define WM_QUERYOPEN	0x0013
#define WM_QUEUESYNC	0x0023
#define WM_QUIT	0x0012
#define WM_RBUTTONDBLCLK	0x0206
#define WM_RBUTTONDOWN	0x0204
#define WM_RBUTTONUP	0x0205
#define WM_RENDERALLFORMATS	0x0306

Table 21-4.   *WM_ Windows Messages Defined in winuser.h* (continued)

Message	Value
#define WM_RENDERFORMAT	0x0305
#define WM_SETCURSOR	0x0020
#define WM_SETFOCUS	0x0007
#define WM_SETFONT	0x0030
#define WM_SETHOTKEY	0x0032
#define WM_SETREDRAW	0x000B
#define WM_SETTEXT	0x000C
#define WM_SHOWWINDOW	0x0018
#define WM_SIZE	0x0005
#define WM_SIZECLIPBOARD	0x030B
#define WM_SPOOLERSTATUS	0x002A
#define WM_SYSCHAR	0x0106
#define WM_SYSCOLORCHANGE	0x0015
#define WM_SYSCOMMAND	0x0112
#define WM_SYSDEADCHAR	0x0107
#define WM_SYSKEYDOWN	0x0104
#define WM_SYSKEYUP	0x0105
#define WM_TIMECHANGE	0x001E
#define WM_TIMER	0x0113
#define WM_UNDO	0x0304
#define WM_VKEYTOITEM	0x002E
#define WM_VSCROLL	0x0115
#define WM_VSCROLLCLIPBOARD	0x030A
#define WM_WINDOWPOSCHANGED	0x0047
#define WM_WINDOWPOSCHANGING	0x0046
#define WM_WININICHANGE	0x001A

Table 21-4. *WM_ Windows Messages Defined in winuser.h* (continued)

Windows divides this long list of identifiers into several different categories, including window creation, resizing, moving, iconization, menu item selection, mouse manipulation of scroll bars, client area repainting, and destroying a window.

Notice that the **WndProc()** callback function uses the LRESULT CALLBACK calling convention. Like many Windows functions, the first parameter to **WndProc()** is *hWnd*. *hWnd* contains the handle to the window that Windows will send the message. Because it is possible for one window function to process messages for several windows created from the same window class, this handle is used by the window function to determine which window is receiving the message.

The second parameter to the function, *messg*, specifies the actual message being processed as defined in the windows.h or winuser.h header files. Both of the last two parameters, *wParam*, and *lParam*, are involved with any additional information needed to process each specific message. Frequently, the value returned in these parameters is NULL, meaning they can be ignored; at other times they contain a two-byte value and a pointer or two word values.

The **WndProc()** function continues by defining several variables: *hdc*, for the display context handle, and *ps*, a PAINTSTRUCT structure needed to store client area information. The main purpose of the callback function is to examine the type of message it is about to process and then select the appropriate action to be taken. This selection process usually takes the form of a standard C/C++ switch statement.

The WM_PAINT Message

The first message **WndProc()** will process is WM_PAINT. This message calls the Windows function **BeginPaint()**, which prepares the specified window (*hWnd*) for painting and fills a PAINTSTRUCT (&*ps*) with information about the area to be painted. The **BeginPaint()** function also returns a handle to the device context for the given window.

The device context comes equipped with a default pen, brush, and font. The default pen is black, one pixel wide, and draws a solid line. The default brush is white with a solid brush pattern. The default font is the system font. The device context is very important, because all of the display functions used by Windows applications require a handle to the device context.

Because Windows is a multitasking environment, it becomes quite possible for one application to display its dialog box over another application's client area. This creates a problem whenever the dialog box is closed, namely a hole on the screen where the dialog box was displayed. Windows takes care of this problem by sending the application a WM_PAINT message. In this case, Windows is requesting that the application update its client area.

Except for the first WM_PAINT message, which is sent by a call to the **UpdateWindow()** function in **WinMain()**, additional WM_PAINT messages are sent under the following conditions:

■   When a window needs resizing.

- When forcing a WM_PAINT message by calling the **InvalidateRect()** or **InvalidateRgn()** functions.

- When the application's client area needs repainting due to a recently closed menu or dialog box that has hidden a portion of a client area.

- When using scroll bar functions.

Whenever a portion of an application's client area has been corrupted by the overlay of a dialog box or menu, that part of the client area is marked as invalid. Windows manages the redrawing of the client area by keeping track of the diagonal coordinates of this invalid rectangle. The presence of an invalid rectangle prompts Windows to send a WM_PAINT message.

Windows is extremely efficient in how it processes multiple invalidated rectangles. Should the execution of statements invalidate several portions of the client area, Windows will adjust the invalid rectangle coordinates to encapsulate all invalid regions. Therefore, it sends only one WM_PAINT, rather than one for each invalid region.

An application can force a WM_PAINT message by making a call to the **InvalidateRect()** function which marks the application's client area as being invalid. By calling the **GetUpdateRect()** function, an application can obtain the coordinates of the invalid rectangle. A subsequent call to the **ValidateRect()** function validates any rectangular region in the client area and removes any pending WM_PAINT messages.

The **WndProc()** function ends its processing of the WM_PAINT message by calling the **EndPaint()** function. This function is called whenever the application is finished outputting information to the client area. It tells Windows that the application has finished processing all paint messages and that it can now remove the display context.

The WM_DESTROY Message

When the user selects the Close option from the application's system menu, Windows posts a WM_DESTROY message to the application's message queue. The program terminates after retrieving this message.

The DefWindowProc() Function

The **DefWindowProc()** function call in the default section of **WndProc()**'s switch statement is needed to empty the application's message queue of any unrecognized (and therefore unprocessed) messages. This function ensures that all of the messages posted to the application are processed.

Why Use Project Files?

Compilers, such as your Borland C/C++ compiler, used to rely on command-line make files when compiling and linking applications. These make files were difficult to understand and to create. Fortunately, the Windows graphics environment has helped compiler manufactures produce more user-friendly compilers.

The Borland C++ compiler is fully integrated with the Windows GDI environment. From within this integrated environment, Windows applications can be written, compiled, debugged, and executed.

The key to success, when working within the integrated environments, is to properly configure and create a project file. Borland's project files use an .ide file extension. In the following section, you'll learn specific tips for creating project files.

Creating Project Files

First create and write your application code. When the application is completed, select the File menu and chose the New menu item then select Project... from the supplied list of options, as shown in Figure 21-1.

This process will invoke the New Target dialog box, shown in Figure 21-2.

Here you may set the project's location and name. Borland uses the .ide file extension for projects. This example will be built for the Win32 platform and use the GUI model. Select the libraries shown earlier in Figure 21-2. Now, click on Advanced

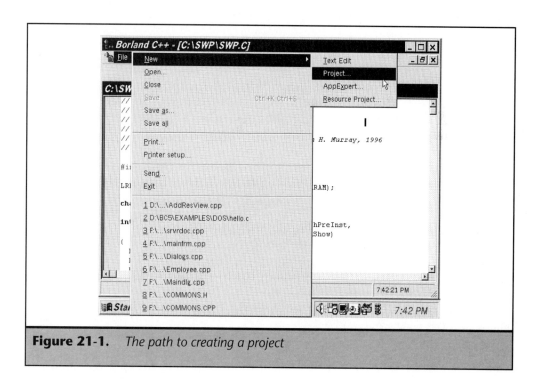

Figure 21-1. *The path to creating a project*

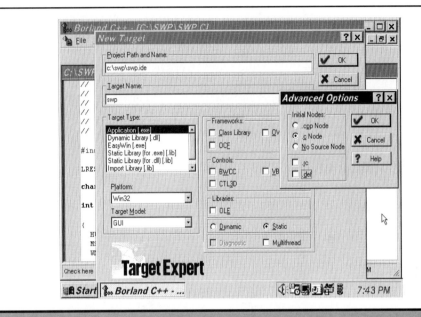

Figure 21-2.   *The New Target dialog box allows project options to be set*

when the previous selections are complete. From the Advanced Options dialog box, also shown in Figure 21-2, it is possible to change whether the application will be built from a C or C++ source code file. This project does not use a resource script file (.rc) or a module definition file (.def), so those options are not checked.

> **NOTE:** *When building 16-bit applications for Windows 3.x a module definition file is needed. Your Borland C++ compiler will prompt you in these cases and suggest the use of the default module definition file. The default choice is satisfactory.*

Click on the OK buttons in the dialog boxes to return to the editor. From the Project menu, select the Build all menu item, as shown in Figure 21-3. This selection will build the executable file for this project.

Every Windows application in this book will need a project file. All project files are built in essentially the same manner. As applications become more complicated, it will be possible to add additional items to the project's file list. These additional items can include multiple source files and resources.

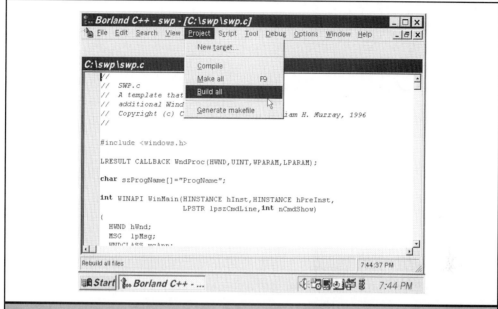

Figure 21-3. *The executable file can be built by selecting the Build all menu item from the Project menu's options*

The Executable (swp.exe)

The Build all menu item, discussed in the previous section, invokes the compiler, the resource editor (if needed), and the linker. Together they will create an executable file for your application.

If the build process goes well, several new files, including swp.obj and swp.exe, will appear on the hard disk. Execute the swp.exe file from within the Borland C++ compiler by using the Debug menu and selecting the Run menu item. Figure 21-4 shows how the program looks when it is executed under Windows 95.

Use the Template Again

Frequently it is important to have an application determine which operating system it is operating under. In the next application, the SWP template application will be modified to return information on the operating system. This program is named OpSys.c. OpSys is a mnemonic for Operating System.

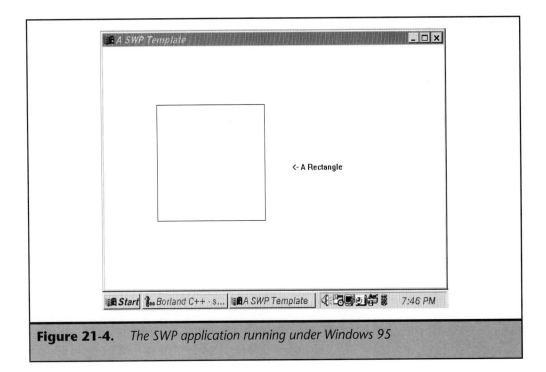

Figure 21-4.   *The SWP application running under Windows 95*

The following listing contains the complete code for the OpSys.c application. The code that differs from SWP code is shown in bold. If you have a copy of SWP.c, just edit the code and rename the application OpSys.c.

```
//
//  OpSys.c
//  What Operating System is this?
//  Copyright (c) Chris H. Pappas and William H. Murray, 1996
//

#include <windows.h>
#include <stdio.h>
#include <string.h>

LRESULT CALLBACK WndProc(HWND,UINT,WPARAM,LPARAM);

char szProgName[]="ProgName";
```

```
int WINAPI WinMain(HINSTANCE hInst,HINSTANCE hPreInst,
                   LPSTR lpszCmdLine,int nCmdShow)
{
  HWND hWnd;
  MSG  lpMsg;
  WNDCLASS wcApp;

  wcApp.lpszClassName=szProgName;
  wcApp.hInstance    =hInst;
  wcApp.lpfnWndProc  =WndProc;
  wcApp.hCursor      =LoadCursor(NULL,IDC_ARROW);
  wcApp.hIcon        =0;
  wcApp.lpszMenuName =0;
  wcApp.hbrBackground=GetStockObject(WHITE_BRUSH);
  wcApp.style        =CS_HREDRAW|CS_VREDRAW;
  wcApp.cbClsExtra   =0;
  wcApp.cbWndExtra   =0;
  if (!RegisterClass (&wcApp))
    return 0;

  hWnd=CreateWindow(szProgName,"Operating Systems",
                    WS_OVERLAPPEDWINDOW,CW_USEDEFAULT,
                    CW_USEDEFAULT,CW_USEDEFAULT,
                    CW_USEDEFAULT,(HWND)NULL,(HMENU)NULL,
                    (HANDLE)hInst,(LPSTR)NULL);
  ShowWindow(hWnd,nCmdShow);
  UpdateWindow(hWnd);
  while (GetMessage(&lpMsg,NULL,0,0)) {
    TranslateMessage(&lpMsg);
    DispatchMessage(&lpMsg);
  }
  return(lpMsg.wParam);
}

LRESULT CALLBACK WndProc(HWND hWnd,UINT messg,
                         WPARAM wParam,LPARAM lParam)
{
  HDC hdc;
  PAINTSTRUCT ps;
  DWORD dwVersion;
  char szVersion[30];
```

```
      dwVersion = GetVersion();

    switch (messg)
    {
      case WM_PAINT:
        hdc=BeginPaint(hWnd,&ps);
//--------- your routines below ---------

        if (dwVersion < 0x80000000) {
          wsprintf(szVersion, "Windows NT Version %u.%u",
                  (LOBYTE(LOWORD(dwVersion))),
                  (HIBYTE(LOWORD(dwVersion)))));
          TextOut(hdc,300,300,szVersion,strlen(szVersion));
        } else if (LOBYTE(LOWORD(dwVersion)) <= 3) {
          wsprintf(szVersion, "Windows 3.x Version %u.%u",
                  (LOBYTE(LOWORD(dwVersion))),
                  (HIBYTE(LOWORD(dwVersion)))));
          TextOut(hdc,300,300,szVersion,strlen(szVersion));
        } else {
          wsprintf(szVersion, "Windows 95 Version %u.%u",
                  (LOBYTE(LOWORD(dwVersion))),
                  (HIBYTE(LOWORD(dwVersion)))));
          TextOut(hdc,300,300,szVersion,strlen(szVersion));
        }

//--------- your routines above ---------
        ValidateRect(hWnd,NULL);
        EndPaint(hWnd,&ps);
        break;

      case WM_DESTROY:
        PostQuitMessage(0);
        break;

      default:
        return(DefWindowProc(hWnd,messg,wParam,lParam));
    }
    return(0);
}
```

This application will need a project file similar to the one you created for the previous SWP application.

The trick to this application is obtaining the version information from the Windows function **GetVersion()**. This function returns a DWORD value. If the MSB (most significant bit) is a zero, the operating system is Windows NT. Thus, a check is made to see if that bit is not set with the hexadecimal number 0x80000000. The major release version number, such as the "3" in Windows 3.1, is contained in the LOBYTE of the LOWORD. The minor version number, such as the "1" in Windows 3.1, is contained in the HIBYTE or the LOWORD. How did we know this? We used the Help utility supplied with the Borland C++ compiler to learn more about this function. Give it a try on your system.

Now, build the OpSys.c application. If the build is successful, execute the application. If you are running under Windows 95, you should see a screen similar to the one shown in Figure 21-5.

In the Next Chapter...

Now that you understand the basic components of a Windows application and how to navigate yourself through all of the required files and Borland C++ compiler options, it's time to add some functionality to the program.

In the next chapter you will learn how to add several resources to an application.

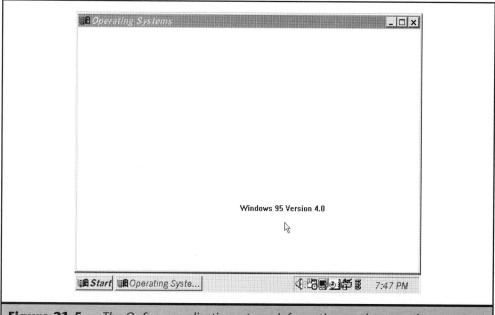

Figure 21-5.   *The OpSys.c application returns information on the operating system*

Chapter Twenty-Two

Adding Resources to Windows Programs

In this chapter, you'll learn how to add menu and dialog box resources to two practical Windows applications. The first application will draw a scientific waveform, and the second will allow you to plot a line chart.

Ideas and concepts are often expressed in a plotted format. Engineers, mathematicians, and scientists use charts and graphs, just as business professionals do, for this purpose. Business data is frequently plotted to familiar pie, bar, and line charts. Sometimes chart data is generated by an equation while at other times the data points are entered by the user. The first application will use a mathematical equation to generate the data points, and the second application will allow the user to enter data points. In both cases, Windows resources will help make the application more user interactive.

View both of the applications in this chapter as models you can develop further. They were designed to operate under the Windows 3.*x*, Windows 95, and Windows NT platforms. They are complete in themselves but are ready for your individual touch. Study the code for each application, learn what it can do, and then customize the code to suit your needs.

A Scientific Waveform

An interesting scientific application involves the fairly complicated calculation of a Fourier series. The French mathematician Baron Jean Baptiste Joseph Fourier (1768-1830) observed that almost any periodic waveform can be constructed by simply adding the correct combinations of sine wave harmonics together. His results produce a wide variety of waveforms, from square to triangular. Electrical engineers are often interested in square wave reproduction, because square waves are made from a fundamental sine wave and its associated overtones. The quality of amplifiers and other communication devices depends on how well they can reproduce these signals. (For a more detailed treatment of the Fourier series, refer to college-level physics or electrical engineering textbooks.) Fourier's formal equation is usually expressed this way:

$$y = A + A1(\sin wt) + A2(\sin 2wt) + A3(\sin 3wt) + A4(\sin 4wt)...$$

Periodic waveforms can include odd or even harmonics only; in others, all terms are included. And in some periodic waveforms, the signs alternate between + and - for adjacent terms. This example constructs a square wave by adding the odd harmonic terms in a Fourier series together. The more terms that are used in the series, the more the final result will approach a precise square wave. For a square wave, the general Fourier series equation becomes:

$$y = (\sin wt) + (1/3)(\sin 3wt) + (1/5)(\sin 5wt) + (1/7)(\sin 7wt)...$$

Notice that only odd harmonics will contribute to the final result. Notice also, from the equation, that if only one harmonic is chosen, the result will be a sine wave. Also notice that each successive term uses a fractional multiplier—in other words, each successively higher harmonic affects the waveform less and less.

In order to appreciate what this application is about to accomplish, remember that each term in a Fourier series will be calculated separately by the program, with the sum of these individual terms being continuously updated. Therefore, if you ask it to draw 2000 harmonics, 2000 separate sine values will be scaled, calculated, and added together to form a single point for the waveform. But this must be repeated for each point that is to be plotted on the window. Therefore, 2000 calculations times 360 points = 720,000 (one point for each degree in a full sine wave) calculations. How fast your application can calculate the points depends on two factors: the clock speed of the microprocessor and whether a coprocessor is present in your computer. If you are running this application on a 16-megahertz 80386 computer without a math coprocessor, expect rather sluggish results. However, if you are running this on a 80486 or Pentium computer at clock rates above 90 megahertz, you can expect the calculations to be almost instantaneous.

This application uses a header file and resource script file. Here is the code for the fourier.h header file:

```
#define IDM_FOUR    200
#define IDM_EXIT    201

#define IDD_TITLE   300
#define IDD_TERMS   301
```

Techniques for designing menus and dialog boxes were discussed in Chapter 20. When these items are designed, a resource script file (a text file) is generated to describe the graphical results from the Borland resource editors.

This application requires a simple menu and dialog box. Here is the resource script file, fourier.rc, generated for this application:

```
#include "windows.h"
#include "fourier.h"

FourierMenu MENU
{
  POPUP "Data Entry"
  {
    MENUITEM "Fourier Data...",   IDM_FOUR
    MENUITEM "Exit",              IDM_EXIT
  }
```

```
}

FourDiaBox DIALOG 74,21,142,70
  STYLE DS_MODALFRAME|WS_POPUP|WS_VISIBLE|
        WS_CAPTION|WS_SYSMENU
  CAPTION "Scientific Information"
  FONT 8, "MS Sans Serif"
{
  LTEXT "Title: ",-1,6,5,28,8
  CONTROL "Title ",IDD_TITLE,"edit",
          WS_BORDER|WS_TABSTOP,
          33,1,106,12
  LTEXT "Number of terms: ",-1,6,23,70,8
  CONTROL "1",IDD_TERMS,"edit",WS_BORDER|WS_TABSTOP,
          76,18,32,12
  PUSHBUTTON "Okay",IDOK,25,52,24,14
  PUSHBUTTON "Cancel",IDCANCEL,89,53,28,14
}
```

The source code for this example, fourier.c, follows the programming guidelines from previous applications. Here is the source code for fourier.c:

```
//
//  fourier.c
//  Plotting a scientific waveform.
//  Copyright (c) Chris H. Pappas and William H. Murray, 1996
//

#include <windows.h>
#include "fourier.h"
#include <string.h>
#include <math.h>

LRESULT CALLBACK WndProc(HWND,UINT,WPARAM,LPARAM);
BOOL CALLBACK FourDiaProc(HWND,UINT,WPARAM,LPARAM);

char szProgName[]="ProgName";
char szApplName[]="FourierMenu";
char mytitle[20]="Title";
int  nterms=1;
```

```
int WINAPI WinMain(HINSTANCE hInst,HINSTANCE hPreInst,
                   LPSTR lpszCmdLine,int nCmdShow)
{
  HWND hWnd;
  MSG  lpMsg;
  WNDCLASS wcApp;
  if (!hPreInst) {
    wcApp.lpszClassName=szProgName;
    wcApp.hInstance     =hInst;
    wcApp.lpfnWndProc   =WndProc;
    wcApp.hCursor       =LoadCursor(NULL,IDC_ARROW);
    wcApp.hIcon         =NULL;
    wcApp.lpszMenuName =szApplName;
    wcApp.hbrBackground=GetStockObject(WHITE_BRUSH);
    wcApp.style         =CS_HREDRAW|CS_VREDRAW;
    wcApp.cbClsExtra   =0;
    wcApp.cbWndExtra   =0;
    if (!RegisterClass (&wcApp))
      return 0;
  }
  hWnd=CreateWindow(szProgName,"A Scientific Waveform",
                    WS_OVERLAPPEDWINDOW,CW_USEDEFAULT,
                    CW_USEDEFAULT,CW_USEDEFAULT,
                    CW_USEDEFAULT,(HWND)NULL,(HMENU)NULL,
                    (HANDLE)hInst,(LPSTR)NULL);
  ShowWindow(hWnd,nCmdShow);
  UpdateWindow(hWnd);
  while (GetMessage(&lpMsg,NULL,0,0)) {
    TranslateMessage(&lpMsg);
    DispatchMessage(&lpMsg);
  }
  return(lpMsg.wParam);
}


BOOL CALLBACK FourDiaProc(HWND hdlg,UINT messg,
                          WPARAM wParam,LPARAM lParam)
{
switch (messg)
  {
```

```
      case WM_INITDIALOG:
        return FALSE;
      case WM_COMMAND:
        switch (LOWORD(wParam))
        {
          case IDOK:
            GetDlgItemText(hdlg,IDD_TITLE,mytitle,80);
            nterms=GetDlgItemInt(hdlg,IDD_TERMS,NULL,0);
            EndDialog(hdlg,TRUE);
            break;
          case IDCANCEL:
            EndDialog(hdlg,FALSE);
            break;
          default:
            return FALSE;
        }
        break;
      default:
        return FALSE;
  }
  return TRUE;
}

LRESULT CALLBACK WndProc(HWND hWnd,UINT messg,
                         WPARAM wParam,LPARAM lParam)
{
  HDC hdc;
  PAINTSTRUCT ps;
  static int xClientView,yClientView;
  static FARPROC fpfnFourDiaProc;
  static HWND hInst;
  double y1,y2,yp;
  int i,j,ltitle;
  int angle;

  switch (messg)
  {
    case WM_SIZE:
      xClientView=LOWORD(lParam);
      yClientView=HIWORD(lParam);
      break;
```

```
      case WM_CREATE:
        hInst=((LPCREATESTRUCT) lParam)->hInstance;
        fpfnFourDiaProc=MakeProcInstance((FARPROC)FourDiaProc,
                                         hInst);
        break;

      case WM_COMMAND:
        switch (LOWORD(wParam))
        {
        case IDM_FOUR:
          #ifdef _WIN32    // Windows 95 & NT
            DialogBox((HINSTANCE) GetModuleHandle (NULL),
                      "FourDiaBox",hWnd,
                      FourDiaProc);
          #else
            DialogBox(hInst,"FourDiaBox",hWnd,fpfnFourDiaProc);
            FreeProcInstance(fpfnFourDiaProc);
          #endif
          InvalidateRect(hWnd,NULL,TRUE);
          UpdateWindow(hWnd);
          break;
        case IDM_EXIT:
          SendMessage(hWnd,WM_CLOSE,0,0L);
          break;
        default:
          break;
        }
      break;

      case WM_PAINT:
        hdc=BeginPaint(hWnd,&ps);
//--------- your routines below ---------

        SetMapMode(hdc,MM_ISOTROPIC);
        SetWindowExtEx(hdc,600,600,NULL);
        SetViewportExtEx(hdc,xClientView,-yClientView,NULL);
        SetViewportOrgEx(hdc,xClientView/8,yClientView/2,NULL);

        angle=0;
        yp=0.0;
```

```
        // draw x & y coordinate axes
        MoveToEx(hdc,0,200,NULL);
        LineTo(hdc,0,-200);
        MoveToEx(hdc,0,0,NULL);
        LineTo(hdc,450,0);
        MoveToEx(hdc,0,0,NULL);

        for (i=0; i<=450; i++) {
          for (j=1; j<=nterms; j++) {
            y1=(200.0/((2.0*j)-1.0));
            y2=sin((((j*2.0)-1.0)*0.01397*angle);
            yp+=y1*y2;
          }
          LineTo(hdc,i,(int) yp);
          yp-=yp;
          angle++;
        }

        ltitle=strlen(mytitle);
        TextOut(hdc,200-(ltitle*8/2),250,mytitle,ltitle);

//--------- your routines above ---------
        ValidateRect(hWnd,NULL);
        EndPaint(hWnd,&ps);
        break;

    case WM_DESTROY:
        PostQuitMessage(0);
        break;

    default:
        return(DefWindowProc(hWnd,messg,wParam,lParam));
    }
  return(0);
}
```

This application will compile as a 16- or 32-bit application and execute properly under the Windows 3.*x*, Windows 95, or Windows NT environments.

In addition to the header, resource script, and source code files, you will need to create a project file for the Borland C++ compiler. Additionally, for 16-bit builds you will have to edit the default module definition file and name the two dialog box procedures under the EXPORTS statement.

A Closer Look at the Application

The request for the data entry dialog box is made through the menu. A simple **case** statement is used to check for IDM_FOUR. The function is responsible for drawing the dialog box on the screen. This particular application will work for 16-bit and 32-bit applications, as you can see from the following partial listing:

```
case WM_COMMAND:
      switch (LOWORD(wParam))
      {
      case IDM_FOUR:
        #ifdef _WIN32    // Windows 95 & NT
          DialogBox((HINSTANCE) GetModuleHandle (NULL),
                   "FourDiaBox",hWnd,
                   FourDiaProc);
        #else
          DialogBox(hInst,"FourDiaBox",hWnd,fpfnFourDiaProc);
          FreeProcInstance(fpfnFourDiaProc);
        #endif
        InvalidateRect(hWnd,NULL,TRUE);
        UpdateWindow(hWnd);
        break;
        .
        .
        .
```

FourDiaProc() processes returned dialog box information when a WM_COMMAND message is received. The WM_COMMAND message can be generated, for example, by selecting the OK button in the data entry dialog box.

```
BOOL CALLBACK FourDiaProc(HWND hdlg,UINT messg,
                          WPARAM wParam,LPARAM lParam)
      .
      .
      .
  case WM_COMMAND:
    switch (LOWORD(wParam))
    {
      case IDOK:
        GetDlgItemText(hdlg,IDD_TITLE,mytitle,80);
        nterms=GetDlgItemInt(hdlg,IDD_TERMS,NULL,0);
        EndDialog(hdlg,TRUE);
```

```
      break;
    case IDCANCEL:
      EndDialog(hdlg,FALSE);
      break;
    default:
      return FALSE;
         .
         .
         .
```

In this example, we are interested in two items: the label for the scientific waveform and the number of terms to plot for the scientific waveform. Can you see where these values are returned in the previous listing?

The actual dialog box is shown in Figure 22-1.

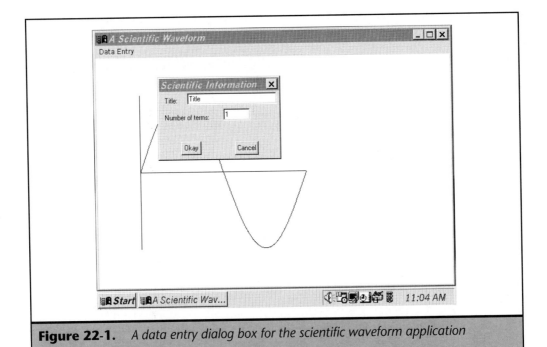

Figure 22-1. *A data entry dialog box for the scientific waveform application*

Now, return to the complete listing, fourier.c. Examine the code that is processed when a WM_PAINT message is received. The actual Fourier calculations are made within two **for** loops and drawn with the **LineTo()** function:

```
for (i=0; i<=450; i++) {
    for (j=1; j<=nterms; j++) {
        y1=(200.0/((2.0*j)-1.0));
        y2=sin(((j*2.0)-1.0)*0.01397*angle);
        yp+=y1*y2;
    }
    LineTo(hdc,i,(int) yp);
    yp-=yp;
    angle++;
}
```

The outer loop, using the *i* index, increments the horizontal plotting position across the window. This value represents the scaled angle for one complete cycle, as in the preceding example. The inner loop, using the *j* index, calculates the appropriate number of Fourier values for each angle. For example, if *i* is pointing to a value representing 40 degrees and the number of Fourier terms is 20, then 20 calculations will be made in the inner loop for each *i* value. Because this deals with a simple series, those 20 values are algebraically added to form the resulting Fourier value. Remember, if the number of Fourier terms is 2000, then 2000 values must be calculated and added together for each *i* value.

Figure 22-2 shows a sine wave produced by using the dialog box to select one harmonic.

Figure 22-3 shows a 200-harmonic plot.

The greater number of harmonics drawn, the more the scientific plot will approach a square wave.

Why not change the Fourier equation so that you plot just even harmonics or both odd and even harmonics? You might be surprised at the results.

The Line Chart

Line charts are very popular in business for plotting trends in various areas. It is typical to see line charts with one or multiple lines showing sales figures, products manufactured, employment rates, and so on. This application will allow the user to enter numerous (positive) data points (x,y pairs) from a dialog box. The data is captured as a string, parsed, and then scaled to the plot dimensions. The maximum Y

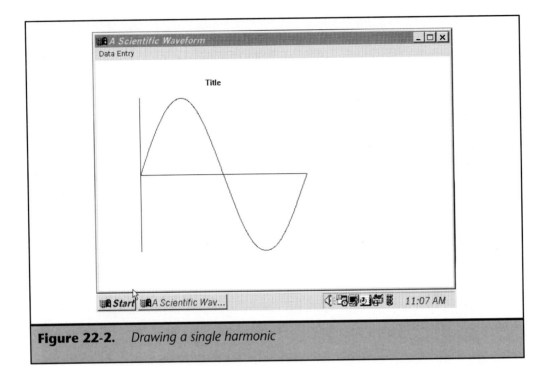

Figure 22-2. *Drawing a single harmonic*

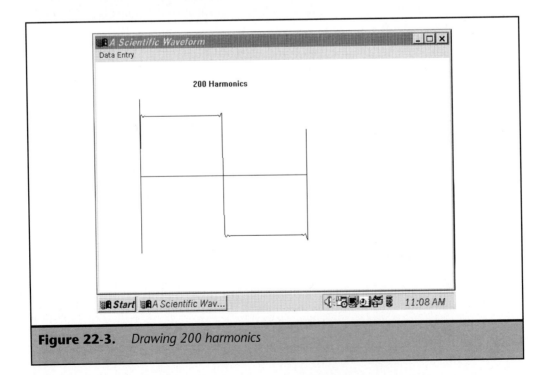

Figure 22-3. *Drawing 200 harmonics*

value will be plotted at the top of the chart and the maximum X value at the extreme right of the chart. The data entry dialog box is shown in Figure 22-4.

The maximum values for the x and y data points are printed on their respective axes. The line chart application uses tick marks on both the X and Y axes. Three labels can be added to this application, as was done in the bar chart application. At each point plotted on the chart, a small plus (+) symbol is drawn to represent the point. The **LineTo()** function then draws a line between each of these symbols.

This application could be changed to permit the use of negative numbers. If you make this change, data could be plotted into all four quadrants.

Here is a listing of the line.h header file:

```
#define IDM_ABOUT    200
#define IDM_INPUT    201
#define IDM_EXIT     202

#define IDD_TITLE    300
#define IDD_XLABEL   301
#define IDD_YLABEL   302
#define IDD_XVALUES  303
#define IDD_YVALUES  304
```

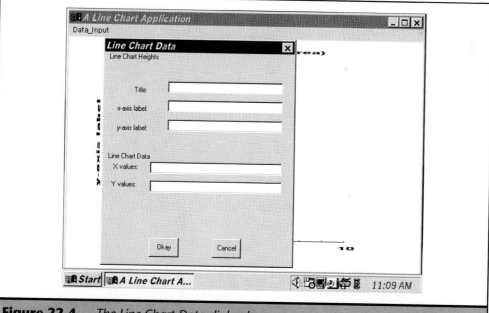

Figure 22-4. *The Line Chart Data dialog box*

The number of ID values in the header file is small because all data entry will be achieved with strings.

Here is a line.rc resource script file that describes the menu and dialog box created with the Borland resource editors described in Chapter 20. Examine this listing and see if you can determine which edit boxes accept x and y values:

```
#include "windows.h"
#include "line.h"

LINEMENU MENU
{
  POPUP "Data_Input"
  {
    MENUITEM "About...",        IDM_ABOUT
    MENUITEM "Input...",        IDM_INPUT
    MENUITEM "Exit",            IDM_EXIT
  }
}



ABOUTDIABOX DIALOG 6,18,160,100
  STYLE DS_MODALFRAME|WS_POPUP|WS_VISIBLE|
        WS_CAPTION|WS_SYSMENU
  CAPTION "About Box"
  FONT 8, "MS Sans Serif"
{
  CTEXT "A Line Chart Application",-1,34,10,91,8
  CTEXT "by",-1,61,25,32,8
  CTEXT "Chris H. Pappas and",-1,38,42,86,8
  CTEXT "William H. Murray",-1,45,59,70,8
  PUSHBUTTON "Okay",IDOK,58,80,40,14
}

LINEDIABOX DIALOG 41,0,223,223
  STYLE DS_MODALFRAME|WS_POPUP|WS_VISIBLE|
        WS_CAPTION|WS_SYSMENU
  CAPTION "Line Chart Data"
  FONT 8, "MS Sans Serif"
{
  LTEXT "Line Chart Data",-1,5,105,212,81
  LTEXT "Line Chart Heights",-1,5,0,212,98
  LTEXT "Title: ",-1,35,35,28,8
```

```
    EDITTEXT IDD_TITLE,75,30,135,12,ES_AUTOHSCROLL
    LTEXT "x-axis label:",-1,15,55,55,8
    EDITTEXT IDD_XLABEL,75,50,135,12,ES_AUTOHSCROLL
    LTEXT "y-axis label:",-1,15,75,60,8
    EDITTEXT IDD_YLABEL,75,70,135,12,ES_AUTOHSCROLL
    LTEXT "X values: ",-1,12,116,40,8
    LTEXT "Y values: ",-1,10,135,40,8
    EDITTEXT IDD_XVALUES,55,115,155,12,ES_AUTOHSCROLL
    EDITTEXT IDD_YVALUES,55,135,155,12,ES_AUTOHSCROLL
    PUSHBUTTON "Okay",IDOK,55,195,35,20
    PUSHBUTTON "Cancel",IDCANCEL,130,195,34,20
}
```

The line.c source code listing is shown next. In this listing you should be able to identify the string parser for both the X and Y axes:

```
//
//  line.c
//  A line chart application.
//  Copyright (c) Chris H. Pappas and William H. Murray, 1996
//

#include <windows.h>
#include <string.h>
#include <stdlib.h>
#include <math.h>
#include "line.h"

#define maxnumpts 10

LRESULT CALLBACK WndProc(HWND,UINT,WPARAM,LPARAM);
BOOL CALLBACK AboutDiaProc(HWND,UINT,WPARAM,LPARAM);
BOOL CALLBACK LineDiaProc(HWND,UINT,WPARAM,LPARAM);

static char szProgName[]="ProgName";
static char szApplName[]="LineMenu";
static char szCursorName[]="LineCursor";
static char szTString[80]="(line chart title area)";
static char szXString[80]="x-axis label";
static char szYString[80]="y-axis label";
char szXValues[80]="10,20,30,40,50";
```

```
char szYValues[80]="20,30,5,40,80,50";

int WINAPI WinMain(HINSTANCE hInst,HINSTANCE hPreInst,
                   LPSTR lpszCmdLine,int nCmdShow)
{
  HWND hWnd;
  MSG  lpMsg;
  WNDCLASS wcApp;
  if (!hPreInst) {
    wcApp.lpszClassName=szProgName;
    wcApp.hInstance     =hInst;
    wcApp.lpfnWndProc   =WndProc;
    wcApp.hCursor       =LoadCursor(hInst,szCursorName);
    wcApp.hIcon         =NULL;
    wcApp.lpszMenuName  =szApplName;
    wcApp.hbrBackground=GetStockObject(WHITE_BRUSH);
    wcApp.style         =CS_HREDRAW|CS_VREDRAW;
    wcApp.cbClsExtra    =0;
    wcApp.cbWndExtra    =0;
    if (!RegisterClass (&wcApp))
      return 0;
  }
  hWnd=CreateWindow(szProgName,"A Line Chart Application",
                    WS_OVERLAPPEDWINDOW,CW_USEDEFAULT,
                    CW_USEDEFAULT,CW_USEDEFAULT,
                    CW_USEDEFAULT,(HWND)NULL,(HMENU)NULL,
                    (HANDLE)hInst,(LPSTR)NULL);
  ShowWindow(hWnd,nCmdShow);
  UpdateWindow(hWnd);
  while (GetMessage(&lpMsg,NULL,0,0)) {
    TranslateMessage(&lpMsg);
    DispatchMessage(&lpMsg);
  }
  return(lpMsg.wParam);
}

BOOL CALLBACK AboutDiaProc(HWND hdlg,UINT messg,
                           WPARAM wParam,LPARAM lParam)
{
```

```
  switch (messg)
  {
    case WM_INITDIALOG:
      break;
    case WM_COMMAND:
      switch (wParam)
      {
        case IDOK:
          EndDialog(hdlg,TRUE);
          break;
        default:
          return FALSE;
      }
      break;
    default:
      return FALSE;
  }
  return TRUE;
}

BOOL CALLBACK LineDiaProc(HWND hdlg,UINT messg,
                          WPARAM wParam,LPARAM lParam)
{
  switch (messg)
  {
    case WM_INITDIALOG:
      return FALSE;
    case WM_COMMAND:
      switch (wParam)
      {
        case IDOK:
          GetDlgItemText(hdlg,IDD_TITLE,szTString,80);
          GetDlgItemText(hdlg,IDD_XLABEL,szXString,80);
          GetDlgItemText(hdlg,IDD_YLABEL,szYString,80);
          GetDlgItemText(hdlg,IDD_XVALUES,szXValues,80);
          GetDlgItemText(hdlg,IDD_YVALUES,szYValues,80);
          EndDialog(hdlg,TRUE);
          break;
        case IDCANCEL:
          EndDialog(hdlg,FALSE);
          break;
        default:
```

```
          return FALSE;
      }
    break;
  default:
    return FALSE;
  }
  return TRUE;
}


LRESULT CALLBACK WndProc(HWND hWnd,UINT messg,
                         WPARAM wParam,LPARAM lParam)

{
  HDC   hdc;
  PAINTSTRUCT ps;
  static HFONT hOFont,hNFont;
  static HPEN hOPen,hNPen;
  static FARPROC fpfnAboutDiaProc,
                 fpfnLineDiaProc;
  static HWND hInst1,hInst2;
  static int xClientView,yClientView;
  int i,iNPts,iPtxMax,iPtyMax;
  static int ilenMaxYLabel,ilenMaxXLabel;
  int x,y,xtic,ytic;
  float fPtxScaled[maxnumpts];
  float fPtyScaled[maxnumpts];
  char sxbuffer[10],sybuffer[10];
  static char *n,*p,*strxptr,*stryptr;
  int iPtxSize[maxnumpts];
  int iPtySize[maxnumpts];

  switch (messg)
  {
    case WM_SIZE:
      xClientView=LOWORD(lParam);
      yClientView=HIWORD(lParam);
      break;

    case WM_CREATE:
      hInst1=((LPCREATESTRUCT) lParam)->hInstance;
      hInst2=((LPCREATESTRUCT) lParam)->hInstance;
      fpfnAboutDiaProc=MakeProcInstance((FARPROC)AboutDiaProc,
```

```
                                                    hInst1);
        fpfnLineDiaProc=MakeProcInstance((FARPROC)LineDiaProc,
                                         hInst2);
        break;

    case WM_COMMAND:
      switch (wParam) {
        case IDM_ABOUT:
          #ifdef _WIN32    // Windows 95 & NT
            DialogBox((HINSTANCE) GetModuleHandle (NULL),
                      "AboutDiaBox",hWnd,
                      AboutDiaProc);
          #else
            DialogBox(hInst1,"AboutDiaBox",hWnd,
                      fpfnAboutDiaProc);
            FreeProcInstance(fpfnAboutDiaProc);
          #endif
          break;
        case IDM_INPUT:
          #ifdef _WIN32    // Windows 95 & NT
            DialogBox((HINSTANCE) GetModuleHandle (NULL),
                      "LineDiaBox",hWnd,
                      LineDiaProc);
          #else
            DialogBox(hInst2,"LineDiaBox",
                      hWnd,fpfnLineDiaProc);
            FreeProcInstance(fpfnLineDiaProc);
          #endif
          InvalidateRect(hWnd,NULL,TRUE);
          UpdateWindow(hWnd);
          break;
        case IDM_EXIT:
          SendMessage(hWnd,WM_CLOSE,0,0L);
          break;
        default:
          break;
      }
      break;
```

```
case WM_PAINT:
      hdc=BeginPaint(hWnd,&ps);
//--------- your routines below ---------

      // Set View Port and Map Mode
      SetMapMode(hdc,MM_ISOTROPIC);
      SetWindowExtEx(hdc,640,400,NULL);
      SetViewportExtEx(hdc,xClientView,yClientView,NULL);
      SetViewportOrgEx(hdc,0,0,NULL);

      // Print Labels to Screen
      hNFont=CreateFont(12,12,900,900,FW_BOLD,
                        FALSE,FALSE,FALSE,
                        OEM_CHARSET,
                        OUT_DEFAULT_PRECIS,
                        CLIP_DEFAULT_PRECIS,
                        DEFAULT_QUALITY,
                        VARIABLE_PITCH|FF_ROMAN,
                        "Roman");
      hOFont=SelectObject(hdc,hNFont);
      TextOut(hdc,50,200+(strlen(szXString)*10/2),
              szYString,strlen(szYString));

      hNFont=CreateFont(12,12,0,0,FW_BOLD,
                        FALSE,FALSE,FALSE,OEM_CHARSET,
                        OUT_DEFAULT_PRECIS,
                        CLIP_DEFAULT_PRECIS,
                        DEFAULT_QUALITY,
                        VARIABLE_PITCH|FF_ROMAN,
                        "Roman");
      hOFont=SelectObject(hdc,hNFont);
      TextOut(hdc,(300-(strlen(szTString)*10/2)),
              15,szTString,strlen(szTString));
      TextOut(hdc,(300-(strlen(szXString)*10/2)),
              365,szXString,strlen(szXString));
      TextOut(hdc,(500-(ilenMaxXLabel*12/2)),
              355,strxptr,ilenMaxXLabel);
      TextOut(hdc,(90-ilenMaxYLabel*12),
              45,stryptr,ilenMaxYLabel);
```

```
// Draw Coordinate Axis
hNPen=CreatePen(PS_SOLID,1,PALETTERGB(0x00,0x00,0xFF));
hOPen=SelectObject(hdc,hNPen);
MoveToEx(hdc,100,50,NULL);
LineTo(hdc,100,350);
LineTo(hdc,500,350);


// parse the x string
iNPts=0;
i=0;
n=szXValues;
p=strtok(n,",");
while ((n != NULL)) {
  iPtxSize[i]=atoi(n);
  p=strtok(NULL,",");
  n=p;
  iNPts++;
  i++;
}

// parse the y string
i=0;
n=szYValues;
p=strtok(n,",");
while ((n != NULL)) {
  iPtySize[i]=atoi(n);
  p=strtok(NULL,",");
  n=p;
  i++;
}

iPtxMax=0;
// Find point in array with maximum X value
for (i=0;i<iNPts;i++)
  if(iPtxMax<iPtxSize[i]) iPtxMax=iPtxSize[i];

strxptr=itoa(iPtxMax,sxbuffer,10);
ilenMaxXLabel=strlen(sxbuffer);
```

```
iPtyMax=0;
// Find point in array with maximum Y value
for (i=0;i<iNPts;i++)
  if(iPtyMax<iPtySize[i]) iPtyMax=iPtySize[i];

stryptr=itoa(iPtyMax,sybuffer,10);
ilenMaxYLabel=strlen(sybuffer);

// Scale all X values in array.  Max X=400
for (i=0;i<iNPts;i++)
  fPtxScaled[i]=(float) (iPtxSize[i]*400.0/iPtxMax);

// Scale all Y values in array.  Max Y=300
for (i=0;i<iNPts;i++)
  fPtyScaled[i]=(float) (iPtySize[i]*300.0/iPtyMax);

// Print Axis values
TextOut(hdc,(500-(ilenMaxXLabel*12/2)),
        355,strxptr,ilenMaxXLabel);
TextOut(hdc,(90-ilenMaxYLabel*12),
        45,stryptr,ilenMaxYLabel);

// Draw X axis tic marks
xtic=140;
for (i=0;i<10;i++) {
  ytic=350;
  MoveToEx(hdc,xtic,ytic,NULL);
  ytic=347;
  LineTo(hdc,xtic,ytic);
  xtic+=40;
}

// Draw Y axis tic marks
ytic=50;
for (i=0;i<10;i++) {
  xtic=100;
  MoveToEx(hdc,xtic,ytic,NULL);
  xtic=103;
  LineTo(hdc,xtic,ytic);
  ytic+=30;
}
```

```
      // Plot a + symbol for each point
      hNPen=CreatePen(PS_SOLID,1,PALETTERGB(0xFF,0xFF,0x00));
      hOPen=SelectObject(hdc,hNPen);
      for(i=0;i<iNPts;i++) {
        x=100+(int) fPtxScaled[i];
        y=350-(int) fPtyScaled[i];
        MoveToEx(hdc,x-5,y,NULL);
        LineTo(hdc,x+5,y);
        MoveToEx(hdc,x,y-5,NULL);
        LineTo(hdc,x,y+5);
      }

      // Plot Lines between Points
      hNPen=CreatePen(PS_SOLID,1,PALETTERGB(0xFF,0x00,0x00));
      hOPen=SelectObject(hdc,hNPen);
      x=100+(int) fPtxScaled[0];
      y=350-(int) fPtyScaled[0];
      MoveToEx(hdc,x,y,NULL);
      for(i=1;i<iNPts;i++) {
        x=100+(int) fPtxScaled[i];
        y=350-(int) fPtyScaled[i];
        LineTo(hdc,x,y);
      }

      SelectObject(hdc,hOFont);
      SelectObject(hdc,hOPen);

//--------- your routines above ---------
      ValidateRect(hWnd,NULL);
      EndPaint(hWnd,&ps);
      break;

    case WM_DESTROY:
      DeleteObject(hNPen);
      DeleteObject(hNFont);
      PostQuitMessage(0);
      break;

    default:
```

```
        return(DefWindowProc(hWnd,messg,wParam,lParam));
    }
  return(0);
}
```

To build this application, you will need a project file for your Borland C++ compiler in addition to the line.h, line.rc, and line.c files. This application can be built as a 16- or 32-bit application and will execute under the Windows 3.*x*, Windows 95, and Windows NT environments. Remember, if you are building a 16-bit application, add the names of both dialog box procedures to the EXPORTS statement of the module definition file.

A Closer Look at the Application

The menu and dialog boxes for this application are processed in a manner similar to the previous example. However, the line chart application has become more involved. This application will allow the user to enter three labels (title, X-axis, and Y-axis). Additionally, the dialog box will allow numerous x,y data pairs to be entered. You'll also see the use of a unique string parser for separating data points. Once the data points are parsed, they will be scaled and plotted to the positive X and Y axes. The largest x point will be scaled to the maximum horizontal value; the largest y point will be scaled to the maximum vertical value on the screen.

Everything is ready for plotting titles, labels, marker symbols, and lines when a WM_PAINT message is received. The mapping mode, window extent, viewport extent, and viewport origin are set to allow the chart to be scaled as the window size is increased or decreased.

The dialog box returns a string of numeric values which are parsed, converted, and placed in two global arrays: *iPtxSize[]* and *iPtySize[]*. Because data is entered in pairs, it is necessary only to count *iPtxSize[]* entries in order to determine the actual number of data points entered by the user.

The following portion of code is responsible for parsing the x string. The multiple data values for plotting on the x axis were entered as a string in the dialog box. They must now be separated (parsed) with a routine:

```
// parse the x string
    iNPts=0;
    i=0;
    n=szXValues;
    p=strtok(n,",");
    while ((n != NULL)) {
      iPtxSize[i]=atoi(n);
```

```
        p=strtok(NULL,",");
        n=p;
        iNPts++;
        i++;
    }
```

The parser routine uses the **strtok()** function. Used correctly, this function will save you hours of work. Used incorrectly, it will cost you hours of work! Unfortunately, Borland chose the easier road in its programming examples and did not demonstrate the real power of this function.

The **strtok()** function allows you to parse one string (in this case, *n*) with characters found in another. For this example, we'll only use a comma (,) to separate numbers, so that value is *hardwired* in the function. The string to be parsed is only identified the first time the function is called. For all other calls to the function, a NULL value is used.

We are assuming that the numeric values are separated by commas. The **strtok()** function is called within a **while** loop. The string will be parsed until a NULL value is returned, marking the end of the string. Now here is the trick for efficiently using this function: the string pointer must be updated, or the scan for the next comma will begin at the start of the string! Some programming gymnastics are used to accomplish this. Another, less interesting technique would be to fill the delimiter string with enough commas to match the string being searched. Wasn't that easy?

The maximum x and y values are needed for properly scaling the data points. These values, *iPtxMax* and *iPtyMax*, are determined with the use of a **for** loop. Each data array, *iPtxSize[]* or *iPtySize[]*, is scanned until the maximum value is found. It is this value that is returned to *iPtxMax* and *iPtyMax*.

```
iPtxMax=0;
// Find point in array with maximum X value
for (i=0;i<iNPts;i++)
   if(iPtxMax<iPtxSize[i]) iPtxMax=iPtxSize[i];

strxptr=itoa(iPtxMax,sxbuffer,10);
ilenMaxXLabel=strlen(sxbuffer);

iPtyMax=0;
// Find point in array with maximum Y value
for (i=0;i<iNPts;i++)
   if(iPtyMax<iPtySize[i]) iPtyMax=iPtySize[i];

stryptr=itoa(iPtyMax,sybuffer,10);
ilenMaxYLabel=strlen(sybuffer);
```

The maximum x and y values are important for another reason; they will be printed at the far end of both the X and Y axes. In order to accomplish this, the numeric values must be converted to strings. This is done with the familiar **itoa()** function. The X-axis string is referenced with *strxptr*, and the Y-axis string with *stryptr*. The lengths of the strings are saved in two variables: *ilenMaxXLabel* and *ilenMaxYLabel*.

The values in each data array are scaled to fit the graph. The scaled points are saved in two new arrays of type **float**: *fPtxScaled[]* and *fPtyScaled[]*. Scaling is achieved with the use of a simple equation:

```
// Scale all X values in array.  Max X=400
for (i=0;i<iNPts;i++)
  fPtxScaled[i]=(float) (iPtxSize[i]*400.0/iPtxMax);

// Scale all Y values in array.  Max Y=300
for (i=0;i<iNPts;i++)
  fPtyScaled[i]=(float) (iPtySize[i]*300.0/iPtyMax);
```

Tick marks are drawn to both the vertical and horizontal axes. The tick marks are actually short line segments drawn with the **MoveToEx()** and **LineTo()** functions on each axis:

```
// Draw X axis tic marks
     xtic=140;
     for (i=0;i<10;i++) {
       ytic=350;
       MoveToEx(hdc,xtic,ytic,NULL);
       ytic=347;
       LineTo(hdc,xtic,ytic);
       xtic+=40;
     }

     // Draw Y axis tic marks
     ytic=50;
     for (i=0;i<10;i++) {
       xtic=100;
       MoveToEx(hdc,xtic,ytic,NULL);
       xtic=103;
       LineTo(hdc,xtic,ytic);
       ytic+=30;
     }
```

This is the same approach used to form the small plus symbol (+) drawn at each x,y data pair:

```
// Plot a + symbol for each point
hNPen=CreatePen(PS_SOLID,1,PALETTERGB(0xFF,0xFF,0x00));
hOPen=SelectObject(hdc,hNPen);
for(i=0;i<iNPts;i++) {
  x=100+(int) fPtxScaled[i];
  y=350-(int) fPtyScaled[i];
  MoveToEx(hdc,x-5,y,NULL);
  LineTo(hdc,x+5,y);
  MoveToEx(hdc,x,y-5,NULL);
  LineTo(hdc,x,y+5);
}
```

When two or more symbols are in place, lines are drawn between each point by using **MoveToEx()** and **LineTo()**. In this chart the lines are drawn in red:

```
// Plot Lines between points
      hNPen=CreatePen(PS_SOLID,1,PALETTERGB(0xFF,0x00,0x00));
      hOPen=SelectObject(hdc,hNPen);
      x=100+(int) fPtxScaled[0];
      y=350-(int) fPtyScaled[0];
      MoveToEx(hdc,x,y,NULL);
      for(i=1;i<iNPts;i++) {
        x=100+(int) fPtxScaled[i];
        y=350-(int) fPtyScaled[i];
        LineTo(hdc,x,y);
      }
```

Figure 22-5 shows the default line chart produced by values initially stored in *iPtxSize* and *iPtySize*.

Figure 22-6 shows the data entry dialog box for this application with information on sales figures for Windows 95 (just kidding).

Examine the resulting line chart in Figure 22-7. Apparently Windows 95 is doing very well.

Now that you know how to add resources to a Windows application, why not alter this application to allow the user to draw two line charts on the same graph?

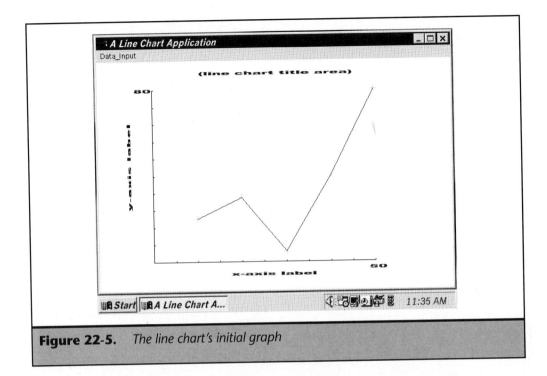

Figure 22-5. The line chart's initial graph

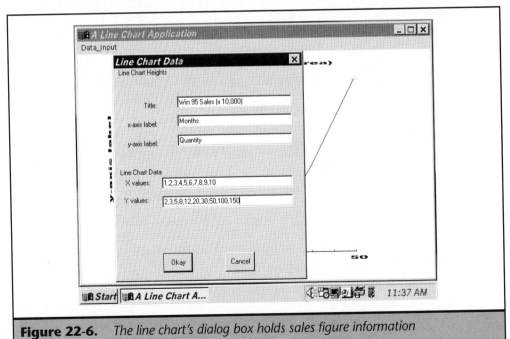

Figure 22-6. The line chart's dialog box holds sales figure information

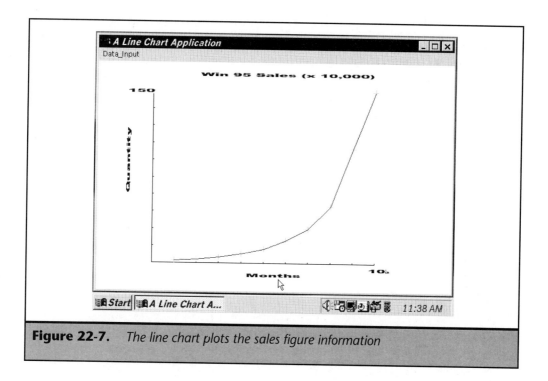

Figure 22-7.   *The line chart plots the sales figure information*

In the Next Chapter...

In the next chapters, you'll learn how to build Windows applications in an object-oriented environment. In Chapter 25, you'll learn how resources can be added to these applications.

PART SIX

Using Object Libraries for Win32 Programming

Chapter Twenty-Three

Borland's ObjectWindows Library (OWL)

Chapters 20 through 22 showed you the traditional form of Windows programming, using the procedure-oriented approach. In this and the remaining chapters of this book, you will work with an alternative, and perhaps better, programming technique. This and the next two chapters discuss Borland's solution to object-oriented programming with the Object Windows library (OWL). Chapters 26 and 27 concentrate on Microsoft's solution with the use of the Microsoft Foundation Class library (MFC). All examples make extensive use of C++ and Windows-based class libraries.

Using Windows-based class libraries can simplify the creation of Windows programs. There are two major Windows class libraries versions, as mentioned earlier: Borland's ObjectWindows Library (OWL) and Microsoft's Foundation Class library (MFC). Normally, you will chose one or the other for your developing environment.

Class Libraries

Supporters of C++ claim that the use of class libraries, sometimes called object libraries, can speed application development, make maintenance (upgrades, etc.) of applications easy, make maintenance more cost effective, and reduce overall program code size. Proponents of the object-library approach have suggested that all Windows code should be written with object libraries.

There is, however, a down side to the object-library approach. These disadvantages include a steep learning curve to C++ and object-oriented programming concepts, a steep learning curve to using any object library, the fact that Borland's OWL and Microsoft's MFC library are not compatible, and the fact that, regardless of the manufacturer, once you develop an application with an object library, your application will be tied to that product and its advantages and disadvantages.

Even the simplest Windows applications, when created with the standard API procedure-oriented functions calls, can be difficult and time-consuming to develop. For example, most applications require at minimum of two or three pages of code just to establish a window on the screen. Although Windows applications are a joy to use, they are certainly not easy to write.

The object-oriented programming approach and a library of objects designed for Windows will speed up program development and shorten program code, as you will see. Because it is easier to develop and because of its shorter size, it will be easier to understand and maintain, too.

The use of the Borland ObjectWindows Library requires a firm grasp of C++ and object-oriented programming concepts. Before starting this section, you may wish to review Chapters 15 through 18.

The ObjectWindows Library Environment

You have learned that the window contains the essential elements for support of an object-oriented programming language such as C++. Borland has added another optional, but important, tool to their integrated development environment. Borland's ObjectWindows Library (OWL) provides a powerful object-oriented alternative to the standard procedure-oriented approach to developing Windows applications. ObjectWindows is a mature collection of objects that describe standard Windows features. By using the properties of inheritance, you can now take advantage of pre-written code that performs the repetitive work required to develop applications.

ObjectWindows makes development cycles shorter, applications easier to write, and errors easier to find and remove. All of the Windows features that you have used in earlier chapters can be applied to programs written with Borland's ObjectWindows.

The ObjectWindow Library (OWL) can be accessed from the command line with the Borland command-line compiler (bcc.exe for 16-bit applications and bcc32.exe for 32-bit applications) or from the integrated programming environment with the Borland IDE (bcw.exe). If you chose the integrated environment, everything from design to execution can be done directly under Windows.

TIP: *If you choose to use ObjectWindows with your Borland C++ compiler, install all files to the suggested default subdirectories.*

Again, before getting into the meat of this chapter you may decide that brushing up on object-oriented terminology is in order.

Three Object-Oriented Features

A true object-oriented language has three important features: abstraction, encapsulation, and message response. ObjectWindows provides object libraries that enable the Windows programmer to take advantage of these object-oriented features.

Encapsulation with Interface Objects

Borland uses the term *interface object* when referring to ObjectWindows objects. This term comes about because of the way these objects interface with the visual components of Windows. For similar reasons, the visual components of a window are called *interface elements*. Interface objects, contained in ObjectWindows, instruct Windows on how to generate interface elements. ObjectWindows provides the objects for defining the behavior of Windows properties and the data storage necessary for their use.

Abstraction

ObjectWindows provides objects with member functions that abstract many of Windows' hundreds of function calls. Because many parameters for Windows functions also can be stored in the object's data members of interface objects, ObjectWindows places related Windows function calls into groups. These

ObjectWindows groups can then supply parameters to other related functions in the same group. This streamlines the programming process. For example, **WMCommand()** and **WMSize()** are related functions that share the (TMessage& Message) parameter, so they are grouped together.

Message Response

Windows is a message-based environment. With the procedure-oriented approach, all Windows communications is done directly with messages which are sent to Windows functions. Windows must be able to intercept and process hundreds of messages. In procedure-oriented applications, message processing is frequently based on the use of **case** statements.

With ObjectWindows, however, messages are processed by objects designed for the task. More precisely, ObjectWindows converts Windows messages into object member function calls. These object-oriented applications now have a unique object member function to respond to each Windows message a program might generate or encounter. For example, if a Windows message is generated by an action such as a key press, mouse move, or mouse button click, a specific member function will respond to the message. For example, the messages that were processed by WM_SIZE and WM_COMMAND are now handled by the member functions **WMSize()** and **WMCommand()**. Borland has attempted to keep member function names as close to their procedure-oriented counterparts as possible.

An ObjectWindows Object

The ObjectWindows Library is actually made of a collection of individual library files. This collection of files is contained in the LIB\OWL library subdirectory. The library houses objects that programmers can incorporate into their programming application. The member function prototypes for the library are described in various header files found in the INCLUDE\OWL include subdirectory. The owlall.h. file is the gateway to all necessary object header files. In other words, owlall.h. gives your program access to all other object header files. The TWindow object, for example, is used by almost every Windows application. Its prototype can be found in the window.h header file.

Here is a small portion of the TWindow class definition, edited for easier viewing:

```
class _EXPORT TWindow:public TWindowsObject
{
public:
  TWindowAttr Attr;
  PTScroller Scroller;
  HANDLE FocusChildHandle;
  TWindow(PTWindowsObject AParent,LPSTR ATitle,PTModule
         AModule = NULL);
```

```
   TWindow(HWND AnHWindow);
   virtual  TWindow();
virtual BOOL AssignMenu(LPSTR MenuName);
virtual BOOL AssignMenu(int MenuId);
virtual BOOL Create();
virtual classTypeisA() const
  {return windowClass;}
virtual Pchar nameOf() const
  {return "TWindow";}
static PTStreamable build(); protected:
virtual LPSTR GetClassName()
  {return "OWLWindow";}
virtual void GetWindowClass(WNDCLASS _FAR & AWndClass);
virtual void SetupWindow();
virtual void WMCreate(RTMessage Msg)=[WM_FIRST + WM_CREATE];
   .
   .
   .

virtual void WMVScroll(RTMessage Msg)=[WM_FIRST +
                                       WM_VSCROLL];
virtual void WMPaint(RTMessage Msg)=[WM_FIRST + WM_PAINT];
virtual void Paint(HDC PaintDC, PAINTSTRUCT _FAR
                  & PaintInfo);
virtual void WMSize(RTMessage Msg)=[WM_FIRST + WM_SIZE];
virtual void WMMove(RTMessage Msg)=[WM_FIRST + WM_MOVE];
virtual void WMLButtonDown(RTMessage Msg)=[WM_FIRST +
                                       WM_LBUTTONDOWN];
TWindow(StreamableInit) : TWindowsObject(streamableInit) {};
virtual void write (Ropstream os);
virtual Pvoid read (Ripstream is); private:
virtual const Pchar streamableName() const
  {return "TWindow";}
};
```

Use this listing as a reference and use either the Help Utility provided with your Borland C++ compiler or the ObjectWindows reference manual. Examine the description of TWindow's properties and components. Do you notice any similarities between the TWindow components and message-based Windows functions used in earlier chapters? Now, as an experiment, repeat the same steps for the TApplication prototype. TApplication is another important object class that will be used repeatedly in our examples. TApplication is prototyped in the applicat.h header file in the INCLUDE\OWL subdirectory.

In the next sections, you'll see how these and other key objects are used to form a basic Windows window.

A Simple ObjectWindows Application

In Chapter 21 you learned how to build a very simple Windows application that provided the essential Windows elements, such as a border, title bar, system menu, and so on.

In this section, you'll learn how to develop an equally simple object-oriented application with the use of ObjectWindows. The application is named swpo.cpp. SWPO stands for Simple Windows Platform with ObjectWindows. SWPO contains all of the Windows components of the initial procedure-oriented application of Chapter 21.

If you are working through the examples in each chapter, you will need to enter the following program listing for swpo.cpp. If your application is to be compiled as a 16-bit application, you will also need a module definition file. The default module definition file offered by the Borland C++ compiler will work in this case. When you are ready to build the application (compile and link), you will need to create a project file for this application.

Here is a module definition file that can be used to build 16-bit applications. Remember, this file is not needed for 32-bit builds.

```
NAME            SWPO
DESCRIPTION     'SWPO for 16-bit Borland OWL apps.'
EXETYPE         WINDOWS
CODE            PRELOAD MOVEABLE DISCARDABLE
DATA            PRELOAD MOVEABLE SINGLE
HEAPSIZE        1024
STACKSIZE       5120
```

The source code file, swpo.cpp can be used to build 16-bit or 32-bit applications without modification. The OWL takes care of all differences; you just select 16-bit or 32-bit versions when creating the project file. Take a minute to examine the following source code listing:

```
//
// SWPO.CPP
// Simple Windows Platform with Objects.
// An application for all versions of Windows that
// use Borland's ObjectWindows Library (OWL).
// Copyright (c) Chris H. Pappas and William H. Murray, 1996
//
```

```
#include <owl\owlall.h>

class TMainWindow : public TFrameWindow {
  public:
     TMainWindow(TWindow* parent, const char far* title);
     void EvPaint();

  DECLARE_RESPONSE_TABLE(TMainWindow);
};

DEFINE_RESPONSE_TABLE1(TMainWindow, TFrameWindow)
  EV_WM_PAINT,
END_RESPONSE_TABLE;

TMainWindow::TMainWindow(TWindow* parent,
                         const char far* title)
          : TFrameWindow(parent, title)
{
  Attr.X = 0;
  Attr.Y = 0;
  Attr.W = 639;
  Attr.H = 479;
}

void TMainWindow::EvPaint()
{
  TPaintDC paintDC(HWindow);
  // GDI graphics commands below


  // GDI graphics commands above
}

class TMainApp : public TApplication {
  public:
     TMainApp() : TApplication("Main")
     {
     }
     void InitMainWindow();
};
```

```
void TMainApp::InitMainWindow()
{
  MainWindow = new TMainWindow(0, "An OWL Application");
}

int OwlMain(int /*argc*/, char* /*argv*/ [])
{
  return TMainApp().Run();
}
```

If you are working from within the integrated development environment (IDE) remember to set your include and library directories. For example, our include and library files were found at these locations:

include	c:\bc5\include\owl;
	c:\bc5\include\classlib;
	c:\bc5\include
library	c:\bc5\lib\16BIT;
	c:\bc5\lib\32BIT;
	c:\bc5\lib

The project file, created from within the IDE for this application, must include the swpo.cpp source code file and the swpo.def module definition file (for 16-bit builds).

Once you've entered the application, build the executable file with the project utility. Now run the swpo.exe program template. What appears on the screen? If your application is successful, you should see a blank window with a border, system menu, and so on, as shown in Figure 23-1.

The source code file, swpo.cpp, contains the essential objects for placing a window on the screen. It can be used as the foundation of any graphics program you wish to develop or experiment with later in this book.

Although the application makes use of Borland's ObjectWindows library, it is still possible to make ordinary message-based function calls as you did in earlier chapters. You'll learn how later in this chapter. This mix-and-match approach gives you the best of both programming worlds. There is additional good news, in that resource files for dialog boxes, menus, icons, cursors, and other window attributes will not change in the ObjectWindows environment.

Even if you don't fully understand (yet) how the various objects work in this application, you can see that the results are similar to earlier applications written with a procedure-oriented approach.

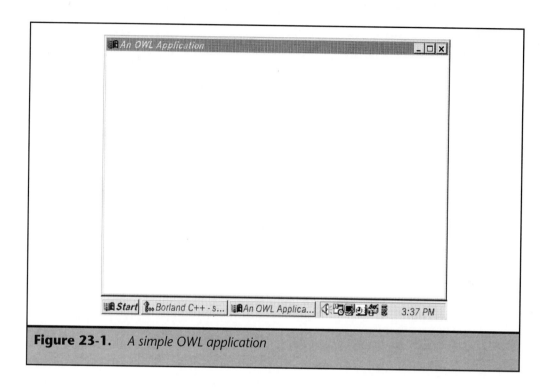

Figure 23-1.   *A simple OWL application*

Were there any advantages to this object-oriented approach? Did you notice that the source code for this application was only about a page long, whereas the procedure-oriented source code application in Chapter 21 was about two and a half pages long? Did you notice that this application could be converted from a 16-bit to 32-bit application with nothing more than a simple recompile?

Using Objects in the Application

Object-oriented applications do not use a top-down programming approach, as do procedure-oriented programs. An important section of the application's code appears at the end of the code listing. **OwlMain()** is the entry point for the application:

```
int OwlMain(int /*argc*/, char* /*argv*/ [])
{
  return TMainApp().Run();
}
```

Here **Run()** is responsible for initializing the instance, calling **InitApplication()** for the first executing instance and **InitInstance()** for all instances. If successful, **Run()**

then calls **MessageLoop()** and executes the application. When an error occurs during the creation of a window, **Run()** signals a TXWindow exception.

You will find that these lines of code do not change significantly from one ObjectWindows applications to another. Your Borland manuals provide a diagram of the ObjectWindows' class hierarchy, if you wish to study how the various ObjectWindow classes are utilized.

Creating a Window with TApplication

Each program that uses ObjectWindow objects must define a new class derived from **TApplication** (TApplication is derived from **TModule**), the ObjectWindow class. **TApplication** member functions can create instances of a class, create main windows, and process messages.

```
class TMainApp : public TApplication {
  public:
      TMainApp() : TApplication("Main")
      {
      }
      void InitMainWindow();
};
```

Can you tell the portion of procedure-oriented code from Chapter 21 that achieved the same results?

TApplication describes the Windows behavior that all applications must adhere to. Our class **TMainApp** is derived from Borland's **TApplication** class.

You know about this derivation by the syntax used:

```
class TMainApp : public TApplication
```

The single colon (:) indicates a derived class. In the **TMainApp** class description, "Main" is the *name* parameter passed to the class constructor. Class constructors are often used for initialization purposes.

In this application, **TMainApp** uses one protected member function from **TApplication**, **InitMainWindow()**. However, TApplication is much more versatile in what it can do. For example, its public and protected data members include:

```
// public data members
HACCEL HAccTable;
HINSTANCE hPrevInstance;
int nCmdShow;
```

```
//  protected data members
bool BreakMessageLoop;
int MessageLoopResult;
```

You can see that **TApplication** can use an acceleration table, check instances, make the window visible, and maintain a message loop.

Here are the public constructors and destructor for **TApplication**:

```
// constructors
TApplication(const char far* name = 0,
             TModule*& gModule = ::Module,
             TAppDictionary* appDict = 0);
TApplication(const char far* name,
             HINSTANCE hInstance,
             HINSTANCE hPrevInstance,
             const char far* cmdLine,
             int cmdShow,
TModule*& gModule = ::Module, TAppDictionary* appDict = 0);

//destructor
~TApplication();
```

You will see how to use the constructors shortly. Remember, in C++ constructors and destructors are called automatically when the class is invoked.

TApplication also provides numerous public member functions:

```
int BeginModal(TWindow* window, int flags = MB_APPLMODAL);
bool BWCCEnabled() const;
virtual bool CanClose();
void Condemn(TWindow* win);
bool Ctl3dEnabled()const;
void EnableBWCC(bool enable = true, uint Language = 0);
void EnableCtl3d(bool enable = true);
void EnableCtl3dAutosubclass(bool enable);
void EndModal(int result);
bool Find(TEventInfo &, TEqualOperator = 0);
TModule* GetBWCCModule() const;
TModule* GetCtl3dModule() const;
TDocManager* GetDocManager();
TFrameWindow* GetMainWindow();
```

```
TWindow* GetWindowPtr(HWND hWnd) const;

void GetWinMainParams();
virtual int MessageLoop();
void PostDispatchAction();
virtual void PreProcessMenu(HMENU hmenu);
virtual bool ProcessAppMsg(MSG& msg);
bool PumpWaitingMessages();
int QueryThrow();
void ResumeThrow();
virtual int Run();
static void SetWinMainParams(HINSTANCE hInstance,
                             HINSTANCE hPrevInstance,
                             const char far* cmdLine,
                             int cmdShow);
void SuspendThrow(xalloc& x);
void SuspendThrow(xmsg& x);
void SuspendThrow(TXOwl& x);
void SuspendThrow(int);

void Uncondemn(TWindow* win);
```

Here are protected member functions for **TApplication**:

```
virtual bool IdleAction(long idleCount);
virtual void InitApplication();
virtual void InitInstance();
virtual void IniTMainWindow();
TFrameWindow* SetDocManager(TDocManager* docManager);
TFrameWindow* SetMainWindow(TFrameWindow* window);
virtual int TermInstance(int status);
```

Recall that a derived class (**TMainWindow**) inherits all components of the parent class (**TApplication**). In this example, our template uses the **InitMainWindow()** member function:

```
void TMainApp::InitMainWindow()
{
  MainWindow = new TMainWindow(0, "An OWL Application");
}
```

Member functions can be defined within the class itself or outside the class. When they are defined outside the class, a special syntax is used:

```
void TMainApp::InitMainWindow()
```

The double colon (::) indicates a member function definition. The *new* operator provides dynamic storage allocation in C++. The operator is considered superior to the standard C library function **malloc()**.

TFrameWindow—A Window Style

TMainWindow is a class derived from an ObjectWindows class, **TFrameWindow**. **TFrameWindow** is, in turn, derived from an ObjectWindow class named **TWindow**.

```
class TMainWindow : public TFrameWindow {
  public:
      TMainWindow(TWindow* parent, const char far* title);
      void EvPaint();

  DECLARE_RESPONSE_TABLE(TMainWindow);
};
```

TFrameWindow controls specific window behavior such as keyboard interaction, command processing, restoring input focus, adding menu bar and icon support, etc. It also defines the frame area of a window including the window's border, system menus, optional toolbar, status bars, and so on. For example, in this application, **TMainWindow** is derived from **TFrameWindow**. It sets the initial size of the window's frame to 640 x 480 (a full VGA screen) with the following code:

```
TMainWindow::TMainWindow(TWindow* parent,
                         const char far* title)
            : TFrameWindow(parent, title)
{
  Attr.X = 0;
  Attr.Y = 0;
  Attr.W = 639;
  Attr.H = 479;
}
```

Attr is a structure that holds various window attributes that can be set during the construction of a window. The public data members of this structure include:

```
TResId AccelTable;
uint32 ExStyle;
int Id;
TResId Menu;
char far* Param;
uint32 Style;
int X, Y, W, H;
```

Here x and y are the coordinates for the upper-left corner of the window. w and h represent the height and width of the window. **TFrameWindow** does not describe the client window where applications draw graphics and text.

TFrameWindow provides versatility. The public and protected data members of **TFrameWindow** include:

```
// public data members
bool KeyboardHandling;

//  protected data members
TWindow* ClientWnd;
int DocTitleIndex;
HWND HWndRestoreFocus;
TModule* MergeModule;
```

These are the constructors and destructor for **TFrameWindow**:

```
// constructors
TFrameWindow(TWindow* Parent,
             const char far* title = 0,
             TWindow* clientWnd = 0,
             bool shrinkToClient = false,
             TModule* module = 0);
TFrameWindow(HWND hWnd,
             TModule* module = 0);

//destructor
~TFrameWindow();
```

TFrameWindow also provides numerous public member functions:

```
virtual bool AssignMenu(TResId menuResId);
void EnableKBHandler();
virtual TWindow* GetClientWindow();
virtual HWND GetCommandTarget();
const TMenuDescr* GetMenuDescr();
bool HoldFocusHWnd(HWND hWndLose,
                   HWND hWndGain);
void IdleAction(long idleCount);
bool MergeMenu(const TMenuDescr& childMenuDescr);
bool PreProcessMsg(MSG& msg);
bool RestoreMenu();
virtual TWindow* SetClientWindow(TWindow* clientWnd);
bool SetDocTitle(const char far* docname,
                 int index);
bool SetIcon(TModule* iconModule, TResId iconResId);
virtual bool SetMenu(HMENU newMenu);
void SetMenuDescr(const TMenuDescr& menuDescr);
```

Protected member functions for **TFrameWindow** include:

```
LRESULT EvCommand(uint id, HWND hWndCtl, uint notifyCode);
void EvCommandEnable(TCommandEnabler& ce);
bool EvEraseBkgnd(HDC);
HANDLE EvInitMenuPopup(HMENU hPopupMenu, uint index, bool sysMenu);
void EvPaint();
void EvParentNotify(uint event, uint childHandleOrX, uint childIDOrY);
HANDLE EvQueryDragIcon();
void EvSetFocus(HWND hWndLostFocus);
void EvSize(uint sizeType, TSize& size);
void Init(TWindow* clientWnd, bool shrinkToClient);
void SetupWindow();
```

You'll learn how to use various member functions in this and the next chapter. Remember that ObjectWindows include files give complete prototypes for these classes. Your compiler's Help facilities can often answer questions that you might have about various class components.

Did you notice an additional line of code in the definition of the **TMainWindow** class? It was the declaration to define a message response table.

```
DECLARE_RESPONSE_TABLE(TMainWindow);
```

In order to handle events for a class, a response table is defined for that class. *Response tables* provide the interface between Windows messages and a corresponding event-handling function. This application is designed to respond to WM_PAINT messages.

```
DEFINE_RESPONSE_TABLE1(TMainWindow, TFrameWindow)
  EV_WM_PAINT,
END_RESPONSE_TABLE;
```

TFrameWindow response tables can include: EV_WM_ERASEBKGND, EV_WM_INITMENUPOPUP, EV_WM_PAINT, EV_WM_PARENTNOTIFY, EV_WM_QUERYDRAGICON, EV_WM_SETFOCUS, and EV_WM_SIZE.

Here the **TFrameWindow::EvPaint** (a member function) responds to Windows WM_PAINT messages. The response is necessary in order to permit drawing in the client area:

```
void TMainWindow::EvPaint()
{
  TPaintDC paintDC(HWindow);
  // GDI graphics commands below


  // GDI graphics commands above
}
```

The **TPaintDC** class, a device context DC class, is derived from the **TWindowDC** class. It wraps the begin and end paint calls (see use of WM_PAINT in procedure-oriented applications) for use in a WM_PAINT response function. **TPaintDC** has a single public data member:

```
PAINTSTRUCT Ps;
```

This class has a single constructor and destructor:

```
TPaintDC(HWND wnd);
~TPaintDC();
```

Here *wnd* is a protected data member of this class. Borland's Help facilities provide extensive resources to help you understand which objects are available in the OWL, how they were derived from other objects, and how they are used.

In the Next Chapter...

The SWPO application that was created in the previous sections establishes a window by drawing a frame, setting up communications with Windows, and preparing the client area for receiving drawing commands. In other words, it is like opening a store without merchandise on the shelves.

In the next chapter, however, you'll discover that this application can be modified to allow you to experiment with fonts and various GDI graphics drawing functions.

Chapter Twenty-Four

Using Borland's Object-Windows Library (OWL)

In this chapter, two simple applications will be developed. Both of these applications are simple extensions of the program developed in Chapter 23. The font.cpp application will draw text to the window in a variety of fonts. The damp.cpp application draws a scientific wave form to the window. Neither application requires the use of menus, dialog boxes, or additional Windows resources.

Experimenting with Fonts

In this section, you'll learn how to expand the application developed in the previous chapter into a program that will allow you to experiment with various Windows fonts. This program, named font.cpp, will allow you to manipulate and alter various font parameters.

Designing the font.cpp Application

In this example, the application from Chapter 23 is used to create a program that allows us to change the size of text fonts on the screen. This application will use the **CreateFont()** function to set font parameters. In this case, a single string is printed to the window several times while changing the height and width property of the selected font.

Examine the following modified code, named font.cpp:

```
//
// Font.cpp
// Changing font properties.
// This application uses Borland's ObjectWindows Library (OWL).
// Copyright (c) Chris H. Pappas and William H. Murray, 1996
//

#include <owl\owlall.h>

class TMainWindow : public TFrameWindow {
  public:
    TMainWindow(TWindow* parent, const char far* title);
    void EvPaint();

  DECLARE_RESPONSE_TABLE(TMainWindow);
};

DEFINE_RESPONSE_TABLE1(TMainWindow, TFrameWindow)
  EV_WM_PAINT,
```

```
END_RESPONSE_TABLE;

TMainWindow::TMainWindow(TWindow* parent,
                         const char far* title)
           : TFrameWindow(parent, title)
{
  Attr.X = 0;
  Attr.Y = 0;
  Attr.W = 639;
  Attr.H = 479;
}

void TMainWindow::EvPaint()
{
  TPaintDC paintDC(HWindow);
    static LOGFONT lf;
    HFONT hNFont;
    static char szTextString[] = "The Object-Windows Library";
    int i, ypos;

    lf.lfWeight = FW_NORMAL;
    lf.lfCharSet = 0;          //Arial Font Char Set
    lf.lfPitchAndFamily = 34;  //Arial Font Family
    ypos = 0;

    for (i = 1; i < 9; i++) {
      lf.lfHeight = 6 + (6 * i);
      hNFont=CreateFontIndirect(&lf);
      paintDC.SelectObject(hNFont);
      paintDC.TextOut(0, ypos, szTextString,
                      strlen(szTextString));
      ypos += 12 * i;
    }
}

class TMainApp : public TApplication {
  public:
    TMainApp() : TApplication("Main")
    {
    }
```

```
      void InitMainWindow();
};

void TMainApp::InitMainWindow()
{
   MainWindow = new TMainWindow(0,"A Borland OWL Application");
}

int OwlMain(int /*argc*/, char* /*argv*/ [])
{
   return TMainApp().Run();
}
```

Build and execute the modified application. This application will draw several rows of the same message on the screen. Each time the string is drawn, it will be in a larger point size, as shown in Figure 24-1.

An Arial TrueType font is used for this example. The first time through the loop, a point size of 12 is requested. The second time, 18 is requested, and so on. Windows

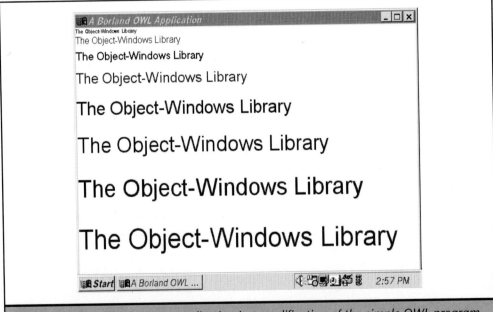

Figure 24-1.   *The font.cpp application is a modification of the simple OWL program shown in Figure 23-1*

will attempt to supply the application with the point size requested or select the closest size based on internal calculations.

This application contains one major change over the simple program in Chapter 23: the inclusion of a call to the **EvPaint()** function. The **EvPaint()** function allows the text strings to be drawn in the client area. What did you think when you saw these three lines of code?

```
        .
        .
        .

hNFont=CreateFontIndirect(&lf);
paintDC.SelectObject(hNFont);
paintDC.TextOut(0, ypos, szTextString, strlen(szTextString));
        .
        .
        .
```

Did you notice that two function calls are proceeded by paintDC while the other function call is not? The first parameter for normal procedure-oriented function calls is the handle to the device context. This is usually designated as *hdc*. However, when using the OWL, the handle is *not* the first parameter. For functions that require the device context, that information is now passed with the following syntax:

```
paintDC.[function] (parameter list);
```

That is the reason both **SelectObject()** and **TextOut()** used paintDC. However, **CreateFontIndirect()** does not use a handle to the device context, which is why it is not preceded with this syntax.

Designing the damp.cpp Application

The application you just saw, font.cpp, was designed with only minor modifications to the simple application from Chapter 23. The damp.cpp application allows you to draw various GDI graphics shapes in the client area of the window. For this example, a damped sine wave curve and its damping envelope will be drawn in different colors.

Here is the code that will draw the graphics in the client area. Notice how similar it is to the font.cpp application:

```
//
// Damp.cpp
// This application draws a mathematical wave form
```

```
// using Borland's ObjectWindows Library (OWL).
// Copyright (c) Chris H. Pappas and William H. Murray, 1996
//

#include <owl\owlall.h>
#include <math.h>

class TMainWindow : public TFrameWindow {
  public:
    TMainWindow(TWindow* parent, const char far* title);
    void EvPaint();

  DECLARE_RESPONSE_TABLE(TMainWindow);
};

DEFINE_RESPONSE_TABLE1(TMainWindow, TFrameWindow)
  EV_WM_PAINT,
END_RESPONSE_TABLE;

TMainWindow::TMainWindow(TWindow* parent,
                        const char far* title)
          : TFrameWindow(parent, title)
{
  Attr.X = 0;
  Attr.Y = 0;
  Attr.W = 639;
  Attr.H = 479;
}

void TMainWindow::EvPaint()
{
  TPaintDC paintDC(HWindow);
  HPEN hNewPen;
  double y;
  int i;

  // create a blue pen
  hNewPen = CreatePen(0,1,0xFF0000L);
  paintDC.SelectObject(hNewPen);
```

```
  // draw damping envelope
  paintDC.MoveTo(100,240);
  for (i=0;i<500;i++) {
    y=180.0*(exp(-i*0.01));
    paintDC.LineTo(i+100,240-(int) y);
  }
  paintDC.MoveTo(100,240);
  for (i=0;i<500;i++) {
    y=180.0*(exp(-i*0.01));
    paintDC.LineTo(i+100,240-(int) -y);
  }

  paintDC.TextOut(250,30,"A Damped Sine Wave",18);

  // create a green pen
  hNewPen=CreatePen(0,1,0x00FF00L);
  paintDC.SelectObject(hNewPen);

  // draw x & y coordinate axes
  paintDC.MoveTo(100,50);
  paintDC.LineTo(100,430);
  paintDC.MoveTo(100,240);
  paintDC.LineTo(600,240);
  paintDC.MoveTo(100,240);

  // draw sine wave in envelope
  for (i=0;i<500;i++) {
    y=180.0*(exp(-i*0.01))*sin(M_PI*i*(1440.0/500.0)/180.0);
    paintDC.LineTo(i+100,240-(int) y);
  }

  // delete new pen
  DeleteObject(hNewPen);
}

class TMainApp : public TApplication {
  public:
    TMainApp() : TApplication("Main")
    {
    }
```

```
      void InitMainWindow();
};

void TMainApp::InitMainWindow()
{
  MainWindow = new TMainWindow(0,
                        "Damped Wave form and Envelope");
}

int OwlMain(int /*argc*/, char* /*argv*/ [])
{
  return TMainApp().Run();
}
```

If you build and execute this application, you should see a screen very similar to the one shown in Figure 24-2.

In this example, two pens were created. The next portion of code shows how the blue pen is defined for drawing the damping envelope.

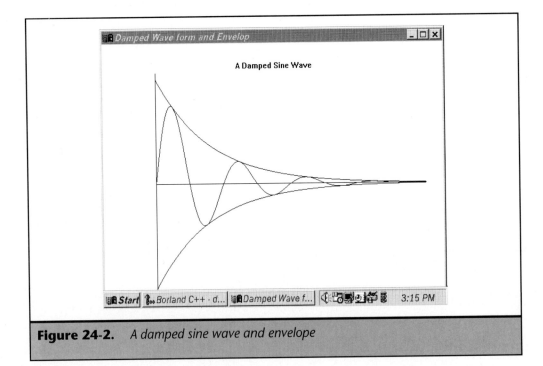

Figure 24-2. *A damped sine wave and envelope*

```
// create a blue pen
  hNewPen = CreatePen(0,1,0xFF0000L);
  paintDC.SelectObject(hNewPen);
```

The new pen is selected into the device context with a call to the **SelectObject()** function.

The **MoveTo()** and **LineTo()** functions are used to draw the damping envelope. Here is a portion of that code:

```
// draw damping envelope
  paintDC.MoveTo(100,240);
  for (i=0;i<500;i++) {
    y=180.0*(exp(-i*0.01));
    paintDC.LineTo(i+100,240-(int) y);
  }
     .
     .
     .
```

The envelope is generated by an equation that uses the **exp()** function. This function is prototyped in the math.h library. The **for** loop is repeated twice in order to generate the top and bottom envelope lines.

The sine wave is then drawn between the two constraining envelope lines:

```
// draw sine wave in envelope
  for (i=0;i<500;i++) {
    y=180.0*(exp(-i*0.01))*sin(M_PI*i*(1440.0/500.0)/180.0);
    paintDC.LineTo(i+100,240-(int) y);
  }
```

You'll notice, in the previous listing, the inclusion of the **exp()** function once again. If this function were not used, a normal sine wave would be drawn across the screen. The use of the **exp()** function "squeezes" the sine wave between the damping envelope.

In the Next Chapter...

The next chapter shows how to add Windows resources to produce Windows applications that are fully functional and have a professional appearance. You'll find that the information you learned in Chapter 22 can be directly applied to OWL Windows applications with regard to resources.

Chapter Twenty-Five

Adding Resources to OWL Applications

In the previous two chapters, you learned how to build simple OWL applications with Borland's ObjectWindows. In this chapter, you will learn how to expand these simple applications to include resources such as menus and dialog boxes. These additional resources will help you produce professional-looking Windows applications.

The good news, for the object-oriented programmer, is that these resources are exactly the same as their procedure-oriented counterparts. All you'll need to learn is how to use them with object-oriented code and the ObjectWindows Library.

The first application is an OWL drag-and-drop application. This application uses a simple menu resource that allows filenames to be selected from the file manager and dragged into the client area of the drag-and-drop application. The second OWL application makes use of GDI graphics primitives, but includes menu, keyboard accelerator, and cursor resources. The third application is an OWL graphics program that incorporates cursor, menu, and dialog box resources.

All three applications use Borland's OWL. When you create your project files for each application, these options must be indicated. Figure 25-1 shows the options used for the PieChart project file.

You will find that these OWL applications parallel the procedure-oriented applications designed in Chapters 21 and 22.

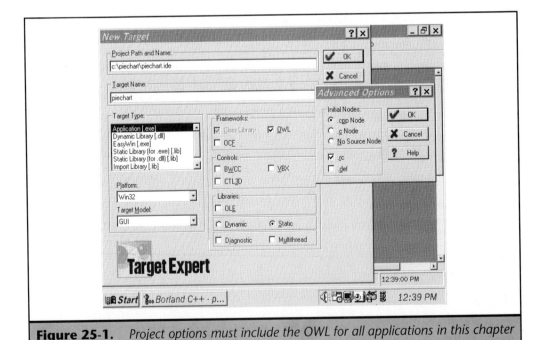

Figure 25-1. *Project options must include the OWL for all applications in this chapter*

A Drag-And-Drop OWL Application

Drag-and-drop simply means that you can select an item in one window and paste it in another window. Typically, items are first selected with a click of the left mouse button. Next, with the left mouse button held down, the selected item is "dragged" to another window. When the item is correctly positioned in the new window, the button is released. The selected item is now "pasted" in the new window.

The dragdrop.cpp application will illustrate the drag-and-drop concept by allowing you to select filenames in the File Manager or Explore and drag the selection to the DragDrop window for display.

Remember, this application is designed to help you understand how menu resources can be added to OWL applications. The application is built upon the simple applications discussed in Chapters 23 and 24.

Here is the code for the menu resource, dragdrop.rc:

```
WIPEMENU MENU
{
  POPUP "Wipe"
  {
    MENUITEM "&Wipe Screen", 100
    MENUITEM "&Exit",        101
  }
}
```

As you can see from the listing, there will be two menu items; one menu item will allow the user to wipe the screen of previous entries, while the other will permit the user to exit the application.

The dragdrop.cpp source code is a straightforward expansion of earlier OWL applications, as the following listing shows:

```
//
// DragDrop.cpp
// Drag-And-Drop concepts are introduced while
// showing how to include menu resources in an
// OWL application.
// (c) Chris H. Pappas and William H. Murray, 1996
//

#include <owl\owlall.h>
#include <stdio.h>
#include <dir.h>
#include <classlib\bags.h>
```

```
class TPlaceFile {
  public:
    operator==(const TPlaceFile& other) \
              const {return this==&other;}
    char* FileName;
    TPlaceFile(char*);
    ~TPlaceFile() {delete FileName;}
    char* FileInfo();
};

typedef TIBagAsVector<TPlaceFile> TFiles;
typedef TIBagAsVectorIterator<TPlaceFile> TFilesIter;
typedef TBagAsVector<TFiles*> TFilesList;
typedef TBagAsVectorIterator<TFiles*> TFilesListIter;

TPlaceFile::TPlaceFile(char* NameFile)
{
  FileName=strcpy(new char[strlen(NameFile)+1],NameFile);
}

char* TPlaceFile::FileInfo()
{
  static char namebuff[80];
  sprintf(namebuff,"%s",FileName);
  return namebuff;
}

static void DoDelete(TFiles*& list,void*) {
  delete list;
}

class TMainWindow : public TFrameWindow {
  public:
    TMainWindow(TWindow* parent, const char far* title);

  protected:
    void SetupWindow();
    void CleanupWindow();
    void EvDropFiles(TDropInfo);
    void EvSize(UINT,TSize&) { Invalidate(); }
    void EvPaint();
```

```
    void GetWindowClass(WNDCLASS& WndClass);
    void CmWipe() {
      EachFile->ForEach(DoDelete,0);
      EachFile->Flush();
      Invalidate();
    }
    void CmExit() {
      DestroyWindow(HWindow);
    }

  protected:
    TFilesList* EachFile;

  DECLARE_RESPONSE_TABLE(TMainWindow);
};

DEFINE_RESPONSE_TABLE1(TMainWindow,TFrameWindow)
  EV_WM_PAINT,
  EV_WM_DROPFILES,
  EV_COMMAND(100,CmWipe),
  EV_COMMAND(101,CmExit),
END_RESPONSE_TABLE;

TMainWindow::TMainWindow(TWindow* parent,
                         const char far* title)
          : TFrameWindow(parent,title)
{
  Attr.X = 0;    // set window to 1/4 VGA size
  Attr.Y = 0;
  Attr.W = 319;
  Attr.H = 239;
  EachFile=new TFilesList;
}

void TMainWindow::EvDropFiles(TDropInfo drop)
{
  int i;
  int NumFiles=drop.DragQueryFileCount();

  TFiles* files=new TFiles;
```

```
  for (i=0; i < NumFiles; i++) {
    UINT LenFile=drop.DragQueryFileNameLen(i)+1;
    char* NameFile=new char[LenFile];
    drop.DragQueryFile(i,NameFile,LenFile);

    files->Add(new TPlaceFile(NameFile));
  }
  EachFile->Add(files);
  drop.DragFinish();

  Invalidate();
}

void TMainWindow::SetupWindow()
{
  TFrameWindow::SetupWindow();
  DragAcceptFiles(TRUE);
}

void TMainWindow::CleanupWindow()
{
  delete EachFile;
  TFrameWindow::CleanupWindow();
}

void TMainWindow::EvPaint()
{
  TPaintDC paintDC(HWindow);

  TFilesListIter FullList(*EachFile);
  int i=0;

  // draw list
  while (FullList) {
    if (FullList.Current()) {
      TFilesIter SmList(*FullList.Current());
      while (SmList) {
        char* str=SmList.Current()->FileInfo();
        paintDC.TextOut(5,20*i,str);
        i++;
        SmList++;
```

```
        }
        FullList++;
      }
    }
}


class TMainApp : public TApplication {
  public:
    TMainApp() : TApplication("Main") {}
    void InitMainWindow();
};

void TMainWindow::GetWindowClass(WNDCLASS& WndClass)
{
  TWindow::GetWindowClass(WndClass);
  WndClass.style=0;
  WndClass.hbrBackground=CreateSolidBrush(RGB(0,0,150));
}


void TMainApp::InitMainWindow()
{
  MainWindow=new TMainWindow(0,"A Drag-And-Drop Application");
  MainWindow->AssignMenu("WIPEMENU");
}

int OwlMain(int /*argc*/,char* /*argv*/ [])
{
  return TMainApp().Run();
}
```

If you decide to build this as a 16-bit application for Windows 3.1, you will need a module definition file. The default module definition file offered by the Borland C++ compiler is acceptable. A 32-bit build for Windows NT or 95 will not require a module definition file.

Build and execute the application. Figure 25-2 shows an example of how several files can be dragged to the application's window from the Windows 95 Explorer.

In order to better understand this program, we'll divide the discussion into two parts. The first section will discuss the requirements for adding a menu resource to an OWL application. The second section will discuss the requirements of adding drag-and-drop capabilities.

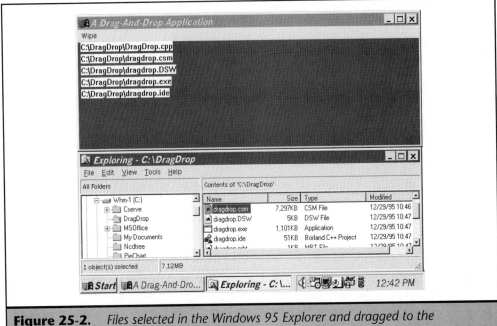

Figure 25-2. *Files selected in the Windows 95 Explorer and dragged to the application's window*

Adding a Menu

The menu for the DragDrap application is quite simple. Figure 25-3 shows the menu items available to the user.

The menu resource is brought into the application with a call to the **AssignMenu()** function, as shown in the following portion of code:

```
void TMainApp::InitMainWindow()
{
  MainWindow=new TMainWindow(0,"A Drag-And-Drop Application");
  MainWindow->AssignMenu("WIPEMENU");
}
```

The menu allows the user to wipe the screen clean or exit the application. Because both options can be programmed with a small amount of code, the member functions

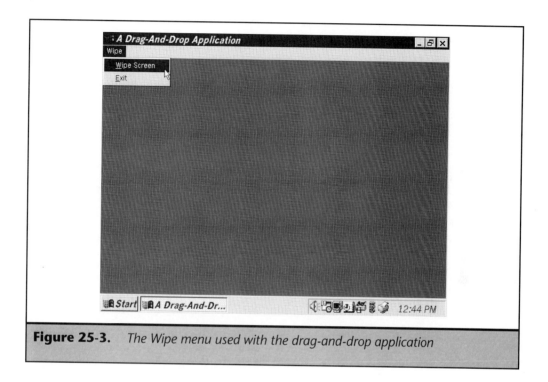

Figure 25-3. *The Wipe menu used with the drag-and-drop application*

are described in the class definition itself. The required code is shown in the following partial listing:

```
class TMainWindow : public TFrameWindow {
  public:
    TMainWindow(TWindow* parent, const char far* title);

  protected:
        .
        .
        .
    void CmWipe() {
      EachFile->ForEach(DoDelete,0);
      EachFile->Flush();
      Invalidate();
    }
    void CmExit() {
      DestroyWindow(HWindow);
    }
```

```
          .
          .
          .
    DECLARE_RESPONSE_TABLE(TMainWindow);
};
```

In **CmWipe()**, the code will delete each file from the file list, flush the buffer, and call the **Invalidate()** function. With no files in the list, the window is repainted as a clean window. The **CmExit()** function simply calls the **DestroyWindow()** function, which allows the user to exit from the application.

Both menu options are processed by command messages. Thus, the response table must include two EV_COMMAND statements, as shown here:

```
DEFINE_RESPONSE_TABLE1(TMainWindow,TFrameWindow)
  EV_WM_PAINT,
  EV_WM_DROPFILES,
  EV_COMMAND(100,CmWipe),
  EV_COMMAND(101,CmExit),
END_RESPONSE_TABLE;
```

By following these simple steps, you will find that adding any number of menu items to an OWL application is a straightforward process.

The Drag-and-Drop Connection

The implementation of drag-and-drop code requires an extensive number of functions that most users are not familiar with. You'll find an additional drag-and-drop application provided in the example files for your Borland C++ compiler. You should examine this application for more drag-and-drop concepts.

This application will use the bags.h header file, found in the classlib subdirectory, in addition to the normal header files:

```
#include <owl\owlall.h>
#include <stdio.h>
#include <dir.h>
#include <classlib\bags.h>
```

The bags.h header file defines templates, such as:

```
template  <class Vect, class T>  class
```

Bag containers are used to manage bags of objects. (A bag is a container that holds objects. These objects can be held in any order and be of any value.) **TBagAsVectorImp** can be used to implement a bag with this template. This bag uses a vector as the underlying implementation. *Vect* gives the form of the vector which can be a **TCVectorImp<T0>** or a **TICVectorImp<T0>**. *T* gives the type of object being put in the bag.

```
class TPlaceFile {
  public:
    operator==(const TPlaceFile& other) \
              const {return this==&other;}
    char* FileName;
    TPlaceFile(char*);                    // constructor
    ~TPlaceFile() {delete FileName;}  // destructor
    char* FileInfo();
};
```

The **TPlaceFile** class is responsible for maintaining the *FileName* information on the drag-and-drop file list.

```
typedef TIBagAsVector<TPlaceFile> TFiles;
typedef TIBagAsVectorIterator<TPlaceFile> TFilesIter;
typedef TBagAsVector<TFiles*> TFilesList;
typedef TBagAsVectorIterator<TFiles*> TFilesListIter;

TPlaceFile::TPlaceFile(char* NameFile)
{
  FileName=strcpy(new char[strlen(NameFile)+1],NameFile);
}
```

Review the previous listing to see the actual **typedef** statements for implementing the bag. Bags are considered the least structured of all the data structures used by containers in a container class. A bag includes four container classes and their corresponding iterator classes. Containers used here manage the objects and the pointers to those objects. It is usual practice to use **TStandardAllocator**, the default memory manager. The bag contains the following container classes:

TBagAsVector	**TMBagAsVector**
TBagAsVectorIterator	TMBagAsVectorIterator
TIBagAsVector	TMIBagAsVector
TIBagAsVectorIterator	TMIBagAsVectorIterator

A vector is used as the underlying implementation. In this example, **TBagAsVector** holds the collection of filename objects, whereas **TBagAsVectorIterator** is the iterator used to traverse those objects. In a similar manner, **TIBagAsVector** holds a bag of pointers to objects of type **TPlaceFiles**. **TIBagAsVectorIterator** uses an iterator object to traverse the **TIBagAsVector** objects.

File information is obtained with the next small portion of code:

```
char* TPlaceFile::FileInfo()
{
  static char namebuff[80];
  sprintf(namebuff,"%s",FileName);
  return namebuff;
}
```

The file information is passed to the **FileInfo()** class member function. **CmWipe()** uses **DoDelete()** to delete the file list with the following code:

```
static void DoDelete(TFiles*& list,void*) {
  delete list;
}
```

TMainWindow is derived from **TFrameWindow** in this example. Examine the complete listing for this application. Notice that the application contains several protected member functions used to implement the drag-and-drop features. The member functions include:

```
          .
          .
          .
      void SetupWindow();
      void CleanupWindow();
      void EvDropFiles(TDropInfo);
          .
          .
          .
```

The **SetupWindow()** member function contains a call to the **DragAcceptFiles()** function:

```
void TMainWindow::SetupWindow()
{
  TFrameWindow::SetupWindow();
  DragAcceptFiles(TRUE);
}
```

When the **DragAcceptFile()** uses a TRUE as its parameter, a window can process dropped files. When the parameter is FALSE, the window can no longer process dropped files.

The **CleanupWindow()** member function deletes each file in the file list, with the following portion of code:

```
void TMainWindow::CleanupWindow()
{
  delete EachFile;
  TFrameWindow::CleanupWindow();
}
```

The dropped file list is managed by **EvDropFiles()**:

```
void TMainWindow::EvDropFiles(TDropInfo drop)
{
  int i;
  int NumFiles=drop.DragQueryFileCount();

  TFiles* files=new TFiles;

  for (i=0; i < NumFiles; i++) {
    UINT LenFile=drop.DragQueryFileNameLen(i)+1;
    char* NameFile=new char[LenFile];
    drop.DragQueryFile(i,NameFile,LenFile);

    files->Add(new TPlaceFile(NameFile));
  }
  EachFile->Add(files);
  drop.DragFinish();
}
```

```
    Invalidate();
}
```

As you examine the previous listing, notice that it contains four drag-and-drop function calls. **DragQueryFileCount()** is used to return the number of dropped files in the **TDropInfo** object. **DragQueryFileNameLen()** is used to return the length of the filename in the **TDropInfo** object for the given index. **DragQueryFile()** is used to obtain the name of the file and any related information for the object. For example, if the index is -1, the number of dropped files will be returned. Finally, **DropFinish()** is used to release memory that has been allocated for transferring the objects that have been dragged.

The code contained under **EvPaint()** is used to draw the dragged file list to the application's client area:

```cpp
void TMainWindow::EvPaint()
{
  TPaintDC paintDC(HWindow);

  TFilesListIter FullList(*EachFile);
  int i=0;

  // draw list
  while (FullList) {
    if (FullList.Current()) {
      TFilesIter SmList(*FullList.Current());
      while (SmList) {
        char* str=SmList.Current()->FileInfo();
        paintDC.TextOut(5,20*i,str);
        i++;
        SmList++;
      }
      FullList++;
    }
  }
}
```

This application uses the **TextOut()** function to draw each drag-and-drop file name in order. This information is drawn, starting horizontally at 5 pixels on the horizontal and 0 pixels on the vertical. For every filename in the list, the y coordinate is incremented by 20 pixels.

NOTE: *This application was designed to show you how easy it is to implement menu resources in an OWL application! Don't let the concepts of drag-and-drop interfere with your understanding of how to add menu resources.*

The next application will also use menu resources to reinforce these concepts.

A Graphics Application with Multiple Resources

This application, named sketch.cpp, is designed to draw simple graphics figures in a window and give the user the ability to change background colors. In order to allow the program to be interactive, a menu and accelerator keys need to be added.

Remember that resource information remains virtually the same even with OWL applications. Here is the header file for the application, named sketch.h:

```
// sketch.h header file

// size information

#define IDM_SMALL      101
#define IDM_MEDIUM     102
#define IDM_LARGE      103

// background colors

#define IDM_BLACK      201
#define IDM_WHITE      202
#define IDM_RED        203
#define IDM_ORANGE     204
#define IDM_YELLOW     205
#define IDM_GREEN      206
#define IDM_BLUE       207
#define IDM_MAGENTA    208
#define IDM_LTGREEN    209
#define IDM_LTBLUE     210
#define IDM_LTRED      211
#define IDM_LTGRAY     212
```

The sketch.h header file contains the ID information used by the menus and accelerator keys.

The resource script file, sketch.rc, contains the descriptions for two pop-up menus; Rectangle_Size and Background_Colors. The application will allow the user to select three rectangle sizes and up to a dozen different background colors:

```
#include "windows.h"
#include "sketch.h"

CURSOR_1 CURSOR sketch.cur

Change MENU
{
  POPUP "&Rectangle_Size"
  {
    MENUITEM "&small",        IDM_SMALL
    MENUITEM "&Medium",       IDM_MEDIUM
    MENUITEM "&LARGE",        IDM_LARGE
  }

  POPUP "Ba&ckground_Colors"
  {
    MENUITEM "BLAC&K\tF1",     IDM_BLACK
    MENUITEM "&WHITE\tF2",     IDM_WHITE
    MENUITEM "&RED\tF3",       IDM_RED
    MENUITEM "&ORANGE\tF4",    IDM_ORANGE
    MENUITEM "&YELLOW\tF5",    IDM_YELLOW
    MENUITEM "GREE&N\tF6",     IDM_GREEN
    MENUITEM "&BLUE\tF7",      IDM_BLUE
    MENUITEM "&MAGENTA\tF8",   IDM_MAGENTA
    MENUITEM SEPARATOR
    MENUITEM "Lt GR&EEN\tF9",  IDM_LTGREEN
    MENUITEM "Lt BL&UE\tF10",  IDM_LTBLUE
    MENUITEM "Lt RE&D\tF11",   IDM_LTRED
    MENUITEM "Lt GR&AY\tF12",  IDM_LTGRAY
  }
}

Change ACCELERATORS
{
  VK_F1,   IDM_BLACK,   VIRTKEY
  VK_F2,   IDM_WHITE,   VIRTKEY
  VK_F3,   IDM_RED,     VIRTKEY
  VK_F4,   IDM_ORANGE,  VIRTKEY
```

```
    VK_F5,    IDM_YELLOW,   VIRTKEY
    VK_F6,    IDM_GREEN,    VIRTKEY
    VK_F7,    IDM_BLUE,     VIRTKEY
    VK_F8,    IDM_MAGENTA,  VIRTKEY
    VK_F9,    IDM_LTGREEN,  VIRTKEY
    VK_F10,   IDM_LTBLUE,   VIRTKEY
    VK_F11,   IDM_LTRED,    VIRTKEY
    VK_F12,   IDM_LTGRAY,   VIRTKEY
}
```

Notice, in the previous listing, that the 12 function keys (F1..F12) will be used as accelerator keys for changing background colors.

The following listing is the complete source code listing for the sketch.cpp application:

```
//
// Sketch.cpp
// This application draws simple graphics shapes and
// uses menus, accelerator keys, and cursor resources.
// (c) Chris H. Pappas and William H. Murray, 1996
//

#include <owl\owlall.h>
#include "sketch.h"

HBRUSH hBrush;
HMENU hmenu;

static int wSize=25;
static int wColor;
static int wColorValue[12][3]={{0,0,0},            //black
                               {255,255,255},      //white
                               {255,0,0},          //red
                               {255,96,0},         //orange
                               {255,255,0},        //yellow
                               {0,255,0},          //green
                               {0,0,255},          //blue
                               {255,0,255},        //magenta
                               {128,255,0},        //lt green
                               {0,255,255},        //lt blue
                               {255,0,159},        //lt red
```

```
                                    {180,180,180}}; //lt gray
int xClientView,yClientView;

class TMainWindow : public TFrameWindow {
  public:
    TMainWindow(TWindow* parent, const char far* title);
    void CmIDM(WPARAM);
    void EvPaint();
    void EvSize(UINT,TSize&);

  DECLARE_RESPONSE_TABLE(TMainWindow);
};

DEFINE_RESPONSE_TABLE1(TMainWindow,TFrameWindow)
  EV_WM_PAINT,
  EV_WM_SIZE,
  EV_COMMAND_AND_ID(IDM_SMALL,CmIDM),
  EV_COMMAND_AND_ID(IDM_MEDIUM,CmIDM),
  EV_COMMAND_AND_ID(IDM_LARGE,CmIDM),
  EV_COMMAND_AND_ID(IDM_BLACK,CmIDM),
  EV_COMMAND_AND_ID(IDM_WHITE,CmIDM),
  EV_COMMAND_AND_ID(IDM_RED,CmIDM),
  EV_COMMAND_AND_ID(IDM_ORANGE,CmIDM),
  EV_COMMAND_AND_ID(IDM_YELLOW,CmIDM),
  EV_COMMAND_AND_ID(IDM_GREEN,CmIDM),
  EV_COMMAND_AND_ID(IDM_BLUE,CmIDM),
  EV_COMMAND_AND_ID(IDM_MAGENTA,CmIDM),
  EV_COMMAND_AND_ID(IDM_LTGREEN,CmIDM),
  EV_COMMAND_AND_ID(IDM_LTBLUE,CmIDM),
  EV_COMMAND_AND_ID(IDM_LTRED,CmIDM),
  EV_COMMAND_AND_ID(IDM_LTGRAY,CmIDM),
END_RESPONSE_TABLE;

TMainWindow::TMainWindow(TWindow* parent,
                         const char far* title)
          : TFrameWindow(parent, title)
{
  Attr.X=0;
  Attr.Y=0;
  Attr.W=639;
  Attr.H=479;
```

```
  AssignMenu("Change");
}

void TMainWindow::EvSize(UINT sizeType,TSize& size)
{
  xClientView=size.cx;
  yClientView=size.cy;
  Invalidate(TRUE);
}

void TMainWindow::EvPaint()
{
  TPaintDC paintDC(HWindow);
  TSize oldVExt,oldWExt,newWExt,newVExt;
  TPoint oldOrg,newOrg;

  paintDC.SetBkMode(TRANSPARENT);
  paintDC.SetMapMode(MM_ISOTROPIC);
  newWExt.cx=500;
  newWExt.cy=500;
  paintDC.SetWindowExt(newWExt,&oldWExt);
  newVExt.cx=xClientView;
  newVExt.cy=-yClientView;
  paintDC.SetViewportExt(newVExt,&oldVExt);
  newOrg.x=xClientView/2;
  newOrg.y=yClientView/2;
  paintDC.SetViewportOrg(newOrg,&oldOrg);

  paintDC.Rectangle(-wSize*2,-wSize,
                wSize*2,wSize);
  paintDC.Rectangle(-wSize,-wSize*2,
                wSize,wSize*2);
  paintDC.TextOut(-60,200,"New Background Colors",21);
}

class TMainApp : public TApplication {
  public:
    TMainApp() : TApplication("Main")
    {
    }
  void InitMainWindow();
```

```
};

void TMainWindow::CmIDM(WPARAM WParam)
{
  switch (WParam)
  {
    case IDM_SMALL:
      wSize=25;
      break;
    case IDM_MEDIUM:
      wSize=50;
      break;
    case IDM_LARGE:
      wSize=75;
      break;
    case IDM_BLACK:
    case IDM_WHITE:
    case IDM_RED:
    case IDM_ORANGE:
    case IDM_YELLOW:
    case IDM_GREEN:
    case IDM_BLUE:
    case IDM_MAGENTA:
    case IDM_LTGREEN:
    case IDM_LTBLUE:
    case IDM_LTRED:
    case IDM_LTGRAY:
      hmenu=GetMenu();
      CheckMenuItem(hmenu,wColor,MF_UNCHECKED);
      wColor=WParam;
      CheckMenuItem(hmenu,wColor,MF_CHECKED);
      #ifdef WIN32
        wColor=WParam;
        CheckMenuItem(hmenu,wColor,MF_CHECKED);
        SetClassLong(GCL_HBRBACKGROUND,
                     (int) CreateSolidBrush(RGB
                     (wColorValue[wColor-IDM_BLACK][0],
                     wColorValue[wColor-IDM_BLACK][1],
                     wColorValue[wColor-IDM_BLACK][2]))));
      #else
        wColor=WParam;
```

```
        CheckMenuItem(hmenu,wColor,MF_CHECKED);
        SetClassWord(GCW_HBRBACKGROUND,
                    (int) CreateSolidBrush(RGB
                    (wColorValue[wColor-IDM_BLACK][0],
                    wColorValue[wColor-IDM_BLACK][1],
                    wColorValue[wColor-IDM_BLACK][2])));
    #endif
      break;
    default:
      break;
  }
  Invalidate(TRUE);
}


void TMainApp::InitMainWindow()
{
  MainWindow=new TMainWindow(0,"Simple Graphics Manipulations");
  MainWindow->SetCursor(this,"CURSOR_1");
  HAccTable=LoadAccelerators("Change");
}

int OwlMain(int /*argc*/, char* /*argv*/ [])
{
  return TMainApp().Run();
}
```

This application can be compiled as a 16-bit or a 32-bit application. If you are building the 16-bit version for Windows 3.1, you will need a module definition file. The default module definition file offered by the Borland C++ compiler is acceptable. The 32-bit version designed here does not require this file and will execute under Windows NT or 95.

You will need to create a cursor for this application. Design this cursor in the resource editor and name the file sketch.cur.

Examining the Source Code File

Return to the full source code listing for this application. Find the **AssignMenu()** and **LoadAccelerators()** function calls. These two functions are responsible for implementing the menu and accelerator resources. Notice that the cursor resource is added with a function call to the **SetCursor()** function.

Menu selections will be processed with our **CmIDM()** member function, as you can see in the following portion of code:

```
class TMainWindow : public TFrameWindow {
  public:
    TMainWindow(TWindow* parent, const char far* title);
    void CmIDM(WPARAM);
    void EvPaint();
    void EvSize(UINT,TSize&);

  DECLARE_RESPONSE_TABLE(TMainWindow);
};
```

In the previous listing, **TMainWindow** is derived from Borland's **TFrameWindow** class.

This application must process messages, therefore, there is also a response table. A portion of the response table is shown next:

```
DEFINE_RESPONSE_TABLE1(TMainWindow,TFrameWindow)
  EV_WM_PAINT,
  EV_WM_SIZE,
  EV_COMMAND_AND_ID(IDM_SMALL,CmIDM),

        .
        .
        .

  EV_COMMAND_AND_ID(IDM_LTGRAY,CmIDM),
END_RESPONSE_TABLE;
```

Examine the response table and notice the three categories of responses: EV_WM_PAINT, EV_WM_SIZE, and EV_COMMAND_AND_ID. You have already learned that EV_WM_PAINT enables the processing of WM_PAINT messages. In a similar manner, EV_WM_SIZE processes WM_SIZE messages. These messages are generated when the window's size changes. Likewise, EV_COMMAND_AND_ID processes command messages whenever a menu selection is made.

The EV_COMMAND_AND_ID information is passed to **CmIDM()** and processed in a manner similar to the procedure-oriented application of Chapter 22. Here is a small portion of that code:

```
void TMainWindow::CmIDM(WPARAM WParam)
{
  switch (WParam)
```

```
   {
     case IDM_SMALL:
       wSize=25;
       break;
         .
         .
         .

     case IDM_LTGRAY:
     hmenu=GetMenu();
     CheckMenuItem(hmenu,wColor,MF_UNCHECKED);
     wColor=WParam;
     CheckMenuItem(hmenu,wColor,MF_CHECKED);
     #ifdef WIN32
       wColor=WParam;
       CheckMenuItem(hmenu,wColor,MF_CHECKED);
       SetClassLong(GCL_HBRBACKGROUND,
                    (int) CreateSolidBrush(RGB
                    (wColorValue[wColor-IDM_BLACK][0],
                    wColorValue[wColor-IDM_BLACK][1],
                    wColorValue[wColor-IDM_BLACK][2])));
         .
         .
         .
```

The **EvSize()** member function returns information on the size of the window. If the window size changes, the coordinates of the window are returned in a **TSize** structure. The *cx* member variable is passed to *xClientView* and the *cy* member variable is passed to *yClientView*.

```
void TMainWindow::EvSize(UINT sizeType,TSize& size)
{
  xClientView=size.cx;
  yClientView=size.cy;
  Invalidate(TRUE);
}
```

EvSize() forces a redraw of the entire window if the size changes. Otherwise, portions of the old screen would overwrite portions of the new screen.

EvPaint(), as you know, draws the graphics shapes to the screen. However, notice that the size of the window is taken into account when drawing figures. The following portion of code illustrates how this is to be accomplished:

```
void TMainWindow::EvPaint()
{
  TPaintDC paintDC(HWindow);
  TSize oldVExt,oldWExt,newWExt,newVExt;
  TPoint oldOrg,newOrg;

  paintDC.SetBkMode(TRANSPARENT);
  paintDC.SetMapMode(MM_ISOTROPIC);
  newWExt.cx=500;
  newWExt.cy=500;
  paintDC.SetWindowExt(newWExt,&oldWExt);
  newVExt.cx=xClientView;
  newVExt.cy=-yClientView;
  paintDC.SetViewportExt(newVExt,&oldVExt);
  newOrg.x=xClientView/2;
  newOrg.y=yClientView/2;
  paintDC.SetViewportOrg(newOrg,&oldOrg);
        .
        .
        .
```

The functions **SetWindowExt()**, **SetViewportExt()**, and **SetViewportOrg()** use **TSize** or **TPoint** structures for passing or setting window size information.

Executing the Application

Build either a 16-bit or 32-bit version of this application. Figures 25-4 and 25-5 show the pop-up menus for this application during execution.

Figure 25-6 shows a sample screen with a light gray background and a medium pair of rectangles.

A Pie Chart Application with Multiple Resources

In Chapter 22, we developed a professional-quality line chart application using traditional procedure-oriented programming. In this chapter, we'll develop a pie chart application that integrates cursor, menu, and dialog box resources into an OWL application.

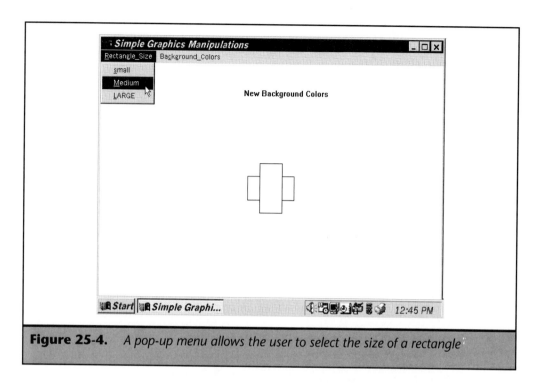

Figure 25-4. A pop-up menu allows the user to select the size of a rectangle

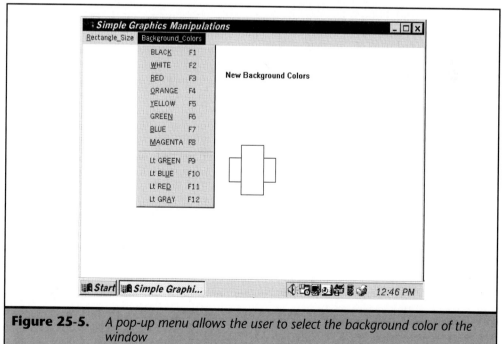

Figure 25-5. A pop-up menu allows the user to select the background color of the window

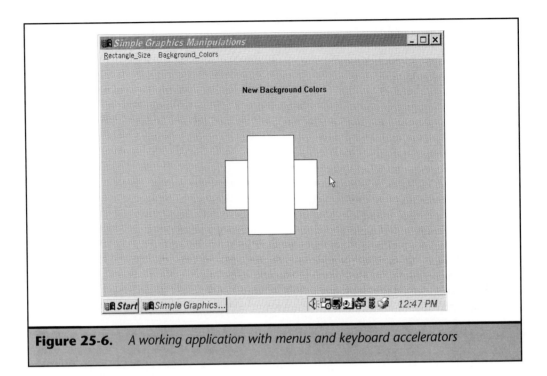

Figure 25-6. *A working application with menus and keyboard accelerators*

The piechart.h header file contains constants for each menu and dialog box option. The values IDM_ABOUT through IDM_EXIT are constants used for menu options. The values IDD_TITLE through IDD_L10 are for the various dialog box options:

```
#define IDM_ABOUT    200
#define IDM_INPUT    201
#define IDM_EXIT     202

#define IDD_TITLE    300
#define IDD_P1       301
#define IDD_P2       302
#define IDD_P3       303
#define IDD_P4       304
#define IDD_P5       305
#define IDD_P6       306
#define IDD_P7       307
#define IDD_P8       308
#define IDD_P9       309
#define IDD_P10      310
```

```
#define IDD_L1      401
#define IDD_L2      402
#define IDD_L3      403
#define IDD_L4      404
#define IDD_L5      405
#define IDD_L6      406
#define IDD_L7      407
#define IDD_L8      408
#define IDD_L9      409
#define IDD_L10     410
```

The header file indicates that up to ten pie slices (IDD_P1..IDD_P10) are available on the chart. Additionally, the user can label each pie slice (IDD_L1..IDD_L10).

The piechart.rc resource script file contains information for the menu (PieMenu), and two dialog boxes (AboutDiaBox and PieDiaBox).

```
#include "piechart.h"

PieCursor CURSOR piechart.cur

PieMenu MENU
{
  POPUP "Pie_Chart_Info"
  {
    MENUITEM "About...",  IDM_ABOUT
    MENUITEM "Data...",   IDM_INPUT
    MENUITEM "Exit",      IDM_EXIT
  }
}

AboutDiaBox DIALOG 6,18,160,100
  STYLE DS_MODALFRAME|WS_POPUP|WS_VISIBLE|
        WS_CAPTION|WS_SYSMENU
  CAPTION "About Box"
  FONT 8, "MS Sans Serif"
{
  CTEXT "OWL Pie Chart for Windows",-1,30,10,95,8
  CTEXT "by",-1,61,25,32,8
  CTEXT "Chris H. Pappas and",-1,38,42,86,8
  CTEXT "William H. Murray",-1,45,59,70,8
```

```
   PUSHBUTTON "Okay",IDOK,58,80,40,14
}

PieDiaBox DIALOG 72,4,250,233
  STYLE DS_MODALFRAME|WS_POPUP|WS_VISIBLE|
        WS_CAPTION|WS_SYSMENU
  CAPTION "Pie Chart Data"
  FONT 8, "MS Sans Serif"
{
  LTEXT "Pie Chart Title:",-1,6,4,130,30
  LTEXT "Pie Chart Slice Sizes and Labels",-1,6,39,236,173
  LTEXT "Title: ",-1,10,17,22,8
  LTEXT "A Pie Chart for Windows",-1,144,16,94,8
  EDITTEXT,IDD_TITLE,35,15,95,12,ES_AUTOHSCROLL
  LTEXT "Slice #1:",-1,8,55,30,8
  LTEXT "Slice #2:",-1,8,70,30,8
  LTEXT "Slice #3:",-1,8,85,30,8
  LTEXT "Slice #4:",-1,8,100,30,8
  LTEXT "Slice #5:",-1,8,115,30,8
  LTEXT "Slice #6:",-1,8,130,30,8
  LTEXT "Slice #7:",-1,8,145,30,8
  LTEXT "Slice #8:",-1,8,160,30,8
  LTEXT "Slice #9:",-1,8,175,30,8
  LTEXT "Slice #10:",-1,8,190,35,8
  EDITTEXT,IDD_P1,45,55,30,12,ES_AUTOHSCROLL
  EDITTEXT,IDD_P2,45,70,30,12,ES_AUTOHSCROLL
  EDITTEXT,IDD_P3,45,85,30,12,ES_AUTOHSCROLL
  EDITTEXT,IDD_P4,45,100,30,12,ES_AUTOHSCROLL
  EDITTEXT,IDD_P5,45,115,30,12,ES_AUTOHSCROLL
  EDITTEXT,IDD_P6,45,130,30,12,ES_AUTOHSCROLL
  EDITTEXT,IDD_P7,45,145,30,12,ES_AUTOHSCROLL
  EDITTEXT,IDD_P8,45,160,30,12,ES_AUTOHSCROLL
  EDITTEXT,IDD_P9,45,175,30,12,ES_AUTOHSCROLL
  EDITTEXT,IDD_P10,45,190,30,12,ES_AUTOHSCROLL
  LTEXT "Label #1:",-1,120,55,33,8
  LTEXT "Label #2:",-1,120,70,33,8
  LTEXT "Label #3:",-1,120,85,33,8
  LTEXT "Label #4:",-1,120,100,33,8
  LTEXT "Label #5:",-1,120,115,33,8
  LTEXT "Label #6:",-1,120,130,33,8
  LTEXT "Label #7:",-1,120,145,33,8
```

```
    LTEXT "Label #8:",-1,120,160,33,8
    LTEXT "Label #9:",-1,120,175,33,8
    LTEXT "Label #10:",-1,120,190,38,8
    EDITTEXT IDD_L1,155,55,80,12,ES_AUTOHSCROLL
    EDITTEXT IDD_L2,155,70,80,12,ES_AUTOHSCROLL
    EDITTEXT IDD_L3,155,85,80,12,ES_AUTOHSCROLL
    EDITTEXT IDD_L4,155,100,80,12,ES_AUTOHSCROLL
    EDITTEXT IDD_L5,155,115,80,12,ES_AUTOHSCROLL
    EDITTEXT IDD_L6,155,130,80,12,ES_AUTOHSCROLL
    EDITTEXT IDD_L7,155,145,80,12,ES_AUTOHSCROLL
    EDITTEXT IDD_L8,155,160,80,12,ES_AUTOHSCROLL
    EDITTEXT IDD_L9,155,175,80,12,ES_AUTOHSCROLL
    EDITTEXT IDD_L10,155,190,80,12,ES_AUTOHSCROLL
    PUSHBUTTON "Okay",IDOK,66,214,33,14
    PUSHBUTTON "Cancel",IDCANCEL,165,214,34,14
}
```

Figure 25-7 shows the About Box dialog box described in the previous code listing
Figure 25-8 shows the data entry dialog box.

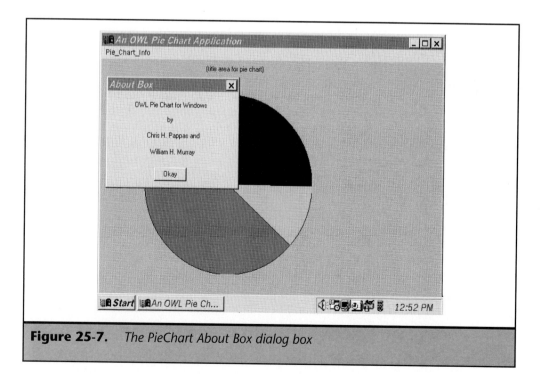

Figure 25-7. *The PieChart About Box dialog box*

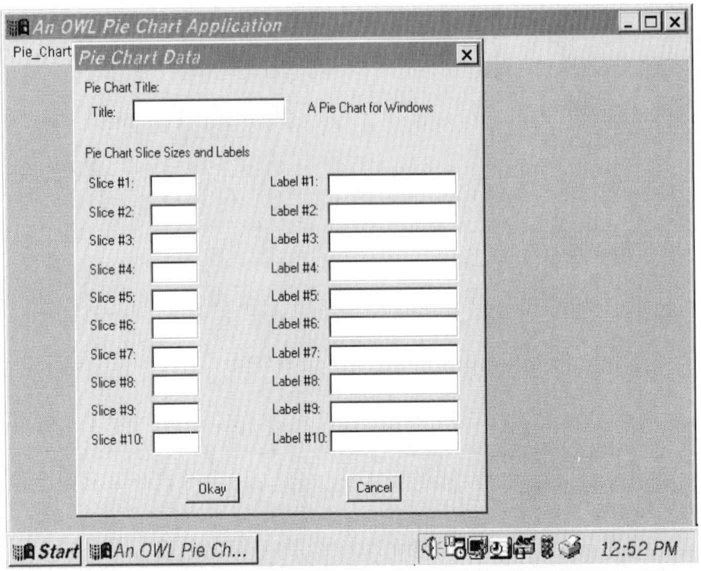

Figure 25-8. *The Pie Chart Data dialog box accepts data for the PieChart application*

The piechart.rc file, described in the previous listing, was created by designing the menu and dialog boxes within the Borland Resource Workshop and saving the file in both a script (.RC file extension) and compiled (.RES file extension) format. If you are creating your own custom dialog boxes for this application, you must have a fairly clear idea of how you want to represent items such as the various data fields.

This application uses a dialog box for user input. The data entry dialog box will prompt the user to enter up to ten integer numbers which will define the size of each pie slice or wedge. These numbers are then scaled in order to make each "pie slice" proportional in the 360-degree pie chart. Slices are colored in a sequential manner. The sequence is defined by the programmer and contained in the global array *lColor[]*. This application also allows the user to enter a title for the pie chart. The chart title is centered just above the pie figure. Legend labels are optional and are drawn to the right of the pie chart.

Here is the piechart.cpp source code:

```
//
// PieChart.cpp
// This application draws a quality pie chart
// with up to ten pie slices and labels.
```

```
// (c) Chris H. Pappas and William H. Murray, 1996
//

#include <owl\owlall.h>
#include <math.h>
#include <string.h>
#include "piechart.h"

#define radius 180
#define maxnumwedge 10
#define pi M_PI

char szProgName[]="ProgName";
char szApplName[]="PieMenu";
char szCursorName[]="PieCursor";
char szTString[80]="(title area for pie chart)";
static char szTLabel[10][20];
static UINT iWedgesize[maxnumwedge]={30,25,60,15,0,0,0,0,0,0};
static COLORREF crColor[maxnumwedge]={0x0L,0xFFL,0xFF00L,
                                      0xFFFFL,0xFF0000L,
                                      0xFF00FFL,0xFFFF00L,
                                      0xFFFFFFL,0x8080L,
                                      0x808080L};
int xClientView,yClientView;

class TPieDialog : public TDialog
{
  public:
    TPieDialog(TWindow* parent,const char far* name);
    void CmOk();
    void CmCancel();
  DECLARE_RESPONSE_TABLE(TPieDialog);
};

DEFINE_RESPONSE_TABLE1(TPieDialog,TDialog)
  EV_COMMAND(IDOK,CmOk),
  EV_COMMAND(IDCANCEL,CmCancel),
END_RESPONSE_TABLE;

TPieDialog::TPieDialog(TWindow* parent,const char far* name)
          : TDialog(parent,name),TWindow(parent)
```

```
{
}

class TMainWindow : public TFrameWindow {
  public:
    TMainWindow(TWindow* parent,const char far* title);
    void EvSize(UINT sizeType,TSize& size);
    void CmIDMABOUT();
    void CmIDMINPUT();
    void CmIDMEXIT();
    void GetWindowClass(WNDCLASS& WndClass);
    void EvPaint();

  DECLARE_RESPONSE_TABLE(TMainWindow);
};

DEFINE_RESPONSE_TABLE1(TMainWindow,TFrameWindow)
  EV_COMMAND(IDM_ABOUT,CmIDMABOUT),
  EV_COMMAND(IDM_INPUT,CmIDMINPUT),
  EV_COMMAND(IDM_EXIT,CmIDMEXIT),
  EV_WM_SIZE,
  EV_WM_PAINT,
END_RESPONSE_TABLE;

TMainWindow::TMainWindow(TWindow* parent,
                         const char far* title)
          : TFrameWindow(parent,title)
{
  Attr.X=0;
  Attr.Y=0;
  Attr.W=639;
  Attr.H=479;
}

void TMainWindow::EvSize(UINT sizeType,TSize& size)
{
  xClientView=size.cx;
  yClientView=size.cy;
  Invalidate(TRUE);
}
```

```
void TPieDialog::CmOk()
{
  GetDlgItemText(IDD_TITLE,szTString,80);
  iWedgesize[0]=GetDlgItemInt(IDD_P1,NULL,0);
  iWedgesize[1]=GetDlgItemInt(IDD_P2,NULL,0);
  iWedgesize[2]=GetDlgItemInt(IDD_P3,NULL,0);
  iWedgesize[3]=GetDlgItemInt(IDD_P4,NULL,0);
  iWedgesize[4]=GetDlgItemInt(IDD_P5,NULL,0);
  iWedgesize[5]=GetDlgItemInt(IDD_P6,NULL,0);
  iWedgesize[6]=GetDlgItemInt(IDD_P7,NULL,0);
  iWedgesize[7]=GetDlgItemInt(IDD_P8,NULL,0);
  iWedgesize[8]=GetDlgItemInt(IDD_P9,NULL,0);
  iWedgesize[9]=GetDlgItemInt(IDD_P10,NULL,0);
  GetDlgItemText(IDD_L1,szTLabel[0],20);
  GetDlgItemText(IDD_L2,szTLabel[1],20);
  GetDlgItemText(IDD_L3,szTLabel[2],20);
  GetDlgItemText(IDD_L4,szTLabel[3],20);
  GetDlgItemText(IDD_L5,szTLabel[4],20);
  GetDlgItemText(IDD_L6,szTLabel[5],20);
  GetDlgItemText(IDD_L7,szTLabel[6],20);
  GetDlgItemText(IDD_L8,szTLabel[7],20);
  GetDlgItemText(IDD_L9,szTLabel[8],20);
  GetDlgItemText(IDD_L10,szTLabel[9],20);
  EndDialog(HWindow,TRUE);
}

void TPieDialog::CmCancel()
{
  EndDialog(HWindow,FALSE);
}

void TMainWindow::CmIDMINPUT()
{
  TPieDialog(this,"PieDiaBox").Execute();
  Invalidate(TRUE);
  UpdateWindow();
}

void TMainWindow::CmIDMABOUT()
{
```

```
    TPieDialog(this,"AboutDiaBox").Execute();
}

void TMainWindow::CmIDMEXIT()
{
  DestroyWindow(HWindow);
}

void TMainWindow::EvPaint()
{
  TPaintDC paintDC(HWindow);
  static HBRUSH hNBrush;
  static HFONT hNFont;
  static LOGFONT lf;
  TSize oldVExt,oldWExt,newWExt,newVExt;
  TPoint oldOrg,newOrg;
  int i,y1,y2,iNWedges;
  unsigned int iTotalWedge[maxnumwedge+1];

  iNWedges=0;
  for (i=0;i<maxnumwedge;i++) {
    if(iWedgesize[i]!=0) iNWedges++;
  }

  iTotalWedge[0]=0;
  for (i=0;i<iNWedges;i++)
    iTotalWedge[i+1]=iTotalWedge[i]+iWedgesize[i];

  paintDC.SetMapMode(MM_ISOTROPIC);
  newWExt.cx=500;
  newWExt.cy=500;
  paintDC.SetWindowExt(newWExt,&oldWExt);
  newVExt.cx=xClientView;
  newVExt.cy=-yClientView;
  paintDC.SetViewportExt(newVExt,&oldVExt);
  newOrg.x=3*xClientView/8;
  newOrg.y=yClientView/2;
  paintDC.SetViewportOrg(newOrg,&oldOrg);

  paintDC.SetBkMode(TRANSPARENT);
```

```
    lf.lfCharSet=0;
    lf.lfPitchAndFamily=34;
    lf.lfHeight=xClientView/40;
    hNFont=CreateFontIndirect(&lf);
    paintDC.SelectObject(hNFont);
    paintDC.TextOut((-50-(strlen(szTString)*lf.lfWidth/2)),
                   240,szTString,strlen(szTString));

    y1=-100;
    y2=y1+15;
    for(i=0;i<iNWedges;i++) {
      hNBrush=CreateSolidBrush(crColor[i]);
      paintDC.SelectObject(hNBrush);
      paintDC.Pie(-180,180,180,-180,
                  (int) (radius*cos(2.0*pi*iTotalWedge[i]/
                  iTotalWedge[iNWedges])),
                  (int) (radius*sin(2.0*pi*iTotalWedge[i]/
                  iTotalWedge[iNWedges])),
                  (int) (radius*cos(2.0*pi*iTotalWedge[i+1]/
                  iTotalWedge[iNWedges])),
                  (int) (radius*sin(2.0*pi*iTotalWedge[i+1]/
                  iTotalWedge[iNWedges]))));
      if ((strlen(szTLabel[0])>0) && (xClientView>300)) {
        paintDC.Rectangle(190,y1,205,y2);
        paintDC.TextOut(210,y2+2,szTLabel[i],
                        strlen(szTLabel[i]));
        y1=y2+5;
        y2+=20;
      }
    }
}

class TMainApp : public TApplication {
  public:
    TMainApp() : TApplication("Main")
    {
    }
  void InitMainWindow();
};

void TMainWindow::GetWindowClass(WNDCLASS& WndClass)
```

```
{
  TWindow::GetWindowClass(WndClass);
  WndClass.style=0;
  WndClass.hbrBackground=CreateSolidBrush(RGB(180,180,180));
}

void TMainApp::InitMainWindow()
{
  MainWindow=new TMainWindow(0,"An OWL Pie Chart Application");
  MainWindow->SetCursor(this,"PieCursor");
  MainWindow->AssignMenu("PieMenu");
}

int OwlMain(int /*argc*/,char* /*argv*/ [])
{
  return TMainApp().Run();
}
```

The piechart.cpp application can be built as a 16-bit or 32-bit application. In addition to the three files just listed, you will need to create a unique cursor for this application. If you are building a 16-bit version for Windows 3.1, the project will also need a module definition file. The default module definition file offered by the Borland C++ compiler is acceptable.

The previous two applications have shown you how to add menu resources to an application. Our discussion for this application will concentrate on the inclusion of the dialog box resources.

Dialog Boxes

Examine the complete listing for this application shown earlier. Here you will notice the use of two Borland classes: **TFrameWindow** and **TDialog**. You have already learned the purpose of **TFrameWindow**. The **TDialog** class is the gateway to including dialog box resources in your application.

TDialog objects can be used for both modal and modeless dialog box elements. A *modal* dialog box disables operations in the parent's client window while it is open. *Modeless* dialog boxes are more like child windows. The focus of a modeless dialog box can be on the dialog box or the parent.

The **TDialog** class contains the following public data members:

```
TDialogAttr Attr;
bool IsModal;
```

Its constructor and destructor take on the following form:

```
TDialog(TWindow* parent,TResId resId,TModule* module=0);
~TDialog();
```

Its public member functions include:

```
void CloseWindow(int retValue=IDCANCEL);
void CmCancel();
void CmOk();
virtual bool Create();
virtual void Destroy(int retValue=IDCANCEL);
virtual bool DialogFunction(uint message,WPARAM wParam,LPARAM lParam);
virtual HWND DoCreate();
virtual int DoExecute();
void EvClose();
HBRUSH EvCtlColor(HDC hDC,HWND hWndChild,uint ctlType);
virtual bool EvInitDialog(HWND hWndFocus);
void EvPaint();
virtual void EvSetFont(HFONT hfont,bool redraw);
virtual int Execute();
uint GetDefaultId() const;
HWND GetItemHandle(int childId);
bool PerformDlgInit();
bool PreProcessMsg(MSG& msg);
uint32 SendDlgItemMsg(int ChildId,uint16 Msg,uint16 WParam,uint32 LParam);
void SetCaption(const char far* title);
void SetDefaultId(uint Id);
```

TDialog also contains several protected member functions:

```
char far* GetClassName();
void GetWindowClass(WNDCLASS& wndClass);
void SetupWindow();
```

The **TPieDialog** class, for this application, is derived from Borland's **TDialog** class and inherits its properties.

```
class TPieDialog : public TDialog
{
```

```
public:
  TPieDialog(TWindow* parent,const char far* name);
  void CmOk();
  void CmCancel();
  DECLARE_RESPONSE_TABLE(TPieDialog);
};
```

Examine the description of **TDialog**'s public member functions and observe that this application will use three member functions from the group: **CmOk()**, **CmCancel()**, and **TPieDialog()**.

Because **CmOk()** and **CmCancel()** must respond to Windows messages, a response table is required:

```
DEFINE_RESPONSE_TABLE1(TPieDialog,TDialog)
  EV_COMMAND(IDOK,CmOk),
  EV_COMMAND(IDCANCEL,CmCancel),
END_RESPONSE_TABLE;
```

A dialog box is created when requested by the member function. Here is the required code for establishing the Pie Chart Data and About Box dialog boxes:

```
void TMainWindow::CmIDMINPUT()
{
  TPieDialog(this,"PieDiaBox").Execute();
  Invalidate(TRUE);
  UpdateWindow();
}

void TMainWindow::CmIDMABOUT()
{
  TPieDialog(this,"AboutDiaBox").Execute();
}
```

An **Invalidate()** and **UpdateWindow()** function call is made when data entry is completed in the Pie Chart Data dialog box. These two functions update the client area on the user's screen.

The Pie Chart Data dialog box also uses a Cancel button. In this case, the dialog box is removed from the screen without updating the client area with new data. This portion of code is easy to implement with a simple call to the **EndDialog()** function.

```
void TPieDialog::CmCancel()
{
  EndDialog(HWindow,FALSE);
}
```

When users enter data, they are allowed to enter a pie chart title and data for the pie slices. This information is accepted when the Okay button is selected in the data entry dialog box. The title, and any optional labels, are returned as text strings with separate calls to the **GetDlgItemText()** function. Numeric information is returned with the **GetDlgItemInt()** function. This function translates the "numeric" string information entered by the user into an integer value which can be a signed or unsigned number.

```
void TPieDialog::CmOk()
{
  GetDlgItemText(IDD_TITLE,szTString,80);
  iWedgesize[0]=GetDlgItemInt(IDD_P1,NULL,0);
  iWedgesize[1]=GetDlgItemInt(IDD_P2,NULL,0);
         .
         .
         .

  GetDlgItemText(IDD_L1,szTLabel[0],20);
  GetDlgItemText(IDD_L2,szTLabel[1],20);
         .
         .
         .
```

The implementation of this code is fairly straightforward. Successful dialog box integration depends upon properly deriving the dialog class used in your application from Borland's **TDialog** class.

Application Details

The pie chart application is similar in structure to the line chart application presented in Chapter 22. However, because we are now working in an object-oriented environment there are a few details that must be addressed.

Examine this portion of the **EvPaint()** function:

```
TSize oldVExt,oldWExt,newWExt,newVExt;
TPoint oldOrg,newOrg;
int i,y1,y2,iNWedges;
unsigned int iTotalWedge[maxnumwedge+1];
```

The pie chart application changes the mapping mode, viewport, extent, and the origin. With a procedure-oriented approach, such as the line chart application in Chapter 22, individual variables are used to change the various function parameters. With Borland's OWL, a new approach is used—parameters are passed through either a **TSize** or **TPoint** structure.

Here is a portion of program code for setting these values:

```
paintDC.SetMapMode(MM_ISOTROPIC);
newWExt.cx=500;
newWExt.cy=500;
paintDC.SetWindowExt(newWExt,&oldWExt);
newVExt.cx=xClientView;
newVExt.cy=-yClientView;
paintDC.SetViewportExt(newVExt,&oldVExt);
newOrg.x=3*xClientView/8;
newOrg.y=yClientView/2;
paintDC.SetViewportOrg(newOrg,&oldOrg);
```

Here, the mapping mode is changed to MM_ISOTROPIC. The default drawing mode is MM_TEXT, which draws in "pixel" coordinates. Under MM_TEXT, point (0,0) is in the upper-left corner of the screen. MM_ISOTROPIC allows us to select the extent of both the X and Y axes.

The mapping mode is changed by calling the function **SetMapMode()**. When the function **SetWindowExt()** is called, it is passed the height and width of the client. These are logical coordinate sizes, which Windows adjusts (scales) to fit the physical display device. The display size values are used by the **SetViewportExt()** function. The negative sign for the -*yClientView* coordinate specifies increasing y values from the bottom of the screen. It should be no surprise that these are the values previously obtained by a WM_SIZE message. This application will place the pie chart on a traditional x, y coordinate system, with the center of the pie chart positioned at half the vertical distance and moved just a little to the left of center for the horizontal position. This positioning is necessary to accommodate the optional legend labels. The **SetViewportOrg()** function accomplishes this task.

The pie chart is created a slice at a time. The first slice is drawn starting on the positive X-axis and moving in a counterclockwise direction. The values in the *iTotalWedge[]* array have been scaled in order to form a complete (whole) pie regardless of the number or size of the slices. Here is the portion of code that draws the pie chart:

```
for(i=0;i<iNWedges;i++) {
   hNBrush=CreateSolidBrush(crColor[i]);
   paintDC.SelectObject(hNBrush);
   paintDC.Pie(-180,180,180,-180,
               (int) (radius*cos(2.0*pi*iTotalWedge[i]/
               iTotalWedge[iNWedges])),
               (int) (radius*sin(2.0*pi*iTotalWedge[i]/
               iTotalWedge[iNWedges])),
               (int) (radius*cos(2.0*pi*iTotalWedge[i+1]/
               iTotalWedge[iNWedges])),
               (int) (radius*sin(2.0*pi*iTotalWedge[i+1]/
               iTotalWedge[iNWedges]))));
   .
   .
   .
```

If legend labels are entered by the user, they will be drawn to the right of the pie chart. However, they will only be drawn if the pie chart is sufficiently large. If you examine the following portion of code, you will see that a check is made for the size of the *xClientView* variable. Do we need to check the size of *yClientView*, too?

```
   .
   .
   .
   if ((strlen(szTLabel[0])>0) && (xClientView>300)) {
      paintDC.Rectangle(190,y1,205,y2);
      paintDC.TextOut(210,y2+2,szTLabel[i],
                      strlen(szTLabel[i]));
      y1=y2+5;
      y2+=20;
   .
   .
   .
```

This check is necessary because the figure can be scaled to a very small size, and tiny little characters would be impossible to read.

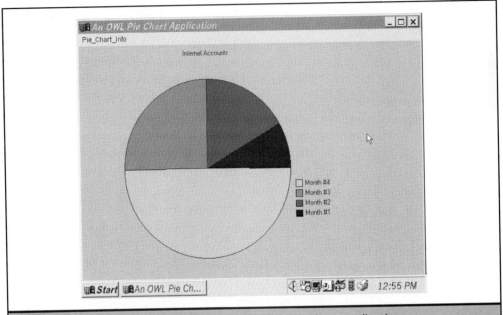

Figure 25-9. *A pie chart created with the OWL PieChart application*

Executing the Application

Use the Borland C++ compiler to build the pie chart application as either a 16-bit or 32-bit program. Figure 25-9 shows an example pie chart.

In the Next Chapter...

Borland's OWL offers just one solution to using libraries of objects when programming in an object-oriented environment. In the next two chapters we'll examine Microsoft's solution and learn how to use the Microsoft Foundation Class (MFC) library.

Chapter Twenty-Six

Using Microsoft's MFC Library

C lass or object libraries are unique and belong to the manufacturer of the C++ compiler. Although Borland's ObjectWindows Library (OWL) is perhaps the oldest object library on the market, it is not the only successful object-oriented library.

Microsoft also has an object-oriented solution, named the Microsoft Foundation Class library, or MFC. The Microsoft Foundation Class library is available in 16 and 32-bit versions. The 16-bit version is used for older Windows 3.1 applications, whereas the 32-bit version is designed exclusively for Windows 95 and Windows NT applications. The 32-bit version of the MFC has been expanded to include additional class support for control bars, property sheets, OLE, and so on.

Interest in the MFC library has increased dramatically over the past few years. It now appears that the MFC library will most likely become the defacto standard of object-oriented Windows libraries. Where does this leave the Borland C++ programmer? The answer is between a rock and a hard place. The current version of the Borland C++ compiler supports the Microsoft Foundation Class library but is not shipped with it. This is probably an indication that Borland will eventually license the MFC library from Microsoft. The question is, will they continue to support the OWL? Our prediction is that Borland will eventually ship both libraries, and over a period of time, de-emphasize the use of the OWL. The only catch to this is if Microsoft will not license the MFC to a manufacturer shipping a competing library.

At the present time, a programmer would be wise to understand how Borland's and Microsoft's class libraries are constructed and how they are used. This chapter examines the Microsoft Foundation Class (MFC) library for Windows code development. It discusses terms, definitions, and techniques that are common across all Microsoft Foundation Class versions. In the next chapter, you will see more detailed programming examples using the MFC.

To build the applications in this and the next chapter with the Borland C++ compiler, you will have to have access to the header and library files shipped with the Microsoft Visual C++ compiler.

What Is the Microsoft Foundation Class Library?

The MFC library is a collection of easy-to-use objects for the programmer. Windows, from its very inception, has followed many principles of object-oriented programming design within the framework of a non-object-oriented language like C. These features were discussed in Chapters 20 and 21. The use of the C++ language and Windows is a natural that can take full advantage of object-oriented features. The MFC library development team designed a comprehensive implementation of the Windows Application Program Interface (API). This C++ library encapsulates the most important data structures and API function calls within a group of reusable classes.

Class libraries such as the MFC library offer many advantages over the traditional function libraries used by C programmers. These advantages include the elimination of function and variable name collisions, encapsulation of code and data within the class, inheritance, reduced code size, and classes that appear to be natural extensions of the language.

By using the MFC, the code required to establish a window has been reduced to approximately one-third the length of a conventional application. This allows you, the developer, to spend less time communicating with Windows and more time developing your application's code.

Design Goals

The design team set rigorous design principles that had to be followed in the implementation of the MFC library. These guidelines include:

- Mixing traditional functions calls with the use of new class libraries
- Balancing power and efficiency in the design of the libraries, making the transition from standard API function calls to the use of class libraries as simple as possible
- Designing a library that can migrate easily to new platforms, such as Windows 95 and NT
- Using the power of C++ without overwhelming the programmer

The C++ foundation classes are designed to be small in size and fast in execution time. Their simplicity makes them very easy to use, and their execution speed almost matches the speed of the bulkier function libraries of C.

These classes were also designed to require a minimal amount of relearning of function names. This feature was achieved by carefully naming and designing class features. The MFC library also permits a "mixed-mode" operation. Here, classes and traditional function calls can be intermixed in the same source code.

The development team designed the original class library to be dynamic rather than static. Thus, the MFC library is fully integrated across all platforms, including Windows 3.1, Windows 95, and Windows NT.

The CObject Parent Class

All class libraries have a root parent class, as you saw in Chapter 23. When working with Borland's OWL, for example, we often used TFrameWindow as the parent for our derived classes. Microsoft also uses a few classes as parent classes with additional classes being derived from them. **CObject** is one MFC parent class used extensively in developing Windows applications. The MFC library header files provide a wealth of information on defined classes.

CObject is defined in the Microsoft afx.h header file. The following portion of code has been edited for clarity, but is essentially the same for both 16-bit and 32-bit versions:

```
class CObject
{
public:
  virtual CRuntimeClass* GetRuntimeClass() const;

virtual ~CObject();
  void* operator new(size_t, void* p);
  void* operator new(size_t nSize);
  void operator delete(void* p);
  void* operator new(size_t nSize, LPCSTR lpszFileName, int nLine);

protected:
  CObject();

private:
  CObject(const CObject& objectSrc);
  void operator=(const CObject& objectSrc);

public:
  BOOL IsSerializable() const;
  BOOL IsKindOf(const CRuntimeClass* pClass) const;
  virtual void Serialize(CArchive& ar);
  virtual void AssertValid() const;
  virtual void Dump(CDumpContext& dc) const;

public:
  static CRuntimeClass AFXAPI_DATA classCObject;
};
```

Notice the components that make up the **CObject** class definition. First, **CObject** is divided into public, protected, and private parts. **CObject** also provides normal and dynamic type checking and serialization. Dynamic type checking allows the type of object to be determined at run time. The state of the object can be saved to a storage medium, such as a disk, through a concept called *persistence*. Object persistence means that object member functions will be persistent, permitting retrieval of object data.

Child classes are derived from parent classes. **CGdiObject** is an example of a class derived from **CObject**. Here is the **CGdiObject** definition as found in the Microsoft afxwin.h header file. Again, this listing has been edited for clarity.

```
class CGdiObject : public CObject
{
  DECLARE_DYNCREATE(CGdiObject)

public:
  HGDIOBJ m_hObject;
  HGDIOBJ GetSafeHandle() const;
  static CGdiObject* PASCAL FromHandle(HGDIOBJ hObject);
  static void PASCAL DeleteTempMap();
  BOOL Attach(HGDIOBJ hObject);
  HGDIOBJ Detach();
  CGdiObject();
  BOOL DeleteObject();
  int GetObject(int nCount, LPVOID lpObject) const;
  BOOL CreateStockObject(int nIndex);
  BOOL UnrealizeObject();

public:
  virtual ~CGdiObject();

#ifdef _DEBUG
  virtual void Dump(CDumpContext& dc) const;
  virtual void AssertValid() const;
#endif
};
```

CGdiObject and its member functions allow drawing items such as stock and custom pens, brushes, and fonts to be created and used in Windows applications.

It is not necessary to know how the various classes are defined in order to use them efficiently. For example, in procedure-oriented Windows applications, the **DeleteObject()** function can be called in the following manner:

```
DeleteObject(hBRUSH);   /*hBRUSH is the brush handle*/
```

In C++ the same results will be achieved by using the MFC library in the following manner:

```
newbrush.DeleteObject(); //newbrush is current brush
```

Switching between procedure-oriented function calls and MFC library objects can be intuitive. Microsoft has used this approach in developing all Windows classes, making the transition from traditional function calls to MFC library objects very easy.

Additional Parent Classes

Table 26-1 lists additional 32-bit MFC library classes. These classes are derived from the parent, **CObject**.

```
Cobject
      CException*
            CMemoryException*
            CFileException*
            CArchiveException*
            CNotSupportedException*
            CUserException*
            COleException*
                  COleDispatchException*
            CDBException*
      CFile*
            CStdioFile*
            CMemFile*
            COleStreamFile*
      CDC*
            CClientDC*
            CWindowDC*
            CPaintDC*
            CMetaFileDC*
      CGdiObject*
            CPen*
            CBrush*
            CFont*
            CBitmap*
            CPalette*
            CRgn*
      CMenu*
      CArray
      CByteArray*
      CWordArray*
      CDWordArray*
      CPtrArray*
      CObArray*
```

Table 26-1.   *Classes Derived from Microsoft's CObject*

```
        CStringArray*
        CUIntArray*
        CList
        CPtrList*
        CObList*
        CStringList*
        CMap
        CMapWordToPtr*
        CMapPtrToWord*
        CMapPtrToPtr*
        CMapWordToOb*
        CMapStringToPtr*
        CMapStringToOb*
        CMapStringToString*
        CDatabase*
        CRecordSet*
        CLongBinary*
        CCmdTarget
            CWinThread
                CWinApp
            CDocTemplate
                CSingleDocTemplate
                CMultiDocTemplate
            COleObjectFactory
                COleTemplateServer
            COleDataSource
            COleDropSource
            COleDropTarget
            COleMessageFilter
            CDocument
                COleDocument
                    COleLinkingDoc
                        COleServerDoc
            CDocItem
                COleClientItem
                COleServerItem
    CWnd
        CFrameWnd
            CMDIChildWnd
            CMDIFrameWnd
```

Table 26-1. *Classes Derived from Microsoft's CObject (continued)*

```
                        CMiniFrameWnd
                        COleIPFrameWnd
                CControlBar
                        CToolBar
                        CStatusBar
                        CDialogBar
                        COleResizeBar
            CSplitterWnd
            CPropertySheet
            CDialog
        COleDialog
            COleInsertDialog
            COleChangeIconDialog
            COlePasteSpecialDialog
            COleConvertDialog
            COleBusyDialog
            COleLinksDialog
                COleUpdateDialog
    CFileDialog
    CColorDialog
    CFontDialog
    CPrintDialog
    CFindReplaceDialog
    CPropertyPage
    CView
        CScrollView
            CFormView
                CRecordView
    CEditView
    CStatic
    CButton
        CBitmapButton
    CListBox
    CComboBox
    CScrollBar
    CEdit
```

*These classes are also supported by the 16-bit MFC library.

Table 26-1. *Classes Derived from Microsoft's CObject (continued)*

Additionally, the MFC library offers run-time object model support. Table 26-2 lists 32-bit run-time object model support classes.

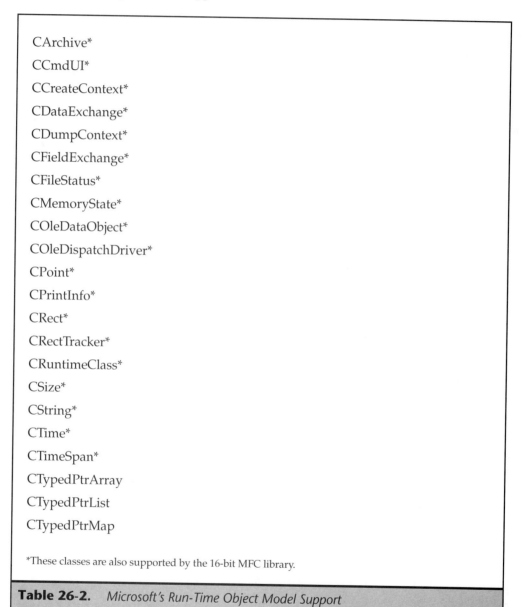

CArchive*

CCmdUI*

CCreateContext*

CDataExchange*

CDumpContext*

CFieldExchange*

CFileStatus*

CMemoryState*

COleDataObject*

COleDispatchDriver*

CPoint*

CPrintInfo*

CRect*

CRectTracker*

CRuntimeClass*

CSize*

CString*

CTime*

CTimeSpan*

CTypedPtrArray

CTypedPtrList

CTypedPtrMap

*These classes are also supported by the 16-bit MFC library.

Table 26-2.   *Microsoft's Run-Time Object Model Support*

These tables will help you as you continue to study the MFC library in Chapter 27.

A Simple MFC Application

When using the MFC library there is a minimal amount of code necessary just to establish a window on the screen. You'll soon see that this minimal amount of code is about one-third the size of an equivalent procedure-oriented application.

In this section, we'll examine the simplest possible Windows application, named simple.cpp. This application will create a window on the screen and place a title in its title bar area.

Creating a Window

If this application is to be compiled as a 16-bit application, you will need to create a module definition file along with the source code file. If the application is to be compiled as a 32-bit application, the module definition file is not needed. Here is a sample module definition file for 16-bit builds named simple.def:

```
NAME            Simple
DESCRIPTION     'Creating A Window with MFC'
EXETYPE         WINDOWS
STUB            'WINSTUB.EXE'
CODE            PRELOAD MOVEABLE DISCARDABLE
DATA            PRELOAD MOVEABLE MULTIPLE
HEAPSIZE        2048
```

The source code file, although initially strange in appearance, is much shorter than its procedure-oriented counterparts. Here is the source code listing for simple.cpp:

```
//
//  Simple.cpp
//  The minimum object-oriented code needed to establish a
//  window with the Microsoft Foundation Class library.
//  To build this application with the Borland C++ compiler
//  you will need access to Microsoft's MFC header and
//  library files.
//  Copyright (c) Chris H. Pappas and William H. Murray, 1996
//

#include <afxwin.h>

class CTheApp : public CWinApp
{
public:
  virtual BOOL InitInstance();
```

```
};

class CMainWnd : public CFrameWnd
{
public:
  CMainWnd()
  {
    Create(NULL,"Using the MFC library",
           WS_OVERLAPPEDWINDOW,rectDefault,NULL,NULL);
  }
};

BOOL CTheApp::InitInstance()
{
  m_pMainWnd=new CMainWnd();
  m_pMainWnd->ShowWindow(m_nCmdShow);
  m_pMainWnd->UpdateWindow();

  return TRUE;
}

CTheApp TheApp;
```

Once these files are entered, you can compile this application from the integrated environment by creating a project file that includes the use of the MFC library.

The following sections examine how each piece of code works in establishing the resulting window on the screen.

The afxwin.h Header File

The Microsoft afxwin.h header file is the gateway to Windows programming with the MFC library. This header file calls all subsequent header files, including windows.h, as they are needed. Using one header file also aids in creating precompiled header files. Precompiled header files save time when repeated compilation is being done during application development.

You might want to print a copy of afxwin.h for your reference as you continue to study the MFC library. This header file has grown to almost 100 pages in the 32-bit version of the Visual C++ compiler!

Deriving CTheApp from CWinApp

This application derives our class, **CTheApp**, from the MFC parent class **CWinApp**. The **CTheApp** object is defined by the programmer.

```
class CTheApp : public CWinApp
{
public:
  virtual BOOL InitInstance();
};
```

The **CTheApp** class overrides the member function, **InitInstance()**, of the **CWinApp class**. You will find that overriding member functions occurs frequently. By overriding **InitInstance()**, you can customize the initialization and execution of the application. In **CWinApp**, it is also possible to override **InitApplication()**, **ExitInstance()**, and **OnIdle()**, but for most applications this will not be necessary.

Here is an edited portion of the **CWinApp** class description, as found in the Microsoft afxwin.h header file:

```
class CWinApp : public CObject
{
  DECLARE_DYNAMIC(CWinApp)
public:
  CWinApp(const char* pszAppName=NULL);
  void SetCurrentHandles();

  const char* m_pszAppName;
  HANDLE m_hInstance;
  HANDLE m_hPrevInstance;
  LPSTR m_lpCmdLine;
  int m_nCmdShow;

  CWnd* m_pMainWnd;

  HCURSOR LoadCursor(LPSTR lpCursorName);
  HCURSOR LoadCursor(WORD nIDCursor);
  HCURSOR LoadStandardCursor(LPSTR lpCursorName);
  HCURSOR LoadOEMCursor(WORD nIDCursor);

  HICON LoadIcon(LPSTR lpIconName);
  HICON LoadIcon(WORD nIDIcon);
  HICON LoadStandardIcon(LPSTR lpIconName);
  HICON LoadOEMIcon(WORD nIDIcon);

  BOOL PumpMessage();
```

```
    virtual BOOL InitApplication();
    virtual BOOL InitInstance();

    virtual int Run();

    virtual BOOL PreTranslateMessage(MSG* pMsg);
    virtual BOOL OnIdle(LONG lCount);
    virtual int ExitInstance();

protected:
   MSG m_msgCur;
};
```

The **CWinApp** class is responsible for establishing and implementing the Windows message loop. Message loops, which were discussed in Chapters 2, 3, and 4, eliminate many lines of repetitive code.

The CFrameWnd Class

The window created by the **CMainWnd** class is defined in the **CFrameWnd** base class, as shown in the following segment of code:

```
class CMainWnd : public CFrameWnd
{
public:
   CMainWnd()
   {
     Create(NULL,"Using the MFC library",
            WS_OVERLAPPEDWINDOW,rectDefault,NULL,NULL);
   }
};
```

The constructor for the class, **CMainWnd()**, calls the **Create()** member function to create initial window parameters. For this application, the window's style and caption are provided as parameters. In Chapter 27, you'll see that it is also possible to specify a menu name and an accelerator table when this member function is used.

Here is an edited portion of **CFrameWnd**, also found in the Microsoft afxwin.h header file:

```
class CFrameWnd : public CWnd
{
  DECLARE_DYNAMIC(CFrameWnd)

protected:
  HANDLE m_hAccelTable;

public:
  static const CRect rectDefault;

  CFrameWnd();

  BOOL LoadAccelTable(const char FAR* lpAccelTableName);
  BOOL Create(const char FAR* lpClassName,
              const char FAR* lpWindowName,
              DWORD dwStyle = WS_OVERLAPPEDWINDOW,
              const RECT& rect = rectDefault,
              const CWnd* pParentWnd = NULL,
              const char FAR* lpMenuName = NULL);

public:
  virtual ~CFrameWnd();
  virtual CFrameWnd* GetParentFrame();
  virtual CFrameWnd* GetChildFrame();

protected:
  virtual BOOL PreTranslateMessage(MSG* pMsg);
};
```

The first parameter used by the **Create()** function allows a class name to be given in compliance with the traditional Windows API **RegisterClass()** function. Normally, this will be set to NULL in the applications you develop and a class name will not be required.

Member Functions

Recall that the derived **CTheApp** class object overrode the **InitInstance()** member function. Here is how this application implements **InitInstance()**:

```
BOOL CTheApp::InitInstance()
{
  m_pMainWnd=new CMainWnd();
  m_pMainWnd->ShowWindow(m_nCmdShow);
  m_pMainWnd->UpdateWindow();

  return TRUE;
}
```

The **new** operator invokes the class constructor **CMainWnd.** The m_pMainWnd member variable (m_ indicates a member variable) holds the location for the application's main window. The **ShowWindow()** member function is used to display the window on the screen. The parameter, m_nCmdShow, is initialized by the application's constructor. The **UpdateWindow()** member function displays and paints the window being sent to the screen.

The Constructor

The last piece of code invokes the application's constructor at startup:

```
CTheApp TheApp;
```

The code is very simple and straightforward. The application creates a window; but does not permit you to draw anything in the window.

Running the Application

Figure 26-1 shows a window similar to the one that will appear on your screen. Although the application didn't draw anything in the client area of the window, it did give the application a new title!

This code forms the foundation for all MFC library applications in this chapter and in Chapter 27.

A Template Application

Let's expand the previous application so that we can draw in the window's client area. This application, named Template, draws a message in the window's client area. The code used in the Template application will make it easier for us to build applications in the next chapter.

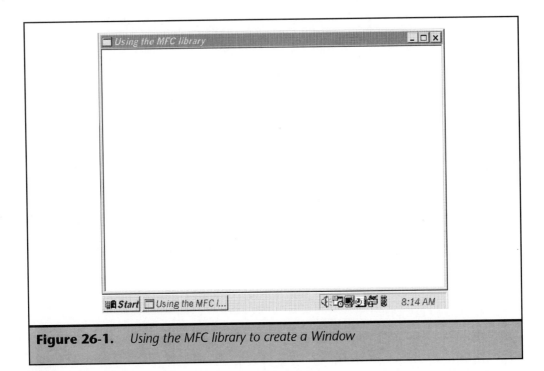

Figure 26-1. *Using the MFC library to create a Window*

 NOTE: If you are building a 16-bit version of this application, you will need a module definition file similar to the one shown in the previous section.

The Template.h header file contains information on how the application's classes were derived from the MFC library. This is a style of coding that is promoted by Microsoft. Here is the Template.h header file listing:

```
class CMainWnd : public CFrameWnd
{
public:
  CMainWnd();
  afx_msg void OnPaint();
  DECLARE_MESSAGE_MAP();
};

class CTemplateApp : public CWinApp
{
public:
  BOOL InitInstance();
};
```

The C++ source code file is straightforward. As you examine the following Template.cpp file, pay particular attention to the length of the listing:

```cpp
//
//  Template.cpp
//  A complete Windows application using the MFC library.
//  This code can serve as a template for the development
//  of other MFC applications.
//  To build this application with the Borland C++ compiler
//  you will need access to Microsoft's MFC header and
//  library files.
//  Copyright (c) Chris H. Pappas and William H. Murray, 1996
//

#include <afxwin.h>
#include "Template.h"

CTemplateApp theApp;

CMainWnd::CMainWnd()
{
  Create(NULL,"A Complete MFC Windows Application",
         WS_OVERLAPPEDWINDOW,rectDefault,NULL,NULL);
}

void CMainWnd::OnPaint()
{
  CPaintDC dc(this);
  dc.TextOut(150,200,"Drawing in the Client Area",26);
}

BEGIN_MESSAGE_MAP(CMainWnd,CFrameWnd)
  ON_WM_PAINT()
END_MESSAGE_MAP()

BOOL CTemplateApp::InitInstance()
{
  m_pMainWnd=new CMainWnd();
  m_pMainWnd->ShowWindow(m_nCmdShow);
  m_pMainWnd->UpdateWindow();

  return TRUE;
}
```

This source code listing gives you a chance to examine all of the code necessary to produce this working template application. The next sections examine those details that are unique to this application.

The Header File

The header file used in this example indicates class definitions that are unique to the application. As a matter of style, this type of header file type will always be identified by the filename and the .h file extension—for example, Template.h. In Chapter 27, you'll see another type of header file. This header file can contain menu and dialog box resource identification values. When this second style of header file is used, we will identify it with an additional *R* (for resource) at the end of the filename. For example, if the application in this section had used a resource ID header file, it would have been named TemplateR.h.

The definitions for two classes are contained in the Template.h header file. **CMainWnd** is derived from **CWinApp**, and **CTemplateApp** is derived from **CFrameWnd**:

```
class CMainWnd : public CFrameWnd
{
public:
  CMainWnd();
  afx_msg void OnPaint();
  DECLARE_MESSAGE_MAP();
};

class CTemplateApp : public CWinApp
{
public:
  BOOL InitInstance();
};
```

NOTE: *These classes were contained in the body of the Simple.cpp application and were explained earlier in this chapter. Putting class descriptions in a separate header file is a matter of style – a style encouraged by Microsoft.*

As you examine the previous listing, notice that **CMainWnd** contains a function declaration, **OnPaint()**, and the addition of a message map. For member functions such as **OnPaint()**, the **afx_msg** keyword is used instead of **virtual**. **OnPaint()** is a member function of the **CWnd** class that the **CMainWnd** class overrides. This allows the client area of the window to be altered. The **OnPaint()** function is automatically called when a WM_PAINT message is sent to a **CMainWnd** object.

DECLARE_MESSAGE_MAP is used in virtually all MFC Windows applications. This line states that the class overrides the handling of certain messages. (See the body of the application.) Microsoft uses message maps, instead of virtual functions, because they are more space efficient.

The Source Code File

The majority of this application's code is the same as the code found in Simple.cpp. The difference is the addition of the **OnPaint()** message handler function. Examine the piece of code shown here:

```
void CMainWnd::OnPaint()
{
  CPaintDC dc(this);
  dc.TextOut(150,200,"Drawing in the Client Area,26);
}
```

A device context is required for handling the WM_PAINT message. Any Windows GDI functions that are encapsulated in the device context can be used when drawing in the client area. When the **OnPaint()** function has ended, the destructor for **CPaintDC** is called automatically.

This application uses a fairly short message map, as the following code indicates:

```
BEGIN_MESSAGE_MAP(CMainWnd,CFrameWnd)
  ON_WM_PAINT()
END_MESSAGE_MAP()
```

Two classes are specified by BEGIN_MESSAGE_MAP: **CMainWnd** and **CFrameWnd**. **CMainWnd** is the target class, and **CFrameWnd** is a class based on **CWnd**. The **ON_WM_PAINT()** function handles all WM_PAINT messages and directs them to the **OnPaint()** member function just discussed. In Chapter 27, you'll see many additional functions added to the message map.

The biggest advantage of using message maps is the elimination of many switch/case statements that are error prone and typical of procedure-oriented applications.

Running the Application

When you create the project file for this application, you'll have to provide access to the MFC header and library files. Once you have entered the application code and received an error-free compilation, run the program. The screen should be similar to the one shown in Figure 26-2.

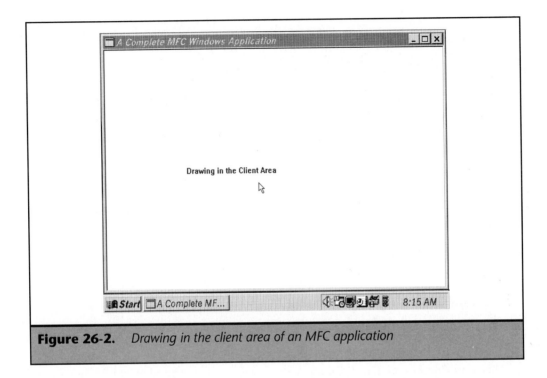

Figure 26-2.   *Drawing in the client area of an MFC application*

If you want to experiment with other GDI primitives, just remove the **TextOut()** function call and insert the GDI function of your choice into the template code. You can choose from functions such as **Ellipse()**, **LineTo()**, **MoveTo()**, **Rectangle()**, and so on.

In the Next Chapter...

In the next chapter, you will learn how to build MFC applications with resources. You will find that adding resources to a MFC project is just as easy as adding them to an OWL application.

Chapter Twenty-Seven

Adding Resources to MFC Applications

763

In this chapter, you'll learn how to add resources to Microsoft Foundation Class (MFC) library applications. These resources include menus, dialog boxes, keyboard accelerators, and so on. Chapter 26 described the theory and specifications of the Microsoft Foundation Class library and taught you how to build simple applications.

The program listings for each application are quite long, so enter them carefully. Notice how much shorter these listings are than their procedure-oriented counterparts in Chapters 21 and 22.

The applications in this chapter will require access to Microsoft's MFC header files and library files when compiled with the Borland C++ compiler. At the time of this writing, they were not being supplied with the Borland C++ compiler.

A Fourier Waveform Application

The nice thing about this object-oriented Fourier Series application is that you can compare the overall program code with its procedure-oriented counterpart in Chapter 22. You'll be able to see, firsthand, if there are advantages to object-oriented coding. This application uses two Windows resources: a menu and a dialog box. You may want to refer to Chapter 22 for the details on the techniques for creating each of these resources.

As the complexity of each application grows, so does the list of files required for compiling and linking. This application requires a module definition file (for Windows 3.1 builds only) named fourier.def, a header file named fourier.h, a resource header file named fourierr.h (note the addition of the extra *r*), a resource script file named fourier.rc, a dialog script file named fourier.dlg, and the source code file named fourier.cpp.

Enter each file carefully. When all the files have been entered, the application can be built from the Borland IDE, if the Microsoft MFC header and library files are available.

REMEMBER: Also include fourier.def, fourier.rc, and fourier.cpp in your project file's list of files required for the build process.

Here is a module definition file, fourier.def, used for 16-bit builds only:

```
NAME          Fourier
DESCRIPTION   'Drawing A Fourier Series Waveform'
EXETYPE       WINDOWS
STUB          'WINSTUB.EXE'
CODE          PRELOAD MOVEABLE DISCARDABLE
DATA          PRELOAD MOVEABLE MULTIPLE
HEAPSIZE      4096
```

Next, remember that one header file is used for class information, as you can see in the fourier.h file, which follows:

```
class CMainWnd : public CFrameWnd
{
public:
  CMainWnd();
  afx_msg void OnPaint();
  afx_msg void OnSize(UINT,int,int);
  afx_msg int  OnCreate(LPCREATESTRUCT cs);
  afx_msg void OnAbout();
  afx_msg void OnFourierData();
  afx_msg void OnExit();
  DECLARE_MESSAGE_MAP()
};


class CFourier : public CWinApp
{
public:
  virtual BOOL InitInstance();
};


class CFourierDataDialog : public CModalDialog
{
public:
  CFourierDataDialog(CWnd* pParentWnd=NULL)
                    : CModalDialog("FourierData",pParentWnd)
                    {  }
  virtual void OnOK();
};
```

Another header file contains the traditional ID values needed by menus and dialog boxes. This file is named fourierr.h:

```
#define IDM_FOUR    200
#define IDM_ABOUT   210
#define IDM_EXIT    220
#define IDD_TERMS   300
#define IDD_TITLE   310
```

The resource script file, fourier.rc, for this example includes a description for a menu and a call to include the dialog box script file:

```
#include <windows.h>
#include <afxres.h>
#include "FourierR.h"

FourierMenu MENU
BEGIN
  POPUP "Data Input"
  BEGIN
    MENUITEM "Fourier Data...",   IDM_FOUR
    MENUITEM "Fourier About...",  IDM_ABOUT
    MENUITEM "Exit",              IDM_EXIT
  END
END


rcinclude Fourier.dlg
```

There are two dialog box descriptions contained in the fourier.dlg script file. A simple About box and a data entry dialog box are described here:

```
DLGINCLUDE RCDATA DISCARDABLE
BEGIN
  "FourierR.h\0"
END

ABOUTBOX DIALOG DISCARDABLE  14,22,200,75
  STYLE WS_POPUP | WS_CAPTION
  CAPTION "About Box"
BEGIN
  CTEXT "A MFC Fourier Series Application",-1,30,5,144,8
  CTEXT "By Chris H. Pappas and William H. Murray",
        -1,28,28,144,8
  CTEXT "(c) Copyright 1996",201,68,38,83,8
  defPUSHBUTTON "OK",IDOK,84,55,32,14,WS_GROUP
END

FOURIERDATA DIALOG DISCARDABLE 74,21,142,70
  STYLE WS_POPUP | WS_CAPTION
  CAPTION "Fourier Data"
BEGIN
  LTEXT "Title: ",-1,6,5,28,8,NOT WS_GROUP
  EDITTEXT IDD_TITLE,33,1,106,12
```

```
       LTEXT "Number of terms: ",-1,6,23,70,8,NOT WS_GROUP
       EDITTEXT IDD_TERMS,76,18,32,12
       PUSHBUTTON "OK",IDOK,25,52,24,14
       PUSHBUTTON "Cancel",IDCANCEL,89,53,28,14
   END
```

The source code file, fourier.cpp, is slightly more complicated than the templates of
the previous chapter because it must handle a menu and two dialog box resources. See
if you can find this additional code as you examine the following listing:

```cpp
//
//  Fourier.cpp
//  An MFC Fourier Series application.
//  To build this with the Borland C++ compiler
//  requires access to Microsoft's MFC header
//  and library files.
//  Copyright (c) Chris H. Pappas and William H. Murray, 1996
//

#include <afxwin.h>
#include <string.h>
#include <math.h>
#include "FourierR.h"    // resource IDs
#include "Fourier.h"

int m_cxClient,m_cyClient;
char mytitle[80]="Title";
int nterms=1;


CFourier theApp;


CMainWnd::CMainWnd()
{
  Create((AfxRegisterWndClass(CS_HREDRAW|CS_VREDRAW,
        LoadCursor(NULL,IDC_CROSS),
        (HBRUSH) (GetStockObject(WHITE_BRUSH)),NULL)),
        "A MFC Fourier Series Application",
        WS_OVERLAPPEDWINDOW,rectDefault,NULL,"FourierMenu");
}


void CMainWnd::OnSize(UINT,int x,int y)
```

```
{
  m_cxClient=x;
  m_cyClient=y;
}

void CMainWnd::OnPaint()
{
  CPaintDC dc(this);
  int i,j,ltitle,ang;
  double y,yp;
  CBrush newbrush;
  CBrush* oldbrush;
  CPen newpen;
  CPen* oldpen;

  // create a custom drawing surface
  dc.SetMapMode(MM_ISOTROPIC);
  dc.SetWindowExt(500,500);
  dc.SetViewportExt(m_cxClient,-m_cyClient);
  dc.SetViewportOrg(m_cxClient/20,m_cyClient/2);

  ang=0;
  yp=0.0;

  newpen.CreatePen(BS_SOLID,2,RGB(0,0,0));
  oldpen=dc.SelectObject(&newpen);

  // draw x & y coordinate axes
  dc.MoveTo(0,240);
  dc.LineTo(0,-240);
  dc.MoveTo(0,0);
  dc.LineTo(400,0);
  dc.MoveTo(0,0);
  // draw actual Fourier waveform
  for (i=0; i<=400; i++) {
    for (j=1; j<=nterms; j++) {
      y=(150.0/((2.0*j)-1.0))*sin(((j*2.0)-1.0)*0.015708*ang);
      yp=yp+y;
    }
    dc.LineTo(i,(int) yp);
    yp-=yp;
```

```
    ang++;
  }

  // prepare to fill interior of waveform newbrush.
  newbrush.CreateSolidBrush(RGB(127,127,127));
  oldbrush=dc.SelectObject(&newbrush);
  dc.ExtFloodFill(150,10,RGB(0,0,0),FLOODFILLBORDER);
  dc.ExtFloodFill(300,-10,RGB(0,0,0),FLOODFILLBORDER);

  // print waveform title
  ltitle=strlen(mytitle);
  dc.TextOut(200-(ltitle*8/2),185,mytitle,ltitle);

  // delete brush objects
  dc.SelectObject(oldbrush);
  newbrush.DeleteObject();
}

int CMainWnd::OnCreate(LPCREATESTRUCT)
{
  UpdateWindow();
  return (0);
}

void CMainWnd::OnAbout()
{
  CModalDialog about("AboutBox",this);
  about.DoModal();
}

void CFourierDataDialog::OnOK()
{
  GetDlgItemText(IDD_TITLE,mytitle,80);
  nterms=GetDlgItemInt(IDD_TERMS,NULL,0);
  CModalDialog::OnOK();
}

void CMainWnd::OnFourierData()
{
  CFourierDataDialog dlgFourierData(this);
  if (dlgFourierData.DoModal()==IDOK) {
```

```
        InvalidateRect(NULL,TRUE);
        UpdateWindow();
    }
};

void CMainWnd::OnExit()
{
    DestroyWindow();
}

BEGIN_MESSAGE_MAP(CMainWnd,CFrameWnd)
    ON_WM_PAINT()
    ON_WM_SIZE()
    ON_WM_CREATE()
    ON_COMMAND(IDM_ABOUT,OnAbout)
    ON_COMMAND(IDM_FOUR,OnFourierData)
    ON_COMMAND(IDM_EXIT,OnExit)
END_MESSAGE_MAP()

BOOL CFourier::InitInstance()
{
    m_pMainWnd=new CMainWnd();
    m_pMainWnd->ShowWindow(m_nCmdShow);
    m_pMainWnd->UpdateWindow();
    return TRUE;
}
```

The Application's Header File

Examine the code segment below. Notice that **CMainWnd** now contains several function declarations and a message map. The member functions include **OnPaint()**, **OnSize()**, **OnCreate()**, **OnAbout()**, **OnFourierData()**, and **OnExit()**. The **afx_msg** keyword is used instead of **virtual**. **OnPaint()** is a member function of the **CWnd** class that the **CMainWnd** class overrides. This allows the client area of the window to be altered.

```
afx_msg void OnPaint();
afx_msg void OnSize(UINT,int,int);
afx_msg int  OnCreate(LPCREATESTRUCT cs);
afx_msg void OnAbout();
```

```
afx_msg void OnFourierData();
afx_msg void OnExit();
```

The **OnPaint()** function is automatically called when a WM_PAINT message is sent to a **CMainWnd** object by Windows or the application. **OnSize()** is called whenever a WM_SIZE message is generated by a change in the size of the window. This information will be useful for scaling graphics to the window size. **OnCreate()** points to a structure that contains information about the window being created. This structure contains information on the size, style, and other aspects of the window. **OnAbout()**, **OnFourierData()**, and **OnExit()** are user-defined functions that respond to WM_COMMAND messages. WM_COMMAND messages are generated when the user selects an option from a menu or dialog box.

DECLARE_MESSAGE_MAP is used again to state that the class overrides the handling of certain messages. (See the body of the application.) Recall that this technique is more space efficient than the use of virtual functions.

The MFC library supports regular and modal dialog boxes with the **CDialog** and **CModalDialog** classes. For very simple dialog boxes such as About boxes, the Foundation Class can be used directly. For data entry dialog boxes, however, the class will have to be derived. The dialog box for this example will permit the user to enter an optional graph title and an integer for the number of harmonics to be drawn in the window. The **CFourierDataDialog** class is derived from the **CModalDialog** foundation class. Modal dialog boxes must be dismissed before other actions can be taken in an application, as shown here:

```
class CFourierDataDialog : public CModalDialog
{
public:
  CFourierDataDialog(CWnd* pParentWnd=NULL)
                   : CModalDialog("FourierData",pParentWnd)
                   { }
  virtual void OnOK();
};
```

Member variables and functions can be added to specify the behavior of the dialog box in a derived modal dialog class. Member variables can also be used to save data entered by the user or to save data for display. Classes derived from **CModalDialog** require their own message maps. The exceptions are the **OnInitDialog()**, **OnOK()**, and **OnCancel()** functions.

The **CFourierDataDialog** constructor supplies the name of the dialog box, FourierData, and the name of the parent window that owns the dialog box. There is no owner for this modal dialog box.

The dialog box will return data to the application when the user clicks on the OK dialog box button. If either the OK or the Cancel button is clicked, the dialog box closes and is removed from the screen. When the dialog box closes, the member functions access its member variables to retrieve information entered by the user. Dialog boxes requiring initialization can override the **OnInitDialog()** member function for this purpose.

The Application's Resource Header, Resource Script, and Dialog Script Files

The resource header file (fourierr.h), the resource script file (fourier.rc), and the dialog script file (fourier.dlg) are all used by the resource compiler to produce a single compiled Windows resource.

The resource header file contains five identification values. IDM_FOUR, IDM_ABOUT, and IDM_EXIT correspond to menu selections, whereas IDD_TERMS and IDD_TITLE are used by the data entry dialog box.

The resource script file also contains a description of the application's menu, which is shown in Figure 27-1. Compare the menu title and features to the text used to create the menu in the resource file.

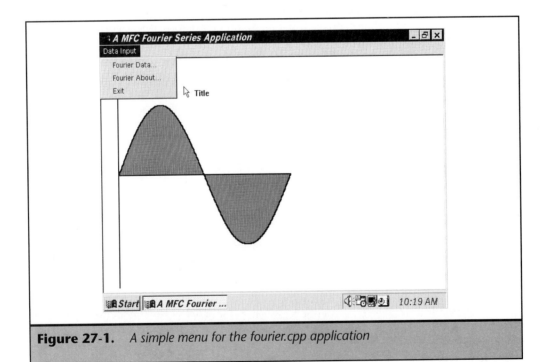

Figure 27-1.   *A simple menu for the fourier.cpp application*

It is possible to merge dialog box script information with the resource script file, however, in this example they are separate files. In large applications, it is often desirable to leave the dialog script file as a separate entity and combine it with other resources when it is compiled by the resource compiler. Here, fourier.dlg contains the script information for the About Box and FourierData dialog boxes. Figure 27-2 shows the About box for this application.

Figure 27-3 shows the data entry dialog box for this application.

Compare the contents of the fourier.dlg file with the actual screen figures. Remember that the dialog box resources are constructed with the dialog box editor supplied with the Borland IDE.

The Application's Source Code File

The source code file for this example has increased in size and complexity because of the inclusion of menu and dialog box resources. Additionally, you'll see how to select a new cursor, set the background color, determine the size of the current window, set a new viewport and origin for drawing, and draw and fill an object in the window.

Let's examine these features and resources as they appear in the program.

Designing a CMainWnd Class

The **CMainWnd** class can be customized by using **AfxRegisterWndClass** to create a registration class. A registration class has many fields, but four are easily altered: style, cursor, background, and the minimize icon.

The following portion of code shows the syntax for changing the cursor to a stock cross shape (IDC_CROSS) and setting the brush that paints the background to a WHITE_BRUSH:

```
CMainWnd::CMainWnd()
{
  Create((AfxRegisterWndClass(CS_HREDRAW|CS_VREDRAW,
        LoadCursor(NULL,IDC_CROSS),
        (HBRUSH) GetStockObject(WHITE_BRUSH),NULL)),
        "A MFC Fourier Series Application",
        WS_OVERLAPPEDWINDOW,rectDefault,NULL,"FourierMenu");
}
```

Notice, too, that the menu name is identified in the **Create()** member function.

Finding the Window's Current Size

The current size of the window can be determined with a call to the **OnSize()** member function. A WM_SIZE message is generated whenever the window is resized. The

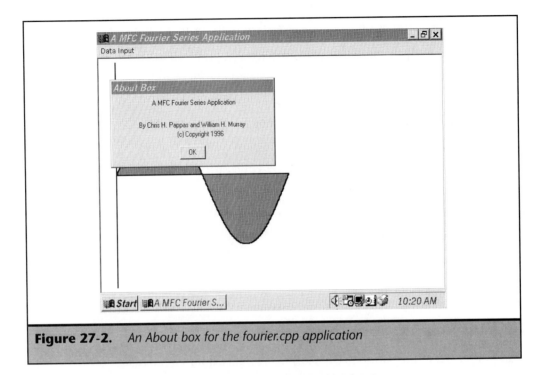

Figure 27-2. *An About box for the fourier.cpp application*

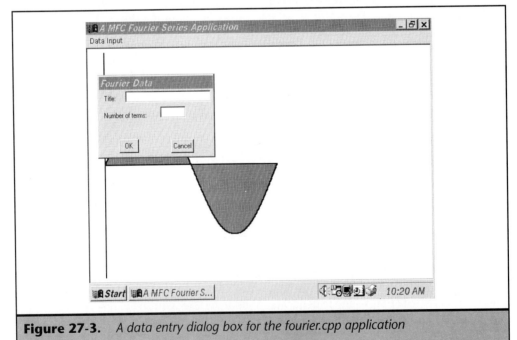

Figure 27-3. *A data entry dialog box for the fourier.cpp application*

current window size is saved in two variables, *m_cxClient* and *m_cyClient*:

```
void CMainWnd::OnSize(UINT,int x,int y)
{
  m_cxClient=x;
  m_cyClient=y;
}
```

These values are helpful because they can be used to scale the graphics in the current window's dimensions.

Drawing in the Client Area

The graphics shape can be scaled to the window size. A scaleable drawing surface is created by setting the mapping mode to MM_ISOTROPIC with a call to the **SetMapMode()** function. The MM_ISOTROPIC mapping mode uses arbitrary drawing units:

```
dc.SetMapMode(MM_ISOTROPIC);
```

Next, the window's extent is set to 500 units in both the X and Y directions:

```
dc.SetWindowExt(500,500);
```

This means that the X and Y axes will always have 500 units, regardless of the size of the window. The viewport extent is set to the currently reported window size, as shown here:

```
dc.SetViewportExt(m_cxClient,-m_cyClient);
```

This means that all 500 units will be visible in the window. The negative value, attached to *m_cyClient* means that y will increase in the upward direction.

The viewport origin is set midway on the Y axis, a short distance from the left edge of the X axis:

```
dc.SetViewportOrg(m_cxClient/20,m_cyClient/2);
```

The X and Y coordinate axes are drawn in the window. Compare the values shown here to the axes shown in screen shots later in this section:

```
// draw x & y coordinate axes
dc.MoveTo(0,240);
dc.LineTo(0,-240);
dc.MoveTo(0,0);
dc.LineTo(400,0);
dc.MoveTo(0,0);
```

The technique for drawing the Fourier wave, shown below, uses two **for** loops. The *i* variable controls the angle used by the sine function, and the *j* variable holds the value for the current Fourier harmonic. Each point plotted on the screen is a summation of all the Fourier harmonics for a given angle. Thus, if you request that the application draw 40,000 harmonics, 1.6 million separate calculations will be made:

```
// draw actual Fourier waveform
for (i=0; i<=400; i++)
{
  for (j=1; j<=nterms; j++)
  {
    y=(150.0/((2.0*j)-1.0))*sin(((j*2.0)-1.0)*0.015708*ang);
    yp=yp+y;
  }
  dc.LineTo(i,(int) yp);
  yp-=yp;
  ang++;
}
```

The **LineTo()** function is used to connect each calculated point. This will form a waveform drawn with a solid line. This waveform will have its interior region filled with a gray color by the **ExtFloodFill()** function. The **ExtFloodFill()** function requires the coordinates of a point within the fill region and the bounding color that the figure was drawn with. The FLOODFILLBORDER parameter fills to the boundary color. You can see how these functions are used with the following code:

```
// prepare to fill interior of waveform newbrush.
  newbrush.CreateSolidBrush(dwColor[7]);
  oldbrush=dc.SelectObject(&newbrush);
  dc.ExtFloodFill(150,10,dwColor[0],FLOODFILLBORDER);
  dc.ExtFloodFill(300,-10,dwColor[0],FLOODFILLBORDER);
```

A title is printed in the window and the brush object is deleted once all drawing is completed:

```
// print waveform title
ltitle=strlen(mytitle);
dc.TextOut(200-(ltitle*8/2),185,mytitle,ltitle);

// delete brush objects
dc.SelectObject(oldbrush);
newbrush.DeleteObject();
```

All objects drawn within the client area will be scaled to the viewport. This program eliminates the sizing problem of earlier examples and requires only a little additional coding.

Working with the About Box

About boxes are easy to create and implement. About boxes are used to communicate information about the program, the program's designers, the copyright date, and so on.

A modal dialog box is created when the user selects the Fourier About... option from the application's menu. The **OnAbout()** command handler requires only a few lines of code:

```
void CMainWnd::OnAbout()
{
  CModalDialog about("AboutBox",this);
  about.DoModal();
}
```

The constructor for **CModalDialog** uses the current window as the parent window for the object. The **this** pointer is used here and refers to the currently used object. The **DoModal()** member function is responsible for drawing the About box in the client area. When the OK button is clicked, the dialog box is removed and the client area is repainted.

Working with the Data Entry Dialog Box

Dialog boxes that allow user input require more programming than simple About boxes. In this example, a data input dialog box can be selected from the application's menu by selecting the Fourier Data.... option.

The data entry dialog box allows the user to enter a chart title and an integer representing the number of Fourier harmonics to draw. When the user clicks on the OK button, the data entry dialog box is removed from the window and the client area is updated:

```
void CMainWnd::OnFourierData()
{
  CFourierDataDialog dlgFourierData(this);
  if (dlgFourierData.DoModal()==IDOK)
  {
    InvalidateRect(NULL,TRUE);
    UpdateWindow();
  }
};
```

The **CFourierDataDialog** class is derived from the **CModalDialog** class. You can see this in the fourier.h header file discussed earlier. Notice, however, that it is at this point in the application that data is retrieved. This data was entered in the dialog box by the user. Here is a portion of code that returns this information when the dialog box's OK push button is clicked:

```
void CFourierDataDialog::OnOK()
{
  GetDlgItemText(IDD_TITLE,mytitle,80);
  nterms=GetDlgItemInt(IDD_TERMS,NULL,0);
  CModalDialog::OnOK();
}
```

The **GetDlgItemText()** function returns chart title information to *mytitle* in the form of a string. The dialog box location for this information is identified by IDD_TITLE. Integer information can be processed in a similar manner with the **GetDlgItemInt()** function. Its dialog box identification value is IDD_TERMS, and the integer retrieved by the function is returned to *nterms*. The second parameter is used to report translation errors but is not used in this application. If the third parameter is nonzero, a check will be made for a signed number. In this application, only positive numbers are possible.

Terminating the Application

The final application menu option is Exit. Exit will destroy the client window by calling the **DestroyWindow()** function:

```
void CMainWnd::OnExit()
{
  DestroyWindow();
}
```

This application menu option gives the user a method of exiting the application without using the system menu.

Examining the Message Map

Two classes are specified in BEGIN_MESSAGE_MAP: **CMainWnd** and **CFrameWnd**. **CMainWnd** is the target class, and **CFrameWnd** is a class based on **CWnd**. The **ON_WM_PAINT()** function handles all WM_PAINT messages and directs them to the **OnPaint()** member function. Here **ON_WM_SIZE()** handles WM_SIZE messages and directs them to the **OnSize()** member function. The **ON_WM_CREATE()** function handles WM_CREATE messages and directs them to the **OnCreate()** member function. Note that there is an **ON_COMMAND()** function for each of the application's menu items. Message information on menu items is processed and then returned to the appropriate member function. Here is the message map for this example:

```
BEGIN_MESSAGE_MAP(CMainWnd,CFrameWnd)
  ON_WM_PAINT()
  ON_WM_SIZE()
  ON_WM_CREATE()
  ON_COMMAND(IDM_ABOUT,OnAbout)
  ON_COMMAND(IDM_FOUR,OnFourierData)
  ON_COMMAND(IDM_EXIT,OnExit)
END_MESSAGE_MAP()
```

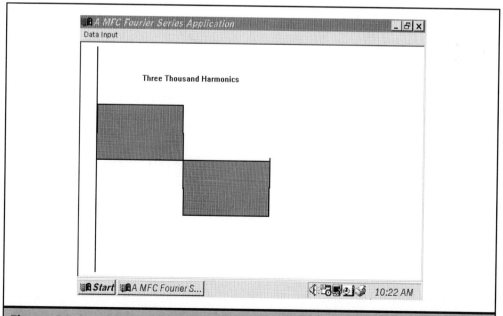

Figure 27-4.   *A screen showing 3,000 harmonics drawn with the Fourier application*

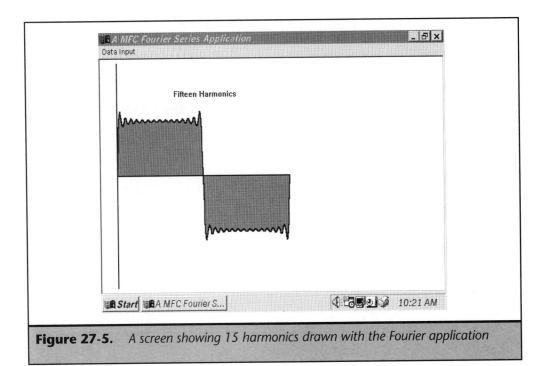

Figure 27-5. *A screen showing 15 harmonics drawn with the Fourier application*

The use of message maps has eliminated the need for the error-prone switch/case statements found in procedure-oriented applications.

Running the Application

Build this application from within the Borland IDE as you have done for past examples. When the application is executed, a default waveform is drawn in the client area. A default value of one harmonic produces a sine wave. Figure 27-4 shows 15 harmonics, and Figure 27-5 shows 3000 harmonics.

As the number of harmonics increases, the figure drawn in the client area will approach a perfect square wave. You can experiment with various values and see how the drawing time increases for very large numbers of harmonics.

A Bar Chart Application

The barchart.cpp application will draw a bar chart in the window's client area. This application makes use of several Windows resources, including a menu, an About box, and a data entry dialog box. Many aspects of this bar chart application are similar to the procedure-oriented line chart application of Chapter 22 and the object-oriented pie chart application of Chapter 25. This bar chart allows up to 12 bars to be drawn in the client area and uses a parser routine for entering data and labels.

The complete application is built with up to five separate files. These files include the module definition file, barchart.def (for Windows 3.1 only), the header file, barchart.h, the resource header file, barchartr.h, the resource script file, barchart.rc, and the source code file, barchart.cpp.

Enter each file carefully. You also will need to create a project file. The barchart.rc and barchart.cpp must be named in the project file's list of files to include for the build. When all files have been entered, the application can be built. When building this application with the Borland C++ compiler, you must have access to the Microsoft MFC header and library files. These are not currently provided with the Borland C++ compiler.

Here is the code for the module definition file, barchart.def, used when making a 16-bit Windows 3.1 executable:

```
NAME            BarChart
DESCRIPTION     'A MFC Bar Chart Application'
EXETYPE         WINDOWS
STUB            'WINSTUB.EXE'
CODE            PRELOAD MOVABLE
DATA            PRELOAD MOVEABLE MULTIPLE
HEAPSIZE        4096
```

The barchart.h header file gives the class descriptions for CMainWnd, CBarChart, and CBarDataDialog. These classes are children of MFC library classes:

```
class CMainWnd : public CFrameWnd
{
public:
  CMainWnd();
  afx_msg void OnPaint();
  afx_msg void OnSize(UINT,int,int);
  afx_msg int  OnCreate(LPCREATESTRUCT cs);
  afx_msg void OnAbout();
  afx_msg void OnBarData();
  afx_msg void OnExit();
  DECLARE_MESSAGE_MAP()
};

class CBarChart : public CWinApp
{
public:
```

```
  virtual BOOL InitInstance();
};

class CBarDataDialog : public CModalDialog
{
public:
  CBarDataDialog(CWnd* pParentWnd=NULL)
                : CModalDialog("BarDlgBox",pParentWnd)
                { }
  virtual void OnOK();
};
```

The barchartr.h resource header file contains the ID values that will be used for the menu and two dialog boxes:

```
#define IDM_ABOUT    200
#define IDM_INPUT    210
#define IDM_EXIT     220

#define IDD_TITLE    300
#define IDD_XLABEL   310
#define IDD_YLABEL   320

#define IDD_P        400
#define IDD_L        410
```

The barchart.rc resource script file defines the application's menu and dialog box descriptions:

```
#include "windows.h"
#include "afxres.h"
#include "BarChartR.h"

BARMENU MENU DISCARDABLE
BEGIN
  POPUP "Data_Input"
  BEGIN
    MENUITEM "About Box...",   IDM_ABOUT
    MENUITEM "Bar Values...",  IDM_INPUT
    MENUITEM "Exit",           IDM_EXIT
```

```
   END
END

DLGINCLUDE RCDATA DISCARDABLE
BEGIN
   "BarChartr.h\0"
END

ABOUTDLGBOX DIALOG DISCARDABLE 14,22,200,75
   STYLE WS_POPUP|WS_CAPTION
   CAPTION "About Box"
   FONT 8, "System"
BEGIN
   CTEXT "A MFC Bar Chart Application",
         -1,30,5,144,8
   CTEXT "Experimenting With The MFC Library",
         -1,30,17,144,8
   CTEXT "By Chris H. Pappas and William H. Murray",
         -1,28,28,144,8
   CTEXT "(c) Copyright 1996",-1,68,38,83,8
   defPUSHBUTTON "OK",IDOK,84,55,32,14,WS_GROUP
END

BARDLGBOX DIALOG DISCARDABLE 42,-10,223,222
   STYLE WS_POPUP|WS_CAPTION
   CAPTION "Bar Chart Data"
   FONT 8, "System"
BEGIN
   GROUPBOX "Bar Chart Labels",100,5,11,212,89,WS_TABSTOP
   GROUPBOX "Bar Chart Heights",101,5,105,212,85,WS_TABSTOP
   LTEXT "Title: ",IDC_STATIC,40,35,20,8,NOT WS_GROUP
   LTEXT "x-axis label:",IDC_STATIC,15,55,55,8,NOT WS_GROUP
   LTEXT "y-axis label:",IDC_STATIC,15,75,60,8,NOT WS_GROUP
   LTEXT "Bar values: ",IDC_STATIC,20,155,40,8,NOT WS_GROUP
   LTEXT "Bar labels:",IDC_STATIC,20,170,45,10,NOT WS_GROUP
   EDITTEXT IDD_TITLE,75,30,135,12
   EDITTEXT IDD_XLABEL,75,50,135,12
   EDITTEXT IDD_YLABEL,75,70,135,12
   EDITTEXT IDD_P,75,150,135,12,ES_AUTOHSCROLL
   EDITTEXT IDD_L,75,170,135,12,ES_AUTOHSCROLL
   PUSHBUTTON "OK",IDOK,50,200,35,14
```

```
    PUSHBUTTON "Cancel",IDCANCEL,120,200,34,14
    CTEXT "Enter values, separated by a comma",IDC_STATIC,
      15,125,195,8
END
```

It took a while to get here, but we're now ready to look at the source code for the barchart.cpp application. Examine this code and note the inclusion of various resources such as menus, dialog boxes, and so on:

```cpp
//
//  BarChart.cpp
//  A MFC bar chart application.
//  When building this application with the
//  Borland C++ Compiler, you will need access to
//  the Microsoft MFC header and library files.
//  Copyright (c) Chris H. Pappas and William H. Murray, 1996
//

#include <afxwin.h>
#include <string.h>
#include <math.h>
#include <stdlib.h>
#include "BarChartr.h"    // resource IDs
#include "BarChart.h"

#define maxnumber 12
static char szTString[80]="Chart Title";
static char szXString[80]="x-axis label";
static char szYString[80]="y-axis label";
static char szGHValues[80]="25,20,10,40";
static char szGLValues[160]="#1,#2,#3,#4";
int m_cxClient,m_cyClient;

CBarChart theApp;

CMainWnd::CMainWnd()
{
  Create((AfxRegisterWndClass(CS_HREDRAW|CS_VREDRAW,
        LoadCursor(NULL,IDC_CROSS),
        (HBRUSH) GetStockObject(WHITE_BRUSH),NULL)),
        "MFC Bar Chart Application",
```

```
            WS_OVERLAPPEDWINDOW,rectDefault,NULL,"BarMenu");
}

void CMainWnd::OnSize(UINT,int x,int y)
{
  m_cxClient=x;
  m_cyClient=y;
}

void CMainWnd::OnPaint()
{
  CPaintDC dc(this);
  static DWORD dwColor[12]={RGB(0,0,0),          //black
                            RGB(255,0,0),        //red
                            RGB(0,255,0),        //green
                            RGB(0,0,255),        //blue
                            RGB(255,255,0),      //yellow
                            RGB(255,0,255),      //magenta
                            RGB(0,255,255),      //cyan
                            RGB(0,120,120),      //blend 1
                            RGB(120,0,120),      //blend 2
                            RGB(120,120,0),      //blend 3
                            RGB(120,120,120),    //blend 4
                            RGB(255,255,255)};   //white

  CFont newfont;
  CFont* oldfont;
  CBrush newbrush;
  CBrush* oldbrush;
  int i,iNBars,iBarWidth,iBarMax;
  int ilenMaxLabel;
  int x1,x2,y1,y2,z1,z2;
  char szLValues[160];
  char szHValues[80];
  static int iBarSize[maxnumber];
  int iBarSizeScaled[maxnumber];
  char sbuffer[10],*strptr;
  char szBarLabel[12][20];
  static char *n,*p;

  // make copies of data for re-drawing
```

```
strcpy(szHValues,szGHValues);
strcpy(szLValues,szGLValues);

// parse string to get bar heights
iNBars=0;
i=0;
n=szHValues;
p=strtok(n,",");
while ((n!=NULL)) {
  iBarSize[i]=atoi(n);
  p=strtok(NULL,",");
  n=p;
  iNBars++;
  i++;
}

// parse string to get bar labels
i=0;
n=szLValues;
p=strtok(n,",");
while ((n!=NULL)) {
  strcpy(szBarLabel[i],n);
  p=strtok(NULL,",");
  n=p;
  i++;
}

iBarWidth=400/iNBars;

// Find bar with maximum height and scale
iBarMax=iBarSize[0];
for(i=0;i<iNBars;i++)
  if (iBarMax<iBarSize[i]) iBarMax=iBarSize[i];

// Convert maximum y value to a string
strptr=_itoa(iBarMax,sbuffer,10);
ilenMaxLabel=strlen(sbuffer);

// Scale bars in array.  Highest bar = 270
for (i=0;i<iNBars;i++)
  iBarSizeScaled[i]=iBarSize[i]*(270/iBarMax);
```

```
// Create custom viewport and map mode
dc.SetMapMode(MM_ISOTROPIC);
dc.SetWindowExt(640,480);
dc.SetViewportExt(m_cxClient,m_cyClient);
dc.SetViewportOrg(0,0);

// Draw text if window is large enough
if ((m_cxClient>300)&&(m_cyClient>200)) {
  newfont.CreateFont(12,12,900,900,FW_BOLD,
                     FALSE,FALSE,FALSE,
                     OEM_CHARSET,OUT_DEFAULT_PRECIS,
                     CLIP_DEFAULT_PRECIS,
                     DEFAULT_QUALITY,
                     VARIABLE_PITCH|FF_ROMAN,
                     "Roman");
  oldfont=dc.SelectObject(&newfont);
  dc.TextOut(50,200+(strlen(szXString)*10/2),
             szYString,strlen(szYString));

  newfont.CreateFont(12,12,0,0,FW_BOLD,
                     FALSE,FALSE,FALSE,OEM_CHARSET,
                     OUT_DEFAULT_PRECIS,
                     CLIP_DEFAULT_PRECIS,
                     DEFAULT_QUALITY,
                     VARIABLE_PITCH|FF_ROMAN,
                     "Roman");
  oldfont=dc.SelectObject(&newfont);
  dc.TextOut((300-(strlen(szTString)*10/2)),
             15,szTString,strlen(szTString));
  dc.TextOut((300-(strlen(szXString)*10/2)),
             365,szXString,strlen(szXString));
  dc.TextOut((90-ilenMaxLabel*12),70,strptr,ilenMaxLabel);
}

// Draw coordinate axis
dc.MoveTo(99,49);
dc.LineTo(99,350);
dc.LineTo(500,350);
dc.MoveTo(99,350);
```

```
  // Initial values
  x1=100;
  y1=350;
  z1=50;
  z2=z1+15;
  x2=x1+iBarWidth;

  // Draw each bar
  for(i=0;i<iNBars;i++) {
    newbrush.CreateSolidBrush(dwColor[i]);
    oldbrush=dc.SelectObject(&newbrush);
    y2=350-iBarSizeScaled[i];
    dc.Rectangle(x1,y1,x2,y2);
    x1=x2;
    x2+=iBarWidth;

    // Draw labels
    if ((strlen(szBarLabel[0])!=0)&&(m_cxClient>300)&&
        (m_cyClient>200)) {
      dc.Rectangle(545,z1,560,z2);
      dc.TextOut(565,z1,szBarLabel[i],
                 strlen(szBarLabel[i]));
      z1=z2+15;
      z2+=30;
    }
  }

  // Delete objects
  if (m_cxClient >= 200) {
    dc.SelectObject(oldfont);
    newfont.DeleteObject();
  }
  dc.SelectObject(&newbrush);
  newbrush.DeleteObject();
}

int CMainWnd::OnCreate(LPCREATESTRUCT)
{
  UpdateWindow();
  return (0);
}
```

```
void CMainWnd::OnAbout()
{
  CModalDialog about("AboutDlgBox",this);
  about.DoModal();
}

void CBarDataDialog::OnOK()
{
  GetDlgItemText(IDD_TITLE,szTString,80);
  GetDlgItemText(IDD_XLABEL,szXString,80);
  GetDlgItemText(IDD_YLABEL,szYString,80);
  GetDlgItemText(IDD_P,szGHValues,80);
  GetDlgItemText(IDD_L,szGLValues,160);
  CModalDialog::OnOK();
}

void CMainWnd::OnBarData()
{
  CBarDataDialog dlgBarData(this);
  if (dlgBarData.DoModal()==IDOK) {
    InvalidateRect(NULL,TRUE);
    UpdateWindow();
  }
};

void CMainWnd::OnExit()
{
  DestroyWindow();
}

BEGIN_MESSAGE_MAP(CMainWnd,CFrameWnd)
  ON_WM_PAINT()
  ON_WM_SIZE()
  ON_WM_CREATE()
  ON_COMMAND(IDM_ABOUT,OnAbout)
  ON_COMMAND(IDM_INPUT,OnBarData)
  ON_COMMAND(IDM_EXIT,OnExit)
END_MESSAGE_MAP()

BOOL CBarChart::InitInstance()
```

```
    {
      m_pMainWnd=new CMainWnd();
      m_pMainWnd->ShowWindow(m_nCmdShow);
      m_pMainWnd->UpdateWindow();
      return TRUE;
    }
```

When all of these files are entered, build the application with the Borland C++ compiler's Project Utility. Remember to specify the location of the Microsoft MFC header and library files.

The Application's Header File

This application will use many of the features of the previous application. For example, note the similar function declarations in **CMainWnd** and the message map:

```
    afx_msg void On Paint();
    afx_msg void OnSize(UINT,int,int);
    afx_msg int  OnCreate(LPCREATESTRUCT cs);
    afx_msg void OnAbout();
    afx_msg void OnBarData();
    afx_msg void OnExit();
```

The creation of the About and data entry dialog boxes parallels the Fourier example. In this application, the data entry dialog box will process more user input than in the previous example.

The Application's Resource Header and Resource Script Files

The barchartr.h and barchart.rc files are combined by the resource compiler into a single compiled Windows binary, barchart.res.

The barchartr.h resource header file contains three menu identification values: IDM_ABOUT, IDM_INPUT, and IDM_EXIT.

Several identification values are included for use by the modal dialog box. Three of these values include IDD_TITLE, IDD_XLABEL, and IDD_YLABEL. The remaining two values, IDD_P and IDD_L, are for retrieving the height and labels for the individual bars. These values are returned as strings.

The resource script file, barchart.rc, contains a description of the application's menu and two dialog boxes. The application's menu is shown in Figure 27-6.

The application's About box is shown in Figure 27-7.

The data entry dialog box has a very neat appearance because bar data and bar labels are entered in individual edit boxes. Figure 27-8 shows the application's data entry dialog box.

The Borland dialog box editor was used to construct both the About box and the data entry dialog box.

The Application's Source Code File

This section concentrates on those features of the bar chart application that were not addressed in the previous Fourier application. The barchart.cpp application will allow the user to draw a bar chart in the client area of a window. With the use of a modal dialog box, the user can specify a chart title, axis labels, and the heights of up to 12 bars. The chart will then be correctly scaled to the window, with each bar's color selected from an array of predefined values.

The maximum number of bars, *maxnumbar*, is set to 12 at the start of the application:

```
#define maxnumbar 12
```

This value can be changed, but you shouldn't crowd too many bars onto a chart.

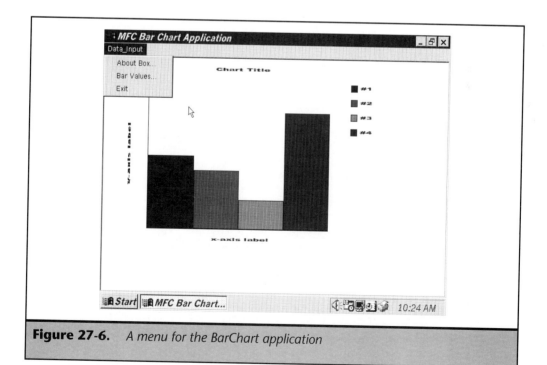

Figure 27-6. *A menu for the BarChart application*

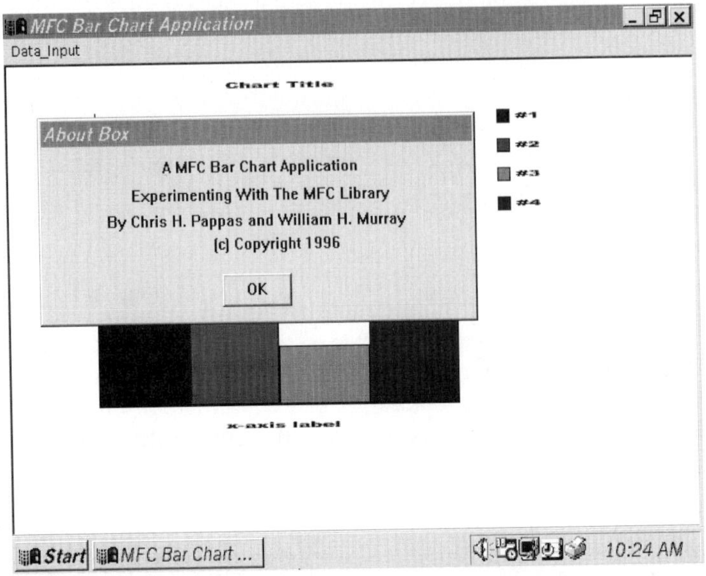

Figure 27-7.   *An About box for the BarChart application*

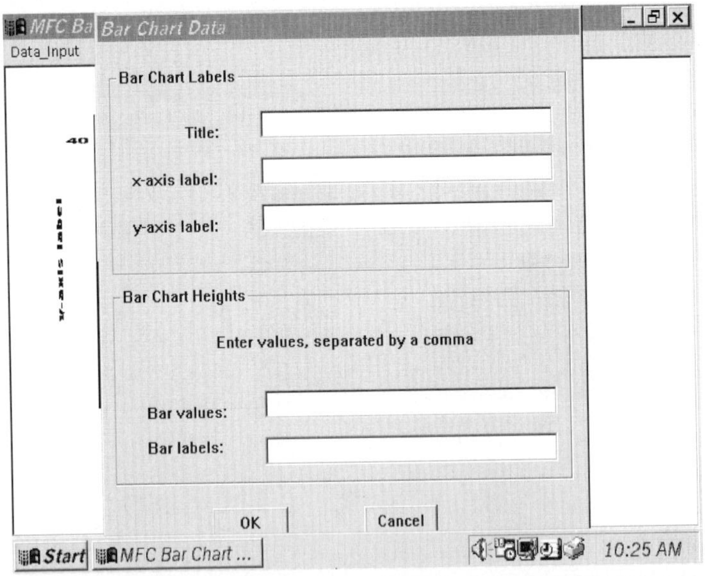

Figure 27-8.   *A data entry dialog box for the BarChart application*

As you can see in the following code, global data types hold initial bar chart values for titles, axis labels, and bar heights and labels:

```
static char szTString[80]="Chart Title";
static char szXString[80]="x-axis label";
static char szYString[80]="y-axis label";
static char szGHValues[80]="25,20,10,40";
static char szGLValues[160]="#1,#2,#3,#4";
int m_cxClient,m_cyClient;
```

The size of the client area will also be saved in global values. These are the same variable names used in the Fourier application. Because the application keeps track of the client area size, this bar chart can be scaled to fit the current window size.

Bar colors are selected from the *dwColor* array in a sequential manner. If the bar chart has four bars, they will be black, red, green, and blue. If you like, you can exchange colors in the array.

The **CFont** and **CBrush** classes permit a font or brush object to be passed to any CDC (base class for display context) member function. New fonts will be needed to draw the chart title and axes labels. Brushes are used to fill the rectangular bars. Here is the syntax used to create a new font and brush object:

```
CFont newfont;
CFont* oldfont;
CBrush newbrush;
CBrush* oldbrush;
```

Calculating Bar Chart Data

Before plotting a bar chart, you must first obtain individual bar values and then calculate how many bar values are being used. The values for each bar's height will be obtained by parsing the *szHValues* string. The number of bars is held in the global array *iBarSize*. The following portion of code shows a parsing routine. This routine parses the string containing the heights of the bars. A similar parser is used to parse the individual bar labels.

```
// parse string to get bar heights
iNBars=0;
i=0;
n=szHValues;
p=strtok(n,",");
while ((n!=NULL)) {
  iBarSize[i]=atoi(n);
  p=strtok(NULL,",");
```

```
      n=p;
      iNBars++;
      i++;
   }
```

This parsing routine is built around the **strtok()** function. For more information on this function's use, see the line chart application in Chapter 22. Individual bar chart heights are saved in the *iBarSize[]* array. Individual bar labels are saved in the *szBarLabel[][]* array.

The actual number of bars is determined by incrementing *iNBars* each time the parser finds a new bar value. The width of each bar, drawn in the chart, is dependent upon the total number of bars. The chart will always be drawn to the same total width. Individual bar widths, *iBarWidth*, are determined by using this:

```
iBarWidth=400/iNBars;
```

The height of each bar is determined relative to the largest bar value entered by the user. The largest bar value is always drawn to the same chart height. The size of the largest bar value is easy to determine:

```
// Find bar with maximum height and scale
iBarMax=iBarSize[0];
for(i=0;i<iNBars;i++)

   if (iBarMax<iBarSize[i]) iBarMax=iBarSize[i];
```

This chart will also print the height of the largest bar value next to the vertical axis. The **_itoa()** macro is used to convert this value to a string:

```
// Convert maximum y value to a string
strptr=_itoa(iBarMax,sbuffer,10);

ilenMaxLabel=strlen(sbuffer);
```

The remaining bars in the array are then scaled to the largest bar's value:

```
// Scale bars in array. Highest bar = 270
for (i=0;i<iNBars;i++)
   iBarSizeScaled[i]=iBarSize[i]*(270/iBarMax);
```

Creating a Custom Client Area

This application will scale the graphics to fit the client area of the window. Before drawing begins, the mapping mode, window extent, viewport extent, and origin are set with this code:

```
// Create custom viewport and map mode
  dc.SetMapMode(MM_ISOTROPIC);
  dc.SetWindowExt(640,480);
  dc.SetViewportExt(m_cxClient,m_cyClient);
  dc.SetViewportOrg(0,0);
```

The bar chart can be scaled all the way down to an iconic size, with all of the bars still clearly visible.

Drawing Text to the Client Area

The Fourier application drew its text to the screen by using Windows default font. When several fonts or orientations are required, special font functions must be used. This application requires several font sizes and orientations. In this section, we'll review how these fonts can be created.

There are two functions with which you create and manipulate fonts in Windows: **CreateFont()** and **CreateFontIndirect()**. This example uses the **CreateFont()** function.

Working with the CreateFont() Function

The **CreateFont()** function uses a logical font from the GDI's pool of physical fonts. The actual font, selected by Windows, will be the font that most closely matches the characteristics specified by the developer in the function call. Once created, this logical font can be selected by any device. This is the syntax for the **CreateFont()** function:

```
CreateFont(Height,Width,Escapement,Orientation,Weight,
           Italic,Underline,StrikeOut,CharSet,
           OutputPrecision,ClipPrecision,Quality,
           PitchAndFamily,Facename)
```

The first time **CreateFont()** is called in this application, the parameters are set to the following values:

Height = 12
Width = 12
Escapement = 900
Orientation = 900
Weight = FW_BOLD

```
Italic = FALSE
Underline = FALSE
StrikeOut = FALSE
CharSet = OEM_CHARSET
OutputPrecision = OUT_DEFAULT_PRECIS
ClipPrecision = CLIP_DEFAULT_PRECIS
Quality = DEFAULT_QUALITY
PitchAndFamily = VARIABLE_PITCH | FF_ROMAN
Facename = "Roman"
```

This font will be used to print a vertical string of text in the window. Notice that *Escapement* and *Orientation* are set to 900. Both of these parameters use angle values specified in tenths of a degree. Here, a value of 900 represents an angle of 90.0 degrees. The *Escapement* parameter rotates the line of text from horizontal to vertical. *Orientation* rotates each character in this application by 90.0 degrees.

The second call to the **CreateFont()** function uses the following parameters:

```
Height = 12
Width = 12
Escapement = 0
Orientation = 0
Weight = FW_BOLD
Italic = FALSE
Underline = FALSE
StrikeOut = FALSE
CharSet = OEM_CHARSET
OutputPrecision = OUT_DEFAULT_PRECIS
ClipPrecision = CLIP_DEFAULT_PRECIS
Quality = DEFAULT_QUALITY
PitchAndFamily = VARIABLE_PITCH | FF_ROMAN
Facename = "Roman"
```

Again, an attempt will be made by Windows to find a match to the preceding specifications. This font is used to print the horizontal labels.

Here is the code used to draw the vertical axis label:

```
// Draw text if window is large enough
  if ((m_cxClient>300)&&(m_cyClient>200)) {
    newfont.CreateFont(12,12,900,900,FW_BOLD,
                       FALSE,FALSE,FALSE,
```

```
                      OEM_CHARSET,OUT_DEFAULT_PRECIS,
                      CLIP_DEFAULT_PRECIS,
                      DEFAULT_QUALITY,
                      VARIABLE_PITCH|FF_ROMAN,
                      "Roman");
     oldfont=dc.SelectObject(&newfont);
     dc.TextOut(50,200+(strlen(szXString)*10/2),
                szYString,strlen(szYString));
```

Because the windows can be scaled, it is best to check and make sure it can support readable text. When the fonts are scaled, they can quickly become unreadable.

Drawing the Axes and Bars in the Client Area

Simple X and Y coordinate axes are drawn with the use of the **MoveTo()** and **LineTo()** functions:

```
// Draw coordinate axis
  dc.MoveTo(99,49);
  dc.LineTo(99,350);
  dc.LineTo(500,350);
  dc.MoveTo(99,350);
```

The application then prepares for drawing each bar. The first bar always starts at position 100,350 on the chart. This position is defined by *x1* and *y1*. The position/width of the first bar and all subsequent bars is calculated from the last drawing position and the width of each bar. The second x value is defined by *x2*.

```
// Initial values
  x1=100;
  y1=350;
  z1=50;
  z2=z1+15;
  x2=x1+iBarWidth;
```

Individual bar chart bars are drawn by retrieving the scaled bar height value from **iBarSizeScaled[]**. This scaled value, saved in *y2*, is used in the **Rectangle()** function. Because the **Rectangle()** function draws a closed figure, the figure can be filled with the current brush color. The color value, selected from the array, is incremented during each pass through the loop. Examine this small portion of code to learn how this is achieved.

```
// Draw each bar
   for(i=0;i<iNBars;i++) {
      newbrush.CreateSolidBrush(dwColor[i]);
      oldbrush=dc.SelectObject(&newbrush);
      y2=350-iBarSizeScaled[i];
      dc.Rectangle(x1,y1,x2,y2);
      x1=x2;
      x2+=iBarWidth;

      // Draw labels
      if ((strlen(szBarLabel[0])!=0)&&(m_cxClient>300)&&
         (m_cyClient>200)) {
        dc.Rectangle(545,z1,560,z2);
        dc.TextOut(565,z1,szBarLabel[i],
                    strlen(szBarLabel[i]));
        z1=z2+15;
        z2+=30;
      }
   }
```

After each bar is drawn, the values in *x1* and *x2* are updated to point to the next bar's position. A legend and bar label are also drawn in each pass through the loop. This process is repeated in the **for** loop until all the bars, legend icons, and legend labels are drawn.

Running the Application

Build and run the barchart.cpp application. A default bar chart, similar to the one in Figure 27-9, will be drawn in the window.

A custom bar chart, as shown in Figure 27-10, can be created by entering a chart title, axis labels, and unique bar values.

This application can be enhanced by adding axis tick marks, axis values, and so on.

In the Next Chapter...

Now that you've learned how to develop procedure-oriented and objected-oriented applications, it is time to investigate Borland's Experts. In the next two chapters you'll learn how Borland's Experts can actually generate program code for you. Experts will make your first introduction to OLE much easier than developing the code yourself.

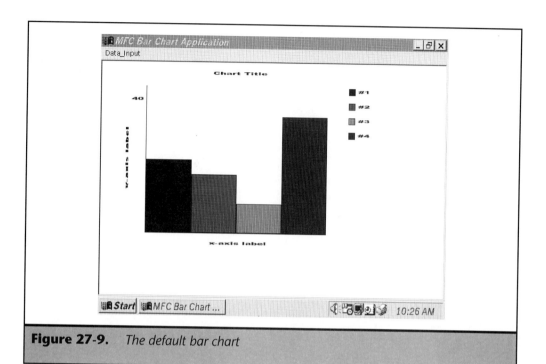

Figure 27-9.   *The default bar chart*

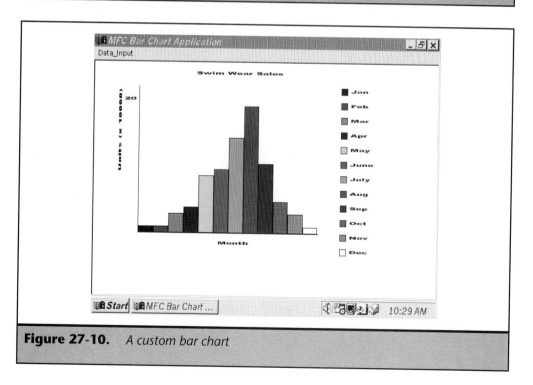

Figure 27-10.   *A custom bar chart*

PART SEVEN

Borland Experts

Chapter Twenty-Eight

Win32
Development with
Borland Experts

In Chapters 20 through 27 you learned how to develop Windows applications with both a procedure-oriented and object-oriented approach using Borland and Microsoft Object libraries. These chapters relied heavily on the repeated use of the same or similar code for establishing a window and adding resources to applications. This code could be copied and pasted from one application to another.

When programming, simple cut and paste operations are not always sufficient for generating a new project. Borland's solution to the problem of redundant but ever-changing code was the development of a program generator capable of creating *dynamic* templates or base applications. A code generator asks programmers what basic features they want included in their project, then generates the base template code. The programmer then inserts the remaining code into the template to complete the application. Borland's program generator is called the *Application Expert*. Microsoft's Visual C++ compiler is shipped with the *Application Wizard*.

This chapter will explore the basic use of Borland's Application Expert and help you understand how it can be put to work for you. Simple applications will be generated as examples. You will find this program generator easy to use, but be warned, it only generates object-oriented code and relies heavily on the OWL.

There is also a learning curve that you must overcome before you will be comfortable using this new tool. We strongly recommend that you review object-oriented programming in Chapters 15 through 18 and Chapters 23 through 25. These are the chapters that deal with the fundamentals of object-oriented programming and the use of Borland's ObjectWindows Library (OWL).

Borland's Application Expert

The AppExpert can be started from within the Borland C++ compiler's IDE by selecting the File menu and choosing the New and AppExpert... menu items, as shown in Figure 28-1.

When the previous selection is made, the New AppExpert Project dialog box will request a filename, as shown in Figure 28-2.

For this example, this project will be created in the c:\bex subdirectory and will use the filename bexpert.ide.

At this point, the AppExpert will start a step-by-step process that allows you to select specific features for the project. After the project is complete, your job will be to add the specific code to the project to make it a unique application.

The next section continues the step-by-step process of using AppExpert. The end result will be a simple wordprocessor application.

Designing Applications

The AppExpert builds an application by asking the programmer to make a number of decisions concerning the final project. In this section, we'll go through these steps one at a time. If you follow along and actually create this application, make sure your responses match those shown in the figures that follow in this section.

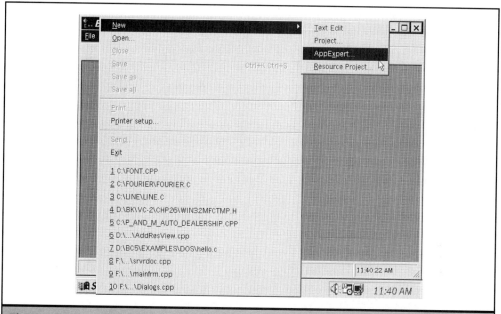

Figure 28-1.   *The AppExpert is started from the compiler's File menu*

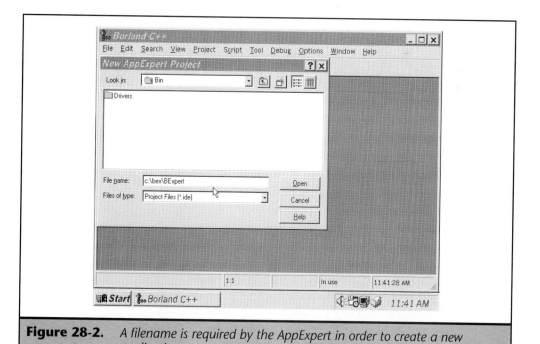

Figure 28-2.   *A filename is required by the AppExpert in order to create a new application*

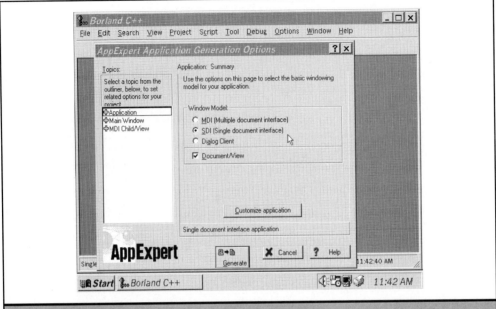

Figure 28-3. *Various options are set for the basic windowing model from the Application Generation Options screen*

Once you have named the project, as shown earlier in Figure 28-2, the AppExpert switches to the AppExpert Application Generation Options dialog box, as shown in Figure 28-3.

For this example, the SDI or single document interface is selected in the Window Model box. This will create an application, such as a word processor, that allows you to work on a single document at a time. A Printing feature will be added from the Features Group.

At this point, you could generate the application by selecting the Generate pushbutton or you could add more features.

To customize various aspects of the application, select the Customize application pushbutton. When Application is boxed in the Topics Group, the customization selection will allow you to change various Application options, such as Basic Options, Advanced Options, OLE 2 Options, Code Gen Control and Admin Options. Figure 28-4 shows these options.

In this example, only the Printing option is accepted under Basic Options. Under Advanced Options, the default window style is accepted.

If OLE 2 Options is selected from the Topics Group (by clicking with the mouse), a dialog box, such as the one shown in Figure 28-5, will be displayed.

In this example, neither container nor server options will be built into our application, so the suggested defaults are accepted.

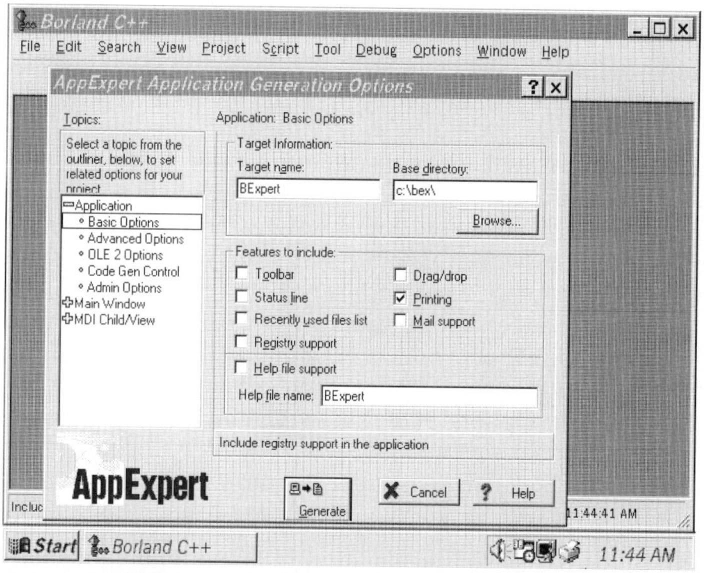

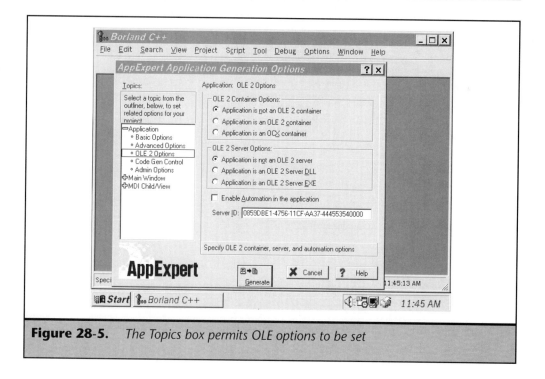

Figure 28-4.   *The Customization application pushbutton allows application options to be changed before code is generated*

Figure 28-5.   *The Topics box permits OLE options to be set*

It is possible to use the Topics box to set new Code Gen Control options, as shown in Figure 28-6.

Administrative options, as shown in Figure 28-7, allow version number, copyright notification, a brief description of the project, and the owner's identification to be recorded.

The information entered in the Administrative Options dialog box is used by the AppExpert in various source code files and in the project's About box.

If the Main Window is boxed in the Topics box, features relating to this window can be customized by selecting the Customization main window pushbutton. Figure 28-8 shows the use of this option. The window's title is set to "BExpert". The background color is not changed in this example, so the default is accepted.

When the Customization main window pushbutton is selected with the mouse, the Topics box expands under the Main Window topic, as shown in Figure 28-9.

In Figure 28-9, the Basic Options allows the programmer to set various Window Styles. New options include Basic Options, SDI Client, MDI Client, and Dialog Client.

Double-clicking SDI Client (single document interface) shows you the various names that the AppExpert will use with the SDI Client Window, as shown in Figure 28-10.

All of the defaults were accepted for the SDI Client. This project does not use the MDI Client or Dialog Client options. However, Figures 28-11 and 28-12 show the

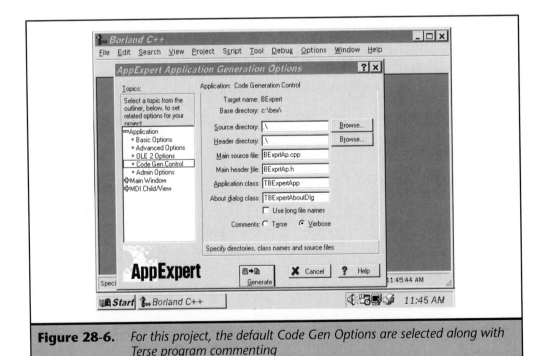

Figure 28-6.   *For this project, the default Code Gen Options are selected along with Terse program commenting*

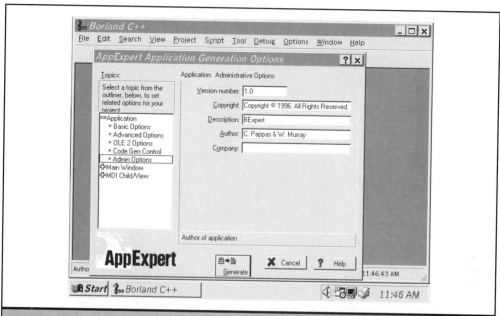

Figure 28-7.   The Admin Options selection in the Topics box lets you enter administrative details, such as name and copyright information

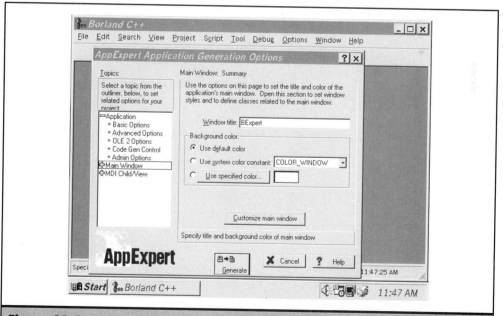

Figure 28-8.   Use the Main Window dialog box to enter the text for the window's title bar and to set the background color for the client area

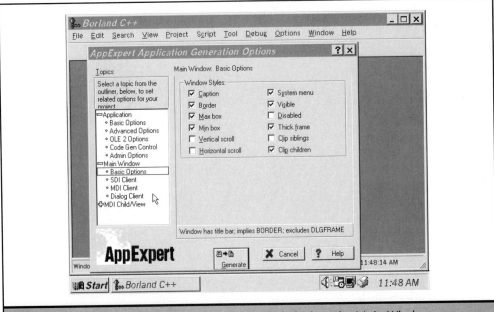

Figure 28-9. *Four additional options are included when the Main Window is expanded*

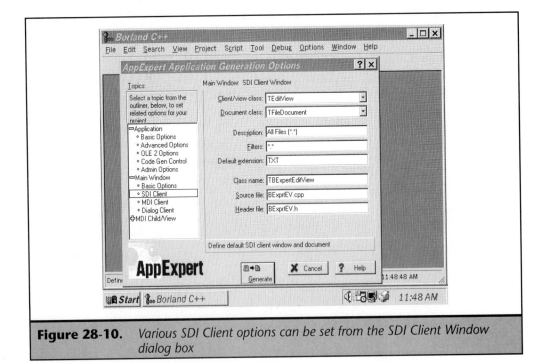

Figure 28-10. *Various SDI Client options can be set from the SDI Client Window dialog box*

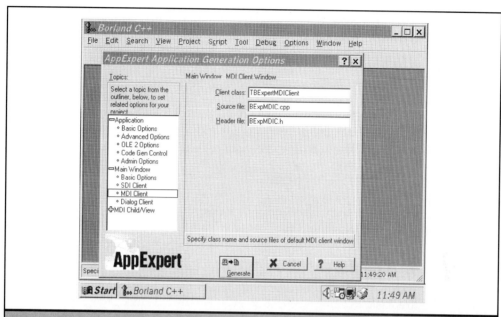

Figure 28-11. *The AppExpert would have used these class names and filenames if the Multiple Document Interface (MDI) had been selected*

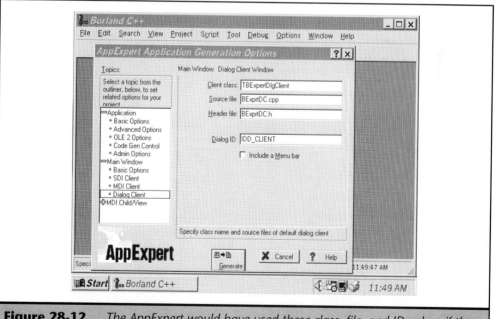

Figure 28-12. *The AppExpert would have used these class, file, and ID values if the Dialog Client had been selected*

names that the AppExpert would have used if these options had been selected at the start of the project.

The last topic in the Topics box is MDI Child/View. Figure 28-13 shows a summary of default options.

In this application, these options will not be used because a SDI interface was selected at the start of the project.

When all of the customization features for your project have been entered, select the Generate pushbutton with the mouse to begin automatic program generation.

Once the Generate pushbutton has been selected, you will have one final opportunity to halt the process. Figure 28-14 shows the AppExpert's warning box. To build the application, select the Yes pushbutton.

The AppExpert will now generate all of the header, resource, module definition, resource script, and source code files required by the project. Figure 28-15 shows the list of generated files for our sample application.

Building the AppExpert Application

The files generated by the AppExpert are syntactically correct and complete. They can be compiled into a basic working application even without the inclusion of your specific project code. To build this application, select the Build all option from the Project menu, as shown in Figure 28-16.

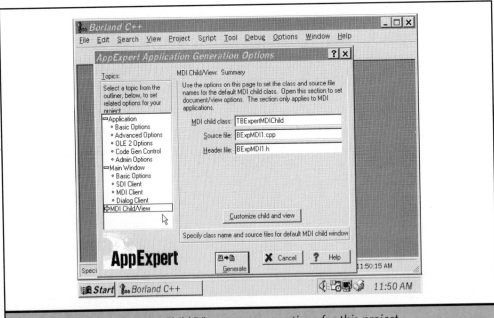

Figure 28-13.   *The MDI Child/View summary options for this project*

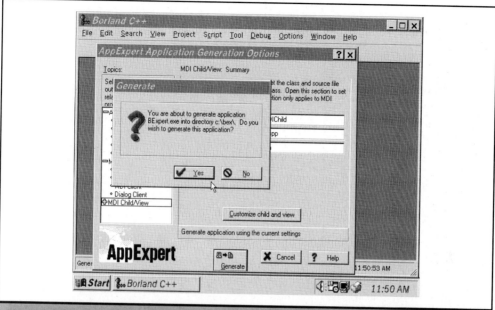

Figure 28-14. *A warning box is the last step before the AppExpert generates program code*

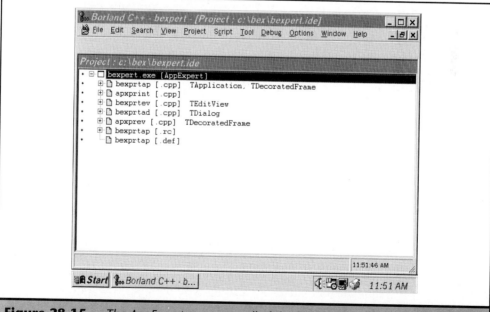

Figure 28-15. *The AppExpert generates all of the files needed by the application*

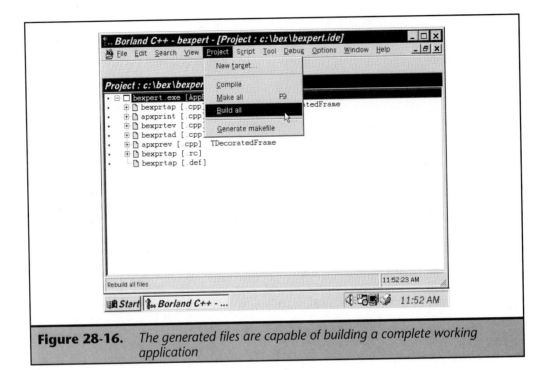

Figure 28-16. *The generated files are capable of building a complete working application*

These files will produce a project with the essential programming features you requested. In this case, the application allows the user to load, edit, and print documents written in ASCII format. Figure 28-17 shows one of the project files, apxprint.cpp, loaded into the application.

Isn't this great? You now have a full-featured OWL application and you haven't written one line of code!

Understanding the AppExpert Code

In this section, we will take a brief look at some of the most important sections of code in each of the C++ source code files generated by the AppExpert. For our example these include: bexprtap.cpp, bexprtad.cpp, bexprtev.cpp, apxprint.cpp, and apxprev.cpp. This project also uses header files, resource script files, and module definition files, which will not be discussed because they are so similar to the files we've used in previous chapters.

The Borland AppExpert will create five source code files to implement all of the features you requested for the project. We will not discuss these source code files line by line, but rather approach each source code file in terms of what it adds to the project. As you examine the following code listings, you'll see several bolded sections of code that will be discussed immediately after the listing.

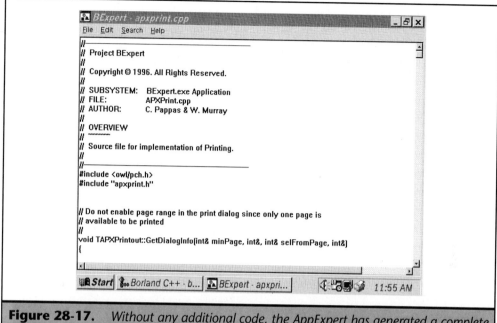

Figure 28-17.   *Without any additional code, the AppExpert has generated a complete SDI application capable of simple text editing*

What Is the Purpose of the bexprtap.cpp File?

The purpose of the bexprtap.cpp source code file is to implement the **TApplication** class for the project. Here **TBExpertApp** is derived from Borland's **TApplication** class.

NOTE: The printing items shown in this listing will not be present if the printing option was not checked in the Application Summary shown earlier in Figure 28-3.

```
//------------------------------------------------------------
//   Project BExpert
//
//   Copyright © 1996. All Rights Reserved.
//
//   SUBSYSTEM:     BExpert.exe Application
//   FILE:          BExprtAp.cpp
//   AUTHOR:        C. Pappas & W. Murray
//
//   OVERVIEW
```

```
//   ~~~~~~~~
//   Source file for TBExpertApp (TApplication).
//
//------------------------------------------------------------

#include <owl/pch.h>

#include <owl/docmanag.h>
#include <owl/filedoc.h>

#include "BExprtAp.h"
#include "BExprtEV.h"     // Definition of client class.
#include "BExprtAD.h"     // Definition of about dialog.


//{{TBExpertApp Implementation}}


//{{DOC_VIEW}}
DEFINE_DOC_TEMPLATE_CLASS(TFileDocument,
                          TBExpertEditView, DocType1);
//{{DOC_VIEW_END}}


//{{DOC_MANAGER}}
DocType1 __dvt1("All Files (*.*)", "*.*", 0, "TXT",
                dtAutoDelete | dtUpdateDir);
//{{DOC_MANAGER_END}}


DEFINE_RESPONSE_TABLE1(TBExpertApp, TApplication)
//{{TBExpertAppRSP_TBL_BEGIN}}
  EV_OWLVIEW(dnCreate, EvNewView),
  EV_OWLVIEW(dnClose,  EvCloseView),
  EV_COMMAND(CM_HELPABOUT, CmHelpAbout),
  EV_COMMAND(CM_FILEPRINT, CmFilePrint),
  EV_COMMAND(CM_FILEPRINTERSETUP, CmFilePrintSetup),
  EV_COMMAND(CM_FILEPRINTPREVIEW, CmFilePrintPreview),
  EV_COMMAND_ENABLE(CM_FILEPRINT, CmPrintEnable),
  EV_COMMAND_ENABLE(CM_FILEPRINTERSETUP, CmPrintEnable),
  EV_COMMAND_ENABLE(CM_FILEPRINTPREVIEW, CmPrintEnable),
  EV_WM_WININICHANGE,
//{{TBExpertAppRSP_TBL_END}}
END_RESPONSE_TABLE;
```

```
TBExpertApp::TBExpertApp() : TApplication("BExpert")
{
  Printer = 0;
  Printing = 0;

  SetDocManager(new TDocManager(dmSDI, this));

  // INSERT>> Your constructor code here.
}

TBExpertApp::~TBExpertApp()
{
  delete Printer;

  // INSERT>> Your destructor code here.
}

//  Initialization of the main window.
void TBExpertApp::InitMainWindow()
{
  if (nCmdShow != SW_HIDE)
    nCmdShow = (nCmdShow != SW_SHOWMINNOACTIVE) \
               ? SW_SHOWNORMAL : nCmdShow;

  SDIDecFrame* frame = new SDIDecFrame(0, GetName(), 0,
                                       false, this);

  frame->SetIcon(this, IDI_SDIAPPLICATION);

  frame->AssignMenu(IDM_SDI);
  frame->Attr.AccelTable = IDM_SDI;

  SetMainWindow(frame);

  frame->SetMenuDescr(TMenuDescr(IDM_SDI));
}

void TBExpertApp::EvNewView(TView& view)
{
  GetMainWindow()->SetClientWindow(view.GetWindow());
  if (!view.IsOK())
```

```
      GetMainWindow()->SetClientWindow(0);
  else if (view.GetViewMenu())
    GetMainWindow()->MergeMenu(*view.GetViewMenu());
}

void TBExpertApp::EvCloseView(TView&)
{
  GetMainWindow()->SetClientWindow(0);
  GetMainWindow()->SetCaption("BExpert");
}

//{{SDIDecFrame Implementation}}
SDIDecFrame::SDIDecFrame(TWindow* parent,
                         const char far* title,
                         TWindow* clientWnd,
                         bool trackMenuSelection,
                         TModule* module)
  :
  TDecoratedFrame(parent, title, clientWnd,
                  trackMenuSelection, module)
{
  // INSERT>> Your constructor code here.

}

SDIDecFrame::~SDIDecFrame()
{
  // INSERT>> Your destructor code here.

}

void TBExpertApp::CmFilePrint()
{
  if (!Printer)
    Printer = new TPrinter(this);

  TDocument* currentDoc = GetDocManager()->GetCurrentDoc();

  char docName[_MAX_PATH];

  if (currentDoc->GetTitle())
```

```
      strcpy(docName, currentDoc->GetTitle());
   else
      strcpy(docName, "Document");

   TAPXPrintout printout(Printer, docName,
                         GetMainWindow()->GetClientWindow());
   printout.SetBanding(true);

   Printing++;

   Printer->Print(GetWindowPtr(GetActiveWindow()),
                              printout, true);

   Printing--;
}

void TBExpertApp::CmFilePrintSetup()
{
   if (!Printer)
      Printer = new TPrinter(this);

   Printer->Setup(GetMainWindow());
}

void TBExpertApp::CmFilePrintPreview()
{
   SDIDecFrame* sdiFrame = TYPESAFE_DOWNCAST(GetMainWindow(),
                                             SDIDecFrame);

   if (sdiFrame) {
      if (!Printer)
         Printer = new TPrinter(this);

      Printing++;

      PreviewWindow* prevW = new PreviewWindow(sdiFrame,
                              Printer,
                              sdiFrame->GetClientWindow(),
                              "Print Preview",
                              new TLayoutWindow(0));
      prevW->Create();
```

```
    BeginModal(GetMainWindow());

    Printing--;

    GetMainWindow()->SetRedraw(true);
    GetMainWindow()->Invalidate();

    prevW->Destroy();
    delete prevW;
  }
}

void TBExpertApp::CmPrintEnable(TCommandEnabler& tce)
{
  if (!Printer) {
    Printer = new TPrinter(this);
      tce.Enable(!Printer->GetSetup().Error);
  }
  else
    tce.Enable(!Printer->GetSetup().Error);
}

// Menu Help About BExpert.exe command
void TBExpertApp::CmHelpAbout()
{
  TBExpertAboutDlg(GetMainWindow()).Execute();
}

void TBExpertApp::EvWinIniChange(char far* section)
{
  if (strcmp(section, "windows") == 0) {
    if (Printer) {
      const int bufferSize = 255;
      char printDBuffer[bufferSize];
      LPSTR printDevice = printDBuffer;
      LPSTR devName;
      LPSTR driverName = 0;
      LPSTR outputName = 0;
      if (::GetProfileString("windows", "device", "",
                             printDevice, bufferSize)) {
        devName = printDevice;
```

```
        while (*printDevice) {
          if (*printDevice == ',') {
            *printDevice++ = 0;
            if (!driverName)
              driverName = printDevice;
            else
              outputName = printDevice;
          }
          else
            printDevice = ::AnsiNext(printDevice);
        }

        if (Printer->GetSetup().Error != 0  ||
            strcmp(devName,
                    Printer->GetSetup().GetDeviceName())!=0 ||
            strcmp(driverName,
                    Printer->GetSetup().GetDriverName())!=0 ||
            strcmp(outputName,
                    Printer->GetSetup().GetOutputName())!=0) {
          // New printer so get new printer device now.
          //
          delete Printer;
          Printer = new TPrinter(this);
        }
      }
      else {
        // No printer installed(GetProfileString failed).
        //
        delete Printer;
        Printer = new TPrinter(this);
      }
    }
  }
}

int OwlMain(int , char* [])
{
  TBExpertApp   app;
  return app.Run();
}
```

This is the main file for the application. At the end of the previous listing is the traditional call to the **OwlMain()** function, which activates the application in Windows.

This portion of code performs a number of operations. First, it is responsible for the initialization of the main window. As with earlier Borland OWL applications, this window is based upon the **TApplication** class. This is a normal window with icon, menu, acceleration table, and so on. If you are interested in the actual class derivations from their parent classes, you can refer to the header files associated with each of the source code files. For example, in the bexprtap.h header file, you'll see how the **TBExpertApp** class was derived from Borland's **TApplication** class. Here is an edited portion of this file:

```
//-----------------------------------------------------------
//   Project BExpert
//
//   Copyright © 1996. All Rights Reserved.
//
//   SUBSYSTEM:    BExpert.exe Application
//   FILE:         BExprtAp.h
//   AUTHOR:       C. Pappas & W. Murray
//
//   OVERVIEW
//   ~~~~~~~~
//   Class definition for TBExpertApp (TApplication).
//
//-----------------------------------------------------------
#if !defined(bexprtap_h)
#define bexprtap_h

#include <owl/printer.h>

#include "apxprint.h"
#include "apxprev.h"

#include "BExprtAp.rh"    // Definition of all resources.

//{{TDecoratedFrame = SDIDecFrame}}
class SDIDecFrame : public TDecoratedFrame {
  public:
    SDIDecFrame(TWindow* parent, const char far* title,
                TWindow* clientWnd,
                bool trackMenuSelection = false,
                TModule* module = 0);
    ~SDIDecFrame();
```

```
};      //{{SDIDecFrame}}

//{{TApplication = TBExpertApp}}
class TBExpertApp : public TApplication {
  private:

  public:
    TBExpertApp();
    virtual ~TBExpertApp();

    // Public data members for print menu and Paint
    //
    TPrinter*        Printer;
    int              Printing;

//{{TBExpertAppVIRTUAL_BEGIN}}
  public:
    virtual void InitMainWindow();
//{{TBExpertAppVIRTUAL_END}}

//{{TBExpertAppRSP_TBL_BEGIN}}
  protected:
    void EvNewView(TView& view);
    void EvCloseView(TView& view);
    void CmHelpAbout();
    void CmFilePrint();
    void CmFilePrintSetup();
    void CmFilePrintPreview();
    void CmPrintEnable(TCommandEnabler& tce);
    void EvWinIniChange(char far* section);
//{{TBExpertAppRSP_TBL_END}}
DECLARE_RESPONSE_TABLE(TBExpertApp);
};      //{{TBExpertApp}}

#endif  // bexprtap_h sentry.
```

The derived class, **TBExpertApp,** provides file and printer support to child classes.
    A little further down the main listing, notice that the **SDIDecFrame** class is derived
from Borland's **TDecoratedFrame** class. A class derived from **TDecoratedFrame** positions
its client window to be the same size as the client rectangle. This allows items such as
toolbars and status lines to be added to the window.
    The remaining code forms a group of member functions that describe editing,
printing, or help capabilities for the application.

REMEMBER: *Additional code commenting is possible by selecting the Verbose radio button at the bottom of the box, shown earlier in Figure 28-6, while setting project specifications.*

What Is the Purpose of the bexprtev.cpp File?

The purpose of the bexprtev.cpp source code file is to implement the **TEditView** class. Here **TBExpertEditView** is derived from Borland's **TEditView** class.

```
//----------------------------------------------------------
//  Project BExpert
//
//  Copyright © 1996. All Rights Reserved.
//
//  SUBSYSTEM:    BExpert.exe Application
//  FILE:         BExprtEV.cpp
//  AUTHOR:       C. Pappas & W. Murray
//
//  OVERVIEW
//  ~~~~~~~~
//  Source file for TBExpertEditView (TEditView).
//
//----------------------------------------------------------

#include <owl/pch.h>

#include "BExprtAp.h"
#include "BExprtEV.h"

#include <stdio.h>

//{{TBExpertEditView Implementation}}

DEFINE_RESPONSE_TABLE1(TBExpertEditView, TEditView)
//{{TBExpertEditViewRSP_TBL_BEGIN}}
  EV_WM_GETMINMAXINFO,
//{{TBExpertEditViewRSP_TBL_END}}
END_RESPONSE_TABLE;

TBExpertEditView::TBExpertEditView(TDocument& doc,
                                   TWindow* parent)
:
```

```
    TEditView(doc, parent)
{
  // INSERT>> Your constructor code here.


}


TBExpertEditView::~TBExpertEditView()
{
  // INSERT>> Your destructor code here.


}


void TBExpertEditView::Paint(TDC& dc, bool, TRect& rect)
{
  TBExpertApp* theApp = TYPESAFE_DOWNCAST(GetApplication(),
                                          TBExpertApp);
  if (theApp) {
    if (theApp->Printing && theApp-> \
        Printer && !rect.IsEmpty()) {
      TSize    pageSize(rect.right - rect.left,
                        rect.bottom - rect.top);

      HFONT    hFont = (HFONT)GetWindowFont();
      TFont    font("Arial", -12);
      if (!hFont)
        dc.SelectObject(font);
      else
        dc.SelectObject(TFont(hFont));

      TEXTMETRIC   tm;
      int fHeight = dc.GetTextMetrics(tm) ? tm.tmHeight + \
                    tm.tmExternalLeading : 10;

      int linesPerPage = MulDiv(pageSize.cy, 1, fHeight);
      if (linesPerPage) {
        TPrintDialog::TData& printerData = \
                            theApp->Printer->GetSetup();

        int maxPg = ((GetNumLines() / linesPerPage) + 1.0);

        printerData.MinPage = 1;
```

```
          printerData.MaxPage = maxPg;

          int    fromPage = printerData.FromPage == -1 ? 1 : \
                             printerData.FromPage;
          int    toPage = printerData.ToPage == -1 ? 1 : \
                             printerData.ToPage;
          char   buffer[255];
          int    currentPage = fromPage;

          while (currentPage <= toPage) {
            int startLine = (currentPage - 1) * linesPerPage;
            int lineIdx = 0;
            while (lineIdx < linesPerPage) {
              if (!GetLine(buffer, sizeof buffer,
                           startLine + lineIdx))
                break;
              dc.TabbedTextOut(TPoint(0, lineIdx * fHeight),
                               buffer, strlen(buffer),
                               0, 0, 0);
              lineIdx++;
            }
            currentPage++;
          }
        }
      }
    }
  }
}

void TBExpertEditView::EvGetMinMaxInfo(MINMAXINFO far& \
                                        minmaxinfo)
{
  TBExpertApp* theApp = TYPESAFE_DOWNCAST(GetApplication(),
                                          TBExpertApp);

  if (theApp) {
    if (theApp->Printing) {
      minmaxinfo.ptMaxSize = TPoint(32000, 32000);
      minmaxinfo.ptMaxTrackSize = TPoint(32000, 32000);
      return;
    }
  }
  TEditView::EvGetMinMaxInfo(minmaxinfo);
}
```

Here the **TBExpertEditView** class, derived from Borland's **TEditView** class, implements editing capabilities in the application.

Paint() is called by base classes when responding to a WM_PAINT message. It is here that the editing capabilities of the application are implemented. You might recall that the procedure-oriented applications in Chapters 21 and 22 drew their text to the window when WM_PAINT messages were received. Although the code in this listing gets a little convoluted because it is written to handle a number of situations, the actual approach to page and line handling is the same as for those earlier examples.

What Is the Purpose of the bexprtad.cpp File?

The purpose of the bexprtad.cpp source code file is to implement the **TDialog** class. Here **TBExpertAboutDlg** is derived from Borland's **TDialog** class.

```
//----------------------------------------------------------
//   Project BExpert
//
//   Copyright © 1996. All Rights Reserved.
//
//   SUBSYSTEM:    BExpert.exe Application
//   FILE:         BExprtAD.cpp
//   AUTHOR:       C. Pappas & W. Murray
//
//   OVERVIEW
//   ~~~~~~~~
//   Source file for TBExpertAboutDlg (TDialog).
//
//----------------------------------------------------------

#include <owl/pch.h>
#include <stdio.h>
#if defined(BI_PLAT_WIN16)
# include <ver.h>
#endif

#include "BExprtAp.h"
#include "BExprtAD.h"

TProjectRCVersion::TProjectRCVersion(TModule* module)
{
  char      appFName[255];
  char      subBlockName[255];
  uint32    fvHandle;
```

```
      uint    vSize;

   FVData = 0;

   module->GetModuleFileName(appFName, sizeof appFName);
   OemToAnsi(appFName, appFName);
   uint32 dwSize = ::GetFileVersionInfoSize(appFName,
                                            &fvHandle);
   if (dwSize) {
     FVData = (void far *)new char[(uint)dwSize];
     if (::GetFileVersionInfo(appFName, fvHandle,
                              dwSize, FVData)) {
       // Copy string to buffer so VerQueryValue will work
       // under Win16.
       strcpy(subBlockName, "\\VarFileInfo\\Translation");
       if (!::VerQueryValue(FVData, subBlockName,
                            (void far* far*)&TransBlock,
                            &vSize)) {
         delete[] FVData;
         FVData = 0;
       }
       else
         *(uint32 *)TransBlock = MAKELONG(HIWORD(*(uint32 *) \
                                 TransBlock),
                                 LOWORD(*(uint32 *)TransBlock));
     }
   }
}

TProjectRCVersion::~TProjectRCVersion()
{
  if (FVData)
    delete[] FVData;
}

bool TProjectRCVersion::GetProductName(LPSTR& prodName)
{
  uint    vSize;
  char    subBlockName[255];

  if (FVData) {
```

```
      sprintf(subBlockName, "\\StringFileInfo\\%08lx\\%s",
             *(uint32 *)TransBlock,(LPSTR)"ProductName");
      return FVData ? ::VerQueryValue(FVData,
                                      subBlockName,
                                      (void far* far*) \
                                      &prodName, &vSize) : false;
  } else
    return false;
}


bool TProjectRCVersion::GetProductVersion(LPSTR& prodVersion)
{
  uint    vSize;
  char    subBlockName[255];

  if (FVData) {
    sprintf(subBlockName, "\\StringFileInfo\\%08lx\\%s",
           *(uint32 *)TransBlock,(LPSTR)"ProductVersion");
    return FVData ? ::VerQueryValue(FVData,
                                    subBlockName,
                                    (void far* far*)  \
                                    &prodVersion,
                                    &vSize) : false;
  } else
    return false;
}


bool TProjectRCVersion::GetCopyright(LPSTR& copyright)
{
  uint    vSize;
  char    subBlockName[255];

  if (FVData) {
    sprintf(subBlockName, "\\StringFileInfo\\%08lx\\%s",
           *(uint32 *)TransBlock,(LPSTR)"LegalCopyright");
    return FVData ? ::VerQueryValue(FVData,
                                    subBlockName,
                                    (void far* far*) \
                                    &copyright,
                                    &vSize) : false;
  } else
```

```
      return false;
}

bool TProjectRCVersion::GetDebug(LPSTR& debug)
{
  uint    vSize;
  char    subBlockName[255];

  if (FVData) {
    sprintf(subBlockName, "\\StringFileInfo\\%08lx\\%s",
            *(uint32 *)TransBlock,(LPSTR)"SpecialBuild");
    return FVData ? ::VerQueryValue(FVData,
                                    subBlockName,
                                    (void far* far*)&debug,
                                    &vSize) : false;
  } else
    return false;
}

//{{TBExpertAboutDlg Implementation}}

TBExpertAboutDlg::TBExpertAboutDlg(TWindow* parent,
                                   TResId resId,
                                   TModule* module)
:
  TDialog(parent, resId, module)
{
  // INSERT>> Your constructor code here.
}

TBExpertAboutDlg::~TBExpertAboutDlg()
{
  Destroy();

  // INSERT>> Your destructor code here.
}

void TBExpertAboutDlg::SetupWindow()
{
  LPSTR prodName = 0, prodVersion = 0, copyright = 0,
        debug = 0;
```

```
   TStatic* versionCtrl = new TStatic(this, IDC_VERSION, 255);
   TStatic* copyrightCtrl = new TStatic(this, IDC_COPYRIGHT,
                                        255);
   TStatic* debugCtrl = new TStatic(this, IDC_DEBUG, 255);

   TDialog::SetupWindow();

   TProjectRCVersion applVersion(GetModule());

   if (applVersion.GetProductName(prodName) &&
 applVersion.GetProductVersion(prodVersion)) {
     //
     char     buffer[255];
     char     versionName[128];

     buffer[0] = '\0';
     versionName[0] = '\0';

     versionCtrl->GetText(versionName,
                          sizeof versionName);
     sprintf(buffer, "%s %s %s", prodName,
             versionName, prodVersion);

     versionCtrl->SetText(buffer);
   }

  if (applVersion.GetCopyright(copyright))
    copyrightCtrl->SetText(copyright);

  if (applVersion.GetDebug(debug))
    debugCtrl->SetText(debug);
}
```

This listing makes use of various class member functions to retrieve the information you entered in the AppExpert's Administrative Options, shown earlier in Figure 28-7. If you look at the associated header file, bexprtad.h, you can see exactly how **TBExpertAboutDlg** is derived from Borland's **TDialog** class.

What Is the Purpose of the apxprint.cpp File?

The purpose of the apxprint.cpp source code file is to provide printing capabilities for the application. This file will not be present if the printing option was not checked in the Application Summary shown earlier in Figure 28-3.

```
//------------------------------------------------------------
//   Project BExpert
//
//   Copyright © 1996. All Rights Reserved.
//
//   SUBSYSTEM:    BExpert.exe Application
//   FILE:         APXPrint.cpp
//   AUTHOR:       C. Pappas & W. Murray
//
//   OVERVIEW
//   ~~~~~~~~
//   Source file for implementation of Printing.
//
//------------------------------------------------------------
#include <owl/pch.h>
#include "apxprint.h"

void TAPXPrintout::GetDialogInfo(int& minPage, int&,
                                 int& selFromPage, int&)
{
  minPage = 1;
  selFromPage = 0;
}

void TAPXPrintout::BeginPrinting()
{
  TRect clientR;

  BeginPage(clientR);

  HFONT    hFont = (HFONT)Window->GetWindowFont();
  TFont    font("Arial", -12);
  if (!hFont)
    DC->SelectObject(font);
  else
    DC->SelectObject(TFont(hFont));
```

```
    TEXTMETRIC  tm;
    int fHeight = DC->GetTextMetrics(tm) ? tm.tmHeight \
                        + tm.tmExternalLeading : 10;

    DC->RestoreFont();

    int linesPerPage = MulDiv(clientR.Height(), 1, fHeight);

    TPrintDialog::TData& printerData = Printer->GetSetup();

    MINMAXINFO minmaxinfo;
    Window->SendMessage(WM_GETMINMAXINFO, 0, (long)&minmaxinfo);
    int maxPg = (minmaxinfo.ptMaxSize.y / linesPerPage) + 1.0;

    printerData.MinPage = 1;
    printerData.MaxPage = maxPg;

    EndPage();

    TPrintout::BeginPrinting();
}

void TAPXPrintout::BeginPage(TRect& clientR)
{
  TScreenDC screenDC;
  TSize screenRes(screenDC.GetDeviceCaps(LOGPIXELSX),
         screenDC.GetDeviceCaps(LOGPIXELSY));
  TSize printRes(DC->GetDeviceCaps(LOGPIXELSX),
          DC->GetDeviceCaps(LOGPIXELSY));

  clientR = Window->GetClientRect();
  Window->MapWindowPoints(HWND_DESKTOP, (TPoint*)&clientR, 2);

  OrgR = Window->GetWindowRect();
  int adjX = OrgR.Width() - clientR.Width();
  int adjY = OrgR.Height() - clientR.Height();

  if (Scale) {
    clientR = Window->GetClientRect();
    PrevMode = DC->SetMapMode(MapMode);
    DC->SetViewportExt(PageSize, &OldVExt);
```

```
    clientR.right = MulDiv(PageSize.cx, screenRes.cx,
                           printRes.cx);
    clientR.bottom = MulDiv(PageSize.cy, screenRes.cy,
                            printRes.cy);

    DC->SetWindowExt(clientR.Size(), &OldWExt);
  }

  Window->SetRedraw(false);
  Window->SetWindowPos(0, 0, 0, clientR.Width() + adjX,
                       clientR.Height() + adjY,
                       SWP_NOMOVE | SWP_NOREDRAW | \
                       SWP_NOZORDER | SWP_NOACTIVATE);
}

void TAPXPrintout::PrintPage(int page, TRect& bandRect,
                             unsigned)
{
  TRect clientR;

  BeginPage(clientR);

  if (Scale)
    DC->DPtoLP(bandRect, 2);

  TPrintDialog::TData& printerData = Printer->GetSetup();
  int fromPg = printerData.FromPage;
  int toPg = printerData.ToPage;

  printerData.FromPage = page;
  printerData.ToPage = page;

  Window->Paint(*DC, false, bandRect);

  printerData.FromPage = fromPg;
  printerData.ToPage = toPg;

  if (Scale)
    DC->LPtoDP(bandRect, 2);
```

```
    EndPage();
}

void TAPXPrintout::EndPage()
{
   Window->SetWindowPos(0, 0, 0, OrgR.Width(), OrgR.Height(),
                        SWP_NOMOVE | SWP_NOREDRAW | \
                        SWP_NOZORDER| SWP_NOACTIVATE);
   Window->SetRedraw(true);

   if (Scale) {
     DC->SetWindowExt(OldWExt);
     DC->SetViewportExt(OldVExt);
     DC->SetMapMode(PrevMode);
   }
}

bool TAPXPrintout::HasPage(int pageNumber)
{
   TPrintDialog::TData& printerData = Printer->GetSetup();

   return pageNumber >= printerData.MinPage && pageNumber <=
printerData.MaxPage;
}
```

This listing is created to manage the page to print transfer for the application. Member functions are used to manage the size of the frame window and perform a conversion to the size of the printer. This is a fairly standard file that is added to all dynamic templates requesting printing capabilities.

What Is the Purpose of the apxprev.cpp File?

The purpose of the apxprev.cpp source code file is to provide print previewing for the application. This file will not be present if the printing option was not checked in the Application Summary shown earlier in Figure 28-3.

```
//----------------------------------------------------------
//   Project BExpert
//
//   Copyright © 1996. All Rights Reserved.
//
//   SUBSYSTEM:    BExpert.exe Application
```

```
//   FILE:          APXPrev.cpp
//   AUTHOR:        C. Pappas & W. Murray
//
//   OVERVIEW
//   ~~~~~~~~
//   Source file for implementation of Print Preview.
//
//-------------------------------------------------------
#include <owl/pch.h>

#include <owl/buttonga.h>
#include <owl/textgadg.h>
#include <stdio.h>

#include "apxprev.h"
#include "BExprtAp.rh"

//{{PreviewWindow Implementation}}

DEFINE_RESPONSE_TABLE1(PreviewWindow, TDecoratedFrame)
  EV_COMMAND_ENABLE(APX_PPR_PREVIOUS, PPR_PreviousEnable),
  EV_COMMAND_ENABLE(APX_PPR_NEXT, PPR_NextEnable),
  EV_COMMAND(APX_PPR_PREVIOUS, PPR_Previous),
  EV_COMMAND(APX_PPR_NEXT, PPR_Next),
  EV_COMMAND(APX_PPR_ONEUP, PPR_OneUp),
  EV_COMMAND_ENABLE(APX_PPR_TWOUP, PPR_TwoUpEnable),
  EV_COMMAND(APX_PPR_TWOUP, PPR_TwoUp),
  EV_COMMAND(APX_PPR_DONE, PPR_Done),
//{{PreviewWindowRSP_TBL_BEGIN}}
//{{PreviewWindowRSP_TBL_END}}
END_RESPONSE_TABLE;

PreviewWindow::PreviewWindow(TWindow* parentWindow,
                             TPrinter* printer,
                             TWindow* currWindow,
                             const char far* title,
                             TLayoutWindow* client)
 :
   TDecoratedFrame(parentWindow, title, client)
{
   CurrWindow = currWindow;
```

```
    Printer = printer;
    Client = client;
    Page1 = 0;
    Page2 = 0;
    FromPage = 1;
    ToPage = 1;

    TPrintDialog::TData& data = Printer->GetSetup();
    PrnDC = new TPrintDC(data.GetDriverName(),
                         data.GetDeviceName(),
                         data.GetOutputName(),
                         data.GetDevMode());

    PrintExtent = new TSize(PrnDC->GetDeviceCaps(HORZRES),
                            PrnDC->GetDeviceCaps(VERTRES));
    Printout = new TAPXPrintout(Printer, "Print Preview",
                                currWindow, true);

    SetBkgndColor(::GetSysColor(COLOR_APPWORKSPACE));

    PreviewSpeedBar = new TControlBar(this);
    PreviewSpeedBar->Insert(*new TButtonGadget(APX_PPR_PREVIOUS,
APX_PPR_PREVIOUS, TButtonGadget::Command, true));
    PreviewSpeedBar->Insert(*new TButtonGadget(APX_PPR_NEXT,
                                               APX_PPR_NEXT,
                                               TButtonGadget:: \
                                               Command,
                                               true));
    PreviewSpeedBar->Insert(*new TSeparatorGadget(6));
    PreviewSpeedBar->Insert(*new TButtonGadget(APX_PPR_ONEUP,
                                               APX_PPR_ONEUP,
                                               TButtonGadget:: \
                                               Exclusive,
                                               true,
                                               TButtonGadget:: \
                                               Down));
    PreviewSpeedBar->Insert(*new TButtonGadget(APX_PPR_TWOUP,
                                               APX_PPR_TWOUP,
                                               TButtonGadget:: \
                                               Exclusive, true));
    PreviewSpeedBar->Insert(*new TSeparatorGadget(12));
```

```
  PreviewSpeedBar->Insert(*new TTextGadget(APX_PPR_CURRPAGE,
                                           TGadget::Recessed,
                                           TTextGadget::Left,
                                           10, "Page 1"));
  PreviewSpeedBar->Insert(*new TSeparatorGadget(20));
  PreviewSpeedBar->Insert(*new TButtonGadget(CM_FILEPRINT,
                                             CM_FILEPRINT,
                                             TButtonGadget:: \
                                             Command, true));
  PreviewSpeedBar->Insert(*new TSeparatorGadget(20));
  PreviewSpeedBar->Insert(*new TButtonGadget(APX_PPR_DONE,
                                             APX_PPR_DONE,
                                             TButtonGadget:: \
                                             Command, true));
  Insert(*PreviewSpeedBar, TDecoratedFrame::Top);

  Attr.Style = (WS_VISIBLE | WS_POPUP);

  Attr.X = 0;
  Attr.Y = -1;
  Attr.W = Parent->GetClientRect().Width();
  Attr.H = Parent->GetClientRect().Height() + 1;
  parentWindow->MapWindowPoints(HWindow, (TPoint *)&(Attr.X),
                                1);
}

PreviewWindow::~PreviewWindow()
{
  delete Page1;
  delete Page2;

  delete PrnDC;
  delete PrintExtent;
  delete Printout;
}

void PreviewWindow::SetupWindow()
{
  TDecoratedFrame::SetupWindow();

  TPrintDialog::TData& data = Printer->GetSetup();
```

```
Page1 = new TPreviewPage(Client, *Printout, *PrnDC,
                         *PrintExtent, 1);
Page1->SetPageNumber(1);
data.MaxPage = 1;

Page2 = 0;

TLayoutMetrics metrics1;

metrics1.X.Set(lmLeft, lmRightOf, lmParent, lmLeft, 15);
metrics1.Y.Set(lmTop, lmBelow, lmParent, lmTop, 15);

TRect r = Client->GetClientRect();
long ratio;

if (PrintExtent->cx > PrintExtent->cy)
  ratio = ((long)PrintExtent->cy * 100) / PrintExtent->cx;
else
  ratio = ((long)PrintExtent->cx * 100) / PrintExtent->cy;

bool xMajor = ((r.Width() * ratio) / 100) > r.Height();
if (xMajor){
  metrics1.Height.Set(lmBottom, lmAbove, lmParent,
                      lmBottom, 15);
  metrics1.Width.PercentOf(Page1,
                           (int)((long)PrintExtent-> \
                           cx * 95 / PrintExtent->cy),
                           lmHeight);
}
else {
  metrics1.Height.PercentOf(Page1,
                            (int)((long)PrintExtent-> \
                            cy * 95 / PrintExtent->cx),
                            lmWidth);
  metrics1.Width.Set(lmRight, lmLeftOf, lmParent,
                     lmRight, 15);
}

Page1->Create();
```

```
  Client->SetChildLayoutMetrics(*Page1, metrics1);
  Client->Layout();
}


void PreviewWindow::SpeedBarState()
{
  TTextGadget* cpGadget = TYPESAFE_DOWNCAST \
                          (PreviewSpeedBar-> \
                          GadgetWithId(APX_PPR_CURRPAGE),
                          TTextGadget);
  if (cpGadget) {
    char    buffer[32];
    if (Page2 && FromPage != ToPage)
      sprintf(buffer, "Page %d - %d", FromPage, ToPage);
    else
      sprintf(buffer, "Page %d", FromPage);
    cpGadget->SetText(buffer);
  }
}

void PreviewWindow::PPR_PreviousEnable(TCommandEnabler& tce)
{
  tce.Enable(FromPage != 1);
}

void PreviewWindow::PPR_NextEnable(TCommandEnabler& tce)
{
  TPrintDialog::TData& printerData = Printer->GetSetup();
  tce.Enable(ToPage != printerData.MaxPage);
}

void PreviewWindow::PPR_Previous()
{
  TPrintDialog::TData& printerData = Printer->GetSetup();

  if (FromPage > printerData.MinPage) {
    FromPage--;
    ToPage--;

    Page1->SetPageNumber(FromPage);
```

```
    if (Page2)
      Page2->SetPageNumber(ToPage);
  }

  SpeedBarState();
}

void PreviewWindow::PPR_Next()
{
  TPrintDialog::TData& printerData = Printer->GetSetup();

  if (ToPage < printerData.MaxPage) {
    FromPage++;
    ToPage++;

    Page1->SetPageNumber(FromPage);
    if (Page2)
      Page2->SetPageNumber(ToPage);
  }

  SpeedBarState();
}

void PreviewWindow::PPR_OneUp()
{
  if (Page2) {
    Client->RemoveChildLayoutMetrics(*Page2);

    delete Page2;
    Page2 = 0;

    Client->Layout();

    ToPage = FromPage;

    SpeedBarState();
  }
}

void PreviewWindow::PPR_TwoUpEnable(TCommandEnabler& tce)
{
```

```cpp
    tce.Enable(PrintExtent->cx <= PrintExtent->cy);
}

void PreviewWindow::PPR_TwoUp()
{
  if (!Page2) {
    Page2 = new TPreviewPage(Client, *Printout, *PrnDC,
                             *PrintExtent, PageNumber + 1);

    Page2->Create();

    TLayoutMetrics metrics2;

    metrics2.X.Set(lmLeft, lmRightOf, Page1, lmRight, 30);
    metrics2.Y.SameAs(Page1, lmTop);

    metrics2.Width.SameAs(Page1, lmWidth);
    metrics2.Height.SameAs(Page1, lmBottom);

    Client->SetChildLayoutMetrics(*Page2, metrics2);
    Client->Layout();

    TPrintDialog::TData& printerData = Printer->GetSetup();

    if (FromPage == printerData.MaxPage) {
      if (FromPage > 1) {
        FromPage--;
        ToPage = FromPage + 1;
        Page1->SetPageNumber(FromPage);
        Page2->SetPageNumber(ToPage);
      }
      else
        Page2->SetPageNumber(0);
    }
    else {
      ToPage = FromPage + 1;
      Page2->SetPageNumber(ToPage);
    }

    SpeedBarState();
  }
}
```

```
void PreviewWindow::PPR_Done()
{
  GetApplication()->GetMainWindow()->SetRedraw(false);
  GetApplication()->EndModal(IDCANCEL);
}
```

This listing includes the code to handle the print preview listings you see on the screen. Various member functions check the length of the document and compare it to the view requested. Again, this is a standard implementation for viewing documents that doesn't change greatly from one dynamic template to another.

Building Unique Applications

The Borland AppExpert and C++ compiler have created a complete working application. What needs to be added? In this example, the AppExpert actually created a mini-word processor application, but it is void of distinctive features that make it uniquely yours. To extend this project, you will want to customize the code with specific features.

As a programming challenge, why not consider adding another menu that will provide the user with system information such as time/date and disk resources? Simply use the information you learned in Chapters 19 and integrate it into the code.

PART EIGHT

Appendix

Appendix A

Java Application Development with Borland BCWJAVA

J ava is the newest and coolest way to create interactive, multimedia Web pages. Using Java *applets*, small programs that you include on your HTML pages, you can build dazzling Web sites that will keep people coming back for more. In this section, you will be shown everything you need to know about quickly writing and adding Java applets to your Web site.

Borland International worked furiously to negotiate the legal issues involved in incorporating Sun Microsystems' Java language and testing Java's integration with the Borland IDE so that this powerful new language would be immediately available to you. Borland has done a superb job of making the use of Java as straightforward and seamless as possible. Whether it is the easy automatic Java installation or the familiar way the IDE responds in this Java world, you will almost feel as if you've programmed in Java before. Borland provides a complete suite of development tools—from a Java compiler/interpreter to an integrated debugger and Applet Viewer—all of which use the same command structure and sequences you've used throughout this book to enter, edit, compile, debug, and test C/C++ programs!

So, what's all the buzz about Java? This high-powered programming language is object-oriented and architecture-neutral, enabling you to build Web pages that execute distributed code—securely—across the Net's patchwork of platforms. So now your once-static Web pages can feature live news feeds and video, animation, interactive three-dimensional imagery, and more. This appendix is just a quick introduction to a whole new world of programming.

Java is C/C++-like, making it very easy for a C/C++ programmer's migration. However, there are differences between C++ and Java. Java does *not* have any of these C/C++ features:

- **#define**s or **typedef**s
- Automatic conversions
- **goto**
- Individual functions
- Multiple inheritance
- Operator overloading
- Pointers
- Standalone functions—all coding must be encapsulated within class methods
- Structures or unions

Java is *both* compiled and interpreted. Java code is first compiled into what is officially called *byte-code*. Byte-code is architecturally neutral, allowing the same byte-code file to run on any architecture supporting Java. Technically, this is possible because Java is the same language on every computer. For example, simple types don't vary: an integer is always 32 bits and a long is always 64 bits. It is at run time that the Java interpreter executes this byte-code in real time.

Although Java is both a compiled and interpreted language capable of creating small, standalone *application*s designed to run dedicated hardware, such as yet-to-be designed TVs, VCRs, telephones, and even futuristic programmable dishwashers, the following sections describe how to install, create, and test a simple Java applet using BCWJAVA.

Unlike Java applications, Java applets are programs invoked by HTML on your Internet Web home page. Naturally, in order to fully test the applet you will need to have an Internet account. You will also need to have your operating system's Internet connection settings initialized. This is usually accomplished by going to the Control Panel | Internet Utility. You need to have done this ahead of time because BCWJAVA automatically dials and connects to your Internet account whenever you enter the debug phase of the Java applet development cycle.

 NOTE: *The Java Language, though similar to C/C++, has its own unique syntax and logical use beyond the scope of this appendix. The same holds true for HTML, Hyptertext Markup Language. Although you can use Java to write standalone applications, you need HTML to generate Internet Java applets.*

Installing BCWJAVA

Installing BCWJAVA is as simple as running the setup.exe program on your installation CD-ROM, clicking on the Add-on for Java button with the official Sun Microsystems, Inc., "Duke" icon (the red-nosed, hand-waving icon), and following the simple install instructions.

Java Syntax Highlighting

You can add Java syntax highlighting options to your active button list by following these steps:

1. Choose Options | Environment from the main menu.
2. Select Speedbar | Customize from the Topics list.
3. Select Editor in the Window drop-down list box.
4. Select the Java highlighting from the Available Buttons and move them both to the active buttons list.

Your First Java Project

The following example program demonstrates the steps necessary to write a simple Java applet, because the majority of readers will want to use Java immediately to spice up their World Wide Web home pages. The applet demonstrates how to add the traditional program number one's "Hello World!" message, only for a slight twist this applet outputs: "Hello Again!" Follow these steps:

1. Choose File | New | Project. The TargetExpert appears.

2. In the Project Path and Name input box, type **bc5\bin\HelloAgain.ide**. (Don't type the ending period.) The Target Name box automatically shows "HelloAgain".

3. In the Target Type list box, scroll down and select Java [.class].

NOTE: *Because this example applet is straightforward, there is no need to use the AppExpert for Java. Figure A-1 shows a completed Java TargetExpert dialog box.*

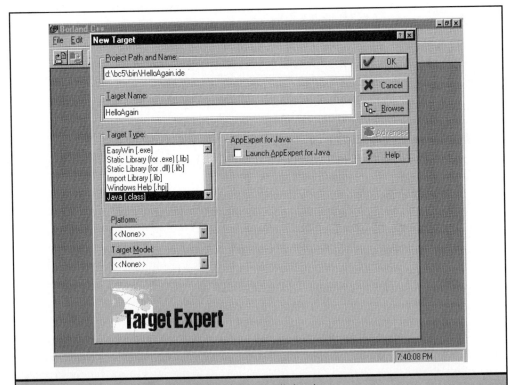

Figure A-1.   *A completed Java TargetExpert dialog box*

4. Click OK. The TargetExpert dialog box closes. The Project window appears (as shown in Figure A-2), displaying your HelloAgain project, which has the following nodes:

HelloAgain.class – The applet, an executable file.
HelloAgain.java – The Java source code.
HelloAgain.html – The HTML document that displays the applet.

5. Choose File | Save.

The bc5\bin\HelloAgain\ directory is created. The HelloAgain.ide project file is saved into this directory. You are now ready to write your Java code.

Writing the Java Applet

You begin a Java applet just like any C/C++ program. First choose File | New | Text from the main menu and enter your source code, which in this case uses Java syntax. To write the HelloAgain applet, follow these steps:

1. Enter the following Java code to create a program (as shown in Figure A-3):

```
import java.awt.*;
import java.applet.*;

public class HelloAgain extends Applet {

  public void init() {
    resize(200,25);
  }
```

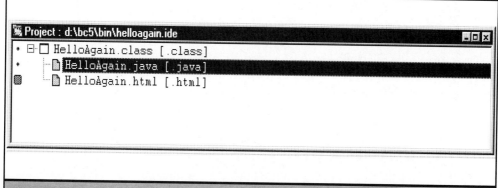

Figure A-2. *The HelloAgain Project window*

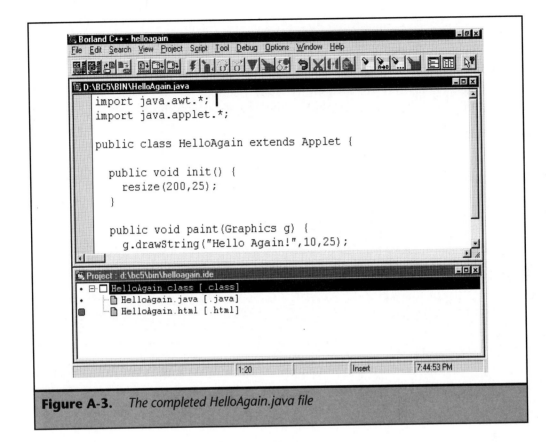

Figure A-3. *The completed HelloAgain.java file*

```
public void paint(Graphics g) {
   g.drawString("Hello Again!",10,25);
}
}
```

2. Choose File | Save.

The source code file HelloAgain.java is saved into the bc5\bin\HelloAgain directory. You are now ready to "Java Compile" the applet, generating the HelloAgain.class. Java files with *.class extensions, which are similar to C/C++ *.exe files.

Compiling "HelloAgain.java"

In the bc5\bin\HelloAgain Project window, select the HelloAgain.java file. Right-click to show the SpeedMenu and choose Java Compile. The compiler window appears (as shown in Figure A-4), and the compiler runs.

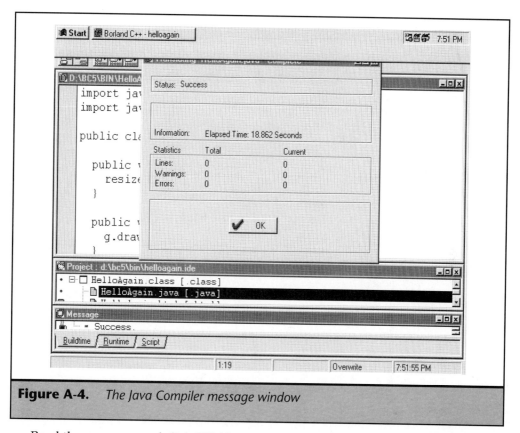

Figure A-4. *The Java Compiler message window*

Read the messages and click OK. You can view your applet either by choosing
View | Java View from the SpeedMenu or by browsing your HTML file with a
Java-enabled browser. To view your applet with the debugger for Java, follow the
steps in the next section.

Debugging HelloAgain.class

Once you compile a *.java file, the Java compiler generates the *.class file, which is
equivalent in many ways to a C/C++ *.exe file. To debug your applet, click the right
mouse button on HelloAgain.class in the Project window. On the SpeedMenu, choose
View | Debug Java Code. (Make certain the Project | Options | Java | Compiler -
Generate debug information check box is checked.)

The good news is that the same commands you have always used to debug a
standard C/C++ program are identical to those used to debug Java applets (see Figure
A-5).

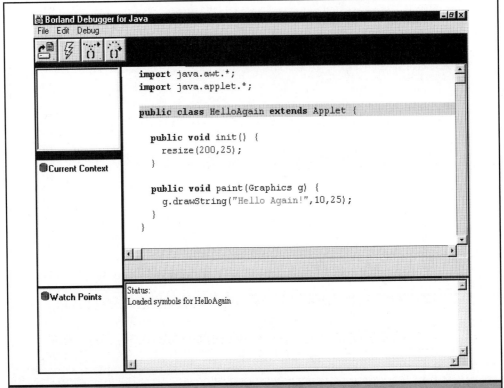

Figure A-5. *Running the Borland Integrated Java Debugger on HelloAgain.class*

Creating the HTML Page

Java applets must be embedded in HTML pages and used with a browser. You embed a Java applet by using the APPLET tag. The following HTML file demonstrates the relative simplicity of HTML syntax. Enter the file exactly as you see it.

1. Double-click the HelloAgain.html node in the Project window. The HelloAgain.html editing window appears.

2. Enter the following HTML code (as seen in Figure A-6):

```
<HTML>
<HEAD>
<TITLE>Hello Again</TITLE>
</HEAD>
<BODY>
<p>Below this line is the Java Applet you wrote:
```

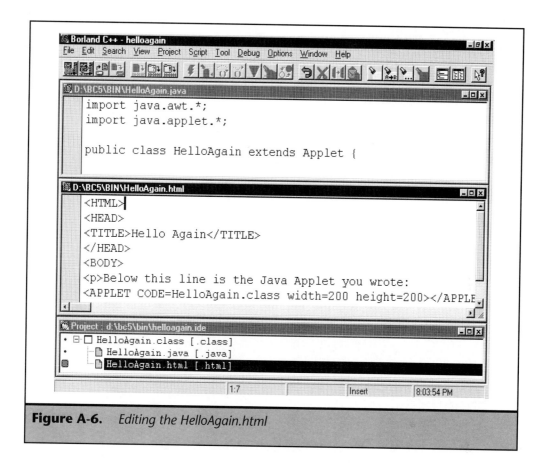

Figure A-6. *Editing the HelloAgain.html*

```
<p><applet code=HelloAgain.class width=200 height=200></applet>
</BODY>
</HTML>
```

NOTE: The *<p><applet...width=200 height=200></applet>* statement links the *HelloAgain.class applet to the home page and dimensions the outputs width and height.*

3. Choose File | Save.

The HTML file is saved into the bc5\bin\HelloAgain\ subdirectory. At this point you are ready to run the applet.

Running "HelloAgain.class"

1. Select the HelloAgain.class node in the Project window and click the right mouse button.

2. Select the Java view option. This starts the Borland IDE Applet Viewer.

3. Wait while the Borland IDE dials your Internet connection and runs the applet (see Figure A-7).

Your HelloAgain page appears with the line "Hello Again!" in the Applet Viewer. For a full-fledged demonstration, connect to the Internet with a Java-compatible browser such as Netscape 2.0 or HotJava, and run the home page.

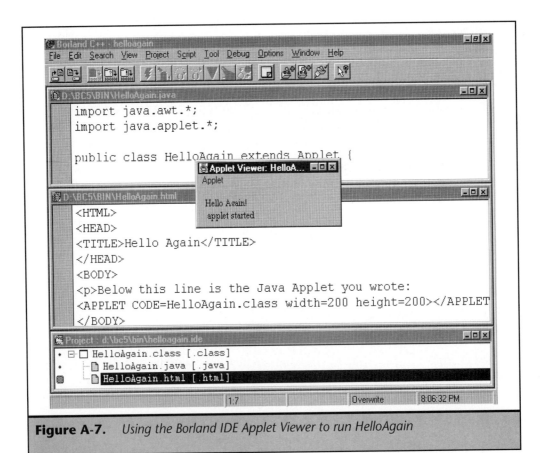

Figure A-7. *Using the Borland IDE Applet Viewer to run HelloAgain*

Although the similarities between C++ and Java make learning this new language straightforward for a C/C++ programmer, there are still many dissimilarities and Java-specific issues that make it impossible to cover this unique environment in an appendix. Complicating the issue is the need to understand HTML, which is the stage for your Java applets.

However, with this said, Appendix A has shown you everything you need to know about activating the Borland C++ IDE's Java utilities and everything necessary to enter, edit, compile, debug, and test Java applets. At this point you are ready to purchase an HTML and a Java Language reference manual and follow the examples. Just as today's programmer cannot ignore C and C++, anyone who wishes to stay current in computer-related issues needs to know how to use the Internet's World Wide Web and its Java compatriot.

Up-to-the-Minute Java

Java is still in a state of evolution with many new features being added. As of this writing, there is still no definitive Java standard. The following World Wide Web sites have been included in order for you to obtain the latest information on this fascinating language:

http://www.java.sun.com/

This Internet address sends you directly to Java's home page, which gives you the latest releases and information on Java.

http://www.sun.com/

This Internet address provides access to the *Sun Online Magazine*. Here you will find information on the behind-the-scenes development of Java.

http://www.javasoft.com/

This World Wide Web site provides up-to-the-minute information on Java, Java applets, and HotJava.

http://www.javasoft.com/applets/

This World Wide Web site lets you jump ahead to sample Java applets. This is an excellent source for experimenting with all that Java applets are capable of doing and for direct access to the Java applet source code.

Java Language Summary

This is a Java Language summary in a form similar to BNF grammar (BNF stands for Backus-Naur Form). You can use this summary to see the similarities between C/C++ and Java and to begin writing Java applications and applets.

```
VariableDeclaration =
  Modifier* Type VarDclr(, VarDclr)* ;

VarDclr =
  Identifier([ ])*(=VarInitValue)?
;

VarInitValue  =
  Exp
| {(VarInitValue( ,VarInitValue)*,?)?}
;

StaticInit =
  static{Statement*}
;

ParamList =
 Parameter(,Parameter)*
;

Parameter =
 Type Identifier([ ])*
;

Statement =
 VariableDeclaration
   Exp;
   {Statement*}
   if(Exp) Statement (else Statement)?
   while(Exp) Statement
   do Statement while(Exp);
   for(VariableDeclaration | Exp ; | ;)
   Exp ? ; Exp ?) Statement
   try Statement(catch(Parameter)Statement)* (finally Statement)?
   switch(Exp) {(case Exp : | default: | Statement)*
   synchronized Exp) Statement
   return Exp?;
```

```
    throw Exp;
    Identifier : Statement
    break Identifier?;
    continue Identifier? ;
    | ;
;

Exp =
 Exp + Exp
 Exp - Exp
 Exp * Exp
 Exp / Exp
 Exp % Exp
 Exp ^ Exp
 Exp & Exp
 Exp | Exp
 Exp && Exp
 Exp || Exp
 Exp << Exp
 Exp >> Exp
 Exp = Exp
 Exp += Exp
 Exp -= Exp
 Exp *= Exp
 Exp /= Exp
 Exp %= Exp
 Exp &= Exp
 Exp |= Exp
 Exp >>= Exp
 Exp >>>= Exp
 Exp < Exp
 Exp <= Exp
 Exp >= Exp
 Exp == Exp
 Exp != Exp
 Exp instanceof(ClassName | InterfaceName)
 Exp ? Exp : Exp
 Exp[Exp]
 ++Exp
 --Exp
 Exp++
```

```
Exp--
-Exp
!Exp
|Exp
(Exp*)
(Type)Exp
Character
Exp(ArgumentLst?)
false
FloatNum
Identifier
IntegerLiteral
new ClassName(ArgumentLst?)
new TypeSpecifier
new(Exp)
null
String
super
this
true
;

ArgumentLst =
 Exp(,Exp ) *
;

TypeSpecifier ([  ])*

TypeSpecifier =
  boolean
  char
  short
  int
  float
  long
  double
  ClassName
  InterfaceName
;
```

```
Modifier =
  public
  private
  protected
  static
  final
  native
  synchronized
  abstract
  threadsare
  transient

CompilationUnit =
 PackageStatement? ImportStatement* TypeDeclaration*
;

PackageStatement =
 package PackageName;
;

ImportStatement =
 import  PackageName.*;
 | import(ClassName | InterfaceName);
;

TypeDeclaration =
 Comnent? ClassDeclaration
 | Comment? InterfaceDeclaration
 | ;
;

ClassDeclaration =
 Modifier* class Identifier
 (extends ClassName)?
 (implements InterfaceName( , InterfaceName)*)?
 {FieldDeclaration*}
;

InterfaceDeclaration =
 Modifier* interface Identifier
 (extends  InterfaceName( ,InterfaceName)*)?
```

```
  {FieldDeclaration*}
;

FieldDeclaration =
 Comment? MethodDeclaration
 | Comment? ConstructorDeclaration
 | Comment? VariableDeclaration
 | StaticInit
 | ;
;
MethodDeclaration =
 Modifier* Type Identifier(ParamList?)
 ( {Statement*} | ; }
;

ConstructorDeclaration =
 Modifier* Identifier(ParamList?)
 {Statement*}
;

PackageName =
   Identifier
   | PackageName.Identifier
;

ClassName =
 Identifier
 | PackageName.Identifier
;

InterfaceName =
 Identifier
 | PackageName.Identifier
;

IntegerLiteral =
     (0...9, L, l, 0x, 0X, 'a'...'f', 'A'...'F')
;

FloatNum =
 DecimalNum.DecimalNum? Exponent? FloatTypePrefix?
```

```
 | DecimalNum Exponent? FloatTypePrefix?
 | DecimalNum Exponent FloatTypePrefix?
;

DecimalNum =
 (0...9), +
;

Exponent =
 (E | e)(+ | - )?
;

FloatTypePrefix =
  f, F, d, D
;
```

Index

X